DATE DUE

MAY 16 1980		
JUN 3 1983		
4-22-94		
APR 1 9 1994		
12/21/96		
1/15/98		
GAYLORD		PRINTED IN U.S.A.

PURCHASING MANAGEMENT

PURCHASING MANAGEMENT
MATERIALS IN MOTION

FOURTH EDITION

J. H. WESTING

Professor of Marketing
University of Wisconsin, Madison

I. V. FINE

Professor of Commerce
University of Wisconsin, Madison

GARY JOSEPH ZENZ

Professor of Business
The Florida State University

A WILEY/HAMILTON PUBLICATION

JOHN WILEY & SONS, INC.
Santa Barbara · New York · London · Sydney · Toronto

Library of Congress Cataloging in Publication Data

Westing, John Howard, 1911-
    Purchasing management.

        First-2d ed. published under title: Industrial purchasing.
        Included bibliographical references and index.
        1.   Industrial procurement—Management.
I.   Fine, Isadore Victor, 1918-   joint author.
II.   Zenz, Gary Joseph, joint author.   III.   Title.

HD52.5.W4   1976   658.7'2   75-38969
ISBN 0-471-93632-4

Printed in the United States of America

10 9 8 7 6 5 4 3 2 1

PREFACE

The purchasing function in both business and institutions has been gaining stature over the past decade or two and its role has grown tremendously as a result of the increasing shortage of raw materials and the many products that rely heavily on raw materials. This condition, which promises to continue indefinitely, will further enhance both the number and importance of people engaged in purchasing. The new status accorded the purchasing function will almost certainly elevate purchasing as a component of the materials management operations of a business. For this reason we have retained the title, *Purchasing Management*, in this fourth edition rather than changing to the fashionable title of Materials Management. Purchasing is still a clearly identifiable function in business organizations and this title deals with it as such.

Most of the changes in this edition have been made to update the discussion of the materials with the latest practice in the field. In this sense, there are changes in all of the chapters. More specifically, the role of purchasing in materials management and the relationship between the two is spelled out in several different contexts. In Chapter 4, there is an increased emphasis on the use of specialized purchasing procedures to reflect the increasing use of these techniques as cost savings methods in business practice. In Chapter 12, which deals with purchasing by governmental units, special emphasis is given to the growing practice of intergovernmental cooperative purchasing and the criteria by which the success of such purchasing can be measured. This method of purchasing has been gaining in popularity and promises economies to hard-pressed government agencies. In Chapter 16, which deals with forward buying and speculation, the revision describes in detail the practice of hedging. As is indicated by the phenomenal growth of the volume of transactions on commodity exchanges as well as the rapid increase in the number and variety of

v

products that can be traded on the exchanges, this form of price protection is of great and growing importance.

From a pedagogical point of view, one of the most significant changes in the fourth edition is the addition of a list of questions at the end of each chapter. The list is designed to facilitate a discussion of the chapter and to stimulate the student to ponder some of the issues presented in a broader context. Also, for the convenience of both the instructor and the student, each chapter is followed by a reference to a case or cases that appear in the final section of the book. Each chapter includes references of cases that are appropriate to some subject in that chapter, and several of the cases can be discussed in connection with more than one chapter. Instructors can choose which issues in the case they wish to stress.

Previous editions of this book were written with the active participation of the Milwaukee Association of Purchasing Managers. Through mutual agreement this relationship has been terminated in the present edition. Much of the material still shows the mark of this cooperative effort, but the responsibility for any errors and shortcomings is ours alone.

J. H. Westing
I. V. Fine
G. J. Zenz

Madison, Wisconsin

CONTENTS

PURCHASING MANAGEMENT

PART I
INTRODUCTION

CHAPTER 1
THE FIELD OF PURCHASING AND MATERIALS MANAGEMENT

The effective management of the purchasing activity and the supporting functions relating to materials (inventory levels, shipping, scrap, etc.) is the key to effective business management. Likewise, efficient management by American companies is a prerequisite to U.S. survival in the increasingly interdependent world markets. In this chapter the dimensions of the procurement activities will be defined, and their significance outlined as a preview to the comprehensive chapters that follow.

In business analysis it is common to refer to "the value added by manufacture," which is the margin between the raw material and the finished product. The amount of this differential between the cost of its materials and the value of its end product represents the unique contribution of each manufacturing firm to the economic process. As an economy becomes more complex, individual firms tend to specialize more in the performance of small segments of the entire conversion process. Many companies engage in the manufacture of fabricating materials and parts, equipment, or supplies for other companies. We have reached the point in the United States where the average company now buys slightly more than one half of the dollar value of its sales. In other words, its "value added by manufacture" is slightly less than 50% of its sales. Since the average company must purchase slightly over 50% as much as it sells, it is apparent that management of purchasing and materials is a vitally important activity to any company. Its profit may to a large measure be determined by how effectively it manages its materials.

Materials, supplies, and equipment are the very lifeblood of any functioning industrial concern, governmental agency, or commercial operation. No organization can operate without them. The efficiency of any business is contingent upon having them available in the proper quantity, with the proper quality, at the proper place and time, and at the proper price. Failure on any of these points adds to costs and decreases profit as surely as do outmoded production methods or ineffective selling techniques. This simple—almost obvious—point has only recently come to be properly understood by business. It is the purpose of this book to discuss the principles, methods, and strategies that are considered to represent the current best practices in this expanding and important field of industrial and governmental purchasing and materials management.

Purchasing is a managerial activity that goes beyond the simple act of buying, and it includes the planning and policy activities covering a wide range of related and complementary activities. Included in such activities are the research and development required for the proper selection of materials and sources; the follow-up to ensure proper delivery; the inspection of incoming shipments to ensure both quantity and quality compliance with the order; the development of proper procedures, methods, and forms to enable the purchasing department to carry out established policies; the coordination of the activities of the purchasing department with such other internal divisions of the concern such as traffic, receiving, storekeeping, and accounting, so as to facilitate smooth operations; and the development of a technique of effective communication with top management of the company so that a true picture of the performance of the purchasing function is presented.

In recent years, an organizational concept known as materials management has come into favor. Under this concept industrial purchasing is one of several activities dealing with the planning for, acquisition of, and utilization of materials in the process of producing goods. The ultimate organizational structure is such that all activities included in bringing materials into and through the plant[1] are combined under one head called the materials manager. The rationale for this organizational change is the fact that taken alone these functions often have conflicting objectives, for example, purchasing to assure adequate supply, inventory control to minimize inventory levels, traffic to secure full carloads, and so forth. By giving the materials manager overall authority, responsibility can also be delegated

---

[1] These include purchasing, inventory control, traffic, receiving, and production control.

to assure that the *overall* cost of materials is at the lowest possible level. The expanded use of EDP equipment has made it possible for the materials manager to control by exception this increased level of operations.

The concept of materials management as a function to obtain the lowest overall cost of materials to the purchasing firm will be utilized throughout this text by presenting the principles in each area as they relate to and interact with each other and purchasing operations.

There are few historical records of the origin of purchasing. This would be expected, since the first industrial purchase was made in the dim past when some individual bought materials or supplies to be used in making some article which he sold instead of using himself. Before the turn of the century there were limited instances of purchasing departments separate and distinct from production or some other operating department. Such purchasing departments as existed were found mostly in the railroad field. The first book dealing with the purchasing function specifically was published in 1887.[2] The fact that the earliest writings on the purchasing function were in railroad publications, on railroad purchasing, and written by railroad personnel can be explained by the predominance of railroad organizations in the economy of the country.[3]

At about the same time occasional articles began to appear in some of the technical trade publications dealing with some of the aspects of purchasing. One such article by James M. Cremer appeared in the August 1908 issue of *Cassier's Magazine*, an engineering publication. This article was entitled "The Engineer as a Purchasing Agent." In an article appearing in *Iron Age* in January 1913, John C. Jay, Jr., general manager of sales of the Pennsylvania Steel Corporation, suggested the organization of a group to promote the interests of purchasing agents through more adequate publicity of their activities. Though this article did not result in the immediate organization of the National Association of Purchasing Agents, it serves to indicate the emerging interest in the purchasing function.

The National Association of Purchasing Agents was founded during the early part of World War I—the period during which purchasing really came of age under the impact of the expanded

[2] Marshall M. Kirkman, *The Handling of Railway Supplies—Their Purchase and Disposition*, Chas. N. Trivess, Chicago, 1887, 233 pp.

[3] See "The Purchasing Function within Nineteenth Century Railroad Organizations," *Journal of Purchasing*, August 1965, for a comprehensive discussion of the early literature on purchasing by the railroads.

production brought about by the war. In approximately 60 years this organization has grown to over 18,000 members affiliated with more than 115 local chapters.

At its fifty-second annual convention in Washington, D.C. (May, 1967), this association voted to change its name to the National Association of Purchasing Management in recognition of the managerial status that purchasing agents have attained.

The role of purchasing in a large corporation is indicated by the size of Western Electric's purchasing organization, one of the largest in the nation. Sales in 1971 hit $6 billion. Purchasing and Transportation spent $2.6 billion. That $2.6 billion went to 50,000 suppliers, 90% of them in the small firm category. Over 2,500 people work for the Vice President of Purchasing and Transportation. Purchasing services over 60 field locations—service centers, regional offices, and manufacturing plants—across the country. Buyers place some 3 million orders per year covering 150,000 different items.[4]

Annual reports of industrial concerns frequently picture the importance of purchasing in graphic form by presenting data illustrating the disposition of their sales dollar. Typically, the major proportion of the sales dollar is expended on the purchase of goods and services. For a number of years, The First National City Bank of New York has prepared data in similar form showing the disposition of the sales dollar of the 100 largest U.S. corporations. The patterns have been remarkably consistent in showing that more than half of the sales dollar passes through the purchasing department.

Black and Decker's President Alonzo Decker sees purchasing's role in his company as essential.

> Management depends on purchasing to produce profits through savings developed from well planned and carefully executed purchasing programs. In addition, we count on our purchasing people to choose suppliers who are an extension of ourselves in that they operate their business efficiently .... Through its many contacts purchasing can be a valuable source of marketing information, price trends, competitors' activities as well as early warning of transportation and suppliers' work stoppages.[5]

There will be considerable variance between industries in the proportion of the sales dollar spent on purchasing goods and services. In

---

[4] C. H. Deutsch, "Purchasing at Western Electric: Keeping a Giant From Becoming Muscle-Bound," *Purchasing*, (December 19, 1972), p. 33.

[5] "What Company Presidents Say About Purchasing," *Purchasing*, (December 9, 1971), p. 47.

highly mechanized industries labor costs are low, and this fact tends to increase the proportion spent for goods and services. In mass-production, assembly-line industries there is likely to be a considerable amount of purchasing of fabricated parts and assemblies, and this kind of purchasing tends to keep the proportion of the sales dollar expended for goods and services high. For instance, the automobile industry spends from 50% to 60% of its sales dollar for goods and services. On the other hand, the extractive industries tend to have a low percentage of purchases because they work on their own raw materials. Craft industries, in which skilled labor is important, also tend to have a lower-than-average purchase percentage.

Service industries, such as railroads and public utilities, typically expend a small proportion of their sales dollar for goods and services. Once the original installation has been made—and it certainly involves a large amount of purchasing—labor costs become the predominant cost factor. Since both railroads and utilities supply service, they do not require raw materials as a manufacturing industry does. Most of their purchases, other than capital outlays, are for supplies, and these quite naturally keep the purchase percentage low.

PURCHASING OBJECTIVES

When a purchasing agent says that it is his responsibility to *buy materials of the right quality, in the right quantity, at the right time, at the right price, from the right source, with delivery at the right place*, he is in a general way stating the objectives of sound purchasing.

However, it is possible to be more specific in describing the objectives of purchasing. In most industrial concerns continuity of operations is of critical importance. The purchasing function must be so conducted as to minimize or eliminate disruptions in production resulting from the lack of any materials, equipment, or supplies. Furthermore, this objective must be achieved with a minimum investment in reserve inventories. Achieving this objective of security with a minimum investment demands a nice balancing of the factors of a risk of shutdown, the cost inherent in forward buying, and the economies of quantity purchases. Weighing these factors calls for experience and a high order of executive judgment.

Another objective of sound purchasing is the maintenance of adequate standards of quality for the items purchased. In industrial purchasing, quality refers primarily to the suitability of an item for its intended purpose. The objective is to procure goods that are best suited rather than those that rank highest in absolute quality. The purchasing agent strives to secure the desired quality at the lowest possible cost. His objective is lowest ultimate cost rather than lowest initial cost. In addition to product quality he must consider the services offered by the suppliers and evaluate these in the light of his company's need for the services. He may find that an initial low cost quoted by one supplier should be ignored in favor of a supplier with a higher initial cost whose favorable service factors indicate a lower ultimate cost on the entire transaction.

Still another objective of sound purchasing is the avoidance of duplication, waste, and obsolescence with respect to the various items purchased. The purchasing department can do much to eliminate these risks by viewing each purchase in the light of long-range operating plans as well as the short-range considerations giving rise to the immediate purchase.

The purchasing manager must also have as an objective the maintenance of his company's competitive position. To do this he must constantly examine his specifications to make sure that his company's quality standards are not higher than those of close competitors, particularly if the company's customers do not demand the higher quality in the goods they buy.

As a representative of his company dealing with many suppliers, a purchasing manager should have an external objective. He must be concerned with the suppliers' image of his company because this image may be an asset or a liability in the procurement of goods and services, as well as in many other ways. A good image will enable the purchasing agent to obtain valuable information that will facilitate its purchasing operations to uncover new ideas or materials that could lower its costs or improve its products, and to experience less difficulty in purchasing during periods of short supply.

A final objective of sound purchasing is the development of internal relationships that lead to understanding and harmony among the various organizational units within the company. Because the purchasing manager buys everything from heavy equipment used in production to pencils used by the office force, he does business with every division of the organization. To be successful he must secure the respect and assistance of all his associates and interact in all management decisions areas where materials costs and controls are involved. However, one of the problems faced by purchasing personnel is that of "educating" top management to their overall profit contributing potential. Studies have indicated that purchasing is often left out of generalized corporate decisions, which often might benefit significantly by their input. Table 1-1 illustrates this fact and highlights the need for purchasing personnel to acquaint management with all facets of their skills.

TABLE 1-1. The Role of the Purchasing Manager
in Non-Purchasing Decisions

Purchasing's View (in percent)	Type of Decision	Management's View (in percent)
68	Market and Price Forecasting	41
68	Long-Range Planning	35
61	Major Product Changes	47
58	Acquisition Planning	26
56	Facilities Planning	41
44	Trade Relations	35
40	Financial Planning	23

Source. Dr. Dean S. Ammer, "Management Doesn't See Purchasing the Same Way We See It," *N.A.P.M. Bulletin*, July 1974, p. 3.

MANAGEMENT EXPECTATIONS

To contribute effectively and completely the materials and purchasing manager must act within the framework of management expectations. The following is an excerpt of a speech on this subject.[6]

The most important issue facing Materials Managers is what management expects of the Materials Manager.

Likewise, the productivity of the whole profession hinges on the cooperation and motivation resulting from management meeting the vocational and personal needs of the purchasing employee.

First of all, what does management expect from purchasing?

It seems very obvious that management expects proficiency in basic purchasing expertise and skills. This is a "given"—necessary to continue efficient operation of the manufacturing or service entity. Let me identify some skills I consider important.

---

[6] Dr. G. J. Zenz, "What Management Expects of Purchasing—What Purchasing Expects of Management—1975," Speech to 59th International Purchasing Managers Convention, May 6, 1974. Also reprinted in *Michigan Purchasing Management*, June 1974, p. 22.

Negotiation

First of all, the purchasing man must be able to negotiate effectively with suppliers at all levels of management while at the same time building their respect and confidence. This is an art which requires the ability to know when to stop during an interchange in which both parties attempt to maximize positions. The supplier is attempting to obtain the highest possible price while the buyer must reduce price to the lowest possible level. Therefore, the art of negotiation is to push price into a "reasonable" area while still obtaining respect and cooperation. The act of negotiation naturally also extends to the other purchasing/sales variables such as delivery times, terms, etc.

Contract formulation

Another technical aspect of the purchasing function involves proficiency in contract formulation procedures particularly as to blanket contracts and translating same to multi-plant situations.

EDP

Continuing with purchasing's technical needs include the ability to utilize electronic data processing equipment. This must include knowledge as to applications where the computer can assume clerical burdens and maximize information retrieval. In my experience this is one of the main areas of technical expertise that is being sought in purchasing people.

Materials Management

Management is increasingly concerned with the cost and control of materials as a separate and distinct profit center. Accordingly the material management concept, which incorporates all functions involved in obtaining and bringing materials into the plant is being viewed as the answer to many coordination and cross-control problems. Therefore, management is expecting to find purchasing people who have the necessary expertise to organize and administer all the functions involved in the material flow which includes inventory control, receiving, traffic, purchasing and in some cases production control. The individual who can fill this position needs to understand the fundamentals of the activities involved in each of these areas. Normally, purchasing personnel have close contact with all of the activities but in some cases lack the in depth knowledge of specific techniques particularly in areas of inventory and production control. Therefore, it behooves the purchasing man to be aware of this expertise need and to take the necessary steps to educate himself, either by occupational interaction or by formal educational effort, in these areas.

Commodity Futures/Hedging

As we face the future, the concern of erratic and often violent price changes will be even more pronounced, mainly resulting from an international scarcity of many base raw materials. Therefore, the purchasing man must be knowledgeable in all possibilities of risk avoidance including applications of commodity futures trading. By use of hedging techniques, costs can be predetermined and sales prices protected long before physical stock is received. Likewise, declining inventory values can be cushioned without liquidating physical stock, and in many cases favorable prices can be obtained without need for contracts with specific suppliers. In addition, international purchases can be safeguarded against currency fluctuations by means of international currency hedges. Therefore, tomorrow's purchasing manager should expend the effort necessary to educate himself to the functioning of commodity and currency markets and master the techniques of hedging.

Professionalism

Lastly, and certainly not least in terms of the technical aspects of the purchasing position, management looks for evidence of professionalism on part of the candidate. This includes evidence of affiliation with local and national purchasing organizations, as well as participation in those activities directed toward improving personal abilities such as communication, comprehension, etc.

In addition to the expertise prerequisites, management also expects administrative abilities in its purchasing people. This involves the organizational ability to recruit, direct, and motivate peers and subordinates. Empathy and a keen sense of individual motivation and patience are needed to obtain maximum performance from others. The ability to express oneself effectively in a written manner to management is also necessary to this task. And, I have already indicated the specific organizational and administrative challenge presented by the materials management concept.

Appearance

Such things as a pleasing personal appearance are evidence of concern for his own physical well being. Several studies have recently been announced that something like 80 percent of the people who advance in management ranks are considered to be within 5 pounds of their "ideal" weight. It seems to me that there is a definite discrimination in management circles today against overweight individuals.

Motivation

Other personal considerations include the self-motivating aspect of the individual. Is he a person who waits for direction or does he constantly attempt to find new areas which he can make contributions to the organization?

Ethics

Lastly, very great concern in the management job specification is the high personal ethics on part of purchasing personnel. In the wake of Watergate and other scandals which have been brought to the public's attention in the last several years, management realizes the increasing importance of having individuals safeguarding the purchasing dollar who have only the very highest ethical and moral standards.

To the extent that the expectations of management are met, along with continuing education purchasing's present and potential contributions to overall corporate decisions, efficiency in American corporations will significantly benefit.

PURCHASING FUNCTIONS

There are two approaches that may be taken in analyzing the work performed by a purchasing department. One approach requires a detailed study of the hours spent at the various tasks performed by the personnel of the department. These data can then be classified and tabulated on some meaningful basis. The other approach requires a qualitative study of the activities of a purchasing department. Activities may be divided into those that are almost always assigned to the purchasing department and those that are sometimes assigned to some other department.

In succeeding paragraphs the second approach to what is done in a purchasing department will be followed. In a sense this section is a preview or outline of the entire book.

Recognition of Need

Any purchase transaction starts with the recognition of the need for an item by someone in the company. Generally, the need is recognized by the individual in charge of a using department such as the foreman of one of the manufacturing operations, the office manager, or the maintenance engineer. The need may often be satisfied by a transfer of materials from another department or from a reserve stock storeroom. However, eventually the storeroom must replenish its supplies of the requisitioned item. Thus one can say that directly or indirectly purchases stem from the recognition of need for an item by a using department.

For many items a well-run purchasing department will anticipate the needs of using departments. Anticipating advance needs is one of the considerations that enters into the determination of the size of the order for items that are used with some regularity in a plant. In such cases the purchasing officer buys a quantity sufficient to reduce the likelihood of "rush" orders in case of sudden increases in the rate of consumption of the item. A purchasing officer should also, as a part of anticipating needs, develop alternative sources of supply and potential alternative materials. Though he does not buy alternative materials on his own initiative, he should call such possibilities to the attention of the using departments and make the purchase with their approval if it is indicated.

Description of the Need

Once the need has been recognized, it must be so accurately described that all parties will know exactly what is wanted. An improperly or poorly described need can be costly. Time is lost when it becomes necessary to check back on a requisition. An improper description is especially unfortunate when it is not discovered until after the order has been placed. In some cases the order may be filled and the goods issued from the storeroom to the using department before the error is observed. At this point it may be difficult to convince the supplier that he should accept the goods for return without some price adjustment. Besides such losses there is the cost of handling the goods and freight from and to the supplier's plant.

Securing an adequate and complete description of needs calls for the exercise of tact on the part of the purchasing officer. He must have enough knowledge of the items being purchased to be able to recognize inadequate descriptions. However, under no circumstances should a purchasing officer change a description that appears to him to be inadequate or interpret a description for the seller if he is in doubt about it. He should never substitute something that he thinks is better suited or assume that the using department does not really know what it wants. Even in a case where there is an obvious error on the requisition it should be standard procedure for the buyer to request a corrected requisition from the using department.

It has been found in practice that insistence on accurate descriptions from the using departments promotes harmony in an organization. Such insistence leads the using departments to place greater confidence in the purchasing department. If a purchasing officer assumes responsibility for changing requisitions that he thinks are wrong, sooner or later he will make a mistake, resulting in a shipment of materials that the using department did not want and, perhaps, cannot use. Then friction between the departments is almost inevitable.

Selection of Sources

The next step in the purchase transaction is the selection of the source or sources for the requisitioned item. For branded or patented items there may be but a single source. However, for most purchases there will be a number of alternative suppliers from which one must ultimately be selected. The manner in which the purchasing department selects a source depends to a considerable extent on whether the item is bought regularly or is one that has seldom, if ever, been bought before. In the former case the purchasing officer will have a group of approved sources with which he has dealt in the past. His selection of the one to be favored with the current order will depend on such considerations as price, his desire to allocate his orders so as to maintain the goodwill of alternative sources as a safety factor, his company's reciprocity policies, and similar considerations.

For items that have not been purchased with sufficient regularity for the development of a list of approved sources there are several things that a purchasing officer may do. As a preliminary step he will consult such sources of information as salesmen who call on him, his file of vendor's catalogs, the trade press, and suggestions from the using department, in order to prepare a list of possible suppliers. His next step is to narrow this list down by means of investigations, salesman interviews, and plant visitations until he has a small group of possible suppliers with whom he can carry on further negotiations. These negotiations will eventually lead to the choice of one or more —depending on company policy—to whom the order is awarded.

Ascertaining the Price

During the process of selecting a source the purchasing department must ascertain price information on the item being purchased. Price will be one of the important factors on which the final choice is based. Although some purchasing departments place small orders without specifying the price, the more usual practice is to include the price in the order. This practice is based on the sound premise that price is one of the essential terms of any agreement which must be accepted by both parties to constitute a legally binding agreement.

For items that have been bought repeatedly in the past, sufficient price information is readily available in the records and files of the purchasing department. Even for purchases of the same item from a given source it occasionally is necessary to consult other sources of price information to be assured that the price of the supplier is competitive and that he is not relying on the buyer's lethargy to hold the business.

For many items it is possible to keep current price information in the form of manufacturer's catalogs, price lists, and discount schedules. Such sources of information must be kept up to date. Although catalog prices are not binding on the seller, since they are not legal offers, most manufacturers endeavor to avoid misunderstandings by supplying customers with current price lists and discount schedules.

A second method of securing price information is to negotiate with the seller until agreement is reached in price and terms. This method is especially suited to goods made to the specifications of the buyer. The negotiation method tends to remove the transaction from the area of keen price competition, but, if the supplier has been chosen on a sound basis, the method has certain advantages. It is a more flexible method of buying, in that it permits adjustments in requirements and specifications, that are difficult to effect when standard items are bought from price lists or when items are bought on a bid basis.

A third method that a purchasing department can employ to secure price information is the competitive bid. This method is widely used by governmental purchasing departments because of statutory requirements, but it is occasionally employed also by industrial purchasing departments, especially for buying fabricated parts that are to be incorporated into a finished product. From the point of view of competition among suppliers on an equitable and open basis this method is desirable. However, the time it requires precludes its extensive use. A considerable amount of time is consumed in securing prices in this manner compared with price lists or negotiations.

Placing the Order

Probably the first thought that comes to mind when purchasing is mentioned is the placing of an order with a supplier. However, as we have seen, there is a considerable amount of work that must be done prior to this step. Although this step is a routine culmination of previous purchasing activities and is usually performed in the physical sense by a clerk, it is vital that the head of the purchasing department keep a close control over the activity.

All orders should be in writing and should be on the buyer's purchase order. To avoid the possibility of legal difficulties, it is customary for the buyer to use his company's form rather than the vendor's sales order. There usually are a limited number of individuals authorized to sign and place purchase orders that commit the company to the expenditure of funds.

Follow-Up of the Order

It should not be supposed that once an order has been placed, the purchasing department has no further responsibilities. Almost every purchasing department has the responsibility for following up orders that it places. For example, the seller may not have received the order even though it has been mailed. Also, as has been stated, one of the objectives of purchasing is delivery at the right time and the right place. To insure delivery when and where needed, it is necessary to institute a follow-up procedure for all orders placed with suppliers. Theoretically, follow-up should not be necessary when suppliers have been selected on the basis of their reliability. However, every concern finds that some follow-up of orders is essential.

Responsibility for follow-up is generally assigned to the buyer who placed the order. The clerical work may be done by an expediter or follow-up clerk who keeps the necessary records and forms and takes routine actions. Orders requiring special action are referred to the buyer, and the responsibility is his.

Some companies put the responsibility for follow-up of orders on the production planning or control division. This assignment is based on the logic that delays in receipt of goods must be reflected immediately in production plans. It is reasoned that the production planning or control division will be best able to make the required adjustments and also that this division is likely to be more aggressive in preventing delays. This reasoning, however, is contrary to the sound principle of organization that requires that authority be coequal with responsibility. Since the purchasing department is responsible for delivery at the proper time and place, that department should be given full authority for bringing about such delivery. Furthermore, it is confusing to the supplier to be required to deal with two parties in the buyer's organization.

Follow-up consists essentially of holding a supplier to his promise of delivery. During World War II purchasing departments were unusually concerned over the time of delivery, and the practice of expediting came into general use. Many companies had several expediters constantly traveling among their suppliers. Although many purchasing men use the terms "follow-up" and "expediting" interchangeably, there should be a distinct difference between the two, as is indicated by their dictionary definitions. Follow-up is defined as "pertaining to repeated action"; expediting is defined as "accelerating the process or progress."

The follow-up of a purchase order thus involves regular communication with a supplier until an explicit acceptance of the order is received and a commitment made as to delivery date. At this point, if it is deemed necessary, the purchasing department may attempt to expedite the order—that is, attempt to secure earlier delivery. Ideally, all orders should be followed up to the extent of receipt of an acceptance and, if possible, a delivery promise. However, in practice this is not always done, because some items are so standardized that last-minute deliveries from an alternate source can be secured. Other items are so low in value and so unimportant to the production process as to preclude the expenditure of time and effort in follow-up procedures. In general, it may be said that follow-up procedures should be employed whenever the costs or risks resulting from delayed deliveries or nondeliveries are greater than the cost of the follow-up procedure.

Checking Invoices

There is a difference of opinion as to whether invoices should be checked by the purchasing department or the accounting department. It is recommended here that invoice checking be a part of the purchasing function, since receipt of the invoice constitutes the usual notification that the supplier has made shipment. This notification is essential to the operation of a successful follow-up policy.

A number of other reasons can be advanced for assigning the function of invoice checking to the purchasing department. It is part of a buyer's responsibilities to see that his orders are accurately filled and billed. In the event of errors, it is the buyer's duty to contact the supplier in order to secure a correction or an adjustment. Time is important in these matters, and, if the accounting department makes the invoice check, there will be some delay in referring errors to the purchasing department before they can be taken up with the supplier.

Since the purchasing department is most familiar with its own terms and intentions in placing an order, it can most readily detect discrepancies and can do so in time to institute corrective action before the invoice is paid. Finally, no purchase transaction is completed until the goods have been paid for at the proper price. As was stated previously, securing the proper price is one of the objectives of sound purchasing. The buyer can only be certain of having done so if he sees and checks the invoices for all goods he has purchased.

There is some merit in the arguments advanced in favor of invoice checking by the accounting department. Basically, the checking of invoices is an accounting procedure, which can be handled efficiently by the accounting department. Unfortunately, when an accounting department checks an invoice, the procedure tends to become a routine clerical procedure. Invoice checking should involve more than an examination of footings and extensions. It is equally important to make certain that there has been compliance with the description and specifications contained on the purchase order.

Another argument in favor of assigning invoice checking to the accounting department concerns the need for processing invoices for payment with sufficient promptness to ensure eligibility for cash discounts. This is not a compelling argument, since a procedure can be established and followed by a purchasing department that will assure prompt clearance of invoices.

A final argument in favor of invoice checking by the accounting department is that, with this method, one department is verifying the accuracy of another department's work. Even though a system of checks and balances is recognized as good organizational practice, it does not appear to be necessary in this case, as these invoices will be subject to internal auditing by the accounting department at some later date.

Maintenance of Records and Files

Still another task of a purchasing department is the maintenance of records and files pertaining to purchase transactions. Since a large proportion of all purchases of industrial firms are repeat orders, these files are consulted frequently and are essential to the proper functioning of the purchasing department. The typical buyer will find it necessary many times each week to refer back to the records of previous transactions to guide him in current dealings with suppliers.

They are particularly important in selecting sources of supply for current purchases.

It should be remembered that purchase orders are legal contracts and as such should be preserved for as long as they have legal significance. Requisitions and similar documents should be preserved by the purchasing department, since they constitute the authority on which the purchasing department took its action to buy a given item.

Maintenance of Vendor Relations

An important part of purchasing is the maintenance of good relations with the vendors with whom the company deals. Good relations are based on the mutual trust and confidence. These grow out of dealings between buyer and seller over a period of time.

Too much emphasis cannot be placed on the importance of this phase of purchasing. It has often been said that the worth of a purchasing department can be measured by the amount of goodwill it has with its suppliers. Such goodwill helps the purchasing department to achieve its objectives of buying the right goods in terms of quality, quantity, price, time, and place.

OTHER MATERIALS MANAGEMENT ACTIVITIES

In the pages that follow, those activities that are usually associated with materials management are mentioned briefly. These include traffic, receiving, stores (both storekeeping and inventory control), inspection, and surplus and scrap disposal. No attempt is made at this point to discuss in detail the policies and procedures followed when these activities are carried on in a materials organization. This discussion is devoted primarily to an analysis of the reasons for and against the assignment of these activities to the purchasing of materials.

Traffic

The traffic function is a specialized phase of management dealing with such matters as selection of methods of shipment, routings of shipments, rate schedules, and claims. In any business organization there are traffic problems concerning incoming shipments and outgoing shipments. It is the former that is of primary interest to the purchasing department.

The purchasing officer must have goods available at the time they are needed, at the place they are needed, and at the lowest possible cost. Traffic management is clearly related to the manner in which these responsibilities are met. The incorrect choice of carrier or route can delay a shipment and add to the transportation costs.

The question arises whether traffic management can best be handled as a subsidiary activity of the purchasing department or as a distinct activity in a separate department. If it is assigned to the purchasing department, care must be exercised to see that this responsibility is not slighted. Some of the larger companies that assign the traffic activity to the purchasing department put a particular person in charge of traffic who reports directly to the head of the purchasing department, even though he does most of his work in conjunction with the various buyers. Other companies believe, perhaps rightfully, that traffic management is a specialized and highly technical business activity and as such should not be subordinated to any other division in the company. A separate department seems especially appropriate where the traffic management of outgoing shipments is important.

Receiving

It can be argued that the receipt of incoming materials and supplies is merely a step in the process of securing items for use at the proper time and place. Accordingly, some companies give full control over the receiving function to the purchasing department. However, a larger proportion gives the purchasing department only indirect control. That is, a separate receiving department is established, and the head of this department is organizationally independent of the purchasing department although he must work closely with that department.

The receiving activity is largely clerical in nature. A report must be prepared describing the type and quantity of material in the incoming shipment. Sometimes the receiving clerk also inspects the shipment and includes the inspection results in the receiving report. This report is usually made on specially designed receiving slips or forms, which have space for the vendor's name and the order number so as to permit ready identification of the shipment.

The purchasing department should have control over or close contact with the receiving department for several reasons. Before an invoice is cleared for payment, the buyer has to verify the fact that the shipment agrees in all respects with the description on the invoice. Since it has been advocated that purchasing departments assume responsibility for checking invoices, it follows that the department must have close contact with or control over receiving.

A second reason for close working relations arises from the need for fast action in certain situations that a receiving department may uncover. When goods are damaged in shipment, legal requirements demand prompt action if a claim is to be registered with the vendor or the carrier. If there is close contact with or direct control over receiving, the purchasing department is likely to be notified immediately in such a situation and can take the necessary actions of submitting a claim and locating a substitute supply of the material if the need is urgent. A similar situation would be faced in the receipt of short shipments from the supplier, which, if not acted on promptly, could lead to work stoppages because of lack of materials.

A reason that may be advanced for control of receiving by the purchasing department is that it may lead to a more efficient receiving operation. It frequently happens that incoming shipments of raw materials are so large that they must be anticipated by several days in order to permit planning for space, materials-handling equipment, and personnel. Although such advance information can be supplied by an independent purchasing department to the receiving department, proper planning is more likely to be done if the receiving activity is a direct responsibility of the purchasing department.

Inspection

Inspection of incoming shipments is closely related to the receiving activity and in the case of simple commodities may be done by the receiving clerk. Receiving checks the shipment for quantity and identity, whereas inspection checks the shipment for quality. Inspection responsibility may also be assigned to the production department, to a separate inspection department, or to the purchasing department.

Since the production department specifies what should be purchased, it is argued that the department should also pass on the shipments when they are received. Another reason for assigning this responsibility to production is that this department is held responsible for defects that appear in the finished products, and it should therefore have the right to inspect purchased goods before they enter the process. Furthermore, it is argued that such an independent inspection will minimize the possibility of collusion between buyer and seller. It is also sometimes said that a buyer will hesitate to reject borderline cases of inferior quality, because rejections of incoming shipments reflect unfavorably on the buyer's ability to select a proper source of supply.

The last two arguments may be advanced as well in favor of assigning the inspection activity to a separate department. In addition, it is likely that a separate department will be staffed by expert inspectors who can do a better job and save time in clearing incoming shipments for transfer or the production department. Such individuals are more likely to be developed by an independent inspection department than by the production department.

Where the goods are not technical, there are reasons for assigning inspection to the purchasing department. A close relationship is developed between the inspector and the buyer. This may be important in case of the rejection of a shipment, since the buyer is likely to be notified more quickly and he can take corrective steps at once. When inspection is under the purchasing department, it can be helpful to the buyers in developing specifications and in evaluating quality in relation to price in the process of selecting sources. Also, close relations between inspectors and buyers facilitate the evaluation of samples submitted by salesmen.

Where it is necessary to utilize an outside testing agency or commercial laboratory because inspection requirements are complicated or expensive, the responsibility for inspection is almost invariably placed on the purchasing department. Or, when it is necessary that a shipment be inspected before it is shipped by the supplier, the inspection responsibility is similarly placed on the purchasing department. Such inspection, known as field inspection, takes place at the supplier's plant. The reason for the assignment of field inspection to the purchasing department is the desire to keep all contacts with suppliers within a single department, since it has been found that this contributes to good supplier relations.

Storekeeping

Storekeeping is frequently and erroneously looked on as a clerical activity to be assigned to a poorly paid clerk. This attitude is unfortunate, because the careful handling of stores and the maintenance of accurate control over them are essential to efficient operations. Since storekeeping is closely related to both production and purchasing, it is natural that there should be a divergence of opinion concerning the responsibility for storekeeping.

It is estimated that more than one half of all industrial concerns place stores under the control of the production department. The following reasons can be advanced for this practice. Since stores must be located close to the using departments, they should be under the control of these departments. Certain types of stores require special materials-handling equipment which is generally available in the production department. The assignment of storekeeping to the production department also enables a company to establish an internal check on inventories through the separation of buying from storing of the goods.

A number of sound arguments may be advanced for assigning storekeeping to the purchasing department. Production managers are primarily interested in the production process and might be inclined to minimize the importance of storekeeping. Storekeeping is primarily a supply function, and the purchasing department is interested in the entire supply function of a company's operation. Furthermore, the flow of requisitions on stores eventually necessitates replenishment of stores, and it may be contended that the need for replenishment will be recognized earlier if storekeeping is a responsibility of the purchasing department.

Inventory Control

Closely related to the physical handling of stores is the system of inventory control. The purpose of inventory control is the preservation of an adequate and balanced inventory of materials and supplies with a minimum investment, so as to reduce storage and handling costs, obsolescence and deterioration risks, insurance, and interest charges, and the risks of price level changes.

Here again there is divergence of opinion with respect to responsibility. However, there is general agreement that policy matters with regard to inventory are a top-management responsibility. Procedures for carrying out the policies are delegated.

There is a growing trend among industrial concerns toward the establishment of an independent department to handle the planning and scheduling of materials as a part of its larger responsibility for production planning and control. Such organizational control is especially desirable when the kinds of items purchased change frequently, as in the automobile industry, which changes models annually. Under this plan of organization, the inventory control unit has no policy control over the inventory level of stores. It merely initiates requisitions when the supply of a store's item reaches the reorder point. The requisition is made out for a quantity that will build up the inventory to the preestablished maximum stock level. All requisitions are cleared through this planning and control department before being forwarded to purchasing, where they become the basis for placing orders.

In a substantial number of smaller industrial concerns, inventory control is a direct responsibility of the purchasing department. This is especially true when storekeeping has been put under the purchasing department. In a small company that cannot have an elaborate organization, the assignment of inventory control to the purchasing department has merit, since inventory control deals/with matters closely related to the purchasing process.

Although some concerns have placed inventory control under the manufacturing or production department, there seems to be no real justification for such an assignment. The production executive can be expected to make certain that he/she does not run short of any item used in the production process. The result is that he/she slights the principle of an adequate inventory at a *reasonable cost*. Excess inventory that will add to both cost and obsolescence risk may be anticipated.

It might be argued that, if the purchasing department were responsible for inventory control, the opposite would take place, and inventory shortages would occur. It must be admitted that this likelihood is increased, but under normal business conditions the risk is not unduly serious. For most industrial materials and supplies it is not especially difficult to correct a shortage with but slight delay. The additional costs are likely to be small compared with the continuing costs and risks entailed in regularly carrying excessive inventories.

Scrap and Surplus Disposal

A responsibility frequently assigned to the purchasing department is the disposal of scrap that originates in the production processes, materials that have been classed as surplus, and materials that have become obsolete through technological improvements or changes in the production process.

One could argue that this is not a proper purchasing activity, because it involves a sale and not a purchasing transaction. Many a purchasing agent has humorously suggested that the assignment of scrap disposal is made to the purchasing department because no other department wants it. There undoubtedly is some truth in the jest, although a case can be made for the purchasing department being in charge of scrap disposal.

In the sale of certain nonferrous metals, it is quite common in periods of shortage for the vendor to include a provision in the sales contract requiring that all scrap be resold to the vendor. In such a case the connection between the purchasing department and scrap disposal is obvious. Furthermore, although a certain amount of scrap is inevitable in any production process, it is possible to hold scrap to a minimum by the purchase of the most favorable sizes and qualities, and the purchasing department is in the best position to control these conditions. A few companies hold that the cost of scrap is a part of materials cost and that its original value is chargeable to the purchasing department. This procedure does not seem altogether reasonable since the control of scrap generated in the production process is as much a function of production planning as it is of careful purchasing.

If the goods to be disposed of are surplus or obsolete materials, the facts would appear to indicate a degree of responsibility on the part of the purchasing department. If the surplus or obsolete materials resulted from materials overbuying, the responsibility properly rests with the purchasing department. However, if the cause was a technological change, it could be argued that the purchasing department was the innocent victim. Actually, this is a poor defense, since a well-run purchasing department should be organized so as to learn early of contemplated changes in materials or methods that might bring about surplus or obsolete materials.

Perhaps the soundest reason for assigning disposal to the purchasing department is that the purchasing officer is most thoroughly acquainted with market conditions and price trends. The scrap market is erratic, and one must have current and accurate information if he is to operate successfully in that market. One must also be interested in the proper classification of scrap in order to obtain the highest prices. Experience suggests that the production department tends to be lax in maintaining proper segregation of scrap. A final reason for disposing of scrap through the purchasing department is that materials that are scrap, surplus, or obsolete in one division of a company may be of value in some other division. Since the purchasing department knows about the requirements of each division, it is in the best position to bring about transfers of such materials whenever this solution is possible.

SUMMARY

This chapter has described the role of purchasing and materials management in business management by highlighting the costs and interrelatedness of materials to aspects of the business decision process. Overall effectiveness would be enhanced by better communication of purchasing personnel with top management, and a review of management's expectations was presented. Finally, a brief review of specifics of the purchasing and materials functions was presented to set the framework for the following organizational and procedural chapters.

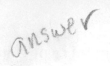

DISCUSSION QUESTIONS

1. Indicate the relationship between the organizational concept of materials management and field of purchasing.

2. Outline the important factors the purchasing manager must consider in order to provide continuity of production.

3. Indicate the rationale for having follow-up handled by purchasing rather than another department.

4. Delineate positive arguments for assigning the invoice checking function to the purchasing department.

5. In what manner does purchasing aid production?

6. Define purchasing in the broad sense as discussed in the text.

7. What is the purchasing agent's responsibility in respect to quality of purchased parts?

8. What are the objectives of purchasing activities?

9. What does management expect of its purchasing department?

10. What are the steps involved in the complete purchasing function?

CHAPTER 2
ORGANIZATION FOR PURCHASING

Organization is needed when people are jointly trying to reach some common goal. A person alone in a wilderness with the goal of survival does not need organization, unless one were to stretch the term to apply to the person's internal integration of plans and actions. Similarly, a group of people relaxing on a beach do not need organization because they have no joint objective. However, if a group of people are put into an inhospitable wilderness from which they wish to save themselves they will quickly devise an organizational pattern. The organization may be thought of as the harness that enables each person to apply his individual effort toward accomplishing the defined goal.

A good organization is essential if the efforts of each individual are to be optimized. In a poor organization the efforts of some may be largely nullified by the efforts of others working at cross-purposes. The efforts of some may be less productive than they might be because their organizational harness may not be properly integrated with that of other parts of the total organization. The secret of good organization, then, is to provide a comfortable harness for everyone and to see that the various segments of the total are so well integrated that everyone is working toward the same goal with maximum effectiveness.

Organization may be thought of in two dimensions. One deals with motivating the individuals and subgroups of the total organization to get them to contribute optimally. The other deals with the pattern of formal interrelationships that tie the members of the group together. These dimensions often find expression in organizational charts. It is this aspect of the organization of purchasing that we shall emphasize.

The most significant recent change in purchasing organization involves a movement toward uniting purchasing with other departments dealing with materials under a single responsible executive. This practice is usually referred to as the materials management concept. In this chapter the elementary considerations involved in organizing a purchasing department are presented, including the need for and advisability of a staff-and-line approach, and centralization versus decentralization of purchasing operations. Next, significant interdepartmental relationships involving purchasing and other functions are examined. The chapter is concluded with a discussion of what the materials management concept means, the extent of its recent growth, and the factors in the business and materials environment that have contributed to its acceptance.

There is much to be derived from sound organization. Responsibilities are clearly assigned to the personnel in the organization, which assures that all activities will be performed, but with no duplication of effort. A sound organization also clearly defines authority so that each individual in the organization knows to whom he reports and who reports to him. This definition of authority tends to lessen friction between individuals. Another benefit of sound organization is the saving in time for executives. With proper assignment of responsibility and authority, most routine decisions can be handled by a subordinate, and the executive can devote her time to broad procedural and policy matters.

Sound organizational structure also permits a chain of promotion to be established. As a concomitant of sound organization it is usual to find the development of job specifications. These in turn facilitate training of individuals for their own positions and for the positions immediately above them. The existence of such a chain of promotion and systematic training for promotion greatly strengthens and improves morale within an organization. Finally, a sound organization will promote harmony among the component parts of the organization. There is less possibility of jealousy or jurisdictional rivalry if the organizational responsibilities are clearly outlined.

It should be recognized that there are distinct limitations to what can be achieved through organization, and there are certain organizational weaknesses to be avoided in setting up a business organization. An inherent limitation to any organization is the personnel who staff it. The best principles of organization are of little value if the personnel who are assigned to carry out the various responsibilities are incapable of doing so. It frequently happens that organizational principles must be compromised so as to assign responsibilities to capable personnel. It is a recognized fact that most company organization charts do not accurately reflect the lines of authority and responsibility which flow through persons as well as their positions.

A second factor to consider is the possibility of overorganizing. There are many organizations in which all duties and responsibilities are so minutely defined that excessive red tape results. Overorganization leads to a slowing down of decision making because the channel to the decision-making executive is too long or too devious. A highly refined organization can be made to run smoothly by retaining policy control at the upper levels, with authority and responsibility delegated to lower levels subject only to reporting and review. On the whole, there is greater risk of poor performance through underorganizing than there is through overorganizing.

In purchasing there are two major organizational problems: (1) the place of the purchasing department in the overall company structure and, (2) the internal organization of the purchasing department. Two basic issues are involved in the first problem: (a) the desired degree of centralization of the purchasing function within the company, and (b) the executive (or division) to whom the purchasing officer should be responsible.

CENTRALIZATION IN THE MULTIPLE-PLANT FIRM

The question arises of decentralizing purchasing activities in each plant of a multiple-plant firm versus centralization at the home office of the firm. There is considerable variation among industrial companies in dealing with this issue. The soundest procedure would seem to be the centralization of all policy matters and the purchase of major raw materials and equipment in the home office. The individual plants then make other purchases in accordance with policies established by the home office.

There are several reasons for a substantial amount of purchasing autonomy by the branch plant. Most branch plants are operated as distinct entities, with the branch manager held responsible for the operations of his plant in an efficient and economical manner. Because materials and supplies used in the plant have a direct bearing on the efficiency and economy of operations, it follows that the branch manager should have control over their purchase.

Another reason for decentralizing purchasing to branch plants is the probable delay if all matters must be channeled through a home office. Such a procedure would require branch plants to maintain higher reserve inventories of materials and supplies to compensate for the extra time involved in purchasing through the home-office purchasing department.

A third reason for decentralization is the better public relations that develop with the communities in which a firm has its plants. Local purchasing tends to be neglected in a centralized purchasing system. Such purchasing has proved to be one foundation of sound community relations for industrial plants and should not be disregarded.

In a multiple-plant firm in which each plant manufactures different products the case for decentralized purchasing is even clearer, since so many of the requirements will differ for each plant. Furthermore, there are frequently local conditions such as transportation facilities, storage facilities, climatic conditions, or local laws and customs that may not be fully understood and appreciated by a home-office purchasing department. Purchases should be made in the light of local conditions, and centralized purchasing in a multiple-plant operation may not be able to cope with all of the local conditions found in widely scattered plant locations. Even in the situations described the home office should get detailed reports of all items purchased so that contracts can be let for standard items that give the company full advantage of quantity discounts.

From the point of view of suppliers, it is costly to have salesmen calling on plant managers or other prospects in branch plants who have no authority to place orders directly but must work through a home-office purchasing department.

Some purchasing agents, however, argue strongly for centralization of purchasing for branch plants, although they usually concede that emergency orders must occasionally be placed locally. Several reasons are advanced for centralization. It is argued that a company should be managed as an entity, and this means that its materials program should also be coordinated. Furthermore, one reason for having a large company is to realize economies of scale. Such economies should be sought in purchasing as well as in other areas. For instance, with home-office control of purchasing, it is possible to transfer surplus materials more readily from one plant to another than when each plant does its own buying.

It is also argued that a centralized organization permits a degree of specialization among buyers that is not possible in a smaller organization. Such specialization leads to greater knowledge of the commodities and market conditions and results in more skillful buying.

ASSIGNMENT OF RESPONSIBILITY
FOR PURCHASING

The second organization problem involving the purchasing department in an industrial concern is: "To whom should the purchasing agent report?" The answer to this question tends to define the status of purchasing in an organization. For the present we shall disregard the materials management form of organization, reserving those special considerations for the last portion of this chapter.

Purchasing has been accepted as a major line activity in a large proportion of business organizations. This means that in a home office organization of a well-managed multiplant company, or the company organization of a large single plant company, the head of purchasing reports to a general management executive rather than to the head of another line department. Where the organization is small enough so that the span of control will permit it, the purchasing executive may report directly to the president of the corporation or to the executive vice-president. In larger organizations he may report to the vice-president in charge of operations or to the controller. These executives then report directly to the president.

When the purchasing executive reports to someone other than the president or executive vice president the responsible executive should have broad enough authority so that he will not be inclined to subordinate purchasing considerations to those of another line activity. It is obvious that purchasing activities have implications for the finance executive or for the manufacturing executive, but it would be unsound to subordinate purchasing (which spends about 50% of a company's revenues) to the limited objectives of the finance or manufacturing executives. Therefore, wherever possible purchasing should report to the president or some executive with a broad view of corporate objectives.

There is some justification for having the head of purchasing report to the top financial officer in an organization that operates under a fixed budget. This would be the case for schools, hospitals, prisons, and government units. In these institutions priority consideration must be given to purchasing within the limits prescribed by the budget.

It should also be noted that the local purchasing executive of a multiplant company will in all probability report to the plant manager who is principally a manufacturing supervisor, since management usually wants to make him responsible for the entire local operation.

Tables of Organization

The tables of organization that follow are designed to graphically illustrate the various ways in which a purchasing department may fit into a company's organization chart. Later in this chapter we shall consider the internal organization of the purchasing department in both large and small firms.

Figure 2-1 presents an example of the type of organization chart most frequently found in medium-sized firms. Purchasing is assigned as a direct line function under the control of the head of the organization. The director of purchases has sufficient status and authority to prevent the likelihood of her activities being subordinated to the operating divisions of the concern.

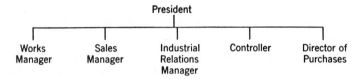

FIGURE 2-1.   Organization chart of medium-sized textile manufacturer.

Figures 2-2 and 2-3 show the organization plans of two large Midwestern manufacturers. In both examples, the head of the purchasing department reports to the production head of the concern. In the case of the electrical goods manufacturer, purchasing is made a direct line activity under operations. In the other case, the general purchasing agent operates in a staff capacity reporting to the vice-president in charge of manufacturing. In the latter company, each of the plant managers has a purchasing agent in his plant directly responsible to him. The general purchasing agent is primarily responsible for making and coordinating company-wide purchasing policies.

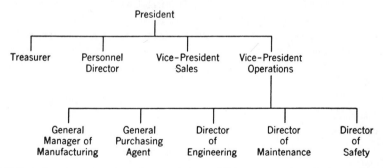

FIGURE 2-2.   Organization chart of large Midwestern electrical goods manufacturer.

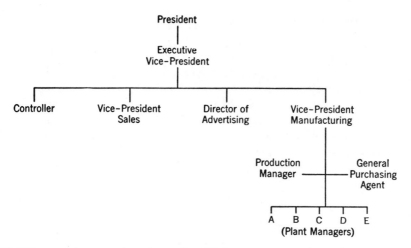

FIGURE 2-3. Organization chart of multiplant textile goods producer.

An illustration of a firm in which the head of the purchasing department reports to the financial officer of the firm is shown in Figure 2-4. As previously noted, this type of organization is occasionally encountered among industrial firms but is most frequently found in institutions that operate under fixed budgets. Occasionally purchasing is assigned to the financial executive as a convenient means of eliminating friction between operating divisions and the purchasing officer in companies where the scope of the purchasing function is not fully understood.

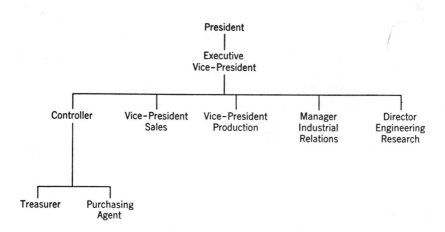

FIGURE 2-4. Organization chart of large Midwestern heavy-equipment manufacturer.

INTERNAL DEPARTMENTAL ORGANIZATION

Purchasing departments are "line" organizations with a purchasing agent, director of purchases, or some similarly designated individual in charge. The typical firm has only a few people assigned to the purchasing department. Two or three buyers are able to handle all of the purchasing for the average industrial concern because there is relatively little diversity or complexity in the items purchased. In such concerns each buyer is directly responsible to the head of the department. A small clerical staff is usually assigned to the department rather than to the individual buyers. A representative internal organization chart for an average size firm would be as shown in Figure 2-5.

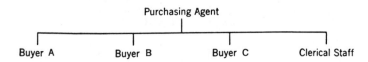

FIGURE 2-5.

The usual procedure is to assign a commodity or group of commodities to a buyer who is held responsible for all purchasing and related activities. This procedure works well because it enables the buyer to become a specialist in a limited area. This practice is also desirable from the seller's point of view because most salesmen sell related products and, if these products are handled by one buyer, the salesman has only one person with whom he must deal. This is more efficient for both parties than for the salesman to interview several buyers in the same company.

Different bases may be used in grouping commodities for assignment to buyers. One common basis is similarity of physical properties. On this basis, for example, nonferrous metals fall into one group and steel and welding supplies into another. A second common basis is similarity in the use to which the items will be put. On this basis one buyer might have raw materials, another operating supplies, and a third might have tools and equipment as his responsibility. A third basis is similarity in sources of supply. Then all items purchased through supply houses might be assigned to one buyer and those bought directly from manufacturers to another buyer.

Whatever the basis of assignment, no buyer should be assigned more commodities than he can handle effectively. If a buyer has too many commodities he will not be able to bargain on even terms with the seller and may buy unsuitable products or pay excessive prices.

The number will depend on their complexity, the variety of items in a class, the number of suppliers, method of placing the purchase order, and extent of the buyer's responsibility for follow-up and expediting.

As a firm increases in size, the structure of its purchasing department changes. There occurs a further subdivision of the commodities assigned to buyers and the assignment of specialists, in a staff capacity, to the head of the department. In matters such as traffic, inspection, expediting, quality control, and salvage and scrap disposal, these staff specialists take over from the buyers some of the responsibility for their specialties.

At about the same stage in the growth of an organization an assistant is frequently appointed to the head of the department. He assumes day-to-day control over the individual buyers and frequently buys one or two of the more important commodities himself. Figure 2-6 is an example of this type of organization for a large public utility. In this organization, it will be noted, the manager of purchases has two staff assistants and an assistant manager of purchases who has the various buyers assigned in a line relationship to himself. It may also be observed that, as the duties of a buyer increase in scope and volume, an assistant buyer is assigned to him. It is also customary in large purchasing departments to assign clerical help to buying groups rather than to the entire department.

One of the more recent organizational developments is the assignment of purchasing responsibilities for a large and special type of project to a team, usually designated a project group. This group has complete responsibility for whatever is needed for its project and consequently its buying will overlap regular buying assignments. This organization is appropriate only when a company wants to give a measure of priority to a major project or must meet stringent quality, cost, or time requirements for such things as a major construction project, a new product development, or a government contract.

Organizationally, the important respect in which governmental and institutional purchasing departments differ from industrial purchasing departments is the multiple authority over the head of the purchasing department. Typically, supervision is exercised by a board. In government the board is usually composed primarily of elected officials, although occasionally the purchasing agent may be directly responsible to a city manager or a similar appointed executive.

Internally the governmental and institutional purchasing departments are organized on lines similar to industrial purchasing departments. There is, however, a greater emphasis on the clerical function

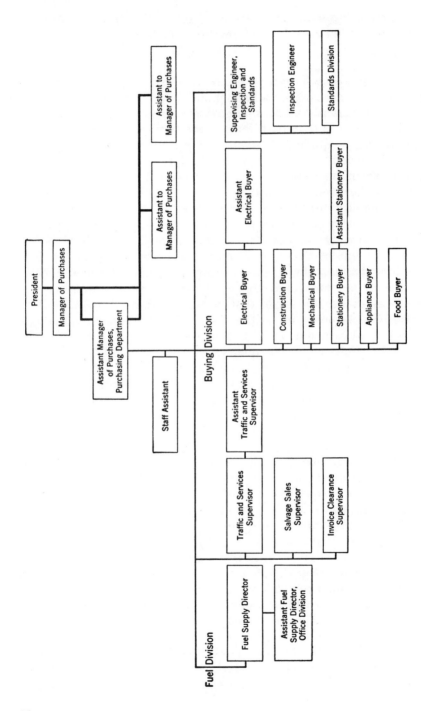

FIGURE 2-6. Administrative organization of purchasing department in large Midwestern public utility.

because of the more detailed procedures required by such statutory requirements as the open-bidding method of purchase.

INTERDEPARTMENTAL RELATIONSHIPS

A purchasing department exists to supply the needs of other departments in the company. To a considerable extent the attitudes and reactions of these other departments toward the purchasing department depend on the degree and kind of service that the purchasing department extends and the nature of the existing interdepartmental relations.

Purchasing is constantly working with the other departments in the company, and thus it is essential that mutual trust and cooperation prevail in order to foster efficiency. There are areas where friction may develop between purchasing and other departments because of misunderstandings over who should do the work. In many companies the materials management form of organization has been introduced to minimize this friction and to improve coordination among the materials departments. An organizational manual that clearly describes the duties and responsibilities of each department helps to minimize conflicts of interest. Such manuals are becoming commonplace today, especially in larger companies. The following paragraphs will be devoted to a brief discussion of some of these interdepartmental relationships.

Production

Production and planning have the common goal of efficient and profitable operations; however, their philosophies differ. A production executive quite naturally thinks in terms of having all he needs of the best materials. This philosophy can easily lead to excessive inventories of unnecessarily high quality. The purchasing executive may find himself in an unpopular position when he must contend for a reasonable quantity of the appropriate quality. To a considerable extent, the relationships between these two departments can be harmonized through the exchange of information which each department develops in the normal course of its operations.

Production must keep purchasing informed as far in advance as possible about production plans and schedules. With such information purchasing is able to plan its procurement program intelligently so as to minimize emergency and "rush" orders. As changes in production plans develop, they should be communicated to purchasing so that time is available for vendor selection, negotiations, and delivery. The production department must be made to realize the "lead time" that exists between the issuance of a requisition and receipt of goods. Efficient purchasing procedures can minimize this time but, at best, production must work closely enough with purchasing in anticipating needs to allow for the minimum "lead time."

On the other hand, purchasing has certain responsibilities toward the production department. The purchasing department must keep production informed of expected arrivals, and must notify the production department promptly of any unusual delays so that production may be rescheduled without plant stoppages.

The purchasing department has a valuable tool for the production department in its file of vendor's catalogs. These should be supplied on call to the production department. Purchasing also has the responsibility of informing the production department about any new materials, machines, or methods that come to the buyers' attention through visiting salesmen or trade literature. A buyer sometimes is instructed to secure samples for testing by the production department. At other times a buyer should secure samples on his own initiative and bring them to the attention of the production department for testing purposes.

In many companies the purchasing and production departments share joint responsibility for development of standards and specifications for materials and supplies to be purchased. In other companies purchasing merely has a voice in the matter, with responsibility in the production department. The important thing is for the purchasing department to make sure that wherever possible, standards conform to materials that are readily available in the market and avoid unnecessary deviations that add to costs.

In the purchase of plant equipment, purchasing and production are but two of many departments involved in the decision. Each, however, has a role to play in the purchase of equipment. Production concerns itself with initiating the action and determining the kind of equipment to be purchased. Purchasing surveys the potential suppliers who will be requested to bid on the order and has an important voice in deciding who gets the order. The treasurer, the engineering department, sometimes the sales department, and often the president participate in the decision.

Engineering

The engineering department is primarily responsible for the design and specifications of the products the company makes and the processes the company uses. Engineers in such departments have definite ideas about the physical and chemical properties required in the end product and know what materials have the desired properties. However, because there frequently are several materials possessing suitable properties, it is important for someone to determine which material can be purchased most advantageously. This is a proper responsibility of the purchasing department.

A close working arrangement must be developed between the engineering and purchasing departments. Engineering should not be so exacting that its demands override price and market considerations, and purchasing must not stress price to the point where it interferes with sound engineering requirements.

The two departments should complement each other, and close cooperation is essential for smooth and successful relationships. Good engineering produces a product up to company specifications, with both technical and market efficiency.

Sales

No company can stay in business for long unless its products can be sold at a profit. The purchasing department can help the sales department by buying at the lowest possible cost so that a company's selling price can be competitive. About 50% of what the typical sales department sells has been purchased from others. The sales department can help purchasing schedule its purchases effectively by apprising the purchasing department of sales quotas and sales expectations. The sales department can be particularly helpful by giving the purchasing department as much advance information as possible during negotiations with customers for special orders and nonstock items.

In many companies the practice of reciprocity calls for the maintenance of close liaison between purchasing and sales in order to properly effectuate the policy.[1]

Accounting

Every purchase transaction initiates a chain of accounting transactions, from charging the transaction to the proper account to the final payment of the bill. In Chapter 1 it was pointed out that in some companies part of the accounting work may be done by the purchasing department. Regardless of where particular accounting tasks were performed, close coordination is essential, since company funds and significant discounts are involved.

[1] See Chapter 6 for a detailed discussion of reciprocity.

Some purchases may be so costly as to necessitate the raising of additional funds. While such transactions are financial rather than accounting in nature, the general practice of placing both financial and accounting matters under the control of a treasurer or coordinator justifies mentioning this as another area in which close coordination between the purchasing and accounting departments is vital.

In the case of purchases by budgetary institutions and governmental agencies there is a clear need for close relationships between the two departments. In most such organizations all transactions must be strictly regulated according to the budget. Therefore, it is routine procedure for all purchase requests to clear through the accounting department to ascertain that there is an uncommitted balance in the proper account equal to the contemplated purchase.

Stores

If the stores department is independent of the purchasing department, the relationship between the two is closer and more continuous than those between any other two departments. On all shelf stock items the stores department initiates the purchase requests on which the buyer acts. The buyer's decision concerning a purchase is based on such factors as rate of use, number of defective parts, and trends in the rate of use. This information is most easily secured through the records of the stores department. The buyer must keep the stores department informed on minimum stocks and reorder points so that the stores department can keep its inventories at proper levels.

International

Today a large proportion of the major firms throughout the world sell to a worldwide market. An increasing number of these companies are becoming truly multinational in the sense that they look upon the entire world as their market—any geographical location that will optimize production costs is a possible site for plant location, and any country that can supply raw materials or parts reliably and at a low cost is a likely resource. The last point is particularly relevant to purchasing. In a truly interdependent world, political boundaries should not be a barrier to the free flow of raw materials and supplies. However, a long history of nationalism and company policies and practices based upon nationalistic thinking, as well as certain laws and government policies, have inhibited the movement and development of certain sources of supply. For example, a recent study of United Kingdom manufacturing companies indicated that these companies tended to restrict their supply horizons until a change was motivated either by (1) a price or availability threat to existing supplies, or (2) a threat to sales brought about by national reciprocity pressure.[2] A well-managed company should look upon the trend toward freer world trade as an opportunity to improve its supply capability. This may well mean giving the manager of purchasing greater responsibility in policy-making matters. If this is done at an early date it can give the company a competitive advantage. If the response is delayed, it will eventually be forced upon a company by competition since its profit implications are compelling.

MATERIALS MANAGEMENT

The term *materials management*[3] came into common usage and practice in business during the 1960s. Its essential significance is that it highlighted for management the fact that there were economies to be gained by coordinating the related activities of production planning and scheduling, purchasing, shipping, storing, handling, and controlling of materials put into the manufacturing process.

The idea was not new. Military organizations have unified their logistical activities since the seventeenth century. However, the principle of specialization in business organizations led to these activities being placed under control of different managers, often with conflicting objectives. For example, production scheduling was under the control of the production manager, whose interest was in minimizing production cost through long runs regardless of the effects on carrying costs, which were the concern of the manager of storage and transportation.

From a company-wide point of view, it is only reasonable that these considerations should offset each other and divisions made that will be in the best interests of the company rather than for the departments. It was such "trade-off" considerations and the development of operations research techniques to quantify them that led to the adoption and popularization of MM.

Utilizing Automated Facilities

Companies that use automated facilities have found that these systems work best with an even and regular work flow. Exceptions

[2] David H. Farmer, "Corporate Planning and Procurement in Multi-National Firms," *Journal of Purchasing*, vol. 10, no. 2, May 1974, pp. 55–67.

[3] In accordance with common practice the term *materials management* will hereafter be abbreviated to MM in this chapter.

must be programmed into them in advance. By providing coordination and control of all materials subfunctions, MM levels the work flow and provides the advance information necessary to allow the systems to function efficiently.

Facilitating "Make and Hold" Purchases ? Question to ask

Buyers are increasingly requesting suppliers to "make and hold" finished goods inventory, causing suppliers to carry inventories that previously were held by the buyers. Effective utilization of this service requires that supplier inventories be closely coordinated to developments in the buying company's materials departments such as production and inventory control. Therefore, MM is often adopted to coordinate supplier inventory management to the other internal materials operations.

Behind all these reasons for adopting MM is the fundamental point that it provides improved coordination and control of the materials subfunctions by centralizing materials authority.

Limitations of MM

Critics of the MM form of organization emphasize that it is difficult, if not impossible, for one person effectively to coordinate and control the many variables involved in materials handling, and that effective coordination is too difficult to achieve merely by establishing a new organizational structure. Others feel that the production control and purchasing departments will be neglected under such an organization. In a study of both users and nonusers of MM, the following limitations were suggested:[4]

A 1970 survey of 106 large manufacturing companies showed that 55% of those responding were operating under some form of MM organization and that those purchasing a higher percentage of their output were much more inclined to employ the MM concept than those purchasing a lower percentage.[5] Several studies have also shown that the trend toward MM is increasing rapidly (see table on page 45).

Organizational Variations within MM

Essentially any manufacturing process consists of altering raw materials and partially processed materials to make them into some

---

[4] Gary J. Zenz, "The Economics of Materials Management," unpublished doctoral dissertation, University of Wisconsin, 1967.

[5] R. Baer and J. Centamore, "Materials Management: Where it Stands ... What it Means ...," *Purchasing*, January 8, 1970, p. 53.

more valuable form. This process consists of obtaining and moving the materials and of processing them as they are moved through the operation. Logically, then, the process could be organized into MM and manufacturing, and this would be the ultimate in MM. One organizational unit would have the responsibility for buying and moving materials, parts, and supplies from outside sources; controlling them throughout the storage and processing stages; and warehousing the finished product and supervising its movement to the customer.

This inclusive kind of logistical control could someday be achieved, but today it encompasses too many diverse activities to be efficiently managed by one authority. Usually the storage and shipment of finished goods (frequently called physical distribution) is excluded from MM. In a fully developed MM organization the responsibility for the other movement, storage, and control functions are included. However, there are many organizational variations, and partial consolidations of an interim nature are more common than fully developed MM plans. The following organizational chart would typify a rather complete MM plan.

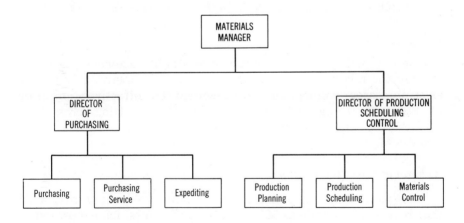

FIGURE 2-7.

Another way of viewing the MM operation is to note the several functions that come under its purview, regardless of where they are located in the organization. The following is a typical list of such functions:

1. Planning the types and qualities of materials and parts required by production operations.
2. Planning the quantities to be purchased and controlling inventories at defined levels.

3. Acquiring the necessary materials, parts, and supplies.
4. Researching materials, sources, and methods.
5. Contracting for and supervising transport services for incoming items.
6. Checking incoming items to make certain of quantities and condition of goods.
7. Measuring the testing incoming items to make sure they meet contract standards.
8. Physically controlling and protecting inventories.
9. Scheduling the production time and rate, and specifying the rates at which materials and supplies will be required for production.
10. Moving goods from point of storage or receipt to the production line.
11. Disposing of scrap materials and unneeded equipment.

Reasons for Adopting MM

The essential reason for uniting materials departments under a materials manager is to provide improved coordination and control of the following issues involved in making materials decisions.

Utilizing Control Tools

One reason for the growing use of MM is management's desire to employ the relatively new control tools such as operations research, electronic programming, and profit centers. The effective application of such tools to materials problems necessitates cutting across functional lines, which requires the coordination and control available under MM.

Achieving Cost Reductions

Another reason is the simple need to improve control over areas that represent as much as 50% of production costs. Large cost reductions typically are available in inventory reduction, transportation, and purchasing as a result of improved coordination of these activities.

Reconciling Conflicting Objectives

Another important reason for the increasing acceptance of MM is the realization that the materials departments often have conflicting objectives that must be coordinated to optimize results. For example, the desire of purchasing and traffic to buy and ship in large quantities in order to cut cost conflicts with the objective of production control for high inventory turnover and low obsolescence. There is the danger that conflicts of this type may be resolved by compromises that are more political than economic. When a decision must be made among conflicting objectives, there must be someone available to make that decision—under the MM organization the materials manager performs this function.

In a study of both users and nonusers of MM the following major limitations were suggested:[6]

Major Limitations of MM

Qualified personnel are too difficult to find	29.9%
Coordination is too difficult	25.2%
Production control is too important to be subordinated	15.7%
Purchasing is too important to be subordinated	13.4%
Too expensive to administer	6.0%
All of the above	3.0%
Other	6.7%

The difficulty in obtaining personnel qualified to handle the requirements of the subfunctions and particularly the difficulty in finding personnel to manage the materials organization are significant limitations to the use of MM. This has important implications for persons employed in the materials subfunctions; they should broaden their knowledge of the entire materials operations. It also indicates a need for management development programs—particularly taking specialists from the subfunctional areas and providing them with total materials knowledge.

The extent of recent growth and the persuasive reasons for its adoption indicate that MM could prove to be one of the significant organizational developments of the last decade.

DISCUSSION QUESTIONS

1. What is the role, function, or purpose of organization in a company?

2. What is over-organization? Give an example of it in purchasing. Discuss the general effects of over-organization.

3. Discuss the argument for centralization of purchasing for branch plants.

[6] Lénz, *op. cit.*, p. 67.

4. How does one determine the number of commodities a buyer should handle?

5. How can the purchasing department be of assistance to the sales department?

6. What unusual problems does a multinational company face in the area of purchasing?

7. What functional areas are included under materials management?

8. What are the basic reasons for adopting the materials management form of organization?

9. The production department should be responsible for the design and specification of products and processes. Discuss.

10. What are the most important limitations on materials management as a mode of organization?

SUGGESTED CASES

Expediting Problems

The Geer Company

The Janmar Company

Powers Company

John Roberts Manufacturing Company

Radmer County

CHAPTER 3

THE PROCEDURES, FORMS, AND RECORDS OF PURCHASING

The purchasing manual, which will generally cover both policy and procedures, is a keystone to the understanding of what transpires in the purchasing department and how it is accomplished. In a survey reported in *Purchasing Magazine* in January 1972, it was found that more than 100 different aspects or areas of the purchasing function were covered. The typical manual will set forth the policy adopted by the company on a specific aspect of the purchasing function within the company and then detail the procedures to be followed in adhering to that policy.

The survey reported that the major benefits of the manual as seen by the respondents were that it provided support for the authority of the purchasing department; it kept other departments within the company advised of purchasing policies and procedures; it kept purchasing personnel advised of policies and procedures; and, it aided in the training of purchasing personnel.

Since each company will have its own individually designed set of policies consistent with its company objectives, it is obvious that procedures will likewise be individualized to companies rather than uniform or standardized.

The variations in company organization, size, and operating policies give rise to the needs for the many variations in purchasing departments. Therefore, most of this book is devoted to a consideration of purchasing policies and the means of implementing these policies. The emphasis on policies rather than procedures is intentional as a means of stressing the important role of purchasing in most business organizations. In any purchasing department, there is always the hazard of so emphasizing forms and procedures that the vital functions of the department are overlooked.

However, in order to provide a realistic background against which to picture the purchasing policies and procedures discussed in the following chapters, this chapter is devoted to a description of the usual steps in the purchasing process and a brief description of the most generally used forms in a purchasing department. In addition, some of the more recent techniques developed to meet the expanding load of frequent but low-value purchases are discussed in Chapter 4.

Electronic data-processing equipment is used in an increasing number of companies that have a heavy load of paper work. Several manufacturers offer such equipment, and a number of systems of automating the procedural processes have been developed. To be successful, such systems must be tailored to the requirements within the company. Some overview of what can be accomplished with EDP is presented in Chapter 23. In this chapter we shall concentrate on the simple nonautomated approaches to procedure.

PURCHASING PROCEDURE

By procedure, in this context, we refer to the way in which a purchase transaction is carried through from its inception to its conclusion. Company policies and purchasing department policies outline the broad objectives to be accomplished and the guidelines within which the procedures must accomplish the desired results. Procedures outline in detail the functions to be performed by the people involved in the purchasing operation. Forms and records are the tools used to implement procedures and policies. In the first part of this chapter, we deal with procedures—the way in which the purchasing function is conducted in a typical purchasing department.

Steps of Purchasing

Since there are wide variations among industries, companies, products, and personnel, it would not be feasible to establish a single set of procedures that would apply to all cases. The following steps, however, must be taken, in one way or another, to complete a purchasing transaction. These may be called the basic steps of the operation.

1. Recognition of need.
2. Description of requirement.
3. Selection of possible sources of supply.

4. Determination of price availability.
5. Placing the order.
6. Follow-up and expediting of the order.
7. Checking the invoice.
8. Processing discrepancies and rejections.
9. Closing completed orders.
10. Maintenance of records and files.

This list might be criticized as incomplete, since related activities such as receiving, storekeeping, or inspection are often a part of the purchasing procedure, particularly in smaller companies. However, it was considered advisable to restrict the list to the functions performed by the purchasing departments in a large majority of industrial concerns.

Recognition of Need

The recognition of need refers to the means by which a needed item is officially brought to the attention of the purchasing department. Two procedures are followed. One involves the issuance of requisitions by the using department or the stores department. The other involves the issuance of a bill of materials.

A purchase requisition describes the needed item and becomes the basis for action by the purchasing department. This form is usually prepared in duplicate, with the carbon copy being retained by the issuing department as a record of its action. Requisitions must be signed by authorized individuals in order to avoid irresponsible purchase requests. In some companies, requisitions for inventory items, as opposed to immediate-use items, are initiated in the department responsible for maintaining inventory. Such requisitions are issued when stocks diminish to the reorder point and are sent to the purchasing department for action.

Requisitions from using departments are commonly routed through the stores department, and if the item is in inventory, it is supplied from stock instead of being purchased. Requisition for items not in inventory are sent on to the purchasing department for action. In governmental agencies and institutions that operate on a budget, the requisition is generally routed to the purchasing department through the financial officer in order to ensure that funds are available.

A bill of materials is a list of all items to be incorporated into a finished product that the company produces. Such bills are generally prepared at the time engineering blueprints for the item are made. Under this method of establishing need, the purchasing department is notified of the manufacturing schedule by the production planning department. The buyer then multiplies the items listed in the bill of materials by the total units planned for production to determine total requirement. After the total needs have been adjusted to make use of existing inventories, the quantity to be purchased is known. The bill of materials procedure is primarily applicable to the purchase of standard parts and small expendable tools. Supplies and similar needs are usually handled by the requisition procedure.

Description of Requirement

The requisition describes the required item. Sound procedure provides a standardized requisition form which indicates the normal amount of detail to be used in stating the requirement.

In order to assure complete and accurate information for ordering, the requisition must include all necessary information in a form that can be readily checked and verified. Since a bill of materials is usually prepared by the engineering department as a part of the original plan for the product, it contains a description that is adequate for ordering purposes.

The buyer must check a requisition carefully on the basis of his own knowledge of the item, records of past purchases, and vendor catalogs. The buyer should not change an inadequate requisition, interpret sketchy descriptions, or in any way make judgments about a questionable requisition. He should refer it back to the party originating the requisition. Even what appear to be obvious errors should be checked with the using department, because production can be delayed if the user wanted an item for some purpose different from that assumed by the buyer, and such delays can be very costly.

Selection of Possible Sources of Supply

After a need has been recognized and described, the buyer must select the sources of supply from whom to secure prices. Selecting the source, as the term is used here, is the process of narrowing down a large list of potential suppliers to a relatively few. The final choice is made from this short list. The process consists of selecting the desired number of suppliers, in accordance with established guidelines, from whom quotations will be requested.

For items that are purchased frequently or that are obtained through distributors, the purchasing agent usually has a few preferred suppliers from whom he buys regularly. In such cases, he merely picks one, frequently on a rather arbitrary basis, as the source for the requested purchase.

For nonroutine purchases, the procedure involves a careful survey of potential sources of supply. The extent and thoroughness of the survey should be determined by the cost of the item and its possible effect on production. The more important the item, the more careful should be the survey of the potential suppliers of that item.

The second step consists of narrowing the list of potential suppliers to the few with whom negotiations are to be conducted. The buyer consults many sources of information during this stage of the purchase transaction. He reviews his records of supplier performance; he may visit and inspect the prospective supplier's plant; he talks to the supplier's salesmen, and may check with fellow purchasing agents who have had dealings with the supplier in question. The procedures of industrial and governmental purchasing departments are quite different on this point. In most cases, governmental purchasers are required by law or regulation to grant all qualified suppliers an opportunity to bid for the business. The industrial buyer chooses from the many suppliers only the ones with whom he wishes to negotiate.

Determination of Price and Availability

The next step in the purchasing transaction is to secure the price for the items to be purchased. This may be accomplished in several ways. For standard items, suppliers' catalogs and price lists are available and for such items the buyer need only check current listings to obtain the price.

Negotiation is a second method of establishing price. Negotiation implies bargaining between buyer and seller. No one technique of negotiating can be used for all types of transactions. The buyer should approach the process of negotiation with an open mind and with as much information as possible about the commodity under consideration—his rate of use, the production facilities of the supplier, market conditions, and any other factors that may bear on the outcome of the negotiations.

The third method of securing price is through a request for bids. Governmental purchasing agents must allow bidding by all qualified suppliers, but industrial purchasing agents may restrict the number of bidding firms in any way they see fit. It is standard practice to solicit bids from prospective suppliers by means of a "bid request" or some similar form that specifies the requirements. At the end of a period of time, usually stated on the bid requests, the bidding is closed and the bids are analyzed and compared. The purchase order is then issued to the chosen bidder.

Bids are generally opened at a specified time and a tabulation of the bids is prepared. In governmental purchasing it frequently is required that this be done publicly, with the award to be made to the lowest qualified bidder. In purchasing for industry there is no such requirement. However, if the buyer has carefully selected the suppliers from whom bids are requested, and the bids are responsive to the specifications, there is no economic reason why he should not accept the lowest bid. Practice varies as to whether unsuccessful bidders are notified and the notification procedure used.

Placing the Order

The legal order is placed with the supplier on a form known as a purchase order. Most companies insist that every purchase be placed in this manner. When an order is placed by telephone or telegraph, it is the practice to confirm the order by sending the supplier a regular purchase order. Such an order should be clearly marked "confirming" to avoid the possibility of the supplier assuming that the order form represents a second order. Occasionally a supplier may insist that the buyer sign a sales order form instead of his own purchase order, but this is an exception ordinarily reserved for large contracts.

It is typical procedure for the buyer to record on the original requisition the name of the company to receive the order, the price, the quantity, and other pertinent data. This annotated requisition then goes to an order-writing clerk who prepares the purchase order for the signature of the authorized individual in the purchasing department.

Companies vary in their practice as to the number of copies of a purchase order prepared. Variation from two to eighteen copies have been found. The number of copies depends largely on the complexity of the purchaser's organization as well as a company's ingenuity in developing an efficient system. Invariably, the original copy is sent to the supplier. This may be accompanied by one carbon known as the acknowledgment copy. On this copy, the vendor is expected to signify his acceptance of the order and the date on which delivery is to be made. Copies may also be sent to the receiving department, the accounting department, the using department, the inspection department, the stores department, and the follow-up section of the purchasing department. One copy is always retained for the files of the purchasing department. Some companies make an even wider internal distribution of copies than indicated above.

Follow-Up and Expediting Order

The method employed in following up an order also varies widely from one company to another. The following description is a simple routine used by a small machine-tool manufacturer in the East.

Purchase orders are prepared in quadruplicate. Two copies, the official copy and an acknowledgment copy, are sent to the vendor (both white). A pink copy is placed in a loose-leaf folder in chronological sequence. The fourth copy (blue) is filed alphabetically by vendor in an unfilled order file. The file of pink copies is checked weekly, and if the acknowledgment copy has not been received after the lapse of a short period of time, a reminder is sent to the supplier.

When the acknowledgment copy is received, it is filed in a loose-leaf folder of unfilled orders which are arranged chronologically. At this time the pink copy of the purchase order is removed from the folder and permanently filed as a record of purchase orders placed. At regular intervals the folder of acknowledgment copies is reviewed and, if the buyer thinks it necessary, past due orders are followed up by further communication with the supplier.

Follow-up procedures may be more elaborate than the one just described, but the basic elements are the same. First, it is necessary to secure an acceptance and a promise of delivery. Then, it is necessary to review outstanding orders at regular intervals and to communicate with suppliers as required. There is considerable variation in the method of filing and reviewing purchase orders on which delivery has not been made, and in the methods of securing action on unshipped orders.

Checking the Invoices

Invoice checking consists of verifying the data on the seller's invoice against the buyer's records. The seller's invoice must be compared with the original order and the receiving slip that is made out when the material is received.

The invoice quantity is checked against the quantity specified on the purchase order and the quantity indicated as received by the receiving slip. Terms and prices are checked against the purchase order. Description of the goods is verified with both forms. It is common practice at this time to check extensions and footings to avoid over- or underpayments resulting from clerical errors, although in some companies this step is left to the accounts payable department. If an invoice is correct in all respects, it is given to the accounting department for payment.

Processing Discrepancies and Rejections

If discrepancies are found, the buyer who initiated the order is notified and he takes appropriate action. If the invoice is in error, the buyer usually returns it to the vendor for correction. In such a case, it is normal to insist that, for discount purposes, the invoice date be changed to the date on which the corrected invoice is received.

When material is rejected it is necessary for the buyer to get the vendor's authorization for return and replacement. It usually is necessary to issue a replacing order to the seller and a debit slip to the accounting department for the defective material. If the production department needs the material urgently, the buyer may subject it to 100% inspection and reject only that part which fails to pass inspection.

Closing Completed Orders

Since most purchasing departments maintain a file copy of unfilled orders, it is necessary to have a procedure for closing orders when they are completed. Before an order is closed the purchase order must be checked against both the receiving reports and the vendor's invoice. The checking of invoices has already been described. There may be only one receiving report to check. However, when partial shipments are involved, there may be several receiving reports. All except the last one should be marked "partial," and the last one, which completes the shipments on the order, should be marked "final."

After the invoices and receiving reports have been checked against the file copy of the order, a notation of this fact should be made on it. It should then be removed and stored in the file of closed orders. In most departments closed orders are filed according to the purchase order number sequence so that they may be readily located if reference is required.

Maintenance of Records and Files

The final step in the purchasing process consists of filing the records of the transaction. This step is routine in nature and, once the method is established, it becomes the responsibility of a clerical employee of the department.

Many companies maintain a file of completed purchase orders in addition to the closed order file mentioned in the preceding paragraph. The second file is arranged according to vendors. With this copy of the purchase order may be filed such records as the original requisition, the receiving slip, and inspection or rejection reports.

Decisions concerning the records to be maintained in the purchasing department, how long they are to be maintained, and the form in which they are to be kept are policy matters to be determined by general management on the basis of legal as well as management principles. The guideposts in such decisions will be a balancing of the cost of maintaining the files and the legal and business risks involved in not having access to historical records.

AUTOMATING PURCHASING PROCEDURES

The large volume of orders processed through the typical purchasing department, many of which are repeated several times during a year, has led purchasing executives to seek ways of minimizing the paper work. These efforts are generally known as the automating of paper work.

Some indication of the benefits to be derived from automating purchasing processes may be found in the following statement of what the use of a computer has done for one company:

. . . an inventory control run is made four days each week, each covering about half of the 30,000 inventoried items. As a result of each run, about 90 purchase orders are printed in about 30 minutes.

. . . many stock items have automatically "gone on order" without any manual assistance. (E.g., for one family consisting of 19 related items, the machine has produced 31 purchase orders during a 14-month period, consisting of anywhere from one to five items per order. No manual orders of any kind were written.)

. . . both automatic and hand-written orders are fed to the machine's follow-up routine. This run is made every day—the machine reviewing some 5,000 open orders each day in about 45 minutes. Tracer letters are generated automatically at an average rate of 80 per day, which are printed in about 20 minutes.

. . . during the same follow-up run, about 200 invoices are being referred to the computer for verification, producing an average of 150 checks each day (which are printed out in about 15 minutes).

. . . important information, heretofore difficult to compile, is being obtained that will help in value analysis, appraisal of vendor performance, reports to management, studies of stock obsolescence, etc. The program is by no means complete: it is easy to visualize hundreds of ways in which it can be improved and made to provide useful information for purchasing and management.[1]

[1] "Purchasing Enters Computer Age," *Purchasing*, January 6, 1968, p. 79.

Perhaps the simplest development in this field is the traveling requisition. This is a form that contains identifying information with respect to an item that is repeatedly purchased and includes the names and addresses of approved suppliers as well as prices paid on previous purchases. Whenever a purchase of the item is to be made, the traveling requisition is forwarded by the using department to the purchasing department with information entered thereon with respect to rate of usage, quantity on hand, and quantity requisitioned. The purchase order is then prepared. The use of the traveling requisition eliminates the need for repeated copying of detailed information.

Another development in this area of automating purchasing procedures is the use of special typing equipment which is operated by punched tapes containing information that is repeated on many purchase orders. This equipment eliminates much manual typing and the use of reproduction methods—for example, the ditto process—from original requisitions. Automatic typing eliminates copying from requisition to purchase order form, with the verified requisition serving as the master for copies of the purchase order and any other forms needed.

A second area where automation of paper work has made great strides in the field of purchasing is the maintenance of inventory stock record cards. Several machines and techniques have been developed to simplify and speed up the entering of inventory receipts and disbursements and to secure reports on inventory levels. The use of such equipment saves considerable time and clerical effort and brings to the attention of the purchasing authorities current information on inventories of materials. Under the earlier hand-tabulating methods, companies frequently found inventories at dangerously low levels before the information reached the proper parties.

It should be noted that automation of record keeping is not profitable for all concerns; the cost of the equipment is high. Top-management and purchasing executives should weigh carefully the benefits against the costs of automation. Although it may be sound to secure as much information as possible, one should not incur the cost of securing information that will not be used.

PURCHASING FORMS

Forms are the tools of the purchasing department. Without forms it would be impossible to run a purchasing department efficiently. The problem for the purchasing executive is to have as many forms as will be used effectively and not so many as to create confusion and red tape. The number of forms required depends on such factors as the size of the firm, the purchasing system employed, and the accounting and internal control methods in effect.

Regardless of the number of forms in use, it is important that they incorporate the principles of good design. The more important of these principles may be stated as follows:

1. The form should facilitate the entering of data required.
2. The form should impress those who use it as being significant.
3. The form should make it easy for those who use it to obtain the data from it.
4. The form should minimize the possibility of errors in entry or use of data.
5. The form should be economical to reproduce.

Since a form is designed to centralize data on which decisions are to be made, it is important that it be so designed as to make the entry of the data as easy as possible. It should allow sufficient space for entering the information and should be so arranged that the data can be entered in a logical and proper sequence. It should also be designed with adequate and properly placed instructions for filling it out.

A good form will create a favorable mental attitude on the part of the individuals who must use it. Consequently, its physical appearance is important. Good appearance can be achieved by proper original design and good reproduction. If a form looks crowded or is poorly reproduced, it tends to create an indifferent attitude in the individual who fills it out.

After a form is filled out, it is submitted to someone as the basis for business action. If the information is hard to read or comprehend, the form is not a good one. Since data on forms are generally both statistical and descriptive, it is important to design the form in such a manner that both types can be readily read and understood, even though the space requirements for each type of data differ markedly. Actual use of a sample form is helpful in designing a form that will serve its intended purpose.

Clerical errors in filling out forms must be kept at a minimum, since they can be very costly. A form will tend to reduce errors if it includes only essential data, clearly segregates columns where statistical data are involved, simplifies reading lines across the page, and generates an attitude of respect from the clerk who enters the data by suggesting that management has planned the form carefully and reproduced it with quality.

The last and one of the most important criterion in designing a form is the economy in paper and printing costs. Economy can be achieved by combining forms to eliminate unnecessary duplication in gathering data, by utilizing standard-size dimensions of paper stock, by eliminating unnecessary duplicate copies, and by using paper stock of a durability consistent with the use to which the form will be put.

Although only four forms are reproduced in this chapter for illustrative purposes, it should be emphasized that any firm will probably have a much greater number of forms. In selecting illustrative forms, an attempt was made to use the simplest types available, since they illustrate the principles without presenting the complicating details that many of the larger companies put into their form for purposes of internal administration. The forms selected for illustration are not intended to illustrate the ideal form, but rather a simple variety and type that will frequently be encountered.

Purchase Requisition

In many companies, two basic types of purchase requisition are used. One of these, frequently called a "traveling requisition," is used for inventory items that are ordered repetitively and was mentioned previously as constituting the simplest step toward automation. The second, which is used for all other requirements, might be called a "descriptive requisition."

As stated earlier, the traveling requisition includes a complete description of the item to be ordered, a listing of the preselected vendors, a space to record the purchase order number, date ordered, and the vendor selected. The quantity to be ordered may be specified by the stores department or may be determined by the purchasing department in accordance with EOQ procedure.[2] The buyer selects the vendor to be used and the price to be paid. The requisition is then forwarded to the typist who prepares the order. After the purchase order has been prepared, the traveling requisition is returned to the person originating it.

A simple form of descriptive requisition includes space for the purchase order number, the date, the description of the required item, date when the item is needed, the signature of the individual originating the requisition, and the action taken by the purchasing department.

The form is usually prepared in duplicate, the original copy going

[2] See Chapter 8 for a detailed discussion of economic order quantity (EOQ) procedures.

THE HOWADORE COMPANY
161 FOURTH STREET,
PROVIDENCE R. I.

INQUIRY— NOT AN ORDER

TO_____

_____

_____

THIS IS A REQUEST FOR QUOTATION ON THE ITEMS ENUMERATED BELOW-

INQUIRY NO.

ON OUR REQ. NO.

DATE

CLASS

SUBJECT

SPECIAL NOTICE TO BIDDER

1. TO RECEIVE CONSIDERATION, THE ORIGINAL COPY OF THIS INQUIRY WITH YOUR BID FILLED IN, MUST BE SIGNED AND RETURNED WITHIN 15 DAYS.

2. ALL PRICES AND CONDITIONS MUST BE SHOWN. ADDITIONS FOR PACKING OR OTHER ITEMS NOT SHOWN ON THIS BID WILL NOT BE ALLOWED.

3. ATTACH COMPLETE SPECIFICATIONS FOR ANY SUBSTITUTIONS OFFERED, OR WHEN AMPLIFICATION IS DESIRABLE OR NECESSARY.

4. THE SELLER AGREES TO PROTECT AND SAVE HARMLESS THE PURCHASER FROM ALL COSTS, EXPENSES OR DAMAGES ARISING OUT OF ALLEGED INFRINGEMENT OF PATENTS.

FOR SHIPMENT TO

VIA

F. O. B.

DELIVERY

TERMS

PLEASE QUOTE US YOUR BEST PRICE ON:

INQUIRY NOT AN ORDER

THIS INQUIRY IS IN DUPLICATE.
FILL OUT AND SIGN THE ORIGINAL AND RETURN TO US.
KEEP THE DUPLICATE FOR YOUR FILES.

IF FAVORED WITH AN ORDER, WE AGREE TO FURNISH THE ITEMS ENUMERATED HEREON AT THE PRICES AND UNDER THE CONDITIONS INDICATED.

SIGNED_____

DATE_____19___ BY_____

BIDDER

FIGURE 3-1. Request for quotation form.

to the purchasing department, and the carbon copy being retained for the files of the requisitioning department. Some companies use a more elaborate form of requisition in which the original copy can be forwarded directly to the vendor as a purchase order for items of small value. In other cases, the original of the requisition may be used as a master for the reproduction of purchase orders and related forms. The requisition usually bears the prominent heading or title "purchase requisition" to differentiate it from other similar forms or the actual purchase order.

Request for Quotation

The request for quotation form is shown in Figure 3-1. This form is used when a potential supplier is asked to furnish prices and terms on a contemplated purchase. To make sure that it will not be mistaken for an order, it bears very clearly across its face an imprint to that effect.

The request for quotation form describes the proposed purchase in detail, including a description of the item, the quantity required, the time and place of delivery, and the terms. Like other forms, it bears an identifying serial number and may also bear a number identifying the purchase requisition that initiated the inquiry.

The form ordinarily specifies a date by which the bid must be received in order to be considered. Many companies permit a prospective supplier to quote on the basis of alterations or substitutions in the original specifications, provided that such changes are clearly denoted and accompanied by complete specifications. This practice permits a supplier who may have a good alternative to make the suggestion without prejudicing his chance to secure the order. In such a case it may be necessary to permit all bidders to quote on the new basis, although the one who made the suggestion would tend to be favored.

A comparable form, usually called an "Invitation for Bid," is extensively used in purchasing for governmental units. Legislative requirements generally specify that public bidding open to all qualified suppliers is required of public agencies. Unlike industrial purchasing, governmental requests for quotations do not permit variations from the specifications on the form.

In governmental purchasing it is sometimes necessary to solicit proposals that do not have the legal status of *offers* capable of being accepted, and thus create a contract per se. This is done through the use of an Invitation for Proposal form.

When a completed request for quotation or an invitation to bid form is submitted by a supplier, it has the legal status of an offer. The purchasing agent can complete the contract by promptly notifying the vendor that he accepts the offer. He may do this by letter and follow the letter with a copy of his own purchase order.

Purchase Order

A purchase order is the commitment by a buyer to pay for goods ordered and the seller's authority to charge the buyer for them. It becomes a legal contract if it is submitted in acceptance of a formal

PURCHASE ORDER
THE HOWADORE COMPANY
161 FOURTH STREET,
PROVIDENCE, R. I.

Order No.

Please refer to above No.
on all your invoices and
Correspondence.

Gentlemen:

Please enter our order for the following material or services and note instructions below.

Yours very truly,
THE HOWADORE CO.

Per ....

Purchasing Agent.

The Number of this order must appear on your invoice, and correspondence in reference to this order.
PLEASE RETURN ATTACHED ACKNOWLEDGMENT OF THIS ORDER AND STATE WHEN SHIPMENT WILL BE MADE.
Render invoice promptly after shipping.
This order must not be filled at higher prices than last charged us unless prices are entered or a quotation is referred to on this sheet.
We reserve the right of cancelling above order, if not filled within a reasonable time.

FIGURE 3-2. Purchase order form.

quotation or offer. It becomes such a contract in other cases when it is accepted by the seller.

The purchase order varies from the simple form illustrated in Figure 3-2 to highly complex and detailed documents. At various times efforts have been made to standardize purchase order forms. These efforts have failed and probably always will fail because the purchase order is a legal document and business concerns differ widely in the degree of legal precaution they desire in their purchasing activities.

Even the simplest type of purchase order should contain space for the date of issue, a purchase order number for identification purposes, the name and address of the vendor, the quantity, the description, the price of the goods, the signature of the buyer, and the conditions or terms that govern the purchase. On the illustrated form the conditions and terms are at the bottom.

The more complex purchase order forms typically have many more conditions or clauses governing the purchase.[3] Many companies leave a space for the number of the requisition that initiated the purchase and other intracompany identification that might be helpful at a later date. Larger companies often include space for indicating desired routings and shipping instructions on their purchase order forms. The buyer has the right to specify such matters, but generally the smaller companies leave this to the judgment of the seller who usually has more experience in traffic matters. Some purchase order forms leave an assigned space for the buyer to indicate the date by which the shipment should be made. Others, such as the form reproduced, require that the buyer type in such information on purchases where a specific delivery date must be met. For standard items the shipping date can safely be left to the discretion of the vendor who will ship as promptly as possible to avoid the risk of the buyer canceling the order.

The distribution of copies of purchase order forms was discussed earlier in the chapter. The basic information on the original copy of the form will be reproduced almost in its entirety on the various carbon copies. The acknowledgment copy is generally clearly labeled as such to indicate its purpose. Frequently in the space in which the conditions of sale are printed on the original copy there will be a substitute section on the acknowledgment copy which will read somewhat as follows:

> Your order is hereby acknowledged and accepted with the understanding that shipment will be made as follows:. . . . .
> Will make partial shipment . . . .
> Will make complete shipment . . . .
> We understand that, if we cannot comply by the date stipulated, deferred shipment must be arranged for in writing.
>
> Signed. . . . .

Follow-Up Forms

Although it should not be necessary to follow up a purchase order to secure acceptance and compliance, it frequently becomes necessary to do so. It is an important responsibility of the purchasing department to obtain the material at the time required. This makes it

---

[3] See Chapter 17, "Legal Aspects of Purchasing," for a more detailed discussion of the types of clauses.

essential to establish a follow-up procedure that can be used effectively by staff people.

For routine follow-up, where adequate time is available, specially designed form postcards are frequently used. Such cards include the purchase order number, the date the material is required, space for the promised shipping date, and the signature of the individual making the promise. Some companies use a double postcard so that half of it may be torn off and returned to the customer with the requested information.

On urgent orders, or where special problems may be involved, the follow-up is often done by telegram or telephone. The follow-up may be by an expediter or by the buyer personally if its importance justifies it.

Receiving Forms

On all incoming shipments the receiving department lists the items received on a receiving-slip form. This form is dated to show when the shipment was received. It contains space for the name of the vendor and the common carrier who made the delivery. Space is provided for noting the amount paid the carrier if the shipment was not prepaid.

The body of the form reports the quantity and kind of materials received. Usually no special space is provided for reporting damaged goods, but a notation of the damage is written across the face of the form when it is discovered during the receiving operation. The form has a space for the signature of the checker.

Rejection Forms

Many companies require that all material received be forwarded to the receiving inspection department. This department makes a detailed inspection of the material against the specifications on the order. If it does not meet the specifications, the material is rejected or must be modified. The purchasing department is notified of this situation by some type of rejection form, frequently called an "inspection report." This report may suggest the return and replacement of the material, or it may state that the material is usable but request that the vendor be notified of the discrepancies involved so they will not occur on future orders.

Other Forms

The forms described above are used by most industrial concerns. However, a discussion of purchasing forms should at least mention

several others that are used by some purchasing departments. Among
such forms are:

Bin card stock form
Change of order notice form
Inspection report form
Purchase contract form
Sample test result form
Stock record form
Stores requisition form

PURCHASING RECORDS

Well-organized records are one of the most effective tools available
to a purchasing department for conducting efficient operations, since
the purchasing process is repetitious in nature. Past experience can be
a valuable guide in repeating successes and avoiding mistakes. A good
record system will add to the cost of operating a purchasing department, but this cost is more than compensated for by the savings it
produces through aiding the buyers in their buying activities.

Many of the records of a purchasing department consist of file
copies of the forms that have been discussed in the preceding paragraphs. In addition to these records there are others that deserve
mention.

Purchase Record

The purchase record is maintained to indicate each purchase of all
commodities bought. It is sometimes combined into a single file with
the perpetual inventory records, and the combined record shows, in
addition to the orders placed, receipts and disbursements of all commodities.

The purchase record is made up of a separate card for each item in
use, although cards are not made out for nonrepeat purchases. The
record includes in the heading a description of the item and a list of
suppliers. The body of the record contains data on orders placed, including purchase order number, quantity, date, vendor, and price.

Vendor Record

The vendor record is a file maintained primarily as an aid to the
order-writing clerk. It is a list of all vendors and their complete mailing addresses. This file is intended to simplify the work of the buyer

when he notes on purchase requisitions the vendor who is to receive the order. If a vendor record is kept, the buyer can merely write the name of the supplier, and the order-writing clerk can fill in the complete name and address from the file.

Blueprint and Specification Record

In metalworking and similar industries many items are purchased by blueprint specification. Such specifications often are very detailed and cannot be reproduced on the purchase order. Even if they could be, there would be risk of errors in transcribing from the master copy. Such items are ordered by writing a brief description of the part on the purchase order with a reference to blueprints and specifications that are enclosed with and made a legal part of the order.

To facilitate the forwarding of such specifications a purchasing department may maintain a file of blueprints and specifications covering all parts in current use. Generally, blueprints and specifications are kept in separate files, with an index showing their location and where the copies have been sent. Thus for repeat orders to old suppliers it is not necessary to send new copies of the specifications. The record is also helpful in mailing corrected copies when a change is made in a blueprint or specification.

Contract File

Certain goods may be bought under a term contract; if so, the purchasing department must maintain a record of such contracts. This record is especially important if the contract is an open one, against which orders may be placed within the contract quantity.

Printed Forms Record

Every industrial concern uses printed forms. It is usually desirable to set up a record of all printed forms in use. This record resembles the purchase record described above. The printed forms record is usually kept in a loose-leaf binder and includes a sample and description of each form used by the company. It also contains information about the sources from which the forms have been purchased. Data on the rate of use and cost are also included. On the basis of this record, it is a simple task for a buyer to replenish the supply of forms.

Tool and Die Record

The tool and die record, sometimes known as a pattern record, is used by companies that purchase fabricated parts, castings, and the like, which are made with a tool, die, or pattern furnished by the buyer. Such patterns are the property of the buyer, and it is important for him to maintain a record of their location at all times. Frequently the record will also show the amount of use already made of the tool or die. Such information is a guide in determining the replacement requirements for tools and dies.

Purchase Order Journal

A few purchasing departments maintain a daily journal where all purchase orders placed during the day are entered. The name of the vendor and the dollar value of the order are entered. This record has a dual purpose: It is useful to the purchasing officer in preparing reports on the activity of his department, and it is sometimes used by the finance department as an indication of the amount of expenditure to which the company is being committed. The record is especially useful in a purchasing department that is operated on a budget. It can be used to show whether purchases comply with the budgeted figures.

SPECIALIZED PURCHASING METHODS

In recent years, many managers of purchasing departments have developed specialized purchasing methods and procedures that reduce or eliminate some high-cost, repetitive clerical operations. Much material is currently being published in trade magazines about such procedures, and some of them will be described briefly in the chapter that follows.

DISCUSSION QUESTIONS

1. What is the difference between a purchase order and a requisition?

2. Define a "bill of materials" and indicate its use.

3. What methods are available to buyers to ascertain price?

4. Are there differences between follow-up and expediting procedures?

5. What procedure is involved in closing an order?

6. What benefits are derived from automating purchasing procedures?

7. Should all firms automate their purchasing procedures? Why or why not?

8. What are the basic concepts involved in designing a good business form?

9. What is the difference between a purchase record and a vendor record?

10. Describe what you consider to be the three most important forms used in a purchasing department.

SUGGESTED CASES

Ajax Sewing Machine Company

Evans Corporation

Expediting Problems

Howell Chuck Company (A)

King County

Roberts Fibre Products Company

The Wagner Corporation (A)

CHAPTER 4

SPECIALIZED PURCHASING PROCEDURES

Specialized purchasing procedures were developed to deal with the problems that arise in purchasing the vast multitude of articles that are small in value but constitute the greatest number of total articles bought by a purchasing department. These are generally items known as maintenance, repair, and operating supplies (MRO). The cost of purchasing MRO items in terms of manpower and paperwork is disproportionately high relative to their value. Thus, buying techniques were developed and are constantly being improved to reduce such costs without impairing the quality of the product or the service connected with securing the product.

Based on the experience obtained in using such specialized buying procedures, some firms are moving in the direction of applying them to other categories of purchases.[1]

NEED FOR SPECIALIZED PROCEDURES

The majority of purchase orders involve small sums of money. Since a substantial part of the operating costs of a purchasing department involves the paper work required to place orders, any reduction in this paper work produces worthwile savings. Some of the new procedures have almost eliminated the paper work.

[1] Peter Wulff, "3 Order Systems Blanket the Field," *Purchasing*, March 19, 1970, pp. 70-72. This article reports that one firm's entire purchasing budget is accounted for by three blanket contracts.

Inventory ownership costs are another category of costs that are of concern to the purchasing manager. Owning and storing inventories may cost as much as 30% of the value of the inventory. These costs include interest on the investment, the cost of the storage space, the physical handling and protection cost, and the costs involved in deterioration or obsolescence of the inventories. Some of the procedures to be described completely eliminate the carrying of inventory by the purchasing company and, thus, eliminate this cost for the purchaser. To the extent the carrying cost is reduced for the seller as well, this procedure lowers the total cost of the products.

The time spent by a purchasing agent on the standardized commodities such as MRO items is time that he cannot spend on more significant aspects of his job. Procedures that reduce routine purchasing make time available for more productive and rewarding work.

As an outgrowth of some of the specialized purchasing techniques to be described, steps may be taken that lead to a decrease in the material costs as well as in operating costs. These steps include a reduction in the number of varieties of items purchased; a reduction in the number of quotations by suppliers; a reduction in the number of suppliers for a given item; and, because of the time saving previously discussed, better purchasing of other types of products. All of these steps bring about a reduction in costs for all purchases.

Blanket Orders

The blanket order is the most popular alternative to the single-item, fixed-price order. A blanket order may be an agreement to provide a designated quantity of specified items for a period of time at an agreed price. If the price is not specified, a method of determining it is made a part of the contract. Deliveries are then made under a specified "release" system. A second type of blanket order is an agreement to furnish all of the buyer's needs for particular items for a designated period of time. Under this type of blanket order the quantity is not fixed until the time period has elapsed.

The unique purpose of a blanket order is to purchase a variety of items for which there are frequent deliveries from one source, typically a middleman. The blanket order is best for items with low unit value, but high annual usage, whose rate of usage cannot be accurately planned.

Typically, a blanket order covers a 12-month period, although other time periods may also be used. A purchasing department employing the blanket order procedure usually finds it advantageous to stagger the expiration dates of its blanket orders to avoid concentrating the work involved in negotiating new orders.

The description of products covered by a blanket order may be handled in one of three ways. The order may completely itemize and describe each product covered. In other instances blanket orders may be written to cover categories of goods that are broadly described, for example, fasteners. Occasionally a blanket order specifies that it covers all items that the supplier is able to furnish.

Price is also handled in a number of ways in a blanket order. Firm prices may be negotiated for each item covered. The blanket order may specify "market price" and include a method of determining such price. In some cases a ceiling price is established and the actual price of a sale is designated each time the supplier releases a product under the order. If the price exceeds the ceiling figure, the transaction is treated as a new and separate purchase which requires the buyer and seller to negotiate it as a single-purchase transaction.

A consideration in establishing blanket orders is arranging the procedure to be employed in releasing goods under the order. The buyer must retain his basic responsibility for providing materials when needed and controlling the dollar spent for them. Releases must be arranged so that the buyer does not lose his control even though the authority to issue releases is delegated to some other department.

Advantages of a Blanket Order Procedure

A blanket order system offers important benefits to the buyer:

1. Greatly simplified paper work routines in ordering and invoicing.
2. Assures regular supply for the buyer. A release quantity, agreed in advance, can be held in the distributor's stock and shipped immediately on release.
3. Cuts buyer's inventory investment because he can rely on the release quantity to be immediately available.
4. Frees purchasing manager's time to deal with the 20% of her orders that commit 80% of her dollars. These are the nonrepetitive capital goods or raw materials purchases that may not be suitable for supply contracts.
5. The distributor can reduce his sales calls or make the same number of calls be more productive and creative. A reduction in unproductive sales calls is an advantage to the buyer.

The Carborundum Company says that seven years of experience in their own MRO supply contracts has resulted in true savings of at least 16% on certain products and more on others.

If the theory sounds so good, why do many distributors look askance at contracts preferred by their customers? Or, alternately, why don't more distributors develop their own contract ordering plans? Unfortunately, the theory breaks down too frequently in actual practice.

Some of the disillusioning experiences of distributors include:

1. Unrealistic inflated figures on estimated annual usage on which the distributor bases his price.
2. Corollary to the above, when actual usage is below the estimate, the distributor is stuck with special inventory at the end of the contract and has no sales outlet for it.
3. One-sided terms drawn up by the buyer's corporate attorney that fail to provide mutual benefits to both contact parties. In some instances, distributors have felt compelled to take such contracts from large accounts in order to cover some percentage of fixed costs and retained good will of their manufacturer-supplier.
4. Demands for cost plus pricing that require the distributor to open his books to the prospective purchaser. How many buyers' companies allow their customers to know their production costs?
5. A large contract causes the distributor to gear his service efforts in that direction, thus leaving him with a large gap in his sales picture when the subsequent contract is given to a competitor at a fractionally low bid.
6. The buyer usually operates an EDP system and requires, as part of the contract, that the distributor gear his paper work to accept the customers' special system and nomenclature, thus creating a costly separate paperwork procedure for the distributor.
7. Overemphasis on price savings on subsequent contract terms as opposed to true cost savings for both parties through increased efficiency and paper work routines.

Blanket orders are of interest to suppliers in that they also may achieve cost savings from such arrangements. Once a supplier has been selected and the negotiations leading to a blanket order contract are concluded, his selling costs are almost eliminated. Furthermore, the assurance of a specified or estimated volume of sales enables the supplier to plan his production and inventory more accurately. Since most blanket order contracts specify monthly invoicing, it follows that the supplier's paper work can be significantly reduced.

The risks or disadvantages in utilizing blanket orders are those that are inherent in vendor selection and those that are avoidable—the selection of a supplier who does not meet the requirements of the blanket contract. However, since most items under blanket contract are readily available on short notice from other middlemen, the risk does not seem too great.

Suppliers have reported various problems with blanket orders. In some instances the buyer presented unrealistic or inflated data on potential quantities involved. This may cause losses to the supplier who based his price quotation on the high usage and may also result in overstocked inventory for the supplier. Since most suppliers under blanket contracts tend to be much smaller firms than the buying firm, they may develop an unhealthy dependency relationship.

Groeneveld sees a number of important implications in the growth of blanket contracting.[2] He believes that inevitably there will be a merging of the pertinent systems involving purchasing and inventory between the two firms. Just how far the integration can proceed is a matter of speculation at this time. EDP communication between buyer and seller under which stipulated stock levels at the buyer's plant trigger order releases at the seller's plant already exist. At this point in time, it is almost impossible to predict the consequences of such integration of buyer and seller systems under our existing antitrust legislation.

Another implication of blanket ordering on existing purchasing policy is the greater reliance on single rather than multiple sourcing for needs. In fact, many of the blanket orders being written require such single sourcing as part of the arrangement.

Other implications projected by Groeneveld include: the stimulation of greater service from the supplier to include assembly, acquisition of related items, and technical service; a significant increase in standardization of requirements by the buying firm; the tendency to remain with the same supplier for a much longer period of time; the need to develop much more comprehensive supplier evaluation systems since blanket orders cover a wide range of products rather than a limited number; the obsolescence of the economic-order-quantity concept (EOQ) since the cost of purchasing input to the formula will no longer be valid, and finally, management as opposed to the line buyer and seller will be involved as part of the team negotiating the blanket order.

[2] Leonard Groeneveld, "The Implications of Blanket Contracting For Industrial Purchasing and Marketing," *Journal of Purchasing*, November 1972, pp. 51-58.

National Contracts

The multiplant company will do some of its purchasing through a master or nationwide contract. Such a contract (generally referred to as a national contract) is normally negotiated by corporate purchasing staff.[3] The purpose of such contracts is to apply the overall company purchasing strength through consolidation of requirements to the task of minimizing costs.

Once the national agreement has been signed, the individual plant purchasing managers are notified as to its existence and how they may proceed to place orders (releases) against the master agreement. A number of companies have begun to adopt the use of preprinted release forms which are provided to the plant purchasing manager with details of the agreement.[4]

The use of the national contract is not an attempt to completely centralize the purchasing function at the corporate level. Most companies recognize that there are major advantages to allowing the individual plants to do their own purchasing.

"Stockless Purchasing" Procedures

Under a stockless purchasing system the buying company has no financial responsibility for inventory of the goods being purchased. The inventory is owned by the supplier. The goods may be located either at the supplier's or the buyer's location. The term *consignment buying* is often used to designate the latter arrangement.

For a stockless purchasing system to succeed, it is necessary for the buyer and the supplier to work together very closely. In selecting the supplier, an evaluation of the likely service of the alternative suppliers becomes vital. If inventories are to be maintained at the supplier's location, nearby suppliers are generally preferred.

Under a stockless purchasing system it is possible that prices will be slightly higher, since the supplier assumes most of the warehousing and inventory costs. However, the cost at the point of use may well be lower, because the seller may be able to perform these functions more economically than the buyer since he is a specialist in the products and handles his own inventory in any case. Another cost saving is generated because the supplier may well be serving a number of "stockless" buyers and thus be in a position to consolidate and lower

---

[3] For a report on how the Sperry Rand Corp. permits local plant purchasing managers to negotiate such contracts see *Purchasing*, June 18, 1974, p. 103.

[4] For an example of one such system see "Master Contracts Make Plant Buying a Snap," *Purchasing*, May 7, 1974, pp. 75-77.

the total inventory maintained for backup or safety purposes. The backup inventory is the extra stock that a using firm maintains to protect itself against unforeseen production delays, interruption of deliveries, or unpredicted increases in requirements. With inventory carried by the supplier a smaller safety stock need be carried, since not all of his customers would be likely to have unforeseen changes in demand at the same time.[5]

The first step in instituting a stockless buying procedure is the identification of the items to which it should apply. In general they will be standard "off-the-shelf" items that are used by several industries. Such items are typically purchased at frequent but irregular intervals. Prices among suppliers do not vary greatly. It should be noted, however, that the stockless buying procedure, especially consignment buying, is being expanded to cover an increasing range of purchased materials.

The buyer will organize items to be purchased into related groups and request qualified suppliers to submit bids on the prospective business. The lists submitted to the bidders will contain full descriptions of the items and data on the rate of usage of each.

Some companies are now incorporating into their stockless buying contract a clause requiring the supplier to maintain a stipulated "backup" inventory for the buyer's protection. Where this is done it is usual to include an agreement by the buyer to purchase the backup stock when the contract is terminated for items that are special to his needs or have become obsolete.

Advantages of Stockless Purchasing

Stockless buying is advantageous to both parties and therefore is likely to continue to spread and become a standard rather than a specialized purchasing procedure.

The buyer gains significantly in that he no longer is required to tie up capital in inventory. Purchasing routine is significantly reduced. Personnel in the purchasing department are freed to devote time to other elements of their jobs. Since the vendor's salespersons do not have to solicit orders, they can devote more time to aiding buyers through various service activities. Obsolescence of inventory is

---

[5] Los Angeles-based Ducommum, Inc., a pioneer in stockless purchasing, is providing the service to a growing list of manufacturers, including Rockwell International, Hughes Aircraft, and the Solar Division of International Harvester. "By eliminating 30,000 sq. ft. of storage space and all the overhead associated with it," says Solar purchasing specialist Bud Barber, "we figure our savings the first year at $150,000." *Business Week*, May 12, 1973, p. 128.

reduced under stockless buying. Lead time tends to be significantly reduced and may even be eliminated under consignment buying. Finally, the buyer is likely to get a lower price, not only because of inherent economics but also because the seller is willing to make price concessions when he knows that he will have all of a customer's business for the contract period.

The advantages to the seller are equally significant. Since the successful bidder on stockless contract has the assurance of the customer's business during the contract period, he can devote his selling efforts to other customers. The seller, as well as the buyer, has a significant reduction in paper work. If the consignment buying version of stockless purchasing is employed, the seller may reduce his warehouse space requirements. Where the product involved is in the equipment category, customers are more likely to acquire new equipment as it becomes available, since they do not have stocks of spare parts. The supplier can also eliminate more rapidly from his inventories spare parts that have become obsolete. The seller, with knowledge of the future requirements of his customers, can schedule his production of contracted items on the most efficient basis. If the seller is a middleman, he can buy in the most advantageous quantities and at the most advantageous times within the constraints of the contract.

Systems Contracting

"A Systems Contract is a total corporate technique designed to assist the buyer and seller to improve reordering of repetitive-use materials or services with an absolute minimum of administrative expense and with the maintenance of adequate business controls."[6]

The concept of the systems contract is generally credited to the Carborundum Company and was first used by that company in 1962. There is some confusion as to whether a systems contract is different from blanket order buying, national purchase agreements, automatic purchasing arrangements, and similar ideas. The essential difference is that in practice the systems contract has been long-term in its operations, whereas the other arrangements are of shorter duration, with changes in suppliers being relatively frequent.

Some of the specific points of difference between a systems contract and these other methods of purchasing lie in the following areas.

[6] Ralph A. Bolton, *Systems Contracting*, American Management Association, 1966.

Choice of Vendor

Under the systems concept not only will the agreement be of longer duration, but a much more formal method of selecting the vendor will be employed to eliminate personal considerations. The service requirements imposed on the vendor by the contract are more stringent and a specified price is more commonly an integral part of the arrangement. The *total* costs for all items and services covered in a systems contract are the determining factor. The chosen vendor should be a specialist in the materials covered by the contract so as to be able to offer maximum quantity to a large buyer of such items and discounts to the buyer.

Materials Covered by the Systems Contract

A selected vendor will generally be used to assist the buyer in analyzing his requirements of the materials covered by the contract so that her purchases will reflect the product variations and prices most suitable to her needs. The prior rate of usage of particular products must be determined as well as the frequency of reordering over some past period.

Since such analyses require a study of closed purchase orders, a policy question arises as to the wisdom of providing access to the vendor to such records. The records show not only transactions with that supplier but also previous purchases from competitive sources. One could argue that transactions have no bearing on the choice of systems contractor which has already been made. In addition, it is likely that the systems supplier was a major supplier in the past and is already in possession of much of this information.

Standardization

Under a systems contract the buyer receives only the brands produced or sold by the contractor. This generally means that a standardization program must be adopted, but for most companies this is desirable for its own sake.

Catalogs

The catalog is vital to a systems contract, since all of the items must be identified. The catalog is usually prepared by the vendor, hence the numbering system is his. Typically, unit packaging is specified to facilitate requisitioning in economic order quantities (EOQ).[7]

[7] See Chapter 8 for explanation.

The negotiated price is listed in the catalog, and this obviates the prior need to provide the accounting department with a copy of all purchase orders as a basis for checking the price at which items are invoiced.

Catalogs with confidential information such as price are given to the purchasing, accounting, and auditing departments. Unpriced catalogs are distributed to the requisition points.

Requisitioning

Since a systems contract vendor guarantees delivery, and, to remain a contractor, must perform dependably, there is no need to requisition more than the buyer's immediate needs. The requisition, properly countersigned by the purchase approval agent, is forwarded to the contractor. There is no need for multiple copies of a requisition as is the case with most purchasing procedures.

Order Filling by Vendor

The systems contracts vendor assigns a number to a requisition when it is received. The numbers are consecutive under each contract, and this numbering system permits much better control than the usual numbering sequence in which all vendors' requisitions are intermingled.

The vendor prices the requisition, since it comes to him unpriced, and he selects the method of shipment, because on-time delivery is a crucial element in the systems contract arrangement. Most vendors agree to deliver on 24-hour notice, which is about the same as requisitioning from a company storeroom.

Payment

A periodic payment is customary even though each requisition technically constitutes an invoice. The periodic payment is made on the basis of a simple tally sheet of all transaction with a vendor for a stipulated period of time. The consecutive numbers on the requisitions ensure to both parties that the periodic payment is complete.

Advantages of Systems Contracting

The foregoing comparison of systems contracting with regular purchasing procedures illustrates that there are significant advantages to a systems contract.

The majority of repetitively purchased items are delivered within a 24-hour work period, which is often faster delivery than is made from a company controlled inventory. The systems contract substantially reduces stores records, requests for quotations, bids, purchase orders, follow-up, and expediting procedures, shipping notices, invoices, and so on. In addition, the sales representative is able to devote more time to service, and if the total time spent with the buyer is reduced, the cost saving can be reflected in a lower price.

The reduction in storeroom requirements nets a saving in personnel and space cost.

The opportunity for errors in ordering is reduced, since the original requisition is used as the notification to the supplier to ship. None of the error opportunities inherent in a system requiring the copying or typing or orders, packing slips, invoices, and so on, are present.

Companies that have adopted systems contracting claim inventory reductions in the magnitude of 80%. This is accomplished by eliminating all nonessential items and carrying a bare minimum of essential items in inventory, which are then stocked and requisitioned from the supplier's warehouse. Both reductions mean a significant lessening of capital investment. Floor space is also saved.

Obsolescence due to changes in requirements is reduced. In addition, without the risk of materials in inventory, changes that would have obsoleted such materials are made more rapidly. If the supplier is required to maintain inventory for the buyer, the contract will generally provide for a means of compensating him if he suffers obsolescence because of a change in requirements on the part of the buyer.

A systems contract has significant advantages to the vendor as well as the buyer.[8] Salespersons' efforts can be directed to work designed to solidify the relationship instead of being spent on order-taking. The supplier can concentrate attention on new ideas and materials not covered under the contract.

If the vendor performs in accordance with the agreement, he is likely to retain the contract for an indefinite time period. He is also likely to be given the first opportunity for expansion of the coverage of materials under the contract.

There are also significant savings in paper work for the vendor under a systems contract. All pricing is done from the catalog. Individual invoices, packing lists, and so on, do not have to be prepared. Quantities sold to a customer are greater, since the vendor furnishes all of the buyer's requirements for the items under contract.

---

[8] For conflicting views on the benefits of systems' contracts to vendors see "Systems Contacts: Do They Work?" *Purchasing*, May 7, 1974, p. 47.

Small-Order Procedures

Probably no procurement subject has received as much attention in recent years as the small-order problem. *Purchasing*, one of the leading magazines in the procurement field, published at least thirteen articles on this subject during 1964. *Purchasing Week* and *Electronic Procurement* likewise have devoted many feature stories to the problem. The National Association of Purchasing Agents has established a Development Project Committee on Small-Order Problems, and has published a booklet on the subject and sponsored Small-Order Workshops throughout the country. The American Management Association also recognized the growing importance of the small-order problem and made it a major topic in several of its purchasing workshops and seminars. A recent *Electronic Procurement* survey found that small-orders are second only to insufficient lead time as the number one problem facing purchasing agents.[9]

All companies have a significant volume of purchase transactions that are of a nonrecurring nature and involve insignificant sums of money for an individual transaction. The specialized techniques already described in this chapter cannot usually be adapted to meet this problem. Since one cannot increase the value of the transaction in relation to the handling costs involved, the alternative of reducing the handling costs per purchase transaction must provide the answer.

The specialized techniques described in the following pages have the common objective of reducing the costs of buying without greatly impairing the services received.[10]

It is difficult to anticipate the need for small, nonrecurring purchases because the situations that generate such needs are usually unrelated to one another. Frequently, the item involved can be bought only from a single supplier, thus precluding the possibility of combining orders to increase total value. Furthermore, such requirements are generally needed promptly. Therefore, one cannot hold and accumulate orders to increase total value of the transaction.

When the nonrecurring purchase is a special part of or tool for a single department in the company, it may be possible to develop specialized procedures that bypass the usual receiving, inspection, storage, and similar functions. This short-cutting not only reduces the amount of paper work but also speeds up the purchasing cycle.

---

[9] William B. Collings, "The Big Small-Order Problem," *Journal of Purchasing*, February 1966, p. 43.

[10] For a more detailed discussion of these specialized techniques, see *The Small Order Problem*, The National Association of Purchasing Agents, New York, 1964.

Petty-Cash System

Petty cash is another system that virtually eliminates paper work. Petty cash is a sum of money set aside to meet minor expenses of a business. This procedure is most effective for purchasing small orders from local sources and works best where a "roving buyer" or chauffeur is available.

Under this procedure a requisition is given to the roving buyer, with the source indicated. The buyer then makes the pickup and pays for the item immediately. The sales slip becomes both the receiving document and the petty-cash voucher. Invoicing and accounts payable as well as the purchase order procedures are eliminated.

Where this technique is employed, the general petty-cash fund or a special fund for small purchases must be under the control of the purchasing department to preserve the advantages of centralized purchasing. Using departments should not be authorized to purchase against petty cash, since they would be inclined to expand this procedure to include larger transactions that ought to be more closely supervised in the interests of sound purchasing procedures.

Cash on Delivery (C.O.D.) Ordering System

Although some companies have argued against the use of the C.O.D. system because it may be interpreted as a reflection on their credit standing, such a position can be costly. A C.O.D. system can reduce paper work significantly. The savings are primarily in connection with invoice and accounts payable procedures, although some companies have also utilized telephone ordering of C.O.D. items to eliminate purchase order writing. A major consideration in the adoption of a C.O.D. system is determining whether any C.O.D. fees paid are less than the costs of the paper work that is eliminated.

Telephone Orders

The use of telephone ordering of small-value nonrecurring purchases is thoroughly logical. Frequently when a buyer receives a requisition from a using department he must, in any event, telephone a supplier to determine the availability and price of the item. When telephone orders are authorized, he merely goes one step further and places the order over the telephone, providing the supplier with an order number that is also used to identify the requisition. The writing of purchase orders is eliminated.

Carbons of requisitions are given to both the receiving and accounting departments. The accounting department is usually authorized to use this requisition, which contains the price data obtained over the telephone, as the invoice for payment purposes.

Some companies realize further savings in paper work by agreeing with the suppliers on a charge account system for telephone orders. Instead of paying for each order, they are accumulated and paid for periodically, in most instances bimonthly, without the seller rendering an invoice.

The state of California adopted a streamlined telephone system in January 1974 and planned to use it for more than 25,000 separate purchases with a value of less than $1000.

The items involved about 80% of all transactions of the state's purchasing departments but only 15-20% of the dollar value. Under the system, competitive quotation will be secured by phone and a decision will then be made and the order placed. The time elapsed between the writing of the requisition and the issuance of the written purchase order will be cut to less than ten days.

The Western Division of GTE Sylvania has adopted what might be called a "paperless buying system."[11]

The remaining essential is that the supplier has agreed *in writing*, to our standard terms and conditions and has agreed that confirming Purchase Orders are not necessary.

The only document involved in the entire process is the Purchase Requisition, which may be hand-written or computer-generated. Prepared by the Material Control Department, it shows the part type and part number, order quantity, date needed, internal destination and some accounting data.

After a buyer number has been assigned by the Purchasing Supervisor, a copy of the requisition is removed and used as the input document to establish these specifics in the computer memory. The requisition, in the meantime, goes to the Buyer, who places an order by phone advising the supplier that no written Purchase Order will be issued. The Purchase Order number, the name and address of the supplier, price quoted, promised delivery date, discount terms, F.O.B. point, method of shipment and the fact that this was a paperless transaction are recorded on the requisition by the Buyer. Additional computer instructions are also coded onto the requisition at this time, which determines the later use of the data for departmental statistics reports.

The requisition is now torn down and distributed, one copy to the requisitioner for his permanent records, one copy becomes the

[11] Lysle D. Brown, "Breaking up the Paperwork Log Jam," *Pacific Purchaser*, March 1974, pp. 9-10.

input document to the computer and is then forwarded to Accounts Payable on which accounting clerks record all invoices received and payment data.

The original copy, with an attached expediting record card, becomes the expediting copy and is used to record status information just as a typewritten copy of the Purchase Order would be used. Upon completion of the order, all documentation associated with the order, receiving, rejection and shipping reports are filed with the requisition in the purchasing closed order file.

When a shipment arrives, the receiving clerk gets the Purchase Order number from the packing slip, refers to an open Purchase Order log, generated daily by the computer and determines for which Purchase Order line items a receiver is required. The computer-generated log is in part number sequence by Purchase Order Number which makes this operation quite fast. If only one or a few line items of the full order are in the shipment, the clerk keys into a keyboard terminal located at the receiving desk, the Purchase Order number and the computer-generated item number associated with the part numbers on the packing slip. Two "slave" terminals located adjacent to the keyboard almost instantaneously generated a four-part receiving report for each item.

Should the shipment contain all or most of the Purchase Order line items the clerk requests all receiving reports for the Purchase Order and simply discards those not needed.

Check Payment Ordering System

This specialized purchasing procedure is frequently called "paperless purchasing." The purchase order draft system is a combination of purchase order and blank check for payment purposes. Besides the product description, the purchase order section will contain shipping instructions, account number, unit price, quantity, applicable sales tax, discounts, and the terms of payment.

The supplier completes the presigned blank check, which bears a notation that it is limited to a fairly low dollar maximum, such as $500. A duplicate copy of the blank check is sent and returned to the buyer. Partial shipments are not permitted under the system. It frequently is possible to negotiate an additional cash discount because of the immediate payment feature on such orders.

The Kaiser Aluminum Company, which was one of the first to use this procedure and gave it the name, "Kaiser Instant Money Plan,"[12] claims a reduction in its operating costs of approximately 28%. In

[12] "The Instant Money Plan," *Business Week*, October 12, 1963, p. 90.

July 1964 this company issued 81% of its orders under this plan, although they accounted for about 16% of the dollars committed.

Kaiser imposes three limitations not found in conventional checks. The checks are limited to $1000 each, they are void after 90 days, and they are made payable only to the account of the payee whose name is typed on the check. The company has found no evidence of dishonesty in connection with its "Instant Money Plan."

Its principal advantage, of course, is in the reduction of the paper work associated with accounts payable.

General Conclusions

Specialized purchasing procedures deal almost exclusively with reducing the cost of handling small purchase orders. The small-order problem is not one that can be solved by the elimination of all small orders. The very nature of the needs that cause small orders is inevitable in the business enterprise. In the case of small orders for nonrecurring types of items, the effort of the analyst who seeks to minimize the problem must be to reduce costs connected with the procedure for handling such orders. The order itself cannot be eliminated, but if several steps in the purchasing process can be combined or bypassed, savings can be effected. As we have pointed out throughout the chapter, the greatest opportunities for effecting economies are in connection with the steps involved in the payment for such purchases.

Small orders for the recurring type of purchases can be handled in a number of ways that would minimize the cost and reduce the size of this problem. Better planning and scheduling can reduce such small orders by combining several into a single-purchase transaction. Special arrangements for combining invoices on the part of the supplier can reduce the paper work usually connected with handling a large volume of invoices.

It must be emphasized that whatever procedures are adopted by a firm to meet its small-order problems, such procedures must be designed to meet the specific needs of that firm. No standard answer can be applied to all firms and all situations.

It should be pointed out that many small orders occur because of carelessness, errors, and ignorance on the part of purchasing personnel or related departments. This chapter has not discussed steps that might be taken to reduce small orders. Improvements in internal efficiency and management of the purchasing function would automatically improve this problem at the same time that other purchasing practices are being corrected.

The proper approach to solving the problems created by small orders involves at least three steps:

1. Analyze and categorize the small orders that have been processed in the department for a specific period of time to determine whether the orders had to be small orders.
2. Determine if any procedure could be adopted that would reduce the costs of handling such orders, the clerical function within the purchasing department, the clerical or operating functions within any other departments of the company, or the related functions in the supplier's plant.
3. Exercise ingenuity in proposing and testing alternative procedures for handling small orders.

DISCUSSION QUESTIONS

1. Why is it necessary to develop specialized purchasing procedures?

2. What is the purpose of a blanket order?

3. How does the buying firm benefit from use of the blanket order?

4. What are some of the problems that have developed with blanket order systems? Can you suggest solutions to those problems?

5. What are national contracts?

6. What is meant by "stockless purchasing"? What are its benefits?

7. What is a system's contract?

8. Describe the petty cash system of purchasing. For what types of purchases should it be used?

9. Describe the check payment order system. For what types of purchases should it be used?

10. Describe the "paperless buying system."

SUGGESTED CASES

The Janmar Company

John Roberts Manufacturing Company

PART II
PURCHASING ACTIVITIES

CHAPTER 5
SELECTION OF SOURCES OF SUPPLY

If there is one activity which, more than any other, epitomizes the purchasing process, it is the selection of sources of supply. All of the other activities of purchasing come to focus and fruition in the crucial decision as to whom shall be selected as the supplier of goods and services. The selection process includes the continuing surveillance of the relationship between the supplier and the buyer to maintain mutually satisfactory conditions of cooperation and interest.

In selecting a source of supply the purchasing officer makes decisions that influence not only the firm's economic success, but the livelihood of the supplier and the efficiency of the entire economy. The purchase decision directly influences the financial ability of the supplying firm, and ultimately the economic welfare of hundreds or thousands of employees and their families. The vitality of the entire economy is involved because proper functioning of our free enterprise economy depends on sound product choices. The consumer by his dollar "votes" (i.e., purchases) determines the economy's production and the resulting allocation of resources. The purchasing official represents the consumer by carrying these votes back to the original producers. The efficiency exhibited in vendor selection stimulates the competition, which results in the development of better products and services for the economy.

Authority for Selection

As selection is the essence of the purchasing process, it is imperative that final authority rest with the purchasing department. In some companies improper selection, causing inferior goods and services, has resulted in authority being shared with the using department. Under these circumstances a large measure of control over purchasing is lost by the purchasing department, friction develops, and morale suffers. Therefore, proper source selection must be exercised by the purchasing department to avoid possibilities of interdepartmental conflict.

Procedure

The procedure of source selection involves the preparation of an exhaustive list of prospective suppliers and the successive elimination from this list on various grounds until the number has been reduced to the one or few to be favored with the business. The procedure is therefore one of searching and sorting—searching for all likely suppliers and then sorting for the one or ones with whom to do business. This chapter will evaluate methods of building up a list of possible suppliers and the criteria and techniques to use to narrow the number down to the chosen sources.

Preparing a Prospective Supplier List

The first step in the process of selecting a supplier is to prepare a complete list of prospective suppliers. The thoroughness with which this list is prepared depends on the importance of the business to be transacted. Quite naturally, the purchasing department will not make an exhaustive search for suppliers unless the value of orders to be placed warrants the cost. The following discussion should therefore be read with the realization that very seldom would any buyer consult all of the named sources. However, in any given case any or another of the sources might prove helpful. The list below gives the more important sources from which a buyer may build his list of prospective suppliers:

Experience
Salesman interviews
Catalogs
Trade directories
Trade journals
Associates
Trade shows and conventions
Requests for quotations

Each of these sources will now be evaluated as a source of supplier information.

Experience

Past experience with suppliers is perhaps the most available and widely used source of information about prospective suppliers. Since so much purchasing is repetitive in nature, a wealth of information is available to the buyer on the basis of which the performance of suppliers can be judged. When a new item is under consideration, a buyer should, therefore, first inquire whether any of the present or past suppliers are likely prospects.

Some buyers rely on their memory for facts about their relationships with suppliers. Since human memory is short-lived, uncertain, and sometimes biased, it is much more satisfactory to have records available for reference on these matters. Most purchasing departments maintain vendor files that contain the names and addresses of all vendors with whom the company has dealt throughout its history as well as a notation of the classes of goods that have been purchased from each vendor. Frequently the files are set up to include additional data on such things as the reliability of the supplier in meeting commitment dates, willingness to handle emergency and rush orders, and defect or reject ratios on shipments received in the past. Companies with computers frequently record experience with vendors in the computer's memory bank which can reproduce this information in complete detail upon demand. Such use of the computer is one of its important functions for purchasing.

Some companies expand their vendor files to include information on all suppliers investigated, as well as the ones with whom the company has done business. Such information may be useful, provided it is still current enough to be pertinent.

Salesman Interviews

The salespeople who call on purchasing agents are extremely valuable sources of information about suppliers for particular products. In most cases their information relates to their own companies and their own products, but often a salesman is also able to tell the buyer about a source of supply for an item that his company does not make.

In an attempt to provide visiting salesmen with the greatest possible amount of information about their requirements, many firms display their finished products and purchased components in reception or special display rooms. The salesman is then able to determine items he can supply and provide technical assistance. Supplementary information relating to standards of quality expected are also provided. The more a salesman knows of his prospective buyer's needs, the better are his chances of being a good source of supply.

Because salesmen are such valuable sources of information, many buyers make it a practice to see every salesman who calls, if it is physically possible to do so. A buyer never knows when a salesman may have either a product or information about a product that will prove beneficial to the buyer's company. Many buyers jot down information that may later prove valuable after each salesman has been interviewed and maintain a file of such data for each salesman who calls and for each supplying company.

In evaluating the salesman as a source of information about the value of a company as a supplier, one must recognize the strong impression that is left in the mind of the buyer by the character and personality of the salesman. Generally, the salesman is the only point of contact between the two companies, and the buyer tends to identify the company with its salesman. If the salesman is reliable, cooperative, and competent, the buyer is inclined to assume that the company he represents is also reliable, cooperative, and competent. This is not necessarily true. Some poor companies have good salesmen and some good companies have poor salesmen. Consequently, a good buyer will attempt to evaluate the factual information given by a salesman as objectively as possible. However, a buyer should not rely solely on representations of the salesman in evaluating a supplier where the amount of the purchase transaction is large.

Catalogs

The catalogs published by vendors in which they list and describe the various items they make for sale constitute a valuable source of information about possible suppliers. For standard production items such catalogs frequently are one of the most effective and efficient sources of potential suppliers. A number of studies have been made in order to learn the extent to which purchasing agents use their catalog files. These studies show that almost all buyers make some use of their catalogs and a substantial percentage of buyers use them extensively.

Although there still is a great diversity of catalog sizes, steps are being taken by such groups as the National Association of Purchasing Management and by trade magazines to bring about more uniformity. The usual catalog file system provides for the insertion of one or a few catalogs into numbered jackets or envelopes for identification purposes. A master card is then prepared for each catalog, listing the catalog by the vendor's name, and a second card on which the catalog is indexed according to the vendor's major product lines. Under this indexing system a purchasing agent can readily locate a catalog if she knows either the vendor's name or the product line in which she is interested. The usefulness of a catalog file depends to a large extent on how up-to-date it is kept. Many larger companies appoint a librarian who maintains the catalog file as one of his official duties.

Trade Directories

A trade directory is a publication that lists and classifies suppliers according to the products they make. Frequently it gives a minimum amount of information on such matters as the financial status of the companies, their method of distribution, and location of sales offices. Usually a trade directory is prepared and published by some private company as a commercial undertaking, and it includes a large amount of advertising by the listed firms, designed to call attention to their offerings. Some trade directories are specialized by industries as, for example, a directory of all companies manufacturing paper and paper products. The better-known directories, however, cover all industries. The two best-known general directories are Thomas' Register of American Manufacturers and MacRae's Blue Book. One should not overlook the yellow pages of the telephone directory as a localized general directory of industrial suppliers. The telephone company has been promoting this use of the telephone directory, and in most of the metropolitan cities of the United States the yellow pages are a rather complete source of supplier information. In some areas it is possible to make use of directories prepared by Chambers of Commerce. Such directories frequently list small local suppliers who do not have the resources to make themselves known through ordinary channels.

Either the general or the specialized trade directories contain enough information to enable a purchasing agent to prepare a first tentative list of possible suppliers. The specialized directory is likely to contain somewhat more pertinent information than a general directory, but, whichever directory is used, the purchasing agent will have to go to other sources to be sure that the companies whose names she has are worth considering as suppliers. So, in general, it may be concluded that trade directories are a prolific but very uncritical source of supplier leads.

Trade Journals

Trade journals—or business magazines—are other very fruitful sources of supplier names. There are thousands of such publications, and no purchasing department can subscribe to more than a small fraction of the total number. A company's choice must be limited to those fields in which it has a primary interest. A metalworking plant would probably subscribe to such magazines as *Iron Age* and *American Machinist*. In addition, most purchasing agents subscribe to magazines such as *Purchasing* which are directed specifically to their interests.

As sources of information on suppliers, the value of trade journals depends on the regularity and thoroughness with which they are read. In general, they are not useful as directories to be consulted as the need arises. Rather, they are general sources of information on new products, developments, and methods that are described in the editorial and advertising pages.

It is frequently contended that industrial advertisements do not have great value to the purchasing agent, since they do not contain sufficient information to serve as the basis for a decision about a product or a company. It undoubtedly is true that few advertisements are so complete that they carry a buyer to the point of decision. However, if they condition the buyers to give a more ready welcome to the advertiser's salesman or if they remind the buyer to inquire about the advertising company's product before buying, they have served a profitable purpose. It is an established fact that the typical purchasing agent reads many trade journals and pays close attention to industrial advertisements because she cannot afford to overlook any information about new products or suppliers.

Suggestions from Associates

Many a buyer has found a truly valuable reservoir of information on potential suppliers in the circle of purchasing associates with whom she has become friendly through business relationships or through meetings of his local purchasing agents' association. They are especially useful in developing sources for materials or supplies that the buyer has not previously had to procure for his company. This is an indirect method of utilizing past experience—the experience of an associate rather than the buyer herself. Its reliability depends on the confidence the buyer places in the associate and the assurance she has that her associate is giving a full disclosure of the facts.

Trade Shows and Conventions

Another source of information about suppliers that is available to all buyers is the trade show or convention. Practically all important industrial groups hold such shows at various times during the year.

At the trade show the members of an industry display their wares in an attempt to attract buyers, build up their interest, and, if possible, make sales. The convention, by contrast, is usually a trade association meeting designed primarily as a forum for the exchange of ideas. However, many such conventions arrange to have display space which they rent to suppliers of their trade for the display of equipment and materials of interest to members. Such conventions are ideal places for a supplier to show his line to a concentrated group of interested prospects and, at the same time, offer a convenient way for a buyer to learn about new products and suppliers.

Some of the local associations of purchasing agents sponsor industrial shows in their cities. At these shows one can find items ranging from office supplies to heavy-duty equipment. A buyer attending such shows can talk to representatives of many firms making similar products and get a good idea of whether the suppliers are worthy of further investigation.

Miscellaneous Sources of Information

Foreign sources for various materials have become more important in recent years with the improvement of manufacturing skill in many areas of the world. Lower labor costs in conjunction with this technical skill frequently have made such products fully competitive with domestic products. Many foreign countries have trade representatives and agencies in the major cities of the United States. These agencies put buyers in touch with potential foreign sources of supply.

Occasionally vendors may be located by requesting information from the manufacturer of the basic material regarding firms that process his material. For example, if a company needs a metal that has been prefinished with a flexible coating to withstand bending in processing, it might be advantageous to get in touch with the manufacturer of the flexible coating and ask for the names of processors who specialize in coating metal with his flexible finishes.

Requests for Quotations

Finally, information on prospective suppliers can be secured through a request for quotation form. A written request to a supplier to quote price and delivery on a named part is referred to as a request for quotation or request for bid. Such requests contain a blueprint or written specifications including quality requirements and estimated usage. This procedure is usually used annually on all significant parts and services that are being purchased. Bids are solicited from at least three potential suppliers, thereby providing an opportunity for equitable comparisons among competitors. Government buyers are required by law to employ such open-bidding procedures.

Factors to Be Considered in Supplier Evaluation

After the list of possible suppliers has been compiled, the next step is to evaluate each supplier so that the list may be narrowed down to the predetermined number with whom the buyer chooses to place her business. This process of evaluation is conducted by comparing the suppliers in terms of their ability to provide the desired quality, quantity, price, and service.

In the purchasing context, *quality* refers to the suitability of an item for its intended purpose. In purchasing, therefore, the *best* quality is not necessarily the highest quality; in fact, sometimes the best quality may be the lowest quality. Quality must always be judged in the light of the use to which the product will be put. In purchasing parlance, *quantity* also has a somewhat specialized meaning. It refers not only to the total amount required but to the schedule according to which the goods are required. Thus a supplier who might be able to supply the desired quantity *during* the time period specified but could not supply that quantity *on* the dates specified would not be a satisfactory supplier from the point of view of quantity. In purchasing, as in all economic activity, price is a measure of value. The important thing to keep in mind is that price is meaningless considered by itself. A price is a *good* price only if it is the lowest price offered for a desired quality, in right quantity, and accompanied by sufficient useful services. When talking in general terms about comparing quality, quantity, and price, it is difficult to say much more than it is highly important for a buyer to make certain that he has considered these three factors carefully and in combination with each other. The exact comparisons that are made will depend to a large extent on the commodity at issue. However, it is possible to discuss the service factor in greater detail and to draw some generalizations about service that are pertinent to all purchases.

Location

The geographical location of the supplier is an important consideration in evaluating service. Shipments from a supplier located at a great distance from the buyer's plant are subject to more and greater risks of interruption such as accidents, strikes, and floods, because of the distance and time involved in transportation. At the same time, the possibility of using substitute modes of transportation is lessened as distance increases. For example, if there has been a disruption to rail transportation on a short haul, it is easier to substitute truck transport than if the shipment involves a long haul. This difficulty of finding substitute transportation for the long haul is still greater if the commodity to be transported is bulky or heavy.

Some companies overcome part of their geographical disadvantage by providing pool car shipments, branch warehouses, and make-and-hold services. Pool car shipments refer to the practice of collecting a number of small orders from a given geographic region and combining them into one shipment, thereby economizing on freight by obtaining the full car rate rather than the much higher LCL (less than carload) rate. A usual practice is to have such shipments once or twice each week. Pool car shipments may be used in conjunction with branch warehouses which act as distributing points for shipments originating at the home plant. For example XYZ Company, located in Waterbury, Connecticut, may utilize a branch warehouse in Chicago. Orders for customers in the Milwaukee-Chicago area are pooled and shipped on Wednesdays and Mondays to the Chicago branch from which final distribution is accomplished. Public warehouses can be used in instances where a privately operated branch is not economically feasible.

The make-and-hold service refers to the practice of the seller producing in anticipation of buyer's needs and storing the merchandise. This allows the seller to ship immediately upon word from the buyer, and thereby minimizes total order time. The increased flexibility in providing immediate shipments may offset the disadvantage of a geographically inferior seller.

Reserve Facilities

The reserve facilities that a supplier has available are another consideration to be taken into account in evaluating a potential supplier's service. This issue is of special importance during periods of high industrial activity. A supplier with a good reserve of productive facilities is in the best position to meet increased demand and to assure his customers that their demand will be met in terms of both quality and quantity. In evaluating reserve facilities one should consider technical and managerial skills as well as physical plant and facilities. If a potential supplier's engineering and management staff is spread thin, it is questionable whether he could make use of extra physical capacity in a seller's market when manpower is often at more of a premium than goods. Thus, in comparing suppliers, it is important to analyze in detail the facilities that the various companies have to offer as a criterion of the service they will supply.

Internal Facilities

The stage of a supplier's technological development and his interest in keeping up with current methods are also considerations affecting service. While it might be argued that a buyer is interested only in whether a supplier can supply the quality requested, this is a short-sighted attitude. As improvements and developments are made by competitors, the buyer is certain to want better products from his suppliers, and, if their technological capabilities do not enable them to keep up with competitors, the buyer will suffer from having chosen a technologically inferior supplier.

The inspection methods and the quality-control standards maintained by the prospective supplier are also important in evaluating service. Since assurance of supply means not only that the goods will be delivered, but also that they will be in usable condition, it is important that these two criteria—inspection and quality control—be carefully checked before the choice of supplier is made. A supplier who is careless about inspection will ship many items that must eventually be rejected and returned because they are not satisfactory for the purpose. If such a supplier is also lax in his production quality control, the problem is aggravated because of some of these imperfections which may not be discovered until after the item has been incorporated into the finished product.

A closely related consideration that bears on supplier service is the "housekeeping" or plant-maintenance standards carried out by the supplier. A supplier who is careful and thorough in his plant-maintenance practices is likely to suffer from a minimum number of production disruptions resulting from machinery breakdowns and similar mishaps. Since production disruptions frequently lead to delays in shipments to customers, they decrease the assurance of supply which is an important consideration in service.

Labor Relations

Another possible interference with the continuity of production in a supplier's plant may originate with the workers themselves. These stoppages may be in the form of strikes or slowdowns and are the by-product of the labor relations of the supplier. To a considerable extent, the possibility of such delays can be determined by observing the morale of the working force, the labor policies as expressed by general management of the prospective supplier, and the degree of responsibility of the leadership of the union associated with the plant. The history of past strikes will reflect the labor-management climate. A final important point is to determine the length of time

remaining on the present labor contract. The possibility of labor difficulties can then be assessed by taking all these factors into consideration.

An indirect clue to anticipated service may be gained from noting
the kind and form of warranty and service that the supplier offers
with his products. One should consider the willingness of the supplier
to give an adequate express warranty with his products, his offer to
install where necessary and to replace where indicated, and his willingness and ability to make available replacement parts as needed.
Assurance of supply means not only that deliveries are made as
promised but also that the product delivered should be usable
throughout its normal life. A supplier who does not stand behind his
product or who is not equipped to service his product satisfactorily
cannot be rated high on the point of service.

The vendor relations of the supplier must also be evaluated in determining his service rating. A good supplier on this score is one who
will meet occasional unusual requests, such as the need for emergency shipments or a sudden slight change in specifications. A buyer
needs assurance that a supplier will willingly accept such situations
if he can be satisfied that the emergency is a real one and that such
emergencies do not arise with undue frequency. It is as important
that the buyer not subject the supplier to a succession of emergencies
as it is that the supplier accept an occasional emergency graciously.

A visit to the plants of prospective suppliers is an important means
of evaluation. Plant visitation is also important in the periodic re-
examination of present suppliers. It is quite customary for a representative of the production department or the engineering department to accompany the buyer on his plant visitations. This is especially desirable if the supplier makes technical products. By having a
technical expert with him the buyer is able to arrive at a sound judgment on the equipment and capabilities of the supplier.

Plant Visitations

Although there is no one list of things to be considered on all
plant visitations, it is possible to generalize somewhat with regard to
the things that should be observed and examined on such visits.

1. *Facilities.* The examination should include not only production
machinery and plant layout but also such facilities as the receiving
room where the supplier handles his incoming shipments, the shipping room where he prepares his own products for delivery, the internal materials-handling system, the supply rooms and tool rooms

where he maintains his reserve stocks, and the office facilities where he processes the necessary paper work and records.

2. *Personnel.* The survey should include observations on the degree and type of supervision by foremen and other supervisors, state of morale of the workers as it may bear on possible work stoppages or strikes, and degree of technical competence shown by all individuals whose work in any way has a bearing on the purchased goods. Particular attention should be paid to union relations. If a supplier is having labor trouble, this will affect his ability to meet required delivery dates.

3. *Housekeeping.* The inspection should include plant maintenance and general cleanliness, as these provide useful clues to the efficiency and steadiness of output that may be expected of the supplier.

4. *Procedures.* It is well to study the manner in which the supplier processes an order from the time it is received until the shipment leaves his plant. Such an analysis will establish the level of efficiency that is maintained and will also acquaint the buyer with any special procedural problems the supplier may have that could affect service.

5. *Production Specialization.* The buyer should attempt to determine during a plant visitation if there are any areas of production in which the supplier tends to specialize. It is in such specialized areas that the supplier is likely to prove to be the most satisfactory source.

Credit and Financial Analysis

Another method of evaluation of suppliers, which is sometimes overlooked by purchasing agents, is the analysis of credit reports. Most concerns have available, through their comptroller's offices, reports of the Dun and Bradstreet credit service. At little or no additional cost to the company, the purchasing agent is able to secure information from this source that will assist in supplier evaluation. Credit reports contain information on a supplier's facilities. Where the report is unfavorable a trip to a supplier's plant can be saved. The reports often give an insight into the experience and character of a potential vendor. By establishing the credit rating of a vendor, the purchasing agent is able to estimate the financial risk of dealing with that vendor. The reports also list the products made by the vendor, giving the purchasing agent some insight into his capabilities. Since the reports show the vendor's profits, the purchasing agent has a clue to the efficiency of the vendor's operations.

A supplementary related procedure involves independent analysis of the vendor's financial statements. Although accounting statements vary with fiscal periods, and details of accounting procedures, the purchasing official can obtain information regarding the financial stability, pricing cushion, and general operating efficiency by applying the tools of ratio analysis to the balance sheet and income statements of the vendor. A short account of the more popular ratios and their use follows.

Current ratio relates current assets to current liabilities. The usual "rule of thumb" acceptable ratio is 2—1. As current assets and liabilities are those that can be turned into cash within a short period of time (one year or less), this ratio measures the financial ability of the firm to continue in the short-run. In recent years, companies often maintain less than a 2—1 current ratio to avoid having idle and unproductive assets; so this ratio should not be overemphasized.

Acid test ratio is a variant of the current ratio in that it relates current assets less inventories to current liabilities. Inventories are omitted from current assets because they often are difficult to turn into cash readily. A rule of thumb acceptable ratio here is 1—1. Like the current ratio, it is a reflection of the ability of the firm to function in the short-run.

Sales-receivable ratio is determined by dividing sales by accounts receivable; it indicates whether customers are paying their bills promptly or whether too much of the vendor's assets are tied up in receivables. This ratio is related to the seller's standard terms of payment. For example, if the terms are 90 days, not much more than this amount of total sales should be in receivables. A firm with sales of $6 million and 90-day terms should not have much more than $1.5 million in accounts receivable.

Net profit to sales is an overall measure of the profitability of the firm after all expenses have been deducted. The size of the profits gives an indication of the possibility of successful price negotiations.

Cash flow is obtained by adding net profit after taxes to depreciation charges. It measures the amount of dollars the firm is receiving. Cash flow assists profit evaluation, as it is a measure of how much cash a company is likely to have to meet expenses in the short-run.

Inventory turnover ratio is the cost of goods sold divided by average inventory. It indicates efficiency in inventory management, and freshness and salability of the inventory. If the ratio is low, the firm is either "overinventoried" or "undersold." A high turnover ratio is usually preferable to a low one.

Supplier Evaluation Plans

Usually the most important measure of a supplier's service is his record of performance in previous transactions. The standard of actual performance is tangible and concrete, whereas the other yardsticks measure performance only by inference and often very tentatively. In recent years increasing attention has been directed to determining objective standards and procedures to evaluate and compare existing suppliers. Three evaluation techniques have been developed: the categorical method, the weighted-point method, and the cost-ratio method.

The Categorical Method

The categorical plan is the least precise of the evaluation techniques. It relies heavily on the experience and ability of the individual buyer. Essentially it consists of a procedure whereby the buyer keeps a record of all vendors and their products. After establishing a list of factors for evaluation purposes, the buyer assigns a grade indicating performance in each area. A marking system of plus, minus, or neutral is usually used. In addition, evaluation lists are given to all departments involved with the supplier's merchandise, such as the quality control, production, and receiving departments. At periodic evaluation meetings the buyer discusses the ratings with representatives of these departments. Later, those suppliers with composite high or low ratings may be notified, and future business allocated accordingly.

Although this system is nonquantitative, it does provide a means of systematic record keeping of performance criteria. It also is inexpensive and requires a minimum of performance data. However, it relies heavily on the memory and judgment of the individuals doing the rating, and the possibility exists that rating will become a routine chore performed with a minimum of critical thought.

The Weighted-Point Method

The weighted-point method provides for quantifying the evaluation criteria. Any number of evaluation factors can be included, and their relative weights can be expressed in numerical terms so that a composite performance index can be determined and supplier comparisons made.

For example, assume that it has been decided to use the following evaluation criteria: quality of shipments, accuracy of delivery promises, frequency of cost reduction suggestions, and price. Assuming

Composite Rating Schedule

Part number_____   Month ended_____

	Total Shipments Received	Percentage Accepted	Quality Rating (% x 40)	Percentage on Schedule	Delivery Rating (% x 30)	No. Cost Reduction Suggestions	Percentage of Total	Cost Reduction Rating (% x 20)
Vendor A	100	90	36	80	24	1	20	4
Vendor B	60	80	32	90	27	1	20	4
Vendor C	50	70	28	100	30	3	60	12

	Average Price/Unit	*Lowest Price*/Actual Price	Price Rating (Price % x 10)	Total Composite Rating (Quality, Delivery, Cost Reduction, and Price)
Vendor A	$40.00	40/40 = 100	10	74
Vendor B	50.00	40/50 = 80	8	71
Vendor C	60.00	40/60 = 67	7	77

Composite Rating Comparison

	Quality (40 points)	Delivery (30 points)	Cost Reduction (20 points)	Price (10 points)	Composite Rating
Vendor A	$36.00	24	4	10	74
Vendor B	32	27	4	8	71
Vendor C	28	30	12	7	77

that quality and delivery are the most significant, a point rating system such as the following might be used: quality 40 points, delivery 30 points, cost reduction suggestions 20 points, and price 10 points. Based on hypothetical performance figures, an evaluation might be as shown in Figure 5-1.

Acceptable and unacceptable ranges could be applied to the composite rating, such as: excellent—85 up; acceptable—84 to 70; unacceptable—69 under.

Among the advantages of the weighted-point plan is the fact that a number of evaluation factors can be included and they can be assigned relative weights corresponding to the needs of the firm. Subjective evaluation is minimized. Finally, if the weighted-point plan is used in conjunction with the categorical plan, suppliers can be evaluated on a quantifiable basis without overlooking the intangible aspects of service.

The Cost-Ratio Method

The third evaluation technique, the cost-ratio method, relates all identifiable purchasing and receiving costs to the value of shipments received from respective suppliers. The higher the ratio of costs to shipments, the lower the rating applied to that supplier.

The choice of costs to be allocated depends somewhat on the products involved. However, quality, delivery, service, and price are the usual categories. Costs associated with quality usually include costs of visits to vendor's plants and sample approval, inspection costs of incoming shipments, and costs associated with defective products such as unusual inspection procedures, rejected parts, and manufacturing losses attributed to defective parts. The costs associated with routine qualifying of a supplier and routine inspection tend to be approximately equal for all vendors of like products. However, the costs associated with defective products will vary substantially from vendor to vendor.

Quality costs can be tabulated by the quality control department, with the aid of information from production regarding the possible reworking costs associated with defective parts. An alternative procedure is to have a specific account established whenever a defective shipment is received, and to have departments forward, for posting to this account, their excess costs incurred as a result of the defective shipment. In either case, total quality costs are related to total dollar purchases to determine the quality-cost ratio as shown in Table 5-1.

The usual costs associated with delivery include expediting, telephone, telegrams, emergency transportation (e.g., air shipments), and

TABLE 5-1.   Quality Costs

Vendor_____	Month of January, 19__
Visits to vendor plant	$ 200
Sample approval	300
Incoming inspection	75
Manufacturing losses	0
Reworking costs	0
Value of rejected parts	425
Other	0
Total costs	1,000
Total value of purchases	100,000
Quality-cost ratio (total costs/purchases)	1%

miscellaneous. The same tabulating procedure would be followed as described for quality costs. A typical tabulation is shown in Table 5-2.

TABLE 5-2.   Delivery Costs

Vendor_____	Month of January, 19__
Telephone calls	$ 300
Telegrams	175
Expediting (visits to plant)	200
Premium shipments	125
Miscellaneous	200
Total delivery costs	1,000
Total value purchases	100,000
Delivery-cost ratio	1%

Measuring the intangible aspects of a supplier's services is the most difficult part of any evaluation procedure, but these considerations are at least as important as delivery and quality. The cost-ratio method of evaluation reduces the subjective element common to other methods, establishes a "norm" of supplier services, and evaluates suppliers above and below the norm in relation to price. The following procedure is suggested to integrate service into the cost ratio:

1. Determine the subjective service factors that the buying company thinks it should evaluate, such as research and development facilities, capacity for future production expansion, field service facilities, stability of labor relations, warranty provisions, geographical

location, financial stability, inventory-storing service, and flexibility in providing short lead times.

2. Assign numerical weights to each factor in accordance with its importance to the buying firm.

3. Establish a premium over quoted price that the total subjective service "package" is worth. A firm producing highly technical electronic components might value this "package" at 10% of quoted price whereas a buyer of standard fasteners might value it at only 1%.

4. Determine an *acceptable* norm. For example, out of a total of 100 possible service points, 70 might be considered as acceptable.

5. Rate the suppliers according to the service factors.

6. Determine the percentage by which the supplier being rated is over or under the acceptable norm.

7. Apply this percentage to the value of the total service package to determine the cost ratio of service. For example, if the total service package is valued at 10% of price and total possible points are 100, with 70 being acceptable, a vendor with 90 service points would have a service-cost ratio of −3%, whereas a vendor with 50 points would have a service-cost ratio of +3%. This final value is obtained by

TABLE 5-3. Service Rating

Vendor_____		Month of January, 19__
Maximum Point Value	Factors	Rating
20	Financial stability	20
10	Field service facilities	9
15	Research and development facilities	10
10	Flexibility in providing short lead time	10
10	Labor stability	8
10	Geographic location	10
5	Potential expansion of capacity	3
5	Warranty provisions	5
5	Inventory-storing service	5
10	Miscellaneous	10
100	Total points	90
	Maximum value service package 10% of price	
	Acceptable service rating = 70	
	Present rating = 90	
	Over acceptable by 30 (minus)	
	Under acceptable by (plus)	
	Service cost ratio = −3% (over acceptable of 30 × value of package, 10%)	

relating the actual number of service points earned to the acceptable level and subtracting the result from 100%. In this example 90/70 = 130% — 100% = 30% over norm. This value (30%) multiplied by 10% (the total value of the service package) equals the service ratio of 3%. As the final value is over the average, the service-ratio cost is —3%.

A tabulation chart such as Table 5-3 could be used.

The quality, delivery, and service cost ratios are now combined with the vendor's quoted prices to determine the net cost. Assuming that the rating procedure already described has been applied to four competing firms, the comparison would be as shown in Table 5-4.

The flexibility of the cost-ratio method allows it to be adopted by any company for any products. The relation of evaluation criteria to quoted price provides for complete vendor selection.

TABLE 5-4. Summary: Cost Comparison

Part					Month of January, 19		
	Quality Cost Ratio	Delivery Cost Ratio	Service Cost Ratio	Total Cost Penalty	Quoted Price/Unit	Net Adjusted Cost
Z Company	1%	1%	—3%	— 1%	$87.00	$86.13
F Company	2	2	+3	+ 7	83.25	89.08
W Company	3	1	+6	+10	85.10	93.61
P Company	2	1	+1	+ 4	85.00	88.40

All three evaluation plans are designed to aid buyer judgment, and in some cases quantify what would otherwise be subjective analysis. However, they are suggested to be used as aids to, and not a replacement for, buyer judgment. Important supplier variables such as integrity, initiative, and ethics are not quantifiable. In addition, many of the quantifiable variables are dependent initially on subjective decisions. Properly used these techniques can make supplier selection more scientific and rational.

Factors That Limit Supplier Evaluation

Even though it is always desirable to evaluate prospective suppliers on the basis of the preceding considerations, such evaluation is not always practicable. In the first place, not all purchases warrant the expenditure of time and money required to do even a moderately good job of evaluation. The differences among several suppliers of small-volume purchase items may not be great enough to justify a careful evaluation of their relative merits. In such cases the usual practice is to place the business with a particular supplier so long as his performance is satisfactory. If the first supplier falls below expectations, a second supplier is selected on the same informal basis.

In a few instances a buyer may face an industry in which all the suppliers operate under a rather rigid sales contract and a standardized code of practice. The legality of such practices is open to question, but that matter is beyond the scope of this discussion. In terms of evaluating suppliers, a situation of this kind means that the buyer is faced with a limited choice. One supplier may still be better than another in terms of his geographical location, his reserve facilities, and his internal operating methods, but all suppliers are likely to deal with buyers on much the same contractual terms.

Another consideration that serves to restrict the objectivity of supplier evaluation is that personal friendship between a buyer and seller sometimes enters into the selection process. Although friendship should not influence business decisions, it occasionally happens that a purchasing agent cannot avoid the situation. Sometimes he may receive instructions from top management to buy from a particular supplier. It also happens at times that the influence of friendship is so insidious that a buyer may think that he has made an objective evaluation, although his judgment has been biased by the personal goodwill he feels toward one of the suppliers.

In other situations company policy will serve to limit the free play of supplier evaluation. When a company follows a policy of reciprocal relations,[1] the buyer is not free to place orders strictly in accordance with the conclusions reached through objective evaluation. In many cases reciprocity is practiced only if all other conditions and terms are equal. Where this is the rule, reciprocity does not interfere seriously with the evaluation process. It should be recognized, however, that under a reciprocity policy there is always a tendency to favor present customers of the company for fear of incurring their ill will. Consequently, it is very difficult to adhere strictly to a policy of reciprocity "only when all other things are equal." It should be recognized that even a company that consciously follows a policy of reciprocity does not do so with respect to all of the products it buys. Therefore, evaluation of suppliers must still be carried on for the many items not affected by the reciprocity policy.

The human element sometimes acts as a factor that prevents complete objectivity in source selection. Now and then a personality conflict develops between the buyer and the representative of the seller. At most, one can recommend that a good buyer check his impulse to let emotion override his good judgment. When all has been said on

[1] See Chapter 6 for a more detailed discussion of reciprocity.

the subject, the fact remains that occasionally supplier selection will be adversely influenced by the personal incompatibility of two people.

Special Considerations Affecting Source Selection

Size

Frequently the buyer is faced with the alternative of buying either from a large supplier or from a relatively small one. Although size alone is no criterion of effectiveness nor an assurance of supply, there are at least two advantages in dealing with the larger firm.

Size provides some measure of the reserve facilities of the supplier. A large company cannot work so close to the limit of its capacity as a small company can and is therefore usually able to manage some increase in its output to meet commitments to its customers. But perhaps even more significant is the fact that a large concern will ordinarily maintain a large technical and research staff and be more interested in the technological improvement of its products and processes than the smaller concern.

On the other hand, there are impressive advantages that can be cited in favor of the small supplier. He is more likely to be appreciative of his customers, since he has fewer of them and cannot afford to advertise or travel extensively to find new ones. He will probably give greater consideration to special or unusual requests from his customers. The relationships between supplier and customer tend to be more personalized, and there is greater understanding of each other's requirements.

"Direct" or Distributor

Sometimes the buyer has a choice of purchasing directly from the manufacturer or through an industrial distributor. The preference for buying direct is rather general among purchasing personnel. Not only is this preference based on the prestige of buying direct and the possibility of extra profit, which may accrue to the buyer through the absorption of the middleman's margin, but also very often on the fact that the volume bought by an industrial firm is greater than that bought by the average industrial distributor. In such a case one may question why the purchasing advantage of quantity buying should not accrue directly to the buyer. Furthermore, if the item requires contact between the maker and the user on specifications or other technical details, it seems altogether superfluous to interpose a distributor between the parties.

In other situations one can make a strong case for the use of the distributor. The existence of the industrial distributor is necessary. Many standard items are purchased by many buyers in such small quantities that they do not warrant the cost to the manufacturer of direct sale. Also, because many of these items are not carried in stock by users, there is need for storage of such items near the point of use so that orders can be filled promptly. The buyer who bypasses the distributor for most of his purchases weakens the position of this middleman. If this occurs too frequently, there may not be enough volume left to support the distributor, and finally the users will have to carry larger inventories of small-use items, thereby increasing their costs. Therefore, it may pay a company to patronize the distributor for certain borderline items in order to ensure his existence.

Because an industrial distributor combines the needs of many buyers, it is often possible to effect economies of scale in providing specialized services. For example, steel distributors are increasingly providing metal slitting and blanking services for customers whose limited individual needs do not warrant the most economical volume or the most efficient equipment.

Another factor that argues for the use of the industrial distributor when feasible is the public relations issue. Most distributors are local firms, and purchasing from a distributor means that the buyer is favoring home industry. Such loyalty to the community tends to improve the firm's position in the community in which it is located.

Single or Multiple Suppliers

Frequently a company has a policy of placing orders where possible with several suppliers rather than a single supplier. In some respects this makes the problem of source selection more difficult, since it frequently is easier to choose the best out of a group than several comparable suppliers.

Deciding on the best policy as between one or a number of suppliers is difficult, since good reasons can be advanced for either choice. Occasionally there may be no alternative as, for example, when a supplier has an item protected by patent. He then is the only source unless the buyer can develop an acceptable substitute.

Frequently, because of quantity discounts or lower shipping rates on carload quantities, it is more economical to concentrate purchases with a single supplier. In still other instances the total requirement may be too small to justify splitting the order among suppliers because it would increase per-unit handling and processing costs or because no supplier would willingly accept the small order.

Occasionally one supplier so far excels all others in his field in quality or service as to make it impractical to consider splitting the order. Still another situation that encourages the use of a single supplier is purchase of parts manufactured by a process that uses expensive tools or dies. Since the buyer pays the cost of tools and dies, he hesitates to provide separate sets for several suppliers but rather concentrates his purchases with a single supplier.

Last, but not least important, one should consider the effect on supplier service of concentrating the order. It is much easier to plan deliveries on an orderly basis when there is only one supplier. Also, the supplier who knows that he is getting all of a buyer's business tends to favor that buyer over one who splits his business. In times of material shortage this can lead to greater assurance of supply to the buyer who has concentrated his purchases with a single supplier.

"Pro's" for Multiple

On the other side of the issue, it can be argued that the buyer who splits his orders among several suppliers has greater assurance of uninterrupted supply because he is more protected against such occurrences as fire, flood, or strike which might disrupt the operations of a single plant. Even if all suppliers were subject to the same mishap, there would still be a greater chance of getting some shipments, since the buyer would presumably have access to the reserve supplies of all of them.

Another important reason for splitting orders is that this is one means that buyers have of encouraging keen competition among suppliers in order to secure the best possible price and superiority in the products being purchased. The typical buyer favors having multiple sources for most of the significant items he buys. He tends to justify this preference on the grounds of the greater security this policy affords in terms of assurance of supply, the fostering of competition, and the flexibility of choice it permits.

It should be observed that the decision to split orders among suppliers immediately raises certain problems. Among how many suppliers should the order be split? On what basis should the business be divided? How does a policy of reciprocity affect the split of the order?

There are no simple answers to these questions. To a considerable extent, the number of suppliers will be dictated by the size of the requirement and the relative size of the suppliers available. The evaluation plans described will aid greatly in this determination and provide impetus for spirited competition. Probably the most common split of orders is between two favored suppliers. Sometimes the business is divided equally between the two, but more often one supplier will be selected to fill the greater part of the order on the basis of past performance. The second supplier is given a portion of the business for goodwill reasons. This basis of splitting is an attempt to get some of the advantages of multiple sources without sacrificing all of the advantages of a single supplier.

Supplier development must be a continuous undertaking. Constant changes in production technology and material development require periodic review of existing and potential suppliers.

DISCUSSION QUESTIONS

1. Do you agree that the selection of suppliers is the primary responsibility of the purchasing officer? Why or why not?

2. From what sources may the buyer obtain information about prospective suppliers? Evaluate these sources.

3. For what reasons is the geographical location of the supplier an important consideration in the selection process?

4. What things can a purchasing officer learn through a plant visit that he is not likely to learn through other means?

5. Would you recommend that suppliers be evaluated in all cases? Discuss.

6. Under what conditions is the industrial distributor a likely source of supply?

7. What are the advantages of the weighted-point plan of supplier evaluation? Does this method of evaluation have any limitations?

8. What ratios are important in judging the financial stability of a supplier? Which of these do you consider the most important?

9. Give the pros and cons of depending upon a single supplier.

10. How can data processing equipment be useful in connection with supplier evaluation?

SUGGESTED CASES

Ajax Sewing Machine Company

ABC Corporation (A)

ABC Corporation (B)

Berg Raingear, Inc.

Evans Corporation

Household Cleaners Corporation

Howell Chuck Company (A)

Sharpe Machine Corporation

Smith Electronic Corporation

CHAPTER 6
OTHER CONSIDERATIONS IN SOURCE SELECTION

Chapter 5 dealt with the more measurable factors that are important in the selection of suppliers. The chapter demonstrated how these measurable factors might be quantified in various ways as a means of improving the precision of the process of identifying the best source or sources. However, after this has been done there are a number of considerations that must be taken into account and which largely defy quantification. These various policy issues will be considered in the present chapter.

Among the more important questions related to source selection are: Shall local suppliers be favored? Shall reciprocity with suppliers be practiced? To what extent should personal influences affect the choice of a source of supply. Shall gifts from suppliers be accepted? What cancellation policy should be expected of the supplier? Shall the policy of purchasing materials jointly with a supplier be practiced? Shall the purchasing department do any purchasing of personal items for company personnel? How shall samples furnished by suppliers be handled?

Local Purchases

The geographical location of the suppliers is a matter of real significance to the purchasing agent. The general tendency among smaller industrial concerns is to buy as much as possible from local sources of supply. To some extent this follows from the fact that the smaller concerns generally purchase from mill supply houses and other middlemen who are willing to sell in smaller quantities than the manufacturers.

In the larger concern there is a greater tendency to buy directly from the manufacturer instead of through a middleman. However, a substantial number of items may still be bought from local suppliers if it is company policy to favor local sellers. A firm operating several plants in scattered locations may encourage local purchasing as a part of its policy of decentralization of the purchasing function. Where such a policy is followed, it is customary to limit the items purchased locally to certain categories that can be easily procured in any industrial community. Operating supplies constitute the most important category of industrial goods that can be readily procured on a local basis. It should be pointed out that even those plants that have definite policies against local purchases occasionally, because of emergencies or rush orders, will make some local purchases.

There are certain distinct advantages to buying from local sources. Frequently a local source can render better service to the buyer because of its personal knowledge of the buyer's needs or because this information can be personally communicated to the supplier. A second advantage is likely to be the saving of freight costs which result from small quantity deliveries that cover only a short distance. It should be observed, however, that such savings can be negligible if the purchase is from a mill supply house because the freight costs have already been added into the local supplier's cost and price. There may be a small saving if the mill supply house buys in a larger shipping unit than the buyer would.

Service tends to be better from local suppliers. Prompt deliveries are possible because of the short distances involved and the possibility of using truck transportation. The buyer is also better able to inspect the facilities of a local supplier and, thus, to evaluate his ability to meet requirements.

An additional advantage to the buyer stems from the goodwill that local buying instills in the community in which both the buyer and seller are located. Through this support of local enterprise, the buyer is strengthening the economic base of his community. When local industry and commerce are thriving, the tax burden on individual concerns for the support of schools and other municipal services tends to be lower. Buying locally generates good local public relations because local citizens feel that the concern is contributing to the welfare of their community. This is an especially important consideration for a large concern operating branch plants in many different communities. Often such a concern is looked on as an outsider taking advantage of a locality and contributing little to the well being of the community.

However, too great a reliance on local sources of supply can be a disadvantage to the purchasing department. Such a policy leads to an undue restriction on the number of sources being used by the buyer and is not consistent with sound purchasing policy. Furthermore, reliance on local sources may mean reliance on less efficient sources than those available to a buyer who is not restricted by geographical considerations.

Legal Constraints

In governmental and other institutional buying there is a wide divergence of policy on local purchases. Some states have so-called "home-preference" laws of various types.

One class of home-preference laws directs that preference be given to bidders doing business within the state. Contracting and printing seem to be especially singled out by a number of states for such preferential laws. Several state laws direct their purchasing agents to give preference to bidders from the state when the quality and price of products are approximately the same. These laws provide for various means of determining which concerns are doing business within the state. All three or any combination of the following clauses are to be found in the various state laws dealing with preferences in buying: (1) must have paid taxes in the state, (2) must be licensed in the state, (3) must maintain plants or stores in the state.

A second group of state purchasing preference laws directs that products rather than persons or businesses be given preference. Such laws give preference to products raised, grown, or manufactured within the home state. A few of these laws provide for such purchases only in cases of "all things being equal." Without such a clause, these laws are obvious examples of unsound purchasing policy.

One other group of state laws that affects local buying is directed at specific commodities. Seven states specify that state institutions must use coal mined in their respective states. Other products that have been singled out by particular states are limestone in Indiana, green marble in Maryland, and products of its own "mines, forests, and quarries" in Missouri.

Reciprocity

The dictionary defines reciprocity as a state of exchange, a cooperation for a return in kind. In a business context it refers to the practice of buying from a company that buys from you *because* this company buys from you. The simple fact of two companies buying from each other does not constitute reciprocity unless each company's buying can be explained, at least in part, by the other company's buying. In its simplest form reciprocity might be illustrated by a paper mill that places its order for chemicals required in the papermaking process with a producer of chemicals who buys his paper products from the paper mill buying the chemicals. In practice, it has often been found that far more complex arrangements have been established in order to effect a policy of reciprocity. In the foregoing illustration, if the paper mill were producing boxboard and selling it to boxboard manufacturers who made the containers needed by the chemical concern, a more complicated form of reciprocity might require that the chemical concern buy its box requirements from one of the paper mill's customers before the paper mill would buy its chemicals from that concern. Such an indirect relationship is referred to as secondary reciprocity.

Trade relations is a phrase often used in lieu of and sometimes incorrectly as a synonym for reciprocity. However, trade relations involves the formalization of planning and the establishment of procedures that provide the background for the actual reciprocal purchase. Essentially trade relations include the practice of maintaining records of sales, purchases, and other pertinent information classified by vendors and commodities. This information is then analyzed in terms of possible sales-purchase relationships that will provide maximum reciprocal returns. Reciprocity, on the other hand, refers to the actual physical performance of the purchase act which is the result of formal or informal interpretation of trade relations considerations.

In some firms trade relations procedures are handled informally through the passing of information from the sales to purchasing executives and vice versa. In other firms, particularly those of large size, a formal assignment of responsibilities for these matters is made to a trade relations director. The director may function in an advisory capacity to the sales and purchasing executives, coaching them in regard to potential contracts, the overall profit picture, and risks and practicability of reciprocal agreements. In other cases the trade relations director has line authority over purchasing and/or sales to the extent of directing specific sources for reciprocal purchases.

Reciprocity has been the subject of much debate among purchasing managers and has given rise to a number of basic policy questions. Should it be practiced? How far should a purchasing executive compromise conditions of quality, service, and price in following a practice of reciprocity? What effect will it have on the morale of the purchasing and sales departments? What are the legal ramifications of the practice?

The first issue to be settled is whether or not a company should practice reciprocity. It will readily be admitted by most purchasing agents that, if other things are equal, they will buy from their customers. They will also admit that they buy from these customers *because* they are customers. In part, this reciprocal buying comes about at the urging of the sales department, but, even without such urging, it would be reasonable for the purchasing agent to patronize a friendly supplier where the offerings were alike in all other respects. Since the object of all business is to make a profit, it is sound judgment to increase the prospects for profit of a customer so that he may continue as a customer and may become a better one. Therefore, it seems unlikely that anyone would question either the ethics or the economic soundness of this pure form of reciprocity.

There is more question about the soundness of reciprocity where the buyer either pays more or receives less when buying from a customer than he would if he bought from a noncustomer. In theory, one could still justify the practice if it could be shown that the buying company gained more from the sales made to the customer (and would not have made these sales without practicing reciprocity) than it lost through the higher price or poorer quality and service. In a complicated business economy such proof is impossible, and one can demonstrate that, with imperfect knowledge and the general practice of reciprocity, costs are raised without compensating benefits. Therefore, a purchasing agent should not practice reciprocity on his own initiative when other terms and conditions are not equal and should discourage the general practice of such reciprocity wherever possible.

In the final analysis, the decision on a policy of reciprocity is one for top management rather than for the purchasing or sales departments. Management itself must evaluate the potential advantages of such a policy against its probable disadvantages. Reciprocity is strictly a competitive device, since it does not in any way increase the total demand for a product. The less efficient producers and distributors are likely to gain the most from reciprocity, since they secure sales that they could not obtain on the basis of quality and price. It is sometimes said to be possible, through reciprocity, to establish very close relationships with one's suppliers. However, it would seem likely that stronger relationships could be established through the practice of normal vendor relations, since such business is secured through merit alone. In fact, there have been many instances in which a policy of reciprocity has led to close, but not harmonious, relationships between buyer and vendor.

Who Practices Reciprocity

Earlier studies indicated that more than 50% of all firms practice reciprocity.[1] A more recent study[2] indicates that in one state the percentage may now be closer to 25%. Either of these figures must be taken with a slight reservation. Reciprocity is a practice that companies are seldom proud of and which they therefore do not discuss freely. So the true figure may well be higher than any survey, which depends upon a free and voluntary admission, may indicate. The decrease suggested by the recent survey in Virginia could indicate a change in business practice with regard to reciprocity, or it could merely mean that since the federal government has taken a more emphatic position against the practice, companies are somewhat more disinclined to admit their involvement with it.

Reciprocity is practiced more extensively in producer goods industries than in industries producing consumer goods, primarily because there is much more opportunity for large-scale buying and selling between the companies involved. In the study cited above, 100% of the respondents in the chemical, petroleum, and iron and steel industries reported reciprocity to be a major factor in their buyer-seller relations, whereas only 36% of the respondents in the consumer goods industry practiced reciprocity. In consumer goods firms the amount of products that can be reciprocally exchanged is usually limited to the small amount that any one individual can use. For example, a leather firm selling to a shoe producer can only reciprocate to the extent of encouraging its employees to purchase the certain brand of shoe—the results would at most be limited in amount. In producer goods industries the sales increases from reciprocity can be substantial as indicated by a leading chemical company which reported that sales to its 100 largest suppliers were $29,414,000 one year, an increase of $7,032,000 from the previous year. The increase represented sales to new customer-suppliers and greater volume with old customers with whom ties were strengthened by reciprocal activities.[3]

There is a close relationship between the use of reciprocity, stage of the business cycle, and excess capacity. During recession periods when substantial excess capacity exists, management exerts pressure on sales departments to increase volume. Reciprocal attempts are

[1] "Reciprocity: Where Does the P.A. Stand?" *Purchasing*, November 20, 1961, p. 76.

[2] "The Purchasing Agent's Role in Trade Relations", *Guide to Purchasing*, National Association of Purchasing Agents, 1965.

[3] M. M. Bird and C. W. Shepard, "Attitudes of Industrial Marketers Toward the Use of Reciprocity", *Purchasing*, November 1973, p. 32.

often among the first that are tried. Most firms reported a substantial increase in reciprocity during the 1960—1961 business recession, and some even reported purchasing agents accompanying salesmen on calls to suppliers who were potential customers.

Reciprocity Problems

Reciprocity has often been attacked as a practice that negates objective considerations in supplier selection—price, quality, and service —and therefore raises the cost of purchased material. Costs may be directly raised because competition among suppliers is reduced, quality standards for customer-suppliers are lowered, and the morale and efficiency of the purchasing department are diminished.

A company that buys extensively from its customers inevitably becomes known for this practice. Companies that are not customers soon lose their desire to compete and discontinue submitting bids for business that they know will be awarded on the basis of reciprocal considerations. Fewer suppliers, higher prices, and less assurance of supply are the result. The following statement illustrates not only the strength that reciprocity can exert in giving preference to customers, but also that this preference can result in higher prices:

> . . . according to court exhibits, one U.S. chemical company that had been buying methyl parathion, a chemical used in insecticides, from another American chemical firm, decided to switch to a foreign producer offering methyl parathion at a lower price. The American firm that stood to lose the business was, in the words of a vice president of the other U.S. concern, "very upset" because it feared it might "be forced to reduce the price to at least the level of the material coming to us."
>
> But the domestic producer of methyl parathion was not without recourse. It happened to be a major customer of the vice president's firm for another chemical, and it threatened to cut orders for this chemical drastically. The upshot was that the vice president's company halted its purchases of methyl parathion from the foreign supplier and resumed buying the chemical from the U.S. producer for 83.6 cents a pound—about six cents more than the foreign price.[4]

Reciprocity can also raise costs and downgrade quality standards by permitting customer-suppliers to submit material that is less subject to rejection than would be the case if no reciprocal ties were

---

[4] "Swapping Business," *Wall Street Journal,* December 5, 1963, p. 10.

involved. Buyers and inspectors tend to make allowances for the favored supplier.

It is questionable whether the competitive spirit of the buyers will be maintained when they know that any advantages uncovered from potential new suppliers will be undone by providing the customer-supplier the opportunity to meet the new conditions. The result is a lack of aggressiveness and accompanying low morale in the purchasing operation, which will inevitably result in higher material costs.

It is important to note that a dollar saved in purchasing is much greater than an equivalent increase in sales. Assuming an average pre-tax profit margin of 10%, a $1 savings on purchases is equivalent to a $10 increase in sales. If a buyer can save $1000 by purchasing from a noncustomer source, it would require $10,000 in sales from supplier-sources to match the profit.

A final problem associated with reciprocity is the unstable nature of the relationship. When there are great differences between the volume of goods required by Company A of Company B and the volume that Company B can possibly buy from Company A, the jockeying for additional volume creates an unstable environment. This is indicated in the following account by a chemical company executive to this firm's vice-president in charge of reciprocity:

> Scotty was in to see me the other day attempting to obtain the 2,000 tons of extra ash business we had dangled before him several weeks ago. I repeated our stand that we could not give them any additional ash unless we obtained additional phosphate business. In a roundabout way Scotty mildly threatened to take away our one million pounds of phosphate business . . . unless we purchased more ash. . . .[5]

Antitrust Laws Relating to Reciprocity

Continued use of reciprocity as a business practice is being increasingly challenged by governmental agencies such as the Federal Trade Commission and the Justice Department. Recent court decisions have indicated that in many instances reciprocal trading interferes with the successful operation of the free enterprise system that the antitrust laws were enacted to preserve.

The sections of the major antitrust laws that may apply to reciprocity and the significance of recent court decisions are discussed in the following paragraphs.

[5] *Ibid.*

Sherman Act, Section 1. Every contract, combination . . . or conspiracy, in restraint of trade or commerce . . . is . . . illegal.

To prove violation of this law, it must be demonstrated that reciprocity practices are restraining trade—a difficult task because of the oral nature of the typical sales transaction. In deciding the legality of a given case, surrounding circumstances, such as the amount of competition in the industry and freedom of entry, would be considered in an attempt to determine if the practice was significantly interfering with and restraining trade.

However, in a suit brought by the government against General Dynamics,[6] the presence of reciprocal buying leverage to restrain trade was assumed from the existence of a formal trade relations department and the practice of using purchasing agents to call on supplier-customers. The facts of the case were as follows. General Dynamics acquired the Liquid Carbonic Division in 1957. In 1962 the Justice Department charged that General Dynamics violated both the Clayton Act and the Sherman Act by forcing its suppliers to reciprocate for orders received from General Dynamics by buying carbon dioxide and industrial gases from Liquid Carbonic. In denying the defendants' motion to dismiss the case, the trial court used the existence of a separate trade relations department (called "Special Sales Program") and the fact that a list of potential firms to be "contacted" for reciprocal business was established (called "SSP Accounts") as evidence that reciprocal pressures were being exerted.

In related evidence the court took note of the fact that purchasing agents were bypassed in favor of higher-placed executives in an attempt to effect reciprocal agreements. The Court said:

> The interference is clear that to by-pass the purchasing agent—seemingly solely concerned with price, quality and service—and go above his head, was designed to accentuate an element the purchasing agent either could not, would not, or was not able to appreciate—the existence of the supplier-customer relationship and the advantage of reciprocal trading.

The significance of this case is that the government built its claim without relying on documentary evidence, which is difficult and often impossible to gather. Instead the government was able to prove that the techniques of reciprocity—a special trade relations department and unusual selling practices—were evidence of trade restraint. Therefore, the existence and functioning of a trade relations department would seem to constitute a strong indication of restraint of

[6] Trade Reg. Rep. (S.D.-N.Y., April 9, 1965).

trade, and any large company using such an organizational structure would be vulnerable to legal attacks. The decision can be expected to influence the number of organized trade relations departments in the future and the extent to which reciprocal selling pressures will be exerted.

> *Sherman Act, Section 2.* Every . . . attempt to monopolize . . . any part of trade or commerce . . . shall be punished.

This portion of the Sherman Act has not yet had application to reciprocity cases. However, it is likely that it could be applied in instances where the practice of reciprocity has proceeded to such an extent that monopoly effects are imminent.

> *Clayton Act, Section 7.* That no corporation . . . shall acquire . . . the whole or any part of the stock or other share capital, and no corporation . . . shall acquire the whole or any part of the assets of another corporation . . . where the effect of such acquisition may be substantially to lessen competition, or to tend to create a monopoly.

The most significant recent case involving reciprocity, and the only one to reach the Supreme Court, was decided under this section of the Clayton Act which prohibits mergers where the effect may be to lessen competition. The case, the *Federal Trade Commission* v. *Consolidated Foods Corporation,*[7] involved the acquisition of Gentry Foods, a producer of dehydrated onions and garlic, by Consolidated Foods, a very large producer and distributor of food products. Although only seven instances of reciprocal pressure on suppliers of Consolidated to buy from Gentry were found over a 10-year span, the Court ruled that the facts of the case were such that the opportunities to effect reciprocal buying arrangements were sufficient to allow seven documented occasions to prove the effects. The Court also made an unusual qualitative evaluation in this case as it noted that although Gentry had not improved its market position as a result of the merger, the fact that a competitor of Gentry Foods had put a superior product on the market indicated that if it had not been for reciprocity Gentry would have suffered a loss of its market position.

The significance of the Consolidated case is that the FTC won by using reciprocity as its main argument, which suggests that the Court will need only minimal evidence of actual reciprocal trading pressure

[7] *Federal Trade Commission* v. *Consolidated Foods Corp.,* 380 U.S. 592, 594 (1965).

to prove the likelihood of substantial lessening of competition when a merger involves a dominant firm. The mere possibility of reciprocal pressures can be used to prove that the merger may lessen competition in the industry. The fact that the Court made a qualitative appraisal of the consequences of the practice also indicates that the difficulty of proving reciprocal effects will be decreased. Finally, this case is the first time that a merger under the Clayton Act has been nullified without finding "horizontal" (among competitors) or "vertical" (buyer-supplier) competitive effects. It represents a new attack on mergers and indirectly on reciprocal practices.

Federal Trade Commission Act, Section 5. Unfair methods of competition in commerce, and unfair or deceptive acts or practices in commerce, are hereby declared unlawful.

The Federal Trade Commission issued three cease-and-desist orders under this section, involving reciprocity in the 1930s. Two of the cases involved the purchase of railroad supply companies by meat-packing company officials, who then used their control over rail shipments of meat to induce the railroads to purchase equipment from the supply companies.[8] A third case involved a large food packer that used its buying of raw materials for processing to induce sellers to employ the shipping facilities that it also owned.[9]

To prosecute reciprocity under this law requires that the practice be found to constitute an "unfair method of competition." Some authorities feel that the decision in the Consolidated Foods case implicitly condemns reciprocity as an unfair method of competition, and that Section 5 may be used in the future as the foundation for a direct attack on reciprocity.

The present actions with respect to reciprocity seem to be limited to aggressive reciprocity in which one party is attempting to coerce the other to some degree. Existing laws do not appear to cover the great multitude of cases where reciprocity is practiced willingly by both parties and where small to medium-sized firms are involved. However, as previously noted, legal impediments are only one of the dangers inherent in reciprocal relationships. The possible adverse effect on a firm's profits should be reason enough for not depending on reciprocity as the primary motivation in a company's purchases.

Reciprocity can be useful to a company attempting to broaden its sales base by securing new customers, but the risk is great, and such a

---

[8] *Waugh Equipment Co. et al.*, 15 F.T.C. 232 (1931); *Mechanical Manufacturing Co. et al.*, 16 F.T.C. 67 (1932).

[9] *California Packing Corp. et al.*, 25 F.T.C. 379 (1937).

policy is advisable only if each reciprocal arrangment is judged on its own merits by a representative of management who is able to take a broad view of all its possible effects.

Personal Influence

Whether purchasing agents admit it or not, personal influence plays an important part in normal business relations. However, personal relationships should not become the prime basis for purchasing decisions. Unfortunately, in practice, it frequently happens that a salesman is the personal friend or close acquaintance of an executive of the buying firm, and, because of this fact, the purchasing agent is told that, all things being equal, preference should be given to that salesman's company. It is difficult in most situations to determine just when "all things are equal."

In other cases the sympathy of the purchasing agent injects the element of personal influence into the transaction. The buyer may feel sorry for the salesman because of knowledge of some personal difficulty facing the salesman and may award orders on that basis. The presence of such personal considerations impairs the effectiveness of the buyer.

Salesmen occasionally attempt to make a sale by presenting such arguments as their need to reach a quota or their participation in a sales contest. The alert purchasing agent will ignore such considerations. He is interested in buying a product that will best achieve certain desired results in his plant. He cannot successfully reach this goal if part of his interest is in achieving benefits for the seller and his representatives.

Where personal influences on purchasing matters originate with higher levels of management, serious problems of policy and internal goodwill arise. Although it is generally condeded that it is unsound policy to permit personal considerations to influence buying decisions, it is difficult to adhere to this principle in the face of a direct request from a top executive to favor a given supplier, even though it is suspected that the request is the result of personal influence. In such a case the purchasing agent should carry out instructions. However, he should protect himself from later repercussions by maintaining a complete file on the transaction in which the direct instructions are clearly indicated. He should further gather from other sources any price, quality, and service data that are pertinent to the item being bought so that he can place such full information before management in the event of later requirements of the same commodity. Where personal influences are permitted to enter into buying transactions, frequent review of the decisions should be made by someone not subject to the same influences.

The alert purchasing agent will do everything within his power to avoid biases resulting from a clash of personalities. It is a recognized fact that all people have likes and dislikes, and purchasing agents are no exception. However, a good purchasing agent will do his best to keep emotions and personal feelings from entering into business relationships. The purchasing agent should spend his company's money as if it were his own. This attitude will make him stop and consider every transaction closely before committing his company, and should minimize the importance of personal influences.

Supplier Gifts and Bribery

The practice of giving gifts, particularly at the holiday season, is quite widespread although there is evidence to indicate that basically it is a costly nuisance. Most sales managers do not believe their sales or earnings would be hurt if they eliminated gift giving. In addition, most purchasing agents do not believe the goodwill generated is worth the cost to the donor. In the light of disbelief in the practice, one might ask why it persists. The only explanation seems to be a feeling that it is risky to go against the prevailing practice in an industry. And the antitrust laws do not permit competing firms to agree to eliminate collectively a practice that apparently few wish to retain individually.

A commercial bribe may be described as a price, gift, or favor bestowed or promised to pervert or corrupt a person in a position of trust in a commercial transaction. Outright commercial bribery is illegal, and most purchasing agents and sellers would not consider practicing it. The difficult questions arise in connection with borderline cases in which neither the giver nor the receiver will admit that a bribe exists, but in which there is some reason to suspect that a gratuity may have subtly influenced the purchasing decision. Gift giving is present in all fields of business activity, and many such gifts are meant as tokens of goodwill on the part of the giver. Unfortunately, what the seller intends as a token of appreciation may take on a different significance in the mind of the recipient. If he originally gave the business to the seller on strictly commercial considerations, the purchasing agent will not feel that the seller is in any way obligated to him. After he has received the gratuity, the balance will tend to swing in favor of the seller, and, with the best of intentions, the purchasing agent will find it difficult to be absolutely unbiased in future transactions.

Policy Areas

Many companies have established a definite policy on gifts and entertainment offered to their personnel by vendors. Some companies permit the acceptance of gifts that are clearly advertising pieces such as pencils, memo pads, and calendars. Still other companies permit the recipient to determine whether the proffered gift is a bona fide goodwill gesture or an attempt at commercial bribery. Obviously, they expect that the latter will be rejected.

The problem of accepting gifts becomes especially acute during the holiday season of each year. In some fields the volume of holiday gifts is so great that a morale problem is created among nonpurchasing employees of the receiving firm. In an effort to avoid this situation, some companies have adopted the practice of pooling all gifts and distributing them on some equitable or chance basis among all employees of the purchasing department or the entire office force. This has the double advantage of aiding morale and so obscuring the identity of the giver that there is little danger of the gifts influencing the buyer.

Some suppliers have attempted to avoid company-imposed restrictions on accepting gifts by sending gifts to the buyer's home, often addressing them to the buyer's wife. In such cases it is extremely difficult to enforce company policy, and the integrity of the purchasing department personnel must be relied on to carry out the official company policy. Where such a practice is employed, it is unlikely that the gift is intended only as a goodwill gesture.

Gift and Entertainment Problems

Arguments can be advanced against the industrial practice of giving gifts. The gifts represent a cost of doing business to the donor firm and will ultimately be reflected in the selling price of its goods. This means that the buyer pays for gifts he receives from suppliers.

Another reason for opposing the practice of gift giving and gift receiving in industry is the course to which such a practice frequently leads. If one firm begins the practice of giving gifts, its competitors generally feel impelled to follow. This in turn leads to competition among the firms concerning the value of the gifts given. In periods of business prosperity this leads to giving gifts of substantial value. The purchasing agent who receives such gifts is sure to find it difficult to maintain a completely objective viewpoint in evaluating one supplier against another. Competition in gifts leads to a diminution of competition in quality, service, and price—factors that should dominate the purchasing agent's decision.

Eventually unbridled gift giving can lead to commercial bribery and its attendant legal problems. The purchasing agent acts in the capacity of an agent for his firm. The laws of agency prohibit any action on the part of the agent that is detrimental to the interests of his principal. A number of states make commercial bribery a specific criminal offense.

Frequently salesmen resort to excessive entertainment in an effort to secure an order. Exactly what constitutes excessive entertainment is hard to say. It is generally agreed that the buying or acceptance of lunch or dinner is not excessive entertainment. However, if the dinner is followed by the theater or other entertainment, the intent becomes suspect. Fortunately, excessive entertainment can usually be recognized and can be stopped by a purchasing agent who wishes to avoid the undue influence of a supplier. The buyer who accepts excessive entertainment is likely, consciously or subconsciously, to have compromised his integrity as an objective agent of his company.

Proponents of the gift giving and entertainment practices argue that gifts enhance morale and contribute to a better climate for business transactions. However, there is little justification for any functional department of a firm to engage in such practices. Certainly one would be concerned if auditing firms received gifts and lavish entertainment from an accounting department. The same concern should exist over gift giving and entertainment directed toward purchasing officials. A purchasing executive cannot perform his job with maximum efficiency if he compromises business sense with overtures expressed through gifts and favors.

Purchasing executives have been active in recent years in attempting to upgrade their profession—a first step in this direction should be the abolishing of all forms of extraordinary entertainment and gifts from suppliers. If a company believes that gifts must be given at times such as Christmas, they might take the form of donations to a charity in the buyers' names. A means of control over entertainment is for the director of purchasing to require a monthly report of all after-working-hour contacts between buyers and suppliers. The report may also include gifts received from vendors and an estimate of their value.Written reports put the buyer on record, and a failure to report any such activities places the buyer in the position of concealing material facts. Company policy can be made and changed in the light of such reports.

Tax Law

The practice of entertaining and gift giving to the purchasing official and his family involves tax considerations in addition to the policy and ethical issues just discussed.

Before October 1962 expense and entertainment tax law was lax and was governed by the Internal Revenue Code of 1954. The interpretation of questionable cases was governed by the so-called Cohan Rule, formulated in 1930. This interpretation provided that, when accurate records of travel and expense expenditures were not available, expenses could be estimated and deducted as a business expense if they were related to business. This gave wide latitude for businesses to deduct many questionable, nondocumented expenditures.

To correct this situation a provision was introduced into the tax law of October 9, 1962. The new provision requires that records be kept to substantiate travel, entertainment, and gift expenses. Included in the supporting records must be the amount of the expense, the time and place of the expenditure, the specific business purpose involved, and the business relationship between the person on whom favors are bestowed and the taxpayer. So-called lavish and extravagant expenses are not allowed, and a maximum of $25 per year is set for business gifts to any one person in any one year. The law as interpreted by the Internal Revenue Service, is as follows:

1.   All expenditures for entertainment and gifts in excess of $25 must be substantiated by adequate records.

2.   Lavish or extravagant expenses are not to be deducted.

3.   Expenses for entertainment, amusement, and recreation must be directly related to the active conduct of the trade or business, and in the case of such activities, directly before or after a substantial bona fide business discussion, the expense must be associated with the active conduct of trade or business.

4.   Facilities such as yachts, country clubs, summer homes, etc., are not deductible for tax purposes unless the facility is used more than 50% of the time for entertaining in connection with the trade or business. Only that portion of the expense associated with the trade or business may be used for tax purposes.

5.   Business meals furnished to an individual under conditions that are conducive to business discussions may be deducted, but so-called reciprocal meals may not. The surroundings and the relationship of the person receiving the meal will be considered in determining tax deductibility.

6.   Business gifts may not exceed $25 per person per year for tax purposes. Certain exceptions will be permitted in the use of advertising matter, signs, display racks, or gifts awarded to employees because of length of service, or for safety achievement.

7.   If a taxpayer travels for more than a week on a trip, and 25% of the time away from home is spent for personal pursuits, the ex-

penses of such to and from the destination, otherwise allowable, must be allocated and the portion allocable to personal pursuits will not be deductible.

8. Expenses for the wife on a business trip will not be allowable unless the taxpayer can establish that her presence served a bona fide business purpose.[10]

The effect of the law should be to reduce the magnitude of entertainment and gift offers made to purchasing personnel.

Splitting Commissions

An indirect form of commercial bribery that is also to be condemned is the practice of splitting commissions with salesmen or accepting "kickbacks" from the supplier. A buyer who accepts compensation from the seller may find it impossible to give her complete loyalty to her employer, which is a legal obligation in the employee-employer relationship.

A good buyer will be vigilant against any possible effort of vendors to bribe her directly or indirectly. She will conduct herself in a manner that conveys the unmistakable impression that she cannot be "bought." Once she opens the door to an unscrupulous vendor, she will find it hard to close it. Some purchasing agents who have fallen into such situations have been forced by the notoriety, once they were discovered, to leave the locality and attempt to start over again. They often have found that their reputations preceded them and that it was impossible for them to continue in a fiduciary capacity in the business world.

Purchasing for Suppliers

Occasionally, a buyer finds that his supplier is unable to secure the materials needed to produce an item he has contracted to supply. Or the supplier may not be able to secure a price that will enable him to sell an item at a price low enough to satisfy the buyer. One way of coping with this situation is for the buyer to procure the materials for the supplier. This practice is sometimes called "joint purchasing."

---

[10] U.S. Treasury, Internal Revenue Service, 5049-1-63, "Rules for Deduction of Travel and Entertainment Expenses," p. 10, as reported by B. Perkins and J. Taylor, "Travel, Entertainment, Expense Regulations, and Comment," *Journal of Purchasing*, November 1965, p. 44. Proof that these rules have not changed much is evident from an article by Carol Brierly entitled, "Don't Trip Over Entertainment Expenses," *Purchasing*, November 1972, pp. 28–56. There is the likelihood that the tax status of entertainment expenses will be further restricted in the next revision of the income tax law.

Typically it involves a large buyer and a small supplier. The small supplier may not have an allocation when materials are in short supply or may lack the buying power to negotiate favorable prices. The buyer may have a liberal allocation or may have a source of materials at a favorable price. In addition to the possibility of securing a lower net price on the item, the buyer has the advantage of closer control over the quality of the materials that the supplier uses.

Before deciding on a policy of joint purchasing, the buyer should be aware of the risks inherent in his policy. First, there will be a temptation for the buyer to concentrate his purchases with this one supplier in order to maximize the benefits derived from joint purchasing. Such concentration will result in a reduction of the number of suppliers serving him. In the preceding chapter, it was pointed out that there are risks entailed in limiting the number of suppliers. Second, joint purchasing, to be highly effective, requires extremely close cooperation between the parties. If the supplier is serving the buyer's competitors, this close relationship may entail revealing more trade secrets than the buyer considers safe. In certain situations there might also be a question of the legality of such an arrangement under the antitrust laws.

Purchasing for one's supplier may raise the operating costs of one's own purchasing department through its assumption of additional duties. This additional cost must be balanced against the savings achieved by joint purchasing. Joint purchasing is not widely practiced; it seems to work best where a large buyer is involved with subcontractors.

Purchasing for Company Personnel

Every purchasing agent at some time faces the problem of having to make personal purchases for members of the executive staff or her company or their families. In some companies she may be called on to make personal purchases for all employees (e.g. major appliances, automobile tires, or small tools).

Few would take exception to the practice of a manufacturer selling goods that he produces himself to his employees at a discount. However, it is highly debatable whether the long-term best interests of our economy are served by companies buying from others for their employees. The practice amounts to a circumventing of normal channels of distribution for the goods involved. If normal channels are generally bypassed, the volume of trade left to regular middlemen will decline to the point where costs and prices must rise. Eventually this process could lead to the shifting from an efficient to an inefficient channel of distribution. It is doubtful whether anyone would seriously contend that purchasing departments could distribute consumer goods more efficiently than retailers.

Another disadvantage of the practice is that personal purchases may place the buyer at a disadvantage in dealing with the supplier. This may be the case where the supplier of the items bought for company personnel is also a supplier of items that the company buys for its own use. The vendor considers that he has granted a favor to the buyer and can reasonably expect to be given an order for the industrial items that he makes and the buyer uses.

Still another disadvantage is that the services ordinarily available to a purchaser of consumer goods cannot be secured when the regular channels are bypassed. If a defective item is obtained, an employee will assume that he has recourse to his own purchasing department for adjustment. However, the purchasing department is not equipped to handle adjustments, repairs, returns, and allowances.

One might ask why, in view of these disadvantages, so many companies engage in personal purchasing. A company operating in an isolated location may find it imperative to supply many of the needs of its employees. This may be the only way in which such a company can secure and retain employees. The operation of a company store in a mining or lumbering community can be completely justified on this basis.

Most purchasing for company personnel does not fall into this category, however. When the request for such purchases originates with an executive and involves a personal purchase for himself, it represents an attempt to get something at a lower price by transferring part of the cost to the company. The ethics of such a transaction are questionable. If the policy is extended to all employees, the ethical question disappears but the soundness of the policy as a business strategy is questionable.

The practice may be adopted as an attempt by management to increase the real income of its employees at little extra cost to the company. Any practice that aids in bettering the standard of living of one's employees has merit. However, there is reason to question whether such a company is fully aware of the additional costs incurred. Furthermore, all employees will not take advantage of the policy to the same extent. Thus, if personal purchasing is adopted as a substitute for a wage increase, one may question its equity, and a company may find that it generates more ill will than goodwill.

One final disadvantage that should be considered concerns the reaction that a policy of personal purchasing may have on local merchants. The practice obviously will cost such merchants some of their customers. Their hostility can make itself felt through adverse regulations by local governing agencies such as refusing to grant requests for zoning changes or similar favors that an industrial plant will require during the course of normal expansion or development.

Several state legislatures have passed laws prohibiting the practice of buying for company personnel. The first of these laws, generally known as "trade diversion laws," was enacted in Wisconsin in 1939. These laws prohibit the sale to employees of articles not of the employer's own production or not handled in the regular course of his trade. Typically they exempt "meals, candy bars, cigarettes, tobacco and such items as may be required for the employees safety or health."

Samples

The examination of samples is an important part of the process of source selection. The willingness of a supplier to furnish samples on request may be a deciding factor in the final choice of the source. Likewise, the fact that many suppliers furnish samples without being specifically requested to do so may exert a favorable influence on a buyer. Therefore, the handling of samples is another matter on which policy decisions should be established by management and the purchasing department.

A policy must be established specifying whether samples are to be accepted free or paid for in every case. Policies must be established on testing methods and procedures. A policy covering the reporting or nonreporting of test results to the vendor must also be established. It is advisable to decide from which suppliers samples will be either accepted or requested.

While it is a common practice to request samples for the buyer's inspection, it is especially true in the purchase of technical items where adherence to close tolerances from specifications is vital for satisfactory results. In most instances a reputable vendor is glad to submit samples, since they will serve to establish his claims and simplify his selling task. A sample, properly tested, will furnish much useful information to the buyer. She should be able to determine whether the vendor is qualified to produce the item in question. Her engineering department can often use samples to check the suitability and accuracy of its original specifications and, if necessary, can then revise them before the changes entail great additional expense. Frequently an order is placed with a vendor with the request that his initial output be forwarded immediately to the buyer's plant for testing, before full-scale production on the order is begun. Sometimes such a procedure can save thousands of dollars.

In requesting samples, the buyer incurs certain obligations to the vendor that should be met. A buyer should request samples of only those suppliers with whom she is willing to place an order. It is a questionable business practice to request samples of a supplier for comparative purposes when the buyer knows that she would not award an order to that supplier.

The number of suppliers from whom to request samples also poses a problem for the buyer. It is unwise to place orders for one item with too many different suppliers. The number of firms that are requested to furnish samples of a given item will depend on the value of the item, the amount that will eventually be purchased, and the extent to which company policy permits the splitting of orders. This means that there will always be some limit on the number of firms submitting samples of any given item.

Some companies have attempted to regulate the flow of samples into their purchasing department by requiring that all samples be paid for by the company. With such a policy the buyer tends to be less demanding in his requests for samples, since he knows that he will have to sign the purchase order issued for the sample. A seller dealing with a firm having such a policy will be less insistent on urging buyers to accept samples, for he knows that he cannot override stated company policy.

The tests to which samples are submitted vary greatly from one company to another. Some companies maintain elaborate laboratories where complete technical tests are performed. Others rely on results obtained from using the sample under normal conditions to prove its merits. Still others rely on a casual visual inspection to reveal the merits of the sample submitted. In general, the more thorough tests are made by those companies that pay for the samples submitted.

Regardless of the type of tests performed, a company must establish some policy on announcing the results of the tests to suppliers who have furnished samples. There is great variation among purchasing departments in the amount of test information reported.

A record should be maintained by the purchasing department of all samples accepted, especially if testing is employed. The maintenance of such records will serve to deter improper sample acceptance and will aid in the use of test results for the selection of suppliers.

Cancellations

Once an order has been placed by a buyer and accepted by the seller, it constitutes a legal and binding contract on both parties.[11]

[11] See Chapter 15 for a detailed discussion of the legal aspects of contracts.

However, there are occasions when it will be necessary for the buyer to seek to cancel a contract. Therefore, he should know in advance something about the cancellation policies of prospective suppliers. Such information should be a factor in choosing among various suppliers.

Cancellations arise from two causes. Those that are occasioned by a default or noncompliance with the terms of a contract impose no procedural problems, because the terms of the contract will provide the proper procedure to be followed in such cases. However, cancellations by the buyer when the seller stands ready to discharge his part of the contract present several problems. Such cancellations may become necessary because of an excessive accumulation of inventory, an engineering or design change in the buyer's finished product, or a basic change in the products being made. Sometimes cancellations are required because of events beyond the control of the buyer such as the situation that arises at the close of wars when government requirements are abruptly curtailed.

From most cancellations that are for the convenience of the buyer the seller stands to suffer financial loss. He may have begun production of the materials required, he may have refused alternative orders because of this commitment, or he may have expended funds in purchasing materials specifically designed for the order. The seller cannot be expected to sustain the loss where the cancellation was for the convenience of the buyer. However, in the degree of reasonableness exhibited by the seller, the buyer finds clues to the desirability of dealing with him for future orders. If the seller is reasonable in his requests for compensation for the costs incurred, the buyer should consider this evidence of the supplier's good faith and his worth as a future source.

Cancellation charges are usually arrived at through negotiations between the buyer and the seller after the cancellation has been made. Occasionally, one will find formulas governing cancellation charges as part of the contract. In general, the governing factor is the amount of actual loss or cost incurred by the seller because of the cancellation. If the cancellation relates to standard material or a product regularly sold by the seller, there is, naturally, less presumption of loss than if it relates to special-order goods. If the amount of the loss cannot be established through negotiations, the next step may be formal arbitration. If the parties cannot agree on arbitration procedure, the final recourse is a court trial.

The federal government has been placing huge orders with industry since 1940. The effects of these orders have been felt throughout industry, because in many cases the prime contractor with whom the government deals must contract with his suppliers to fill his requirements before he can complete the government order. In order to protect themselves against loss, many prime contractors include clauses in their contracts that set forth procedures to be followed in the event of cancellations or terminations that they may be forced to make by reason of cancellation or termination by the government.

SUMMARY

The general import of this chapter has been to emphasize the need for planned policies on many points where it is so easy to make individual, and often inconsistent, decisions. The very process of establishing policies subjects the problem areas to systematic analysis, which often brings to light important factors that might otherwise be overlooked. In the establishment of policies, businesspeople are finding that practices that are firmly based on accepted moral and ethical principles usually are in the long-run interest of business.

DISCUSSION QUESTIONS

1. Any supplier considerations that cannot be quantified are probably not worth worrying about. Discuss.

2. What are the arguments in favor of buying from a local suplier? How important are the various arguments?

3. What are the so-called "home preference" laws? What variations of such laws can you differentiate?

4. Do these laws apply to industrial purchasing as well as to purchasing for government agencies?

5. What is reciprocity, and what degrees or kinds of reciprocity can you distinguish?

6. Distinguish trade relations from reciprocity.

7. What is the legal status of the practice of reciprocity?

8. If you were president of a company would you establish a precise policy with respect to your employees being entertained and accepting gifts from suppliers? What would your policy be?

9. What is joint purchasing? Under what conditions is it likely to be practiced?

10. Should a company expect its purchasing department to buy items for its employees? Why or why not?

SUGGESTED CASES

Pressure Tanks, Inc. (A)

The Wagner Corporation (A)

The Wagner Corporation (B)

CHAPTER 7
QUALITY—DETERMINATION AND CONTROL

The determination of appropriate quality of materials and components influences all aspects of production and performance. However, quality determination is an elusive pursuit, being essentially a function of the manner in which the component or material is used. It is as much an error to provide too high a level of quality and incur the resulting cost premiums as it is to utilize too poor quality for a given application. In somewhat more precise terms, quality is an expression of the measured properties, conditions or characteristics of a product or process, usually stated in terms of grades, classes, or specifications and determined by the application that is involved.

A simple example will serve to illustrate the meaning of the term *quality* as it is understood by the purchasing agent. If the purchasing agent is buying lumber for crating purposes, there are many grades he could purchase that would be of straight grain and free from defects, blemishes, knot holes, and similar imperfections. Such lumber, however, would not be the best quality for crating. Instead, the purchasing agent would buy a grade of lumber that would be considered low-quality by the general public, although such lumber would be suitable for the intended purpose. It is important for the purchasing agent to keep this concept of suitability clearly in mind when considering quality. Many companies waste money by making a fetish of high quality.

In Chapter 5, supplier evaluation plans were outlined which considered quality as one evaluation criterion. In this chapter three more basic quality considerations are discussed. First, there is the matter of determining what quality is the right quality for a given purpose. Second, there is the matter of defining this quality in such a way that it is clearly understood by both buyer and seller. Finally, the method of measuring the quality of goods delivered to see that it conforms to specified quality, is considered.

Development of Standards

The systematic control of quality and development of standards had their inception with the industrial revolution and the mass-production techniques that accompanied it. Before that time, it was a relatively simple matter for a single workman or a small group, such as a guild, to control quality by first-hand inspection of materials as the articles were being made. With the industrial revolution bringing the spread of machines, factories, and enterprises throughout the world, the change of emphasis from hand methods to machine methods made it necessary to manufacture materials without the artisan's personal observation and inspection. Means of precise description of products had to be devised, and this led to the use of samples, brands, and specifications to illustrate the quality of the products.

Mass production had its origin when Eli Whitney discovered that he had contracted to deliver 12,000 muskets to the Army in an impossibly short time. He found that the only way of meeting his contract would be to make all components sufficiently alike to be interchangeable. This decision created the assembly line and with it the possibility of mass production, placing new emphasis on rigid inspection, control, and, perhaps most important, standardization of quality.

Control of quality was no longer accomplished principally through visual inspection of raw materials and finished product. This new development opened up a broad new field calling for sorting, gauging, metering, and various other methods of assuring that the materials and component parts conformed to preestablished standards. The need for consistent quality of process materials led to the setting up of standards that described the chemical and physical characteristics, such as the size, color, hardness, weight, finish, and purity, that the buyer would accept.

Standardization has continued to play an important role in advancing America's technical progress. It has substituted common measurement methods for rule-of-thumb criteria, enabling parts made in Illinois to be interchangeable with those produced in New York and providing an economical means for industrial buyers to specify and measure levels of quality without excessive cost.

Standards Defined

A standard is the description of an acceptable level of quality, design, and composition of a particular item, which evolves as a result of study and experience by industrial firms, sometimes in cooperation with governmental agencies.

Commercial standards are compiled by the U.S. Department of Commerce, with the National Bureau of Standards as the guiding agency. Other groups develop their own standards or develop them jointly with the American Society for Testing Materials, the American Society of Mechanical Engineers, the Society of Automotive Engineers, the American Institute of Electrical Engineers, the American Institute of Mining and Metallurgical Engineers, the Underwriters Laboratory, the National Safety Council, the Canadian Engineering Standards Association, and the American Institute of Scrap Iron and Steel. Similar work is carried on at the international level in cooperation with the International Standards Association and with agencies of the UNited Nations.

Standards are widely publicized and are readily available to any buyer who wants to use them or to any supplier who needs them to develop a quotation. Most buyers find that they can adapt industry or government standards to their use.

Standardization and Simplification

Standardization is the process of establishing agreement upon quality, design, and composition, the end result of which is the so-called standard.

Simplification in an industrial sense involves reducing the number of sizes and types of parts used. It is, therefore, a sorting and selection process that is usually carried on as part of an overall company standardization program.

An attempt to simplify and standardize is illustrated by the programs of Classified Parts Specifications developed by various industries. Classified parts and materials are commercially available and standard in an industry. They consist of items that can be described without the use of drawings or blueprints, such as brand-name items, standard raw materials, hardware, and pipe fittings. As the need for new items develops, their specifications are checked against the classified parts lists before new part numbers are assigned to them.

Informal standardization programs are carried on by all firms. Sometimes such efforts are the responsibility of buyers, inventory control, production control, quality control, and engineering personnel. However, in many firms, formal standardization committees are established with representation from these departments. Savings resulting from formal standardization programs have been reported, ranging from $3-$12 for every dollar spent on standardization efforts. Regardless of whether a formal or informal effort is involved, purchasing employees should be alerted to question every requisition to see if a standard item, with its usual lower purchase price and greater availability, can be substituted for a "special."

Sometimes it is necessary for the buyer to develop his own specifications because the commercial standards are so broad that they will not meet his requirements. Other standards may not be sufficiently accepted to result in economies. It is worth noting that some standards can be used even when certain features require unique specification. For example, a firm may find that a specially threaded bolt is required in an application to withstand excessive vibration. The bolt will be a "special" because of its unique threading, but in describing the material composition standards can be used. In this case, a standard steel can be specified such as #1010, to indicate temper, hardness, and composition.

Metric Measurement

The customary units of standards and measurement used in the United States are due for a radical change during the next decade. The reason is the probable change to the system known as metric-SI, that is, the International System of Units. Its adoption will reflect the desire to have a common, universal worldwide measuring system, thereby facilitating worldwide communication and trade.

The United States and Britian have customarily used a measurement system that is essentially fractional in character, and is identified as the English or Customary system. Elsewhere in the world, for over 160 years, developing nations have been adopting the so-called metric system, which is based on the use of decimals.

The limitations of the English system primarily hinge on its precision particularly when products and their component parts are to be duplicated. When fractions beyond one sixty-fourth are being used, the fractions prove unwieldly to use or communicate.

The meter is generally assumed to be one ten-millionth part of a quadrant of the earth's meridian extending between specified points north and south of the 45th parallel. The system uses seven basic units which are interrelated and all other units derive from them and are expressed in multiples of ten.

The conversion to the metric measurement will be gradual and extended over a long period of time, with the federal government providing guidance and assistance. Segments of the business community are already metric. In Spring of 1973, General Motors and Ford introduced American-made engines built entirely to metric dimensions. The pharmaceutical industry has been on a metric measurement system for several years, and others such as the computer manufacturers and farm equipment industry are converting.

Methods of Describing Quality

There are several ways in which a purchaser can describe the quality of product desired. The description may be simply a brand name or market grade. For specialized or intricate articles, it may be detailed specifications or a blueprint. In some cases, it may be necessary to use a sample. Occasionally, for basic products market grades may be used to describe quality. We shall consider these methods individually, with their advantages and disadvantages.

Brand or Trade Name

A brand name is the mark or designation that a manufacturer uses to distinguish a product and to identify its origin. In putting a brand name on the product, it is the manufacturer's intention to ensure proper credit to the product for any goodwill developed in satisfied customers. To build and retain this goodwill, it is important for the manufacturer to provide consistent quality.

In ordering by brand, the purchaser is depending on the integrity and reputation of the supplier. If a first purchase has proved satisfactory for the intended use, it is reasonable to expect that subsequent purchases of the same brand will prove equally satisfactory. Where the manufacturer with an established record of quality can provide satisfactory materials and products, the purchaser is saved the trouble and cost of writing specifications. There are situations in which it is desirable or necessary to purchase by brand.

Purchase by brand is necessary if an essential part or material is patented. It might also be desirable if a product to be used as a fabricated part had been so successfully advertised that its inclusion in a finished good makes that good more salable. In one case a small appliance company purchased G.E. cord sets for use on appliances because the sales department could then use the G.E. name in its selling efforts. A similar situation exists when the purchaser's production staff develop a strong preference for a particular branded product. Unless the additional cost is great, it may be advisable for the purchasing agent to buy such products by brand in order to please the other departments. Purchase by brand is also to be recommended where the brand owner has managed to make what is recognized to be a superior product although analysis fails to reveal the basis for its superiority. The difference may lie in labor skill or excessive care in manufacture, and these elements cannot always be reduced to specification. Another instance where purchase by brand is desirable for the sake of economy arises when the quantity to be bought is so small that the cost of preparing specification would be unduly costly.

However, there is the possibility of some difficulties with purchase by brand. First, because the supplier has many customers for a branded item, it is possible that he may alter quality slightly from time to time to meet specific needs of users. These variations may aid some buyers, but cause difficulties in other buyers' operations because of different processing procedures. A related difficulty is the fact that the buyer's inspection department normally will not put branded items to rigorous tests. If a specification names a brand, the inspection department merely ascertains that the brand received is the brand specified.

Frequently the price of branded products may be sufficiently higher to induce the purchaser to seek unbranded substitutes or to establish his own specifications. The nature of the required products and the cost of quality testing that would be necessary are important elements in deciding this issue. A purchaser buying by brand will usually do well to develop alternative sources for brands of equal quality. He is also well advised to use caution in buying so-called "off-brand" items that frequently sell at a lower price but also often are of lower or variable quality.

Specifications

Specifications are a detailed description or listing of the characteristics of an item. Compiling specifications often requires considerable time and may prove costly by comparison with other methods of communicating to the supplier what is desired. Nevertheless, buying by specifications is one of the most common methods because a great majority of business purchases require its use.

Dimensional and Material Specifications. Specifications may take the form of a listing of the physical or chemical properties desired in the product. These are sometimes called dimensional specifications because they state the desired properties in measurable terms. Such commodities as metallic raw materials, oil, and paint are examples of items for which this type of specification are frequently used. Conformity to dimensional and material specifications can usually be checked quite simply.

Another form of specification is the minute prescribing of both material and method of manufacture. This method is sometimes used in military purchasing, but in industry it is rarely used except when unique requirements exist. Ordinarily, if the vendor knows the use of the good, he is in better position than the buyer to determine what materials and methods of manufacture are necessary. The buyer assumes a heavy responsibility under this procedure, since he has no recourse if the products are unsatisfactory, as long as his specifications were met by the supplier. The buyer incurs the further risk of losing the benefits of new and improved methods of production with which he may not be familiar. Also, costly inspection at the vendor's plant may be involved.

Performance Specifications. Specifications may detail the performance or use of the purchased item. Here the purchaser indicates interest in the service that the product will give, and he tests the end result rather than the product. If the vendor accepts the specifications, the responsibility for a satisfactory product is his. For example, a part may be specified as capable of being bent to a 90-degree angle and subjected to an 80-degree temperature. These are the least difficult specifications to formulate. The method is especially suitable for purchase of machines or tools about which the purchaser has little technical knowledge. It leaves the seller free of restrictive prescriptions of materials and processes, and he may take advantage of the most up-to-date knowledge to provide the best product at the lowest cost. Satisfactory use of performance specifications requires securing reliable suppliers and developing competition. Otherwise the seller's responsibility for results may cause him to suggest a better but more expensive item than is needed.

Blueprints. Use of the blueprint or dimension sheet is an important corollary of many specifications. The blueprint usually accompanies some descriptive text in the purchase order. It is the most precise and probably the most accurate of all forms of description, and is applicable where close tolerances or a high degree of mechanical perfection is required. Its use is expensive, not only because of the cost of the blueprint but also because it isually describes an item of special design that is costly to manufacture. However, for items that call for extreme accuracy, such as casting, forgings, tools and fixtures, punchings, and machine parts, it is the most feasible method of description. Blueprints also provide the basis for an accurate check on compliance with specifications by the inspection department when material is received.

It is important to remember that an inspector will be governed only by the purchase order and any drawing or specifications indicated thereon. He may only inspect to see that the items comply with the drawing and the written specifications. Therefore, any verbal agreements that have been made may become a source of difficulty when a shipment is received, and care should be taken to make sure that all special conditions and agreements are made a part of the purchase order.

Specifications should be revised as conditions change. In one instance, in the purchase of steel, a situation developed in which a purchasing agent and supplier informally agreed that steel supplied under certain specifications could vary from the specifications. The specifications called for a thickness tolerance of $\pm.003$. The informal agreement was that the supplier would aim at this tolerance but that actual shipments might occasionally vary up to $\pm.005$. The agreement worked successfully for eight years, but when a new buyer was apprised of the agreement by the supplier, he was unable to get the using department to accept the terms of the informal agreement. After considerable time, however, the specifications were changed because adherence to the stated requirements threatened to raise the cost so much that the company would have been unable to compete in the sale of the final product. All this could have been avoided if the informal agreement had been expressed in revised specifications.

Advantages and Disadvantages of Specifications

The following points summarize the primary advantages and disadvantages of purchasing according to specifications.

The main advantages of specification buying are:

1. Drawing up the specifications requires careful thought and a review of the buyer's needs. This frequently results in a simplification of the variety of products purchased, and often reveals the possibility of using less costly items. Both factors result in economies.
2. Buying according to specifications frequently induces more suppliers to bid on an order because all suppliers know exactly what is wanted and that their chances are as good as those of other suppliers because they are bidding on identical items. This increased competition for the business often results in lower prices.
3. Specifications ensure the identical nature of items purchased from two or more sources. Where the purchaser has more than one supplier of an item, this identity is essential, and specification buying is a virtual necessity.

4. Purchasing to specifications gives the buyer's inspection department an exact standard against which to measure the incoming materials and results in accurate inspection and a uniform quality of materials.
5. If specification buying is combined with quality control on the part of the supplier, it may be possible for the buyer to save money by doing a less complete inspection.
6. Specification buying is a necessary step toward industry-wide standardization, and standardization programs hold the promise of substantial savings.

The principal disadvantages of specification buying are:

1. It is not economical to prepare specifications for small-lot purchases. This rules out the possibility of specification buying for many items.
2. Specification buying adds to the purchaser's responsibilities. He must be able to state precisely what he wants, and the supplier's obligation extends only to complying with those terms. If the product does not live up to expectations, the liability rests with the buyer. This disadvantage does not apply to performance specifications.
3. In specification buying the cost of inspection is greater than in purchasing items by brand. Items purchased to specification must be examined, whereas branded items need little more than a casual check and count.
4. There is always the danger of becoming overrefined in preparing specifications and, as a consequence, paying more than necessary for items.
5. There is also the danger of assuming that, after specifications are established, the characteristics of the item have been permanently set. Unless specifications are periodically, reviewed, there is the chance that the buyer will lose out on product improvements.
6. Some products defy specification buying. Certain products are patented or manufactured by patented processes, and others depend so largely on the unique skill of the maker that specifications are inappropriate.

Market Grade

Another method of describing quality is by the use of market grades. This method is largely confined to primary materials such as cotton, wheat, and lumber. The market grade indicates the relative purity, lack of defects, or differences in quality of a particular class or kind of material. For example, the purchaser knows that, when "No. 1 Pine" is the specification, he will get the lumber that differs from other grades in that it has fewer knots and imperfections.

This type of grading must be suitable to the purchaser's need to be useful to him. Differences within a single grade of wheat make it necessary for millers to buy only after examing a sample of the wheat itself. Similarly, cotton-exchange contracts, which permit delivery of various grades of cotton with subsequent adjustment of price according to a prescribed scale of premiums and discounts, may suit the cotton merchant, but not a textile manufacturer. The accuracy of the grading confidence in the ability and honesty of those responsible for grading, and the ability to ascertain differences in grade by inspection are important factors in determining the suitability of this method of purchase description.

Samples

Where none of the preceding methods of defining quality satisfy, the purchaser may submit a sample of the item desired. Difficulties may arise if the sample is subject to physical or chemical change. However, for replacement of mechanical parts, where age or use has obliterated the identification marks, it may be the only feasible way of assuring receipt of the correct item.

In one instance, difficulties in the proper shape and fit of a brake band for a tractor were overcome by attaching a sample brake drum to a mental template indicating the proper placement of the brand. By using this pattern as a guide the vendor was able to provide the length, shape, and conformance needed.

A large proportion of commercial orders employ a combination of the various methods of describing quality. The method must be adapted to the product that a company makes and to the importance of quality in the item being purchased.

Responsibility for Quality Control

With the growing importance of quality control, the question of organizational responsibility is a paramount consideration. The responsibility for defining the quality of purchased materials should rest with that department whose function it is to establish the standards of quality to be maintained in production. Ordinarily, this is the engineering department or the production engineering department. Where the decision involves equipment and supplies not used in production process, the responsibility usually lies with the department that will use the material. For example, office equipment and supplies are largely the concern of the office manager or general management, whereas laboratory equipment and supplies are of primary interest to the laboratory director, and these officials should be responsible for defining quality for their own equipment.

In large companies where responsibilities may be divided among several departments the joint interests of sales, research, production, purchasing, inspection, and engineering may enter into the decision. The same considerations must be taken into account in smaller companies, but the number of individuals concerned will be smaller.

Determining Quality—Inspection

At this point we shall assume that the purchaser has determined the proper quality of the item to be bought, that he has satisfactorily defined this quality in terms of specifications, blueprint, part number, market grade, or sample, and that the purchasing agent has accordingly placed an order with the chosen supplier. However, since the supplier has not certified the quality of his shipment, it now becomes the duty of the inspection department to ensure compliance with the standard of quality. The inspectors are the monitors who see that incoming material is of the proper quality.

Places of Inspection. Inspectors' responsibilities sometimes require visits to the vendor's plant. If the product is complicated and manufactured to precise standards, its high cost may justify stationing an inspector in the vendor's plant to oversee the production process. Or if the cost of transportation is great in relation to the value of the goods, final inspection may be made before shipment in order to avoid return transportation costs in the event of rejection. Some large companies find it economical to maintain inspectors at or near the source of subcontracted items, special items such as heavy forgings and castings, and goods bought in large quantity. Perhaps the most extensive use of inspection at the source is by the U.S. Department of Defense for military purchases.

Where conditions dictate inspection at the source, independent testing laboratories or inspection agencies can sometimes be employed. When the cost of securing and maintaining specialized inspection equipment is prohibitive, the purchaser may also choose to rely on an outside agency for inspection. One possible drawback is that an outsider, not having complete and accurate knowledge of the application or needs, may not be able to exercise informed judgment in borderline cases. The cost involved in hiring an outside agency and the level of quality needed usually will be the determining factors in deciding whether to employ an independent inspection agency.

In the usual situation purchased material is inspected when shipments arrive at the purchaser's plant, with detailed practices varying depending upon the nature of the product and the production processes involved.

Benefits of Quality Control

A good quality-control system will usually benefit both buyer and seller. Effective quality control by the vendor reduces inspection costs of the buyer; zero defects programs, to be discussed in the next section, are dependent on excellent quality control programs. The use of scientific sampling methods based on the laws of probability cut inspection time and effort for both purchaser and vendor, which results in getting the material to the user in shorter time and at lower cost.

Most authorities agree that mutual interest in quality-control methods improves user-supplier relationships. The user desires a product to meet the quality standards set up by his engineering department. If his knowledge of quality-control methods is superior to that of his supplier, the benefits from providing such information to the supplier can be important for both parties. In one case where such cooperation existed, poor quality standards from one vendor, which jeoparded the renewal of his contract, improved within 30 days to the point where it surpassed the quality of other vendors of the same product. In another case rejects were running 16%, but, after quality control was applied in that vendor's plant, rejects were reduced to 2.5%, with further improvement expected.

In achieving such results the vendor is able to reduce the quantity of scrap and rework in his own operations. This means savings that may result in better prices for the purchaser. A foundry reported that control of mold hardness, core hardness, pouring temperatures, and several other operations resulted in cutting the amount of scrap by 32.5%, and controls on machining operations resulted in an improvement of 47% in rework and 56% in scrap reductions. When the statistical checks show a trend toward unsatisfactory limits, corrective measures can be taken before scrap pieces are made. The assurance that defective shipments will be held to a minimum increased the buyer's confidence.

A vendor who has put quality control over production into effect will find that fewer difficulties and problems arise with his customers, and a mutual feeling of goodwill will result. There are many instances where the vendor's certification of statistical results and submittal of quality-control data with each shipment have resulted in the virtual elimination of inspection upon receipt of his material.

INSPECTION METHODS

Certified Quality Control

The vendor may issue a statement certifying that the shipment meets the specifications set forth in the purchase agreement. Thereafter only periodic inspections need be made of shipments for assurance and to prevent a major slip in quality. This practice is called "certified quality control" or "quality certification." The basic objective is to reduce the duplication of quality-control procedures performed by the vendor, which is the case when the traditional inspection procedures are followed by the buying firm's inspection department.

The program is best applied to precision components whose large volume and critical tolerances make inspection costs significant. Naturally a high degree of correlation between buyer and seller is required, including an interchange of inspection tools and techniques. However, when effectively executed, the purchaser's inspection department is relieved of the need for duplicating work already performed by the vendor's inspection department. If vendors were generally to adopt satisfactory programs of production quality control, incoming inspection could become of minor importance.

Zero Defects

A program that originated in the missile-producing industry, aptly called a Zero defects program, is based on the premise that no defects are permitted. It aims at preventing defects by developing a deep concern and personal awareness on the part of each employee—in most cases by employee identification with each unit produced. While all firms would naturally prefer to have the results of such a program, the intense concern for quality and in-process safeguards make it most appropriate for those industries where defects can result in huge losses and high human risks because of malfunctions. These are conditions found in the missile and similar industries.

Statistical Quality Control (Acceptance Sampling)

The growing use of statistical methods of quality control and acceptance sampling plans in inspection resulted from the gradual realization of the inadequacy on the one hand of such rule-of-thumb methods as inspecting ten pieces per shipment, or inspecting a flat 5% or 10% of receipts, and the impossibility on the other hand, because of time and expense, of 100% inspection of all incoming shipments. Even 100% inspection does not eliminate all defective items because of monotony, inspection fatigue, and at times, ineptitude of some of the sizable staff necessary for the task. The basic goal of statistical sampling is to inspect the minimum sample that will be characteristic of the entire lot.

Inspection recognizes the fundamental fact that no two things are identical in all respects, and it attempts to determine what degree of variability is acceptable for the process and rejects items that are not within these limits of variability. Any standard text on quality control will contain sampling inspection tables.

To use statistical sampling, the practioner does not need to understand the mathematical theory, only the underlying assumptions involved. The purchaser, buying on the basis of the samples, assumes a risk that the sample may not contain defects that are in fact present in the lot. This risk is called the consumers risk. On the other hand, some defects may show up in the sample that are not present in the remaining lot, and the buyer might therefore reject the lot unjustly. This is aptly identified as the producers risk in sampling. While these risks do exist, sampling statistics are based on the law of large numbers and instances of these types of error are correspondingly rare.

Sampling inspection tables prescribe for various lot sizes the size of the sample which often enables the buyer to limit his risks. While they do not provide absolute certainty, they prescribe the dimensions of the sampling plan which keeps the sample size to a minimum and correspondingly reduces inspection costs.

When incoming material arrives, the receiving department first checks the quantity and identity of the shipment to verify the shipping papers, to determine whether any damage in transit has occurred, and to record the pertinent information for reports to all departments involved in control or use of the material. If the shipment is in good order, the next step is to determine its quality. Where acceptance sampling is used, the inspector will be guided by the sampling tables. Four facts are needed in determining the plan to be followed from these tables:

Lot size: Number of parts in the shipment.
Acceptable quality level (AQL): Lowest lot quality that
    can be accepted.
Sample size: Number of pieces drawn from the lot that

will be inspected to determine the quality of the entire lot.

Acceptance number: Maximum number of defective pieces allowed in the sample if the lot is to be accepted on the basis of the month.

For example, to judge a lot of 75 pieces with an acceptable quality level of 0.3%, the table would show that 20 pieces would have to be inspected. To accept the lot at 0.3% defective AQL, no defectives may appear in this sample of 20 pieces. If one or more defectives were found in the sample the entire lot would be rejected. This procedure is called single sampling and is employed mainly on small lots where the desire is to maintain a very high quality level.

Double Sampling

On the basis of the four facts listed above, the sampling tables may call for double sampling, a procedure similar to single sampling, except that a decision can often be made with much less inspection. In double sampling the sample can be smaller, but the tables safeguard against accepting or rejecting a doubtful lot by using a second sample to prove the quality of the doubtful lot.

In single-sampling plans the decision to accept or reject a lot is based on the results of inspection of a single group of specimens drawn from the lot. In double-sampling plans, a smaller initial sample is drawn, and a decision to accept or reject is reached on the basis of this group of specimens if the number of defectives is either quite large or quite small. A second sample is taken if the results of the first are not decisive. Since it is only necessary to draw and inspect the second sample in borderline cases, the average number of pieces inspected per lot is generally smaller with double sampling.

For example, to judge a lot of 4000 pieces to be accepted only if the acceptable quality level (AQL) is 1% or less defective, the first sample size is 150 pieces with 3 defectives permissible. The second sample size is 300 pieces with 7 defectives permissible. Thus, if 3 or less defectives appear in the check on the first 150 pieces, the entire lot will be accepted. If 8 or more defectives appear, the lot will be rejected. Should 4, 5, 6, and 7 defectives be found in the first sample, the second sample of 300 pieces is drawn from the lot and the number of defectives in it is added to the defectives found in the first sample. With a total of 7 or less, the lot is acceptable; 8 or more, the lot is rejected.

Sequential Sampling

Another procedure for acceptance inspection is called sequential sampling. Here the decision to accept, reject, or continue inspection is made as the test or observation of each piece is made. Where lots are comparatively large and homogeneous, as for many hardware items, less inspection may be involved with sequential sampling.

If single sampling requires 100 pieces, double sampling will ordinarily accomplish the same result with 74 pieces, and sequential sampling with 55 pieces. However, emphasis must be laid on homogeneity or uniform distribution of defects in a lot where sequential sampling is used, for the smaller sample size might cause acceptance of a lot practically all of whose defects might happen to be segregated in a portion of the lot not deeply tapped by the random sampling.

As a method of inspecting it is rather common practice to provide the inspectors with sequential-sampling charts, which are the diagrammatic expression of mathematical formulas that take into account the acceptable quality level and the sample size. The two parallel diagonal lines define the limits for acceptance or rejection. As each piece is checked, the inspector plots a cross on the chart, continuing horizontally across the sheet until a defect is found. Thereupon he begins a new series of crosses on the next step above. If the line of crosses intersects the lower parallel line, the lot is proved acceptable. If the plotted line intersects the upper prallel, the lot is rejected.

Sample Selection

Obtaining a truly representative sample is an important part of the sampling procedure. Since many materials are received in cartons, crates, and boxes, a part of the sample should be taken from each container. Skimming the top may give an untrue picture of the lot. A random sample in which each unit has an equal chance of being included in the sample is the ideal objective of inspection by sampling.

The acceptability of a part may depend on several distinct features of the part. For instance, a rocker arm for a tractor must have correct bore size, correct overall width, parallel surfaces, polished surface on an adjusting screw, and a certain degree of hardness. A particular piece may have more than one defect when all these requirements are checked. However, it is considered only one defective in the count of the sample. Thus, a defective is a part that has one or more defects.

Figure 7-1 illustrates how one company records the results of an inspection of a rocker arm. The inspector enters the total quantity

Dwg. No. 54369				Part Name Rocker Arm						
Vendor Howadore Company										
Critical Requirements:						Sample Lot	Total Pcs. Rcd.	Date	OK or Reject	
Bore 0.811	Width 0.946	Parallel 0.003	Finish	Hardness Rockwell 54c min						
0	0	0	0	0		35	300	6/10	OK QR	
0	0	0	1	0		35	300	6/19	OK QR	
0	0	0	0	0		35	300	6/26	OK QR.	
2	0	0	0	0		105	302	7/6	OK QR	
0	0	0	0	0		35	300	7/14	OK QR	

FIGURE 7-1. Control sheet—sample inspection. Form inspection department files, Allis-Chalmers Manufacturing Company, West Allis, Wisconsin.

received in the shipment as well as the sample size called for by the sampling table. As the pieces are checked for the critical requirements, the number of defects is listed under each heading. A copy of this form is retained in the inspector's file.

After several lots have been received from a supplier, it is possible to compute the average quality of the lots received. This represents the supplier's process average, which can be used as a guide in determining the degree of inspection needed for that supplier's later deliveries. If the average is good, less inspection may be necessary, resulting in a saving of time and cost. If the average is bad, tighter inspection may be called for. The compiling of all this information into graphs and charts provides pictorial data for easy understanding. Such resumes are one of the advantages of quality-control systems. Recently some large companies with data-processing equipment have begun to put inspection results on punched cards from which they can draw a variety of reports for the purchasing department and the supplier.

Where the cost of inspecting each piece is substantial, a reduction in the number of pieces inspected may justify use of sequential sampling despite its greater complexity and higher administrative costs. On the other hand, where it is not practicable to hold the entire lot of parts while sampling and inspection are going on, it becomes necessary to set aside the full number of items that may need to be inspected before the inspection begins. Single sampling may also be preferable if the cost of selecting, unpacking, and handling, parts is appreciable. It is of course simplest to train personnel, set up records, and administer a single-sampling plan. A crew of inspectors hastily thrown together cannot easily be taught all the intricacies of the more elaborate plans. However, double-sampling plans have proved to be simple to use in a wide variety of conditions, are economical in cost, and are psychologically acceptable to both producer and user.

The necessity of close cooperation between inspection and purchasing has been mentioned. An example of the type of information that inspection can make available on vendor performance is the following.

During the year Company X had purchased 94,318 magnet coils. The accompanying table was submitted by the inspection department showing the results of these purchases.

Vendor A furnished more production coils than vendor B but fewer types of coils. Therefore, the percent requiring inspection and the percent rejected should be less. The quality of work of vendor A was excellent, and it was considered the preferred source of supply.

Vendor B furnished a large percentage of small-lot business, but the quality of product was not equal to that of vendor A.

Vendor	% of Total Purchased	% of Coils Furnished Requiring Inspection	% of Coils Furnished Rejected
A	58.0	24.3	0.85
B	32.5	53.8	3.06
C	7.1	38.3	1.45
D	2.4	94.9	22.4

Vendor C was furnished only two types of coils, each in reasonable quantity. However, the figures were considered of little value in determining the over-all quality that might be expected if he were furnishing the same variety and quantities as vendor B.

Vendor D had furnished coils largely on rush orders and in small quantities; therefore the rejection rates could not be considered conclusive. A careful study of one coil furnished in quantity showed results comparable to those for vendor A, and it was known that the vendor was furnishing a large quantity of coils to another local manufacturer at a very low rejection rate. It was believed that further study of this vendor's quality on purchases in quantity during the next year would determine its suitability as a regular supplier.

Evaluation can be made from the information that is available from an inspection department which keeps complete records. It serves a valuable purpose in guiding the purchasing department in its consideration and selection of suppliers.

The Operating-Characteristic (OC) Curve of a Sampling Plan

Each sampling plan will incorrectly accept some lots and reject others. By mathematical formulas, once the inspection—lot size, sample size, and acceptance and rejection—numbers are determined, it is possible to compute the percentage of inspection lots of any given quality that will be accepted.

This information is presented in graphic form referred to as the "operating-characteristic curve" (abbreviated to OC curve). The OC curve tells the user how effectively the sampling plan discriminates between good and bad lots.

Figure 7-2 illustrates an OC curve for a lot size (N) of 2000, from which samples (n) of 300 are drawn containing (c) 11 or less defectives.

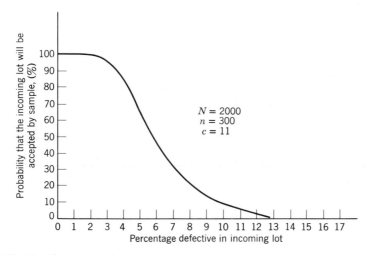

FIGURE 7-2. Operating characteristic curve.

Using probability mathematics one can compute the probability that 11 or less defects will be drawn from the lot in a random sample of 300 if there are a known number of defective items in the lot. It says that using this sampling plan, if the incoming lot contains 4% defective items, there is a 90% probability that the sample will contain 11 or fewer defectives, thus indicating acceptance of the entire lot. There is also a 10% probability that the sample will contain more than 11 defectives, thus indicating rejection of the lot.

Every combination of lot size, sample size, and allowable number of defectives has a different operating characteristic whose values are usually plotted in the form of a curve.

Rejection Procedures

When the inspection department finds that incoming material does not comply with the purchase order, further shipments are temporarily suspended or the goods are sidetracked from the normal flow of goods to the stores or production departments. Notices of rejection are immediately sent to the departments interested in the procurement, use, control, or disposition of the material involved.

There is the possibility that the rejection decision might be reversed if the sampling showed the lot to be close to the borderline of the established tolerance. The time element may enter, since the demands of the buyer's production schedule may not permit the delay caused by returning the material for the vendor to sort, repair, or replace. In an emergency it may be expedient to have the sorting done by the purchaser's inspection department or to make arrangements for defectives to be set aside as the material is used in production.

When faulty items are detected, it may, under some circumstances, be more economical to sort the items at the buyer's plant rather than incur the packing and transportation cost involved to return them to the supplier. The costs involved would usually be assumed by the vendor.

Any negotiations with the vendor about rejections should be handled through the purchasing department. There are several reasons for following this procedure in all situations. First, it is the only way in which good relations between the seller and the buyer can be ensured. If negotiations for purchase are carried on by one person and negotiations concerning rejection by another, the two people may make contradictory statements on certain points which will prejudice the buyer's case. Beyond the possibility of such immediate harm, there is the danger of lessening the goodwill that exists between the seller and the buyer, and goodwill is the foundation of successful business relations; it is as delicate as it is intangible. A curt rejection notice from a person unknown to the supplier may well hurt the buyer's chances of getting materials from him later in a period of short supply. Undiplomatic dealings may also make it more difficult for the purchasing department to secure favorable treatment from the seller in terms of scheduling and service.

Second, a sound organizational reason for handling all rejections through the purchasing department is that this department is responsible for obtaining goods of the specified quality. If it is to be held accountable for procuring goods of the right quality, the purchasing department should be authorized to negotiate with the suppliers about rejections, since these negotiations will have a bearing on future relationships between the buyer and seller.

A third reason for handling rejections through the purchasing department is that this department knows about material requirements throughout the company, and in a large company it is always possible that some other department may be able to renegotiate the price to a level that will make the purchase advantageous and bring about a solution agreeable to both buyer and seller.

Finally, it is always possible that the fault may rest with the buyer rather than the seller. There may have been oral understandings between buyer and seller that could prove that the seller had provided goods according to his agreement. It was mentioned previously that there should be no such oral commitments but, if they exist, it will be less embarrassing to the buyer to admit them than to have them called to his attention by the supplier.

When rejection is necessary, a clear statement of the reasons is vitally important. It should include all pertinent facts and data so as to minimize the possibility of arguments. Protracted discussions over unpleasant subjects are likely to result in ill will on both sides and may jeopardize relationships that could have been mutually beneficial.

SUMMARY

A slogan that has grown up with the quality-control movement is: "Quality cannot be inspected into a product." This being true, the desired quality of purchased material must be in the material when it arrives. Reasonable assurance of this comes through careful attention to all responsibilities in the purchaser's organization. When careful consideration has been given to the exact quality desired, to the development of adequate description or specification of that quality, to making certain that the supplier understands what is needed and is equipped to do the job, and to the application of a suitable inspection program, there is little possibility of failure to achieve the desired results.

Statistical quality control has become a highly profitable industrial development. Most of the large companies have well-developed programs. Since the pioneering work has been done, there is no reason why well-managed smaller companies should not follow similar procedures to equal advantage. The more widely it is practiced, the higher will become the quality level of industrial production and the greater our productivity.

DISCUSSION QUESTIONS

1. If a buyer specifies the material and method of manufacture, what responsibilities does he assume relative to possible rejections if the items prove unfit in the production process?

2. It has been stated that use of performance specifications can result in a supplier's presenting goods of excess quality. Explain.

3. Indicate the alternative methods available to define the quality of a purchased item.

4. What is the basic objective and economic justification for use of certified quality-control procedures?

5. What are the disadvantages associated with the practice of insuring purchase quality by means of brand identification?

6. Indicate the proper use of a simplification policy in conjunction with an overall standardization program.

7. What is the essential difference between the English and metric system of measurement?

8. Under what circumstances might a buyer decide to utilize incoming goods that could actually be rejected and returned to the vendor?

9. What are the benefits of buying by brand name?

10. Which department should handle negotiations or notification of vendor when items are to be rejected? Why?

SUGGESTED CASES

Ajax Sewing Machine Company

ABC Corporation (B)

Selma Instruments Company

CHAPTER 8
QUANTITY-DETERMINATION AND CONTROL

Purchasing and materials management personnel are intimately involved in maintaining the most economical level of inventory consistent with production and safety requirements. The significance of this responsibility is apparent when we consider that frequently one third of the firm's total investment in inventory is involved in either work-in-process, finished goods, or stores, and that materials often account for half of the total production costs. Of the three inventory forms, the stores inventory usually represents the largest share, and this is the area in which the purchasing department, either directly or indirectly, can significantly contribute to company profit by efficient management of quantity and timing of purchases.

There is but one right quantity to buy for any given transaction, but because there are many different kinds of transactions, the determination of the correct quantity is a complicated matter. Similarily, there is only one right time to purchase this quantity.

The issue is an important one because, if too small a quantity is purchased, the unit cost will usually be higher, shortages are likely to increase, expediting work will necessarily be greater, and the relationships between vendor and purchaser will probably suffer. On the other hand, if too large a quantity is purchased, the excess inventory will raise costs, obsolescence will become a more serious problem, and the need for additional storage facilities will create investment problems. Placing orders at the wrong time can be costly in about the same ways.

Factors Affecting Ordering Quantities

Special-Order Manufacturing

The amount ordered depends in large part on the type of manufacturing done. Some firms produce to order, rather than manufacturing in anticipation of orders. Most manufacturers occasionally resort to special-order manufacturing. Where goods are made to order, it is the usual practice to prepare a "bill of materials" for the items being manufactured. This bill of materials will contain a complete list of the component parts and materials required to make the finished goods, including detailed descriptions and quantities needed.

When the sales department receives an order, it notifies purchasing and production scheduling. The purchasing department then secures a copy of the bill of materials covering the order. After checking stocks that may have accumulated in the stores department, the buyer calculates how much must be ordered. When the production scheduling department schedules this order for production, the purchasing department is in a position to buy and control the quantity of goods to be purchased.

Continuous-Run Manufacturing

By contrast to special-order manufacturing, this type of production, exemplified by refrigerator or washing machine manufacturing, consists of producing standardized goods in advance of orders. Bills of materials are established when the product is designed. The purchasing department thereafter can control the quantity of its purchases in accordance with planned production schedules for the various goods. Because of the repetitive nature of production, there is considerable latitude for the purchasing department with respect to quantities and the timing of purchases. This is not true of special-order manufacturing, since a long period may elapse before a given item is manufactured again.

MRO Items (Maintenance, Repairs, and Operating Supplies)

All manufacturing plants use MRO items which, in the main, consist of items that are regularly stocked and used, some of which cannot be purchased in large quantities because of special problems of storage.

Mill supplies such as drills, taps, dies, and files can be bought in the most economical quantities, because they seldom present space, handling, or obsolescence problems that would limit the quantities purchased. Although these are MRO items, they are a special class known as stock items and will be discussed in the next section.

Some MRO items cannot be purchased in the most economical quantities because of the large amount of space they require for storage or because of the fire hazard involved in their storage. Examples of such items are gasoline, naphtha, paint, lubricants, excelsior, other packing materials, and chemicals. Some MRO items are referred to as "shelf-life" items; that is, they tend to deteriorate or waste away during storage. Batteries, cement, and paste are three examples of shelf-life items.

Thus, in buying MRO items, it is necessary to consider the space, hazard, and shelf-life characteristics of the items as well as the most economical unit of purchase.

Stock Items

Stock items present a real opportunity for the purchasing department to exercise its skill in purchasing so as to aid management in increasing profits. In companies where there is a separate inventory-control department, it is important that there be a close working relationship between that department and purchasing to enable purchasing to establish the proper quantity of stock items to be purchased at any given time.

A number of factors should be considered in establishing this correct quantity. These factors are discussed in the following sections of this chapter dealing with the use of mathematical means of determining how much shall be bought. These factors apply even to a concern that does not use the mathematical approach in setting its correct order quantities.

Economic Ordering Quantity (EOQ)

It will be shown at a later point that the correct quantity to buy is the quantity at which the cost of acquisition equals the cost of possession.[1] In the past, it has been difficult to determine this point for the thousands of items handled in a typical purchasing department, especially since this decision often has to be made at the clerical or assistant buyer level.

The EOQ procedure has been simplified by the development of

[1] The concept "economic lot size" has usually been defined as the quantity to make or buy at one time that will achieve the lowest unit cost. EOQ may be defined in the same way, and this term will be used throughout the chapter in the interest of simplicity.

mathematical formulas and tables, which quickly supply the correct answer if certain factors are known. In applying the EOQ concept it is necessary to determine the cost of writing a purchase order (acquisition cost), the cost of stocking material (carrying cost), and the quantity discount available for the item being purchased. Once management has determined these factors, the process of computing the EOQ is largely clerical.

Acquisition Costs

Each time a purchase order is issued, the purchasing, inspection, inventory control, receiving, and accounts payable departments must service it. In determining the economic ordering quantity one must calculate the extra cost of servicing an order. It is the *incremental* cost rather than the average cost per order that is important because, within limits, the fixed costs of these departments continue, regardless of the number of orders written. Since it is important to understand this incremental cost concept, an illustration of a method of computing the cost of a purchase order will be given.

Assume that a purchasing department is now costing $8000 per month. This cost includes salaries, stationery, telephone, telegrams, and so on. The department handles 4000 order per month. Cost analysis indicates that, if one reduced the number of orders to 3000 per month without changing the number of items or the dollar value purchased, the total monthly cost would decrease to $7000. Therefore, the elimination of 1000 orders saves $1000 or $1 per order. This is the figure that is significant.

If cost analysis indicates that inventory control, inspection, receiving, and accounts payable costs, calculated in the same manner, totaled $2 per order, the total incremental cost for the additional order is $3.

Possession or Carrying Cost

The cost of carrying material is expensive, with estimates varying from 10–35% depending on the type of material and varying economic conditions. Table 8-1 illustrates typical ranges of the various cost elements included in carrying charges.

Not all inventory items are subject to the same risk. Stock bought for a single customer's requirement or parts used for a single machine are examples of high-risk inventory. By contrast, stock bought for a general line sold to many customers or parts used on many machines are examples of low-risk inventory. Many companies using formal economic ordering quantity procedures have established at least four

TABLE 8-1. Composition of Carrying Charges

	Percentage ranges
Interest cost	4–15
Obsolescence and deterioration	2– 8
Storage	2– 5
Insurance	1– 4
Taxes	1– 3
Total cost	10–35%

risk categories. In putting a system into effect initially, it is recommended that all items be considered as average risk with refinements incorporated as information becomes available.

After determining the marginal cost of acquiring the material and the possession costs, the purchasing department is in a position to figure the economic order quantity for any stock item not subject to quantity discounts. The effects of quantity discounts will be discussed later.

Mathematical Proof of Economic Order Quantity

It was stated earlier in this chapter, without demonstration, that the least cost quantity is the quantity at which acquisition costs equal the costs of possession. This is the basic principle of quantity buying and is true regardless of the factors used. An example will be given to illustrate this principle.

In the illustration we continue the assumption that the order cost is $3 and will assume that the carrying charges are 15% of one half of the dollar value of the order. We further consider that the illustrated item is used at the rate of $1000 per year. (It is assumed that there are no quantity discounts applicable to the item.)

If the item in question were ordered once every month, the ordering cost per year would be 12 × $3, or $36. If the item were purchased once every 2 months, its per year ordering cost would be 6 × $3, or $18. Costs can be similarly calculated for other order frequencies, as shown in column 2 of Table 8-2.

If the item in question were ordered once every month, the annual carrying charges would be 15% of the average inventory (one-half the dollar value of the order) or $0.15 \times \frac{1}{2} (1000/12) = \$6.25$. If it were purchased once every 2 months, its carrying charges would be $0.15 \times \frac{1}{2} (1000/6) = \$12.50$. Costs can be similarly calculated for other order frequencies, as shown in column 3 of Table 8-2.

By adding the acquisition costs (column 2) and the possession charges (column 3), one arrives at a total annual cost of purchasing

TABLE 8-2.

Order Frequency, Times per Year (1)	Annual Acquisition Costs (2)	Annual Possession Charges (3)	Total Annual Costs (4)
12	$36	$ 6.25	$42.25
6	18	12.50	30.50
4	12	18.75	30.75
3	9	25.00	34.00
2	6	37.50	43.50
1	3	75.00	78.00

the item at different order frequencies per year. These totals are shown in column 4 of Table 8-2. It will be observed that total annual costs for purchasing the illustrated item are lowest when it is bought six times per year. The total annual cost at this frequency is $30.50 per year. At this frequency it will also be observed that the ordering costs are $18 and the carrying charges are $12.50, and that these cost figures are more nearly equal than they are at any other order frequency.

The basic principle is graphically illustrated in Figure 8-1, which is based on the same assumptions with respect to annual usage, acquisition costs, and possession charges. The graphic illustration has the advantage over the table of showing that, at the point where the order-cost curve and the carrying-charge curve intersect, the quantity to be ordered is slightly more than a 2-month supply and that at this point the total cost will be about $30. However, it may be practical to refine purchasing decisions to this point. In practice, one rounds the answer to the closest time unit with which he is working—days, weeks, or months.

The table and graph were constructed on the basis of certain assumptions about ordering costs and carrying charges. It is easily possible to construct other tables and graphs on the basis of different assumptions about these categories of cost. It is also possible to compute the correct ordering quantity algebraically, as follows:

Let A = acquisition costs
B = possession (carrying) charges
C = annual usage in dollar value
X = correct order frequency per year
EOQ = economic order quantity in dollar value

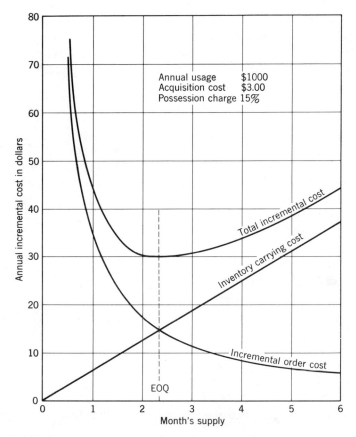

FIGURE 8-1. Economic order quantity graph.

Then, if total order costs equal total carrying charges,

$$AX = \frac{BC}{2X}$$

Solving for X, we obtain

$$X = \sqrt{BC/2A}$$

Economic order quantity $= C/X$

Substituting the $\sqrt{BC/2A}$ for X, we obtain

Economic order quantity $= \sqrt{2AC/B}$

$$EOQ = \sqrt{\frac{2 \times \text{acquisition costs} \times \text{annual use (\$)}}{\text{possession charge}}}$$

The EOQ quantity does not vary directly with usage. It varies with the square root of usage. When usage increases, a shorter time supply is ordered. Therefore, the adoption of a rule for buying a fixed time supply such as one or two months' usage (or sales) can result in extra inventory costs.

Shortcut Method of Calculating EOQ

For the everyday use of the purchasing department it is possible to incorporate EOQ data into tables from which the amount to be ordered of items with varying use rates can be read directly. In order to prepare simple tables for practical use, one must depart from exact mathematics and reduce the figures to reasonable approximations. An example of such a table is Table 8-3. It employs the assumptions of $3 order costs and 24% carrying charges.

TABLE 8-3.

Dollar Value of One Year's Usage	Time Supply to Order	Dollar Value of One Year's Usage	Time Supply to Order
$ 0–10	3 years	$ 101–200	5 months
11–20	1½ years	201–300	4 months
21–30	1 year	301–400	3 months
31–50	10 months	401–600	10 weeks
51–75	7 months	601–1000	8 weeks
76–100	6 months	1000–2000	6 weeks
		2001–up	1 month

Many companies have developed comprehensive tables or charts of this nature which have been used successfully. These tables are based on actual company cost figures but are built on the basic principle that the correct ordering quantity is the amount at which order costs are equal to carrying charges.

Having compiled his own table, the purchasing agent knows the most economical quantity to buy. However, he must modify his decision in light of the following factors:

1. If the item is space-limited, he should not buy more of the item than space limitations permit.
2. If the item has a shelf life, he should not buy more than the shelf life of the item.
3. If a product is about to be discontinued and a last production run is being made, he should limit the quantity to the manufacturing department's level of the last run.
4. He should recognize that the calculations are based on usage or

forecasts of usage as well as on cost calculations that are less than perfectly accurate.

In a given company there may be several other limiting factors, which should also be considered in making the final determination regarding the correct ordering quantity.

Another new version of the EOQ which has the same theoretical and arithmetic justification, but which uses units instead of dollar value is:

$$\text{EOQ (units)} = \sqrt{\frac{2 \times \text{acquisition costs} \times \text{ total annual usage (units)}}{\text{unit cost} \times \text{ carrying charges}}}$$

Assuming the following: $5 acquisition cost per order
1200 units per year
$20 per unit
20% carrying charges per dollar of inventory

$$\text{EOQ} = \sqrt{\frac{2 \times 5 \times 1200}{20 \times 0.20}} = 55 \text{ units}$$

Similar calculations could be made for varying units and the appropriate table constructed.

Purchasing Lot-Size Calculator

The preparation and use of tables for determining the unit of purchase is both time-consuming and tedious. To use such tables requires multiplying the price by the annual usage to determine the dollar value of one year's usage and then multiplying usage by the time supply to obtain order quantity. Much time and effort can be saved and more accurate results achieved by the use of a mechanical device similar to the slide rule. Such calculators are sold commercially. Frequently these may be called a manufacturing lot-size calculator. However, they can be used with equal facility for determining the economical order quantity when discounts are not available. The calculators are prepared in different versions to allow for varying inventory carrying charges.

EOQ Graphs

When a company is purchasing a large number of items of the same category that have similar quantity discounts, it is possible to construct a graph that indicates the economic order quantity by direct reading. This is a further refinement of EOQ and quantity dis-

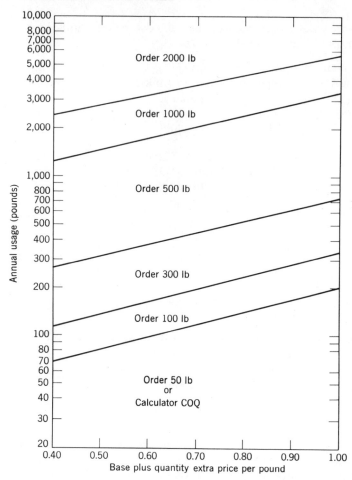

FIGURE 8-2. Economic order quantity chart for repetitive items.

count calculations and does not require a calculator. By plotting annual usage on the vertical scale and price on the horizontal scale, EOQ points can be located by use of the EOQ formula. Although it would not be practical to plot and maintain graphs for every part, it is a timesaver when a large number of parts with similar quantity discounts are involved. Figure 8-2 illustrates such a graph used for various nonferrous materials.

When to Take Advantage of Quantity Discounts[2]

In the example given earlier where the item being bought was not subject to quantity discounts, it was found that the correct ordering

[2] A more detailed discussion of quantity discounts will be found in Chapter 9.

frequency was six times per year. At this frequency the total cost was $30.50 per year. Now assume that a quantity discount of 10% for a $1000 purchase is available. If $1000 worth of this item is purchased once a year, the ordering cost will be $3 × 1, or $3, and the carrying charge will be 0.15 × 500, or $75. Thus, the total cost for buying once a year would be $78. This is an increase of $47.50 over the minimum cost of $30.50. However, since $100 could be saved by taking the 10% discount, the company would spend $47.50 to save $100. This makes a net saving of $52.50, which suggests that the company should take advantage of the discount. Any question of whether to take a quantity discount can be figured in this way.

The purchasing agent for a major metal-fabricating plant has adopted a simplified set of rules for the guidance of his buyers. He assumes a monthly inventory carrying cost of 2% applied to all items purchased. The rules are as follows:

1. If buying an increased quantity does not result in a reduced price, buyers should strive for a minimum of twelve turnovers per year.
2. If the company is now buying a 30-day requirement and an increase in quantity to a 60-day supply effects a cost saving of more than 2%, the larger quantity should be bought.
3. If the company is now buying a 30-day requirement and an increase in quantity to a 90-day supply effects a savings of at least 5%, the larger quantity should be bought.
4. Order quantities should always be based on requirements for periods not exceeding 90 days.

Limitations of EOQ

The original EOQ concept was developed to determine production quantities where the trade-off was made between machine set-up costs and inventory carrying costs. Purchasing adopted the formula by substituting ordering costs for set-up costs. This practice has been criticized by some who state that ordering costs are often trivial and indeterminant. In addition, the formula does not actively take account of such changing conditions as demand variations, seasonal changes, quantity discounts, freight costs, obsolescence risk, or stock-out costs.

The previous discussion of the EOQ indicated possible adjustments to rectify some of these limitations. However, the proper use of the EOQ concept requires a complete understanding of all these limitations.

INVENTORY CONTROL

Inventory control may be defined as the planning, ordering, and scheduling of materials used in the manufacturing process. It is possible to exercise control over the three types of inventories recognized by accountants—raw materials, work in process, and finished goods. However, the purchasing agent is primarily concerned with control over the raw materials inventory, which consists of raw or semiprocessed materials, fabricated parts, and MRO items.

There are four major reasons for maintenance of sound inventory control procedures:

1. Unit costs—quantity purchases (or long production runs) permit lower unit costs.
2. Operating costs—quantity purchases (or long production runs) permit efficient use of manpower, machines, and facilities.
3. Customer service—quantity purchases (or long production runs) assure optimum customer service and provide for efficient scheduling of internal operations.
4. Efficient use of invested capital—the balancing of elements 1, 2, and 3 above with the cost of capital encourages good financial management in the inventory area.

Responsibility for Inventory Control

The broad responsibility for determining inventory policy should rest with general management. This is so because inventories are likely to bulk large on the balance sheet of a company and figure prominently in a company's financial operations. However, the *management* of inventory is usually entrusted to subordinate departments. There is considerable variation as to which department manages the inventory control procedures.

In earlier years the purchasing department most often assumed this responsibility. However, with the introduction of the materials management form of organization, it is expected that inventory control will increasingly be a responsibility of the materials manager. Previously it was noted that a separate inventory control department is quite common under the materials management form of organization.

In the past some companies placed responsibility for inventory control with the stores department. This practice is not desirable. The stores department should have responsibility for the storage and handling of inventory after it has been received. However, the many decisions that must be made in carrying out a sound policy of inven-

CARD NO. _____

AVAILABLE-ACTUAL   FRONT

GROUP NO. _____   PART NO. _____

ACTUAL

DATE	REFERENCE	LOT	RECEIVED	USED	BALANCE		DATE	REFERENCE	LOT	RECEIVED	USED	BALANCE
						1						
						2						
						3						
						4						
						5						
						6						
						7						
						8						
						9						
						10						
						11						
						12						
						13						
						14						
						15						
						16						
						17						
						18						
						19						
						20						
						21						
						22						
						23						
						24						
CULL						25						

S-1326

INVENTORY RECORD CARD

	YEAR	TOTAL	YEAR	TOTAL	YEAR	TOTAL	YEAR	TOTAL
MO.	YEAR	YEAR	YEAR	YEAR	YEAR	YEAR	YEAR	YEAR	YEAR
J									
F									
M									
A									
.M									
J									
6 MO.									
J									
A									
S									
O									
N									
D									
TOT.									

GROUP NUMBER   PART NUMBER

CONTROL CARD—PURCH.   FORM S-1336

CARD NO.   RRBH 6854 (611)

USED ON

SOURCE		DWG. NO.	
DATE STOCKED		PLAN REF.	
NAME	
DESCRIPTION	

P. O.	QUAN.	DUE	VEN.	P. O.	QUAN.	DUE	VEN.

SALES RATIO | ANN. QUAN. | | DATE | RISK |

DEL'Y TIME (FILE 360)

DATE LAST BIN COUNT

BAG RESERVE

STORED AT

AUTO. B. C.

UNIT COST

M	M
LB	LB
T	T

MINIMUM _____

BASED ON _____ PER MO. | PER WK.

POSTING UNIT		DATE	
L. P. QUAN.		CULLING QUAN.	
CONVERSION		

VENDORS

1		6	
2		7	
3		8	
4		9	
5		10	

FIGURE 8-3. Inventory control ledger.

tory control should be the responsibility of a higher level of management. The purchasing department and the production department heads are better qualified to make such decisions.

In a few companies an inventory control committee has been established to initiate broad control policies, with the administration of the policies left to the purchasing department. Such committees contain representatives of all of the company departments affected by inventory control policies.

Records Required for Inventory Control Systems

Basic to a sound system of inventory control is the assembling of pertinent data, on the basis of which necessary ordering points and ordering quantities can be established. With a properly designed inventory control ledger card it is possible to gather the pertinent data in one place.

Inventory ledgers range from relatively simple to extremely complex forms. The nature of the business will determine the complexity of the form adopted. The form illustrated in Figure 8-3 is used by a firm manufacturing in advance of orders from customers. The data included in this form are:

1. Detailed identification of item
2. List of suppliers
3. List of open purchase orders
4. Monthly rate of usage for past several years
5. Delivery time
6. Minimum order quantity
7.. Bin balance available for issue to production

In large companies it is common practice to group the inventory ledger cards into related product lines and assign responsibility for each group to an individual who concentrates on those items and becomes thoroughly familiar with their characteristics. In addition to this separation into product lines, it is often advisable to pick out certain large-volume items and make them the special responsibility of one person.

ABC Analysis

Because most firms find that a small number of purchased items account for the major portion of the purchased value, it is often advisable to classify purchased items according to value—a procedure generally referred to as ABC analysis. Figure 8-4 illustrates a typical classification of this type.

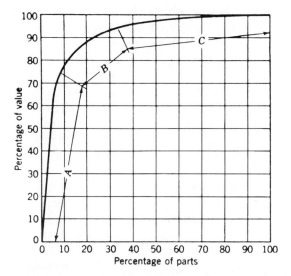

FIGURE 8-4. Distribution of inventory items by inventory dollars. 8% in number, account for 75% of cost; B components, 25% in number, account for 20% of cost; C components, 67% in number, account for 5% of cost.

The large volume A and B items should be controlled with particular care. The A items, which account for approximately 75% of total inventory value, should have continual review of estimated requirements, stock balances, and material on order so as to maintain the inventory level of these important dollar components at an absolute minimum. Lesser concern would obviously be directed to the proportionally lower valued components and materials. For such items it is common practice to establish a simple reordering procedure which can be administered either by the clerical employees in the inventory control section or the stockroom employees in conjunction with the bin records cards.

Minimum-Maximum

One of the most widely used methods of controlling inventory involves the establishment of minimum and maximum inventory levels. Theoretically, the minimum inventory level could be zero. The last unit of inventory would then be used up at the moment a new shipment was received. The maximum inventory would then be the economic or correct ordering quantity.

In practice it would be unwise to follow this extreme policy, since it involves planning that is much too close for safety. In the minimum-maximum system a safety factor is established which becomes the minimum point below which the inventory should not go under normal circumstances. The maximum inventory consists of this safety factor plus the correct ordering quantity.

The safety factor ensures against contingencies such as sudden increases in the rate of usage, failure to receive ordered materials on schedule, receipt of defective materials that cannot be used, and clerical errors in the records of bin balances. The size of this safety factor depends on the importance of the particular item to the process, the value of the investment, and the availability of substitutes on short notice. A high safety factor is indicated for any item, the lack of which would cause production shutdowns.

Under the minimum-maximum system, the rate of usage of an item is determined by past experience and forecasts, and the length of time required to obtain delivery is secured from the inventory control ledger and from studies of alternative sources of supply. An order minimum, or reorder point, is established. This point is equal to the monthly usage multiplied by the delivery time in months plus

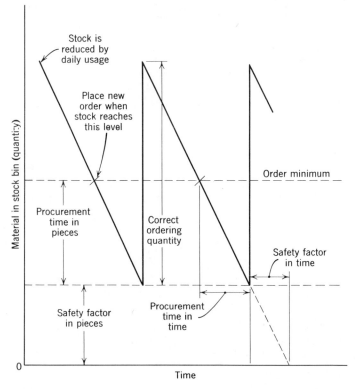

FIGURE 8-5. Graphic illustration of maximum-minimum inventory control.

the safety factor. A graphic illustration of this concept is presented in Figure 8-5.

The system of inventory control described here provides a rather automatic procedure in that at a specified time, in terms of the rate of usage, a reorder is placed. This order quantity is predetermined in accordance with the procedures outlined earlier in this chapter. However, no inventory control system can be a complete substitute for executive judgment. It is applicable only to such items as are purchased routinely. Good judgment is required in establishing the control, and good judgment is required continuously to make adjustments for changes in the size of the safety factor, usage rate, and price. No automatic system can guard against all possible changes.

Inventory Monitoring Systems

Essentially either a continuous or fixed monitoring system is employed in most inventory control procedures. The continuous system utilizes a periodic review of the stock levels of inventories and is accomplished by taking a periodic physical inventory, and monitoring either computer or hand calculated records of receipts and disbursements. The frequency of such inventory review is a function of the importance and value of the specific items. The distinguishing feature of the continuous system is that it has time orientation rather than the quantity orientation of a fixed order system.

The fixed order quantity system makes more direct use of economic order quantity levels rather than a time-dictated review. The desired economic order quantity and safety stock is predetermined, and a "flag" is developed to indicate when a new order is necessary.

Opportunities for Mechanization

During the past decade great strides have been made in the use of electronic data-processing equipment in inventory control systems. The greatest advantage of such equipment for inventory control purposes is that it provides the possibility of reducing the investment in inventory. Use of electronic equipment permits substantial time savings in determining the inventory status and because of this, reduces the size of the reserve or safety element in the inventory. There are many opportunities in the areas of quantity determination and inventory control for the application of data-processing equipment, such as:

Forecasting usage rates
Measuring deviation from forecast of usage

Calculating economic order quantities
Calculating order points with consideration of changing
Forecasts, deviations, and dollars of investment
Scheduling and flagging overdue orders
Calculating physical inventory balances on hand, on order, and
assigned
ABC inventory analysis

The equipment required and the extent of mechanization possible will be largely determined by the circumstances within the individual company. A more detailed discussion of electronic data processing in purchasing will be found in Chapter 22.

DISCUSSION QUESTIONS

1. What is a bill of materials and how is it used?

2. In calculating economic order quantities should the average cost or the incremental cost per order be used?

3. What is the basic principle of the relationship of order costs to carrying charges embodied in the economic order quantity?

4. Of what do MRO items mainly consist?

5. State the formula for the economic order quantity.

6. What factors must be considered by a purchasing agent in modifying EOQ?

7. What are the factors that influence the size of the safety factor to be used in setting minimum-maximum inventory levels?

8. Define inventory control.

9. Discuss the four major reasons for maintenance of sound inventory control procedures.

10. What data is normally included on an inventory ledger form?

SUGGESTED CASES

Gamma Corporation

Gorman Products, Inc.

CHAPTER 9
DETERMINING PRICE

What is price? A simple answer is that price is the amount of money asked for something. A slightly more sophisticated answer is that price is value expressed in terms of money. Value, in turn, is a measure of the utility—or want-satisfying power—of the item being priced. So, in pricing one is striving for an equation between the value of money on the one hand and the value of the product or service being offered on the other hand. While this sounds straightforward and reasonably easy to do, in fact it is so complex that no businessperson ever feels confident of having done it properly.

The money side of the equation presents no problem. Money as the medium of exchange is the standard of value for everything else. However, the other side of the equation—the goods and services— vary in value for every buyer, and their value varies over time. Almost every buyer wants to do something different with the product or service and the value to him varies with the use. Sometimes the quality is better than the buyer needs but if the price is not too high he may buy it anyhow. Or the quality may be too low to suit him but he will buy if the price is correspondingly low.

The buyer will be less demanding if there are a few alternative sources of supply. He also weighs such things as the reputation of the seller and the services that accompany the sale. The seller always has to consider how many people will buy his product or service at the price he has in mind because the volume of sales will influence the cost at which he can produce it. All of the considerations serve to make the pricing process exceedingly difficult for the seller and an endless challenge for the buyer.

Much of the purchasing process focuses on price. However, it is easy to let the price side of the equation occupy undue attention. The alternative possibilities on the other side of the equation seldom are identical, and a buyer should not lose sight of that fact. In fact, it can be said that the essence of purchasing consists of a careful weighing of the suitability of alternative offerings for the purchaser's use and the relating of these values to their prices.

In order to know that the price being quoted is right for him, a purchasing agent must know, for all materials, supplies, equipment, and services used by the company, what quality or quality range is suitable, and he must then familiarize himself with the prices being asked by acceptable suppliers. Only if he knows the price quotations, considers all related cost elements such as transportation, handling, service, and delivery performance, and relates the true cost to his quality requirements, can he intelligently evaluate prices in terms of his needs.

There is a tendency to exaggerate the importance of low price in the function of purchasing. Most purchasing agents would be satisfied if they could equal the market average price on the total of their purchases, provided the purchases were satisfactory in all other respects. An experienced purchasing agent will avoid making a quick decision to buy simply because the seller quotes him a price below the prevailing market. Both the quality of the material and the service offered by the seller are likely to be more important than price. Even a substantial price saving will be less than worthless if the material cannot be used for the intended purpose. Likewise, low prices quickly lose their attractiveness when deliveries are uncertain, adjustments are not made, or other services are below standard. Of course, price is important, but its importance is so universally recognized that throughout this chapter we shall repeatedly emphasize that price is only one of several variables that must be considered in making a purchase.

Price in Relation to Total Purchase Decision

It has been previously stated that the objective of the purchasing department is to buy the right amount of the right kind of goods from the right supplier at the right time and at the right price. Although this is a sound generalization, it assumes away most of the hard decisions by using the term *right*. In this connection, for example, just what is the *right* price? It is not necessarily the lowest price. As mentioned above, the lowest price may not provide the quality and service needed by the company. Even where it does, the lowest price may be offered for buying a substantial quantity in advance of needs. This entails many costs not reflected in the quoted price, as is shown in Chapter 8.

Occasionally, low prices are quoted by suppliers in order to secure orders, even though such prices will cause the supplier to operate at a loss, or the supplier may be unloading an oversupply at less than full cost. Where this is done, it may be a matter of strategic pricing, or it may be desperation on the part of the seller. If the low price is offered as a result of strategy on the part of the seller, the item may represent a good buy. Here the seller is willing to take less than his full average price in order to get established as a supplier of this particular buyer, and the quality and service are likely to be excellent, since the seller is building a reputation. The same would be true in the case of an oversupply that must be sold. On the other hand, the low price may represent the frantic effort of the seller to keep his plant in operation. Then, once he has the order, he might minimize service and cut corners on quality in order to reduce his loss. In evaluating a low price, the purchasing agent has to consider and weigh these possibilities.

Reciprocity, which has been described previously (see Chapter 5), may also enter into the evaluation of a low price. Admittedly, reciprocity should be used with caution. However, if the price differential is small, many companies do buy from their own customers at a slightly higher price. They justify this on the grounds that their continued operations are dependent on the success of their customers, and so they try to help their customers if they can do so at no great cost to themselves. One can argue that the overall result of reciprocity is to raise everyone's costs, but, in the short run and in a restricted marketplace, the appeal of reciprocity is strong.

Right Price

Thus, in deciding what is the right price the purchasing agent must take a broad and objective view of his company. He must examine the prices quoted by different suppliers and attempt to determine which price, in combination with the quality features of the product and the service aspects of the relationship with the supplier, will afford his company the greatest ultimate value.

The importance of sound price determination cannot be overstressed. The purchasing agent is spending a substantial proportion of the funds expended by his company. His decisions can and often do mean the difference between profitable and unprofitable operations. He has a responsibility to his company to see that it gets a full measure of value for the money he spends. This responsibility can be discharged only by constant and careful review of all the prices he can secure. Such review should be made regardless of who the supplier is and the past relationships with that supplier.

A purchasing agent will not find himself designated a "price buyer" in the derogatory sense if he carefully analyzes all quotations in terms of quality, service, and price. It is when price is abstracted from quality and service that the purchasing agent is likely to get into trouble by overemphasizing price.

A sound analysis of price quotations must be based on an understanding of the economic laws governing price making in a free enterprise economy. This understanding must also be accompanied by an appreciation of some of the psychological considerations that enter into the price-making process. In addition, the purchasing agent should be familiar with the various state and federal laws that affect price making, besides knowing how to safeguard his company from difficulties that arise from the contractural nature of any purchase transactions. Each of these areas will be examined in the following sections of this chapter.

Economic Considerations in Price Making

Surprisingly little is known about how businesspersons go about setting prices. Understandably, they want to keep their methods secret from competitors who would gain an important strategic advantage over them if they knew how the prices were determined. It is also probably true that the method has been more haphazard and unsystematic than businesspeople would care to admit.

Cost Approach

Such information as is available suggests that there are two basic approaches to price making. The first might be described as the cost approach and the second as the market approach to price making. The cost approach seems to be the more popular of the two. The central idea of this method is very simple. The price maker adds together the individual cost items as determined by cost-accounting methods. These unit costs include such items as raw material, direct labor, indirect labor, machine time, factory overhead, warehousing, sales, advertising, transportation, office costs, and general overhead. To the total of such costs, the price maker adds an amount representing his desired profit, and this figure represents his price.

At times the cost approach to pricing is reduced to a formula. The price maker observes that there seems to be a definite, rather permanent relationship between certain of the costs and the prices he has been setting. For example, his price may consistently have been approximately twice the raw material and direct-labor costs. Therefore, instead of adding the individual costs, he will use the formula of doubling his raw-material and direct-labor costs. So long as the relationship between costs and prices is close and the relative importance of the cost categories does not change, the method works well and is a simple variation of the cost method of pricing. However, one should keep in mind that cost relationships change over time, and an uncritical adherence to formula pricing may ultimately lead to noncompetitive pricing. The formula method of cost pricing is primarily applicable to a company that makes one product without substantial variations.

Although the cost method of pricing is extremely popular, there is reason to question its economic soundness. It is obviously true that in the long run the prices a company receives for its products must equal or exceed company costs. If the price is less than cost, the company will gradually go bankrupt. However, the mere fact that buyers will not pay a price equal to full average costs does not necessarily mean that a company should hold out for that price or stop producing. In many situations a seller will be better off selling lower than full cost for a time in order to carry out a part of his overhead rather than refusing to sell below cost. Where a company is producing a *line* of products, it may even be advisable to sell one or more of them permanently at less than cost. This might be true, for example, if the company could not find a more profitable product to produce or if the products being sold at less than full costs would aid, from a sales point of view, in selling other products that are profitable. Also, the cost approach gives no consideration to the possibility that a product may have a distinctiveness or quality that makes it worth more than its cost plus a reasonable profit. Thus, although the cost approach to pricing is popular and can be justified under certain circumstances, it should not be used inflexibly or under all circumstances. A price based on cost cannot succeed for long in a competitive market if it is out of line with value, since competitors will force the price down to the value level.

Also, the purchasing agent should not be deceived into thinking that he is getting a bargain simply because the price is set at cost or less. The price should be measured by the value of the product to the buyer, not by its cost to the seller. This is a fundamental principle for the purchasing agent to keep in mind in his buying.

Administered Pricing

In recent years much has been written and spoken about "administered pricing." This is a term that was first used by some economists during the depression of the 1930s in an attempt to explain why prices of certain basic materials did not drop enough to stimulate the demand for greater volume and thereby initiate recovery from the depression. The explanation was that such industries were controlled by a few suppliers who "administered" the prices rather than allowing the free play of supply and demand to determine the level of price. In recent years the issue of administered pricing has been revived because of the government's attempt to hold down prices in the face of rising inflation. Charges are made that such industries as steel, aluminum, or automobiles are raising their prices through administrative action rather than in response to market pressures. The government has been inclined to put the blame on management for "administering" prices to keep them high, whereas management explains the situation by pointing out that costs, made up largely of labor costs, have risen and thus have forced them to maintain or raise prices.

The question raised by the controversy over "administered pricing" is essentially misleading. It assumes that the significant issue is whether large companies today set their prices or have their prices set for them by the impersonal forces of supply and demand. No one can seriously doubt that management sets its prices. In fact, it is doubtful that any industrial economy (as opposed to an agricultural economy) could operate by trying to wait for supply and demand to set prices for all of the infinite variety of products manufactured. The theory of impersonal supply-demand price setting was meant to apply where many small producers all manufactured a few basic, homogeneous products. In our economy we have large companies all trying to manufacture unique products. Under such conditions the manufacturer must name the price. The pertinent issue is whether in doing so he is being responsive to the needs of the market and the value of his product to its users. If a manufacturer thinks too much in terms of unit cost and unit profit, as opposed to total cost and profit, he may set prices that restrict his production and retard the growth of the economy.

Government Controlled Prices. During World War II, and again during the Korean War, the U.S. federal government imposed firm price controls to prevent inflationary price advances. Except for these national emergencies this country has depended on competition to regulate prices and price levels. However, on August 15, 1971, under special legislation passed by Congress, the President imposed a 90-day freeze on all prices followed by periods called Phase I and Phase II, during which prices could be raised only in proportion to cost increases. Since August 15, 1971 a Pay Board has also administered rules governing wage increases.

While the issue is debatable, and cannot be proved, these controls seem to have slightly moderated the pace of inflation. These wage and price restraints are similar to quasi-formal plans called "incomes policies" that have been tried in western European countries and Canada where they have failed to halt long-run inflationary trends.

It has been remarkable to observe how complacently businesspersons have accepted this infringement upon their pricing freedom. Many of them even talk about the possibility of making the controls permanent. If it were possible for this country to succeed with an income policy where others have failed, one should note that to adopt permanent controls would amount to making the cost approach to pricing a matter of law. It would undoubtedly discourage innovation since the high risk could not be compensated by high price and profit. It would also largely forego price as the allocator of our physical resources. The loss would seem large in the light of the dubious gain.

Price controls affect purchasing in a number of ways. First, since prices will usually be pushing against the ceilings, a seller is much more likely to have one price for all buyers. Second, the seller will be less inclined to negotiate prices with a buyer because there will ordinarily not be enough slack in his profit margin to give the seller the required leeway for negotiating. Third, since the buyer can rely less upon price as an indication of value, his responsibility for measuring quality objectively will be greater than usual.

Market Approach

The market approach to pricing essentially consists of putting a price on the product that the market is willing to pay. The method of determining this price will vary. It may be done on the basis of market research designed to reveal through questionnaire or market test what volume can be sold at various possible prices. The market test technique is more commonly applied to consumer goods than to industrial goods because the experimental approach might be upsetting to a narrow industrial market.

Perhaps the commonest approach to market pricing is the technique known as "following the leader." Here the company selects a strong competitor and aims to keep its price in a certain relationship to those of its competitor. This approach recognizes that products must sell competitively and that price differences can succeed only if they measure differences in quality or service.

A third method of market pricing consists of setting a price that will give the seller a certain desired volume of business. This method, as any other method, cannot completely disregard cost considerations, but it explicitly recognizes that making sales in order to use existing facilities may be more important than making a profit on every sale. This method has its principal application to heavy fixed-cost industries in which net profit is highly dependent on large volume production.

Another technique for pricing according to the market is to price in a certain relationship to the price of related products. With the growth of interindustry competition this means of pricing is becoming more common. Glass containers, for example, cannot be priced effectively without taking into account the prices of tin, paper, and plastic containers.

Pricing to the market has a sounder economic basis that cost pricing and will undoubtedly increase in popularity as more study is given to the theory of pricing. It recognizes that price must reflect conditions of demand as well as of supply. Cost pricing overemphasizes the significance of cost in the process of pricing. Market pricing is in the interests of the purchasing agent as well as the seller. If such pricing were perfectly done, it would give the purchasing agent maximum flexibility in buying since prices of all products would be set with a view to their worth to the customer.

A somewhat specialized pricing question arises in cases where a manufacturer wants to buy a part or subassembly for a product he manufactures. Here he is the only buyer and there may be no seller offering the precise item. In such a case the buyer may make inquiries to several suppliers or negotiate with one. In either case his problem is to judge whether the price offered is reasonable. A procedure of fairly recent origin and increasing popularity for judging the price in this situation is known as the "in-plant estimate." Here the buyer has his own specialists carefully plan the part or subassembly in terms of materials and manufacturing operations that must be performed. Costs are then determined for each step of the process. At this point, with the target price in mind, the buyer begins to negotiate with one or more suppliers. Frequently the buyer's specialists assist the supplier in planning his production methods to meet the target prices the buyer had previously worked out. This procedure is a by-product of value analysis.[1]

[1] See Chapter 11 for a more complete discussion of value analysis.

Psychological Considerations in Price Making

One of the fundamental psychological factors bearing on price is the prediction of future supply-demand relationships. At any point in time there is, in addition to the offers and orders that influence price, a market undertone of confidence or uncertainty which has a decided influence on prices. A particular supply-demand relationship coupled with confidence about the future may result in advancing prices, whereas the same supply-demand relationship in an atmosphere of pessimism may bring about declining prices. This attitude about the future cannot be measured, either quantitatively or qualitatively. Through experience a good purchasing agent develops a kind of sixth sense which enables him to evaluate this intangible element and act accordingly. Although it is true that a general attitude about the future cannot be measured, a purchasing agent can do much toward verifying his personal appraisal by talking with other purchasing agents individually or through association meetings.

Another psychological factor has to do with knowing how far to press a bargaining advantage that a purchasing agent may have over a supplier. It is possible under certain circumstances to force a price down to the level that covers little more than the direct or out-of-pocket costs of the seller. If the seller's alternative to taking the order would be to reduce his operations substantially, he might find it advantageous to sell at a price that contributed nothing toward his overhead costs. Superficially it might appear that a purchasing agent accepting such a price had made a very good buy. However, taking full advantage of this situation may ultimately result in driving the supplier out of business, and the consequent reduction in supply may raise the price for that product in the long run. Thirty to forty years ago some industries followed the deliberate policy of getting suppliers to be dependent on them and then forcing the price down until the suppliers were driven into bankruptcy. Such buyers have found that, in time, suppliers avoid them and that their short-run advantage has turned out to be a long-run handicap. Some companies that once followed this policy have had to go to great lengths to convince suppliers that they were reasonable and equitable in their price bargaining. By way of generalization on this point, one might say that the purchasing agent should strive to pay a fair price. A fair price would be one that enables both the buyer and seller to stay in business and to compete effectively.

A third psychological factor in price making is the process of haggling over price. This technique of price determination had, until recently, almost disappeared from the consumer goods field. However, it has been revived for durable consumer goods because of the effect that discount houses have had on the price bargaining of regular dealers. Price haggling has never been absent from the industrial field and probably never can be. If the price can be changed by bargaining, it tends to prolong the selling transactions and raise the cost of buying. It also diverts the attention of both parties from quality and service and concentrates it on price. Finally, after the sale is made, it leaves the buyer with the uneasy feeling that he might have obtained a still better price if he had bargained harder. However, although haggling often creates suspicion rather than goodwill, the process of bargaining over price will probably persist in the industrial goods field. This is likely to be so because price is a more important element in an industrial sale than in a consumer sale, since the industrial buyer must resell a product made from purchased goods at a competitive price. Therefore, a purchasing agent must develop good trading and bargaining skills. Though a part of the trading technique depends on personal qualities, the real basis for success is a thorough knowledge of the market and of price-making forces.

A fourth, and final, psychological consideration in settling on a price has to do with nonbusiness considerations that salespeople sometimes try to inject into negotiations. This may amount to nothing more than the salesman trying to cultivate a friendly feeling between himself and the purchasing agent. So long as the salesman does not try to take advantage of friendship to secure an unwarranted price, this relationship may be mutually helpful. The purchasing agent will do well, however, to be sure that reason always holds the upper hand. At other times nonbusiness considerations may express themselves in terms of entertainment, gifts, or actual bribery. There can be no justification for such activities, and the naive purchasing agent who thinks he is immune to their influence is likely to find that they insidiously distort his thinking. Fortunately, these factors are becoming increasingly less prevalent.[2]

Discounts

An important part of price determination involves the discounts that are available on a given purchase. The purchasing agent must be familiar not only with the discounts available from his suppliers, but must also understand the various types of discounts commonly used in commercial practice.

[2] See Chapter 6 for more complete discussion of gifts and entertainment.

Cash Discounts

At one time most suppliers offered cash discounts that varied both in the amount of discount allowed and the period during which the discount might be taken. Currently suppliers are tending to reduce the percentage discount allowed or are eliminating it altogether. The reason for eliminating the discount is that it is very difficult to enforce when a customer takes the discount after the specified date has passed. To do so creates ill will, and if not enforced uniformly, it results in discriminatory pricing.

The most common cash discount is stated as 2/10, net 30. This means that, if the purchaser pays for the goods within 10 days of the date of shipment or date of invoice, he may deduct a 2% discount from the amount of the invoice. If, however, he delays payment beyond 10 days, he must pay the face amount of the invoice. If the buyer delays payment beyond 30 days, the seller may institute collection procedures and, in some cases, will add interest for the period beyond 30 days.

Although payment within the prescribed discount period is primarily a responsibility of the fiscal department, the purchasing agent should realize that receiving a 2% discount for anticipating the final due date of an invoice by 20 days is equivalent to earning interest on the amount involved in the transaction at the rate of about 36% each year, since there are approximately 18 periods of 20 days each in a year. If the buyer is given 2% discount for anticipating payment by 20 days, this is equivalent to a rate of 2% multiplied by 18 periods, or 36%.

Thus it is vitally important that, in the terms of his transaction, the buyer secure whatever cash discount is customarily granted by the supplier. Cash discounts do not usually vary among the several suppliers of a given type of industrial product. However, there is some variation from industry to industry according to the practice established in the particular industry. The buyer must familiarize himself with the discount practices within the industries with which he deals.

It is frequently said that cash discounts should be thought of primarily as price reductions. It certainly is true that, if a buyer secures a discount that is higher than he had previously been receiving from a supplier, he may consider it to be a reduction in the price of the goods he is buying. Likewise, if the discount is lowered, it effectively increases the price paid for the goods purchased. The latter practice is sometimes resorted to during a period of rising prices to cloak a price rise on a given item.

If the cash discount a buyer receives is the same as he has received in the past from a particular supplier (and also the same as is being offered to other buyers), he should notify the fiscal department of his company. The decision of whether to take or not to take the discount is a fiscal matter rather than one of purchasing policy. However, in many companies it is the responsibility of the purchasing department to make certain that the incoming shipment and all associated paper work are cleared as promptly as possible, so as not to jeopardize the discount by delays in handling.

Trade Discounts

In some lines it is customary for the seller to quote prices to the customer in the form of a price list, from which one or more discounts are deducted before the actual selling price is established. Ordinarily, the list price is considerably higher than the actual selling price. A trade discount represents the compensation of the buyer who assumes certain distribution functions for the seller.

Here is a typical illustration of how a trade discount is rationalized. A manufacturer sells mainly through wholesalers or mill supply houses, but occasionally sells directly to large industrial users. The wholesalers are expected to sell to the small customers in their area and are granted a substantial discount to compensate them for storing goods close to the customers and handling small-size orders. The purchasing agent who buys directly from the manufacturer may expect a discount from list price that nets him a lower price than he would get if he bought through a wholesaler; however, the purchasing agent should not expect a discount as great as that granted to the wholesaler who performs many additional distribution functions for the producer of the goods.

Trade discounts are usually granted for the purpose of protecting a certain channel of distribution. This is accomplished by making it more economical for certain classes of customers to buy from the distributor instead of directly from the manufacturer. If a manufacturer has found that wholesalers are more efficient in the handling of his goods than direct sale by his own organization, he will set up a discount schedule that induces most of his customers to patronize wholesalers. Except under unusual circumstances, purchasing agents will find it profitable to accept the established channel instead of attempting to secure undue trade discounts for direct purchases. Channels that are efficient and perform a needed function should be preserved.

Frequently a seller employs what appears to be a discount plan but in reality is merely an economical method of quoting his price. The seller issues a catalogue illustrating his products and indicating a price, which is an arbitrary price set significantly higher than the prevailing level. He then issues an accompanying discount sheet notifying buyers what discount or series of discounts to apply in calculating the true price. The discount may run as high as 65% or may be a series such as 40-20-10%. When prices are to be changed by the seller he only needs to change the discounts on the accompanying discount sheet. This can be done in less time and at much less cost than reissuing the entire catalogue. Such discounts are frequently called "arbitrary" discounts.

Quantity Discounts

Quantity discounts are discounts granted by sellers to customers who purchase in larger quantities than those to which the regular trade discount applied.[3] They may be calculated on the basis of individual transactions or on the basis of a series of transactions over a period of time. The former are called noncumulative and the latter cumulative quantity discounts.

The seller usually justifies such discounts on the basis of savings that he realizes when he sells in large quantities. He saves on his marketing expenses because marketing costs do not increase in proportion to an increase in the size of an order. The paper work is the same, and the increased costs of packing and shipping are not proportionally larger. There also may be production savings on large orders, especially if they are placed well in advance of delivery and thus permit more orderly production planning and scheduling.

From the buyer's point of view, the quantity discount is closely related to his inventory control policies (see Chapter 8). He must compare the costs of carrying the larger inventory with the savings realized through the reduction in price because of the quantity discount. In addition, the buyer who emphasizes quantity discounts in his purchasing strategy will find that the number of his suppliers tends to decrease, since he concentrates his purchases in order to buy in the largest quantities practicable. In the chapters dealing with source selection (Chapters 5 and 6), it was pointed out that restriction of the number of suppliers entails certain risks.

When quantity discounts are judiciously taken, they effectively lower price. Therefore, the buyer should inform himself of the availability of all quantity discounts and take them whenever indicated.

[3] Sometimes, for civic reasons, sellers grant discounts to governmental agencies regardless of the size of the order.

He must, however, try not to secure preferential discounts lest he find himself in violation of legislation that prohibits price discrimination.

Legislation Affecting Price

Robinson-Patman Act

The Robinson-Patman Act makes illegal those quantity discounts that for "commodities of like grade and quality" are not based on "differences in the cost of manufacture, sale, or delivery resulting from the differing methods or quantities in which such commodities are to such purchasers sold or delivered."[4] The law not only provides that the seller is in violation of the law when he offers quantity discounts that cannot be justified under the provisions of the law, but that the buyer is also guilty for knowingly accepting such discounts.

Under a provision of this law it is legal for a seller to meet in good faith an illegal low price offered by a competitor. This so-called "good faith" defense against price discrimination is legal as interpreted by the U.S. Supreme Court.[5] Congress has made repeated attempts to limit the seller's right to meet the low prices of competitors to cases where meeting such prices would not substantially tend to lessen competition. Such a change would prevent large companies from meeting lower prices of small competitors. This change in the law is opposed by the executive branch of the federal government and by a large segment of business, and thus is not likely to be made.

While the primary burden of justifying discounts as legal rests with the seller, a buyer may be held responsible if he knowingly induces the seller to grant him a discriminatory discount. After 1953, when the *Automatic Canteen Co.* v, *F.T.C.* case was decided, it appeared that the courts would virtually absolve buyers from their responsibility under the law. However, recent cases are tending to place more responsibility upon buyers who are strong enough to influence prices. Therefore, buyers should be cautious in dealing with sellers who are greatly in need of their business.

It should be understood that a discount does not have to equal the full savings accruing to the seller by reason of the buyer's order. It must merely be no more than the saving. Although one of the purposes of this law was to eliminate price discrimination among buyers on the part of the seller, the purchasing agent should not rely on the

---

[4] Public Act 692, 74th Congress, 2d Session, approved June 19, 1936, Sec. 2(a).

[5] *Standard Oil Co.* v. *FTC*, 340 U.S. 231, 71 S. Ct. 240 (1951).

law to guarantee this nondiscrimination. Enforcement of the law has not been entirely effective. He should rely instead on his own knowledge and judgment of the market to obtain fair prices that will enable his company to compete successfully with others.

The question arises as to what a buyer can do under the Robinson-Patman Act if he believes that he has been the victim of unfavorable price discrimination. The following quotation from "Small Business and Regulation of Pricing Practices" prepared by the U.S. Department of Commerce clearly sets forth the possible courses of action that are open.

1. *Informing the seller.* The fact that you are charged more than someone else for an item is not in itself proof of illegal discrimination. You may be able to get your supplier to eliminate discrimination or to show why he is not discriminating against you.

2. *Reporting to the Federal Trade Commission.* The Federal Trade Commission carries the major burden for enforcing the Robinson-Patman Act. Its normal procedures include investigation, complaint, hearing, and—if the facts seem to warrant—a cease and desist order. Orders may be appealed to the Circuit Court of Appeals and finally to the Supreme Court. Procedure is normally slow because the seller does not have to change his pricing practice until an order against him becomes final. Buyer's complaints to the Federal Trade Commission are treated in confidence. Matters are expedited if letters to the commission give definite information about how you think the law is being violated.

3. *Reporting to the Department of Justice.* Since the antidiscrimination section of the Robinson-Patman Act is a part of Clayton Act, Clayton Act procedures can also be set in motion. U.S. district attorneys in the various districts can bring suits for injunction.

4. *Bringing private suit.* You can ask the courts for injunctive relief against threatened damage from illegal price discrimination. You can also bring suit for triple damages for a loss you have sustained because of a discriminatory high price. The courts have ruled that a buyer who is injured by discrimination can collect three times the actual amount of the discrimination. This means that, if you were charged $1 more for an item that a competitor and bought 10,000 items, you can collect $30,000 if you win the case.[6]

[6] "Small Business and Regulation of Pricing Practices," Economic (Small Business) Series 61, U.S. Government Printing Office, Washington, 1947, p. 14.

Frequently, the best remedy for a suspected discrimination against the buyer is to talk the matter over with a seller. Often the seller can explain to his customer the reasons for apparent discrimination, or he will take corrective action if discrimination exists. If the discrimination is not intentional, this method enables both parties to avoid the difficulties and costs of legal proceedings and, in the long run, will result in better relations between the buyer and seller.

Sherman Act, Clayton Act, and Federal Trade Commission Act

The antitrust laws have established the principle that business practices which hinder competition or tend to restrain trade are illegal. These Acts are of interest to the purchasing agent from a price point of view, in that they apply to cases where a number of sellers, through collusion, are quoting identical prices.

When a buyer suspects that prices quoted to him have been the result of collusion, he has several possible courses of action. He may accept the situation temporarily in the belief that there is nothing that he can do about it in the short run and then initiate action on the part of his production or engineering departments to develop acceptable substitute materials that can be secured from other sources. He may begin legal action, but he seldom does because of the time and cost involved in such action. He may select one of the collusive bidders and bring pressure on him to reduce the price. There is some question of the ethics in this course of action, but many buyers consider is permissible to combat an illegal agreement with unethical pressure.

Basically the antitrust laws are premised on the assumption that competitively determined prices will be lower than those that result from monopoly or collusion. While this assumption has strong support in economic theory and common sense, little empirical research has been done to validate the position. An interesting analysis was made of the cost of constructing 112 light manufacturing plants for the Air Force in the 1960-1970 decade.[7] After making adjustments for 28 variables the costs were related to the number of bidders. The conclusion was that a likely saving of $.87 per square foot occurred as the number of competitors increased by one, and this was equal to a 4.4% reduction in cost.

[7] Effect on Number of Competitors on Costs," David N. Burt, *Journal of Purchasing*, vol. 7, no. 4, November 1971, pp. 13-23.

Resale Price Maintenance Laws

These laws, more popularly known as the fair trade laws, are of limited significance to purchasing agents because not many industrial goods are placed under the resale price maintenance laws by the sellers. The fair trade laws are state laws that authorize sellers to specify the minimum price at which resellers may sell their branded products.

A purchasing agent is not likely to buy many items that have been placed under such price protection. When he does buy fair-traded items, he should assure himself that their price is competitive with nonfair-traded items that he might substitute.

Dual Prices

As an outgrowth of Federal Trade Commission and court action, purchasing agents who are buying items for both original equipment use and for resale through company branches as service parts are faced with a dual price problem. It is legal to charge different prices for original equipment and replacement, but it is illegal to allow the lower-priced original equipment to find its way into the replacement market where it could compete unfairly with like items bought at the higher replacement equipment price.

In fields where dual use is common, suppliers insist that the purchase order contain a phrase identifying the end use for the item ordered. In this way they can comply with the requirements of separation of prices between original equipment and replacement parts.

The same requirement also arises in connection with automotive parts that bear a federal excise tax for automotive use but not for nonautomotive use. The purchase order here too must identify the end use.

How Price Is Determined by the Purchasing Agent

The purchasing agent usually wants to enter a specific price on the purchase order that he sends to the selected supplier. He must, therefore, establish a sound procedure for securing this price information. There are a number of sources from which the purchasing agent can secure prices on items that he wishes to buy. His choice will depend on the item he is buying and the type of organization he represents.

Published Price Lists

There are many items that the purchasing agent buys frequently on which price information can be maintained in the purchasing files of the company. These are standard production items for which catalogs and price lists are prepared. The typical purchasing agent has a large collection of such lists and catalogs for a wide range of products from many suppliers.

In using the published price lists the purchasing agent is primarily concerned with making sure that the price lists are current and have not been superseded by newer published lists. This is a problem for the typical purchasing department which receives new and revised catalogs and price lists daily. In the larger companies it may be necessary to employ a clerk to keep the catalog file up to date.

When the purchasing agent receives a requisition for a standard production item, she is likely first to determine from the records when she last bought that item and from which supplier. Often she will then send a new order to the same supplier and specify "price as before." If the item is one that has not been purchased recently, the purchasing agent is likely to use her catalog files to locate possible suppliers and prices quoted for the item.[8]

Salespersons

A second important source of information about price is salespersons. The buyer can learn from salespeople of any price changes or revisions in the price lists and can also secure quotations on modifications of standard stock items. It should be noted that in many instances salespersons cannot bind their companies to prices they quote, but must secure confirmation from their sales managers. Therefore, although the purchasing agent may use salesperson's price information for standard production items, she is well-advised to rely on more direct negotiations for the prices of nonstandard items.

Published Market Data

Most raw materials are traded on well-organized central markets. Business publications such as *Iron Age* and *The Wall Street Journal* publish price information on raw materials that is current, complete, and reasonably accurate. However, since the prices of raw materials tend to fluctuate with almost every sale, such price data are of value to the purchasing agent mainly as a basis on which to begin price negotiations.

The most important factor in determining the price to be paid for raw materials is the price trend of the commodity. Since purchases of raw materials can usually be delayed or advanced to take advantage

---

[8] It should be recognized, of course, that the price list does not constitute a legal offer on the part of the seller at that price.

of a favorable price trend, the purchasing agent is interested not only in current price quotations but also in whatever information is available relative to changes in price over a period of time. It is, therefore, vital that a buy of commodities sold on organized markets keep himself posted on both market price and market trend.

When buying a commodity whose price is related to an organized market quotation, the buyer should first check a dependable source of published market information. Equipped with this information, he should then contact his usual sources, and such new sources as he thinks are worth a trial, to ascertain their prices in relation to the published market price.

It should be recognized that not all suppliers sell at market prices. Some regularly sell above the market, believing that their quality and service is better than average and, therefore, worth more than market price. Others either regularly or occasionally sell under the market for the opposite reasons or because they are especially anxious for business. If the preferred source is found to be above the market without good reason, competitive bids or bargaining may be effective in securing a lower price from this supplier. Personal negotiations have often proved successful in situations of this kind, except for public agencies where the bidding procedure must be followed whenever practicable.

Negotiations

In established concerns sources of supply that have proved satisfactory in quality, service, and price have been developed over the years. These sources tend to be regularly utilized. When the usual source is found to be higher in price or to offer delivery terms that are not as desirable as those offered by a competitor, the buyer will frequently negotiate with the regular source for better price or delivery terms.

These negotiations may be conducted with the supplier's salesman, or they may be carried on by correspondence between the buyer and the seller. Negotiations are most frequently employed with nonstandard items that have to be produced to the buyer's specifications. Negotiations permit a more personalized approach to the problems of agreeing on the terms of the sale than does the formal bid-invitation method described in the following section.

Negotiations are useful whenever compromises are likely to be necessary in arriving at any of the terms of the contract. With open negotiations it is possible to call on any of the departments of the buying and selling companies to bring about a complete understanding and agreement on all factors involved in the transaction. Although such negotiations take more time, their informality and flexibility often are sufficiently important to justify this method rather than buying from catalogs or using the bid process. The time spent in negotiations is time spent in ironing out details that might otherwise lead to trouble at the time of delivery.

Competitive Bids

Still another method of determining price is to secure competitive bids from potential suppliers. Most buying by governmental and other public agencies is done almost exclusively by this method because of statutory requirements. Exceptions are sometimes permitted in emergency situations where time is of the essence or where patented or proprietary items are required. Industry, by contrast, resorts to the competitive-bid procedure to a very limited extent and usually only for certain special purposes.

Bids may be used by a company as a means of developing a list of suppliers for a product not previously purchased or to secure alternative sources of supply. The competitive bid is frequently used by industrial firms in buying special, nonrepeat items such as heavy equipment or machinery. Competitive bids may also be used for term-contract purchases of fabricated parts or materials (items that are to be incorporated into the buyer's finished product with little or no further change). In some instances, industrial firms making goods under government contracts must use the competitive-bid process in order to establish costs to the satisfaction of the government.

Bids are obtained by buyers through the use of a special form which is usually called an "Invitation to Bid" or a "Request for Quotations." Although the form is not a purchase order, and usually explicitly so states, it is similar to a purchase order in form. It describes in detail the item on which bids are sought, including an accurate description, quantity to be purchased, conditions of delivery, end use of the item, and terms of the transaction. Bid requests generally have a statement appended that clearly states the manner in which the bids will be handled, the time during which the bids will be accepted, and other conditions deemed appropriate.

The use of a standard bid request form is necessary in order to secure all quotations on a comparable basis so that accurate comparisons can be made. Since all sellers are equally informed of what is desired and the conditions involved, the buyer may presume that all bids are comparable. However, a careful buyer will make it a practice to verify any bids that seem to be too high or too low relative to the other bids received.

In industrial buying, bid requests are usually sent to a representative list of qualified sources. The buyer should request bids only from sources with which he might place an order. He should not, from either an ethical or practical point of view, request bids from suppliers to whom he has no intention of awarding a contract. Such a practice can actually cause a rise in price. For example, if the buyer seeks quotations on an item that requires a substantial quantity of a scarce material in its production, the firms that have been requested to quote will first ascertain the price they will have to pay for the materials to be used in the manufacture. If a number of market inquiries are received by the supplier of the scarce item, he may misinterpret this interest in his product and raise the price. Thus, an artificial stimulation of demand through a widespread request for quotations can actually raise the price.

The buyer for a public agency is in an entirely different position in the securing of bids. Statutes, ordinances, and local rules of agencies that award contracts generally specify the procedure to be followed. In most instances public agencies are permitted to establish certain standards that bidding firms must meet before their bids will be considered.

When the bids are received from the prospective suppliers, they are listed and tabulated to facilitate comparison. In most public buying, all bids are opened at a stipulated time, and the award made to the lowest responsible bidder whose bid conforms to the conditions stated on the bid request. Invitation to Bid forms of public agencies frequently include a provision that reserves to the buyer the right to reject all bids if he considers the price to be excessive.

An industrial buyer is under no obligation to accept the lowest responsible bid. He is likely to make his decision on the basis of a comparison of service and quality considerations as well as price. Sound policy suggests that an industrial buyer keep all quotations confidential; particularly that he not disclose them to competitors of the bidding firm. He should also follow a policy of "firm" bidding. That is, except under unusual circumstances, he should not permit bidders to change their bids once they have been submitted. It should be recognized, however, that the practice of giving a favored bidder the chance to meet someone's lower price is not uncommon. The practice is sometimes called a "second look." Clearly, the practice undermines the integrity of the bidding process since the preferred supplier is not likely to put in his lowest offer originally, and the other bidders may bid perfunctorily. If the buyer suspects that a bidder has made an honest error in his computations, it would be ethical and proper to call this fact to the attention of the bidder and request him to verify his original bid. Under no circumstances should he be told that this bid is higher or lower than the other bids.

A buyer is not obligated to accept any of the bids submitted if he believes they are too high or if, because of an apparent uniformity of bids, he suspects collusion. He can, in either of these cases, request new bids or enter into direct negotiations with one or more of the bidding firms in order to arrive at a satisfactory contract.

If the bids seem to be in order, the buyer completes the transaction by accepting one of them. Bids submitted in compliance with a request for quotations have the legal status of an offer. The offer is binding on the seller if it is accepted within a reasonable period of time. The buyer sends the successful bidder a purchase order with the notation that it is in accordance with the seller's quotation of a certain date. There is then a legally binding contract between the parties.

Since the industrial buyer does not necessarily accept the lowest responsible offer submitted in answer to a bid request, he has the problem of evaluating the bids in terms of quality, price, and service. Each buyer is likely to have his own approach to this problem, but the following list includes most of the things that should be considered.

1. Are the specifications identical on all bids submitted?
2. Do all suppliers comprehend the manufacturing requirements?
3. Are the specifications accurate and complete?
4. How anxious are the bidders for the business?
5. Have the former dealings with the vendors been satisfactory?
6. How long have the suppliers been in business?
7. Do all the suppliers have technically qualified personnel?
8. Is time of delivery important?
9. Is the proximity of sources a significant factor?

Once the successful bidder has been selected it is customary, as a matter of courtesy, to inform the unsuccessful bidders by correspondence that they have not been selected. There is some disagreement among purchasing agents on whether the unsuccessful bidders should be given reasons for their lack of success. It is also debatable whether they should be given the name of the successful bidder. If the unsuccessful bidder is told why he failed, he may be able to change his methods or procedures and become a successful bidder in future dealings. On the other hand, disclosure of such information may cause resentment if it comes to the attention of his competitors.

Unpriced Orders

There are many items of small value that do not warrant the expenditure of much time or effort in determining their price. Most purchasing departments buy a substantial number of such items. Catalogs may be available for such items, but the typical purchasing department does not maintain a catalog file for them because their low value does not justify the cost.

A common way in which the price of such items is established is for the buyer to send unpriced orders to the supplier. In such cases he places reliance on the integrity of the supplier. Some purchasing departments occasionally check such orders to be certain that the supplier is competitive in his pricing.

Another way such items are priced is for the buyer to add a clause to the purchase order stating that the latest price paid prevails. Here, too, the buyer must rely on the supplier to adjust this price when there has been a downward revision in price. Since many of these small-value purchases are made locally, it is a rather common practice to use the telephone to determine the price.

Special Price Clauses

Situations sometimes arise in which it is necessary to put special clauses in contracts or purchase orders to permit later changes or revisions in price. The two most common types of clauses are the escalator clause and the clause guaranteeing against a price decline. Under normal business conditions such clauses are not widely used. However, if market conditions put either the buyer or the seller in a dominant position, he may insist on the type of clause that affords him protection against price changes.

Escalator Clauses

Escalator clauses are adopted by suppliers during periods of rising costs and prices. Such clauses permit upward revision of a contracted price in accordance with some pre-established formula, to protect the seller from having to comply with a contract signed during a period of lower prices. In estimating his price the seller is governed by current costs and, to a limited extent, future price trends. In a competitive industry he cannot usually add enough to his cost computations to protect himself against extreme price fluctuation. If all suppliers bid on the basis of current costs and include an escalator clause, the seller has protection against inflated cost and the buyer has the assurance that the sellers were bidding on the basis of known rather than assumed costs.

Some purchasing agents believe that such clauses are neither fair nor desirable and that a price arrived at voluntarily should be binding on both parties. Such a stand weakens the position of the purchasing agent who may desire a clause protecting him against a price decline during a period of falling prices. Notwithstanding the opposition, the escalator clause came into common usage during World War II.

If the escalator clause is adopted, it is important that certain problems inherent in the use of such clauses be properly solved. The purchasing agent should avail himself of the legal talent available to his firm before agreeing to such a clause. Among the problems to be solved are the establishment of a basis on which price revisions are to be made (indexes of prices and wage rates), limitations on the number of revisions possible, and of the time at which revisions can be made.

From a legal point of view, a contract must have a definite price, or a means of determining one, in order to be enforceable. There has been considerable litigation concerning the acceptable wording of a contract on this point. Since no one acceptable clause has been developed, it is important for the purchasing agent to consult with legal counsel before signing a contract.

Guarantee against Price Decline

During a period of slack business and general price declines the buyer occupies the dominant position in any transaction. He is in a position to demand and receive from the seller assurances that any decline in the price of the commodity during the life of the contract will be passed on to him. In order to attract business, the seller will frequently offer buyers such price protection for other reasons. The seller finds that a guarantee against price declines keep buyers from holding back orders in the hope of further price declines. Some sellers are also able to even out their production cycle by using such clauses to secure orders in advance of the season. A seller may find that a guarantee against price declines brings in larger orders and fewer cancellations than if no such guarantee is given. It is also contended that, in the long run, such clauses will tend to lessen the extremes of price fluctuations by encouraging the maintenance of demand.

From the buyer's point of view, in addition to preventing loss resulting from price declines, such clauses encourage him to place his orders earlier, thus ensuring his supply, avoiding shipping delays, and building goodwill with the supplier. Buyers quite naturally encourage such clauses whenever possible because there are no inherent disadvantages to them in a clause guaranteeing against a price decline.

Cancellation Charges

Contracts are likely to be cancelled because of a change in the buyer's production plans or because of a substantial decline in price levels which will put the buyer at a competitive disadvantage if he goes ahead with the purchase contract. In the latter event, the purchasing agent is likely to look for a loophole that will enable him to cancel the contract, since he cannot cancel it because of the price decline. Such a practice will not build goodwill for the buyer and should be avoided. Frequently, the seller is willing to renegotiate the contract if his costs have gone down substantially. He realizes that, if he refuses to renegotiate, he is not likely to sell to that buyer in the future.

In the case of cancellations because of changes in plan, it is customary to reimburse the seller for the time and materials that have already been expended on the contract. Such reimbursement is sometimes provided in the contract itself which may set forth the cancellation charges to be levied under certain conditions. If it has not been included in the contract, the buyer and seller must arrive at a mutually satisfactory arrangement through negotiations. Few sellers will hold the buyer to a contract when the reasons are other than a price decline.

DISCUSSION QUESTIONS

1. What is the relationship between price and value?

2. Explain the cost method of pricing? Contrast it with the market approach to pricing.

3. Discuss the pros and cons of buying on the basis of the lowest price.

4. Indicate the method by which you think a firm should establish its price.

5. What can a buyer do when all vendors quote indentical prices?

6. What is meant by a "firm" price?

7. Under what conditions might a buyer expect the seller to insist on an "escalator clause"? Under what conditions would a guarantee against price decline be appropriate?

8. When should cancellation charge be paid? When should they not be paid?

9. How do psychological factors enter the pricing process?

10. Distinguish clearly between a trade discount and quantity discount.

SUGGESTED CASES

Golden City

Household Cleaners Corporation

Hearons Company

Space Systems, Incorporated

CHAPTER 10
PRICE-COST ANALYSIS AND NEGOTIATION

The process of arriving at a price to be paid for purchased materials may be routine as in the case of buying from catalogs or it may involve detailed analysis and direct or indirect negotiations between the buyer and seller. In the preceding chapter the various means by which the purchaser determines the prevailing price were discussed. In this chapter attention is directed to the techniques that have evolved for questioning the quoted price and determining through negotiation what the actual price will be for the precise quality or quantity desired.

The analysis of all of the factors that enter into price, and the attempt to ensure that the final price is a reasonable one in terms of the use to which the material is to be put and the competitive situation faced by the buying and selling firms, is called "price-cost analysis."

Price-cost analysis is a vital activity in industrial buying, and yet it is one that is frequently slighted. In a study of price-cost analysis by the National Association of Purchasing Agents, the following comments were quoted.[1]

"We don't have time."
"Doesn't apply in our business."
"Quality and delivery are too critical."
"We buy sole source."

[1] George Rabstejnek, "Price-Cost Analysis: Proven Techniques," *Guide to Purchasing*, National Association of Purchasing Agents, New York, 1966, p. 1.4.1.

"Why upset a long, stable relationship?"
"My buyers don't have the skills to apply these techniques."

Such objections are based on a lack of understanding of the significance of price-cost analysis and an unawareness of the way in which perceptive negotiations can influence price. Figure 10-1 demonstrates the manner in which price can respond to the economic power of the bargaining parties.

Cost represents the actual costs to the producer to make and sell the item. Frequently he does not know these costs exactly but estimates them. Value represents the utility (in the economic sense) of the item to the buyer. Price falls somewhere between these two levels. The seller tries to push price as close to the value level as possible while the buyer has the opposite motivation. Their relative pressure on price reflects their competitive strength and their bargaining skill.

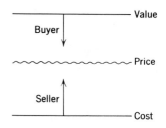

FIGURE 10-1. Price, cost, and value pressures.

Some knowledge of the seller's costs is important to the buyer if he is to exert the appropriate amount of downward pressure, as indicated in the illustration. It should be understood that exerting downward pressure on price is economically, legally, and ethically sound. Such bargaining by the buyer, and resistance by the seller, are fundamental assumptions underlying the marketplace method of price setting.

Price-cost analysis has a number of economic benefits to firms that engage in it. There is the obvious possibility of a reduction of the price that will be paid for materials and supplies. Information developed in such analyses may be shared with the supplier to the mutual benefit of both firms in such matters as production methods, materials used, and improved inventory policies.

Price

It should be recognized that a price quoted by the vendor reflects more than costs and profit. Price is subject to many other influences. Particularly pertinent is competition among both sellers of the commodity and buyers of that commodity. The seller who faces only limited competition from other sellers will react differently in his pricing from the seller who faces active competition from many sellers. Also, he is influenced by whether he has many prospective customers for his products or only a limited number of customers.

Costs furnish a floor for price making, but they do not determine the price. The buyer must acquire knowledge of the seller's productive capacity, the degree to which that capacity is being utilized, and his own company's needs and plans.

The buyer can secure price information through a request for quotation or bid from a potential supplier, as was indicated in the preceding chapter. He may consult published data on prices. Trade journals and other publications provide such information for specific commodities on a regular basis. The government also publishes price information. However, one should note that these data on prices are conglomerate and average data and may not reflect the local conditions that an individual firm faces.

The buyer may also attempt to ascertain from the potential supplier the various cost components that are included in the supplier's price. It should be recognized that there is no legal compulsion on the supplier to furnish such information, but frequently a large buyer through veiled threats or persuasion can induce small suppliers to reveal itemized cost information. Some authorities believe that this practice is contrary to the tenets of the marketplace system, which presumes a reasonable measure of arm's-length bargaining between sellers and buyers. If the buyer knows the intimate facts about a seller's costs, he may be tempted to extort too low a price from the seller.

On the other hand, it has been noted that a seller may stand to gain from a full disclosure of the elements of cost that he has factored into his price. As will be pointed out in succeeding pages, the buyer attempts through price-cost analysis to establish the proper level of costs for the various components of total cost. It is possible that through such analysis the buyer may detect means of lowering costs that had not occurred to the seller. The seller in turn can use this information on all of his production, not just that sold to this buyer.

Costs

Costs are composed of different classes. One traditional grouping has been into direct and indirect costs. The direct costs are those that can readily be attributed to specific units of production, such as direct material cost and direct labor cost. Indirect costs are costs that cannot be directly or accurately attributed to specific units of production, since they tend to be incurred for general purposes and apply to the entire production of the firm. Property taxes, executive salaries, and machinery depreciation are examples of such costs.

Another classification of costs is into fixed, variable, or semivariable costs. For purposes of price-cost analysis this classification has the serious drawback that it is not always possible to differentiate costs as clearly as is implied by the threefold classification.

If a plant were operating at capacity, it is apparent that it would be using such utilities as heat, light, and power to the maximum extent. However, if the plant were completely idle, there would still be need for some utility services, hence some of these costs. Therefore, one would have to classify utility costs as semivariable. But for a man who is on salary and spends most of his time working on a single unit of production, but for a limited period does nothing because he has completed his assigned task on that unit of production, is this cost variable or semivariable? Also, accountants have traditionally treated production supplies, such as cutting oils and grinding wheels, as overhead rather than variable expenses because of the cost involved in identifying the unit of production for which they were used. Logically, however, they are variable costs.

Because of such problems, it is usual to approach price-cost analysis on the basis of a narrower classification of the elements of cost:

Direct materials
Direct labor
Factory overhead
General overhead
Other costs
Profits (although not usually a cost element, by accounts profit is an economic cost and must be considered in a price-cost analysis)

Before discussing these classes of cost, it may be advisable to introduce the "learning curve" concept, since this concept has direct application to many of the cost elements.

Learning Curve

The learning curve is a formalization of the common sense realization that the per unit cost of production of a new item decreases as additional units of that product are manufactured. The cost should decline with each succeeding unit produced, as the supplier becomes more skilled, or learns how to make the product. The more often a worker repeats an operation, the more he improves in speed and efficiency until he reaches the optimum. This leads to reduced labor costs, and the more complex the process, the greater the reduction and the longer the "learning" will continue.

The same reasoning applies within limits to materials used in the product. With experience there is less waste or "off-fall"[2] in the process. Scheduling becomes more efficient. Executive supervision is reduced. Tooling improvements may be expected. In fact, all elements will be lowered according to some learning curve.

Although the concept was developed in connection with new products, one might expect that to a lesser extent the learning curve also exists for products in which a company has had a long history of production. The American productive genius has always prided itself on constantly improving efficiency. A series of synonyms for the learning curve have been developed, including improvement curves, progress curves, cost curves, experience curves, time reduction curves, production functions, and efficiency curves.[3]

The learning curve concepts originated during World War II in connection with studies of aircraft production. Those making the studies developed the hypothesis that as the production quantity of an item was doubled, the man-hours required per unit declined by a constant percentage. Crawford and Straus in their study of aircraft production found a curve with an 80% slope.[4] Later studies have arrived at somewhat comparable conclusions.[5]

In adapting the learning curve concept to an analysis of costs, one must first identify the factors that bring about a lowering of costs (i.e., factors that affect the slope of the curve) and then determine the importance of each of these factors.

The factors most commonly found in such analyses are:[6]

1. Job familiarization and task learning (workers and supervision)
2. Improvement in shop organization and production control
3. Type of work and methods in use
4. Product (stage of development and complexity)
5. The ratio of assembly hours to machine hours
6. Tooling quality and coordination
7. The extent of pre-production planning.

[2] Off-fall is the term used for materials that remain after a piece or pattern is cut from a material, not being large enough to provide material for a second piece or pattern.

[3] S. A. Billon, "Progress Curves and Production Forecasting," *Journal of Purchasing*, November 1965, p. 49.

[4] J. R. Crawford and E. Straus, *World War II Acceleration of Airframe Production*, Air Material Command, Dayton, Ohio, 1947, pp. 9-10.

[5] Werner Z. Hirsch, "Firm Progress Ratios," *Econometrica*, April 1956, p. 139; Reno R. Cole, "Increasing Utilization of the Cost-Quantity Relationship in Manufacturing," *The Journal of Industrial Engineering*, May-June 1958, p. 175; and *The Improvement Curve Trainees Manual*, Air Material Command, Dayton, Ohio, 1958, p. 12.

[6] Billon, *op. cit.*, p. 52.

While it is evident that one can resort to highly sophisticated analyses in arriving at the slope of the learning curve, one can also approach the problem more pragmatically.[7] Bowers says:

> Buyers and P.A.'s sometimes hesitate to use the learning curve as a negotiating tool—either because they're leery of the "higher mathematics" of the technique, or feel that the learning curve is valid only when applied to the manufacture of production-line goods. Actually, anyone with an average knowledge of mathematics can compute learning curve data.

By way of illustration, if the buyer knows that it takes a supplier 100 hours of direct labor to make the first unit of a new item and 80 hours to make the second unit, the average labor hours would be 90 hours. When production doubles to four units, if the third unit requires 73.9 and the four unit 70.1 hours, the average labor for the four units is 81 hours. If each time production doubles the labor hours decline by 10%, this product has a learning curve of 90%.

It is possible to plot the data on regular graph paper or on double logarithmic paper. (See Figure 10-2). The logarithmic curve is a straight line which is easier to read. The learning curves depicted in the first graph are typical in that they gradually flatten out as the number of units increases. At large volumes of production the reduction in labor hours becomes negligible. Because of this tendency the learning curve concept has its greatest application in cost analysis of new products.

Direct Material Costs

The costs of materials that become a part of the finished product can generally be estimated with a high degree of accuracy by a purchasing agent. The bill of materials, which is a listing of all materials and parts included in the finished product, is the basic source of a purchasing agent's information about materials. It is important to recognize that the quantity of materials used will normally exceed the quantity shown in specifications. This is because of the generation of scrap that occurs in most manufacturing processes. Scrap is different from the spoilage of materials, which may also be expected in certain types of production processes. The buyer should include both a scrap and a spoilage factor in his price-cost analysis of direct materials.

[7] W. Bert Bowers, "Who's Afraid of the Learning Curve?" *Purchasing*, March 24, 1966, p. 77.

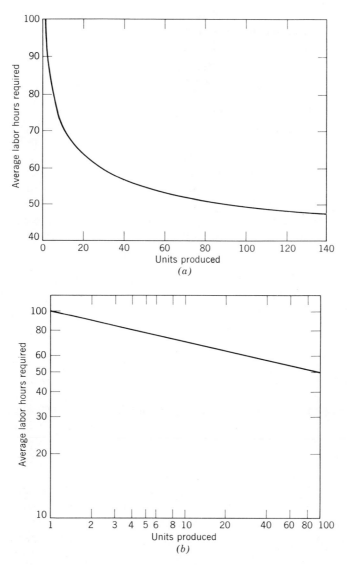

FIGURE 10-2.   Learning curves. *(a)* **90% learning curve on regular graph paper;**
                   (b) **the same learning curve on log-log paper.**

In addition to establishing the quantity of the materials to be used,
it is necessary to establish a price per unit or pound before the direct
material cost is computed. Furthermore, the analyst must recognize
that the scrap and spoiled material will generally have some residual
worth when disposed of through the scrap disposal process (see

Chapter 15), and this amount must be deducted from the direct material costs to arrive at a net cost figure.

Direct Labor Costs

The analyst often finds that it is more difficult to estimate direct labor costs than material costs, since he may be dealing with production processes or methods about which his company's information is quite limited. Engineers can measure materials but at best they can merely approximate the production time required by an outside supplier.

Direct labor costs involve two elements—hours per unit of output and wage rates per hour. Even when the prospective supplier provides a cost breakdown for labor, it is important to separate this figure into its two component elements, as shown in Table 10-1.

TABLE 10-1.

	Supplier 1	Supplier 2
Labor hours	7	6
Rate per hour	$ 1.95	$ 2.20
Direct labor cost	$13.65	$13.20

Although the second supplier is quoting a lower cost per unit, his hourly pay scale is higher. Perhaps in the negotiation process the buyer may be able to convince him that he can use less skilled workers than at present. On the other hand, in dealing with the first supplier he may be able, on the basis of the analysis, to show that supplier how hours per unit might be reduced. Either approach could result in a lowering of the cost of procurement.

As mentioned on the preceding page, the learning curve has its greatest application to labor hours and should not be overlooked by the analyst. The analyst should particularly observe whether the supplier appears to use an average wage rate in making his cost estimates. It may be that the item can be made by less-skilled workers at lower wage rates and lower cost. If production of the item will entail overtime labor, the analyst should be apprised of this fact and treat it accordingly in estimating direct labor costs.

Most price-cost analysts devote more attention to direct labor costs than to any other categories of cost. The reason for this attention is the commonly accepted accounting practice in many firms of computing overhead costs as a percentage of direct labor costs. Thus a reduction in direct labor costs results in a cumulative cost reduction in total costs that far exceeds the direct labor cost reduction when the final price is determined.

Overhead Costs

Overhead costs are costs of an indirect nature that are attributable to the manufacturing, engineering, and research activities of a firm. Sales and administrative costs are generally treated as a separate category in price-cost analysis.

Overhead costs are partially fixed, partially variable, and seldom directly attributable to a given unit of production. Overhead costs tned to be recorded and accumulated for specific time periods, such as annual insurance premiums and monthly utility charges. These are costs that must be shared among all the customers of a supplier and completely covered before he begins to show a profit. Unfortunately, there appears to be no completely "fair" method of spreading such costs, because of inadequacies in the cost allocation process.

Figure 10-3 illustrates some of the more common methods of allocating overhead costs and points out the advantages and disadvantages of each method.

The price-cost analyst must attempt to determine which, if any, portion of the overhead costs were incurred for his benefit. If elements of a supplier's overhead cost are not pertinent to a specific procurement, a buyer may reasonably attempt to negotiate them out of the price. For instance, some companies include their research and development costs as a part of overhead. If a given procurement is based on the buyer's own engineering specifications and drawings, one might question the inclusion of a research and development cost in the price he is asked to pay.

Start-up costs, and occasionally tooling costs, are treated by some accountants as overhead, and thus allocable. The preferred treatment would be to regard them as direct costs chargeable to a given procurement, but this may not be possible if more than one buyer is buying the same item. Furthermore, such costs tend to decrease and may even disappear on future procurements of the item. It is important to identify start-up and tooling costs so as to be in a position to negotiate them out of the cost of subsequent purchases.

General and Administrative Costs

General and administrative costs resemble overhead costs in that they include elements that are fixed, variable, and direct. However, these costs are seldom tied to a given unit of production. They usually are grouped into one large "pool" and allocated at the end of a

METHOD	RATIO	ALLOCATION	REMARKS
Direct Labor Dollar	*Total Overhead* / Total Direct Labor Hours	% Application of Direct Labor Cost	This is the most popular technique. *Advantages* Easily developed. Simple application, plus greatest familiarity. *Disadvantages* Does not consider value added by any other factor than labor. Penalizes operations using highly paid employees over those performed by low wage rate employees.
Direct Labor Hour	*Total Overhead* / Total Direct Labor Hours	$/hr. addition to job costs	Advantages and disadvantages same as Direct Labor Dollar Method.
Machine Hour Rate	*Overhead Expense/ Machine* Estimates Hours of operation (each facility)	Operating time multiplied by machine hour rate added to prime costs	*Advantages* Each machine is a separate entity and can be evaluated as such. Inequitous gross application of O/H can be minimized. *Disadvantages* Requires detailed analysis of overhead factors by machine, e.g., power, space, etc.

Unit of Product	$\dfrac{Total\ Overhead}{\#\ Units\ Produced}$	\$/pc. addition to unit prime costs	*Advantages* Most direct method. Useful where similar products are made with common factors, i.e., weight, volume, etc. *Disadvantages* Relies on historical base which could be quite misleading.
Prime Cost (Total of Direct Labor and Direct Material)	$\dfrac{Total\ Overhead}{Total\ prime\ costs}$	% Application of Prime Costs of Order	*Advantages* Easily developed. Simple application. *Disadvantages* Overhead expense relationship to material or labor content (or both) may be poor. Possible inequitable distribution.
Material Cost	$\dfrac{Total\ Overhead}{Total\ Material}$	% Application of Prime Material costs of order	*Advantages* Above plus particularly useful in bulk industries with uniform product. *Disadvantages* Can result in severe distortion of allocation.

FIGURE 10-3. **Methods of Allocating Overhead.** (From George Rabstejnek, "Price-Cost Analysis: Proven Techniques," *Guide to Purchasing*, National Association of Purchasing Agents, New York, 1966, p. 1.4.26.)

given time period. Typically, they are allocated as a percentage of total manufacturing cost.

To the extent that individual items in a supplier's general and administrative expense are identifiable, there may be the possibility of negotiating some of these costs out of the price. Advertising and certain sales expenses are the two items that are most likely to be negotiable in that a buyer may show that neither cost will be incurred in connection with a purchase he may be making.

Profits

Profits are a normal and necessary part of business transactions. In the short run a supplier may forgo profits for tactical reasons, but ultimately he must incorporate a profit factor in his price if he is to continue in business. The price-cost analyst, therefore, should consider the reasonableness of a supplier's profits along with the various other elements of cost.

As a rule, if effective competition exists in the supplier industry, the analyst need make no detailed study of profits. Competition will exert pressure to keep profit at a reasonable level. Louis DeRose has listed ten considerations helpful in judging a supplier's profits for reasonableness.[8]

1. Competitive price.
2. Initial orders
3. Size of order
4. Amount of values added to a product
5. Kinds of management talent demanded
6. Risks involved in the procurement
7. Efficiency of the vendor
8. Production increases
9. Buyer-furnished property
10. Reliability of cost estimates

If effective competition exists, the vendor with the lowest price is entitled to whatever profit he can make. The profit is a reward for his efficiency. On a first procurement it may be necessary to allow the vendor a higher-than-average profit to induce him to assume the risks and problems of what may be a new kind of production to him.

Profit on small orders will usually be high in order to induce the supplier to accept them. A manufacturer who functions mainly as an

[8] Louis J. DeRose, *Negotiated Purchasing,* Materials Management Institute, Boston, 1962, pp. 10-12 and 10-14.

assembler of components should expect to receive lower profits than a manufacturer who produces the component elements of his finished product.

If a supplier contributes a high degree of technical design and engineering skill or assumes especially difficult production problems, he merits higher profits than a firm engaged in routine production. Likewise, if a supplier assumes unusual risks because of the nature of the product or a long delivery schedule, he should earn a higher rate of profit.

A supplier who has demonstrated extreme reliability in past performances can command a higher profit. An unreliable or unproved supplier may have to prove himself before earning the same profit rate.

Large increments added to the volume of a supplier will justify a lower profit to that supplier. If a buyer furnishes tooling, equipment, or other services to a supplier, he should pay a lower profit rate than to a supplier who does not receive such aid. Lastly, previous experience with a supplier in terms of the accuracy of his cost estimates is a factor in judging the profit allowance. A supplier whose record shows a tendency to inflate cost estimates may be presumed to be trying to increase his profit again.

NEGOTIATION

"The word 'negotiation' as derived from Latin and Civil Law, means 'tradings or deliberations leading to an agreement.' The Pennsylvania Supreme Court has stated that 'negotiations are what pass between parties incident to the making of a contract.' The Florida Supreme Court has interpreted the work 'negotiation' to mean 'to discuss or arrange a business transaction.' "[9] Bloom has said that "negotiation is essentially communication."[10]

Many people assume that negotiations refer to a price discussion. Although it is true that price looms large in any procurement negotiation, it is but one of many elements subject to discussion between the parties. To be legal, any contract must involve agreement by the parties on all aspects of the contract. Thus negotiation should in-

[9] John J. Kennedy, "The Management of Negotiation," *Journal of Purchasing*, August 1967, p. 41.

[10] Harold Bloom, "Principles and Techniques of Negotiation," *Guide to Purchasing*, National Association of Purchasing Agents, New York, 1966.

clude discussion of the quantity, quality, and service elements of the transaction as well as price.

When to Use Negotiation

Not all purchase-sales transaction need involve negotiations. Branded items that are part of the shelf stock of the supplier and are catalog-priced are seldom subject to negotiations. As a rule, negotiations should be limited to cases where there are one or more elements in the transaction which must be discussed and on which compromise or change is possible.

For example, the purchase of a product or service that is being produced or provided to the buyer's specifications lends itself to negotiations. If the purchase involves an item for which, because of a limited number of suppliers, competition appears to be lacking, one would probably use negotiations. If the item being procured does not have fixed or standardized specification, one might negotiate. When the buyer anticipates that during the procurement there will be a large number of design changes and modifications, he will negotiate. Negotiations tend to be used when the purchase covers requirements for a period of time.

Certainly the buyer should negotiate any time he suspects that the prices quoted under one of the other means of determining price yields a price list that does not seem to be reasonable.[11]

Lee and Dobler discuss eight situations in which negotiations appear to be the recommended procedure.[12] Among them are situations in which the buyer suspects that truly competitive bidding did not take place, purchases that include a multiplicity of terms and conditions of sale, high-risk situations where the supplier may have included an excessive factor for risk protection, and purchases involving high tooling or setup costs.

Preparation for Negotiation

In his daily work a purchasing manager may engage in short-term negotiations versus long-term negotiations in a ratio of perhaps 50 to 1. Usually a series of short-term negotiations is necessary before he can engage in complicated negotiations involving vendors as to products, quality standards, sales and service considerations, prices, ven-

[11] Buyers for governmental units must first reject all bids received. Even then they may only negotiate, if permitted by law or statute for that particular procurement.
[12] Lamar Lee, Jr., and Donald W. Dobler, *Purchasing and Materials Management*, 2nd ed., McGraw-Hill Book Company, New York, 1971, pp. 164–165.

dor stocking for his needs, or any one of several such important considerations. Negotiations may be conducted at his place of business, or at the vendor's place of business in conjunction with a plant visit.

The purpose of this sort of long-term negotiation is to improve the position of the company with the vendor so that the lowest possible ultimate cost for the best possible products and service can be achieved.

Long-term negotiations are best conducted when the vendor needs the business badly and when he is seeking to establish a firmer and longer lasting relationship. In order to conduct such important negotiations, the buyer must have as much information as possible and prepare thoroughly, giving due regard to the following:

1. The total quantity of business expressed in dollars.
2. How important is this quantity of business to the vendor?
3. Can he appeal to the vendor as a prestige account?
4. Are buyer requirements so critical that a high rate of waste would occur in production to meet the standards?
5. Is there any way that one can work out major production requirements to coincide with relatively slack schedules of the producer?
6. Is the buyer prepared to see that his company performs properly in receiving shipments, rendering prompt inspection, and promptly pointing out deficiencies if any; promptly paying for acceptable merchandise received, and being sure that personnel inspect to the agreed upon standards?
7. The buyer must be satisfied as to the ability and stability of management and ownership, as well as the operating people through whom the vendor will be handling the business.
8. The buyer must be satisfied that the vendor is financially stable and has good labor relations.
9. If the buyer is to engage in team negotiation, has he selected others from the company who can contribute most to the negotiation? Do they understand who will take the lead and has authority to actually conduct the negotiations and to bring them to fruition?
10. Does the buyer know when to adjourn negotiations for future research by the company with whom he is conducting negotiations, or by his own company?
11. Do all members of the team, understand that overbargaining and seeking to squeeze the last drop of blood out of the turnip can result in less than adequate performance for a contract?
12. Has the buyer, at the outset, negotiated with the right people in the vendor firm?

13. Does the buyer know when to close negotiations successfully, or suspend to the future; or permanently terminate negotiations?

While it is true that the ability to plan, organize, administer, and carry out a negotiation is an art, it is nonetheless possible to train buyers and develop their negotiating skills.[13]

What to Negotiate

By definition negotiations involve discussions between the buyer and seller. Therefore, any element of the transaction on which discussion is needed and where alternative choices exist is an appropriate issue for negotiations. If no alternative choices exist, there can be no negotiations.

It was pointed out in earlier part of this chapter that the cost upon which a seller bases his price quotation is composed of a number of different cost elements, many of which are not precisely attributable to a given unit of production. Thus any aspect of cost and, to a lesser extent, profit is negotiable.

In the area of quality (previously defined as suitability for the intended purpose), many requirements can be met by different qualities of material. A change in dimension of a raw material, a change in composition of a chemical, or merely a change in method of packing a material for shipment that would meet the quality needs of the buyer is negotiable.

Likewise, the quantity of the transaction is negotiable. Whether it be quantity discounts, the commitment for requirements for an extended period of time, or the guarantee of future orders, the quantities involved in the transaction may be discussed and negotiated.

Finally, the service aspects of a transaction are negotiable. Such matters as the handling of rejects and defective materials where this is a reasonably common occurrence (castings) should be discussed and agreement reached prior to making a purchase commitment. In dealings with middlemen such as mill supply houses one can negotiate for monthly invoicing rather than the invoicing of individual shipments.

---

[13] See David H. Farmer, "Training Procurement Personnel in Negotiating Skills," *Journal of Purchasing*, February 1974, pp. 12–21; and Monroe M. Bird, "Research and Training Needs of Industrial Purchasing Managers," *Journal of Purchasing*, February 1973, pp. 70–77.

Strategy and Tactics

The possibility of both strategy and tactics being an integral part of negotiations is generally accepted. Strategy concerns the planning and directing of the negotiations to achieve the negotiator's goals and objectives. Tactics deals with the moves and maneuvers employed to implement strategy.

As an illustration of a strategic consideration one might consider the positions of buyer and seller with regard to downward pressure on prices during a negotiating session. The seller has limited strategic strength when the product under consideration is a product readily available from many sources; when the selling industry is composed of sellers who are smaller and financially weaker than the buyers; when it is relatively easy for new firms to enter the field; and when there are few artificial impediments to price bargaining such as laws, restrictive industry pricing practices, and strong industry or trade associations.

The obverse is also true. The vendor can resist downward pressure when the product is unique or available from a limited number of sources; when the industry is dominated by a few large sellers; when it is not easy to enter the field because of a large initial capital requirement or specialized technical skills; and when there are strong impediments to free and open price negotiation.

Tactics is more than haggling. Tactics, rather, is based on developing as complete knowledge as possible of all elements that are to be discussed between the parties. This includes knowledge of one's own needs, knowledge of the vendor's capabilities, an understanding of the relationship among cost, value, and price, and an understanding of the economic and institutional environment within which both negotiating parties must operate.

Negotiation and the Law

The Robinson-Patman amendment to the Clayton Act has long been excessively feared by purchasing agents as restricting negotiations.[14] This law prohibits preferential pricing. The law requires that buyers of like commodities purchasing under like conditions be quoted like prices. It does not prohibit price differentials among buyers.

---

[14] An overview of the current status of decisions under this law as they affect buyers who negotiate is contained in Lawrence X. Tarpey, Sr., "Buyer Liability under the Robinson-Patman Act: a Current Appraisal," *Journal of Marketing*, January 1972, pp. 38–42.

Price differentials are legal if:

1. Such price differentials are offered because of savings in costs of manufacture, sale, or delivery by reason of variations in quantities sold.
2. There are differences in grade of quality between transactions.
3. Such differentials do not substantially lessen competition.
4. The price differential was made in good faith to meet competition.

Although this law prohibits buyers from *knowingly* accepting discriminatory prices, one should recognize that it is unusual for a buyer to *know* that a price he is paying is discriminatory because such knowledge implies that he has access to the records of his competitors, which is clearly illegal under other provisions of the antitrust laws. This provision of the law is not likely to be invoked against a buyer who is bargaining hard but honestly.

Sellers may legally depart from the prices that are charged in order to keep customers, when forced in good faith by competition. Sellers may also negotiate lower prices by lowering quality specifications. Finally sellers may quote lower prices to buyers whenever cost savings on the transaction can be proved.

DISCUSSION QUESTIONS

1. Explain why price cost analysis is frequently slighted by some purchasing managers.

2. Explain the difference between cost and value.

3. What arguments should a buyer present in trying to convince the seller to disclose his various cost elements?

4. Describe the various elements of total cost that should be included in price-cost analysis.

5. Explain the learning curve and how it is used in price-cost analysis.

6. How do you judge the reasonableness of a supplier's profits?

7. When should negotiation be used?

8. How do you prepare for negotiation?

9. Relate strategy and tactics to the negotiation process.

10. What impact, if any, does the Robinson-Patman Act have on the negotiating process?

SUGGESTED CASES

Berg Raingear, Inc.

Hearons Company

Household Cleaners Corporation

Nelson Auto Parts Corporation

Road Equipment Manufacturing Company

Space Systems, Incorporated

CHAPTER II
PURCHASING RESEARCH

Research is as important to the development and improvement of purchasing activities as it is to all other business activities. New techniques are constantly being developed and tested to improve purchasing performance. Research is being conducted not only in academic circles,[1] but also within the purchasing departments of many firms.

An indication of the concern for purchasing research is evidenced by the fact that the National Association of Purchasing Management organized a standing Research Committee in September, 1965. Its assignment is to foster and to give long-range guidance and financial support to organized purchasing research whenever and by whomever it may be conducted. In this chapter we discuss the manner in which purchasing research efforts are cultivated and some of the new techniques being used.

ORGANIZATION

Purchasing research has as its objective the continuous development and refinement of purchasing techniques designed to contribute profit to a firm. As such, research can be conducted as an adjunct to the regular assignments of the members of a purchasing depart-

---

[1] See *Journal of Purchasing and Materials Management,* published by the National Association of Purchasing Management, New York, for illustration of the types of research that are being conducted.

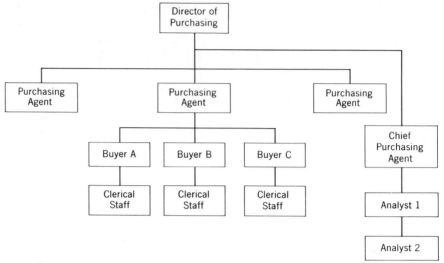

FIGURE 11-1. Purchasing organization chart.

ment, or it can be carried on by specialized staff members, who are usually called purchasing analysts. Although cost considerations will influence the form of organization, the consensus is that purchasing research can be carried on best by individuals who do not have primary responsibility for line buying activities. When research is a supplementary responsibility, there is a tendency to concentrate on the purchasing function, which often appears more urgent.

There is also a problem of evaluating an employee when research is a supplementary activity because it is hard to know the degree to which management should reward the research efforts of line employees. The preferred procedure, therefore, is to have research assigned as a staff responsibility to separate purchasing personnel.

In most companies top management exercises the prerogative of evaluating and approving all profit improvement programs. It is therefore imperative that purchasing research activities report to the chief purchasing officer. The preferred organization form is illustrated in Figure 11-1.

When budget constraints preclude the use of separate staff personnel, research should be considered an important part of each buyer's assignment. Departmental schedules should be arranged to permit time for research and the performance of buyers should be evaluated accordingly. Large research projects will probably have to be instigated by the director of purchasing.

The Purchasing Library

Since a purchasing library provides specialized research references, many of which are unique to the purchasing functions, it should be a supplement to any central library facilities that a firm may have.

Desirable types of purchasing library material would include the following: (1) technical information relating to products and materials, (2) economic data pertaining to supplying industries, (3) vendor and commercial references to sources of supply and industry associations, and (4) purchasing management literature concerning subjects such as job evaluation, profit centers, and organization theory. Library materials will consist of directories, magazines, handbooks, textbooks, and periodicals. Persons using the library should know that specific requests for information may be directed to the recently established library of the National Association of Purchasing Management at its New York headquarters.

Areas of Research

Purchasing research designed to increase profits by improving and refining purchasing planning and procedures may be classified into four groups:

1. Procedural analyses
2. Vendor and commodity research
3. Economic projection
4. Special projects

In practice there is an interrelationship among these areas. A given project could conceivably include all four categories.

Procedural Analysis

This classification involves study of the internal structure and flow of work within the purchasing department and between purchasing and other departments. An illustration of interdepartmental research is provided by the following example. Observation revealed that all purchase orders were accompanied by blueprints of the purchased parts. Though this procedure was acceptable for the initial order, it was needless duplication for repeat orders with the same vendor. Blueprint costs and the costs of delays involved in waiting for blueprints were substantial. Improved procedures were developed between the purchasing and engineering departments whereby repeat orders for purchased parts merely referenced the latest revision number on the blueprint already in the vendor's possession.

Other typical research subjects of a procedural nature include determination of job descriptions and specifications, personnel evaluation procedures, wage payment plans, and receiving and invoice procedures. A consumer products firm reported the following areas of procedural research:

1. Study of the feasibility of contract purchasing, prepaid purchase orders, systems buying, stockless purchasing, data phone, and other new purchasing techniques.
2. More effective use of blanket orders to minimize repetitive ordering.
3. Investigation of the forms generated and processed by purchasing to minimize the number and optimize their use.
4. Research as to the feasibility of establishing the purchasing function as a "profit center."
5. Development of a purchasing manual.

Vendor and Commodity Research

This involves commodity studies, including availability and price trends. A representative listing of such projects would include:

1. Development of information helpful in locating and evaluating sources of supply.
2. Traffic studies of shipments from vendors' plants including the possibility of consolidated shipments, lower cost freight classifications, use of company truck fleets, use of freight forwarding companies, and so on.
3. Elimination of single sources of supply to stimulate competition.
4. Development of vendor evaluation techniques.
5. Studies of terms and discounts from vendors, with a view to obtaining the lowest net cost.

Economic Projections

This includes analysis of probable price changes and availability of purchased commodities, and is an extension of vendor and commodity research. Economic and political developments, such as inflationary trends in nations that are large suppliers for specific commodities and changes in the "cold war," are watched and analyzed to determine their effects on prices and availability.

Special Projects

These, by their nature, can include any type of research involving the purchasing function. Included are studies to determine economic order quantities, lease or buy decisions, quality control procedures, and value analysis.

PERT and CPM

Purchasing planning and research can be aided by use of PERT and CPM techniques. PERT stands for Program Evaluation Review Techniques, and CPM refers to Critical Path Method. Both are control techniques designed to make planning more effective. Although they are principally scheduling and cost control devices, their principles can be used in other areas of purchasing research where complex relationships are involved. An increasing number of applications are being found in subcontracting, development work, construction contracts, and project buying.[2]

The primary advantages of the techniques include: (1) providing a means for more careful planning by specifying all of the variables involved; (2) providing a clearer understanding of the interrelationships involved in projects; (3) assuring a constant review to see that projects are progressing on schedule; (4) identifying potential trouble spots early so that resources can be diverted to avoid cumulative delays; (5) scheduling resources in the most efficient way; and (6) making it possible to predict the completion time of projects with reasonable accuracy.

Development

As commonly used today, the techniques of PERT and CPM are almost identical, differing only in minor details of administration. CPM was originally developed in 1957 by DuPont and Sperry Rand as a means of scheduling plant construction efficiently. PERT was the product of the U.S. Navy, the Booz, Allen & Hamilton consulting firm, and Lockheed Aircraft Corporation as a scheduling technique designed to reduce the development time for the Polaris Ballistic Missile Program and was first described in 1958. At present PERT and CPM are used for scheduling far simpler projects than were originally contemplated, and the techniques have been correspondingly simplified.

[2] For a similar technique which has recently been developed and applied to the negotiating process see Bird, Clayton, and Moore, "Sales Negotiation Cost Planning for Corporate Level Sales, *Journal of Marketing*, April 1973, pp. 7–13.

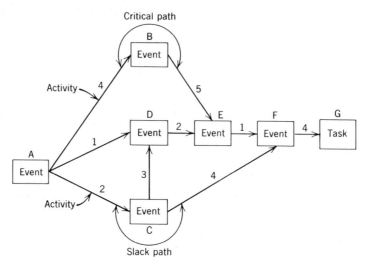

FIGURE 11-2. Simplified network (time in weeks).

Application

The essential part of the system is the network, which is a graphic portrayal of a sequence of tasks that must be performed to complete a project. In PERT terminology, an event is a happening that marks a partial completion of the total task; for example, the completion of a subsection. An activity is the action necessary to produce an event; for example, the procurement of steel for the subsection. The network is thus the master plan showing all events and activities and the times that are necessary to complete each specific task. The network therefore (1) lists all activities necessary to complete the total project, (2) indicates the time required for the completion of each portion of the total (called events) and the total project, and (3) establishes the necessary sequence of activities. Figure 11-2 illustrates a simplified network. In this illustration A, B, C, D, E, and F are events necessary to produce the finished task G.

It should be noted that some activities can be carried on simultaneously, such as AB, AC, and AD; however, activity DE cannot be started until both activities AD and CD are completed. Estimates are made of the amount of time necessary to complete each activity. From this information the critical path is determined. The critical path is the path that takes the longest time between beginning and completion of a project. The total project would be delayed if any of the critical path activities were held up. Therefore, if difficulties develop along the critical path, resources from the other activities should be diverted to the critical path activities to keep the total project on schedule.

In the illustration, path ABEFG is the critical path, as the scheduled time is 14 weeks. A delay of 1 week between event C and event F would not delay the total project, because the total time of ACF is 7 weeks, whereas ABEF requires 10 weeks. Therefore, path ACFG has a slack (or leeway) of 4 weeks. The amount of slack is the difference between the times scheduled for the critical path and those for the noncritical path. However, if path ACFG were to develop a delay of more than 4 weeks, it would become the new critical path.

The determination of time estimates for each activity is as important as properly identifying and sequencing the events. PERT uses three time-period estimates for each activity, while CPM uses only one time estimate (called normal time). The three time estimates of PERT consist of (1) an estimate of the shortest time in which the event can be accomplished under the most favorable conditions, (2) an estimate of the longest time assuming the most unfavorable conditions, and (3) an estimate of the most likely time that an activity will take. These three time estimates may then be put into the following formula to obtain an estimated time to be used for network analysis:

$$\text{Time estimate} = \frac{(\text{most realistic estimate} \times 4) + (\text{shortest and longest estimates})}{6}$$

This formula weights the most likely estimate four times as much as either of the extreme estimates. Table 11-1 illustrates a list of activities, together with optimistic, pessimistic, realistic, and estimated times.

TABLE 11-1. PERT Time Calculations

Activity	Optimistic	Pessimistic	Most Realistic	Time Estimate Used for PERT Analysis
1	8.45	11.00	9.25	9.41
2	4.30	6.25	5.43	5.38
3	9.43	12.65	11.68	11.47
4	1.26	2.95	2.83	2.59
5	5.83	6.13	6.00	6.00
6	21.85	24.63	21.40	22.01
7	13.00	26.83	13.94	15.93

PRODUCT ENGINEERING

Check List Submission	X
Product Committee Approval	X
Engineering Release—Major	2/8
Engineering Release—Minor	3/1

INDUSTRIAL ENGINEERING

Complete Cost Estimate	4/9
Finalize Make or Buy	4/2
Process Authorization Req. By	3/26
Complete Processing	4/16
Complete Tool Design	5/14
Complete Tool Build	7/16
Purchased Tooling In	7/9
Complete Tool Tryout	7/16
Finalize Carton Design	7/9

PRODUCTION—PLANNING

Firm Up Build Schedule By	3/12
Place Material Req. By	3/19

PURCHASING

Place Dies By	2/19
Samples By	6/18
Production Castings By	7/9
Place All Orders By	4/9
Raw Material By	7/2
All Purchased Components By	8/6

MANUFACTURING

Machining—Castings:	
Start Pilot Lot	7/19
Start Production Lot	7/19
Assembly:	
Start Pilot Lot	9/6
Start Production Lot	9/13

WAREHOUSE

Ship Salesmen's Samples	9/17
Stocking Quantities	10/1

MOTOR SCHEDULE (Outside Vendor)

Engineering Release	3/1
Raw Material In	4/23
Shafts and Fans to Vendor	6/4
Motors Required for Assembly	8/6

FIGURE 11-3. New-product time schedule.

232

Figure 11-3 shows a typical time schedule for introducing a new product at the Rockwell Manufacturing Company.[3] It illustrates the interrelationship of a company-wide project.

When a PERT diagram becomes extremely complex, involving thousands of events, the network may be stored on a computer tape. The computer can then be used to provide printouts of segments as working documents.

Purchasing and PERT

As indicated in the preceding illustrations, PERT provides a means of keeping account of critical parts and materials whose delay would hinder production schedules. The writer of the article that accompanied the material in Figure 11-3 described the overall control effected by PERT scheduling as follows:

> The PERT network makes it clear that production cannot start until all raw materials and components are in the plant. Many steps preliminary to production, however, are taken by other departments simultaneously with purchasing's activities. To prevent one material delay from setting back the entire project, the committee splits each new product into several segments.
>
> Each segment is charted separately and given absolute requirement dates. If any date cannot be met, the department concerned reports the fact directly to the committee. At its weekly meetings, the committee reviews the status of each step and decides which should be speeded up and which can be left alone, even should there be some delay.

Without PERT the purchasing department may lose contact with the total project schedule, and only be supplied with specific delivery dates that must be met. When purchasing is supplied with a PERT network analysis, the most economical purchasing and traffic decisions can be made. For example, knowing how much latitude is available on delivery date, purchasing can select low-cost suppliers who may require relatively long lead times. In addition, slower but cheaper forms of transportation may be selected. PERT is also valuable in expediting, because it indicates quickly when a crucial delivery deadline is missed.

In summary, the advantages of PERT in purchasing research consist of (1) careful planning of all steps, including those activities that may precede purchasing; (2) an overview of the entire project; (3) a

[3] Peter Wulff, "PERT Perks Up New Product Buying," *Purchasing*, March 21, 1968, p. 61.

mechanism for systematic review of progress (4) a plan for handling emergencies by diverting resources from a noncritical path to the critical path and activity; and (5) a technique for using computer technology to control the myriad of interrelated events, many of which are remote in their relationships.

Value Analysis

A discussion of purchasing research techniques must include value analysis. There are many names for this procedure, including "purchasing research," "value engineering," "value techniques," "value control," and "product research." Some firms make a distinction between value analysis and value engineering. In such cases value analysis efforts are those directed toward existing products, while value engineering pertains to research involving products and proposals that are still in the research and development stages. Value engineering is considered, therefore, as cost avoidance, and value analysis is cost reduction. In the following discussion the term *value analysis* will be used in the inclusive sense to indicate procedures involving both proposed and actual products.

Definition

Value analysis is the organized, systematic study of the function of a material, part, component, or system, to identify areas of unnecessary cost that can be eliminated without impairing the capacity of the item to satisfy its objective. It begins by someone asking the question: "What is this item worth?" and proceeds to an evaluation of value in terms of the function the item performs. For example, the function of a fastener is to join two or more parts. Value analysis examines the value of this function in terms of alternative methods such as welding, taping, stapling, or gluing, in view of the stresses and vibrations involved in a specific application.

Any component has a primary function, but it may also have a secondary function. In defining a function it is preferable to be as simple as possible, utilizing short definitions such as "indicates temperature" or "controls humidity." One the function has been determined, its appropriateness, cost, and possible alternatives can be analyzed.

History

Organized value analysis can be traced to the late 1940s, when the end of wage and price controls resulted in substantial price escalation. Although generally credited to efforts at General Electric and the Ford Motor Company, purchasing agents throughout the country were being troubled by price increases, and as a countermeasure began critically to examine functional alternatives and supplier alternatives as a means of holding costs down. Although these procedures had always been followed by alert purchasing agents, the evolution of value analysis involved assigning the analytical function to special research personnel to assure that the function was receiving adequate attention and to allow the regular buyers to concentrate on such operational responsibilities as vendor selection and price negotiations. Today, value analysis is practiced somewhat formally by most firms. The extent of its acceptance is indicated by a study which found that 67% of the respondents had a value analysis program in 1968 as compared with 43% 5 years earlier.[4]

Organization

In the typical organizational approach to value analysis, two main areas for research are recognizable—product improvement and new-product design (the latter previously identified as value engineering). By its nature value analysis must be a company-wide effort. Because of the individual company differences, three basic staffing approaches to value analysis are employed: (1) committees with personnel from interested departments to discuss value considerations, (2) staff groups to support line purchasing activity, and (3) staff training programs to make operating personnel conscious of value analysis opportunities.

Committee

The committee approach is most often used by companies practicing value analysis for the first time and by small firms. Usually a coordinator is appointed to direct the efforts of a four-to-eight-man team usually composed of representatives of the following departments: purchasing, manufacturing, engineering, quality control, accounting, and marketing. On important value analysis projects, the departmental operating personnel make investigations in cooperation with their committee member. Results of an investigation are presented to the value analysis committee by the departmental member.

The most serious weaknesses in the committee arrangement are that decisions are difficult to reach because of departmental self-interest or the lack of vigorous leadership by the coordinator and that no one may accept personal responsibility for a joint decision. A re-

---

[4] "VA: More Programs, More Progress," *Purchasing*, May 16, 1968, p. 41.

lated difficulty is that even after decisions are reached, implementation is a major problem, since operating personnel are inclined to resist change. These defects can be partially overcome by a strong coordinator. Therefore, though the committee approach is a simple and inexpensive method of implementing value analysis, it may be seriously limited in reaching decisions and in putting recommendations into action. The most effective committees are usually supported by a small permanent staff, which prepares data for discussion and follows up on committee decisions.

Staff

The commonest type of organization is a permanent staff, usually assigned to the purchasing department. A study of the 500 largest United States industrial firms showed that one third of these firms had one or more staff members assigned to the purchasing department to perform work of a purchase research nature.[5] In this form of organization the staff members concentrate on the research aspect of value analysis while regular purchasing personnel perform the operational functions.

Relating staff specialists to the operating personnel is the key to successful functioning of this form of a value analysis program. Of necessity the staff will participate in studies that involve purchasing procedures. The problem is to determine the respective authority of the staff and the regular purchasing personnel. The staff analyst may be viewed as a threat by the buyer, and consequently may be given only the minimum of information, and that grudgingly. On the other hand, if the analyst is given too much authority over operating matters, a feeling of inferiority may pervade the operating personnel.

Cooperation can best be assured by putting value analysis investigations on an advisory basis and encouraging line personnel to implement the findings on their own initiative. If a firm is organized into divisions, completed value studies can be turned over to the division manager who is given responsibility for seeing that his division complies with recommended changes. Staff personnel can also secure cooperation by providing information aids to departmental personnel to encourage acceptance of recommendations. Such aids might include information about prices, new products, and fabrication methods, and suggested design procedures to reduce cost.

[5] Vincent G. Reuter, "The Success Story of Value Analysis Value Engineering," *Journal of Purchasing*, Vol. IV, No. 2 (May 1968), p. 63—referencing Harold E. Fearon, "Value Analysis/Engineering and the Staff Specialist," *The S.A.V.E. Journal of Value Engineering*, March 1963, p. 9.

Management must be very careful to refrain from relying unduly on staff analysts as a control over operating personnel. Such a procedure will frustrate attempts to secure the staff-line cooperation that is vital to the success of analysis.

Staff Training Approach

This third approach to installing a value analysis program is designed to instill an awareness and appreciation of value analysis principles within the existing organizational structure. An attempt is made to instill an understanding of the concept and its techniques among the personnel that purchase, specify, and use production materials. It is hoped that operating personnel, when apprised of the techniques and benefits of value analysis procedures, will employ them in their day-to-day routines. Most companies using this approach do not have a value analysis staff but rely on personnel within each functional area to conduct regular value analysis sessions. On occasion outside consultants may be used to introduce recent advances in the area and to act as a source of outside stimulus. Although the content of value analysis training programs varies according to a firm's needs, such programs generally include information regarding techniques, cases illustrating successful cost reduction applications, recognition to individuals who have been responsible for successful projects, the creation of a cost reduction attitude, and a cooperative approach to value analysis.

Techniques of Value Analysis

As indicated earlier the basic question involved in value analysis is: "What is this part worth?" To answer this question, function must be related to price. Continuing with the earlier example, a fastener function can be performed by welding, taping, stapling, or gluing. The most desirable alternative for a given application depends on the use to which the product will be put and the attendant conditions of use. The best product is the one that will perform satisfactorily at the lowest cost. Value analysis procedures essentially follow the same pattern in all cases. First there is an analysis of the design of the item and its uses, and then the application of price analysis to the alternatives.

With the advent of materials shortages, value analysts have broadened the scope of their inquiry. The question: "What is this part worth?" is frequently superseded by the question: "How available is this part?" This in turn is leading to much greater attention to substitutability, consolidating and eliminating, simplification and standardization of requirements.

In arriving at the right price the analyst must now attempt to place a monetary value on alternative lead-times of substitutes.

Design Analysis

As a starting point for analysis, it is helpful to visualize both the total functional product and its components. For instance, a panel board assembly may be dismantled and mounted so that each component is adjacent to its mating part on the board. Such an exploded[6] assembly often provides the first opportunity to view each component objectively in relation to the function it performs. During initial design and development components are often developed by designers working individually. Now a value analysis team with members representing different backgrounds are viewing each of the subassemblies in relation to each other and to the total product. The results may include suggestions for an entirely different method of manufacture (e.g., casting versus forging), a new material (e.g., rubber versus copper), or possible elimination of the component altogether as a result of a regrouping of other components.

Check Lists

With the panel board overview as the basic point of reference, the value analysis procedure usually includes the use of a detailed check list to make sure that every pertinent question is asked about each component. Check lists vary in detail, but their basic purpose is to assure that a careful investigation is made. The following questions are indicative of those usually included in value analysis check lists:

1. What is the precise function of the item?
2. Can the item be eliminated?
3. If the item is not standard, can a standard item be sutstituted?
4. Are there any similar items used by the company that can be substituted?
5. Can the item be redesigned to allow greater tolerances?
6. Will a design change permit the item to be made from a lower-cost process or a lower-cost material?
7. Could the item be produced within the firm at less cost?
8. Are the finishing requirements greater than necessary?
9. If different sizes of the item are stocked, can some of these be combined to reduce inventory and take advantage of quantity buying?

---

[6] A term used to denote the breaking apart and pictorial display for analytical purposes of an item into all of its individual elements.

10.   Are there any possible economies available in packaging or shipping techniques?

Relation to Other Firms' Efforts

Included in the value analysis procedure is a study of cost reduction efforts of other manufacturers. In each May issue of *Purchasing* magazine, an annual review of case histories of cost reduction efforts is presented within the categories of metals, chemicals and plastics, component parts, production tools, electrical and electronic equipment, materials handling, packaging and shipping, office equipment and supplies, and MRO and safety. Cost reduction possibilities are often discovered by reviewing the efforts of other firms.

Brainstorming

Brainstorming is a process in which value analysis members throw out ideas as they occur to them during group sessions. It attempts to elicit creative thinking. Suggestions are not evaluated as they are presented, but are written down as fast as they are made. The emphasis is on stimulation or "hitchhiking"—that is, using one person's ideas as a springboard for a completely different idea from others. After the freewheeling brainstorming session, the resulting ideas are evaluated as to their possible contribution in reducing cost. This technique is still employed by some firms, although it has passed its peak of popularity and some firms have not found it to be helpful.

Price Analysis

Although cost is related to all phases of value analysis procedures, it is advisable to have intensive price analysis as a distinct phase of the procedure. Essentially the question to be asked is: "Under optimum conditions, what is the cost to the producer of the item being purchased, and, in view of this estimated cost, how much should the company pay for the item?" The cost of producing the item is established on the assumption that the supplier is thoroughly efficient, equipped with modern facilities, and allowed to make a reasonable return on his investment.

Price analysis must include a thorough study of methods of manufacture as well as the business conditions prevailing in the industry. In order to arrive at a realistic figure, factors such as the following must be considered:

1.   Industry wage rates
2.   Rates of operation of suppliers

REQUEST FOR QUOTE ADDENDUM   ANDREA RADIO CORPORATION

IMPORTANT! In order for your quote to be considered, this form
          MUST BE COMPLETED and returned with your quotation.

ANDREA PART NUMBER

SUBJECT: VENDOR VALUE ENGINEERING

We are Value Engineering all items used in the manufacture of our products; therefore, you are
requested to supply the following information. Please give full consideration to known factors so
that your suggestions will not adversely affect the function or reliability of this item.

QUESTION	YES/NO	BRIEF DESCRIPTION OF SUGGESTION	Approximate savings if suggestion is approved
1. Would a relaxation of any tolerances result in lower manufacturing costs?			
2. Can you suggest any design changes that will lower the cost of the item?			
3. Is there any part of this item that can be produced as a casting, forging, or extrusion, in lieu of machining?			
4. Can you suggest any material substitute?			
5. Are there any finish requirements that could be eliminated, or relaxed?			

6. Are there any test or qualification requirements that appear unnecessary?		
7. Have you any other suggestions which might save weight, simplify the part, or reduce the cost?		
8. Do you have a standard item that can be satisfactorily substituted for this part? What is it? _____ What does it cost? _____ Is it qualified? _____ What would qualification test cost? _____		

Are you willing to attend a meeting at Andrea to discuss your ideas, if requested?   Yes
                                                                                                                                        No

The above information submitted by

Very truly yours,

                                                            Company name

                                                            Signature

P. SAUNDERSON, Director of Purchases   Date

FIGURE 11-4. Request for quote form.

241

3. Excess capacity and its effect on overhead costs
4. Amount of engineering services required
5. Managerial skill and capability required
6. Degree of competition in the industry
7. Rates of profit in the industry
8, Age and condition of industry facilities
9. Changes in productivity and methods of manufacture that may reduce cost

If the conclusion of the price analysis study is that the price being asked for the item is too high, the company may decide to make the item instead of buying it. In other cases the company may decide that it would be preferable to show the supplier how he might produce the item profitably at a lower price. Large companies that have expert engineering and administrative talent often find that it is possible for them to counsel smaller suppliers along these lines to the advantage of both parties.

Supplier Assistance in Value Analysis

Most value analysis staffs enlist the support of present and potential vendors during the evaluation process. They are often in a position to give technical assistance in areas of their specialized competence.

In a study reported in *Purchasing*, 16% of the respondents indicated that their regular suppliers provided them with practical value analysis suggestions and that these ideas saved their firms an average of $58,410 annually. In terms of the areas in which suppliers provide with value analysis help, raw materials were mentioned by 46% of the respondents, and parts and components by 43% of the respondents.[7]

Figures 11-4 and 11-5 illustrate the use of a vendor suggestion form for assistance on specifications, materials, use of substitute parts, standardization, and so forth.

Westinghouse Program

Westinghouse's program illustrates a three-dimensional approach to value analysis including a competitive analysis:

Materials Analysis Techniques (MATS)—An orderly procedure for questioning the functional necessity of all materials used to produce a product. Objective: a potential minimum-material de-

[7]*Purchasing*, April 1972, p. 37.

NEW HOLLAND DIV. OF	SUPPLIER CHECK LIST FOR
SPERRY RAND CORP.	VALUE ANALYSIS STUDY
NEW HOLLAND, PA. 17557	

N. H. part name and number_____

Buyer _____

In order to assure the functional usefulness of the above part, we solicit your help through answers to the following questions:

| QUESTIONS | CHECK | | SUGGESTIONS |
	Yes	No	
1. Do you understand part function?			
2. Could costs be reduced by relaxing requirements:			
Tolerances?			
Finishes?			
Testing?			
By how much?_____			
3. Could costs be reduced thru changes in:			
Material?			
Ordering Quantities?			
The use of castings, forgings, stampings, etc.?			
By how much?_____			
4. Can you suggest any other changes that would:			
Reduce weight?			
Simplify the part?			
Reduce overall costs?			
By how much?_____			
5. Do you feel that any of the specifications are too stringent?			
6. How can we help alleviate your greatest element of cost in supplying this part?			
7. Do you have a standard item that could be substituted for this part?			What is it?_____ What does it cost?_____
8. Other suggestions?			

SUPPLIER: ADDRESS:

SIGNATURE   TITLE   DATE

* If "No," functional information can be obtained from Buyer involved.

FIGURE 11-5. Supplier check list form.

sign. Method: eliminate or reduce the material that is used, as well as the "Off-All" (the 20% of material that is taken off a product, or is not shipped as part of the product).

Competitive Cost Comparison (CCC)—An organized, detailed study of the essential features and costs of the products of Westinghouse competitors. Objective: to capitalize on competitors' solutions to cost and design problems. Method: compare the features of Westinghouse and competitive products, compare the plus or minus costs of each part, then combine the "costs-less' reliable items into a single ideal design.

Verifying the Installation of Products (VIP)—An analytical approach to reducing the distribution, installation, and service costs of Westinghouse products (which in some cases may account for as much as 75% of the customer's dollar). Industrial engineering techniques are used to study such factors as local transportation, material handling, unpacking, check-out procedures, performance tests, clean-up operations, and the installation itself.[8]

Though conditions vary from company to company in actual practice, the application of scientific evaluation principles to each assembly and its components to determine the value of the function performed is the universal principle of value analysis.

Examples of Savings Resulting from the Value Analysis

The following are a few examples of cost reductions resulting from value analysis (VA) programs.

Packaging

An example of how VA can be used to change packaging and shipping is provided in this account of a change in the packaging of carbonless paper. The paper's extreme sensitivity to pressure makes it difficult to ship without damage. It was formerly packaged in a multiroll heavy corrugated drum pack. Customers had to purchase a full pack and rolls had to be uniform. Through the use of a bubble-type cushioning material production, shipping and packaging costs have been reduced 40%. Customers can now buy only what they need and at considerable cost savings.[9]

The same article provided a statistical breakdown on the methods

[8] Paul V. Farrell, "VA at Westinghouse: Better Products, Lower Costs," *Purchasing*, May 5, 1966, p. 46.
[9] "VA '74," *Purchasing*, April 16, 1974, p. 149.

used by purchasing managers to secure value analysis ideas from suppliers and to reward them for such ideas:

TECHNIQUES FOR SOLICITING IDEAS

	Percentage
Ideas are verbally requested during sales interviews	91
Request-for-quote forms solicit ideas	44
Welcome booklet includes such a request	11
Form letters requesting ideas are periodically issued	11
Suppliers are invited to in-house VA seminars	9
VA displays are posted in reception area	4
Suggestion forms are available for supplier use	2

TECHNIQUES FOR REWARDING IDEAS

Supplier is offered more business	71
Supplier gets first order without competition	31
Supplier gets several orders without competition	16
Supplier is paid separately for his technical aid	4
Formal incentive contracts share the savings	4

Raw Materials

The VA savings in cost of raw materials include many accounts of substitution of lower-priced materials without sacrifice of quality. In addition, close analysis of present raw material purchases can often result in cost savings changes.

Conversion to the use of forgings rather than a combination of castings and forgings saved one company 40% on the manufacture of a gear and ring component for automotive twin clutch drive-assemblies.[10] Originally the drive ring and drive plate were castings while the drive gear was forging. Assembling the pieces required four extensive machining operations. By forging with a hot-rolled steel bar, it was possible to combine the drive ring place into a single unit. This eliminated several steps in the production of the part and the uniform structure of the forged part reduced the number of rejects.

Production Parts

Savings in production parts and fittings are illustrated in the following examples. (1) One company switched the manufacture of a metal component of the crank used to raise and lower hospital beds from sand casting to die casting and saved 56% of costs.[11] (2) Another company adopted a plywood palletizing system for the han-

[10] *Purchasing*, April 16, 1974.

[11] *Purchasing*, April 18, 1972, p. 121.

dling of beer kegs at an annual saving of $100,000 over its previous method.[12]

Calculating the Contribution of VA

Accounting for the savings achieved by value analysis programs is important for maintaining the continued support of management. Many companies attempt to establish policies to be followed in accounting for the savings of value analysis. Typical policies might include:

1. Any added costs involved in effecting a cost reduction must be deducted from that reduction.
2. Reductions in costs cannot be claimed retroactively.
3. Change in materials or processes must result in savings that are measurable with reasonable accuracy.
4. The existing materials or processes must have been acceptable or in use at the time the change is made.
5. All reductions in costs are subject to a complete audit.

Concluding Observations

Purchasing research may be formal or informal, depending on the policies of individual firms. The preferred organizational form is to have research as a specific staff assignment, since this ensures that it will receive proper attention. A few of the research techniques in use were discussed in this chapter. With increasing attention being devoted to purchasing research, it is inevitable that many techniques and sophisticated methods of analysis that have been developed in other areas will be applied to purchasing problems.

Linear programming is a mathematical approach to problem solution that can be applied to some aspects of the field of purchasing. For example, a buyer faced with a decision involving the allocation of a given volume of a commodity purchase to several vendors with delivery to more than one location can use this technique to advantage.

The availability of electronic data-processing equipment in more and more companies is forcing management to examine other areas of their operations in which this sophisticated research tool may be used. Purchasing applications are being developed at an accelerated pace, and it is inevitable that purchasing research will become an increasing part of the total purchasing function.

[12] *Purchasing*, April 16, 1974, p. 144.

DISCUSSION QUESTIONS

1. What is the objective of purchasing research?

2. What are the important areas for purchasing research?

3. Discuss the meaning of PERT and its application in purchasing.

4. Define value analysis.

5. What are the problems in using the committee approach to value analysis?

6. Describe the staff training approach to value analysis.

7. Discuss brainstorming and its application to purchasing decisions.

8. How can the supplier become involved in a company's value analysis program?

9. What are the various ways in which the supplier can be rewarded for his aid in value analysis?

10. What are the various policies that a company can adopt to account for savings achieved through value analysis?

SUGGESTED CASES

Ajax Sewing Machine Company

Gamma Corporation

Megalopolis City

Powers Company

Space Systems, Incorporated

CHAPTER 12
PURCHASING FOR PUBLIC AND NONPROFIT AGENCIES

Purchasing of goods and services by federal, state, and local agencies has grown at a pace that far outstrips that of the whole economy. When one adds the purchasing being done by the many nonprofit agencies such as private schools, hospitals, and foundations, it is evident that purchasing for public and nonprofit agencies is a major element in the gross national product of the United States.

Between 1933 and 1959 all purchasing by governmental units increased by approximately $90 billion. During that period the greatest growth by far was in the federal sector. Since that period, as indicated in Table 12-1, most of the growth has been in the state and local sector. It seems reasonable to expect that the growth in public purchasing will continue apace.

Accepted principles for public purchasing have not changed greatly since their formulation in the 1920s. Though procedures and practices have been developed to serve new situations, the fundamental aspects of a well-recognized public purchasing agency are still the same and in many respects do not differ from those of industrial purchasing departments. However, a multitude of legislative and administrative controls have evolved.

An understanding of federal purchasing regulations and procedures has become important to companies that sell to federal agencies. The regulations frequently apply not only to the prime purchase but also to the purchase and subcontracting of materials and supplies for work done on federal contracts.

TABLE 12-1. Purchases of Goods and Services by Governmental Agencies (in Billions of Dollars)

	1959	1969	1970	1971	1972	1973	1974
Federal	53.5	98.8	96.2	97.6	104.9	106.6	113.9
State and Local	44.1	111.2	123.3	136.6	150.8	169.8	189.6
Total	97.6	210.0	219.5	234.2	255.7	276.4	303.5

Source. Federal Reserve Bulletins.

Comparison with Industrial Purchasing

In many respects, there is little difference between governmental and industrial purchasing. Both types involve purchasing for use and processing rather than for resale and frequently both involve substantial quantities and large individual transactions. Both have as their objective securing goods of the right quality, in the right quantity, at the right price, at the right time, at the right place, and with the right service. Nonetheless, there are the following significant differences.

Source of Authority

Authority for governmental purchasing derives from laws. These include federal and state laws and constitutions, and local laws and ordinances. The laws not only create the buying agencies but also levy taxes to secure the funds to provide for their functions. Therefore, the governmental purchasing agent is responsible to a legislative body and ultimately to the voters who elect that body. By contrast, the industrial purchasing agent has no legal responsibility beyond his corporation executives.

Legal Restrictions

Most of the laws that establish the public purchasing agencies also prescribe the regulations under which they must operate. These regulations are intended to protect both the public for whom the buying is being done and the vendor who is selling to the agency.

The regulations are designed to prevent personal favoritism on the part of public officials and to assure all qualified vendors an equal opportunity to bid on governmental business. Usually they require an agency to advertise for bids. In addition, bids must be publicly opened and the award made to the lowest responsible bidder. Industry, by contrast, may negotiate secretly, buy without competitive bidding, award contracts to any vendor, and not divulge information concerning its purchases.

Prices

All public purchasing records are open to the scrutiny of interested parties. All actions taken must be defended against any challenge, necessitating full and complete records. This "fishbowl existence" sometimes results in governmental buyers paying higher prices for comparable goods than industry. Vendors know that quotations to governmental agencies are publicly posted, revealing their offers to all competitors. Consequently, they are less inclined to cut prices to secure governmental orders than industrial orders. However, there is prestige, pride, and advertising value in having governmental agencies use a firm's products or equipment. This is a silent testimonial and attractive bids are sometimes submitted to public agencies, with the price reduction charged to advertising.

The rather common industry practice of granting vendors a second chance to bid in order to meet lower prices quoted by competitors may also lead to industry paying less than public agencies for comparable items. In public buying, unless all bids are rejected, the first bid submitted by each vendor is final.

Absence of Interest Cost

In industrial purchasing, one of the considerations in determining the size of the reserve inventory of materials and supplies is the total cost of maintaining that inventory. One of the important elements in this cost is the financial cost of the investment in inventory. In public purchasing, not much thought is usually given to the cost of carrying inventory, since funds come from taxes which are collected annually. However, as public agencies increasingly invest unspent tax receipts in short-term securities, they are beginning to see the advantage of operating on minimum inventories. However, in governmental purchasing the major considerations are still the favorableness of the quoted price and whether budgeted money is available to pay for the purchase. Of course, when government agencies buy major capital items for which interest-bearing bonds are issued, they foster the interest into their cost considerations.

The necessity of operating within a budget occasionally hinders the governmental buyer. This may restrict purchases to goods that will be consumed within the fiscal year. Toward the close of the year, purchases for stock can be made after the succeeding year's budget becomes available. Without this limitation, many purchases would be made toward the close of a fiscal year to obligate the unexpended funds that had been allocated. Examinations of proposed budgets for public agencies and supervision of their operations are becoming more severe and of wider scope with the large amounts involved.

Other Significant Differences

A public agency purchases against a budget and must encumber funds for each purchase made against the budget. Their industrial counterpart buys against production schedules which have been established by other departments.

The public buyer cannot practice reciprocity, whereas some private buyers require a thorough review of purchases by a trade-relations department, which scans the expenditure from various points of view, including reciprocity.

The private buyer regards his sources of supply and the prices that he pays as trade secrets. By contrast, tabulations of bids received on public purchases are posted for general information. These become sources of competitive information for people in the selling field. Public buyers readily exchange price and source information, but private buyers do not. The posted information is one of the prime sources of information for federal and state authorities charged with detecting and prosecuting instances of concerted action to regulate prices and apportion markets. Patterns of collusion are investigated to protect both the private and public consumer.

While public buying procedures assure free competition, broad exploration of the market, pressure to lower price, and equal opportunity for suppliers to compete, there are certain inherent disadvantages. These are (1) inability to deviate from established procedures when time is important, (2) reluctance of suppliers to furnish technical advice and service, since they cannot be assured of compensation for their efforts, and (3) the inability to favor a deserving supplier who has performed exceptionally well.

Does Competition Exist?

Tax-supported agencies and institutions usually are required by law to request formal bids whenever the amount of a transaction exceeds the established statuatory limit. The Armed Services Procurement Act of 1947, Public Law 413, 80th Congress, liberalized procedures by stipulating 17 exceptions to the advertised sealed-bid procedure. Negotiations can be used in such cases.

One of the premises underlying the sealed-bid procedure is that the procedure fosters competition, for awards must be made to the lowest qualified bidders. It is assumed that all bidders will behave competitively in setting their price, since no influence other than price can be brought to bear.

In detailed study of competition in federal purchasing, Reck concluded that competition varied according to the commodity being
purchased.[1] He analyzed purchases of white enamel paint by studying bids that had been submitted. These showed that prices tended to
cluster around the level of the last government purchase. This was
especially true during periods of oversupply when sellers were particularly interested in the business and were willing to sell at less than
full cost. They seemed to bid below the last transaction price by an
amount they believed necessary to underbid competitors, with their
variable costs as the floor.

Sellers apparently are willing to follow this bid pattern because a
low quotation on one procurement followed by a later high quotation does not prejudice their relationship with governmental buyers,
as it would with industrial buyers, who would be more inclined to
expect the low price to continue. In periods of short supply, they
tended to bid higher than the previous award price for white enamel
because they did not particularly want the business. They evidently
prefered to supply their industrial customers first, expecially those
who had their own branded line of paints and enamels. As a consequence most enamel purchases were made from small paint companies to whom government orders were so important that they were
willing to compete hard for them. Price variations will also be of less
risk to the commercial business of small companies.

Reck also examined purchases of electric lamps and reached the
conclusion that competition was minimal. The electric lamp market
is dominated by a few large producers who make a full line of lamps.
Their pricing policies are clearly established in that they sell through
distributors at list prices, minus clearly defined trade and quantity
discounts. The smaller companies will occasionally grant larger discounts and this appears to be tolerated by the dominant firms. The
government in its buying receives the maximum user discount. Repeated attempts on the part of government buyers to secure better
prices on government contracts have been unsuccessful, according to
Reck's research. Neither of the two largest firms appeared to want all
of the government's business, and this removed any possibility of
granting a single award to one supplier in return for a lower price.

On the other hand, the case has been made that competition does
in fact exist given various reporting requirements and the workings of
the Renegotiation Board.

Renegotiation was first established by law during World War II as

---

[1] Reck, Dickson, *Government Purchasing and Competition*, University of California Press, Berkeley, 1954.

a device for insuring that excessive profits were not realized under contracts which, because of wartime conditions, could not be priced as carefully as might have been desired. After a hiatus of several years, renegotiation was reimposed on a limited basis in 1948. The Korean War prompted enactment of the Renegotiation Act of 1951 which, with some amendments, has been temporarily extended numerous times.

The legislative history of the Act makes it abundantly clear that past difficulties in arriving at close initial pricing because of the lack of available data and urgent need for procurement of military supplies and equipment during World War II and the Korean War were major considerations in enacting renegotiation legislation.

In 1970 out of the 4,400 contractor filings required with the Renegotiation Board, 1029 showed that a contractor had sustained a loss and only 123 contractors were found to have had excess profits. If competition was lacking, far more firms would have shown excess profits since the basic goal of the noncompetitive situation is profits.

The Constitution of the United States authorizes action to ". . . pay the debts and provide for the common defense and general welfare of the United States . . . ."[2] This provision is the authority for federal purchasing. To implement it, Congress passes laws that either directly authorize purchases or authorize them indirectly through the creation of agencies and bureaus which are given authority to engage in the activities required to carry out their prescribed functions.

Authority for purchases and the state level stems from state constitutions. This authority is also supplemented by laws passed by the state legislatures. Some states have established central purchasing agencies. In many states, however, the purchasing function is left to the various departments, bureaus, and institutions of the state.

In most states authority to create purchasing agencies is delegated to counties, cities, towns, and other subdivisions. The exercise of this right is optional with the local governments. In states where by law home rule is granted to cities, the right to establish purchasing agencies is implied.

Education is a legal responsibility of the states and state laws establish the rules and procedures under which schools shall operate at the local level. Authority is usually given to local boards to operate the schools within the framework of the regulations established by the state. Corresponding power to purchase is delegated to these local boards.

The laws establishing purchasing authorities are characterized by

[2] Constitution of the United States, Art. 1, Sec. 8, Cl. 1.

their variations and lack of uniformity. Much study has been given to the formulation of a uniform law. From these attempts two generalizations may be drawn. First, the law establishing a purchasing agency should conform to local conditions. Second, the law should be broad enough to permit details to be worked out by the local agency. The National Institute of Municipal Law Officers has drawn up a model purchasing ordinance which has been adopted by some cities and has served as a guide to the preparation of similar ordinances in other places.[3]

Federal Purchasing

Federal purchasing of goods and services intended for use rather than resale for profit is restricted by budget limitations. Procurement and related laws enacted by Congress are unique to federal procurement, and are calculated not only to safeguard the expenditure of public funds, but to fulfill other missions in the public interest. Federal procurement considerations include encouragement of small business, nondiscrimination in employment, research and the national defense, the use of American-made products, the employment of surplus labor, and the purchase of products of federal prisons and of the blind.

Many of the federal procurement considerations and techniques are not sufficiently different from the considerations and techniques of industrial buying to warrant separate discussion. However, those considerations that are unique to the federal purchasing program are important.

Publicizing Procurement Actions

Bids of $5000 and over must be forwarded for publication in U.S. Government Proposed Procurement, Sales and Contract Awards, except for perishable subsistence requirements, utility services, classified restrictions, and emergency purchases. Defense procurements of $10,000 or more also must be included in this centralized publication ussued by the Department of Commerce.

Business concerns may communicate with the buying agency to secure further information on bid specifications. This permission is granted to increase competition and to broaden industry participation in government procurement. All bid notices, regardless of dollar volume, are forwarded to agency's local post office for public posting.

[3] NIMLO Model Purchasing Ordinance, National Insititue of Municipal Law Officers, Washington, D.C.

Standardized Procurement Forms

Federal procurement agencies employ standardized forms for such use as in Formal Bids (Individual Procurement Actions over $2500), Informal Quotations (Open Market Negotiations under $2500), Construction Contracts (Contracts over $2000 involving Wage Rates prevailing in the Construction Industry), Blanket Purchase Order (Cumulative Purchase Actions), and Imprest Funds (Cash Transactions).

In addition to the economy of using standardized forms and techniques, this uniformity facilitates the government's objective of giving all responsible suppliers an equal chance to bid on federal requirements.

Small Business

It is the policy of the government to aid, counsel, assist, and protect the interests of small business firms and to place with small businesses a fair proportion of government purchases and contracts for goods and services.

This policy was established by legislation in 1953 when the Small Business Administration was created.

For the purpose of the Small Business Act, a small business concern is deemed to be one that is: (1) independently owned and operated and (2) is not dominant in its field of operation. In addition to this criteria the following general size standards have to be met: (1) *Wholesale*—annual receipts from $5-$15 million—depending on the industry; (2) *Retail or Service*—annual receipts from $1-$5 million—depending on the industry; (3) *Construction*—annual receipts of not more than $5 million, averaged over a three-year period; and (4) *Manufacturing*—from 250-1500 employees—depending on the industry.

Most individuals tend to think of SBA solely as a lending institution. However, there are a number of other activities that are quite important and have a direct bearing on procurement activities at the federal level.

First, there is the Prime Contracts Program. Many proposed acquisitions are beyond the capabilities of small businesses. In order to alleviate this situation the SBA developed, in cooperation with various procurement agencies, a set-aside program. Major government purchasing agencies set aside contracts or portions of contracts for small business bidding. Through its own procurement representatives stationed in major military and civilian procurement installations, the SBA recommends additional set-asides, recommends relaxation of unduly restrictive specifications, tries to discover small business competition, closely watches the Certificate of Competency program to ensure its application, when appropriate, and, in general, determines ways and means of increasing the amount of business that small firms may transact with government agencies.

Under the Certificate of Competency program, a contracting officer proposes to reject the bid of a small business firm that is a low bidder because he/she questions the ability of the firm to perform the contract on the grounds of capacity or credit, and the case is referred to the SBA. Upon receipt of the case, the SBA contacts the companies concerned, advises them of the impending decision, and affords them the opportunity to apply for a COC which, if granted, would require the contracting officer to award the contract to the firm. Upon receipt of a COC application, the contracting officer of the procuring agency is notified and a team of financial and technical personnel is sent to the firm to survey its potential. After the survey is completed (and if the SBA concludes that the company has, or can obtain, the contract successfully), it issues a certificate (COC) attesting to these facts, which, in turn is forwarded to the procuring activity and the contract is awarded.

Recognizing the necessity of insuring that "a fair proportion of the total purchases and contracts or subcontracts for property and services for government" is placed with small business enterprises, Congress, in September 1961, passed Public Law 87-305. Under this law the Small Business Administration, the Defense Department, and the General Services Administration were required to develop jointly and cooperatively, a small business subcontracting program. Under the ASPR provisions, contracts in amounts ranging from $5000 to $500,000 must contain a "best efforts" clause which states that the contractor agrees to accomplish the maximum amount of subcontracting with small businesses that he "finds to be consistent with the efficient performance of the contract." In procurements over $500,000 the contractor is required by a mandatory contract clause to undertake a full business subcontracting program.

Another ongoing program is the Disadvantaged Business Development Program-8-A. In order to assist eligible disadvantaged firms to compete effectively in the economic mainstream, the SBA is authorized by Section 8(a) of the Small Business Act to channel government purchases to them. The SBA accomplishes its goals under this program by negotiating contracts with federal agencies for supplies, services, and construction, and then subcontracting to the disadvantaged firm. In effect, the SBA acts as prime contractor.

Labor Surplus Areas

It is the policy of the government to relieve labor surplus areas by placing contracts with firms in such areas to the extent that such purchases are consistent with broader procurement objectives and where such contracts can be awarded at prices no higher than those obtainable in other areas. Under this regulation tie bids may be awarded to concerns in labor surplus area and some government requirements may be "Set Aside" for firms in labor surplus areas.

The Buy American Act

This act allows federal contracts to be awarded to other than the lowest bidder if the bid of an acceptable domestic concern does not exceed the lowest acceptable foreign bid by more than 6%, or by 12% if the domestic bidder operates in a labor surplus area.

Sale and Purchase of Federal Property

There are three categories of property that are offered for sale by the United States when they are no longer needed by *any agency* of the federal government: personal property, real property, and strategic materials no longer critical to the national interest.

Disposal programs are planned to have minimal effect on the market, which is also the reason that products of the Federal Prison Industries are used by the federal government. Prison-made products, with low labor costs, would unfairly compete with products produced at full labor and capital cost.

Purchasing departments of federal agencies may have to perform duties in every area of procurement. Departments may be expected to buy items of rare, exotic, and even secret composition, or their requirements may be very ordinary. They may be requested to buy every type of equipment manufactured and some that is still in the research and development stage. They may become involved in construction contracts for roads and buildings or commodities that employ their own nomenclature and trade practices. Some federal purchasing departments specialize in one method of contracting, but many departments are challenged by all purchasing methods for a wide variety of goods and services.

Civil Departments

The historical development of procurement for the civilian agencies of the federal government indicates that the development of procurement procedures and organization is of recent origin.

Alexander Hamilton, the first Secretary of the Treasury, was given responsibility for procurement of supplies for the federal government in the first law pertaining to government procurement in 1792. Procurement responsibility remained with the Treasury Department until 1949.

It was not until 1861 that Congress recognized the need for additional statutes dealing with federal procurement. At that time a law was passed requiring that there be at least three bids on each purchase. In 1868, Congress established a procedure for the opening of bids and awarding of contracts.

A commission was appointed in 1905 to review federal procurement and recommend improvements. No action was taken on its recommendations. In 1949 another committee, known as the Hoover Commission, made a report with similar recommendations. This report resulted, among other things, in the passage of Public Law 152, the Federal Property and Administrative Services Act of 1949.

The General Services Administration was established under Public Law 152 with authority to develop and organize a method of central buying for most of the civil departments of the federal government. Before this, the only central buying had been under the Treasury Department. The bulk of all buying for civil divisions of the federal government had been handled by the individual bureaus, departments, and administrative agencies. This division of responsibility resulted in duplication, overbuying, and general inefficiency.

Under the present system, the administrator of the General Services Administration has authority to buy for almost all other agencies of the government, to set standards and specifications, to buy and warehouse for future use, and to draw back, store, or transfer supplies and equipment from one department to another in the event of nonuse or oversupply.

Much of today's governmental purchasing is based on contracts covering periods of time rather than individual orders for immediate delivery. The General Services Administration enters into contracts with vendors to supply the needs of the using departments for stipulated periods of time, at prices that have been established through bids or negotiations. All using departments are notified of the contracts that have been placed, and, when their needs arise, they place orders directly with contract vendors.

Most agencies have their own procurement activities in addition to the purchasing done by the General Services Administration. The agency's purchases are usually for items peculiar to its needs. Civil agencies with extensive purchasing programs include Atomic Energy Commission, Department of Agriculture, Department of Commerce,

Department of Health, Education, and Welfare, Department of the Interior, Department of Justice, Department of the Treasury, Federal Aviation Agency, National Aeronautics and Space Administration, Postal Service, Tennessee Valley Authority, and the Veterans Administration.

The pursuit of efficiency in federal purchasing programs has resulted in increased use of data- and machine-processing equipment and the avoidance of duplicated efforts. Drug research conducted by the Veterans Administration, for instance, will improve purchasing by all federal agencies through the negotiation of multiuse contracts placed by that agency in cooperation with the General Services Administration.

Military Departments

Historically, the Army and Navy were assigned responsibility for their own purchases. The Navy Department was given this authority in 1795, and the Army was given similar authority in 1799. The Army decentralized procurement to its technical services, whereas the Navy Department centralized all procurement in Washington, D.C.

Before World War II the total purchasing by the military services was not so large as to have much effect on the economy. Consequently, even though there was waste and duplication, little was done to improve methods of purchasing. During the last two decades, with war and preparation for war playing such a large role in the economy, the reorganization of military procurement procedures became imperative.

Two laws, enacted in 1947 and 1949, were designed to remedy the situation. The Armed Services Procurement Act of 1947 had the following main features:

1. Provision for exceptions to the standard method of purchasing through advertising for bids.
2. Elimination of cost-plus-a-percentage-of-cost contracts.
3. Assignment of a proportion of contracts to small business.

The National Security Act of 1947, as amended in August 1949, has two main provisions bearing on military purchasing.

1. The establishment of an Office of Procurement Methods charged with (a) purchase assignment, (b) procurement regulation, (c) contracting, (d) pricing, (e) cost analysis, (f) contract termination, (g) renegotiation, (h) inspection, (i) standardization, (j) cataloging, and (k) the small-business program.

2. The establishment of a Procurement Policy council, with the responsibility defined in the following paragraph:

It shall be the duty of the board, under the direction of the Secretary of Defense, to recommend assignment of procurement responsibilities among the several military services, and to plan for the greatest practicable allocation of purchase authority of technical equipment and common-use items on the basis of single procurement.[4]

As a result of these laws, most military purchases are now made by a single department for all three military departments. There remain basic differences in the procurement practices of the three departments. The Army has decentralized purchasing to the technical services and field offices, with policy control centralized at the general staff level. The Navy has delegated purchasing responsibility only as far as its bureaus in Washington and maintains policy control in the Office of the Chief of Naval Matériel. The Air Forces have assigned purchasing responsibility to the Air Matériel Command and Dayton, Ohio, with control of policy retained by the Director of Procurement in Washington, D.C.

"The military establishment placed 9,298,954 different orders with business firms for materials, equipment, supplies, and services in the fiscal year 1964. Nevertheless, a few major categories accounted for the vast bulk of the dollars spent."[5] Purchase of weapons systems accounted for two thirds of the expenditures, purchase of standard, commercial types of manufactured goods for 10%, and construction, services, and relatively small orders for the remainder.

More than 80% of all defense contracts are arrived at by negotiations rather than through the sealed bids.[6] Negotiations have become almost inevitable because of the rapid increase in technology, which frequently requires the military to solicit proposals for items that have never been made. The military specifies what it wants the item to do. The proposals submitted by prospective suppliers suggest the nature of item they propose to meet the performance requirements and the price they bid.

Standard procedure on negotiated purchases is to solicit proposals from a number of sources. After the proposals are evaluated, the pro-

[4] National Security Act of 1947, Sec. 213(c).

[5] Murray L. Weidenbaum, "The Federal Government as a Buyer," *Journal of Purchasing*, November 1965, p. 15.

[6] Frederic M. Scherer, *The Weapons Acquisition Process: Economics Incentives*, Harvard University, Division of Research, Boston, 1964.

curing officer calls in the likeliest of the firms and discusses (negotiates) the entire procurement including the price.

There are four types of contracts in common use in military procurement, and one of these is adopted as a result of negotiations.

Cost-No-Fee Contract

These contracts are usually employed in dealing with educational and other nonprofit organizations, primarily for research contracts in which costs are paid to the contractor but no fee or profit.

Cost-Plus-Fixed-Fee Contract

These contracts tend to be used for research performed by industrial concerns and for procurement of new products where considerable developmental work is involved. Such contracts frequently include a ceiling price.

Incentive Contracts

In these contracts the producer is given an incentive to meet or beat specified targets. A target price is established, which includes an allowance for profits. When production is completed, the actual costs are compared with the target. If they are lower than target, the profit allowed is higher by a predetermined percentage of the cost reduction. If the costs are higher than target, the producer has his profit lowered by a predetermined percentage. These contracts are designed to lower costs by the incentive of additional profit and to penalize inefficiency by the threat of reducing profit if costs are over the supplier's estimate.

Firm-Fixed-Price Contract

Here a price is agreed upon and there is no provision for adjustment. The contracts are comparable to most industrial purchase contracts and are used for standard items.

An important difference between federal government and industrial procurement is the required adherence to certain laws governing wages, hours, and nondiscrimination in government purchase contracts. Frequently a prime contractor must make adherence to these provisions a condition of any subcontracts he places under a government contract that he holds.

If a firm violates these laws, it is placed on a "blacklist" and for a time is not permitted to bid on government contracts. The Secretary of Labor maintains a list of ineligible firms. Ineligibility lasts for a period of 3 years.

State and Local Purchasing

Organization

Most state and local government units today have organized purchasing departments. There is considerable variation among states in the extent of authority and the amount of the purchasing done by these departments. In some states the purchasing agent buys almost everything used by the state agencies and institutions. In other states the purchasing agent buys for only a few designated departments, and such agencies as highway departments, airports, prisons, and educational institutions are exempted from centralized purchasing.

There is a growing trend toward centralization of purchasing at the county level, even though counties lag behind both cities and states in this respect. Through the efforts of the National Association of Purchasing Agents, the National Institute of Governmental Purchasing, and other civic-minded bodies that are constantly striving for more efficiency in the spending of taxpayer's money, the number of counties that have centralized their purchasing activities have increased greatly.

In the larger cities purchasing is almost always centered in a department organized to buy for most of their bureaus and divisions. A few departments may be permitted to do their own buying because of the specialized nature of their activities. Expamples of such departments would be libraries, museums, hospitals, schools, and water and transportation utilities.

There is a growing trend toward setting up legislatively some advisory body, such as the county board, the common council, the village board, a commission, committee, or board of top officials, who serve the purchasing agency in an ex officio capacity. This advisory body is usually comprised of five or seven members. The legislation specifies the composition of the group and its authority and function in directing the public buying agency. Such a body is invaluable in insulating the purchasing agent from many pressures and in providing experience and mature judgment in making major decisions.

The group formulates objectives and procedures to guide the purchasing department through by-laws covering all of the phases of public buying. These by-laws also designate committees which function in specific areas.

Prompt action is important for a public agency. Frequent requests for emergency action are received. An executive committee may be appointed to act in emergency situations to give the purchasing agent the authority to proceed without delay.

A standardization committee is frequently established with authority to rule on simplification issues where many makes or brands are requested by the various departments. Reduction to one or a few acceptable items is necessary to achieve savings through quantity purchases. This committee might also give its approval for purchases of items for which standards do not exist.

A specifications committee may review proposed specifications with prospective bidders to determine whether the specifications will unduly restrict competition and whether they will meet the requirements of the agency. Controversial specifications may also be reviewed by the committee with the interested parties.

A valuable authority for a public buying agency is to have the right to call on other departments, boards, and commissions to assist in technical matters. With the growing variety of materials, supplies, and equipment to purchase, drawing up specifications, making inspections, and checking quality often require technical assistance.

Cooperative Purchasing

The advantages of cooperative purchasing are the greater economy and efficiency inherent in the process, especially for the smaller units of government. The larger quantities through combined purchasing lead to lower unit costs, and standardization of requirements provides further savings. The smaller participating units can share the technical skills, the buying skills, and the testing facilities of the larger agencies. Finally, better buyer-vendor relationships are likely to be developed.

Certain legal and political obstacles have inhibited the growth of cooperative buying. There usually are legal restrictions among potential participants in a joint purchasing program, although experience indicates that legal barriers can usually be overcome in time. Political obstacles, such as the desire to favor local merchants, the fear of loss of autonomy, the difficulty of standardizing on items acceptable to all, and the feeling of the larger participants that their percentage of savings will be less than the smaller units, are more difficult to overcome.

A supplementary purchasing technique available to most state and local governmental units is joint purchasing. This technique permits two or more distinct agencies to achieve together the advantages of centralized purchasing that may not be available to them as separate buying jurisdictions.

The various forms of joint buying can be divided into the following categories:

1. Joint buying by various independent public agencies within a specified metropolitan area.
2. Participation in state contracts by governmental units within the state.
3. Utilization by member cities of contract prices negotiated by state municipal leagues.
4. Use of commercial buying services who perform the buying functions for small governmental units on a fee basis.
5. Utilization by educational institutions of contract prices negotiated by national educational associations.

A survey of the extent of cooperative purchasing among municipalities was conducted in 1957 by the International City Managers Association. Eighty-two percent of 1,233 cities with populations of over 10,000 responded to a questionnaire regarding their purchasing procedures. Replies indicated that 104, or 10.3% of the 1,011 reporting cities, were engaged in some form of cooperative buying with one or more governmental units.

Since that early study there has been a proliferation of cooperative plans of various types. Bergen County, New Jersey, might well serve as an example for other local units of government. Of the 145 self-governing municipalities and school districts in the county, 105 were reported as participating in a planned program of Intergovernmental Cooperative Purchasing.[7] The program is effective even though modest in that only 14 commodities are involved. However, the program does result in a saving of approximately $400,000 annually for the participants.

The St. Paul, Minnesota, purchasing department functions as the central purchasing authority for the city and the county as well as other governmental units in both. All units involved share in the operating costs of the St. Paul purchasing department in relation to the services provided to the various participating governmental units. The system has resulted in an estimated savings of $100,000 in staff costs as well as significant savings in material costs through quantity purchasing.

In the state of New York there are 110 commodities purchased by the state, which receives bids and makes the award. The prices are then extended by the bidders to the smaller political subdivisions and school boards. In 1970 such purchases amounted to $330 million.[8]

[7] Robert M. Belmonte, "Intergovernmental Cooperative Purchasing," *Public Works*, July 1970.
[8] George W. Aljian, *Purchasing Handbook*, New York: McGraw Hill, 1973, pp. 20–48.

Such cooperation is also to be found within the hospital field. For 20 years voluntary cooperative purchasing has existed among 78 hospitals in the Greater Boston and Rhode Island area. A central solicitation of bids and awarding of the business is given to each member hospital, which then places its own purchase order, against the award.

When one realizes that there are approximately 81,000 governmental units below the state level it is evident that much can be achieved through various cooperative purchasing arrangements. The surface has only been scratched in this area of purchasing for governmental agencies. Much the same can be said for the various types of nonprofit agencies such as private schools, hospitals, religious organizations, and so forth.

In a detailed study of intergovernmental cooperative purchasing,[9] the author identified ten characteristics of the successful arrangement. These can be summarized as follows:

1. One enthusiastic individual or organization must take the initiative in launching and pushing the program.
2. At the outset only a small number of units should participate.
3. A complete plan must be worked out in the earliest stages.
4. The first commodities covered should be simple, i.e., gasoline, heating fuel, road salt.
5. All participants regardless of size of unit must have co-equal status.
6. When there are two large organizations participating with the smaller units, special arrangements are necessary to accomodate them and secure the benefits of their participation with the smaller units.
7. State legislation should encourage and facilitate cooperative arrangements.
8. Intergovernmental associations and committees of various types tend to exist in regions where cooperative purchasing succeeds.
9. Purchasing in the individual cooperating units must be centralized.
10. The elected and administrative officials of the participating units must firmly back the plan.

Purchasing Procedure

State and local governmental purchasing follows a fairly standard procedure. Small purchases and emergency purchases may be negoti-

[9] Raleigh F. Steinhauer, "IGCP: The Wave of the Future?" *Journal of Purchasing*, August 1972, pp. 34-45.

ated over the telephone. One or two local sources of supply are called.

Larger purchases are usually made only after a written solicitation of bids. The law or the regulations of most buying agencies specify that all purchases above a certian dollar amount must be bought through public advertising and public opening of bids. Award of contracts is usually made at a public meeting where bidders or interested persons may be heard.

To encourage bidders, the buyer must state precisely what he wishes to buy so that all bidders can quote on equal terms. The specifications required for this procedure can ordinarily be obtained from the U.S. Bureau of Standards. It has hundreds of specifications covering almost every item purchased by local governments. The National Institute of Governmental Purchasing also maintains a library of specifications contributed by its members which are available to other members. Many public purchasing agents start with these basic specifications and change them to meet their needs.

Another common method of specifying quality is to name some product by brand and request the bidder to quote on that item "or equal." Although this practice has desirable features, particularly for special equipment, it also has disadvantages. Few companies will admit that their product is not the equal of their competitor's product, and one may find it difficult to prove it inferior, even if it may be so regarded.

A third type of specification buying is called performance specifications. This method sets forth in general what is desired and the use to which the product will be put. Bidders are asked to submit a sample of their standard product which comes closest to meeting the general performance requirements. The request for bids states that the samples will be evaluated by a committee, which will report on the suitability of the items for the intended use. This method has been used by the board of school directors of Milwaukee for buying such items as school desks, pianos, motion-picture projectors, and phonographs, and it has worked very well.

When specifications are properly drawn, it is usually a simple matter to determine the winner. The lowest-cost, responsible bidder meeting the specifications obtains the contract. The "responsibility" of the bidder is determined on the basis of past dealings, information from other purchasing agents, or through prequalification of bidders. Prequalification means that the supplier has assured the buyer of his reliability in advance of bidding.

When specifications are inadequate, or when performance tests are needed to determine the quality of the items offered, a greater element of judgment is required in awarding a contract. In order to justify buying from other than the lowest bidder the public purchasing agent must be able to substantiate his choice. He is on the firmest ground if the bids or samples submitted are examined by a committee of experts, composed in part of those who are to use the goods.

Often in public purchasing more than one bid is required before an award can be made. At one time it was standard practice for the federal government to require three or more bids. It has been legally determined, however, that a single bid may be accepted if the law governing the agency so permits. Single bids become fairly common during periods of scarcity. Single bids are also common in the purchase of patented or proprietary articles made by only one concern.

The state or local purchasing agent is usually authorized to permit using departments to make emergency purchases necessary to maintain essential services. These cases are limited to true emergencies, a maximum expenditure is specified, and such a purchase can be made only when the purchasing department is closed. Written reports are usually required, justifying the emergency procedure.

Many state and local purchasing departments also permit using departments to make small cash purchases where the amount involved is so small that it is more economical to buy for cash than to follow the established procedure. Since it costs from $1 to $5 to issue and pay a purchase order, it is advisable, where permitted by law, to give each department a petty cash fund out of which to make these minor purchases. A careful record of items bought in this manner should be kept and analyzed periodically to note any items purchased often enough to justify carrying it in stock.

Fiscal Aspects

Most public purchasing agencies work under a regulation that prohibits issuing a purchase order unless funds to cover the payment are on deposit with the public treasury and have been appropriated for the purpose. It is, therefore, customary for orders to be cleared through the proper accounting or fiscal agency before being placed. This permits the funds to be encumbered and held for payment of the invoice when due. This clearance is especially important toward the close of the fiscal year when the budget may become exhausted.

In most state and local governments the purchasing departments must obtain the invoices, check them, and then pass them to the auditing department for further checking and payment. Some governmental purchasing departments require that invoices be on their own forms for simplicity of handling and filing. Public agencies sometimes require a notarized statement on the vendor's invoice stating that it is a true and correct copy of the amount due. This statement is being required less frequently, as it serves no important purpose. It may actually be a deterrent to some suppliers who would do business with governmental units if their procedures were more like those of industry.

State and local governments are exempt from federal taxes as well as state and local sales taxes, and the federal government is exempt from state and local taxes. This exemption requires constant checking on the part of the purchasing department to make sure that taxes are not included in invoice totals by vendors who are unfamiliar with the facts. There is much confusion concerning taxes paid at the point of manufacture and added by the manufacturer to the price he charges dealers. Not knowing what taxes they have paid, dealers have trouble getting refunds from manufacturers. Standard forms of tax-exemption certificates are available. These should be included with government purchase orders for any item subject to excise or sales taxes that do not have to be paid by the government.

Federal Internal Revenue Regulations have been changed so that each exempt agency is assigned a number that may be used without an exemption certificate if the purchase is made directly from a manufacturer.

Warehousing

Efficient centralized purchasing requires storage facilities. Widely and frequently used materials and supplies are stored and distributed to using departments as needed. Central warehousing permits quantity purchases at lower prices, allows the purchasing agent to make purchases when the market conditions seem most favorable, facilitates inspection and testing by providing sufficient reserve stock for use during the process of rejection and replacement, and provides a reserve stock from which goods are available when needed.

A perpetual inventory control should be maintained for all stock items so that the supply is never exhausted. Deliveries are usually made to using departments at stated intervals, varying from daily to monthly, and pickups are permitted at the warehouse. Some purchasing departments charge the cost of storage and distribution to the general overhead of their department. Others add a small markup to the cost of the goods so as to make the service self-supporting.

Inspection

Where the volume of purchases warrants it, governmental purchasing departments should have their own testing laboratories. Sometimes these may be maintained jointly by several departments. In smaller governmental units it is possible for the buyer to conduct simple tests and inspections to determine if the goods delivered are as ordered.

Manufacturing, Repairing, and Printing

Some manufacturing processes are conducted, or at least supervised, by the purchasing department. New York City, for example, manufactures drugs and medicines, roasts coffee, and cans food from its own farms. In other cities such items as soap, floor seal, waxes, traffic controllers, and street signs are manufactured. Usually such manufacturing is limited to items that require little equipment and a small capital investment.

A service frequently provided by state and local purchasing departments is the repair and maintenance of equipment. In some cities the purchasing agent is responsible for the shops that repair motor vehicles, water meters, typewriters, office machines, musical instruments, pianos, radios, clocks, and so on. This service has proved profitable for the taxpayer, as many items are kept in service that otherwise would be scrapped or traded before necessary.

Even smaller governmental units have long maintained departments for printing and duplicating under the control of the purchasing department. This trend is growing rapidly, as agencies find that great savings can be made in the cost of printing and duplicating. Central printing and duplicating promote standardization, reduce the number of items to be duplicated, and allow for longer press runs with consequent savings. Service is usually faster than can be secured from outside sources.

Salvage Control

There is probably no better place to centralize the control of salvaged materials and equipment than in the purchasing department. Since the purchasing agent knows the market, he is the logical one to assume responsibility for the sale of items that a governmental unit no longer needs. Salvage control includes the transfer of equipment as well as its sale. If one department has materials or equipment that it no longer needs, they sometimes can be transferred to another department that needs them. This action may change the widespread belief that materials and equipment are the property of the department rather than the public. In a recent survey among 53 large cities, 36 purchasing departments stated that they now have the power to transfer surplus material or equipment between using departments.

When material or equipment cease to be usable by any governmental unit, the purchasing department uses it as a trade-in on a new purchase or sells it for cash. Sales of such items are generally handled through competitive bids in the same manner as purchases.

Supplies and equipment declared surplus by federal agencies are offered to local units of government for use in health, welfare, education, and civil defense. Such items are usually distributed through a state surplus property agency, often under the state educational system.

Nonprofit Agency Purchasing

Certain types of agencies such as schools and hospitals may be either public institutions or private, nonprofit institutions. Occasionally they may be operated for profit. In view of their functions, they are quasi-public institutions.

Purchasing agents in such institutions have some of the characteristics of both the industrial purchasing agent and the public purchasing agent. Their responsibilities tend to resemble those of the public buyer. Generally they are responsible for ordering, pricing, specifications, quality control, value analysis, material control, central storerooms, printing departments, mailrooms, and often auxiliary enterprises such as bookstores and gift shops. Being private, they are not hampered by the restrictive legislation that controls the public buyer, but being supported by many, they have a responsibility to their supporters. Generally they do not open bids in public, but do make vendor and price information available when it is not detrimental to the institution.

Often these institutions spend funds as an agent of the government. Many research and support programs of the federal government are administered by these institutions and are subject to government audit. In such instances they must comply with the regulations and policies of the supporting governmental agency.

Purchasing agents in quasi-public institutions must recognize that there are differences in objectives and philosophy between a profit and a nonprofit institution. Emphasis tends to be on service to the requisitioning individuals and departments rather than on purely economic considerations.

DISCUSSION QUESTIONS

1. What are the significant differences between governmental and industrial purchasing?

2. Describe the responsibilities of the GSA.

3. Does competition exist in governmental procurement?

4. What is the role of the SBA in federal procurement?

5. What is meant by contract renegotiation?

6. The lowest responsible bidder is awarded governmental purchase contracts. What is meant by the responsible bidder?

7. What is the difference between cooperative and joint purchasing at the local level?

8. What are the advantages of cooperative purchasing for local units of government?

9. Does nonprofit agency purchasing differ from other types of purchasing?

10. How can a governmental purchasing agent buy on a brand basis when he is required by law to have free and open bidding for all vendors and a given brand can only be had from a single vendor?

11. Discuss the advantages of central warehousing.

SUGGESTED CASES

Golden City

King County

Megalopolis City

Parktown

Radmer County

Utopia School District

PART III
RELATED PURCHASING ACTIVITIES

CHAPTER 13
MAKE OR BUY

In a very real sense every item is purchased—either from outside suppliers or internally from the using firm's own production department. For many items, outside suppliers compete with the using firm's internal production department to determine who will be the "source." It is the responsibility of the purchasing department to evaluate this option which is known as the make-or-buy decision.

In addition, companies may decide either to do all fabricating and machining in their own plant or to have some of this work done by outsiders. The latter practice, generally called subcontracting, is another form of the make-or-buy decision.

Although the final decision on a make-or-buy question is made by the joint efforts of several departments, the purchasing department will always have an important part in the determination. In this chapter we consider the various issues of a make-or-buy question that should be considered before a decision is reached. It should be emphasized that no simple rule can be applied to all cases. Some decisions are major, such as a paper manufacturing firm deciding whether to build or buy a pulp mill to supply its own raw material, whereas others are minor, such as a metal products firm pondering whether to make a small fitting or purchase it from an outside source. Each instance must be decided on its merits, but the *important* issues may be quite different in the two cases.

HOW MAKE-OR-BUY INVESTIGATIONS ORIGINATE

The procedure of evaluating whether to purchase from one's self —"make," or purchase from outside vendors—"buy" is a continuing process. In all companies, review of previous make-or-buy decisions should be periodically conducted.

The initial make-or-buy investigation can originate in a variety of ways. Vendors may propose the alternative and request permission to submit quotations on components that they are capable of producing. Sometimes the make-or-buy question arises as the result of unsatisfactory vendor performance, such as an emergency created by delivery problems or poor quality. Unreasonable vendor price increases can also trigger an investigation. The addition of a new product or substantial modifications of an existing one typically require make-or-buy analysis; many firms include these studies as an integral part of the steps involved in all new product development decisions. A value analysis study of an existing product may also require a make-or-buy evaluation.

Finally, changes in sales volume and related variations in plant capacity prompt make-or-buy studies. Reduced sales, idle plant, equipment and/or manpower, prompt the firm to consider making items previously purchased from outside vendors. On the other hand, during the periods of rising sales, pressure on existing facilities often prompts management to seek external assistance from outside suppliers and a make-or-buy investigation is required.

As previously indicated, make-or-buy studies should be conducted periodically and the decisions should be reviewed at least once every three years, as the nature of the factors involved in the decision are fluid and constantly changing.

Considerations in Make-or-Buy Investigations

In broad terms, the relevant considerations in make-or-buy decisions are the same as those involved in all purchasing decisions: quality, quantity, cost, and service. An added variable is the expense of tooling. When tooling costs are high, flexibility in changing from make to buy or vice versa is limited unless such tools can be transferred to accommodate the production facilities of the vendor or producer.

In the following discussion each of the purchase factors will be discussed in the make-or-buy context to indicate how they might bear on the decision.

Quality Considerations

Often it will be found that the quality available in an item being purchased differs in no important respects from the quality the company could impart to the same item if it made it. Where this is true, factors other than quality become the basis on which the make-or-buy decision will be made.

However, often there will be sufficient quality differences between the two alternatives to warrant weighing the quality factor in making the decision. An extreme example of quality requiring the producer to select the make option might be the case of a nuclear reactor where conventional manufacturers have not made certain critical parts to the necessary high quality and tolerance requirements.

On the face of it, this appears to be a compelling argument for making the item. However, even here, certain questions should be raised. Why is no supplier making the desired quality? Is the particular quality specified by the engineering department really necessary? Is the failure to find the desired quality on the market a temporary situation which will soon change? Is the company sure that it can produce the desired quality in its own plant?

If no producer is making the desired quality, it may indicate that producers have not had requests for such quality. Most producers will produce to new quality specifications if they have reasonable assurance that the demand is sound and likely to be a recurring one. However, if no producer seems willing to make the item, it may be that the demand is not sound, and questions should be raised as to whether the user could economically and technologically produce the desired quality in his own plant.

Perhaps the specifications drawn up by the engineering department are more exacting than necessary for the proper operation or the expected life of the item. The dimensions or tolerances may be more rigid than the commonly accepted commercial standards for the item. In such cases it is possible that a review of the situation by the proper department will result in a removal of this impediment to purchasing from outside suppliers.

Occasionally an inspection division sets up such rigid inspection standards for a purchased item that suppliers cannot reasonably comply. It then becomes necessary to determine whether such high standards are necessary. Furthermore, before deciding to manufacture rather than buy in order to secure extreme high quality, it is important that there be some assurance that the rigid inspection standards can be met by the making plant.

It is also important to recognize that lack of the desired quality in the product of a supplier may be a temporary situation. This is especially likely if the item is for a new product, and even more likely if the new product is being made by a new industry. Once a decision to manufacture rather than to buy is reached, it can be changed only at great cost or after a period of time. Therefore, it is important to be sure that the reason is not a temporary condition that will correct itself.

Last, before deciding to make an item to get the desired quality, a thorough investigation should be undertaken to make certain that one's own plant can produce to the desired standard. Are the equipment, tooling, and skilled personnel available to produce a better quality than can be bought? There is ordinarily a legitimate reason why suppliers will not furnish items to specifications. If the supplier, who is a specialist in making the item, will not produce to a given specification, this is reason to question whether the buyer, who may be inexperienced, can do any better.

Another reason advanced for making rather than buying is that the maintenance of a desired quality standard for the finished product is so important that it should not be left to the supplier who has a lesser interest in the finished product. This concern over quality may arise in connection with highly technical equipment, or it may arise for promotional reasons. An illustration of the latter reason is the case of a manufacturer of an advertised line of baby furniture who stressed the guarantee on his products. As a protective device his written guarantee contained a clause excluding parts not of his own manufacture. He discovered that the company was incurring much ill will because of the failure of the nonguaranteed parts manufactured by his suppliers. As a consequence, he adopted a policy of making rather than buying in order to ensure his promotional policies.

A reason for making that is sometimes encountered is the need for protection of unpatented process or design secrets. So far as design secrets are concerned, the reason is a weak one, since the product will be available for copying when it reaches the market. At most, such a company is risking the loss of the design at a slightly earlier date. However, with an unpatented process secret the owner has more at risk. If he controls the process in his own plant, he may be able to keep it from competitors indefinitely, whereas the risk of losing the secret is greatly increased if he shares it with suppliers.

Certain positive reasons can be advanced for buying instead of making. In general, they have to do with quality matters and are based on the assumption that considerations of quantity, price, and service are equal.

The strongest reason for buying is that a producer is likely to be particularly skilled in the manufacture of items that constitute his regular line. Thus in buying one can get the benefits of specialization, whereas in making the item it will be a sideline operation in his plant. In time the making plant could also become a specialist, but the outside supplier has already attained that status. Furthermore, since the new item is likely to remain of secondary interest to the maker, there will not be a strong inducement for him to keep up with technological changes relating to that product. A company organized to make the item as a part of its regular line is likely to devote managerial effort and research to the problems of technological improvement of the product and process.

Sometimes the choice in favor of buying is clear-cut from the point of view of quality because of patents or production methods that the supplier controls. Once the engineering decision has been made about an item protected by a product or process patent, the alternative of making the item is eliminated until the patent expires or a change in the quality specifications becomes possible. Sometimes a license can be obtained from the patent holder, authorizing production by the user. This usually involves paying the patent holder a royalty for the privilege.

Still another reason for buying instead of making is the increased flexibility that this policy permits with respect to the quality of the part being purchased. It is a relatively simple matter to change suppliers as quality specifications change. But, if the company is making the part, it is not so simple to alter its production facilities to permit a change in the quality characteristics of the part.

Quantity Considerations

In one omportant respect considerations of quantity differ from considerations of quality in reaching a make-or-buy decision. Desired quality can be accurately and specifically set forth, but this is not true of quantity. In the purchasing context, the concept of quantity must always be considered in relation to time. The correct quantity at a given time under given circumstances can become wrong at another time under changed circumstances. Thus how much to buy is a variable, whereas what to buy is not.

From the viewpoint of quantity, the commonest reason for making rather than buying is that the order would be too small to interest a supplier. Before deciding to make for this reason, a buyer should consider whether buying a sufficient quantity and carrying an inventory for a longer period of time may not be feasible. He should also consider whether it would be possible to change specifications so that several small-use items could be included under common specifications.

Furthermore, it is vital that the implications of making a small-use item in one's own plant be considered. If it is unprofitable for a supplier to accept small-quantity orders, it may be equally unprofitable for the user to make them.

Another reason, in the nature of a quantity consideration, sometimes advanced for making is the possibility it affords of closer coordination between the quantity produced and the quantity required. Since it is difficult to forecast needs accurately, the adjustment of supply to demand as demand shifts can be made more readily if one has control over the production scheduling.

The need for large quantities may be a reason for either making or buying. If no supplier is able to supply an item in the quantities required, it becomes necessary to make it or to split the order among suppliers. The latter alternative often is not practicable if the parts are made with dyes or patterns. The cost of furnishing separate dies or patterns to each supplier might be prohibitive. Thus the requirement of a large quantity sometimes leads to making rather than buying.

On the other hand, if the quantity required is so large that to make it would interfere with production of the regular line of products, it becomes highly desirable to buy from suppliers rather than make the item.

Cost Considerations

In bringing cost into a make-or-buy decision, it is important that all other factors be equal or that reasonable cost estimates of the differences be included to compensate for any inequality. If quality, quantity, and service factors are equal, the cost considerations in a make-or-buy decision become a comparison of a known cost (the price charged by a vendor) with an unknown but estimated cost (the cost of making). For this reason it is possible to generalize by saying that, if all other factors are equal, and if there is but a slight cost advantage in favor of making, the item should be purchased. In most cases a known cost is preferable to a slightly lower estimated cost.

In evaluating the estimated cost of making an item, it should be recognized that the accuracy of the estimate depends on the skill and care with which the cost estimates are compiled. The smaller the item, in terms of either value or quantity, the more difficult it is to arrive at an accurate cost figure.

This problem of estimating accurately the cost of making an item stems from the nature of overhead costs in manufacturing plants. If the make-or-buy decision were concerned with an item that was clearly separate and apart from all other items made in the plant, the allocation of overhead would be a simple matter. However, usually the item is made in a plant from the same types of materials and on the same machines. For example, a firm would be better able to make accurate cost estimates if the decision involved the question of whether or not to set up a foundry to make castings than if the decision concerned the question of whether a certain type of casting should be made in its foundry or bought outside.

Also included is the problem of the current level of production in the plant. A plant operating at or near capacity would have different costs for making an item now being purchased than would a plant that is operating well below capacity. The fixed costs of a plant operating below capacity are a relatively high percentage of total costs. Therefore additional production can be undertaken with only a small increase in total cost. On the other hand, a firm operating at capacity can take on additional production only at substantially increased costs.

Fixed costs do not vary with output and are often referred to as overhead or unavoidable costs. They include such items as management salaries, taxes, depreciation, and insurance. Variable costs fluctuate with output and are often referred to as direct costs. Examples include the direct labor and raw materials required to produce additional units of output.

A plant with excess capacity can increase production by merely adding incremental costs that are variable in nature, whereas a plant being fully utilized can increase production only by increasing its capacity, thereby adding incremental costs of both fixed and variable nature. This point can be diagrammed as in the adaptation of a break-even chart shown in Figure 13-1.

A firm that increases production from 100 to 110% of production incurs incremental costs of $30 ($120 to $150 per unit), because of the increase in fixed and variable costs. However, the same firm could have increased production from 70 to 80% and incurred incremental costs of only $8 per unit ($91 to $98), because in the latter range of output, fixed costs are constant and only direct costs are increased.

When facilities are being employed at less than capacity, the cost of making should be determined by dividing the estimated volume into the increased variable costs. The item then would be purchased only if its unit purchase cost was equal to or less than the unit increase in variable costs. At any higher price the item should be

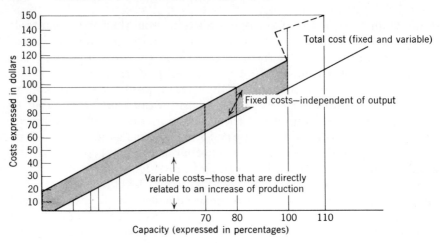

FIGURE 13-1.   Cost-capacity relationships.

made, because it would be contributing something toward overhead costs.

The situation is different when the facilities are being operated at capacity. The choice now is between expansion of the facilities and an outside purchase. In such a case the company is justified in purchasing on the outside at any price less than the unit *total* costs making the item. If the amount requires is not large, the buyer may even be justified in paying a higher price rather than assuming an investment in facilities that might not remain fully utilized.

Although this analysis implies a relatively simple approach to make-or-buy decisions, in reality the cost determinants involve difficult assumptions. A first consideration is the period of time involved. A firm with a plant operating at 70% of capacity would make a mistake in changing from buying to making, if projected sales of its products will require capacity production within a few years. Second, while the calculations used above assume that cost can be neatly classified into fixed and variable categories, the fact is that many cost are partly fixed and partly variable.

If raw materials or supplies are required for making items which have not previously been purchased, the costs of buying them in this short run will be fairly high because of the need for developing and evaluating new sources. Additional personnel may be required for receiving, handling, and storing the materials. If the item to be made is somewhat different from regular production items, it may require new machines or personnel, or at least additional training of present personnel to manufacture it properly.

Another consideration is the probable future course of prices. A

"make" decision that is predicated upon prices of a supplying industry when that industry is unusually busy and, therefore, prices are
unusually high, is obviously incorrect.

An adequate return on investment should be considered as a cost
of making an item because money invested in raw materials and
equipment is tied up and therefore a real cost, since other opportunities must be foregone. Management should ask itself: If, as a result of
a buy decision, we can free money, what return can we expect from
it? On the other hand, if a make decision requires an increase in investment, what will be the implicit or explicit cost of this money?

It must also be remembered that a firm that produces for itself
may have only itself as a customer, and therefore its production runs
must be large enough to take advantage of economies of scale. An
outside supplier may have many customers for the same item and
therefore be able to enjoy production cost advantages. Usually more
inventory (both raw material and finished goods) is required when an
item is made internally than when it is purchased from an outside
source.

The difference in ordered quantities can be illustrated by the use
of the economic ordering quantity formula. To apply EOQ to a
"make" decision, the previously used formula for purchased parts,

$$EOQ = \sqrt{\frac{2AC}{B}}$$

where A = order costs
       C = annual usage in volume
       B = carrying charges
is adapted to read

$$EOQ = \sqrt{\frac{2US}{ID}}$$

where U = expected usage in units over time
       D = cost per unit (direct manufacturing costs when in-plant
            production   is involved)
       I = inventory carrying charge as a percentage (including value
            of money invested, insurance, and other overhead items)
       S = set up costs or purchase costs (materials and supplies)

The only difference in the two formulas is that in the latter formula costs are changed to setup costs, usage in dollar volume is now expressed as usage in units, and the carrying charges are broken down
into inventory carrying charges and cost per unit.

Assuming no significant discount for volume and the same cost, regardless of whether the item is purchased or manufactured, the most economical number of parts to be manufactured will be greater than the number to be purchased, resulting in a heavier carrying cost for the "make" item. The following example illustrates the higher EOQ quantity required for an item with the same purchased cost and make cost.

Economic Lot Size Calculation
Annual Usage: 100 pieces
Purchase Price: $10
Cost to Make: $10

Manufactured Lot:
Carrying Charge—25%
Setup Costs—$100

$$EOQ = \sqrt{\frac{2 \times 100 \times 100}{0.25 \times 10}}$$

$$EOQ = \quad 89$$

Purchased Lot:
Carrying Charge—25%
Purchase Costs—$10

$$EOQ = \sqrt{\frac{2 \times 100 \times 10}{0.25 \times 10}}$$

$$EOQ = \quad 28$$

The higher the setup costs to prepare for production, the greater the disparity between the quantities for making versus buying.

Another cost element that may be higher in making than in buying is the cost of transportation. Because of the greater bulk of raw materials, their transportation costs may be higher than those for finished parts. One offsetting consideration is the fact that the transportation rate per 100 pounds of raw material is usually less than the rate for processed goods.

Finally, to all of the known costs that must be included in arriving at a reasonable estimate of the cost of making an item, there are a number of factors to which only a judgmental value can be assigned. While they are imponderable, these factors must be considered before a wise make-or-buy decision is taken, and even then the decision may be incorrect. These are the intangible considerations that enter into most buying decisions and will be considered in the next section.

Service Considerations

In purchasing parlance, service is often defined simply as reliable delivery, but in a broader sense it includes a wide variety of intangible factors that lead to greater satisfaction on the part of the buyer. It is important that the buyer's company not be given undue credit with respect to service when evaluating it in a make-or-buy decision.

The assurance of supply is an important service consideration. In general, it can be said that there is greater assurance of supply when a company makes an item than when it buys it, and this assurance of an adequate and even flow of materials to the assembly line is often given as a reason for making rather than buying. Decisions based on this particular reason are more plausible for large industrial concerns where a breakdown in the supply line creates greater disturbances, affects more personnel, and results in proportionally larger losses than in small concerns.

Making rather than buying items may enable a firm to give more assured and regular employment to its employees and, in effect, enable a company to serve itself better by stabilizing its organization.

Another situation that may lead a company to make rather than buy is the suspicion of collusion among suppliers. Although collusion is illegal and evidence thereof should be reported to the Department of Justice or the Federal Trade Commission, a company's first reaction to its discovery will usually be to seek alternative sources of needed supply. One likely alternative is the decision to make the item.

Closely related to the collusion issue is the purchasing question that arises when there are but one or two suppliers available to the buying company. Although one cannot be sure that the suppliers will act monopolistically, still a buyer does not have much confidence that they will behave competitively. Furthermore, the buyer is somewhat at the mercy of the seller with respect to assurance of supply during periods of shortage. Thus the existence of a monopolistic condition provides a strong stimulus to make rather than to buy.

A similar situation exists when the buyer is faced with what may be termed a "legal monopoly"—when an item is protected by patents. In such cases a buyer may deem it advisable to try to develop a substitute, which can be made without patent infringement, in order to protect himself against the monopoly power of a supplier's patent.

An imponderable factor to consider is the effect that a decision to make an item will have on suppliers of other items being purchased by the buyer. When a company begins to make items that it formerly bought, its other suppliers begin to wonder whether their items too will eventually be made by the buyer. When a supplier begins to question the continuity of his relations with a customer, he tends to pay more attention to those customers about whom he is more assured. Thus there is the risk that the quality of service and the assurance of supply may be impaired for other items when a make decision is reached for one.

Another service factor to consider before a make-or-buy decision is taken is the effect the decision will have on the buyer's flexibility. When an item is purchased, the buyer is in a favorable position to negotiate with various suppliers. Competition is keen, and he can move from one supplier to another as the occasion demands, in order to secure the right quality, at the right time, and for the right price. However, once a company is committed to making an item, the flexibility is lost. It becomes difficult to adjust quantity, quality, or price (cost).

Other Considerations

A number of miscellaneous factors have a bearing on make-or-buy decisions, but cannot logically be classified under one of the four main headings. Like service considerations, these are difficult to measure quantitatively, but are nonetheless significant to the decision.

The first miscellaneous factor is a proper evaluation of the competence of know-how required to make the item in question. It is, of course, possible for a company to hire or train personnel to produce almost any item. However, the feasibility of doing this depends on the cost of acquiring the necessary competence in relation to the cost of buying the competence in the form of the supplier's organization. Although competence has a bearing on the quality of the item being produced, its primary effect is on the cost in the make-or-buy decision.

A second miscellaneous factor to consider is the environmental tax situation. Since the decision to make an item is usually undertaken as a means of improving one's profit position, it may be important to consider the income tax consequences of increasing one's profits. At times in our tax history the rates have been so high that there was little incentive to increase profits if the venture entailed more than a nominal risk. At other times in our tax history the tax relief afforded to those investing in new plant and equipment was so substantial as to encourage expansion for almost any reason, and it frequently has taken the form of making things that were formerly purchased.

The contingency of war is another consideration bearing on the make-or-buy decision. In some cases war disrupts normal sources of supply. This is particularly true of items purchased abroad. Then, if no acceptable domestic source of supply can be located, it becomes necessary to make the item formerly purchased. In another context, it has been the practice of many large firms to take prime contracts for war materials and to subcontract with smaller concerns for the making of many of the component parts. This permits a large firm to contract with the armed services for larger amounts than would be possible if the "prime contractor" conducted all manufacturing within its own plant. Thus one can say that war and defense business in some situations may lead to making and in others to buying.

Another miscellaneous consideration bearing on make-or-buy decisions is the age of the company considering the two alternatives. In general, a new company that is still growing will tend to buy more items that a company that has reached maturity. The new company understandably concentrates on increasing its output by emphasizing its major production lines while buying components from suppliers. The mature company, on the other hand, tends to have extra facilities, capital, and personnel that can be used for making rather than buying. Actually both companies are expanding in the way most appropriate to their circumstances.

Another consideration, which cannot be measured, classified, or even clearly described, but which is nevertheless a powerful motivating factor, is the emotional element. If a management decides to enlarge its company by making items it formerly bought, in order to have the satisfaction of managing a larger concern, the motivation is very real, but the usual purchasing yardsticks are not pertinent. It occasionally appears that such situations arise, and the most that a purchasing agent can do is to give sound advice where procurement policies are involved. Such expansion or integration may be motivated by thoroughly economic reasons as well as emotional ones. A textbook on purchasing is not the proper place for a discussion of the advantages and disadvantages of size and integration, and we shall pass over the subject with the observation that, although if affects purchasing policies and is affected by purchasing policies, the issue is basically much broader than the question of whether to make or buy.

The increased importance of unions in labor-management relations is reflected in make-or-buy decisions. Unions often attempt to include in their contracts clauses that prohibit management from buying or subcontracting items that can be manufactured in its own plant. In such cases the unions are given the privilege of overruling previous management decisions to purchase. On the other hand, because strikes in vendor plants can cause serious production tie-ups, an unstable history of labor relations in a given industry may dictate making rather than buying.

Subcontracting

Subcontracting is a business practice under which a producer hires another firm to perform some of the manufacturing processes or to furnish subassemblies that will be incorporated into his end product. Since subcontracting is simply one method of buying instead of making, many of the factors previously discussed influence the subcontracting decision. The term subcontracting has come to be particularly associated with contractual arrangements between industrial concerns and governmental agencies, especially during war or active defense periods, and that is the sense in which it is used here.

During national emergencies, large orders are placed by governmental purchasing agents with large suppliers, because it simplifies the process of awarding and administering the contracts. When such prime contractors farm out some of the components to other suppliers who have available facilities, the prime contractor has in effect chosen to buy rather than to make the items subcontracted. Many government contracts favor the use of small businesses, which are identified as those firms employing 500 or fewer employees. Large companies who are prime contractors to the government receive extra considerations if certain proportions of the price contract are subcontracted to small businesses. The government also gives extra consideration in making awards to companies subcontracting orders in so-called "labor distress areas."

There are certain other advantages to subcontracting, which will be briefly discussed. In most cases subcontracting is the fastest method of increasing output. It is a procedure that often enables the prime contractor (the buyer) to use manpower where it is located instead of shifting that manpower into his own plant. It enables him to use engineering and management skills already existing as a functioning unit instead of developing new units. It may avoid the need for new plants and equipment on the part of the buyer, since he, in effect, borrows existing facilities.

Thus one may say that, during an emergency when there is need for utilizing the nation's productive capacity to the utmost, subcontracting is a practice that should be encouraged by purchasing agents and all other industrial officials. It has also been promoted during such periods as a means of assuring the survival of small producers whose availability during normal periods is important to the purchasing agent and the economy. Subcontracting in war production has helped minimize the charges of war profiteering usually made against large firms holding many prime contracts.

Another benefit of subcontracting during periods of forced production is the avoidance of the overexpansion of productive facilities. Such overexpansion can create serious overcapacity if the demand is temporary. Expanding to meet an abnormal demand may subject an industry or the entire economy to heavy fixed charges at a future time when all the facilities are not needed.

There are several practical or operating questions that should be raised by a company considering the possibility of subcontracting. To what extent should the subcontractor permit his facilities to be committed to one prime contractor? To what extent should a prime contractor aid a subcontractor in procuring materials, supplies, and tools? To what extent should engineering assistance be extended? To what extent should a subcontractor be financed? These and many similar questions will arise. No certain answers can be given to these questions. About all one can say is that it is important to raise the questions and to answer them in the light of the particular situation and sound business principles.

The degree of subcontracting that a prime contractor should undertake is influenced by a variety of factors. In a sense these factors are the counterparts of the factors considered in selecting among outside vendors for the purchase of materials or components. One of these factors is time. Subcontracting will generally result in a time savings over doing the work in one's own plant if one has not previously done such work. This results because the subcontractor presumably has a background of skill, equipment, and general know-how already developed.

A second factor concerns the location of the prospective subcontractor. Since subcontracting is basically an extension of one's own plant, it follows that the subcontractor should be in reasonable proximity lest dysfunctions of location be introduced.

Subcontracting will generally save the prime contractor from incurring investment costs in specialized machinery and tooling which may not be usable for his regular production requirements. However, since the subcontractor does incur such costs, his operating costs will reflect them, and to some extent the savings may be more nominal than real. This might be called the comparative cost factor to be considered prior to making the subcontracting decision.

The extent to which the prime contractor is using his own manufacturing facilities to capacity is an influencing factor. Obviously, if he does not have machinery, personnel, or other facilities available in his plant, he will tend toward subcontracting. Expansion of facilities cannot be effected in a limited time period.

Another factor to be considered in whether or not to subcontract is the availability of a "market." If there are subcontractors already engaged in the type of required production, one has a significantly different situation than he would have if no one were presently doing such work. In this case the prime contractor will more readily turn to subcontracting as a reliable source.

Lastly, there is the factor of relative costs between doing the job in the plant and subcontracting for it. If the subcontractor quotes a price reasonably close to the estimated derived for doing that job within the plant, the *known* cost is to be preferred to an estimated one.

The Purchasing Agent in Make-or-Buy Decisions

The make-or-buy problem is primarily one for executive decision. The place of the purchasing officer in solving this problem depends to a considerable extent on his position in the company organization. If he is accorded executive status, he will take an active part in making such decisions, since he will be one of the best-informed on the subject. If his position is below the level at which the decision is made, his responsibility becomes that of gathering data on the basis of which the executives can make an intelligent choice.

Generally the purchasing department will be expected to gather the cost data that are essential to a decision. In gathering these data, it is of extreme importance that there be close coordination between the purchasing and engineering departments on: quality considerations; on such matters as available production facilities, quantity requirements, and production schedules; and on matters of capital availability and returns on capital.

There are quantitative techniques, such as goal programming, that may be employed in arriving at major make or buy decisions. Such techniques are likely to be sponsored by the Engineering Department, but the Purchasing Department may be expected to supply the essential data.

After the data have been gathered and considered by all parties, a decision must be reached. In few cases will the purchasing officer make the final decision on his own authority, although in many companies he will be an important member of the committee that determines the make-or-buy questions for his company.

DISCUSSION QUESTIONS

1. What are the most compelling reasons advanced for buying rather than making?

2. What quality considerations dictate making rather than buying?

3. If all other factors are equal, but there is a slight cost advantage in making rather than buying, what action is recommended? Why?

4. When facilities are being operated at capacity and a make-or-buy decision is being made, what costs (fixed/variable/total) are relevant?

5. Define a "legal monopoly."

6. What negative supplier reaction can be expected to result from a "make" decision?

7. How do tax laws affect the make-or-buy decisions?

8. Indicate the advantages of subcontracting to a prime contractor.

9. What conditions determine the influence of the purchasing agent in make-or-buy decisions?

10. Indicate how the traditional EOQ formula can be adapted to "make" decisions.

SUGGESTED CASES

ABC Corporation (B)

Anson Company

Berg Raingear, Inc.

Road Equipment Manufacturing Company

CHAPTER 14
TRANSPORTATION AND TRAFFIC MANAGEMENT

After labor and materials costs, transportation represents the most important category of costs for the average firm. In 1972 it was estimated that transportation costs of all kinds—public and private, freight and passenger—totaled about $200 million.[1] This amount was only slightly less than 20% of the gross national product for the year. Of course, this overstates the transportation bill of industry because it includes the cost of passenger transportation. Also, industries vary in the amount of transportation they require by reason of the weight of their raw materials and finished products as well as the size of the market they serve. However, by any measure, transportation is the largest industry in the country and is a growing one because of the gradual dispersion of our population and the gradual improvement of facilities, such as the interstate highways, inland waterways, airfreight facilities, and even long distance rail accommodations. Transportation and traffic offer opportunities to a particular firm in two respects. They can be used imaginatively in order to gain an advantage over competitors and they can be employed carefully to save money for the firm.

Transportation is of particular importance to purchasing personnel for several reasons. Firms organized under the materials management concept often include transportation as a function of that depart-

---

[1] Karl R. Rachan, "The Traffic Department: "It's Important in a Corporate Enterprise," *Purchasing Management*, December 1972, p. 45.

ment.[2] Therefore, purchasing personnel who aspire to the materials manager position must be prepared to assume traffic and transportation responsibilities. Second, every order placed includes transportation services. A vendor's quotation has little significance until transportation charges are added to arrive at a delivered price. Often this aspect of purchasing is neglected, and responsibility is placed on the vendor to determine traffic routings and shipping methods.

A major reason for the neglect of traffic matters is a mistaken assumption that traffic rates are fixed by the Interstate Commerce Commission and therefore little can be done to effect savings. In this chapter the fallacy of this assumption is illustrated by indicating the methods used in setting rates, carrier freedom in rate determination, the various class and commodity rates, rates relating to shipping practices, and rates relating to commodity descriptions. The result should be a better appreciation of the challenge presented by the management of the transportation function.

Organization for Transportation

Because of the complexities involved in transportation the responsibility for it is often placed in a separate department designated as the traffic department. This department's responsibilities generally include incoming freight, outgoing freight, and internal plant transportation. The traffic matters of greatest concern to purchasing include:

1. Ascertaining rates.
2. Selecting carriers and routings.
3. Auditing freight charges and preparing claims.
4. Tracing lost or overdue shipments.
5. Determining cost reduction possibilities by consolidation of shipments and the many special arrangements available from shipping concerns.
6. Preparing rate evidence for hearings with the ICC and rate and service negotiations with carriers.

When a separate traffic department does not exist, many of these transportation responsibilities fall upon purchasing personnel. Even when there is a separate traffic department, purchasing often shares a portion of these responsibilities. This fact is illustrated by a study of 1000 purchasing agents which found that 80% of them route some of

---

[2] See Chapter 2 for discussion of materials management. The reported study indicated that 59% of all companies include traffic within the MM organization.

their inbound shipments and 43% route some of their outbound shipments.[3] This study also found that purchasing takes an active role in establishing routing policies. In answer to the question, "Who normally determines the routing on the purchasing order?" the following tabulation of responses was obtained:

Traffic manager	24%
Purchasing agent, buyer	59%
Vendor	10%
Traffic-purchasing combined, other	7%

Vendors often are of little assistance to purchasing personnel in obtaining economical traffic services. One firm estimated that less than 40% of its purchases was shipped from plants of vendors having traffic departments. Most of the remainder came from vendors whose traffic function was handled by persons who had several other duties and had little expertise in traffic. It is unreasonable to expect an untrained clerical employee to judge which carrier will give the best service, with the least time in transit, with transfer points minimized, and at the minimum cost. As a result of its analysis this firm has its traffic department route all incoming shipments. Many large firms follow this practice.

Because the transportation responsibility often cannot be shifted to vendors, it is important that purchasing personnel understand the essentials of traffic rate determination, carrier alternatives, and related considerations, which will be discussed in the following pages.

Transportation Rates

The factors that determine freight rates, the government's role in rate regulation, and the flexibility of rates are some of the least understood areas of purchasing and traffic management. The tendency is to view traffic as a maze of tedious facts that cannot be influenced by the individual firm. The basic principles on which freight rates are predicated are quite simple, even though their application at times may be surprising, and the firm does have some possibility of influencing the rates it pays.

In the days of this country's economic development railroads played the major role in transportation. Because they had so little competition, they could and usually followed the pricing policy of "charging what the market will bear." This is still a starting point in

[3] "Transportation: Purchasing's Bigger Role," *Purchasing*, August 10, 1967, p. 42.

rate-making today. Implicit in this approach is an assumption regarding the price elasticity of demand for the service.[4] If demand is inelastic, rates can be set high without a significant loss in total revenue to the carriers. If demand is elastic, the reverse is true. To make it tolerable in a monopolistic industry the "what the market will bear" policy must be related to other variables, the most important of which is the degree of competition among transportation agencies available to users. In fact, charging what the market will bear is only sound as a procedure for setting the upper limit on rate determinations. For the protection of all parties such factors as the following must also be considered:

1. The value of the product—the more valuable the item the higher its rate can be. The rate of transporting gold can be higher than that of coal, partially explained by the risk involved in handling the higher-value item.

2. The cost of hauling, which in turn is related to:
   a. Density of product. Product density is related to the ability of a carrier to obtain complete loads. The denser a product is, the easier it is to completely load a carrying vehicle and, therefore, the lower the corresponding rate. For example, a shipment of women's hats may occupy 300 cubic inches but weigh only ½ pound. For rating purposes their weight is assumed to be 2 pounds.
   b. Packaging requirements. The greater the requirements, the higher the rates.
   c. Experience of past claims on the commodity.
   d. Space required. Lampshades require a great deal of space and, therefore, carry relatively higher rates.
   e. Geographic factors. Considerations such as traffic density at origin and destination and the terrain between origin and destination influence costs and, therefore, rates. Likewise, distribution of the volume of traffic moving through the territory and physical considerations—for example, overhead or bridge traffic.
   f. Volume of traffic moved. Quantity discounts are universally applied. The type and seasonal movement of traffic are also considered.
   g. The distances goods must be transported.

[4] For a more complete discussion of elasticity of demand see E. F. Brigham and J. L. Pappas, *Managerial Economics*, The Dryden Press, Inc., Hinsdale, Ill., 1972, pp. 94–101.

    h. Special services required, such as special connection and stopover privileges.
3. Competition, which consists of:
    a. Intermodal competition, that is, railroads versus trucks.
    b. Intraindustry competition, that is, number of truck lines.
4. Government regulation, including:
    a. The opinions of the Interstate Commerce Commission.
    b. Policies of state and federal governments with respect to the regulation of transportation.
    c. Economic policy of the carriers or government in the development of industries or regions.
5. Other considerations:
    a. The "rule of analogy." This rule is used for rating a product that has not been classified previously, and simply states that similar items should have similar rates.
    b. The mixture or combination of materials. When an article includes materials of high and low value, the rate tends to reflect the high-value component.

In summary, established freight rates relfect many variables, and charges will vary with the relative importance of the many considerations listed above.

Rate Regulation

The first federal regulation of interstate commerce came with the Interstate Commerce Act of 1887, which established the Interstate Commerce Commission. The initial authority of the ICC to determine whether rates were "just and reasonable" was broadened by the Hepburn Act of 1906 to establish maximum rates for nearly all forms of rail, water, pipeline, and highway transportation, including surface freight forwarders. The Civil Aeronautics Act of 1938 assigned regulatory control of airlines to the Civil Aeronautics Board. Later legislation extended ICC jurisdiction to rule on the reasonableness of *proposed* rates and to establish minimum as well as maximum rates.

The Commission has considerable leeway in determining whether a proposed or actual rate is reasonable, as evidenced by the vagueness of this portion of the Transportation Act of 1958: "In determining whether a rate is lower than a reasonable minimum rate,(the ICC) shall consider the facts and circumstances attending the movement of the traffic by the carrier or carriers to which the rate is applicable."[5] The

---

[5] Interstate Commerce Act, Section 15a(3), as amended by the Transportation Act of 1958.

statutes merely state that rate must be "just and reasonable," without defining the meaning of the terms. The law also states that rates shall be uniformly applied, that is, no common carriers shall receive a greater or lesser compensation for services from one shipper than from another.

The jurisdiction of the ICC is broad and includes authority to:

1. Grant carriers operating authority, which for railroads includes constructing or abandoning lines.
2. Govern rates and determine reasonableness of new or changed rates.
3. Authorize consolidations and mergers, and issuance of securities of carriers.
4. Oversee accounting procedures to evaluate returns to the carriers.
5. Regulate publication and filing of claims.
6. Prescribe and regulate insurance coverage of carriers.
7. Prescribe and regulate safety provisions to be followed by carriers.

In addition, the ICC hears complaints of any alleged rate irregularities, and in general is charged with enforcing the Interstate Commerce Act and succeeding statutes.

In addition to considering the variables listed above in evaluating rates, the ICC also gives some thought to assuring carriers a return on their investments which is consistent with the growth and welfare of the industry and the economy. For example, in February 1968 the ICC approved a $300 million rate increase for the railroads, citing the fact that financial reports ranked railroads 72nd in a list of 73 industries on return on net worth, which was 2.46%.[6] Though, obviously, the consideration of a comparable rate of return on investment did not rank very high, it was, at least, considered.

Because of the ICC regulation of rates there is a tendency for shippers to develop a hands-off attitude regarding the possibility of changing rates. In reality there is considerable latitude in rate determination.

Carriers have considerable freedom in instituting rate changes. On individual rate changes the ICC usually acts on the basis of the carrier's requests, as illustrated in the following statement by the chairman of the ICC:

> Exclusive of schedules involving general increases in rates, more than 50,000 rail tariffs were filed with the Commission in 1957.

[6] "Freight Buyers Will Be Paying 5% More," *Purchasing*, March 21, 1968, p. 36.

These rail tariffs contained hundreds of thousands and probably millions of rates. It is our estimate that 98.3 per cent of these tariffs became effective without protest or restraint by the Commission. Of the remaining 1.7 per cent which were protested, about 85 per cent were nevertheless permitted to go into effect without suspension. This left about one-fourth of one percent of the total in which the voluntary action of the carriers was restrained by the Commission's exercise of its investigation and suspension powers. In almost one-half of the cases suspended pending investigation, the proposed rates were approved upon completion of the proceedings. And so, instead of the spector of a meddling Government unwarrantably preventing what the carriers regard as the proper exercise of their managerial responsibilities, we find that a bare one-eighth of one per cent of their proposals are condemned.[7]

General rate increases that are authorized by the ICC are often altered by the practice of "hold-downs," which limits the amount of increase in some particular markets to less than the general increase. "Hold-downs" are usually applied to long hauls of basic materials. They should be considered before a firm accepts a general rate increase. The posibility of a "hold-down" may also be used as a bargaining device to discourage shippers from applying for a uniform rate increase.

A fact that encourages rate differentials among carriers is that all *intrastate* common carriers, private carriers, specialized commodity carriers, and contract carriers to a certain extent are exempt from ICC regulation. One estimate is that only 35% of the intercity truck ton-miles are performed by carriers regulated by the ICC, with the remaining 65% either intrastate or exempt carriers.[8] Of Course, many of these carriers have their rates regulated by state commissions. It is further estimated that only 11% of the Mississippi River tonnage is subject to ICC regulations.

[7] Testimony of Howard Freas, then Chairman of the ICC, on March 28, 1958, before the Surface Transportation Subcommittee of the Interstate and Foreign Commerce Committee, as reported in National Transportation Policy, Preliminary Draft of a Report Prepared for the Committee on Interstate and Foreign Commerce, U.S. Senate, by the Special Study Group on Transportation Policies in the United States (January 3, 1961), p. 685.

[8] From testimony of E. E. Childe in Proposed Amendments to Federal Transportation Laws—Hearings before the Committee on Commerce, U.S. Senate, 87th Congress, second session, August 22-24, September 10-13, 24-26, 1962, p. 242, as reported by William H. Dodge in "Purchasing Transportation Services," *Journal of Purchasing*, May 1965, p. 33.

Carriers are often very influential in setting their original rates. In addition, those that are exempt from ICC and state regulation are subject to the same type of competitive price bargaining that characterizes the remainder of our free-enterprise economy.

Variations within Established Rate Structures

In addition to differentials existing between carriers, there are also rate variations, which can be classified as (1) class and commodity rates, (2) rates related to specific shipping practices, and (3) rates relating to commodity descriptions.

Class and Commodity Rates

Class rates are overall rates set by grouping commodities into a limited number of classes to which rates are then applied. The result of this process, a freight classification, is an alphabetical list of articles, together with each commodity's "rating." The rating is the class into which the article is placed for rate purposes. The use of this classification system greatly reduces the number of freight tariffs in which rates are published. Tariff is the term used for schedules that contain rates and charges, as well as the special conditions governing the movement of products or persons by commercial means.

A commodity rate, by contrast, is a special rate on a specific article. It is a rate quoted directly instead of through a system of freight classification. Commodity rates are lower than calss rates and are the means whereby carriers quote special "prices" to meet particular conditions—for example, special rates on frequent shipments between two points to meet the needs of a particular buyer and seller or a community, or to meet some competitive situation. Commodity rates, then, are established to facilitate the heavy movement of goods, and most repetitive shipments move under commodity rates. A buyer anticipating such a movement should apply through a regular carrier to have a commodity rate established. The ICC will eventually determine whether the rate request will be granted. Thus commodity rates represent a possible cost reduction available to the transportation buyer under certain circumstances.

Shipping Practices Related to Rates

Quantity Discounts. A commodity will have a lower transportation rate if the quantity shipped meets the carload (CL) or truckload (TL) weight limits. It carries a much higher rate if less than a carload (LCL) or less than a truckload (LTL) quantity is involved. The minimum rates vary with the cubic densities of the commodities and the specific modes of shipping. For example, for steel the truckload weight is 32,000 pounds and the carload weight is 80,000 pounds. Often intermediate quantity rates are also allowed for shipments that reach certain amounts which are less than full load quantities; for example, steel shipments have intermediate quantity breaks at 20,000 and 40,000 pounds for truck and rail hauls, respectively.

Trainload or Multiple-Car Rates.   On occasion rail rates have been established that give discounts for weights in excess of a carload. Iron ore is an example of such a commodity. These rates are usually established to meet competition from other carriers such as water carriers or trucks.

Pool Cars.   If a shipper has a number of small shipments going to the same general destination, he may combine them into one carload and consign the car to an agent for final distribution. Such a combined shipment is called "pool car." The total weight of the combined orders is used to justify quantity rate differentials. Although there are distribution costs for dispersing the goods from the agent to the final customers, the quantity rate reduction normally represents a significant savings.

Commodity Consolidation.   A shipper having several different commodities going to one destination may combine them so as to meet the minimum weights for carload lots. The applicable rate will be that applying to the commodity with the highest CL rate. Shipments may be made to one or more consignees.

Special Shipping Facilities.   In recent years transportation companies, especially the railroads, have been developing special shipping equipment as a means of holding or regaining traffic. One of the first of these developments was "Piggyback" service in which truck trailers are carried on special railroad flatcars. On high density routes these flatcars are made up into special trains that leave at fixed times, run at high speeds, and bypass switching yards. This service combines the low cost service of the railroad with the flexibility of truck pickup and delivery. Piggyback service was initiated in 1926 on the Chicago, North Shore & Milwaukee railroad, but it did not become popular until after World War II. This service is sometimes referred to as TOFC—Trailer on a flat car.

A related, but even more significant, facility development has been containerization. Containers are boxes, usually of metal, that are 8 feet wide, 8 feet high, and 20, 30, or 40 feet long. They can be loaded at the point of origin, closed and locked, and shipped by truck, transferred to rail, to ship, to rail, to truck, and delivered to destination. They avoid the necessity of rehandling the individual pieces of freight and greatly speed the process of loading and unloading. One other big advantage is that containers minimize the loss from pilferage in transit—especially at dockside. In recent years this loss has become substantial. In 1956 the number of flatcars loaded with trailers or containers numbered 207,783 while by 1970 the number had increased to 1,264,501. The growth is continuing, and at present ship lines are adding specially designed container vessels as rapidly as possible. Ports with container handling facilities are in existence in the United States, Europe, and Japan, and this capability is being expanded at a frantic pace. The flexibility and economy of containerization are such that one can safely predict substantial further growth.

The unit train is another quite recent innovation. Here a railroad supplies a customer, such as a utility power plant, with an entire train to carry a full load from origin to destination. This procedure greatly speeds shipment and cuts costs. Between one-third and one-half of the coal in the United States is now shipped in this manner and other products are beginning to use unit trains.

The railroads have also been active in designing special cars for particular uses. Special automobile carrying, three-deck cars have been so successful that the railroads have recaptured most of the long-haul automobile deliveries. Special larger cars for carrying grain from terminals to ports have been designed and gradually are gaining acceptance. New whale-shaped tank cars which hold 30,000 gallons are now in service as well as high-cube box cars and special hopper cars designed to carry large loads of bulk products are available. With these and other new facilities the railroads have been able to speed up deliveries and prevent rates from rising as fast as other prices have risen in recent years.[9]

Freeze Rates. Many trucking companies employ what are known as "freeze rates" or "rate stops." These terms means that a company quoting such a rate will not, for example, carry shipments of fourth-class or lower freight for less than the third-class rate. The term *freeze* here means that the trucking company has frozen its rate at the third-class rate. Since many manufactured articles are subject to less than the third-class rate, a shipper should inquire about freeze rates before employing truck transportation. He should not assume

[9] Many of the facts in this section were drawn from an article by Walter J. Auburn entitled, "The Shipping Revolution," which appeared in *The Chicago Purchaser*, October 1972, pp. 18–30.

that because a trucking company did not employ freeze rates on one date this will continue to be true. Trucking companies change their practices in respect to freeze rates, depending on the availability of different classes of freight.

Shipper Associations. For shippers who do not have an adequate volume to abtain minimum rates, shipper associations exist to combine shipments into carloads or truckloads. The shipper receives an intermediate rate from the association. The shipment moves under the association's name.

Through Rates. A through rate is the rate from point of origin to destination. A long-haul rate is less per mile than a short-haul rate. It is therefore an advantage to the buyer to get a rate on one long haul rather than on two short hauls. For this purpose railroads have developed various forms of through rates, with the privilege of interruption. This means that a commodity can, for example, be shipped from Milwaukee to New York with a break at Pittsburgh, with the basic Milwaukee to New York charges being applied. Through rates are obtained as a result of direct negotiation with the carrier. The three principal forms of rates with interruption privileges are:

1. *Diversion and reconsignment.* Rail carload shipments may be diverted or reconsigned while in transit. Diverting a car means giving the carrier a new destination at some specified point before the car reaches its original destination. Reconsignment refers to the practice of naming a new party as the consignee of the shipment while the car is en route. Frequently diversion and reconsignment are both involved when a shipment of a commodity is sold while it is in transit.

There are a number of commodities that frequently move to market on a diversion and reconsignment basis. For example, lumber, fresh fruits and vegetables, and grain handled by commission merchants are commonly shipped with the knowledge that they will be sold while in transit. New orders must be given the carrier in time to allow the car to move by the most economical route. Freight carriers assess a moderate charge for allowing the privilege of diversion and reconsignment.

2. *In-transit privileges.* A substantial amount of freight cost can be saved by a proper use of the "fabrication in transit," "milling in transit," and "storage in transit" privileges allowed by carriers. Each of these privileges is granted under defined conditions by the carrier, permitting the shipper to stop the shipment at some intermediate point without treating the shipment as if it were made up of two separate movements. Thus a shipper can stop a shipment at an inter-

mediate point for fabricating, milling, or storage and then, at a some-what later date, move an equivalent tonnage to a market beyond the stop-off at the lower long-haul rate, and enjoy a significant cost saving.

These "in-transit" privileges are available only to industries and products for which an agreement exists between the carriers and shippers. They are not blanket rights for all products. Fabrication in transit is quite generally accorded to processors of iron and steel. Milling in transit is most commonly permitted for the malting, milling, and mixing of grain and for the milling of forest porducts. Storage in transit applies to a large number of heavy commodities but is especially characteristic of grain.

The following example illustrates fabrication in transit applied to steel plates and related articles shipped from a steel company to a processor to be made into small bridges for delivery at various destinations. The processor paid the railroad the full amount of freight for shipping the steel from the mill to his plant, and the shipper registered the freight bill with the Western Weighing and Inspection Bureau (an agency supported by the railroads). When the fabricated article was delivered to the buyer (which may be up to one year), the freight cost was calculated from the steel company to the ultimate destination, as if the shipment had not been interrupted. The processor then subtracted the amount he had paid previously, and the balance was the amount due, plus a nominal charge by the carrier for the privilege of fabricating in transit.

In order to take advantage of fabrication-in-transit rates, the processor's plant must be considered to be intermediate between the point of origin of the raw material and the destination of the fabricated product. However, "intermediate" should not be understood literally, since steel shipped from Chicago may be fabricated in Milwaukee and shipped across Lake Michigan to eastern destinations. Also, steel plates from Pennsylvania may be shipped to Milwaukee via car ferry and, after processing, be shipped to southwestern destinations. In both of these examples Milwaukee is considered to be an intermediate point, although it is not geographically between the points of origin and destination.

The principles of an in-transit operation are the same for milling and storing as for fabrication in transit. Although these special privileges were originated by rail carriers, it is possible today to make similar arrangements with motor carriers.

3. *Stop-off privilege.* The stop-off privilege allows a shipper to distribute merchandise along the carrier's route. Although the rate is based on the maximum weight of the shipment, there still are sub-

stantial economies over the alternative costs of small-lot shipments. The privilege may also be applied to shipments where merchandise is picked up rather than distributed. One firm reports that under a stop-off arrangement negotiated with a truck line on castings, pick-ups are made at three suppliers plants on the day before the truck-load is assembled. The combined shipments are above the minimum truckload weight and thus at the lowest rate. There is also a saving in dock space at the buyer's plant, with only one truck making delivery.

Rates Relating to Commodity Description.   Often material changes, description changes, or a regrouping of commodities can result in transportation economies. The possibilities presented in the following discussion show rate-negotiation opportunities available to all shippers.

When components are redesigned to incorporate different materials, the new materials may allow either higher or lower rates. In one example fittings originally made from iron and steel were changed to zinc. The initial effect was to increase the freight charges by raising the LTL classifications from Class 50 to Class 85. However, by appealing to the motor freight classification board, the manufacturer was able to hold the old classification on the grounds that the zinc part was actually cheaper to make.

Some products carry a higher freight classification than necessary because they are designated by their trade name rather than a classification description. A tire inflator was shipped under its trade name at an LTL Class 100 of 3.86/cent. When shipped as a tire-puncture-sealing compound, it carried a LTL Class 85 or 3.36/cent.[10]

When various materials or components are included in a shipment, the highest commodity rate will apply for the entire shipment. Lower rates can often be obtained by careful separation of materials.

Responsibility for Correct Rates.   Anyone using common carriers is assumed to have a knowledge of freight classifications and rates. Carriers are not legally responsible for erroneous quotations of freight rates. For example, if a purchasing agent in deciding between two vendors on the basis of their delivered cost relied on a carrier's erroneous rate quotations, the carrier could not be held responsible if the agent later found he had made the wrong decision because a rate quoted by the carrier was incorrect. This is true even though the error might have resulted in a large loss to the purchaser. For this reason tariff schedules are on file in freight stations, and those using common carriers are well advised to be familiar with the rates.

[10] "What to Do to Get a Lower Commodity Classification," *Purchasing Week*, November 5, 1962, p. 23.

As indicated, freight rates are subject to varying degrees of flexibility, depending on many variables. It is imperative that shippers know enough transportation and traffic management to understand that rate economies can be achieved through a careful classification of goods. They should also be familiar with the various truckload and carload minimum weights so as to compare the advantages of buying in small quantities with the freight savings possible from larger unit shipments. They should further realize that it may be possible to negotiate with the carrier and the regulatory agencies for a commodity rate that may be much lower than the class rate on which the goods otherwise move. Many of these matters will be handled by the traffic department of the company if one exists, but purchasing personnel should know enough about them to initiate actions that may save substantial money.

Carrier Alternatives

Essentially there are three types of carriers: common carriers, contract carriers (sometimes referred to as for-hire carriers), and private carriers. The extent to which each class is regulated varies.

The preponderance of freight in the United States is shipped by common carriers. They serve the general public by providing service either for all commodities or for specified types of commodities. A contract carrier is an independent contractor who operates under individual contracts. He generally provides specialized service for selected commodities to a limited number of shippers. The private carrier provides transportation for his own commodities in company-owned or leased equipment.

Common carriers and contract carriers are regulated by the ICC if they are involved in interstate commerce. However, the regulations pertaining to contract carriers are less stringent than those pertaining to the common carriers. Both must obtain ICC certification in addition to filing their rates. The ICC authorizes the geographical area in which they may operate and approves their rates. State agencies regulate those contract and common carriers who are involved only in intrastate commerce. Private carriers are only regulated in matters pertaining to safety.

Free-on-Board Terms

The designation F.O.B. indicates the point of origin from which freight charges are calculated. The routing of shipments has economic and legal significance to buyers, carriers, and shippers. In general, the designated F.O.B. point determines who pays the freight charges and also who has legal title to the merchandise while it is in the hands of the carrier.

Technically, F.O.B. has no meaning unless a phrase is added to indicate the point at which the goods are free on board, such as F.O.B. shipping point or F.O.B. destination. It is at the F.O.B. point where title changes hands, and from which freight charges accrue to either buyer or shipper. For a shipment proceeding F.O.B. shipping point, title passes to the buyer at the shipping point. Thereafter, the carrier acts as the agent of the buyer who is responsible for damage, freight claims, other complications that may arise during shipment, and paying freight charges. For a shipment made F.O.B. destination, these responsibilities fall upon the seller. If no qualifying phrase is added, the term F.O.B. is generally understood to be at the point of origin of the shipment.

The following outline indicates the respective responsibilities of the seller and buyer under various F.O.B. terms. The seller, Adams Company, is assumed to be located in Milwaukee, Wisconsin, and the buyer, Baker Company, in New York City.

I. F.O.B. (named point of origin, e.g., F.O.B. Adams Company, Milwaukee, Wisconsin, via ABC Transport)
    A. Seller must
        1. Place goods on or in cars or vehicles.
        2. Secure receipted bill of lading from carrier.
        3. Be responsible for loss and damage until goods have been placed in or on cars or vehicles at point of origin and clean bill of lading has been furnished by carrier.
    B. Buyer must
        1. Provide for the movement of goods after they are on board.
        2. Pay all transportation charges to destination.
        3. Be responsible for loss or damage or for filing claims with carrier for loss or damage to shipment while in transit.
        4. Pay any demurrage and storage charges.
    C. Title passes to buyer when shipment is turned over to carrier.

II. F.O.B. (named point of origin with transportation charges allowed to destination, e.g., F.O.B. Adams Company, Milwaukee, Wisconsin, Freight Allowed, via ABC Transport)
    A. Seller must
        1. Place goods on or in cars or vehicles.

    2. Secure receipted bill of lading from carrier.

    3. *Pay transportation charges from point of origin to destination.*

    4. Be responsible for loss and damage until goods have been placed in or on cars or vehicles at point of origin and clean bill of lading has been furnished by carrier.

  B. Buyer must

    1. Provide for the movement of goods after they are on board.

    2. Be responsible for loss or damage or for filing claims with carrier for loss or damage to shipment while in transit.

    3. Pay any demurrage and storage charges.

  C. Title passes to buyer when shipment is turned over to carrier.

III. F.O.B. (named destination, e.g., F.O.B. Baker Company, New York City, via ABC Transport)

  A. Seller must

    1. Place goods on or in cars or vehicles.

    2. Secure receipted bill of lading from carrier.

    3. *Pay all transportation charges until goods have arrived at destination.*

    4. *Be responsible for loss or damage or for filing claims with carrier for loss or damage to shipment while in transit.*

  B. Buyer must

    1. Provide for any movement of the goods after arrival at named destination.

    2. Be responsible for any loss and damage incurred after arrival of goods at named destination.

    3. Pay any demurrage and storage charges.

  C. Title remains with seller until the shipment is delivered to buyer.

Import Shipments

An understanding of the meaning of F.O.B. terms on import shipments is of greater importance than on domestic shipments because additional insurance coverage is required if the goods are purchased F.O.B. a foreign point of origin. Domestic common carriers are required by law to insure all goods carried up to a prescribed minimum value. Thus domestic shipments have a certain insurance protection whether they have been sold F.O.B. point of origin or F.O.B. destination. The only difference is that in the first instance the buyer must file the claim with the insurance company, whereas in the second the seller must file the claim. Of course, if the goods have a value greater than is covered by the carrier's insurance, the seller or buyer may well take out additional insurance on the shipment.

On ocean shipments the carrier does not insure shipments aboard his vessel and, consequently, it is vital that the buyer provide adequate insurance coverage where the purchase terms are F.O.B. point of origin. There is also a marine freight term, known as C.&F. (cost and freight). This term is similar to the domestic term F.O.B. point of origin with transportation charges allowed to destination. Here again it is the buyer's responsibility to cover the shipment with adequate insurance, since neither the seller nor the carrier will provide insurance. The third common marine freight expression is C.I.F. (cost, insurance, and freight). This is similar to the domestic term, F.O.B. destination. If a sale is made C.I.F., it means that the seller will provide the insurance, and the buyer has only limited responsibility for the goods before they are landed in the country of destination.

It is significant that under C.I.F. terms, title to goods passes when they are delivered to the carrier. After that point in time, any losses are the responsibility of the buyer. Most buyers, therefore, prefer C.&F. terms because under these terms the buyer has the choice of insurance companies; that is, he can choose the coverage which best meets his requirements and he can arrange that payment of claims be made in his own country and in his own currency. With large insurance companies in the United States specializing in marine insurance, it is no longer desirable to have foreign shippers select insurance coverages under C.I.F. terms.

The purchasing agent should also know that in marine insurance there are two kinds of coverage that he should provide. One is against "general average" loss and the other is against "particular average" loss. A greatly oversimplified explanation of a general average loss is that a ship's captain may, when faced with a peril of the sea, decide to sacrifice a specific shipment or part of the ship in order to save the remainder. If he makes such a sacrifice, marine law holds that all who had a financial interest in the voyage must contribute a pro rata share toward the loss. Each one must contribute even though his own shipment was in no way harmed by the peril. Insurance against general average loss assumes the insured shipper's contribution.

Insurance against particular average loss protects the insured person against such things as loss or water damage that may befall his shipment without endangering the entire venture. Imports should be protected against both types of risk.

Routing Incoming Shipments

The purchaser has the right to route a shipment that has been purchased F.O.B. point of origin. There are many reasons why he may wish to exercise his right of deciding the route and the carrier for incoming shipments. The purchaser may have arrangements with particular carriers under which the carriers buy the products of the company in return for being given favorable consideration on the routing of incoming freight. Also, a particular carrier may have been helpful to the purchaser in securing favorable rate approval from the Interstate Commerce Commission, and the purchaser may wish to reward the carrier for his help. Such cooperation of carriers in rate matters is extremely helpful to industries and companies. In other instances the purchaser may prefer a particular carrier because in the past it has given him the best service between the points involved.

However, a purchaser at times may do better if he does not insist on his right to route the shipment and permits the seller to select the route. Sometimes there are car shortages, and the best interests of the purchaser may be served if he permits the vendor to use his own judgment in selecting a carrier. At the time the material is ready for shipment, the vendor is in a better position to know which of the carriers has available cars. Furthermore, the vendor is more likely to be familiar with unfavorable traffic conditions, such as floods, snow accumulation, labor difficulties, and other factors which make it inadvisable to use a particular route at a given time. Such conditions are generally not known to the purchaser when he places his order.

In heavy industries particularly, the question of railroad clearances and special equipment such as depressed-center cars, well cars, or heavy-duty cars is important. Not all carriers have the necessary equipment. Even if they have the equipment, it may not be available on their line at the time it is required for the given shipment. Thus, under certain circumstances, the purchaser may only create confusion by insisting on his right to route the shipment.

It is good practice for a purchasing agent permitting the vendor to route his shipment to put a notation on his purchase requisition, "Ship via best and cheapest." If the vendor then ships by a carrier who does not quote the lowest available rate, the purchaser is in a position to charge the vendor for the difference between the actual and the lowest freight rate applicable.

Special Trucking Considerations

Transportation by truck today is becoming a method of great and growing importance to industry. In many respects, truck carriers are governed by the same laws and regulations as rail and water carriers. However, there are certain differences that should be observed if one is to manage truck traffic to the best advantage.

It is usually advisable for a purchaser to select a limited number of responsible carriers for handling his truck shipments. If the purchaser divides his business among too many truck carriers, it will cause congestion at his plant because of the constant arrival and departure of trucks.

A practice that is spreading among large concerns is the establishment of docking facilities at major supply points. Purchase orders placed in that area specify delivery to the company's dock. Employees of the buyer are stationed at the dock and they consolidate the shipments into truckloads, which then carry the minimum rate. In effect, such concerns are operating as their own freight forwarders.

In general, truck carriers would rather deal with companies that give them a reasonable amount of business. Since most truck carriers are classified as common carriers, they are not permitted to refuse to accept undesirable freight, but sometimes, by devious means, they are able to discourage this kind of business. For example, they may be slow in picking up shipments when they are called by the shipper and in this way discourage him from making small shipments.

There are more compelling reasons for a purchaser to route truck shipments than railroad shipments. Since rail carriers are usually larger and financially sounder than truck carriers, the risk of the carrier not making good on claims for loss and damage is much less for the railroads than truck carriers. In the railroad field it has been accepted practice for the receiver or trustee of a bankrupt railroad to pay loss and damage claims as well as claims for overcharges without requiring the claims to be filed through court procedure. Frequently, however, when a trucking company goes into receivership, it is necessary to file claims for loss and damage as well as for overcharges through the court. Claims will then be given consideration based entirely on the assets and the liabilities of the trucking company. With railroads it is a rare occurrence for properly substantiated loss and damage claims not to be paid.

The Interstate Commerce Commission and the various state commissions require trucking companies to carry insurance to cover both cargo and injury to persons or property. The insurance required of a trucking company, however, is a very limited and inadequate amount.

Several years ago, for example, there was a case involving injury to two employees of a large firm which occurred in the delivery of steel plates by a trucking company. One of the company employees was killed in the accident, and a second was seriously injured. The insurance company settled the claim for the employee who was killed for $7500. The injured employee lived for six or seven years in a hospital where he required hospital service and nurses. The court finally a- warded the employee a judgment of $62,500. The trucking company had insurance in the amount of $45,000. Since this trucking company was financially sound, it paid the deficiency of $17,500 al- though the judgment was beyond the insurance required by either the Interstate Commerce Commission or the state commission. If the shipment had been carried by a trucking company without adequate insurance or without ability to pay a court judgment, it would have been obligatory on the purchaser to meet the court judgment. Such contingencies make it apparent that one should select trucking com- panies carefully.

It sometimes happens that an urgent need for material induces a purchaser to lease a truck for carrying a shipment because of inabil- ity to secure the services of a common carrier. It should be kept in mind that such a purchaser is responsible for any accidents that may occur. Since an accident claim may be large, such trucking practices should be followed with great caution.

Tracing

There is a tendency in some purchasing departments to use the terms *expediting* and *tracing* interchangeably. Actually, these terms are not synonymous. Expediting commences at the time the order is placed. Part of it consists of selecting the most direct route in view of prevailing traffic conditions. Also, to expedite a shipment, the carrier should be informed in advance that a particular shipment is urgently needed. Finally, a shipment may be expedited by keeping in touch with the representatives of the carrier to make sure that the purchas- er is being given the best possible service.

Tracing, on the other hand, is a traffic function that is resorted to after the shipment has had sufficient time to reach its destination but has not arrived.

It should be obvious that to expedite or trace all or nearly all ship- ments lessens the effectiveness of expediting and tracing. Carriers soon get to know habitual tracers, and their requests for tracing re- ceive little attention.

Carload Shipments

Tracing carload shipments is relatively simple. When requesting that a car be traced, one should be sure of the date of shipment, the car initial and number, and its complete routing. Railroads maintain records of carload shipments by car initial and number. If several railroads are involved in the routing, the time that has intervened between the date of shipment and the date of tracing will indicate whether the request should be taken up with the initiating, the intermediate, or the delivering carrier. Each railroad has a card record office. When a freight car moves onto the tracks of a given railroad, the record is posted in the car record office. Therefore, by telephoning the proper department of the railroad it can very readily be determined whether and when the carrier has received the car.

The larger railroads in the United States have general agents in all of the large cities. Such railroad offices usually have teletype service through which it is possible to locate a car very quickly. Securing such information for a purchaser is one of the important functions of a general agent's office.

Less-than-Carload Railroad Shipments

In the past, if a carrier were given the waybill (equivalent to invoice) number, date of shipment, and the contents of the shipment, he could tell in what car the shipment had been loaded and to what transfer point that car had been directed. However, in recent years for reasons of economy, many carriers have discontinued keeping records of each shipment.

If it should become possible in the future once again to trace less-than-carload shipments, the procedure would be about as follows. The purchaser would secure from the vendor the date of shipment, the number of packages and pieces, weight of the shipment, waybill number, the car number, and to what transfer point the car was directed. With this information the carrier could locate the shipment.

Truck Shipments

Tracing truck shipments, TL or LTL, is quite simple. The important information for tracing a truckload shipment is the trailer number and whether the trailer is moving direct to the final destination or is to be delivered to an intermediate line. If truckload shipments are not transferred from one trailer to another, it is easy to locate the trailer and keep in touch with the single trucking company that is handling the shipment or the several truck lines involved. Tracing truckload shipments is not much more difficult than tracing carload shipments on railroads.

Less-than-truckload (LTL) shipments are handled in much the same way as rail LCL shipment, except that trucking companies are better able than railroads to supply information about the location of small shipments. Truck companies keep a record of the trailer in which each shipment is loaded and the destination of each trailer. A record is also kept of each shipment at the transfer point, so that it is possible to trace an LTL shipment throughout its entire course.

Other Shipments

Since express companies do not keep records of transfers of shipments from one car to another, or from one depot to another, there is no possibility of tracing express shipments.

Airlines operate in the same manner as trucking companies in tracing shipments. Therefore, it is possible for them to tell a shipper the location of his shipments between point of origin and destination.

Auditing and Paying Freight Charges

The Interstate Commerce Commission rules require that freight charges be paid to railroads within 48 hours of the receipt of the goods and to truck lines or freight forwarders within 7 days. Companies having a high credit rating may be granted 96 hours by the railroads. Failure to adhere to these regulations subjects both the shipper and the railroad to a fine of $1000 for each shipment. Since such fines are frequently assesed, it is extremely important that purchasing agents comply with this provision of the regulations.

Demurrage Charges

Demurrage charges are penalties assessed by carriers on cars or vessels held by or for a consignor or consignee beyond a stipulated free time provided for loading or unloading.

Two days' free time after the first 7 A.M. is permitted before demurrage charges are levied. "After the first 7 A.M." is an important provision because cars usually are delivered to a plant after 7 A.M. Then the receiver has 2 full days plus the amount of time remaining after 7 A.M. of the day on which the car was delivered.

During periods of rail-car shortages, demurrage rates are made punitive so that cars will be unloaded faster.

Most business concerns operate under what is known as an "average agreement" with respect to demurrage charges. The gist of such an agreement is that a receiver is given a credit for each car released before the expiration of the first 24 hours of free time. This credit can be used to offset a debit of one day's demurrage.

Adjustments and Filing of Claims

When a shipment arrives at the plant, an immediate inspection should be made by the purchaser. If loss or damage is discovered, a notation to that effect should be placed on the freight bill, either by the carrier's agent or by a representative of the Inspection Bureau maintained by the carriers. The agent or the representative will then present a loss or damage report to the freight claim agent. Then, when the purchaser files his claim for loss or damage, the carrier will refer to this report and the claim can be settled in a relatively short time.

There are times when damage or loss is concealed or cannot readily be recognized. When such damage is discovered, the agent of the carrier or the Inspection Bureau representative should be requested to submit a loss or damage report for concealed loss or damage.

A properly presented and documented claim will avoid much unnecessary correspondence. Delay in payment of claims is primarily the result of improperly filed claims. Forms for filing claims for loss or damage are available from carriers. They provide for entering data on when the shipment was made, by whom, description of the goods, routing, weight, and so forth. The claim form should be accompanied by the following supporting documents: the original bill of lading, the original freight bill with loss or damage notations, a certified invoice, and a report by the carrier or Inspection Bureau.

Claims must be filed within 9 months after delivery of a damaged shipment, or, if the shipment is presumed lost, within 9 months after a reasonable length of time has been allowed for the shipment to arrive. If it is impossible to file a claim because certain supporting documents are not available, the receiver must notify the carrier within the 9-month period of his intention of filing a claim. A claim may be filed with either the originating carrier or the delivering carrier, but usually it is filed with the delivering carrier.

Overcharge Claims

Claims for freight overcharges may be filed within 3 years of the payment of the freight charges. Errors noted during the month in which they occurred may be referred to the carrier's agent who often is able to make the refund locally. However, claims for overcharges filed after the month in which they occurred must be filed with the auditor of freight overcharge claims who is usually located at the general office of the carrier.

It should also be recognized that a carrier is permitted to collect freight undercharges that have occurred during the same period of time. Not only is the carrier permitted to collect such undercharges, but he must do so, even to the point of bringing suit, or it would be considered an illegal rebate.

DISCUSSION QUESTIONS

1. Which of the traffic matters of greatest concern to the purchasing agent do you consider to be the most important?

2. Distinguish clearly between "class rates" and "commodity rates." Which comes first? What brings about the change from one type of rate to the other?

3. What is the role of the Interstate Commerce Commission in rate setting?

4. Under what conditions should a buyer specify routing instructions and choice of carrier for incoming shipments?

5. Explain the difference between expediting and tracing as these terms are used in traffic management.

6. What do the abbreviations F.O.B. and C.I.F. stand for? Explain the importance of these terms for import shipments.

7. Describe some of the special shipping facilities which have been developed in recent years.

8. What is meant by a pool car, an in-transit privilege, and demurrage?

9. It is widely held that, when truck carriers are used, the buyer should insist upon his right of routing and carrier. Why?

10. What are some of the ways in which a purchasing agent working with his traffic manager can save money for his company through good traffic management?

11. What is a stop-off privilege and how is it used?

SUGGESTED CASE

Bielaw Company

CHAPTER 15
SURPLUS AND OBSOLETE MATERIALS

The efficient management of surplus and obsolete materials is a financial as well as social concern of the industrial firm. High interest rates and low and sometimes managed profit margins make the incremental dollar savings and economical reuse of salvage of special importance.

Society's interest is manifested in the President's report to Congress in August 1970, in which he stated that a major challenge and opportunity for private industry is to develop closed systems to recycle so-called "wastes" back to productive, useful purposes. As a nation we are consuming about one-half of the world's natural resources and becoming the most cluttered country on earth. To overcome this condition, state and federal laws regulating dumping and disposal procedures are being considered, and in many cases, passed.

The importance of the flow of scrap steel from metal working plants back to steel producing mills illustrates the nation's stake in the efficient redistribution of materials. Because scrap is the metalic equivalent of pig iron, every ton used in making steel conserves up to 1½ tons of iron ore, a ton of coke, and a half-ton of limestone—all of which are natural resources in limited supply.

Normally, purchased scrap makes up 40% of the copper produced in the United States, 25% of the steel, and 20% of the aluminum and paper. But even more significant is the fact that when demand for these basic commodities rises rapidly, the producers use extra scrap as an incremental source of raw materials.

The generation of surplus materials is, at least partially, a price

317

paid because of the changing nature of American business. For example, an engineer may discover a new production technique requiring the use of different materials. Although an overall economy is involved, the old raw material inventory is obsolete. Or, after a new product has been on the market for a short time, design improvements may be found that obsolete existing finished goods and some raw material inventory. Finally, production innovations involving technological advances almost always result in obsoleting former equipment and materials. In short, surplus is one of the prices of progress.

In other cases surpluses are the result of human errors such as an overly optimistic market projection and the resulting production schedule that proves to be excessive or an overextension of buying for the future resulting in excessive inventories which then may deteriorate.

Finally, the regular manufacturing process produces scrap residues and spoiled or damaged materials. On the average, approximately 15% of all finished steel products such as sheets, plates, or shapes and 5% of the original weight of all castings eventually end up as scrap during processing.

In many ways, scrap and surpluses are a paradox. Man does not want to produce them, yet they are materials he constantly produces. They are virtually the only resources that are never depleted, but constantly replenish themselves and, with proper processing and redistribution, are a perpetual source of some raw materials vital to the continued existence of our industrial society.

Categories of Disposable Materials

Several terms are used to distinguish the classes of disposable materials commonly comprehended under the broad term *scrap*.

Spoilage consists of those items of production that are found to be defective during the manufacturing or inspection process. Such items are also called "rejects." Occasionally, one finds spoilage referred to as waste. The term *waste*, however, should be reserved for materials that are lost in the manufacturing process or that have no significant recovery value, such as gases, smoke, dust, and unsalable materials.

Scrap, in the narrow sense, consists of the residue of process materials left during a manufacturing operation. This might include such materials as the turnings from a lathe, sprues and "flash" from the foundry or molding process, and paper cuttings from a book bindery. Worn-out equipment and parts are also included in this category.

In recent years, people in the industry have come to find the word *scrap* offensive and have opted for the term *secondary material*. Even this seems to have become undignified and the trade group, the National Association of Secondary Material industries, has changed its name to the National Association of Recycling Industries.[1]

The industry (under whatever name) recognizes three categories of scrap. *Home Scrap* is produced in the mills of the basic industries—trimmings from steel ingots, slag, and skimmings from molten metal. This scrap can be immediately recycled. *Prompt-Industrial Scrap* is what is left over from the manufacturing process—skeleton sheets after stampings have been made from them, paper trimmed in the manufacture of envelopes, turnings and borings from machine shops, and so forth. The terminology is derived from the fact that the manufacturer must dispose of such scrap promptly lest he be inundated by its very volume. Prompt-industrial scrap is a highly desirable commodity because it is likely to be free of contamination. The third type of scrap, *Obsolete Scrap*, consists of items that have been used and are basically worn out—automobile hulks, appliances, old industrial machinery, and so on.

Another category of disposable goods is equipment, materials and supplies that have become obsolete. A well-managed firm considers any item obsolete when the increased efficiency possible from using a more modern item exceeds the added costs of replacing the old with the new item. In many instances an item that is obsolete for one company may still be useful to another firm.

Frequently a company will have supplies and replacement parts on hand when it replaces a piece of obsolete equipment. Such supplies and parts no longer have economic value to the company. However, since many companies may still be using this type of equipment and the supplies and parts can be sold to such users as new materials, it is perhaps more descriptive to call them *surplus*. Recycling is a form of surplus utilization in which the basic chemical and physical properties of solid waste materials are returned as productive inputs in the production process.

In the remainder of this chapter the term *surplus* will be used inclusively to indicate all classes of scrap, spoiled material, or obsolete material that still have economic worth.

Management of Surplus Disposal

From many points of view the management of surplus is a stepchild. The main concern of any company is the production of its finished product. The surpluses originating as a by-product of this proc-

[1] Marilyn Wellemeyer, "For Scrapmen, These Are 'Tinsel Days'," *Fortune*, August 1974, p. 152.

ess are often regarded as a necessary nuisance to be handled as quickly and simply as possible. They are not usually thought of as a source of supplementary income. Their value seldom, if ever, is shown as a separate item on a company's income statement or balance sheet. Usually the income they generate is buried in the "other income" category or treated as an offset to the cost of raw materials. Since the variety of surpluses is great and the amount of each type is likely to be relatively small, the seller does not usually become an expert in the business. In fact, scrap is one of the few items in the world of business about which the buyer is ordinarily better informed than the seller.

Responsibility for the disposal of surplus materials is assigned to the purchasing department, the treasurer, the comptroller, or the production department.

The purchasing department most often has the responsibility for surplus disposal. A study by the National Association of Purchasing Management in 1971 involving 5539 respondents indicated 56% had purchasing responsibility for this activity. However, considerable variation is found, as indicated in a study of industrial firms in Virginia:[2]

Responsibility for Scrap Management

Management Area	Percent of Firms
Purchasing	29
Top Management	13
Production	12
Building and Maintenance	8
Quality Control	6
Shipping	5
Other	15
Non response	10

This variation in assignment of responsibility illustrates the fact that there is confusion as to its proper position in the firm. The financial and accounting officers are sometimes brought into the activity because surplus is a source of revenue and because record keeping is involved. The production department incurs its responsibility because most of the scrap is generated in that department and its employees must classify, handle, and store the scrap.

[2] "Industrial Scrap Management: A Study of Some Current Practices," Monroe M. Bird, *Journal of Purchasing*, February 1971, p. 44.

Purchasing and Surplus

Since the disposal of surpluses is a selling rather than a buying activity, one might well ask why this responsibility is usually assigned to the purchasing department. Some authorities have said that this assignment is simply a matter of convenience. Management assigns responsibility for surplus disposal to the purchasing department primarily because it is a miscellaneous activity that none of the other departments of the organization particularly desire, and the purchasing department is as well-equipped to handle it as any other department.

Actually, there are positive reasons for putting surplus disposal under the purchasing department. In the first place, it is the responsibility of the purchasing department to have comprehensive knowledge of price trends. Prices of scrap and surplus materials fluctuate more than the prices of most raw materials because of the fluctuating demand and the derived nature of their demand. When the consuming industry is having difficulty marketing its output, it cuts back production and reduces its purchases of scrap; for example, if a reduction of steel output occurs when scrap dealers have their yards full of scrap, the steel mills will make sharp reductions in the prices offered for scrap. On the other hand, it also frequently happens that the demand for scrap is exceptionally strong when its supply is low, thus causing the price to rise rapidly. Unfortunately, no one within a typical manufacturing firm is an expert on the prices and grades of scrap and other classes of surplus materials. However, the purchasing agent, through daily contacts with many different markets, can adapt more easily than anyone else to the disposal problems.

Salvage Department

Large companies may find that the amount of scrap and surplus generated in their operations is so substantial that it justifies the establishment of a separate scrap and surplus department. In most instances such a department reports directly to the general manager of the company. However, the following suggested procedure for the establishment of a separate salvage department argues for the salvage director to report to engineering and emphasizes the need for management acceptance and an accurate accounting of the economies resulting from the operation.[3]

[3] "Boost Your Profits with Tool Scrap," *Canadian Metalworking/Machine Production*, July 1967, p. 43.

1. Appoint a salvage director under the supervision of factory engineering. Factory engineering can also determine lost man-hours from improper machining practices which will show up in scrap. Engineering can change methods on the spot, when the salvage director sees too much waste coming in from one department.

2. Key salvage employees should be equipped with a chemical analysis kit (cost approximately $50) to correctly determine each type of metal and trace the most precious ones back to the factory source. After locating the source, on-location separation will keep losses and separation cost down.

3. Containers should be color-coded for all types of material. This will eliminate second handling in the salvage department and prevent the mixing of high and low value scrap.

4. In most cases high cost exotic material is normally distributed from the tool cribs in plant locations. The tool crib operator will find his handling cost will not increase very substantially, but his salvage return will increase considerably if he requires an exchange of worn tools and scrapped materials for new ones.

5. The salvage director should be in a position to tabulate the direct cost and return of all his operations to demonstrate profitability by the ratio of scrap return on sales. As a rule of thumb, industry has found that a dollar returned to the profit column by scrap salvage equals the profit returned by $100 of sales.

6. Salvage departments should always sell direct to the end user of exotic materials to get the greatest possible return. The difference is substantial and can be had for little extra effort.

7. Treat salvage operations the same as production operations. Amazingly, otherwise efficient companies often let lost dollars and manhours go unnoticed in the salvage department. Waste and inefficiency should not be tolerated any more in the salvage department, than in production.

A materials engineer can help to increase the amount of materials for recycling by establishing a close working relationship with others in the technical area. For example, a suggestion to use aluminum in making automotive starters, generators, and alternators to replace copper can significantly reduce the amount of copper that gets into furnace charges through automotive scrap. A separate surplus department would appear to be sound in those cases where the volume of scrap generated warrants the cost of a separate department.

Production and Surplus

A third alternative for organizing the surplus disposal activity is to assign it to production. Because most scrap and surplus originate with the production process, responsibility can reasonably be assigned to the production department. The counterargument is that the production department is usually so dominated by its interest in producing the end product that the surplus disposal program is handled very casually.

Because of the wide range of surplus materials and the relative low quantity of each, proper preparation and segregation are important considerations in obtaining maximum return from their sale. When large amounts of a surplus scrap are involved, a firm may be justified in processing the material, such as performing its own bailing, which will allow the firm to sell the material direct to a user rather than through a middleman.

Segregation involves the sorting of scrap surplus by type, alloy, grade, size, and weight. The specifications for various types and grades of scrap materials are established by trade associations and specify the maximum and minimum size as well as the type of material required to meet the standards for each category. When the size and content of scrap fall within the prescribed limitations, the greatest economic return can be anticipated for the material. However, if sizes are mixed or several categories of scrap are combined, the return is considerably reduced. Frequently scrap that has been mixed commands an even lower price than that paid for the lowest-value item in the mixture. The reason for this is the high cost of separating a contaminated mixture. The scrap dealer must perform this segregation in order to dispose of the scrap to a user. This cost will be passed back to the seller of the scrap in the form of a lower price. The slight additional cost of proper attention to segregation at the point of origin will usually be more than compensated by the increased return from the segregated scrap.

Some indication of the magnitude of the segregation task is the fact that there are 27 grades of aluminum scrap, 44 of copper and brass, 46 of commonly traded wastepaper, and 105 of iron and steel.

Segregation is particularly important when surplus is sold. Valuable stainless steels are worth about 80% less if they are mixed with other steel scrap. In general, ferrous scrap mixed with nonferrous scrap lowers the value of the nonferrous component sharply; steel scrap mixed with aluminum, for example, cuts the value of aluminum scrap 60%. It is therefore profitable to establish a system of in-plant segregation of surplus scrap. Segregation is best handled by the production department as part of its routine safety and maintenance responsibilities.

Some materials have a much higher rate of reclamation than others. Differences in the rate of recycling are due in part to difficulties involved in sorting and collecting the metals once they become part of a complex system. For example, zinc has a low recovery rate because of its heavy use in galvanizing which is not recoverable. Copper is another metal that is very difficult to recover because of its heavy use in magnet wire. Other reasons for differences in reclamation rates include inequitable freight rates and depletion allowances, need for specialized labor and equipment for reclamation, and varying pollution codes between states.

The variation in reclamation is illustrated in the following study of seven classes of metals:[4]

Material	Short Tons Available for Recycling	Percentage Recycled
Aluminum	2,215,000	48%
Copper	2,456,000	61
Lead	1,406,000	42
Zinc	1,271,000	14
Nickel	106,000	40
Stainless Steel	429,000	88
Precious Metals	105,000,000	75

Scrap material and small subassemblies should generally be distorted or dismantled before sale and removal from the seller's premises. There is a reason for such action, in addition to maximizing the return by meeting the specifications on size and composition of scrap. It may be desirable to avoid the possibility of the subassembiles being bought at a low price and used by a competitor of the seller. Some sellers have been surprised to find their scrap items appearing on the market and competing with their products. Protection is available to the seller by specifying as a condition of the sale that the subassembly or part be destroyed or by securing a guarantee against its resale as a usable item. If such security cannot be secured, the seller should have the dismantling job performed before the sale is consummated.

[4] A Battelle Memorial Institute study (Columbus, Ohio), as reported in Robert A. Wilson, "Will Metals' Recycling Need a Social Price Tag?", *Iron Age*, January 27, 1972, p. 55.

The accumulation and preparation of scrap prior to sale is generally supervised by some department other than purchasing. However, the purchasing department should work closely with that department in order to maximize the return.

Disposition of Surplus

Surplus materials and scrap can be disposed of in various ways. The return will vary according to the channel used. For example, the sale of a given surplus item through a surplus dealer will usually bring 15 to 35% of original cost, whereas return of the material to the original supplier typically brings 90 to 95% of original cost. In the following paragraphs the various disposition alternatives are presented.

Use within the Firm

The greatest value is obtained from surplus if it can be reclaimed for further use. One form of reclamation involves reuse of "off-falls." Careful study frequently shows that a smaller piece can be stamped or pressed from the "off-fall." Such use results in a saving equal to the difference between the price of raw material and the price of scrap. Of course, there may be extra incidental costs of processing from scrap instead of from new raw material, but generally the savings are substantial. For example, automobile companies reuse their sheet steel shearings to make such things as flanges and washers. It is estimated that this reuse saves them enough metal to make one extra car for every fifty produced.

Reprocessing is another means of reclaiming scrap materials for reuse. Sometimes this can be done by welding or the use of mechanical joints. Short ends of pipe and bar stock can be joined into working lengths by this process. Defective or spoiled castings and metal parts often can be reclaimed at minimum expense by welding.

When a careful study of the surplus material indicates that it cannot be reclaimed, a further effort should be made to determine whether the material can be modified in a way to make it suitable for some purpose other than that for which it was intended. Such analysis often reveals a part that is similar in shape and size which can be made from the scrap material after inexpensive modification. A related possibility is that parts that have been damaged or spoiled can be reworked. One purchasing agent cited success in reconditioning old valves—as scrap they were bringing $18 a gross ton, but as usable valves they were worth $5050 per ton.

When surplus equipment or usable material is involved, most large firms periodically circulate a list of such equipment to all depart-

SEE BACK OF THIS FORM FOR INSTRUCTIONS

SURPLUS PLANT EQUIPMENT

No. 0177

WORKS AND LOCATION			DATE	
MFG. NAME		MODEL NO.	ASSET NO.	
NAME OF EQUIPMENT				
SIZE OR CAPACITY			SERIAL NUMBER	
OPERATING CONDITION (SEE INSTRUCTIONS)	EXCELLENT	GOOD	FAIR	POOR

ADDITIONAL DESCRIPTION AND MOTOR SPEC., STARTERS, ACCESSORIES, SPECIAL SPARE PARTS

YEAR PURCHASED	PURCHASE PRICE $	PRESENT BOOK VALUE $	ESTIMATED WEIGHT

WHY IS EQUIPMENT NO LONGER NEEDED?

IF OBSOLETE—ESTIMATED COST TO MODERNIZE $	DATE EQUIPMENT AVAILABLE	ESTIMATED COST TO PLACE IN ORIGINAL CONDITION $	CAN NEW PARTS BE PURCHASED AT REASONABLE COST

ESTIMATED COST TO LOAD ON CARS $	ESTIMATED COST TO SCRAP $	ESTIMATED VALUE AS SPARE PARTS OR SCRAP $	RECOMMENDED METHOD OF DISPOSAL	HOLD FOR FUTURE PROJECT	TRANSFER	DONATE	SELL	SCRAP

REVIEWED BY

		REMARKS:
STOREKEEPER	DATE	
PROPERTY ACCOUNTANT	DATE	
REPORT BY	DATE	
DEPARTMENT HEAD	DATE	
CHIEF WORKS ENGINEER	DATE	
WORKS MANAGER	DATE	
DIVISION MANAGER	DATE	

FINAL DISPOSITION	PURCHASE ORDER NO.	DATE

FIGURE 15-1.

ments and branch plants. Often the surpluses can profitably be used by other units of the firm with little or no reprocessing costs. Figure 15–1 illustrates a typical surplus equipment form used to inform departments and plants of available stock.

Return to Supplier

Surplus material often can be returned to the original suppliers either in the same form in which it was purchased or as scrap residue. As previously noted, when the material is returned in its original form, returns may be as high as 90 to 95% of the purchase price.

When surplus scrap is involved, such as scrap copper and other nonferrous metals, arrangements can often be made to return the "off-fall" material at a favorable price. Whether or not the original processor will be interested in the return of the uncontaminated scrap from metal he has sold depends on conditions of supply. During periods of shortage the seller may go so far as to put a clause in the sales contract requiring the return of scrap. Even when supply conditions are "easy," a seller will usually accept the scrap from his customers but will be indifferent about it. Under conditions of surplus supply, a seller may discourage returns by refusing to take more than a certain percentage of new-metal sales in the form of returned scrap.

Some technology changes are directly influencing the attitude of metal processors toward scrap. For example, steel companies, using oxygen in blast furnaces find they can use more iron ore and less scrap. As a consequence, the demand for steel scrap has slackened to the point where its price is low even during periods of relatively heavy demand for steel.

Precious metals, such as silver and copper, and their alloys, can be returned to their original processors for reprocessing into their original form. A charge, commonly called a "toll," is made for such reprocessing.

"As-Is" Sale to Other Users

The sale of scrap materials may be sold to another company that can use it in its existing condition. Such sales often bring relatively high prices, and therefore this possibility should be explored before it is decided to sell the material to middlemen as scrap.

To avoid responsibilities for malfunction or related difficulties, these sales are usually on an "as-is" basis; that is, the selling firm makes no express or implied warranty as to the fitness of the products.

"As-is" transactions are usually effected through the medium of trade journal advertising or as a result of direct exchanges of information between firms in the same or similar industries.

Sale to Dealer Middlemen

Dealers or brokers are specialized middlemen who collect, sort, and process surplus materials, especially surplus scrap. When it has been determined that scrap cannot be used or salvaged and that the quantities are too small to justify direct sale to the supplier, these middlemen are normally utilized for disposition. There are three types of scrap middlemen.

The scrap peddler is the smallest of the three types of middlemen. He collects various kinds of scrap from homes, merchants, and very small manufacturing plants. He does not maintain a scrap yard, but disposes of his scrap to a dealer.

The second type is the scrap dealer, who maintains one or more yards in industrial centers in which he accumulates various classes of scrap. The scrap dealer also often has specialized materials-handling equipment, which he may make available to the buyer from time to time. He may also furnish trailers for scrap collection. He has three objectives in operating his yard. He must accumulate enough of a certain class of scrap so that it can be transported to the user economically. Also, he must try to reclassify the scrap he buys in such a way as to raise its grade and price. This can be done by more carefully segregating the types of scrap or by cutting the scrap into smaller sizes to increase its utility to the scrap user. Furthermore, a dealer will hold scrap he has bought until it brings a more favorable price. This is a speculative function, which serves the useful purpose of somewhat balancing supply and demand. Most manufacturing plants sell their scrap to dealers.

The third type of middleman is called a scrap broker. He is not technically a broker, since he takes title but may not take possession of the scrap in which he deals. The broker's function is to negotiate sales between scrap dealers or scrap generation and scrap users. His profit comes out of whatever difference there may be between the price he pays and the price at which he sells to the users. It is not an assured margin. At times it may be unduly large and at other times may disappear or become a negative margin. In his capacity as a broker this middleman does not operate a yard. Therefore, only very large manufacturers with their own scrap-handling facilities deal directly with a scrap broker.

Alternative sales agreements can be established with these middlemen, which involve variables covering pickup arrangements and price calculations. In all cases the volume of scrap offered affects the price. Infrequent collections of substantial scrap volumes are obviously more economical than frequent small pickups and the return to the seller will be proportionately greater.

Under a term contract with price established as that in effect at time of pickup, provision may be made for the sale of scrap to a middleman for periods varying from one month to one year. The price is the market price at time of removal less a stipulated percentage. Prices are stipulated to be those quoted in such trade publications as *Iron Age, Steel*, or *American Metal Market*. From such price quotations a dealer will deduct an allowance or margin which represents his own cost and profit. Since all dealers determine their base prices in the same way and from the same source, the bidding centers in the allowance of margin that the dealer charges for his functions.

Term contracts with fixed-price agreements usually run for periods up to one year. A set price is established by negotiation between the seller and the buyer. The dealer furnishes a trailer or container and provides periodic pickups. Arrangements are usually made for weighing more valuable types of scrap on the seller's premises in order to minimize the risk of scrap being removed from the container before it reaches the public scales.

The principal advantage of term contracts is that the middleman is obligated to accept scrap regardless of market conditions. This advantage is particularly valuable when conditions are such that mills are not buying. During these periods the middlemen accumulate substantial scrap inventories.

The other middlemen arrangements include (1) the bid or negotiation methods under which each lot of scrap is offered to middlemen either by sealed bids or negotiations and (2) the commission method, under which the middleman periodically removes the scrap and sells it for the highest price obtainable, out of which he is paid a commission.

Unfortunately, current research seems to indicate that many firms are not obtaining the maximum return on scrap sales. Assuming that either negotiated or competitive contracts produce maximum returns, the following are discouraging results:[5]

Methods Used to Determine Selling Prices for Scrap Materials

Methods	Percentage of Firms
Current Market Price	71
Negotiated Contracts	22
Competitive Bidding	13
(Some firms use multiple methods)	

[5] Monroe M. Bird, "Industrial Scrap Management: A Study of Some Current Practices," *Journal of Purchasing*, February 1971, p. 45.

Scrap Consultant

It was mentioned earlier in the chapter that scrap is one commodity class about which the buyer is typically better informed than the seller. This is almost universally true because, though important as a source of revenue, the volume of scrap sales is small in comparison with the sale of a company's regular product line. Furthermore, the kinds and grades of scrap are so numerous as to be bewildering. There are more than 500 different kinds of scrap, including 75 recognized grades of ferrous scrap alone. In order to offset the scrap buyers' expertise some companies employ the services of a scrap consultant.

The scrap consultant is paid a commission on sales of scrap as reimbursement for his services. His services consist of an initial survey of the plant and its scrap-handling procedures. The consultant then makes a report to management, recommending a program for segregating, grading, handling, weighing, and accounting for the company's scrap. If a contract is signed, the consultant proceeds to negotiate the most advantageous sales he can arrange. Thereafter, he audits all scrap sale invoices and makes periodic surveys of the plant to see that the recommended procedures are being carried out. The consultant works with someone designated by management as supervisor of its scrap program.

It is claimed that this method of handling scrap puts the company on a parity with scrap buyers in negotiations, that the designation of a scrap program supervisor with responsibility to top management puts scrap management under unified control, that it frees the purchasing agent to concentrate on his more usual duties, and that it facilitates an audit control over a fringe business activity, which by its inherent nature is peculiarly susceptible to embezzlement.

Direct Sales to Scrap Consumers

Another alternative available to the scrap-generating firm is to process the scrap by compressing and baling it and then selling it direct to scrap users. However, few firms dispose of their scrap in this manner. The volume of scrap generated by a typical plant is not large enough to warrant the substantial expense involved in purchasing specialized equipment and training employees. Specialized scrap dealers have the volume necessary to justify the purchase of specialized equipment (which often costs more than $250,000), in addition to having the specialized knowledge required to handle the wide variety of scrap grades. Finally, scrap dealers typically pay lower wages than do their industry counterparts. Therefore, it usually is impracticable for firms to process their own scrap for direct sales, although automobile manufacturers, railroads, and similar large firms have found it worthwhile to do so.

Economics of the Scrap Industry

The scrap industry is characterized by a market that is in many respects unique. Scrap is said to be bought rather than sold. For practical purposes, demand cannot be created, meaning that the usual tools of advertising, styling, and so on, do not apply to this industry. The demand is a derived demand completely dependent on the sale of final products and the derived need for the raw materials. Therefore, unlike manufacturing firms, which manage to achieve high rates of inventory turnover, the typical scrap dealer must usually maintain large inventories. He is dependent on the mills and foundries, which do not respond to sales, bargain prices, or "hard selling" efforts. When scrap is in demand, however, it must be readily available.

The long ton of 2240 pounds is the basic unit of measurement in the industry although some dealers quote on the basis of a short ton (2000 pounds). The scrap user's weights govern and the scrap must be "suitable and acceptable" to the customer. A few large firms buy scrap on the basis of standards established by the Institute of Scrap Iron and Steel and the National Association of Waste Material Dealers. The specifications are quite loose, and because scrap is a low-priced commodity not readily subject to detailed measurements, few scrap shipments are rejected.

There are thousands of dealers and other middlemen selling undifferentiated products to relatively few large buyers. Therefore, the selling of scrap takes place in a market that resembles perfect competition on the selling side, which means that profit margins often are low.

Usually the performance of a contract is considered complete when the carrier issues a bill of lading rather than upon receipt of the material. A tolerance of 5% is usually accepted in determining tonnage.

The scrap industry association, known as the Institute of Scrap Iron and Steel, is composed of the larger dealers in the field. Before a dealer is admitted to membership he must be approved by the local I.S.I.S. chapter, which is familiar with his facilities and reputation.

The principal scrap markets are located in Boston, New York, Philadelphia, Buffalo, Pittsburgh, Cincinnati, Detroit, Chicago, St. Louis, Birmingham, Los Angeles, San Francisco, Seattle, Portland, Dallas, and Houston. Prices established in these centers form the basis for trading throughout their areas.

DISCUSSION QUESTIONS

1. Why are surplus and obsolete materials sometimes labeled as the price of progress?

2. Distinguish between spoilage, waste, and scrap as applied to the production process.

3. Why is the responsibility for scrap disposal typically assigned to the purchasing department?

4. Under what conditions should disposal of scrap be assigned to the production department?

5. In what ways can scrap be used within the plant?

6. What is an "as is" sale?

7. What is the contribution of scrap dealers in the sale of scrap?

8. How is price determined in scrap disposal activities?

9. What is the role of the scrap consultant?

10. (a) How does a firm determine whether an item is obsolete? (b) What is a surplus item?

11. What are the arguments voiced for and against assigning the surplus disposal activity to the production department?

SUGGESTED CASE

Megalopolis City

CHAPTER 16
FORWARD BUYING, SPECULATION AND COMMODITY MARKETS

One of the primary responsibilities of a purchasing agent involves procurement of the firm's requirements in the most economical quantity. However, determination of this amount is one of the more subjective aspects of the position. Some may interpret the amount as just enough of everything to keep the plant running. Under this definition of requirements, there would be no reserve supply to protect the company against slow deliveries, strikes in suppliers' plants, or transportation interruptions. Such a policy of meeting a company's minimum requirements might be designated as *hand-to-mouth buying*.

At the opposite extreme would be the policy of buying far beyond immediate plant requirements when market prices appear favorable, in the expectation of making an inventory profit on the excess inventories because of advancing prices in the period between purchase and use. This policy could be termed *speculative buying*. Between these two extremes is the area that may best be described by the term *forward buying*, which includes all purchases for contingency reserves but excludes all speculative purchases that have as their objective a profit from price appreciation.

It is the purpose of the first part of this chapter to develop these distinctions somewhat more fully and to suggest what would appear to be sound purchasing policy with respect to buying in advance of minimum needs. Later in the chapter the use of commodity markets for price protection will be discussed in detail.

HAND-TO-MOUTH BUYING

It should be recognized that hand-to-mouth buying is seldom followed in the extreme form described above. In somewhat modified form, however, it became a very popular method of purchasing during the great depression of the 1930s, and it is a policy that may be expected to reappear whenever supplies of goods become plentiful and price declines seem imminent. Its appeal to purchasing agents lies in the fact that hand-to-mouth buying shifts to suppliers all storage and investment costs and the obsolescence risks involved in price-level fluctuations. Hand-to-mouth buying has been facilitated in our economy through speedy communications, rapid transportation, and an increasing degree of decentralization of production facilities.

If, through hand-to-mouth buying, industrial purchasers manage to shift essential costs and risks back to the suppliers, they should recognize that in time the prices charged by the suppliers will be increased enough to cover the greater costs and risks. Thus any gains of this nature from hand-to-mouth purchasing policies are likely to be illusory—or, at most, short-term in nature. Of course, there would be an advantage to the buyer if his product or process were facing alterations in equipment, models, or raw material.

One other way in which purchasers may plan to profit from hand-to-mouth buying is by engaging in such purchasing when it appears that the price of the article in question is likely to decline. Larger purchases are then postponed until the price level is lower, and a saving occurs. If the purchasing agent is able to forecast the price decline accurately, there can be no doubt about his ability to save his company money through this strategy. The real question concerns the ability of any purchasing agent to anticipate price declines with enough certainty and regularity to make the savings that accrue worth the risk.

In point of fact, hand-to-mouth buying in anticipation of a price-level decline is only another form of speculative buying, the merits of which will be considered in a later section of this chapter. The typical speculative purchase is made in anticipation of a rise in price levels, which corresponds to the "long" position on the commodity or stock markets. The hand-to-mouth speculative purchase corresponds to the "short" position in which the speculator hopes to make his profits later by buying at a lower price. A hand-to-mouth speculative purchase is neither better nor worse than the advance speculative purchase, which will be discussed later.

There are quite obvious and substantial risks entailed in a policy of hand-to-mouth buying, aside from the possibility of the price rising instead of falling. First, there is always the risk that, because of slow order-filling, improper quality of materials shipped, or delays in transportation of shipments from the supplier, the plant may be forced to shut down. The cost of a shutdown—or even a slowdown of operations—would greatly exceed any possible savings from lesser warehousing, investment, and risk costs. Sometimes it may be possible for the purchasing agent to borrow from neighboring plants to tide him over, but even this solution is costly and uncertain.

Second, the purchasing agent who follows a policy of hand-to-mouth buying is quite likely to find that he cannot secure as favorable quantity discounts or as low freight rates on the smaller unit quantities that he will be buying under such a policy. These losses should be considered as an offset to whatever savings there may be in hand-to-mouth buying.

Finally, hand-to-mouth buying does not permit so exhaustive a survey of market offerings or so careful an inspection of the materials when received because the plant requirements are so urgent that time is at a premium.

As mentioned before, there are times when hand-to-mouth buying is the proper policy. When model changes are soon introduced or new production methods that might affect the kind of materials used are being contemplated, it would be unwise to stock more than a minimum inventory. Likewise, when there are reports of impending changes in materials that the supplier is contemplating, it is sound policy to buy with caution. However, it may be said that hand-to-mouth buying should be designed to meet exceptional circumstances and is not a recommended policy for normal operations of the typical industrial concern.

Forward Buying

Forward buying includes all purchasing in excess of the minimum stock required to keep the plant operating on a basis of normal output and average delivery times. It excludes advance purchases made with the object of realizing speculative profits. A sound policy of forward buying is essential to successful purchasing, and the purchasing agent in conjunction with top management should define the company's forward-buying policy regarding both its objectives and its extent.

Some of the more common objectives of forward buying are:

1. To provide a margin of insurance against interrupted operations.
2. To purchase in large enough quantities to earn quantity discounts.

3. To purchase in economical transportation units.
4. To protect the company against the risks of prospective shortages of materials.
5. To secure materials of desired qualtities when they are available.

The first of these objectives—buying ahead to ensure against interrupted operations—represents the minimum policy of forward buying. A purchasing agent who does less than this is remiss in the performance of his duties unless he is carrying out an agreed policy of hand-to-mouth buying as a calculated risk. The usual way of determining the margin of safety to ensure continuous operations of a plant is to calculate the quantity of the material that would be needed to operate at capacity during the time that it takes to process and place an order and receive delivery from the most distant supplier by the slowest acceptable means of transportation. A certain percentage of this quantity is then added for a safety factor, and the figure so established becomes the minimum inventory quantity to be stocked at all times.

For the more or less staple materials and supplies, it is then customary to establish a standard unit of order. When the inventory of such materials or supplies falls to the minimum point described in the paragraph above, the purchasing agent, after checking prices, terms, and quality, rather automatically places a reorder for the standard unit of order quantity. The standard unit of order, however, should be determined with care and should be subjected to periodic reexaminations. It should be established by taking into account such considerations as the storage space required and available for use, the amount of money required to buy various quantities, the possibility of physical deterioration during the period of storage, the cost and work entailed in placing orders with suppliers and receiving the goods, the quantity discounts offered with orders of various size, and the applicable freight rates for shipment of various weights and quantities.

It is evident that certain of these considerations conflict with others. For example, the ordering unit that entitles the buyer to the largest possible quantity discount will require the largest investment and take up the most space. Also the most economical shipping quantity may entail the risk of spoilage. Therefore, the decision establishing the standard unit of order is one requiring judgment on the part of the purchasing agent and his staff. Since the considerations mentioned change over time, the decision concerning the unit of order should be reviewed periodically. In the interim, purchases of such staple materials can be entrusted to employees in the purchasing department who hold the lowest ranks and have the fewest policy-making responsibilities.

During periods of shortage or threatened shortage, the purchasing of materials, even staple materials, cannot be made on the basis of rules and formulas, but rather requires the constant exercise of judgment and ingenuity on the part of the purchasing department staff. There are no sure indications of future market conditions, and the purchasing agent can be guided only by his own experience plus the best informed thinking that he can bring to bear on his problems. It is this combination of experience and analysis, which often passes for intuition, that constitutes the true executive talent of the successful purchasing agent.

The final objective of forward buying is the purchase of the right quality at the right time. When the manufacturing processes call for peculiar characteristics in the raw materials and these are available from only certain sources, or at certain seasons of the year, the purchasing agent must take advantage of the offerings when they are made. The ability to make sound decisions on this issue is a by-product of extensive market information. The alert purchasing agent will keep informed of market offerings at all times so that he/she may take advantage of a favorable supply situation when it develops. Of course, one cannot lay down rules about how much forward buying is proper for materials that are in short supply or have special qualities. The decision will depend on the facts in the given situation.

When a company is buying fabricating materials, parts, or subassemblies to its own specifications, forward buying must take a slightly different form. A supplier cannot be expected to set up his production line at frequent intervals in order to fill a small order for the buyer. In such cases requirement contracts are made for a period of time, such as 6 months or a year. The price will be set either by bidding or by negotiation. It is rather common to provide a basis in the contract for altering the price in accordance with some specified index if costs change over the period of the contract. The contract will also usually specify the rate of delivery and permit certain maximum and minimum rates of delivery to accommodate changes that either party may require. In a sense this may be considered forward purchasing because a financial commitment is made in advance. However, such arrangements are dictated by production demands rather than by a decision to purchase according to needs or ahead of needs. Therefore, it is a special variation of forward buying.

Speculative Buying

The distinction between forward buying and speculative buying lies in the reason for making the advance purchases. Forward buying is done because operational considerations or supply conditions suggest the need for an inventory reserve. Speculative buying, on the other hand, is conducted with the hope of profiting from price changes. The factors leading to forward buying are clearly of the kind that the purchasing agent understands and regularly deals with. However, this is not so true of speculative buying. The purchasing agent is not a specialist in forecasting price trends. As a matter of fact, no class of business executives has a very good record of predicting the time and degree of significant price-level changes.

The foregoing reasoning would seem to lead to the conclusion that purchasing agents—and businessmen in general—should avoid speculative purchasing. Probably all business would be more secure and equally profitable if it would concentrate on making manufacturing profits instead of trying to combine speculation with processing. This conclusion is based on the rather evident fact that manufacturing business executives do not have the training or the experience that is required to make them good speculators.

Although this recommendation is believed to be sound, the unfortunate fact is that often a business firm does not have a free hand in deciding whether or not to engage in speculative buying. If one or more firms in an industry follow the practice of speculative buying, they may force the entire industry to speculate. This result is brought about because it seems to be the general practice for a company that speculates successfully in a given instance to take advantage of its success by pricing its products low, on the basis of the actual cost rather than the replacement cost of its materials. Such a company is temporarily in a stronger competitive position with buyers than one that must pay the current higher material prices, and it can use its advantage to lure customers away from less favorably situated competitors.

One might argue that a company that has speculated successfully should take the profit directly by pricing on the basis of the higher replacement cost of the materials it holds. Such a policy would be suggested by the fact that some of its later speculations will turn out unfavorably and entail a loss since the company's finished-goods prices will have to reflect the lower materials costs. In a declining market the pressure for business will force companies to price their finished products on the basis of current materials costs, and this almost inevitably leads to inventory losses. A company should prepare for such losses by taking profits on inventories during periods of price appreciation. But, as was mentioned above, one company in a competitive industry cannot follow this policy by itself, and very frequently a few companies, by their policy of passing on to customers the advantages of successful speculation, will force an entire industry into speculative purchasing.

Where speculative buying is necessary, the question arises as to who should make the policy decision and the buying decisions relative thereto. Since the risks inherent in speculative buying are so great and the financial implications so far-reaching, it seems clear that the *policy* decision should be made by the highest executive authority in the company. In different situations this may be the president, the executive committee, or the board of directors. It is equally apparent that at this executive level the individuals have neither the time nor the close association with market situations to make the *specific* decisions about when and how much to buy. It has already been mentioned that the purchasing agent is not an expert in economic forecasting. He is, however, in close touch with the markets and has a wealth of information about past price trends and relationships. Therefore, he should have an important part in making specific buying decisions. He should, however, be assisted by a committee made up of other interested company officials.

The official in charge of the company's marketing research and sales forecasting should be a member of the committee. He can supply relevant data from sources other than the company's internal records, as well as the statistical means of interpreting both internal and external data. For example, he will be able to construct price indexes, fit trend lines, and compute correlations between what appear to be causally related price series. He will be able to aid the committee in making judgment by selecting the pertinent information bearing on the company's business from the wealth of statistical material published by the federal government and many private research agencies. For example, he can adapt information from the Department of Labor's basic commodity price index, which is published weekly, or its weekly and monthly wholesale price index, or its monthly report on employment and payrolls. He may secure a great variety of business statistics from the *Survey of Current Business* published monthly by the Department of Commerce. He may refer to business information published by the Federal Reserve System in its monthly *National Summary of Business Conditions* or its *Annual Survey of Consumer Finances*. Also, he will find about 30 of the most significant indexes summarized and published monthly in *Economic Indicators* prepared by the President's Council of Economic Advisers. The *Sta-*

tistical Abstracts published annually by the Bureau of the Census and its periodic census reports are similarly invaluable sources of historical data, on the basis of which one may sharpen his forecasting talents. In particular cases of statistician will find much valuable information available from industry trade associations and groups such as the National Association of Purchasing Management.

The financial division of the company has a vital concern about speculative purchasing, since it affects both the working capital position and the net income of the company. Consequently the speculative buying committee should include the treasurer or his deputy. Thus, as a minimum, the committee should have three members: the purchasing agent, the director of marketing research, and the treasurer. Because of its importance to the financial results, in industries where speculative buying is a dominant practice, the president may want to serve on the committee.

Speculative Buying versus Gambling

Frequently speculative buying of an extreme nature is referred to as gambling. If this is a proper statement, the difference between speculative buying and gambling is only one of degree, and the borderline between the two is perhaps impossible to establish. To admit that speculation and gambling are different only in the sense that gambling is an extreme form of speculation has serious ethical implications. In our society gambling generally is held to be socially undesirable, of questionable legality, and unethical in the eyes of many people. To put speculation in the same category with gambling casts doubt on a very pervasive and important business activity.

Actually one can draw a much sharper distinction between speculation and gambling—one that makes the two activities different in kind rather than degree. First, it should be admitted that the two activities are similar in many respects. Both practices involve a prediction of future events. Both involve a substantial element of risk. In both, the gain or loss is measured in monetary terms. The practitioners in either may operate on the basis of much or little knowledge.

However, there are two vital distinctions between them that make one respectable and necessary and the other questionable and unproductive. The first distinction is that speculation involves taking a financial interest in a risk that is in existence, whereas gambling involves the creation of a financial risk so that it may be assumed. In buying ahead for speculative reasons the buyer takes the risk of price changes off the shoulders of some other person who would otherwise be required to carry it. Thus there is merely the substitution of one risk-taker for another. In gambling the participants use the pretext of some uncertain future event as the occasion for creating a financial risk. The event that determines the outcome for the gamblers has no necessary financial implications. A horse race, a ball game, or a card game all have the element of uncertain outcome, but they could all occur with no money loss to anyone caused by the uncertain outcome. Thus the gambler creates new financial hazards, whereas the speculator deals with existing hazards.

One might argue that two speculators on a "futures" market are creating risks because they have no expectation of making or taking delivery of the product. In a sense this is true, and it leads to the second difference between speculating and gambling. There is no economic necessity for gambling and no service to the economy resulting from it. By contrast, the speculators, as an incident to their transactions, are performing a service to the economy. A sound economy requires a reasonable projection of the present price level into the future. In order for future price levels to be related to present price levels, there must be speculators who express their convictions in the form of financial commitment. This is one of the economic functions of the speculator. Another of his functions is the somewhat more specialized one of helping to create an active futures market on organized commodity exchanges so that hedging becomes a sounder and safer technique of price protection. This point will be developed more fully in the following section.

COMMODITY EXCHANGES

One of the major risks of business is the risk of loss through the effect of adverse price fluctuations on raw-material, in-process, and finished-goods inventories. Such risks can be substantially reduced for commodities for which organized futures markets exist through the practice of hedging. It is the purpose of this section to describe some aspects of the operations of commodity exchanges and to discuss some of the ways in which purchasing agents can make use of hedging.

The Nature of Hedging

Hedging[1] is a procedure designed to minimize risks resulting from adverse price fluctuations in a cash commodity. In simplest terms hedging amounts to entering simultaneously into two transactions of a like amount—the one a purchase and the other a sale—in two markets whose prices are known to move up and down together by approximately the same amounts. If one can find any two commodity-price series that move together, he can accomplish the object of hedging—the cancellation of gains and losses from price changes—by buying one commodity, and selling a like amount of the other for purchase and delivery at a later date. If prices go up, he will realize an inventory profit on the commodity he bought, but, since prices move together and in like amount, he will suffer a loss of an equivalent amount in selling the second commodity. If prices go down, the buyer will lose on his purchase but will gain a like amount on his sale for future delivery.

Hedging is, therefore, defined as the process of entering simultaneously into two contracts of an opposite nature—one in the cash market, the other in the futures market—whose primary purpose is to protect operating profit margins. Essentially, it involves the transfer of price risk to a specialist in risk taking—the speculator.

In practice, it is virtually impossible to find two different commodity-price series that move together so closely that they can be used for price protection. For this reason, among others, traders in a number of commodity fields have organized futures markets to serve this purpose.

Historical Development

Trading in futures contracts on an organized basis originated with the Chicago Board of Trade which has been in operation since 1848. Today, there are 40 to 50 commodities traded on a dozen different U.S. commodity exchanges.

The earliest markets and exchanges were developed around agricultural commodities such as wheat and corn. Today commodity trading has been broadened significantly into such nonagricultural products as silver, lumber, copper, and even international currencies. This

---

[1] A complete report of hedging procedures and research on purchasing's role in this procedure is available from either N.A.P.M. or Merril Lynch: G. J. Zenz, "Futures Trading and the Purchasing Executive," (New York: National Association of Purchasing Management and Merrill Lynch, Pierce Fenner & Smith, Inc., 1971), 42 pages.

expanded development has sparked the interest of industrial firms as they attempt to protect fluctuating raw material costs and to stabilize international transactions conducted in an atmosphere of volatile prices and currencies.

In the five-year period 1969–1973, futures volume more than doubled. The tremendous increases in futures trading can be seen from the following charts depicting number of trades and their value.[2]

	Trades (Millions)	Approximate Value (Billions)
1969	22.4	81.3
1970	27.2	135.6
1971	29.1	155.0
1972	36.7	189.4
1973	51.6	399.3

In an attempt to reduce price risks, early American businessmen developed what was known as the "to-arrive" contract. Under terms of this agreement, the seller assured the delivery of his goods at a future date at a price fixed at the time of the initial contract. Hence, the buyer had protection, but the seller bore the brunt of any risks associated with downward changes in price during the interval between the contracting and delivery dates.

These risks increased greatly as American markets expanded, resulting in greater in-transit time, the necessity of carrying larger inventories, extending credit, and so forth. In short, mechanization, industrialization, and large-scale production increased the risk of price fluctuations to the point where the seller often no longer could give the "to arrive" price protection.

It was because of this risk dilemma that futures trading and commodity exchanges developed. Essentially, the exchange provided a physical meeting place for buyers and sellers, and organized and regulated the trading of futures contracts. The exchange itself does not engage in buying or selling contracts; it merely acts as a clearing house for recording transactions. Exchanges gradually expanded their functions to include the role of supervision of some specifics of trading, including such considerations as trading hours, collateral transfer

---

[2] Trades will be approximately double the number of contracts. Figures supplied by Association of Commodity Firms, New York, N.Y.

fees, margin requirements, and contract provisions. By formulating and enforcing trading rules, the exchanges help assure speculators and hedgers that their contracts will be honored.

A futures market is essentially a second market for a commodity, with its transactions limited to purchases and sales for delivery in future months. However, since the commodity concerned is the same in the futures market and in the regular market—usually called the "spot" or "cash" market—the prices will move up and down more or less in accord because both markets are affected by the same price-making forces. The hedger then takes one position (purchase or sale) in the cash market and the opposite (sale or purchase) in the futures market. Thus he can have reasonable assurance that his gain or loss in one market will be offset for the most part by a loss or gain in the other.

Carrying Charges

Usually the price of a futures contract is higher than the cash commodity. The difference is represented by all or part of the charge of carrying (i.e., the cost of storage, insurance, and interest charges) the cash commodity to the futures month. For example, if cash wheat in April is selling for $3.50 a bushel and carrying costs are 2 cents a bushel per month, July wheat futures would theoretically sell for $3.56 per bushel.

However, if enough traders feel that there will be a greatly increased supply of wheat between April and July, it is possible that the futures price could be less than the cash price. This would result in what is called an "inverted" market, a condition that occurs infrequently.

Reasons for Hedging

Hedging has the advantage of safeguarding profit margins when sales contracts with fixed prices are negotiated, but the raw material purchase is postponed. Hedging may also be of benefit in protecting inventory values in a declining market period. Trading in futures can be utilized to guarantee delivery of a raw material without storing physical stock and incurring finance and carrying charges. It may also be used to establish a favorable material price, again without necessitating purchase of actual inventory.

These practices are not included as hedging because they may involve taking a position in futures without having a corresponding physical inventory or an established selling price. Nevertheless, for the purchasing executive, they represent important tactical possibilities which are now being used to a greater extent than in the past. A related benefit of hedging is that banks will usually lend a greater percentage of inventory value pledged for collateral when this inventory is protected by a hedge.

The Buying Hedge

The buying hedge is used to establish raw material costs when a sales contract has been executed which calls for subsequent purchase of raw materials. As an example, assume that on April 1, XYZ Company sells generators for delivery on September 30. It is reasonable to assume that the April 1 sales price is predicated upon raw material prices existing on April 1, of which copper will be used for illustrative purposes.

The selling manufacturer has three choices in this situation. He can buy his copper in April and hold it until September or whenever processing will begin. By doing so, he would establish the price but would incur storage, interest, and insurance costs on the copper until used.

His second alternative is to execute the buying hedge. This action will establish the copper cost with limited risk of price change and without incurring the cost of carrying physical inventory. Simply stated, the buy hedge involves the purchase of a futures contract at the time of the sales transaction (April 1) and the later sale of a futures contract when the physical copper is purchased. Since futures and cash prices tend to fluctuate together, any profit or loss because of the change in cash price of copper between April and September 1 will be largely offset by a profit or loss in the futures contract. Diagrammatically the transactions involved in the buy hedge are as follows:

Cash

April 1—sell 25,000 lb., based on 80¢ prevailing price
  (copper in form of generators)

Futures

April 1—buy 25,000 lb. September futures @ 85¢
  (difference in cash and future prices due to carrying charges)

At this point, the manufacturer has hedged. He has entered into two contracts of an opposite nature, selling in the cash market and buying in the futures market.

Because the futures and cash markets tend to move together, a change in one price will be largely offset by a change in the price of the other market. Let us assume that on September 1, the price of copper has increased to 85 cents per pound. If the manufacturer had not hedged, he would find his profit margin cut considerably as the generators' sales prices were predicated on the 80 cents copper. However, because he has bought a futures contract (in technical terms he is "long" futures), the rise in the cash price of copper will be reflected in a rise in the price of September futures. Therefore, the loss sustained because the cash price advanced from 80 cents to 85 cents will be offset by a gain in the futures transaction when the September futures contract is sold.

Completing the diagrammatic representation:

<table>
<tr><td colspan="3" align="center">Cash</td></tr>
<tr><td>April 1—sell</td><td>25m lb.</td><td>@80¢</td></tr>
<tr><td>Sept. 1—buy</td><td>25m lb.</td><td>@85¢</td></tr>
<tr><td></td><td align="right">Loss</td><td>−5¢</td></tr>
<tr><td colspan="3" align="center">Futures—September Copper</td></tr>
<tr><td>April 1—buy</td><td>25m lb.</td><td>@85¢</td></tr>
<tr><td>Sept. 1—sell</td><td>25m lb.</td><td>@90¢</td></tr>
<tr><td></td><td align="right">Gain</td><td>+5¢</td></tr>
</table>

The hedging transaction is now complete. By taking the profit from the futures transaction and applying it to the cash price paid in August, the XYZ Company has in effect purchased its copper at 80 cents per pound—the price on which its sale was originally predicated.

But what if the price of copper drops, for example, to 75 cents in the cash market? Would not the manufacturer lose in the futures market because he bought at one price (85¢) and will have to sell at a lower price (75¢)? The answer is yes. In this case, there is a loss in the futures market. However, there is a "gain" in the cash market because XYZ Company originally anticipated paying 80 cents for the copper—and they sold it at this 80 cents price in the form of generators. Now in September when they actually buy the copper they have an abnormal profit (selling at 80¢, buying at 75¢) which offsets the futures loss.

The Selling Hedge

The selling hedge is used when the purchasing executive has a physical inventory whose value is declining because the open market price is dropping. Let us assume that XYZ Company normally carries a 60-day inventory of 1 million pounds of copper. Assume further that sales decline because of a cutback in automotive production so that his 1 million pounds now represent four months' average inventory. We can make the example even more realistic by assuming that the firm has forward purchase commitments that will continue to inflate the inventory.

Chances are that the slowdown in XYZ's automotive sales will be reflected elsewhere in the business world and these pressures may result in a declining copper price. What can the purchasing executive do when inventory is excessive and continuing to expand while its value is declining?

The traditional purchasing executive would probably concentrate on the supply side of this inventory problem. He would attempt to defer future shipments from suppliers and allow time to "eat up" his inventory. This procedure will take at least two months (in our illustration) and during that time he will actually be using relatively expensive copper. Sales of XYZ's finished product will probably be predicated on price-in-effect at time of shipment. This means that the firm will be "losing" its normal profit margin by using expensive copper while being restricted in the sales price of generators which are predicated on the prevailing lower copper prices.

Another alternative for the traditional purchasing executive would be to sell the excess inventory in the open market. This is a cumbersome procedure that requires the development of sales contracts, negotiation of sales prices, and related concerns which usually are not within the purchasing domain.

The third alternative is to hedge the physical inventory price by selling futures contracts. Because the futures price will reflect declines in the cash market, the futures profit can be used to offset the diminishing cash value. By doing so, inventory value losses are minimized without moving any physical stock. In a diagrammatic form the sell hedge looks as follows:

Cash

April 1—have 500,000 lb excess inventory at today's value of 80¢/pound. A reduction in price is anticipated.

Futures

April 1—sell 500,000 lb (20 contracts) of July futures at today's price of 85¢.

At this point the firm has hedged its excess inventory. It has entered into simultaneous transactions of an opposite nature—holding physical stock, while selling contracts in the futures market. The loss or gain in one market should offset the loss or gain in the other market.

Let us assume that copper prices do decline so that on June 1, when the excess inventory has been used, the cash price is 70 cents per pound. The firm has lost 10 cents per pound on its physical inventory. However, the futures market will also reflect the lower price. And because this alert executive is short futures, when the futures contract is liquidated he will pay less than his sale price. Consequently, he will have a futures profit to offset the cash loss.

Again, using a diagrammatic illustration, the transaction would be as follows:

Cash

April 1—holds 500,000 excess @ 80¢ lb

June 1—sells the excess inventory in the form of generators at the reduced market price of 70¢ per lb
_____
Loss 10¢ lb

Futures

April 1—sells 500,000 lb of copper (July @ 85¢ per lb

June 1—buys 500,000 lb of July copper @ 71¢ per lb
_____
Gain 14¢

The sell hedge has allowed the XYZ Company to consume its excess inventory in a declining market while tying its price to the lower, declining cash commodity levels. This has been accomplished without moving or selling physical inventory. The purpose of the selling hedge is to keep the actual value of an inventory close to the declining market price.

If the prices of copper had risen between April and June, there would be, leaving basis considerations aside, a corresponding loss on the futures transaction with a gain on the physical inventory value. The hedge will still perform its purpose—establishing the inventory price at a predetermined level and avoiding profits or losses resulting from commodity value changes.

However, if the firm was certain that prices would rise, it is obvious that they would merely enjoy increased profits resulting from the price rise. As indicated in the buy-hedge example, such perfect knowledge is rarely available—and therin lies the rationale for hedging.

Simplifying Assumptions

The transactions just cited contain certain assumptions which should be examined at this time. It was assumed in the buy hedge that the changes in price in the cash and futures markets were equal. When the cash market changed by 10¢, the futures market changed by the same amount. This would constitute an ideal hedge, but in reality the changes between the two markets may not be exactly the same.

In the first illustration, April cash and September futures were used. During the intervening months, between the time the hedge was placed (April in this case), the potential supply/demand picture for copper may change. For example, an election in Chile in May could reduce that country's potential production and influence prospects for future supply. This could cause the futures price to rise more than the cash price, which reflects today's supply and demand. Another influencing possibility is a change in the U.S. tariff policies; this could increase imports and therefore, depress futures to an amount lower than the cash price. These are just some of the factors that could cause the cash and futures markets to deviate from the partial or full carrying charge spread.

In cases when the two markets do not fluctuate proportionately, the hedge may be imperfect. One can generalize, however, and say that prices usually move together and, therefore, hedges provide protection against major price fluctuations. In reality, the benefit of futures hedging is that one avoids the major risk of fluctuations in the price of the commodity, for the much smaller risk involved in the fluctuations between the cash price and that of futures. There is a risk, but it is only a fraction of the risk one faces without a hedge.

A second assumption made in the previous examples was that the contract grade of the futures contract was the same as the grade used by the manufacturer. They may not be exactly the same. The difference determines the imperfection of the hedge. However, we assume the relationship, even if imperfect, is still close enough to eliminate major price risks, which is the hedger's main worry.

Other Uses of Futures Markets

Hedging, in the true sense of the word, involves a cash position (either in plant inventory or a sales contract calling for future material requirements) and an offsetting futures position. Under these conditions, a loss or gain in one market will offset (within the limits already discussed) the gain or loss in the other market. However, futures markets may be effectively used by the sophisticated purchasing executive, providing he/she and management fully recognize the risks inherent in these practices. The use of the futures market for anticipatory pricing and as a supply assurance aid are logical, legitimate tools that the purchasing executive should be prepared to utilize. In this context, one can view the following use of futures trading as a possible exercise of one's best business judgment.

Anticipatory Pricing

The traditional responsibilities of the purchasing executive include obtaining material at the right price, time, quantity, and quality. We shall be concerned with the first two aspects—price and time—in the following review of futures trading. Note that we have now changed terminology. The use of futures trading is being substituted for hedging because the requirement of a cash-and-futures position will not be met in these applications as they were in the previous examples.

A purchasing executive obviously is very knowledgeable about the raw material he buys. By reviewing the trade papers and daily contacts with suppliers, he is constantly aware of existing and impending supply/demand changes. Suppose he is convinced that today's price for one of his materials—silver—is very low, perhaps even artificially low. He would probably check his inventory, review projected sales, evaluate carrying charges, and balance all these variables against the advantages of increasing existing inventory buying at the low price. He may suggest forward buying. Certainly management expects him to continually explore such possible cost savings.

Assuming that approval is received, the executive will contract for additional supplies at the favorable price and negotiate delivery schedules accordingly. If prices rise as anticipated, management is both impressed and pleased. But if prices decline, the firm is faced with an inflated inventory, resulting carrying charges, and is paying a price during the delivery contract which is higher than the market. In effect, the purchasing executive's action has involved the firm in considerable expense.

Traditional alternatives available to the executive are few. He can attempt to cancel the contracts, which probably won't be successful, or he can attempt to sell the excess inventory. The latter alternative is also likely to be unpalatable because of the difficulty in locating buyers and moving stock. In effect, there is likely to be no workable alternative except to wait for time to consume the stock and heal the wounds.

Does this mean that anticipatory pricing is not a sound purchasing procedure? Definitely not—a right price is very often a judgment price and therefore subject to error. With his intimate knowledge of the market, the purchasing executive will have a minimum of such decision mistakes.

But the purpose of this rather lengthy discussion was not to justify buying ahead when conditions are extremely favorable. The point is to illustrate the use of futures trading as an alternate means of establishing a favorable price without carrying the stock, without paying full price for it, and with the flexibility to reverse the decision with minimum cost if conditions change. That is what anticipatory price via the futures market is all about.

Anticipatory pricing in the futures market simply means taking a long position—buying a futures contract when the cash price appears favorable (this assumes, of course, a normal basis differential exists). This will establish the price. Before the futures month reaches maturity, the contract is sold and profits are applied to offset the actual commodity purchase, whose price and value would have risen in the interim.

For example, assume that on February 1, 1971, silver is priced at $1.65 per troy oz, which is considered an attractive price. After a review of anticipated sales, existing inventory, and carrying costs, it is decided to purchase 60,000 troy oz of July futures to establish the price.

Assume further that by May 1, the price has risen to $2.24/oz, and it is decided that this is a normal price level. The futures contract can now be sold and the profit ($2.25-$1.65) used to offset the higher price paid when buying physical silver for actual production requirements.

Diagrammatically, the procedure would look as follows:

Futures

February 1—buy July (assuming normal carrying charges)
@ $1.75

May 1—sell July   @ $2.29

Gain @ $0.54

By taking the 54 cents gain and subtracting this amount from the cash price prevailing on May 1 ($2.25), the cost of silver has almost been reduced to the price prevailing on February 1—the most favorable price.

As can be seen, this low February price was established without incurring physical inventory or carrying costs. Because the margin requirement on such purchases is only a small percentage of the contract value (usually about 10%) and treasury bills can often be used as original margin, allowing the buyer to continue to receive interest, the cost of carrying the futures position from February to May is minimal.

If the price decision pegged in February is incorrect, the executive can liquidate his futures position at any time and absorb the losses. This is in contrast to taking in physical stock in February and then experiencing the disturbing downward price while having no alternative but to go out into the open market and sell the inventory—a procedure that has already been explained as being undesirable and perhaps impossible.

In summary, anticipatory pricing involves the fixing of a favorable price by taking a long position in the futures market. It involves less risk and cost than purchasing physical stock at the favorable price level. The futures market also provides a means to leave the market if the pricing judgment proves incorrect, with a minimum of cost and effort.

Guarantee Supply

By purchasing futures contracts and taking delivery when they come due, the purchasing executive can guarantee supply even during periods of strikes or other shortages. The exchanges place extremely heavy penalties on nonperformance. This guarantees the company, which has a long position, delivery if any of the commodity is available. However, acts of God, civil disturbance, and similar extreme events could result in "force majeur" and necessitate cash settlements rather than physical delivery. These would be rare occurrences.

In contemplating actual delivery an important consideration here is that the grade of the commodity used may not be the same as the contract grade. Also, the delivery point specified in the contract will probably not coincide with the manufacturing location at which the material will be used. However, brokers can usually arrange the exchange of goods and locations necessary to present a usable commodity. Cost premiums to adjust grades and locations are relatively minimal. It should be noted, however, that because of the variables involved (grades, locations, "force majeur," etc.) the use of futures as a partial source of supply should be undertaken only after the purchasing executive has gained considerable expertise in futures trading.

Summary of Characteristics of Hedging

In summary, the futures market provides strategic tools for the purchasing executive in addition to straight price protection of his cash position. By effectively using anticipatory pricing procedures, he can establish prices without incurring inventory and carrying costs. In addition, futures trading provides the flexibility necessary to liquidate his position if the initial pricing decision is in error, or if supply/demand conditions change. Also, supply can be at least partially protected during periods of shortage. Finally, the review of supply/demand information can significantly aid the executive in routine price negotiations as well as providing background for important decisions concerning economical inventory levels.

The essential element in all hedging or futures transactions is the futures contract. It has been indicated previously that these contracts are legally binding agreements to buy or sell a specific quantity and quality of a commodity during a specific month. While this is true, over 97% of all futures contracts are satisfied—not by delivery, but by a procedure known as offset: buying back a futures contract that was previously sold, or vice versa. In other words, the purchasing executive and other futures traders will usually offset their futures position without taking delivery (the exception being the case when the futures contract is entered into as a supply mechanism). The firm pays or receives, as the case may be, the difference in price between the purchase and sale contract.

Basis has been defined as the difference between the cash and futures contract price. By observing the amount and direction of basis changes, favorable profits from futures trades can be enhanced. As has already been stated, futures contracts usually sell at premiums to cash market prices because of the amount of full or partial carrying charges.

In general, then, carrying charges set the theoretical maximum by which futures can exceed the cash price. If this maximum is exceeded, it becomes profitable to buy the cash commodity and simultaneously sell the futures and eventually deliver against the futures contract. The effect of this action is to drive up the price of cash (the result of many people buying) and/or drive down the futures price (resulting from heavy sales). The net effect is to restore a normal carrying charge differential.

On the other hand, there is no automatic mechanism to correct an imbalance if carrying charges are absent. (i.e., if futures should be equal to or less than cash). The cash price can go higher than futures because of predicted changes in supply and demand. For example, a strike or political upheaval in a major foreign producing country. In these cases, perfect sell hedges will not be found and the price protection value will be reduced. The result is that under these conditions it may be better not to use the sell hedge. Of course, the "inversion" creates attractive hedging opportunities for prospective buy hedgers.

Some Difficulties in Hedging

Hedging has been described as the cancellation of gains and losses from price changes. This is an accurate description in the ideal situation. However, the situation frequently is not ideal, and the purchasing agent should be aware of some of the departures from the ideal that he will experience in practice.

Basis versus "Acceptable" Grades

The prices quoted on the futures market are for the basis grade of the commodity. This basis grade is the grade in which the largest volume of business is transacted. All other acceptable grades have their prices set by the exchange in relation to the basis grade. In other words, to find the price of a particular grade one adds the established premium or discount to the price of the basis grade. This works well so long as the trade differentials and the exchange differentials between the grades are the same, or approximately so. However, in a particular year, assume that the highest-quality grade was in short supply whereas the basis grade was in average supply. Suppose that Company A agreed to sell a specified quantity of finished goods requiring the highest-quality grade and price its finished goods on the prevailing price of the basis grade of raw material plus the exchange differential for the highest-quality grade. Company A then bought futures for the amount needed, expecting to buy the actual raw material when it was required for processing. By the time Company A got around to buying its actual raw material, the shortage conditions would have driven the price up, and the cost might be well above that on which it priced its finished goods. According to the theory of hedging, this loss should be offset by the gain Company A would realize on the sale of its futures contracts. But in this case the supply and demand conditions for the basis grades were normal, and so its price would not advance correspondingly. Thus Company A would have lost money, even though it had hedged its short position.

Of course, the outcome would have been the same if Company A had hedged a long spot position of high-quality raw materials by selling futures and then found that either the high-quality materials were in surplus supply or that the high-quality, supply-demand conditions were normal but that the basis grade was in short supply. One can work out several such situations, all of which serve to illustrate that hedging is not perfect price protection because of variations between the basis grade and other grades. The purchasing agent should realize that the function of hedging is to *minimize* losses rather than to eliminate them.

Open Interest

Another point that often causes difficulty for the unskilled hedger is that the price of futures sometimes tends to be erratic during the month when the futures contracts must be fulfilled by completing the round turn—that is, making the opposite contract—or by making or taking delivery. This erratic price behavior is likely to be the result of either of two factors. First, the "open interest" is too small to permit the purchase or sale of a substantial number of contracts without significantly affecting the price. The open interest refers to the number of unliquidated contracts or open commitments. If the open interest in a particular month is 2000 contracts, this means that there are outstanding 2000 contracts to buy (long contracts) and 2000 contracts to sell (short contracts). If a particular hedger has 200 short contracts which he decides must be covered by purchasing 200 contracts, it is evident that his action will tend to raise the price.

Certifiable Inventory

Another factor is the amount of the commodity certified for delivery in the month. If this amount is small, those who are "long" in the particular month will be reluctant to sell until the price has been bid up substantially. Suppose, for instance, that in the example there are 1000 contract lots certified for delivery. It is apparent that only 1000 of the 2000 outstanding contracts can be satisfied by actual delivery of commodity. The remaining "short" traders will have to fulfill their contracts by buying from the "longs." Sensing this situation, the long traders will not sell until the price has advanced as much as they dare force it up. To avoid such squeezes, the experienced and careful hedger will use a futures month far enough ahead so that he can lift his hedge before such price "jockeying" begins. If he has made a mistake and the delivery month approaches before he is ready to lift his hedge, he will transfer the hedge forward by, for example, buying to close out the hedge in the at-hand month and selling in a forward month to reestablish the hedge.

A hedger will also watch the open-interest figures, which are published daily, because they give him a clue to the explanation of price behavior on the futures market. For example, if the price is up and the open interest is increased, this indicates new demand in the market and suggests that the market is strong and the price sound. On the other hand, if the price is up and the open interest is decreased, it suggests that the demand has come from shorts who have entered the market to cover their short commitments. Such a demand does not suggest a basically strong market but rather a technical imbalance in the futures market. If prices are declining and the open interest is decreased, it suggests that the long interests are liquidating their holdings. If prices decline while the open interest increases, it suggests that short selling is the cause. From these clues the purchasing agent can glean information that will aid him in interpreting price changes.

Size of Market

The purchasing agent interested in hedging should also consider the size of the futures market he will use, and its composition in terms of number and types of traders. Many of the futures markets are so small that a fairly large company attempting to use the market for hedging will find that its single influence may be so great that, when it buys or sells, its influence forces prices up or down. Thus it will determine prices rather than having them determined for it. Also, one should be careful about hedging in a market that is dominated by a few large companies even though one may be small himself, because one can never be sure what action the few large companies may take. They might upset normal price relationships at any time by their activity and render the market worse than useless for hedging by other traders.

Dissimilar Products

Another point that should be kept in mind about hedging is that the protection it affords is reasonably complete only when the product for which the price is being hedged is identical with or very closely similar to the product traded on the futures market. If the products are identical, it is reasonable to expect the price series to move together. As the products diverge in characteristics, the expectation of their price series moving together decreases, because unrelated costs intervene. For example, an automobile tire manufacturer using cotton for its fabric will not get much protection from hedging its cotton inventory on the cotton futures market, since the price of tires is quite unrelated to the price of cotton. Similarly, a manufacturer of men's cotton shirts would get only moderate protection from hedging because the costs of labor and processing determine the price of shirts more than the price of cotton does. A manufacturer of cotton sheets would secure more protection because the cost of cotton is a more important part of total cost. A manufacturer of cotton batting would obtain still greater price protection because the price of cotton determines the price of batting to a substantial degree.

It should not be inferred from the preceding paragraph that hedging is inappropriate for the tire and shirt makers. They can protect their cotton prices through hedging. The significant fact is that the protection of the price of cotton is less important to the total operations of the tire and shirtmakers than it is to the sheet and batting makers.

Finally, and obviously, hedging is of the greatest importance to manufacturers who use raw materials that are subject to wide and sudden price fluctuations.

The Role of the Speculator

The speculator has always been the object of suspicion and censure by moralists, politicians, and the uninformed. We shall not attempt at this point to justify his role in society other than to point out that his activity should not be classified as gambling, since he is assuming an existing and necessary risk. He is also a vital factor to the success of hedging. Usually there is not enough hedging activity to support an active, year-round market. This essential market activity is created by the speculator who buys and sells futures contracts on the basis of his personal judgment, in the hope of making a profit from the trading without needing or expecting to take possession of the commodity.

In the hedging process the speculator serves the dual function of creating activity (so a hedger can always find someone to take the other side of the transaction) and of stabilizing prices. The second function is also an important one. The hedger's interest in buying or selling is determined for him by his long or short position in the spot commodity. If several hedgers need protection against long positions, their combined selling of futures will tend to depress the price and destroy the normal relationship of spot and futures prices. The speculator, however, is looking at the price level in the light of its consistency with supply and demand. If several hedgers by their selling activity depressed the price abnormally, the speculator would step in and buy because it would appear to him that the price had gone down without sound underlying reasons. His purchases would tend to restore price to its proper level. This stabilizing influence that he provides for the market is an important economic contribution.

The Purchasing Agent and the Futures Market

It is customary for an officer of a company or a purchasing committee to determine what policy is to be followed in trading on the futures markets. Where this is handled by a purchasing committee, its members generally will consist of the purchasing agent and a representative of general management, finance, sales, and production. It is the responsibility of the purchasing agent to advise this committee with respect to market conditions and to have a knowledge of all other pertinent factors required by the committee. The committee decides on the quantity of coverage, which futures month to trade in, and other details of the hedging process.

In some companies the trading on commodity exchanges is entrusted solely to an officer of the company, who may or may not also be in charge of purchasing, or to the purchasing agent himself. In these instances the person responsible is a specialist and has had long and successful experience in futures trading. He must enjoy the complete confidence of the principals of his company since his actions can have an important effect on the company's financial structure.

Any individual or company contemplating the use of a futures market for hedging should make a careful study of the commodity and its trading practices. There are many costly mistakes that can be made by the novice. A good broker can be of real assistance to the beginner until the latter has built up his own technical knowledge of the operations of the futures market through experience.

DISCUSSION QUESTIONS

1. What is forward buying?

2. In what respect is hand-to-mouth buying similar to speculative buying?

3. Under what exceptional circumstances is hand-to-mouth buying the proper policy and why?

4. What is the principle distinction between forward buying and speculative buying?

5. Explain the following statement: "If one firm in an industry follows the practice of speculative buying, it may force the entire industry to follow suit."

6. What is hedging, and why is the practice undertaken by industrial firms?

7. Discuss how "open interest" figures affect hedging.

8. Explain why the speculator is socially necessary.

9. Why is it that not all commodities can be traded in the futures market?

10. What is the role of the purchasing agent in his company's futures market activities?

SUGGESTED CASES

Gorman Products, Inc.

Hearons Company

Weldon Coffee Roasters, Inc.

CHAPTER 17
LEGAL ASPECTS OF PURCHASING

The purchasing agent's primary responsibility is the procurement of goods or services from his company's suppliers. He does this through the creation of legal and binding commitments between his company and his suppliers. The existence of such contracts may afford protection and in many instances monetary recompense for nonperformance, but do not provide the goods or services needed to keep his company operating. the buyer who concentrates on legal protection at the expense of those decisions that assure delivery is doing a disservice to his company.

The primary interest of a purchasing agent in legal matters is to use a knowledge of the basic principles of law in such a way as to avoid litigation. Litigation is both costly and of uncertain outcome and should therefore be avoided except as a last resort. This is not meant to suggest that a purchasing agent should be a lawyer or that a buyer should rely on his own knowledge of the law in complicated situations or on controversial matters. One effective way in which a purchasing agent can minimize litigation is by investigating new suppliers as to their ability to perform, their financial responsibility, and their record of performance with other concerns. Such an investigation, of course, is a strictly nonlegal activity. It is also advisable for the purchasing agent to request a periodic review of the company's purchase-order terms and conditions by a competent attorney.

The Purchasing Agent and the Lawyer

A purchasing staff that manages to get delivery of precisely the materials and services that its company needs, at precisely the right place and time, and at the right price, has done its job. *How* the job was accomplished often appears to be of secondary importance. From some points of view the less effort, paper work, and detail are involved, the better. Undue precaution is a waste of time and money.

It is the responsibility of a company lawyer, nevertheless, to critically analyze even those transactions on which perfect purchasing results are achieved, in anticipation of the few cases that make legal trouble. One transaction, whether small or large in dollar amount, can mean serious legal problems, involving damage claims and legal costs that may undermine the financial stability of a company.

Legal trouble, like an accident, always seems a remote possibility until it happens. Whether it becomes a major or a minor tragedy for the company, depends principally on two things: (1) the lawyer's ability to resurrect, in a form permitting proof in court, a precise and detailed record of the transaction, including every "tacit understanding," conversation, proviso, fact, and circumstance involved; and (2) the conformity of the company's conduct and procedure, in the transaction in question, to legally established standards of proper performance.

Today many companies employ their own counsel for such work. Those that do not should have independent counsel available through a retainer arrangement. Even where legal counsel is readily available, however, a purchasing agent must know enough about the law to know when to consult the attorney.

A presentation of the legal aspects of purchasing could include many, and perhaps even most, of the major fields of commercial law. However, because of the breadth of subject matter of each of these fields and because many of them are infrequently a factor in purchases, only the more pertinent aspects of law are discussed in this chapter.

No attempt is made to turn the reader into a legal expert. It is believed, however, that a statement of some of the legal principles behind many of the routine practices of purchasing should provide an understanding of the reasons for their existence. Such an understanding should in turn create a respect for proper purchasing routine and a more intelligent handling of it.

Sources of Law

There are five important documentary sources of modern law:

1. Court opinions, reported and published over the years, deciding literally hundreds of thousands of prior legal controversies. Together, these are sometimes referred to as the "common law."
2. Federal and state constitutions, including their various amendments.
3. Federal, state, and local legislative enactments ("statutes" and "ordinances") governing a great variety of subjects. When grouped by subject, these enactments are sometimes referred to as "codes." For example, we speak of the "Building Code," the "Criminal Code," or the "Commercial Code." Especially in the commercial area, there has been a strong effort, not only to codify the law, but to codify it uniformly throughout the country. Since the turn of the century, two national organizations have assumed primary responsibility for this work: the Commissioners on Uniform Laws and the American Law Institute.

The Uniform Sales Act, which originated in 1909 and was subsequently adopted by every state except Louisiana, was for many years the prime source of law relating to purchases and sales of goods. Its principal weakness was its failure to cover a number of collateral subjects such as credit, shipping, inspection, and security terms of the sales transactions. After 10 years of work by the Commissioners and the Institute, the 1958 Draft of the Uniform Commercial Code was produced. With some amendment since 1958, that draft has supplanted more than a dozen earlier codifications of commercial law subjects. The Uniform Commercial Code (hereafter referred to as the UCC) has become the commercial law of every major business center of the country, except New Orleans. Its importance to purchasing can scarcely be exaggerated.

4. Published general orders and rulings of public regulatory or administrative boards, commissions, agencies, and departments.
5. "Secondary" sources, consisting of writings on legal subjects, prepared by attorneys, judges, professors, and the editorial staffs of legal publishing houses, primarily for the continuing education of lawyers.

Substantive and Adjective Law

It is not always possible to completely distinguish between the definition of a legal right in the abstract and a statement of the procedures and processes by which that right is enforced. Nevertheless, the abstract definition is called the "substantive" law of the subject, and the forms and procedures of enforcement are called "adjective" (or procedural) law. For our purposes, we shall largely ignore adjective law and attempt only a brief survey of those substantive principles that have frequent impact on the work of the purchasing agent.

Elements of Legal Claim

There are three basic elements in every legal claim: (1) A factual relationship of the parties, by which each party is entitled to have the other *act or refrain from acting* in a certain way. This is called the right-duty relationship. (2) *Conduct* of one or both parties that violates the right-duty relationship. This is called the "breach." (3) *Injury or damage* to one or both parties resulting from (caused by) the breach.

Kinds of Right-Duty Relationships. Legal rights and duties are classified according to the relationships from which they spring. The two basic relationships are public (the relationship between a citizen and an agency of government) and private (the relationship between two citizens).

Public relationships give rise to rights of government against the citizen (requiring the citizen to act or refrain from acting in certain ways) and to rights of the citizen against the government. In the first group, there are two major subclasses: (1) criminal laws and public regulatory laws and (2) revenue (tax) laws.

Constitutional and political guarantees are of fundamental importance among the laws defining the rights of citizens against their government; however, a host of other rights of the citizen, ranging from police protection to social security, are also included.

Agency

The overwhelming majority of the right-duty relationships in modern commercial law arise "vicariously," that is, through the agency of representatives rather than by direct dealings between natural persons on their personal accounts. A purchasing agent does not ordinarily buy for his own account, nor does a selling agent ordinarily sell for his own account. Before examining the specific rights and duties that arise out of the typical purchase transaction, therefore, we should appreciate the basic rules by which an agent can effectively bind his principal.

The question generally arises in one of three basic patterns. First, there is the case of the "general officer" of the selling or buying corporation, whose authority is very broad but not unlimited. Second, we have the case of the "limited agent" or employee, whose authority to represent the principal is, by definition, relatively specialized. Finally, there is the problem of the broker, distributor, or commission salesman, who may represent a seller in a still more limited manner.

In order for an agent to operate effectively in binding a principal, two things are necessary: The agent's authority must have been *broad enough* to cover the transaction in question, and the agent must have *exercised* that authority in negotiating the particular transaction.

Authority to act in the name or on behalf of a principal most commonly arises by *express* authorization. The principal tells the agent to undertake transactions of a given description in the principal's name, usually as a matter of job assignment. Every *express* authorization gives rise to a number of *implied* authorizations which empower the agent to do those things that are reasonably necessary or customary to carry out the expressly assigned job. No *implied* authority can arise, however, in direct contradiction of an *express limitation* of the agent's authority. Thus if a salesman is expressly prohibited from signing contracts, or from granting credit terms or other concessions not stated in the principal's published lists, or from negotiating with certain buyers, or from handling certain lines, his power in those respects is limited accordingly, regardless of how necessary or customary a broader authority might be.

Both *express* and *implied* authority are legally classified as forms of *actual* authorization. Their basic weakness, in everyday practice, lies in the fact that a person dealing with such an agent has no way, other than by direct inquiry of the principal, of knowing just how far his actual authority extends. The *agent's own assurance may not be used* to prove actual authority unless the principal has somehow *seconded* those assurances.

The last-mentioned possibility—that the principal has *apparently* authorized the agent to contract in the principal's name—represents the most common ground upon which a third party, dealing with an agent who is exceeding his actual authority, can nevertheless hold the principal responsible. The keynote of apparent authority is the third party's *reliance* on appearances of authority for which the principal was responsible. A supplier who, for example, gives a free-lance commission salesperson a set of the supplier's order forms or other restricted sales materials, or who gives such a salesperson an office at the supplier's place of business, or who rather regularly receives and fills orders written by such a salesperson, may well create an appearance of agency despite the fact that the salesperson has no actual authority to bind the supplier. Furthermore, a principal who knowingly accepts the product (sometimes called the "fruit") of an unauthorized transaction *ratifies* the transaction and binds himself as thoroughly as though he had originally authorized it.

Obviously, However, a person claiming either implied or apparent agency cannot ignore a plain contradiction of that claim, which the purported principal has taken pains to circulate. Printed sales materials often contain statements that directly deny the authority of any but certain designated agents to represent the seller, the most common clause being one that states, in effect: "No obligation shall arise against the seller unless this order is accepted at the principal office of the seller."

In summary, purchasing officers should be aware of the agency problem in two respects. First, they should recognize company limitations on their own authority to obligate their own companies and should take pains to inform suppliers' representatives of these limitations in transactions where they may apply. Second, they should routinely verify the authority of purported suppliers' agents, especially where the agent's connection with the supplier is indirect, indistinct, or doubtful. A fully authorized agent will usually have no difficulty in producing satisfactory credentials and will not take offense if he is asked to do so. The representative who resents having his authority questioned is often attempting to "work both sides of the street," legally representing no one.

Contracts—Expressed and Implied

"Claims sounding in contract," as the lawyer often expresses it, are those that arise from rights and duties that the parties have voluntarily undertaken by the terms of an agreement. They arise because one party has either not done something that he agreed to do or has done something that he agreed not to do. Implicit in the concept is the idea that, aside from his agreement, he was under no legal duty to the claimant to act or not to act in that particular way. The *agreement*, then, is the heart of contractual liability. It is its source, its definition, and its limitation.

However, one must be careful not to exaggerate the coverage of the contract itself, so as to suppose that, unless the agreement specifically and *expressly* calls for a given detail of performance, the performance is not required. Nor is it correct, on the other hand, to assume that every specific and express stipulation to which the parties agree invariably raises a corresponding duty of performance in that regard.

Some contracts arise without any express agreement whatever.

They are totally implied, and arise out of the *conduct* of the parties, rather than from their verbal or written agreements. If a supplier, for example, delivers goods that his customer has not ordered, but the customer receives and uses the shipment, a contract to pay for the shipment arises by implication.

Again, under some circumstances, the law will imply certain stipulations not mentioned by the parties in their express agreements. Such implied stipulations are of two kinds: those implied-in-fact and those implied-in-law. Agreements are implied-in-fact when reason and common sense indicate that the parties probably took the matter for granted and simply failed to say anything about it. To determine what terms, conditions, and stipulations will be implied into an agreement in this way, we must consider all of the circumstances under which the agreement was made (at least so far as those circumstances were known to *both* parties), including: (1) the terms of the express agreement, (2) the terms that are standard or customary, either in past dealings between the same parties (called a "course of dealing" in the UCC) or generally in the industry (called a "usage of trade"), and (3) any legal rules of interpretation that may have been established, by statute or judicial decision, to govern questions of that kind.

Stipulations implied-in-law consist of those terms and agreements that the law itself imposes on all contracts because, without them, the agreement would violate public law. For example, an agreement to construct a bathroom implies that the plumber will be licensed, that building and plumbing permits will be obtained, and that the workmanship and materials will comply with applicable codes. An agreement for transport, by rail, road, or air, implies a stipulation that all applicable regulatory rules will be observed, including those requiring licenses and permits, and further implies that the rates are in accordance with approved tariff schedules.

Matters implied-in-law into a given agreement, unlike matters implied-in-fact, may override even express stipulations to the contrary. Put another way, the law will not insist that the parties intended a certain point of agreement, which they expressly stated differently or to the contrary, *unless* the point was one on which they had no real choice, because public law permitted them only one possibility. For example, tariff schedules control the rates that public utilities and regulated passenger and freight carriers may and must charge. Even though a contract stipulates a different rate, it is implied-in-law that the parties intended to contract at the legal rate.

The line between statutes and other laws that are merely interpretative of private agreements and those that are aimed at public regulation sometimes becomes extremely fine. As a result, it may occasionally become a delicate matter to distinguish between contract terms that are inescapable, because they are implied-in-law, and those that are *disclaimable*, because they are implied only where the agreement is not expressly to the contrary. This problem is present when a contract, by its express terms, attempts to *exculpate* (i.e., declare blameless) conduct that is "tortious."

Torts

Private rights and duties "sounding in tort" are legally *imposed* on all persons who stand in a certain relationship to each other, and in that sense arise without regard to any voluntary agreements. "Tortious conduct" is that which violates the legally protected interests of another, either by act or failure to act.

Many acts that violate public law are also tortious when regarded from the standpoint of their private victim. Indeed, the act may also constitute a breach of contract. For example, a drug supplier contracts to deliver a shipment of penicillin. Federal and state Pure Food and Drug laws prescribe certain standards of quality and purity for such drugs, which the supplier violates. The customer, a retailer, resells half the lot before the deficiencies are discovered, and several consumers are injured by reason of the poor quality. By one act, the supplier has "breached":

1. His public duty, subjecting him to fine, imprisonment, or other penalty.
2. His contract duty to his customer, subjecting him to payment of damages to the customer.
3. His tort duty to his retailing customer.
4. His tort duty to the injured consumers with whom he had no direct contact whatever.

It is erroneous to conclude, however, that tort duties are limited to cases in which the prohibited conduct constitutes a violation of public law. There is a vast area of tort law that is strictly private in its applications.

Intentional Torts. Torts are classified into three groups: intentional, unintentional, and strict. Intentional torts are those in which the invasion of another's interests is more or less deliberate. Most of the intentional torts have close parallels in public law crimes, such as theft, embezzlement, obtaining money or property under false pretenses (confidence games), assaults, and various types of fraudulent schemes. But there are a number of other torts that are classified as intentional principally because they are not clearly unintentional. These are less commonly proscribed as crimes, but may have considerable importance in the commercial world. They include:

1. Conversion—the assertion of ownership in the property of another. The subtlety of this tort lies in the fact that an *innocent* mistake as to the rightful ownership is *not* a complete defense.
2. Patent or copyright infringement, of which a person may be guilty despite the fact that the infringing product or process was purely of his own invention.
3. Misrepresentation and deceit, which do not necessarily require that the false statement be uttered as a deliberate lie, but include a number of cases in which one falsely certifies to the truth or accuracy of a matter on which he is innocently mistaken.
4. Defamation (libel and slander) to which the defense, "I honestly believed it was true," is very rarely available. Parenthetically, one should note that the reputation of a company or business may be tortiously defamed as easily as that of an individual, and often involves substantially greater damages.
5. Tortious interference with contract, which consists, essentially, of inducing another to violate his contractual obligations with a third person, the claimant. The battle among business competitors comes under severe restrictions after a contract has been made.
6. Conspiracy to fix prices or control markets, and unlawful price discrimination. Since these are almost purely statutory torts, they merit separate consideration.

Unintentional (Negligent) Torts.   Negligence is defined as a failure to exercise *ordinary care* to avoid *unreasonable* risks of harm to the interests of another. "Ordinary care" is such care as the "ordinarily prudent and careful person" would be expected to exercise "under the same or similar circumstances."

It is a rare case in which accidents happen without someone having been in a position to prevent them by stronger precaution. Nevertheless, one of the more difficult elements to satisfy in a claim based on negligence and arising out of the accidental failure of a product, is proof of *foreseeability*—that the supplier should have anticipated that his product would be used under the particular conditions and circumstances in which it failed. His defense, in essence, is that he took no greater precautions because he could not reasonably have *foreseen* the necessity for greater precaution. He will claim that his product met the specifications of the purchase order and also (largely by the same token) measured up to the standard of ordinary care.

Whose fault, then, is an accident by which someone may have lost life, limb, or fortune? No blanket answer is possible. But it is possible that, if the purchasing office had managed to gather more information about the intended use of the supplier's product and had passed that information on to the supplier, the *unavoidable accident* would have been avoided. At very least, the *unforeseeability* defense would have been effectively nullified.

It is important to understand that, though failure to fulfill a contract specification often constitutes negligence, adherence to contract specifications does not necessarily constitute *ordinary care*. In one case, a purchase order for industrial aprons did not, either expressly or by implication, specify that they be treated for flammability. Yet the supplier of such aprons was held liable for tort to a workman injured when his apron burst into flames. Before assuming that negligence shifts all liability to the supplier, a purchasing agent should realize three things: First, the purchase order *should have* specified nonflammable materials; second, the purchaser's company itself ultimately absorbed a generous portion of the liability; and third, the litigation expense alone far exceeded the cash of the entire order.

Strict Liability Torts.   Until fairly recently, most claims arising out of various types of product failure were based either on breach of contract (including the closely related breach of sales warranty) or on negligence. Today, a sizable segment of product-liability cases—those involving personal injury or property damage caused by "defective" products—are being brought on a newly developing tort theory, *strict liability*.

The legal and commercial implications of the new doctrine are still far from clear, but there is little doubt that strict liability will strongly accentuate the need for careful purchasing practices. This is true primarily because of the heavy inroads that the doctrine of strict liability produces into traditional *privity* limitations.

Assume, to illustrate, the case of a motorist injured when a defective brake cylinder on his automobile fails. Conceivably, the manufacturer of the defective cylinder could be liable to the consumer for negligent design or manufacture; but in contract or warranty, under traditional sales law, he could be liable only to the automobile manufacturer to whom he sold the cylinder. "Privity" does not conventionally reach beyond the immediate contract relationship. The automobile manufacturer, in turn, might conceivably be liable to the consumer for negligent inspection, but he ordinarily cannot be liable for negligent design or manufacture except to the distributor to whom he sold the car. The upshot of that, for all practical purposes, the consumer's warranty claim has not previously been enforceable beyond the person from which he purchased, and his negligence claim required him to prove the particular "want of ordinary care" of which each member of the manufacturing and distributing chain was guilty. Successful claims, needles to say, were relatively rare; claims costs were correspondingly low. Purchasing officials could feel reasonably secure about injury claims.

Strict liability, as a tort principle that masquerades in several states under the misleading title of "implied warranty," makes each *member* of the manufacturing and distributing chain liable to the injured user, irrespective of contract, warranty, or negligence, provided the defect was present when the product passed through his hands. Lack of privity is no defense against such liability.

Warranties

When a purchased item breaks prematurely and fails to fulfill its purpose, someone must stand the resulting loss. Such loss is not necessarily limited to the cost of repair or replacement of the item itself. Nor is the problem eliminated simply because the purchaser has managed to pass the item along to someone else before it goes bad. The claim can return (as breach of warranty, misrepresentation, negligence, or strict liability) from the damaged consumer.

In sales law, as in contract law generally, warranties may be either express or implied. Express warranties may arise otherwise than from direct negotiations between a seller and a buyer. They may arise from statements in catalogs, in advertising, or on brochures or labels. Nor need there be any proven intention to make a warranty in any formal sense. Statements in letters, conversations, or any other type of communication will suffice.

Express warranties are generally preferable to implied ones. This is true because express warranties can be phased in more detailed terms than ordinarily is possible by implication. Express warranties do not easily yield to standard disclaimer clauses. Express warranties, as a matter of practice, tend more routinely to be filed or noted with the papers relating to the particular transaction. Consequently, they are more easily proved and more reliable. The chief difficulty with express warranties is that they take time, effort, and skill to formulate and to negotiate.

By contrast, in purchases of goods (and, to a lesser extent, in contracts for services), a number of *implied* warranties of some value arise out of simple silence, wherever the seller is a dealer in goods or services of the kind. These warranties, collectively called the warranty of *merchantability* in UCC 2-314, are important enough to list verbatim:

Goods to be merchantable must be at least such as:

1. To pass without objection in the trade under the contract description.
2. In the case of fungible goods, are of fair average quality within the description.
3. Are fit for the ordinary purposes for which such goods are used.
4. Run, within the variations permitted by the agreement, of even kind, quality and quantity within each unit and among all units involved.
5. Are adequately contained, packaged, and labeled as the agreement may require.
6. Conform to the promises or affirmations of fact made on the container or label, if any.

In most cases the purchaser will use the goods in an ordinary and conventional way for their ordinary and conventional purpose. In some cases, however, a distinction must be observed between a warranty that goods are fit for ordinary purposes and a warranty that they are fit for a particular buyer's special use. In these cases, the implied warranty arises only if the seller at the time of contracting has reason to know (a) the particular purpose for which the goods are required and (b) that the buyer is relying on the seller's skill or judgment to select or furnish suitable goods.

Offer and Acceptance

The "meeting of the minds" that is the legal keynote of every contract is usually arrived at by the process of *offer* and *acceptance*. Prior to the UCC, conventional sales law declared that no enforceable sales contract could arise until offer and acceptance were in substantially complete agreement with each other, without any variation of material terms between the two. This rule, often called the "mirror image" doctrine, treated a number of common mercantile contract procedures quite unrealistically. Whenever an attempted acceptance or confirmation added a detail of specification not stated in the offer, substituted one detail for another, proposed alternates, or deleted or qualified a term, the nominal acceptance or confirmation was treated as a rejection of the original offer *in toto* and as a counteroffer that required a "mirror image" acceptance of its own.

The "mirror image" rule, thus, requires the parties to agree on 100% of the terms and specifications of a given transaction before the law will recognize an agreement. So long as any detail remains unsettled, the transaction cannot move out of the negotiation stage. Such a rule is not necessarily a bad one, but it is unrealistic and impractical if applied in blanket fashion. It works especially badly when standardized forms of purchase and sales orders are used. Rarely, if ever, will all clauses of one company's purchase order conform to another company's sales-order clauses.

The disagreement may be purely a disagreement of forms. The actual "meeting of the minds" may be fully present on all substantive matters. In such cases, an inflexible "mirror image" requirement may deny legal support to agreements that both parties regard as complete. It is likely that a large percentage of routine sales transactions are completed without a legally enforceable contract having been concluded.

The UCC relaxes the rigidity of the "mirror image" doctrine, permitting the parties to contract either strictly or liberally, as they prefer. In the absence of express stipulation by either party that no contract will arise except upon the terms which that party states, or expressly agrees to, a legally enforceable agreement may arise, at least to the extent of the terms upon which offer and acceptance correspond, even though other terms remain open to further negotiation. Furthermore, in the absence of such stipulation, *failure to object within a reasonable time to certain terms* introduced incident to an acceptance or confirmation makes those terms a part of the contract, even though there may be no affirmative assent to them.

There is one exception to this principle of "assent by silence": it does not apply to "material alterations" of the contract. Unfortunately, the distinction between "material alterations" and mere "additional terms" is not entirely clear. A good rule of thumb is that any significant difference between the *express* specifications of offer and acceptance relating to parties, price, quantity, quality, or credit terms is probably material. But it is bad practice to depend on any such rule of thumb in purchasing practice. The only safe practice is to examine documents of acceptance of confirmation for nonconformity and to send prompt and pointed notices of objection with respect to any nonconforming term that is objectionable.

The other alternative is to state expressly in advance that the other party's nonconforming or added terms are rejected. A clause in the purchase order form, for example, might read: "This order may be accepted only in strict and total conformity with its terms and specifications, without variance, addition, or limitation, and no contract shall arise upon any different terms unless this company expressly assents thereto." Although solving the problem of "material alterations," such a clause requires full "mirror image" procedure and subjects the transaction to the objectionable aspects of that procedure.

Precisely when a transaction leaves the negotiation state and becomes a contract is a matter of great importance, since no legal rights or duties of a contractual sort can ordinarily arise out of mere negotiations.

As a general rule, a contract arises at the moment when a conforming acceptance of an unrevoked offer is *communicated* to the offerer. Communication of acceptance, therefore, generally marks the point of no return in purchase negotiations, after which neither party is entitled to back out of the transaction, by withdrawing or materially changing either his offer or his acceptance without the other's consent.

However, this general rule should not be understood too literally. First, an acceptance may arise without any oral or written expression, in some cases by shipping the goods and in other cases by commencing to produce or acquire the goods. The confirmation in such special cases may follow the offer by a matter of days or weeks, and operate retroactively.

Second, UCC 2-205 now confirms the mercantile practice of making "firm offers," which, unlike the usual offer, cannot be withdrawn during the period during which the offerer has promised to hold them open. Two technical requirements should be noted in this regard: The assurance that the offer will be held open must be written and signed, and it is not binding for longer than three months.

Traditional contract law explicitly condemned practices by which one or more of the material terms of the agreement were either deliberately left open for later settlement or were stated indefinitely in some respect. UCC 2-204 liberalizes that traditional rule, so that commercial standards of dealing, rather than unyielding legal technicality, control the question of whether or not a contract has been reached. No purchasing agent should take this change of law as an invitation to piecemeal, open, or indefinite contracting. However, it is important to understand that the law now allows those possibilities. When negotiations are not intended to create a contract until all details of the transaction have been clearly settled and stated, special care may be required to guard against a possible opposite claim. Therefore, preliminary inquiries and contingent understandings should be plainly labeled as such.

Must It Be in Writing?

The answer is that human memory is fallible, and misunderstandings are inevitable if contracts are not recorded. There are at least two legal reasons why a written record of the purchase transaction is necessary. The first has been mentioned earlier in this chapter when the importance of proof of contract was discussed. The second is the Statute of Frauds, which operates to deny legal enforceability to oral agreements in certain cases.

Different requirements as to the necessity of a written record apply to different types of transactions. The requirements of the UCC relating to contracts for the sale of goods should not be mistakenly applied, therefore, to contracts for services or real estate.

Where UCC 2-201 is in force, there is a general requirement that contracts for purchase and sale of goods for a price of $500 or more are not enforceable unless some writing "sufficient to indicate that a contract has been made between the parties" is signed "by the party against whom enforcement is sought or by his authorized agent or broker." Even a scratch pad memorandum may be sufficient under this requirement, provided that it (1) names a seller and a buyer, (2) is signed, initialed, or otherwise authenticated by (or on behalf of) at least one party, (3) specifies a quantity of goods, and (4) in some manner indicates that it is a memorandum of sale. Of course, such a memorandum would ordinarily be binding only upon the party who prepared it, since it would not contain a signature of the other party. Such a situation, where one party is bound and the other is entitled to withdraw, rarely becomes a matter of practical significance, unless one of the parties seeks to repudiate what the other insists was a firm verbal agreement. A sufficient memorandum or confirmation letter will block the escape of the party who prepared it in such cases.

There are several exceptions to the rule that a party whose commitment is oral can legally repudiate the deal. The UCC has introduced some significant changes in this regard, not all of which have been entirely clarified at this time. Under the new rules:

1. It still is true that a contract for less than $500 need not be in writing; but to what extent it is possible to divide a given transaction into two or more component parts, so that some or all of the parts are under $500, is less clear.
2. Nonresponse, for 10 days after receipt of a written confirmation that binds the sender, also binds the silent party; but this rule applies only "between merchants," and there is some doubt (especially concerning purchasing agents) as to precisely when a party qualifies as a *merchant.*

3. Contracts for goods that are manufactured especially for the buyer, and are of custom design or utility, require no writing when seller has substantially begun manufacture or procurement before buyer repudiates.
4. Payment for or acceptance of goods sold under oral contract waives the rule, at least to the extent of the goods paid for or accepted. Acceptance of part of a "commercial unit" is acceptance of the entire unit.
5. Admission in court that the oral contract was, in fact, made forecloses the admitting party's right to insist upon the statute. In practical terms, then, the requirement of a signed writing has no significance unless the nonsigner claims, under oath or affirmation, that the parties did not come to terms in the first place.

One cannot emphasize too strongly what was previously stated about "open price" and other "open term" contracts. A *sufficient* written memorandum or confirmation need not state any price at all. Businesspersons trained under earlier law and practice may fail to realize that now a casual letter *confirming our discussions* can give rise to a fully enforceable contract. Even memoranda prepared and kept in one's own file, for one's personal use, may acquire strong, and perhaps unintended, significance. Important as it is to be careful of what is said in negotiating a transaction, it is even more important to scrutinize what is written. If a matter is only tentatively settled, subject to further negotiations, every notation of the transaction should expressly say so.

Inspection, Acceptance, Rejection, Returns

Except in rare cases, a purchaser is entitled to inspect goods before paying for them to determine whether they conform to contract specifications. If the contract includes terms prescribing the method, place, or time of inspection, such terms control. Expenses of inspection are the purchaser's responsibility unless the goods prove to be nonconforming and are rejected.

Nonconforming goods may be rejected *in toto*, accepted subject to correction or price adjustment, or accepted in part and rejected in part. The last-named alternative is not available, however, if it requires the splitting of a commercial unit, that is, leaves what is regarded in the business as a broken lot. To whatever extent a shipment is rejected for nonconformity, the purchaser must (1) notify the seller of rejection within a reasonable period of time, (2) hold the goods for seller's disposition, and (3) follow the seller's reasonable instructions with respect to disposition or return. The purchaser is entitled to be paid for expenses incurred in connection with rejected goods, as well as for damages.

The notice of rejection should specify every way in which inspection has revealed the goods to be nonconforming. Failure to specify can waive the unspecified defect. This suggests the advisability of making a complete inspection of any shipment that a purchaser intends to reject. If the principal ground for rejection is clear and uncorrectable, there is no great risk in only specifying it, but should the principal ground be disproved or corrected, the other defects may be needed to justify the rejection.

Whether or not the shipment is inspected, acceptance waives any complaints that a reasonable inspection would have disclosed. An accepted shipment cannot always be rejected on subsequent discovery of defects. Furthermore, a purchaser has only a reasonable time to reject a shipment or he will be presumed to have accepted by his silence.

This is not to suggest that a purchaser who accepts a shipment has no recourse for subsequently discovered nonconformity. If the defect or deficiency of the goods is one that is not reasonably discoverable by ordinary commercial inspection, the purchaser is entitled to claim damages if he notifies the seller of the problem promptly upon its discovery.

In three cases, an accepted shipment can be subsequently rejected for nonconformity that "substantially impairs its value" to the purchaser. One is the case in which the original acceptance was made upon the reasonable assumption that the seller would correct the nonconformity. A typical case would be one in which a machine arrived without specified motors and the purchaser assumed that the motors would follow from a different source. The second situation in which subsequent rejection is possible is one in which the deficiency is not discoverable by ordinary processes of inspection. The third is the case in which a seller's pointed "assurances" induced the purchaser to take the shipment on faith. In no case, however, can an accepted shipment be rejected after its condition has been substantially changed by use. Then the purchaser is limited to a claim of damages.

Some of today's purchases are made "on approval," "sale or return," or "consignment." On-approval arrangements permit the purchaser to return even conforming goods if, after a reasonable period of trial, he/she decides not to accept. Both shipment and return of such goods are, in absence of a different viewpoint, at the seller's risk and cost. From a purchaser's point of view this arrangement seems ideal, but it has its legal and practical limitations. Few sellers are willing to do business on approval without extensive contractual safeguards. If the purchaser accepts part of the goods by using or consuming more than a trial amount, he accepts all of them. If the purchaser delays his decision beyond a reasonable time, he has accepted them. In addition, purchasers are inclined to relax their specification standards too far in buying on approval and therefore are without remedy for nonconformity discovered after acceptance.

Purchases on a sale-or-return or on a consignment basis are usually purchases for resale. Broken lots are not subject to return under these arrangements, the return is ordinarily at the buyer's expense, and the buyer is responsible for the goods if they are not returned. Beyond those restrictions a sale-or-return follows the pattern of outright sales, except that commercial units are subject to return if unsold and special legal consequences for the buyer's creditors arise under a sale-or-return arrangement.

Patent Rights

UCC 2-312 (3) provides some protection against patent infringement in contracting for goods and supplies. Under this section a merchant seller whose contract does not specifically provide otherwise warrants against patent claims by third parties, unless the buyer furnished the infringing specifications. There is no necessity for an express provision that the goods be sold free of patent claims. Nor is the seller's warranty against infringement one that a general disclaimer will eliminate. Under UCC 2-605, should an infringement claim arise against the purchaser, he is required promptly to notify his seller. If the seller demands in writing the right to settle or defend against the claim, the buyer must turn the matter over to him.

Assuming the seller's financial ability to pay damages, these provisions should protect purchasers against infringement claims that do not arise out of their own specifications. Contract language suggesting any disclaimer of the seller's full patent right to the product should be scrutinized with extreme care and usually rejected. A purchaser should be as suspicious of buying an item without guarantee against infringement as he would be if the seller refused to guarantee title.

Protection of his company's trade secrets and patentable ideas may occasionally become a responsibility of the purchasing agent. This presents a problem of special delicacy where a supplier is required to develop a new product meeting functional specifications described in the purchase contract. When the purchaser's development of the idea has not yet progressed to the point where formal patent or copyright protection can be applied for, there is real danger that the supplier will claim for himself the fruit of research suggested to him by the purchase order. He may thus beat the purchaser to rights on his own idea. Where it is necessary to solicit a number of potential suppliers on such an order or where subcontractors are involved, the problem is compounded.

Antitrust Laws

The individual states of the United States have laws regulating monopoly and prohibiting unreasonable restraint of trade. A purchasing agent should be familiar with these state laws in the state where he is located and in states where he makes major purchases. These laws vary significantly in their provisions and the vigor with which they are enforced. Historically the state laws have not been the source of as much litigation as the federal laws, but recently the more industrial states have become increasingly active in prosecuting restraint of trade offenses. Since a company indicted under such laws not only runs the risk of heavy fines and the imprisonment of its responsible officers, but also suffers a form of unfavorable publicity that is hard to counteract, a purchasing executive should be very careful to avoid antitrust involvement.

The federal antitrust statutes apply to transactions that involve interstate commerce. With the broadened definition of interstate commerce, these laws can be invoked in almost any situation in which the federal government wishes to intervene. Of the many types of transactions with antitrust implications, those listed below are the ones with which a purchasing executive is most likely to be involved.

Price-Fixing and Agreements Not to Compete. The first section of the Sherman Act prohibits contracts, combinations, or conspiracies in restraint of trade. Any kind of an agreement among competing buyers or sellers is such a conspiracy and represents the commonest violation of Section 1 of this Act. Many companies do—and all companies should—have firm rules against their executives talking with executives of competing companies about pricing and related matters.

Boycott. Although a purchaser may ordinarily buy from whomever he pleases, an agreement with others not to buy from a particular seller may not be made by the purchaser without serious danger of violating Section 1 of the Sherman Act since a boycott is clearly a combination of conspiracy in restraint of trade.

Price Discrimination. The Robinson-Patman Act not only prohibits sellers from charging different prices to purchasers of goods of like grade and quality, subject to certain limited exceptions, but also prohibits purchasers from knowingly inducing or receiving an illegal discriminatory price.

Aside from bona fide general price changes and distress sales, the only exceptions to the prohibition against price discrimination among competing customers for comparable goods are, for all practical purposes, those permitting differences in price that (a) merely reflect differences in the seller's cost of dealing with the favored customer resulting from differing methods of quantities in which the goods are manufactured, sold, or delivered to such customer, or (b) are granted to meet (not beat) a competitor's bona fide offer to a favored customer.

Discriminatory pricing practices have been detected in various forms of concessions, beyond the obvious practice of "shading" the price itself. Although none of these concessions are illegal in themselves, they are illegal if given under circumstances that tend to produce the prohibited result, that is, injuring a competitor of the buyer or seller without "cost" justification. The common forms of illegal concession are:

1. Quantity differentials not based on demonstrable cost savings.
2. Cumulative volume differentials, in which purchases are aggregated over a period of time, with increasing discounts being granted as the volume rises.
3. Geographic differentials, based on adjustments for shipping and delivery costs, in which the favored purchaser is given a concession on delivery cost not accorded to his competitors.
4. Trade and functional discounts based on a system of customer classification that essentially distinguishes the consuming purchaser from the purchaser for resale, and further arbitrarily distinguishes among classes of purchasers for resale. Trade and functional discounts are of doubtful legality if they are arbitrary and are merely designed to preserve a channel of distribution.
5. Locality differentials, often used as part of a seller's localized promotion campaign and having overtones of predatory price cutting for the purpose of hurting a competitor.
6. Carrier-option discounts, which discriminate between customers served by different modes of shipment (e.g., by rail and by truck) to a degree not justified by the differences in cost.
7. Pooled-order discounts, in which a number of buyers combine their orders but for all other purposes act as independent buyers. The legality of these cooperative purchasing schemes has not been finally settled, but it is fairly well established that

when the pooled orders produce no significant savings to the seller, the arrangement is suspect.

Exclusive Dealing and Supply Contracts.   Section 3 of the Clayton Act, another of the federal antitrust laws, prohibits a sale or lease of goods conditioned upon the purchaser's agreeing not to use or deal in the goods of a competitor of the seller where the effect of such arrangement "may be" to lessen competition substantially or tend to create a monopoly in any line of commerce. An exclusive dealing arrangement that ties up a large dollar amount of business or involves a dominant member of the industry will ordinarily be considered to have the necessary adverse effect on competition. Common examples of exclusive dealing arrangements that violate Section 3 of the Clayton Act are (a) agreements to supply all of a purchaser's requirements of a particular commodity for a substantial period of time and (b) tie-in sales or leases under which the purchaser of one product is also required to purchase a related product from a seller or lessor.

Antitrust violations can have serious and far-reaching consequences, including not only the invalidation of contracts and destruction of patent rights, but also severe criminal fines and imprisonment for individuals, substantial triple damage recoveries by injured private parties, and injunctive decrees and cease-and-desist orders that may jeopardize an entire business operation. Even minor questions of legality under the antitrust laws deserve cautious handling and early consultation with legal counsel.

"OSHA"

The passage of the Occupational Safety and Health Act of 1970 and the creation of the Occupational Safety and Health Administration (both known under the acronum—OSHA) have created a whole range of legal problems for industrial purchasing.

Many of these problems arise from a lack of knowledge on the part of all parties as to what is required. Administrators are still in the process of formulating standards that are to be applied, and as a result, purchases are being made under temporary standards that may later prove unacceptable. Purchasing departments are receiving requisitions for many strange items for which they have no prior buying experience. Similarly, requisitioning departments are quite vague as to what they really need to meet the requirements of the law.

Many buyers have attempted to protect themselves and at the same time shift responsibility to suppliers for compliance by including in their purchase orders a clause somewhat as follows: "Seller agrees to comply with the provisions of the Occupational Safety and Health Act of 1970 and the standards and regulations issued thereunder. Seller certifies that all items furnished and all work performed hereunder will comply with said standards and regulations. Seller further agrees to indemnify and hold harmless Buyer for any loss, damages, fine, penalty, or any expense whatsoever as a result of Seller's failure to comply with the Act and any such standards or regulations issued thereunder."

Whether such clauses get included in purchase agreements seems to depend on the relative bargaining position of the buyer and seller while the contract is being negotiated. Even if there is no OSHA clause in a purchase contract, it is possible that the buyer will have recourse under the implied warranty of merchantability, UCC 2-314. The buyer could argue that failure to comply with OSHA standards which the seller could have discovered is a breech warranty since goods that do not comply with OSHA standards are not *merchantable* goods.

Since there have not been cases covering the above, one cannot as yet say what the *law* really is. It will take a number of years before all the ramifications of OSHA are fully worked out. In the interim, purchasing departments will be well advised to consult with the company lawyers whenever any questions in this area arise.

Purchase Order Clauses

Many companies, in order to avoid legal entanglements with respect to purchased materials, include on the purchase order form carefully worded phrases regarding the requirements placed on the seller. These should be prepared in cooperation with legal counsel. Purchase order clauses almost always include items such as cash-discount terms, billing procedure, number of copies of invoices, bills of lading required, and mailing instructions for such documents. Such clauses, although technically a part of the contract when properly accepted, generally are considered informative and to some extent instructive and may not have legal significance.

There are other clauses, however, relating to patent protection, to proper insurance protection, percentage of overrun, and so forth, which have considerable significance and should be prepared in good legal form. An informal survey of a number of typical purchase order forms showed some degree of uniformity in the types of clauses and their phraseology on the following subjects:

Patent infringement	Time of shipment
Inspection	Billing and B/L

Boxing charge   Replacement of defective goods
Change without written   Payment
   authority   Acknowledgement
Verbal understanding   Routing
Fair labor standards   Insurance
Price   Overrun of quantities

Although it would be desirable to have a standardized set of purchase order contract clauses for use by purchasing departments, such a possibility appears to be remote. There is a wide divergence of opinion among both purchasing and legal personnel on the best means of affording a company protection in its dealings with suppliers. As a result most companies employ those purchase order clauses that they have developed through experience over a period of years and afford them the protection they desire.

DISCUSSION QUESTIONS

1. How much knowledge of law is required of the industrial buyer?

2. What is meant by "implied authority"?

3. What are the specific legal principles to be considered relative to signing a purchase contract?

4. What are the three basic elements to every claim?

5. Name and discuss the three classifications of torts.

6. What should a purchaser do when he rejects a shipment for nonconformity?

7. List the types of transactions that have antitrust implications to a purchasing agent.

8. What is OSHA and how does it affect purchasing?

9. What is meant by purchase order clauses? Are they important?

10. Is it necessary for all contracts to be in writing? Why?

SUGGESTED CASES

ABC Corporation (A)

American Arbitration Association

Court Decisions on Purchasing Issues

Utopia School District

PART IV
CONTROL OF PURCHASING ACTIVITIES

CHAPTER 18
PURCHASING PERSONNEL MANAGEMENT

Many of the functions of purchasing have changed over the past decade. New types of materials are constantly becoming available which must be evaluated as possible substitutes through value analysis. Management is becoming increasingly concerned over the costs and risks of carrying inventories and is keeping pressure on the operating divisions to reduce the inventory-to-sales ratio. The production function is being increasingly planned and scheduled through the application of mathematical decision theory which puts a premium on the assurance of supply. Electronic data processing equipment has become a tool of prodigous power in the maintenance of records and the retrieval of information for managers who are schooled in its use. Rising costs of handling order routines have led to the adoption of practices that balance the advantages of making individual decisions against the cost of carrying out those decisions.

All of these changes, and many more, have put a premium on purchasing managers who have broad backgrounds of experience and sufficient adaptability to be able to adjust to changing circumstances. Today's and tomorrow's purchasing managers will need more breadth and depth than their predecessors if they are going to meet successfully the many opportunities and challenges that face purchasing today.

This chapter deals with personnel management practices as they apply to the purchasing department. Such personnel management may be described as the job of directing and coordinating the personnel of the organization with the objective of securing maximum production with the minimum of effort and friction and with a proper regard for the well-being of the individual. Among the activities examined in this chapter are the following:

1. Types of positions
2. Qualifications for purchasing
3. Sources of purchasing personnel
4. Selection of purchasing personnel
5. Training
6. Compensation
7. Professionalism

Positions in Purchasing

The number of positions in a purchasing department varies greatly from company to company and from industry to industry. The chief factors that explain this variation are (1) size of firm, (2) the degree of centralization, (3) variations in responsibilities, and (4) differing production processes. The more the purchasing activities of a multi-plant firm are centralized, the larger the central purchasing department will be. However, with a centralized purchasing department the total number of man-hours spent on purchasing activities will tend to be lower than in a company that decentralizes its purchasing operations, because centralized control leads to the efficiencies that arise from specialization.

Variations in purchasing responsibilities account for differing department sizes. In some companies the purchasing department buys all materials and services, expedites deliveries, disposes of scrap or waste materials, checks invoices and receipts, maintains records, has its own typists, stenographers, and clerical workers, whereas in other companies the purchasing activity is limited to buying. The related functions are performed in other departments.

The nature of the production process also affects the size of the purchasing department. In a company making a simple product on a high-volume basis, material for a year's operation may be purchased on a few blanket orders or systems contracts with delivery specified at regular intervals. On the other hand, a company producing complex, made-to-order units must go through the entire buying routine for each unit, which requires many people.

Although studies have been made of the sizes of purchasing departments in relation to total work force or dollar volume of purchases, the figures do not constitute a sound basis for comparison for the reasons outlined above. However, some indication of the number of employees assigned to the purchasing activity by typical industrial concerns may be secured from Table 18-1.

TABLE 18-1. Number of Firms Having Purchasing Departments of Various Sizes as Related to Total Size of the Firm

Number of Employees in Purchasing Department	Size of Firms in Terms of Total Employees						Total Number of Firms
	1–150	151–300	301–500	501–1001	1001–2000	Over 2000	
2	7	3	2				12
3	7	4	2	1		1	15
4	2	3	4	3			12
5		4	2	3	2		11
6	1	2	4	4	1	1	13
7				1	1		2
8					1		1
9			2		3		5
10				3			3
11–15				4	5	2	11
16–20				1		1	2
21–35						4	4
26–30				1		1	2
Over 30						2	2
	17	16	17	21	12	12	95

Source: An unpublished study conducted by a graduate student under the direction of the authors.

Among the titles in a typical purchasing department are purchasing agent,[1] assistant purchasing agent, senior buyer, junior buyer, expediter, production coordinator, price clerk, materials controller, and clerical employees. In smaller companies the duties and responsibilities of two or more of these positions frequently are assumed by a single individual. In such situations, it is customary for the individual to carry the title of the highest-ranking position.

No detailed job description of the several purchasing positions is applicable to all companies. However, a generalized description of the most common duties and responsibilities of those occupying the enumerated positions is given in the following paragraphs.

Purchasing Agent (Department Head)

The duties and responsibilities assigned to the purchasing agent depend to a considerable extent on the nature of his company's product and the level of management to which the agent belongs. In many of the largest companies the head of purchasing is a high-level official, frequently a vice-president or a director of purchases. The functions of such an official primarily concern the formulation and supervision of purchasing policy. A subordinate, often called an assistant director of purchases or a purchasing agent, then, has the operating duties and responsibilities that more closely correspond to those of the purchasing agent in a smaller concern. These duties and responsibilities generally include:

[1] See Chapter 1 for the various titles given to heads of purchasing departments.

1. Establishment and supervision of purchasing procedures that are in keeping with company policies. The policies, to which the department procedures must conform, are made by a company's top management in consultation with the operating department affected.
2. Internal organization of the purchasing department, including selection, training, and compensation. In larger companies the personnel department usually works with the purchasing department in these matters.
3. The personnel program of the purchasing department, including selection, training, and compensation. In larger companies the personnel department usually works with the purchasing department in these matters.
4. Supervision of such departmental activities as the selection of vendors, placing of orders, expediting, storekeeping, and the approval of invoices for payment. The operating head of the purchasing department frequently assumes direct responsibility for the purchase of major raw materials or other important purchases.
5. Cultivation of sound supplier relationships.
6. Coordination between the purchasing department and other departments of the company. The head of the purchasing department frequently serves on such company committees as product development, value analysis, and budget committees.
7. Preparing forecasts of supply conditions and price trends. The purchasing agent may also be responsible for establishing forward-buying policies in the light of these trends, or may serve as a member of a company committee that establishes these policies.
8. Such auxiliary activities as disposal of scrap and surplus materials, inspection of incoming shipments, and traffic routing for incoming shipments are also frequently assigned to the purchasing agent.
9. Simplification, standardization, and specification tasks for purchased materials and supplies are sometimes a responsibility of the purchasing agent.

Assistant Purchasing Agent

The assistant purchasing agent, as the title implies, is assigned as many of the duties and responsibilities of the purchasing agent as can be delegated in order to lighten the load of the department head. Depending on company size, its policies, and the nature of its product, one or more assistants may be involved. One may have supervision over the activities of the buyers and another over the clerical activities. Another division of responsibility may find one assistant responsible for procurement of raw material and another for processed materials. The assistant purchasing agent generally is a buyer of certain materials.

In some companies that are major suppliers to the federal government there is need to comply with the multiplicity of governmental regulations relating to materials control. The responsibility for soliciting federal and state authorities, maintaining records, preparation and allocation of priority applications, and compliance with other requirements contained in government contracts may then be delegated to an assistant purchasing agent.[2]

Senior Buyer

The buyer reports to the purchasing agent, or assistant purchasing agent, depending on departmental organization. Although the duties and responsibilities of buyers vary, the following list of duties with the percentage of time devoted to each presents a portrait of the typical buyer:[3]

1. Checking requisitions—5%. (Examining and checking the accuracy of an average of 25 orders per day for correctness of description and manner of disposition.)
2. Placing orders—47%. (Obtaining quotations, selecting vendors, and interviewing salesmen.)
3. Making adjustments—3%. (Checking for discrepancies in invoices and arranging satisfactory adjustments when required.)
4. Following up on delivery—35%. (Checking on the progress of all orders overdue, or about to become due, and reporting to the personnel concerned.)
5. Filing reports and references—2%. (Maintaining lists of products, prices, vendors, and other reference material.)
6. Writing blanket orders—3%. (Making partial releases on large coverage orders.)
7. Maintaining correspondence—5%. (Keeping in contact through correspondence with vendors and interplant personnel as required.)

---

[2] In larger departments a specially qualified individual is placed in charge of this work which entails considerable travel to Washington, D.C.

[3] Unpublished study by Industrial Management Institute, University of Wisconsin.

Junior Buyer

Duties of a junior buyer are in general the same as those of a senior buyer. Commodities purchased by the junior buyer are for the most part lower-value, standard "shelf" items covered by published price lists and readily available for prompt delivery. The junior buyer reports to the purchasing agent or assistant purchasing agent.

Assistant Buyer

The assistant buyer, in companies that have this position, is generally assigned to the more routine aspects of buying, both as a means of lightening the work load of the buyers and training the assistant. The assistant buyer often serves as an expediter in the smaller purchasing department and may also perform follow-up duties. The assistant buyer is under the jurisdiction of the buyer.

Expediter

The duties of the expediter depend largely on the method of expediting and the degree of expediting employed. In many companies this position is primarily clerical, involving the maintenance of tickler files and the follow-up of purchase orders to secure acceptance copies with promised delivery dates. In some companies, especially during periods of short supply, the duties of the expediter are enlarged to include field expediting. This involves contact with the supplier at his plant and may even include contacts with the suppliers of the vendor.

Production Coordinator

The production coordinator is the link between the purchasing and production departments. He maintains summaries of purchase orders issued for each manufacturing order along with delivery dates specified. By comparing delivery promises with required production dates, he is able to advise buyers when follow-up efforts are necessary to assure meeting production schedules. He also advises the production department of the status of purchased material on order. A production coordinator usually reports to the assistant department head.

Price Clerk

The price clerk maintains price record files. He records or posts prices, vendors' acknowledgments, and other pertinent information in appropriate records and on the open purchase orders. Included in his responsibilities may be periodic reports on price changes. He usually works under an assistant purchasing agent.

Materials Controller

The materials controller has physical responsibility for all reserve stocks of materials, supplies, and equipment. He is accountable for their issuance on proper authorization and in some cases for the maintenance of inventory records. He is generally responsible for initiating requisitions that lead to the purchase of stock items. He may also be called stock-room or tool-crib supervisor.

Clerical Employees

The lowest-ranking positions in a purchasing department are the clerical positions. A wide variety of activities is performed by such personnel. Among the duties are the typing of purchase orders and other correspondence with vendors, and the maintenance of vendor lists, requisition files, purchase order files, correspondence files, a vendor catalog library, and inventory records in companies where this is a responsibility of the purchasing department.

Qualifications for Purchasing Positions

The qualifications for individuals who succeed in purchasing may conveniently be grouped into three categories—personal characteristics, educational background, and business experience.

The personal characteristics that promise success in purchasing are no different from those in any other field of business. Any difference is likely to be in the importance attached to some of the characteristics. In the list of personal characteristics that follows no attempt is made to be exhaustive. Rather, it is a list of the more important characteristics, with some indication of the reasons for their importance. It is unlikely that any experienced purchasing agent would agree precisely with this list of traits or the order of importance assigned to them. Rather, it represents a consensus on the subject.

1. *Integrity.* Purchasing agents and buyers expend huge sums of company money. They must be impervious to the financial temptations that accompany such a position of trust, whether in the form of an inordinate gift, a secret "kickback," or outright bribery. Personal integrity is also required to refrain from making unwarranted promises to potential suppliers in order to secure preferential treatment.

2. *Dependability.* This personality trait is important in purchasing personnel because frequently the continuity of operations of an industrial plant depends on the reliability of the purchasing department in following through on requisitions until goods are delivered according to specifications.

3. *Initiative.* Purchasing personnel are constantly faced with situations demanding initiative and imagination. The continual search for alternative sources of supply or alternative materials is but one area where initiative is important. It also frequently happens that unexpected requirements necessitate locating materials and supplies in unusual places and on short notice.

4. *Industriousness.* Knowledge of materials and sources is acquired only after extended training and experience. Because of this fact, a heavy burden tends to be thrown on experienced personnel during periods of rapid business expansion which cannot be relieved until new personnel are trained. During such times the industriousness of purchasing personnel is tested by the long hours they must work. The person who is unwilling to work long hours when the occasion demands is lacking an important trait for success in purchasing.

5. *Cooperation.* Purchasing personnel must possess an unusual ability to cooperate, since almost every item bought is for the use of some other department of the company. Cooperation is essential to minimize the many points of friction that may evolve out of such a situation. It is also important because purchasing personnel must of necessity serve on many policy committees, since the ability to acquire materials and supplies is an important aspect of many policy decisions.

6. *Tact.* Many purchasing agents consider tact the most important single personal characteristic. The reason for this is the crucial importance of maintaining sound and friendly vendor relations. A tactless person may inadvertently antagonize a supplier whose goodwill and cooperation have been cultivated over many years.

7. *Ability to Learn.* A good purchasing agent must have an inquiring mind. He/she must always be seeking information about his/her company's products, materials, and processes and must study the suitability of every supplier's offerings. He/she must constantly learn more about his/her company's requirements and the availability of alternatives for meeting those requirements. An individual who does not have the desire or ability to learn will not make a good purchasing agent.

8. *Ability to Work on Details.* Much of the work in a purchasing department, as in any department, may be classified as detail work. Such work is important, even though it is routine in nature. Persons

who do not have the ability or inclination to perform detail work are not suited to purchasing positions.

Business Experience

Business experience is almost universally considered to be necessary for purchasing personnel in the higher ranking positions. This is not surprising since people in these positions must be knowledgeable about both company affairs and general business practices so that they can deal effectively with other departments and outside suppliers. A somewhat more surprising fact was revealed by a survey of the members of 12 purchasing manager associations.[4] Respondents were asked to rank a list of seven criteria according to their importance for *hiring* to purchasing positions. Table 18-1 shows how the criteria were rank-ordered.

TABLE 18-1. Characteristics Considered Important for Hiring to Purchasing Positions

Rank Order	Criteria	Average Score
1	Business Experience	2.174
2	Business Education	3.172
3	General Education	3.451
4	Personality	3.785
5	Technical Education	4.071
6	Appearance	5.058
7	Tests	5.225

It is significant that business experience is rated one full rank-order higher than the next most important characteristic, business education. It should be noted that this ranking is for initial hiring to the field. One may well wonder whether experience should be considered of such prime importance for getting into purchasing. It would appear to be a reflection of the fact that many purchasing employees are acquired by interdepartmental transfers or are hired from the purchasing departments of other companies. As the next section indicates, there is an increasing emphasis being given to education as a prerequisite for purchasing and this may gradually tend to deemphasize prior experience as the chief prerequisite for entry into a purchasing department.

[4] A 1972 unpublished survey by the authors.

Education

Today, some college education has become a virtual necessity for anyone expecting to get ahead in the field of purchasing. The survey of the 12 purchasing manager associations supervised by the authors in 1972 showed that of the 214 respondents 85.5% had some college education, 32.7% had completed a degree program, and 15.9% had had graduate education. The fact that about one-half of the members of a representative group of purchasing employees had completed college or beyond is indicative of the advisability of higher education for anyone aiming at a high managerial position in this field.

The study also showed that 58.4% of the respondents who had gone to college majored in business administration while 16.9% majored in engineering. The remaining 24.9% had studied in a variety of fields. These percentages suggest that a general business background in education probably offers the likeliest entree into the field. An engineering education is probably best where the purchasing operation involves highly technical products.

Sources of Purchasing Personnel

Sources of purchasing employees may be grouped into two categories. Internal sources include employees from other departments of the company, employees recommended by present members of the purchasing department, and employees recommended by other members of the company. External sources include all sources outside the organization. Some of the more important of these are classified and display advertisements, college and university placement offices, employment agencies, direct solicitation by prospective employees, and recommendations by outsiders.

An indication of the relative importance of these various sources of purchasing employees may be obtained from the data in Table 18-2. In tabulating the responses it was observed that larger firms tended to rely on classified advertisements to a greater extent than smaller firms. The table shows that the two most important sources of purchasing employees were transfers within the organization (35%) and classified advertisements (33%). When the same data are analyzed to determine the source of purchasing employees above the clerical level, a different pattern emerges. For these higher-level employees, internal transfers account for 50% of all placements and classified advertisements for only 21%. The more recent survey of 12 associations in general confirms the figures in Table 18-2.

TABLE 18-2. Percentage of Employees Hired from Various Sources by a Selected Sample of Firms

	Clerks	Assistant Buyers	Buyers	Assistant Purchasing Agent	Purchasing Agent	Total
Transfers within organization	11	42	48	54	63	35
Classified advertisements	51	32	20	16	12	33
Solicitation by employee	13	19	17	11	25	15
Employment agencies	9	7	6	7		7
School placement office	8		4	5		5
Other	8		5	7		5
Total	100	100	100	100	100	100

Source: An unpublished study conducted by a graduate student under the direction of the authors.

Internal Transfers

Hiring from within an organization has much to recommend it, especially when a transfer can be made from a closely related department. Training time can be reduced because there is no need for covering such general matters as company history, organization, and policies. Knowledge of the company's products and familiarity with personnel with whom the employee must work is also an advantage of the internal transfer as a source of purchasing employees. If the transfer is from the production department, the new member of the purchasing department brings considerable knowledge that will be of aid in buying. Finally, it is universally recognized that internal transfers aid in building morale within an organization, especially when the new position is of higher rank than the one from which the individual was transferred.

Recommendations

Purchasing personnel hired through the recommendation of present purchasing employees or others within the company occasionally prove successful. Employees in the department are aware of the characteristics and qualities that are desirable for purchasing work, and if they are persons of sound judgment, their recommendations are likely to have merit. Unfortunately, it is often found that this source results in the hiring of friends and relatives without much regard for ability. It is extremely difficult for a company official to know whether a recommendation is being made in the interest of the company or the interest of the individual.

Newspapers

Advertisements furnish the majority of recruits from external sources. Classified advertisements in local newspapers are of particular value for the lower-ranking positions. Such advertisements generally result in a large number of responses, but frequently not many from promising prospects. Even when great care is exercised in preparing the advertisement to describe the job and the necessary qualifications with precision, there will be a large proportion of unacceptable applicants. Some companies have found that display advertisements are more selective, since specifications can be stated in greater detail. Display advertisements are most widely used for higher-ranking positions and are frequently run in distant metropolitan newspapers.

Display advertisements in newspapers, magazines, and trade journals enable a concern to reach persons who are currently employed and cannot take the time to solicit new employment. Advertisements also reach employees or competitors without the personal solicitation that might be considered improper. The "situations wanted" columns of a newspaper will occasionally obtain a good employee. People placing such advertisements have shown the strong desire for employment that suggests initiative.

Colleges and Universities

The use of college and university placement offices for securing purchasing personnel is increasing in importance as the trend toward employing college graduates in purchasing positions continues. This is a highly specialized form of recruiting, and most of the larger companies that now use this source recruit simultaneously for a number of different divisions within the company. College recruiting is frequently handled by the personnel department of the firm. Many colleges and universities have facilitated the recruiting of employees by establishing placement bureaus, providing facilities for interviews, securing recommendations of faculty members, and compiling records of the scholastic achievement of applicants. A number of secondary and vocational schools today provide similar services for their students. The latter two sources are especially valuable in recruiting clerical and lower-ranking personnel for the purchasing department.

Selection of Purchasing Personnel

The selection process may be divided into three stages: (1) forms, (2) interviews, and (3) tests.

Forms

Application forms are almost universally used by industrial concerns. These forms contain a number of questions designed to obtain background information about the applicant that will be useful in evaluating his qualifications for the position under consideration. These questions relate to such matters as the applicant's personal and family background, health, educational and work experience, and his current family and living conditions. Correctly designed questions, when properly interpreted, aid immeasurably in the evaluation of an applicant.

The use of application blanks before interviews enables a company to weed out those applicants who are obviously not qualified for the position. They further serve as a good starting point for the interviews and provide a basis for verifying the honesty of the applicant. This is accomplished by formal or informal checking on some of the statements made on the blanks and by consulting the references given. Application blanks should not be used as the sole basis on which the decision to hire is made. They are but one of three tools that should be used in the selection process.

Many companies use a form letter to communicate with character references given by the applicant. There is much difference of opinion among experts as to the value of information secured by this means. Most people asked for a reference feel that in the interest of giving everyone another chance they should not report derogatory information. One skilled in the process of selection will, therefore, study a report from a reference for its omissions rather than its explicit statements. A reference letter may also uncover misrepresentations by the applicant about previous employment or similar pertinent facts. Thus its role in the selection process should be to supplement the application blank.

Interviews

The interview is a selection tool that is even more widely used than the application blank. A common practice is to hold a preliminary interview which, together with the application blank, is a part of the screening process for eliminating those who do not merit further consideration. Frequently this preliminary interview is conducted by a member of the personnel department. The second and succeeding interviews are conducted by the purchasing agent. These interviews are much more extensive than the preliminary interview and furnish most of the information on which the final decision is based.

The purpose of interviews is to allow the employer and the applicant to get acquainted so that each can judge whether he has further interest in the other. When conducting an interview, the purchasing agent should remember that it is as important to sell the company to the prospective employee as it is for the applicant to sell himself to the purchasing agent. In order to accomplish both objectives, the purchasing agent must get the applicant to talk freely. This can usually be accomplished by discussing the job and the company for a short time until the applicant feels at ease, and then asking questions designed to get the applicant to talk about himself—the subject he is most familiar with. An important element in a fruitful interview is a detailed plan of the ground to be covered during the interview. Experienced companies prepare interview patterns or guides to aid the interviewers in this matter. It is also important to record all pertinent information as soon as the interview is over. The interviewer should not trust his memory, especially if several applicants are to be interviewed for the same position.

Tests

Many companies use psychological tests as a third tool in the selection of employees. There is a wide difference of opinion among employers concerning the value of tests, and there is a great diversity of tests available. All psychological tests used for selection may be conveniently divided into three catagories: (1) intelligence tests, (2) personality and interest tests, and (3) aptitude or trade tests.

The use of intelligence tests is based on the assumptions that intelligence can be measured and that there is some relationship between intelligence and success in purchasing. It should be understood that neither of these two assumptions has been proved. There are a number of different tests that can be used for measuring intelligence. Some measure mechanical intelligence (the ability to manipulate objects), others measure abstract intelligence, and still others measure the ability to understand people (the so-called social intelligence tests).

Personality tests are used to rate an applicant on such traits as self-confidence, temperament, emotional maturity, and other personality traits that would appear to be important as a measure of success. Interest tests are designed to reveal the extent to which an applicant's interests coincide with those who have been successful in the field. Aptitude tests are designed to measure the natural ability of an applicant in the field for which he is applying and his inherent fitness for the work. Aptitude tests have been found to be quite reliable in measuring mechanical or clerical abilities, but in testing for positions requiring judgment and mental abilities the aptitude tests have not proved reliable.

The selection of personnel through psychological tests is in an early stage of development. Such tests, therefore, should be viewed as a supplement to established procedures, and the results of tests should be compared with later success on the job. If this is done for enough people over a sufficiently long period of time, it may lead to validation of some of these tests, so that at a future date they may become a more reliable selection device.

The use of the lie detector, or polygraph, has been gaining in popularity as a means of verifying the information given by a prospective employee on the application blank. The cost of a polygraph test is only about one-fourth that of a background check and this economy makes it appealing in any company that interviews several applicants for each position filled. There is a growing sentiment against the widespread use of the polygraph because it is thought to constitute an invasion of privacy. This objection should not be controlling where the position is a fiduciary one involving the administration of substantial sums of money.

Training for Purchasing Personnel

There are three types of training for purchasing personnel. First, education by schools, particularly universities and their extension divisions, which can be adapted to the training needs of full-time students, beginners in the field of purchasing, and practicing purchasing men. The second type of training is that given to its own beginners by an individual business concern. This is generally called "job training." The third type of training, "in-service training," is designed primarily as a means of continuing a person's training after the person has progressed sufficiently to no longer be classified a beginner. The subject matter peculiar to each of these three types of training will be considered after a brief discussion of training methods.

One method of training a new employee is by "trial and error." Put the beginner in the water and let him "sink or swim." Many of today's most successful purchasing agents learned their jobs in this manner. No accurate method of measuring the costs of such a training method has been devised. However, it is probable that the costs of this method are disproportionate to the number of good purchasing personnel that it produces. When a company resorts to this method of training, it is probably admitting that it has not taken the trouble to develop a better method.

A second method of training new employees in purchasing is the "big brother" technique. The new employee is assigned to an experienced employee in the department. For as long as necessary the new employee works under the direct supervision of a "big brother." As he develops skill, he is given new responsibilities until he is able to do his job without more than the usual amount of supervision. When this method is employed in the purchasing department, the new employee starts with routine tasks, such as clerical and filing; progresses to invoice checking, requisitions, and stock record checking; and is next permitted to make routine repeat-order purchases to gain buying experience.

A third method of training involves semiformal classes or seminars. This method is well adapted to use by a large company, but it can be utilized by smaller companies also if the beginners from several firms are collected into groups and taught under combined auspices or with the aid of a nearby college or university. The seminar method is usually best for handling the continuing training of experienced personnel. This method works best with a small group of 5 to 25 trainees and relies heavily on group participation in the discussion rather than on the lecture method of teaching.

One variation of this method is known as "role playing." The individuals taking part in the training are assigned specific "business parts" to be acted out in some typical situation which has been previously planned by the instructor. If skillfully planned and executed, the situation can be made so realistic that the participants forget that they are playing a role and act as they would in a real situation. The leader of the seminar session can point out the strong and weak points of the performance after it is over and thereby enable the trainees to learn by doing. Role playing is not suited to all the subjects that must be covered by a training program, but it does serve as a stimulating supplement to the usual methods of presenting training materials. Principles, procedures, and policies are examples of matters that must be covered by use of lectures or round-table discussions.

The study of a purchasing manual is frequently assigned in conjunction with one of the three training methods. Many companies today have prepared such manuals setting forth company policies, procedures, and related matters pertaining to a purchasing department.

University Training

The training afforded both potential and actual purchasing department employees by universities is of three types. The full-time student can pursue a program leading to a degree, with some amount of specialization in the field of purchasing. It is estimated that more than 250 colleges and universities are now offering at least one course in purchasing, either in a school of business or in an engineering school. In the curricula of most universities, many courses offer good training for a student interested in a purchasing career.

The second type of training for purchasing sponsored by colleges and universities consists of extension courses, which are normally run during evening hours and are designed to attract inexperienced employees in the field of purchasing. In some of the larger cities these extension courses are jointly sponsored by the evening school division of a university and the local chapter of the National Association of Purchasing Management. Such courses frequently are taught by a practicing purchasing agent, and their content is more specifically tailored to local industrial interests than a similar course offered to full-time college students.

A few universities have undertaken, independently or in conjunction with the National Association of Purchasing Management, the third type of training for purchasing. This training is designed specifically to meet the needs of experienced purchasing personnel. It usually consists of a seminar presentation, relying heavily on participation by the individuals attending the seminar. The seminar leader is generally a national authority in the field and functions primarily to introduce and direct the discussion of the participants. Such programs tend to deal with policy matters more than with the procedural aspects of purchasing.

Job Training and In-Service Training

This training is basically a program of progression through various purchasing duties until a satisfactory degree of competence has been acquired by the trainee. Thorough job training should be supplemented by written materials and contacts with other departments in the company, so that the trainee learns not only purchasing but also such matters as company history, organization, policies, and interrelationships. In smaller companies a beginner may start immediately with some actual work in the department in order to help earn his salary. In large companies it may be possible to organize a training program in which the new employee's efforts need not be immediately productive.

In-service training is especially effective as a means of increasing the skills and abilities of buyers and assistant buyers to qualify them for advancement to higher-ranking positions within the department. This type of education is a recognition of the fact that learning never ceases. Even with a stable and successful purchasing department it is sound practice to continue the training of personnel throughout their business careers. A person with years of experience can still profit from a well-planned and coordinated training program.

The training of experienced personnel differs in content and method from the training of the newer employee. Primary emphasis must be placed on an interchange of ideas rather than on lectures and demonstrations on how to do things. Continuous training is frequently offered by companies through staff meetings held during company time. Such meetings need to be informal enough not to be resented by older employees and yet coordinated enough so that some actual training is accomplished. Such meetings are good places to discuss or explain matters relating to company purchasing policy.

A second technique of in-service training is job rotation. This practice is primarily applicable to larger companies, which have purchasing departments large enough to permit job rotation. Through rotation an employee, by actual experience, learns the duties and responsibilities of several positions and becomes better qualified for promotion. The experienced purchasing employee of a smaller company generally finds that outside sources must provide most of the advanced training. This employee's training is likely to come through talks by business leaders or professional associates sponsored by such groups as the local chapter of the National Association of Purchasing Management. Trade papers and pamphlets on pertinent purchasing subjects also provide substantial training for experienced personnel. Finally, as mentioned earlier in the chapter, some universities sponsor training sessions and institutes that provide a valuable means of keeping abreast of new developments in the field.

Training of purchasing agents for state and local units of government has lagged behind industrial purchasing training, despite the fact that it is possible for governmental units to establish training programs that are as effective as those of industry. The county of Los Angeles has developed such a program, which might well serve as a model for other governmental units.

Compensation of Purchasing Personnel

The straight salary method of compensation is almost universally used in paying employees of purchasing departments. Under this method of compensation the employee is paid per unit of time worked rather than per unit of work performed. Upward revisions in the rate of compensation may be made from time to time, depending on improvement in the quality of the employee's work, company policy, and business conditions.

In many companies employees are classified into various wage-level groups, with steps in each group denoting the individual's relative proficiency. Improvement in proficiency, gained through application and experience, may justify advancing an employee through the steps of one wage-level group into a higher group, with a higher rate of compensation at each advance in level.

Since purchasing responsibilities are hard to measure, and since the salary of each employee in each level should reflect his relative proficiency in that level, it is important that some measure of ability and performance of each employee be devised and used periodically to rate the individual's progress. On the basis of these ratings, the employee should be advised of his shortcomings or rewarded for his improvement with a salary increase.

Some companies have devised rating scales, which have tended to remove inequities in salary rates within various job levels, and have made possible a relatively close evaluation of each employee's progress and potential. The use of such rating scales removes some of the personal feelings associated with granting or withholding salary increases.

Purchasing executives will normally be included in company-wide incentive or bonus plans. Such plans are almost invariably related to company profits.

The financial opportunities and rewards in the field of purchasing are gradually increasing as greater recognition is given by management to the importance of this business activity. An indication of the range of salaries paid to purchasing agents can be obtained in Table 18-3.

TABLE 18-3.   Salary Levels by Type of Enterprise[a]
(percentage of respondents)

Salary	Manufacturing	Retailing	Public Agency	Financial Institution	Public Utility
Under $10,000	1.7	25.0	2.1	—	—
$10,000–11,999	14.7	16.7	14.6	7.1	—
$12,000–13,999	13.8	8.3	8.3	14.3	36.4
$14,000–15,999	18.0	8.3	12.5	35.7	9.1
$16,000–19,999	27.6	25.0	22.9	14.3	9.1
$20,000–24,999	17.1	8.3	29.2	28.6	27.3
Over $25,000	7.1	8.4	10.4	—	18.1

[a]From a survey by the authors of 12 Purchasing Managers Association in 1972.

Several interesting points are evident from Table 18-3. For practical purposes the starting salary in purchasing departments in 1972 was in the $10–12,000 range, except in retailing where it averaged somewhat less, and in public utilities where it averaged more. There is more evidence of steady upward salary progression in manufacturing than in any of the other categories. The salary ceiling, somewhat surprisingly, is likely to be higher in public agencies than in manufacturing retailing, and financial institutions but less likely to be higher than in public utilities.

Based on the same study a comparison of the responses indicates that job titles and salaries are clearly associated. For example, 88% of the respondents with the title of buyer reported salaries below

$16,000, whereas only 66% of those with the titles of purchasing agent or assistant purchasing agent were paid less than $16,000. Alternatively, 62% of the employees called purchasing managers received $16,000 or more and 78% with the titles of vice-president or director of purchasing reported salaries of $16,000 or more.

The U.S. Bureau of Labor Statistics in its 1967 study entitled "National Survey of Professional Administrative, Technical, and Clerical Pay" included industrial buyer's salaries in its report on salary levels and trends. Unfortunately, the survey does not classify the salaries in terms of department managers or other managerial positions. Instead, employees are classified into categories from Buyer I to Buyer V, according to their degree of buyer skill.

The Buyer I category includes employees whose primary responsibility involves purchasing standard or shelf items. The Buyer V category includes buyers whose purchases are so large that they affect commodity market prices. The study has not as yet included buyers in the Buyer V category.

The median annual salary figures reported for mid-1967, arranged according to two size categories, are shown in Table 18-4. A comparison of this table with Table 18-3 indicates the changes that have taken place during the most recent 5-year period. The report shows that buyers in large companies typically receive more than their counterparts in smaller firms.

TABLE 18-4. Median Purchasing Employee Salaries

Buyer	All Firms	Firms with More Than 2500 Employees
I	$ 6,912	$ 7,500
II	8,088	8,496
III	9,720	10,020
IV	11,640	11,676

Intangible Compensation

Any discussion of compensation for purchasing personnel would be incomplete without mention of the intangible rewards to purchasing agents. First is the challenging and rewarding meetings with salespersons and other representatives of sellers. The buyer is in a position to award business to the seller and as a consequence receives the most courteous and attentive solicitude of the seller's representatives.

Another intangible reward is the satisfaction derived from the fact that buyers are entrusted with the spending of large sums of their company's money. Realization of this responsibility is sobering, and the conscientious fulfillment of this trust is a source of inner satisfaction. Another real benefit received by purchasing personnel is the opportunity to gain an overview of the firm's operations and the interrelationships and interactions of the various departments within the firm.

Because purchasing is closely allied with production, engineering, and sales, its help is constantly enlisted by these departments in finding new or alternate materials, securing technical assistance, determining sales and marketing trends, or even joining with the company's sales representatives in a presentation to a customer who is also a supplier. This variety of endeavor and feeling of accomplishment by sharing in the planning of products and production are interesting, challenging, and rewarding.

Professional Certification for Purchasing Agents

The concept of a program leading to certification of the individual as a professional has been a goal of special-interest groups in various functional areas of business. Today there are such varied certification programs as the Certified Public Accountant, the Certified Professional Casualty Underwriter, and the Certified Professional Secretary. In the field of purchasing the National Institute of Governmental Purchasing has established a program leading to certification as a Certified Public Purchasing Officer. A similar program is in the process of being implemented by the National Association of Purchasing Management.

The program formulated by the National Institute of Governmental Purchasing (NIGP) requires completion of an academic curriculum, a public purchasing curriculum, a written examination, and an oral examination by a three-member board of examiners. In addition, there are age and experience requirements. At various times similar certification programs have been proposed for industrial purchasing agents. Is certification of purchasing agents a desirable objective for those engaged in that activity?

A dictionary's definition of a profession is an occupation in which one professes to have acquired some special knowledge used by way of either instructing, guiding, or advising others or serving them in some art. This definition would appear to exclude purely commercial, mechanical, and agricultural occupations. A professional has been defined as one having the characteristics of or conforming to the technical or ethical standards of a profession or an occupation regarded as such. Under the second definition an individual who behaves professionally and can induce others to regard his work as a profession is a professional. Thus, the matter of professional status for purchasing is, at best, ambiguous.

Various reasons have been advanced for seeking professional designation for purchasing. It may represent a status symbol and be used to deny the fact that many industrial purchasing agents have not achieved the recognition they believe they deserve. Others look upon certification as a means of providing control over individuals entering the field. Because a certification program would probably entail educational requirements, these requirements could be used to guide the preparation of those desiring to enter or advance in the field of purchasing. One cannot quarrel with these objectives, but they may not justify professional certification for purchasing agents. Purchasing agents are not like other professionals such as doctors, lawyers, or professors. They are not even like public accountants who come the closest to having achieved professional status in the field of business.

Three aspects of public accounting distinguish its practitioners somewhat from other business administrators: (1) professional accountants have required that their members possess a certain level of technical knowledge and skill; (2) they render service in an environment of economic independence; (3) the public interest is involved in the nature and results of the accountant's work.[5]

If the foregoing reasons are needed to justify professional designation for an occupation, purchasing and other business activities do not qualify. While industrial purchasing requires some technical knowledge and skill, it is extremely difficult to force upon employers a requirement that only trained and knowledgeable people be employed. Nor do purchasing agents operate in an environment of economic independence. Lastly, the same degree of public interest in the results of the work of the purchasing agent cannot be established.

Those in industrial purchasing can do much to increase the stature of their occupation. They can encourage better performance through higher educational attainments for themselves and for their subordinates. They can foster high ethical standards and condemn the few who do not follow such standards. In other words, they can operate professionally without worrying about professional certification.

[5] Adapted from A. C. Littleton, *Structure of Accounting Theory*, Monograph #5, American Accounting Association, 1958.

DISCUSSION QUESTIONS

1. What are some of the changes in business methods that will require more highly skilled personnel in the purchasing department?

2. What factors influence the size of the purchasing department of a particular company?

3. What two activities take the major share of a buyer's time? Are these also the buyer's most important activities?

4. From what source do most of the purchasing department's personnel come?

5. What use or uses should be made of the application form in hiring for the purchasing department?

6. How would you distinguish between interest tests and aptitude tests? How useful is each in the hiring process?

7. In what part of the training process is the seminar approach usually recommended? What are its advantages?

8. What is role playing? How can it be used in training?

9. What form of compensation is most appropriate for purchasing? Why?

10. Name and discuss some of the intangible rewards of purchasing.

SUGGESTED CASES

Ferner Company

Powers Company

Pressure Tanks, Inc. (B)

The Wagner Corporation (B)

CHAPTER 19
PUBLIC RELATIONS, SOCIAL RESPONSIBILITY, AND ETHICS

Not many years ago the topics mentioned in the title of this chapter were clearly tangential to business operations and quite optional with management. Social responsibility consisted of such things as supporting the Community Chest, sponsoring symphony orchestras, and letting employees serve on civic committees. Ethics was the practice of the golden rule, which was to be commended to all and practiced whenever it did not interfere with efficiency and profit. And public relations was a craft similar to advertising, to be employed whenever the company's reputation had suffered and its image needed a facelift. This view of these activities prevailed at a time when it could safely be assumed that free enterprise and the marketplace economy were beyond question and safe from attack by all but extreme radicals.

Today the situation is changing, and present indications suggest that further changes may be in the offing, particularly with regard to social responsibility. Over the past five years several events have highlighted the growing significance of a new and broader type of social responsibility on the part of corporations. The sudden awareness of pollution, the dwindling of our once plentiful natural resources, and the political implications of the activities of multinational companies in other countries have all served to focus the attention of thinking people on the implications of the unrestrained activities of the business sector of our society.

At present it probably would be more accurate to describe the attitude as one of concern rather than condemnation, but if businessmen do not deal wisely with these issues, it may safely be predicted that our political processes will deal with them one way or another. We seem to have entered a new era in which the old yardsticks of business performance are no longer adequate but new yardsticks are now in the process of being formulated. Operating in such an environment presents an interesting but difficult challenge.

In the coming period public relations will also undoubtedly have to change from what might be described as a "fire-fighting" operation to a "fire-prevention" operation. Business will have to convince the public that whenever it cannot meet the highest expectations with regard to such matters as pollution, use of resources, and ethical behavior, the end-product is worth the price. While this is a reasonable expectation on the part of the public, it is a new one for business and represents a standard to which business has not as yet adapted.

Purchasing may not be in the forefront of this developing role of business, but as an activity that touches various publics, its performance directly affects the total posture of the firm.

The Purchasing Manager and Social Responsibility

Not everyone agrees that business should assume a leadership role in the area of social responsibility. A good case can be made for the position that our economy will achieve its greatest efficiency if managers strive solely for maximum profits and do not voluntarily assume social responsibilities that entail costs. There is little doubt that this would be true if (1) our economy operated in an ethical vacuum and (2) efficiency were the only criterion by which business was measured. Unfortunately, however, business does not operate in a vacuum. The public has certain expectations of business. The economy cannot be sealed off from the rest of life. The public expects and demands a certain kind of performance on the part of the business sector.

The nature of the public's expectations differs from one period to another, and it is important that the business community be sensitive and respond to the demands of the public because through various avenues, especially political, the public determines the orbit of business freedom. At present the public is expressing a strong inclination toward business activism in social and ethical arenas. While such activism may somewhat reduce economic efficiency, that choice seems to have been made by the final arbiters—the public—and business can ignore this message only at considerable risk to its future operational freedom.

One area in which the purchasing manager can play a socially responsible role is in the use of natural resources. There is no denying the fact that a growing population with rising economic expectations will someday exhaust the finite resources of our planet. One can argue endlessly about the date at which this catastrophe will strike but with an exponential growth trend there is no denying the eventual outcome.

To meet the public concern over this issue purchasing managers can play a helpful social and public relations role. Value analysis is an ideal technique to reduce the use of critical materials and to shift as much as possible from the use of nonreplaceable to replaceable resources. Value analysis has been primarily cost-oriented so far, but it could easily be redirected to emphasize the social necessity of conserving resources.

Pollution control is another area in which the purchasing manager may have a role to play. Insofar as the company's own pollution of the environment is concerned the primary responsibility will lie with the company's engineering department. The purchasing department may be of some help in discovering new kinds of pollution control equipment available, but its role here is limited. However, in the area of the use of recycled materials, purchasing managers can be of positive service to their companies.

The energy demands of our society promise to perpetuate our own present energy crisis until we develop sources of energy much more productive and more lasting than the present ones. Here, too, purchasing personnel can be helpful. They can take into account the energy component of the materials and parts they buy and give some advantage to those that minimize the use of power. Such things as the purchase of plastics to replace metals, recycled metals to replace virgin metals, and the use of forms of transportation that minimize the consumption of power are examples of ways in which the purchasing department can improve the company's socially responsible image.

The Purchasing Manager and Ethics

Today there seems to be more concern with, but less understanding of, ethics than formerly on the part of businesspersons. The increased concern probably stems from our relative affluence. As the needs of a society are more adequately met there appears to be some tendency for its members to aspire to higher standards in nonmaterial areas. Over recent years this tendency has been quite evident in a mild revolt of the young against our materialistic society, as well as a feeling of unease on the part of participants in business over the imbalance between the demands of institutions and those of the individual. The concern over ethics is probably fostered by the revelation of many unethical practices on the part of businesspersons and government officials in their dealings with each other.

The lower level of understanding of ethics probably stems from the fact that our society has become so predominantly secular that the typical businessperson has no ethical ideal or standard of reference. The subject of ethics is an exceedingly complex one involving many philosophical and subjective issues which would not be appropriate for a text of this kind. Therefore, all we shall attempt to do is give the reader an exceedingly simplified model of how the subject looks to the authors. It is of the very essence of ethics that everyone must formulate his own system, and what we say about it may serve as a starting point from which readers can begin to formulate their own views.

Business ethics may be defined as a self-generating system of moral standards in the realm of business to which a *substantial majority* of business executives give *voluntary* assent. It is a force within business that leads to industry-wide acceptance of certain standards of practical conduct. Here the standard is a relative one. It is a composite, or a sort of an average, of what the group accepts and practices.

Personal ethics should be distinguished from business, or any other group, ethics. Personal ethics have their source in a person's religion and philosophy of life. Here the standard may be—and in many cases is—absolute. In fact, unless the standard is fixed and is higher than the prevailing group level, the force of competition will lead to its erosion. As the standards and practice of the individuals decline the level of the group ethics declines with it. In time, then, the level of business ethics degenerates and there is no apparent base line or minimum level. There must be some countervailing force such as altruism to offset the eroding effect of selfishness which is inherent in competition. This comes from personal ethics which are derived from clearly defined moral standards.

Figure 19-1 shows the relation of these two kinds of ethics to each other and to the laws of the society in which they operate.

The Purchasing Manager and Public Relations

A business firm has personal relationships running in many different directions. There are relationships between a firm and such groups as the government, the community, the industry, and the entire public. At any particular point in time one or another of these

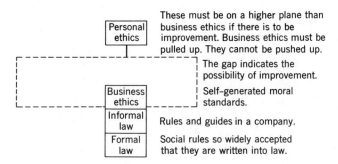

FIGURE 19-1. A model depicting the relationships among personal ethics, business ethics, and the law.

relationships may be of paramount importance, but ordinarily they are not of day-to-day concern to a company. The three groups of greatest and most frequent concern to a firm are its customers, its employees, and its suppliers.

Since the purchasing department is responsible for supplier relationships, it clearly has an important role in building and maintaining good public relations for the firm. In order to do the public relations job well, it is important first of all to have a clear understanding of the nature of the activity.

Some Definitions of Public Relations

While there is no universally accepted definition of the term the following definitions of public relations should serve to delineate its essential meaning. One very simple definition says that public relations is simply good morals and good manners. This definition is placed first because it clearly relates public relations to ethics. It suggests that before a firm can expect its good manners to be appreciated they must be derived from good morals. Public relations, properly understood, is not a matter of putting a good face on bad practices. It consists first of practicing good morals and then conveying this to its public by exhibiting good manners.

Another definition says that public relations is the production and distribution of a good reputation. This definition emphasizes the same point, namely, that public relations involves doing the right thing as well as saying the right thing. While the specialists in public relations may not have a primary role in doing the things that serve as the basis for creating a favorable image, properly understood, public relations is an attitude that must pervade an entire organization if the end result is to be favorable over the long run. In this sense purchasing employees can be effective both in generating and maintaining a good reputation for their company.

A third definition says that public relations is the continuing process by which management endeavors to obtain the goodwill and understanding of its customers, its employees, and the public, inwardly through self-analysis and outwardly through all means of expression. This definition says less about the foundation of public relations although the phrase "self-analysis" hints at its ethical origins. On the other hand, this definition is somewhat more explicit in describing the methods of the practice of public relations. The three definitions are essentially consistent and rather adequately convey the meaning of public relations in business.

It was stated above that the purchasing department practices public relations toward company suppliers. However, in the very broadest sense it might be noted that this cannot be done effectively unless purchasing employees gain the willing cooperation of company employees—minor executives, major executives, and general management. This may be thought of as internal public relations and will be discussed next.

Internal Public Relations

A successful purchasing operation depends heavily on the soundness of its internal relations. Rapport with other functional areas within the company determines to a large extent whether purchasing's external relations will be satisfactory. Understanding the interrelationships between departments is essential to success. The realization that each function is dependent on the other makes for an effective operation. Even though purchasing may have come of age and its contributions may be more widely recognized than formerly, internal public relations will be harmed by an overemphasis of this fact by purchasing personnel.

The interdepartmental problems that inevitably arise can be overcome much more easily if a cooperative attitude exists. Problems of specifications, quality levels, delivery times, and vendor qualification can be much more easily dealt with if purchasing personnel become aware of the fact that there may be more than one solution to a problem. If such an attitude exists in the purchasing department, others in the company will be favorably disposed toward the purchasing function and its efforts on behalf of the company.

A friendly atmosphere can be promoted by certain techniques available to all employees. These may range from formal reports to press releases, to stories in company papers, to bulletin board announcements, to informal visits with personnel in other departments. Every organization has its informal communications network, and employing it is an effective way of achieving good public relations. The informal communications system can also be used to gain useful information for the purchasing department from within the company.

Informal "feedback" channels can efficiently furnish information on acceptability of product or shop problems with materials that are not important enough to get into official reports. Frequently one product is more acceptable to the men in the shop than another for reasons difficult to identify. Such knowledge is important to the purchasing personnel and can be used to avoid irritations that develop from such prejudices. Purchasing people can facilitate these informal communications if they recognize their possibilities.

Formal reports generally relay information to management. They deal with volume of expenditures, volume of materials, and effectiveness of supplier relations. Another kind of management report can also be quite effective—a regular report on markets, price trends, supply trends, substitute materials, improved materials, and new materials. If well written, such reports can be used by other departments as a guide in changing designs and manufacturing processes to accommodate to important shifts in the market.

External Public Relations

Sound external relations are built on a foundation of internal acceptance of the purchasing organization. A purchasing department cannot convey to external publics an image of effectiveness, cooperativeness, and responsibility if its internal position is weak.

An important benefit of a favorable internal climate is the ease with which a vendor can be induced to assist in the solution of problems that require outside help or cooperative research. In many instances the vendor is well enough acquainted with problems that affect an entire industry to make helpful suggestions that will guide the company into avenues of research that achieve the solution to the problem. Thus, good external relations are dependent on good internal relations, and the results of cooperation are expanded through the good relations between the purchasing department and its vendors.

Conversely, the purchasing department's help in the solution of a difficult problem through a vendor's resources is more helpful in improving internal relations than any other single thing. The company begins to look to purchasing for help.

Some Public Relations Tools and Techniques

A company's own public relations department is the best source of assistance in getting a better public relations job done in purchasing.

Next in importance to professional assistance is the use of certain public relations techniques. Perhaps, as mentioned before, doing an honest job in every interview is the best public relations opportunity for every purchasing agent and buyer. Here the purchasing personnel can indicate their appreciation for the information, advice, and services that are being offered by the vendor, and the vendor obtains his most important reaction to the purchaser. Much more important than concerning oneself with such details as calling hours is the effort to make oneself available to the caller so that he will not have to reschedule visits to accommodate the purchasing department.

There is need for the exercise of good judgment in dealing with representatives of companies with whom there is no likelihood of doing immediate business. Explaining the situation as honestly and diplomatically as possible will save the time of both parties and keep open the possibility of later dealings.

Next in importance to the interview is the correspondence between the buyer and the seller. Here again, the proper attitude will show through in the correspondence. Letters are so important to public relations that many companies hire experts to assist them in improving their letter-writing practice. Where it is necessary to write complaints about quality or count deficiencies, price variations, or delivery failures, care must be taken to avoid negative attitudes.

Such devices as welcome folders identifying the persons who buy particular items, listing department heads and their responsibilities, and describing the company's product line, help to initiate first-time callers. A welcome brochure can also be advantageously used to inform visitors of company policies regarding such matters as gratuities, payment for lunches, and acceptance of entertainment, so that embarrassment can be prevented.

It is the responsibility of the purchasing department to see to it that a salesperson's time is not wasted in needless waiting. Prompt admission to the interview area, or an acknowledgement of his presence with advice as to the amount of delay to be anticipated is proper procedure. Another appointment may be arranged if the day is inconvenient for the buyer. Such consideration is appreciated by the salesperson and conveys the impression that the buyer is aware of the value of the salesperson's time.

An important public relations tool that has come into service in recent years is vendor analyses which, when combined with an informative report to vendors, is extremely helpful in advising them how they rate in the areas of service and delivery.

Another important means available to the purchasing agent is visiting vendors' plants. If visitation is done with proper preparation and by mutual agreement, good public relations will result. The purchasing representative should make a complete plant tour, noting such things as methods of manufacture, testing methods, shipping preparation, maintenance procedures, and new equipment. The representative should inquire about such things as open orders, lead time to be anticipated, and trends in the price levels, which bear on present and future relationships with the vendor.

Professional Relations

The purchasing profession has a strong national organization. The National Association of Purchasing Management, composed of local associations in all major industrial areas of the country, has a membership of more than 18,000 purchasing executives in all types of industrial and institutional purchasing. One of the active committees of NAPM is that on public relations. This committee has as its objectives "to improve purchasing's image to its significant publics" and "to improve understanding of the professional quality and importance of the Purchasing profession."

An advantage of membership in NAPM is the opportunity it provides for members to talk to groups other than purchasing people or to write articles on purchasing subjects for various periodicals. Some chapters have well-developed speakers' bureaus that allow the purchasing agent to contribute to the improvement of the stature of the profession through this kind of service. NAPM chapters often have arrangements with educational institutions for the organization of purchasing conferences, institutes, seminars, and courses that influence public relations.

A former National Chairman of the Public Relations Committee on NAPM said: "Every member of the Purchasing profession lives in a goldfish bowl—twenty-four hours a day—every day—both on and off the job. Everything he says or does is watched by the general public. It is just human nature for everyone to watch any person who is spending someone else's money." In view of this public interest, ethics is a matter of great interest to the purchasing profession.

Although ethics tend to be codified into neat little compilations of "do's" and "don'ts," it is more than this. Rules and regulations will always be superficial because truly ethical conduct, coming from within a person, is the result of a conscious resolution of an inner conflict between what persons are tempted to do and what they ought to do.

Ethics deals with man in society. Most people conform to the law, written and informal. This might be called the sphere of practical ethics. But many issues confronting a person transcend what society has reduced to rules. Also, new situations arise when a person has to resolve the conflict between what society does and what his ideal decree.

These considerations explain the endless discussions of how much of a gift is allowable, who pays for the lunch, and whether the buyer should pay the cost of transportation on a plant visit. Attempts to reconcile the real with the ideal usually result in rules for guidance. These rules developed by a department, a company, or an association, have the practical effect, at least, of raising the minimum standard of ethics for a profession, although they may leave unresolved many difficult problems for the individual who has the urge to be ethical.

Examples of rules of conduct to be found in the Principles and Standards of Purchasing Practice of NAPM are:

1. To consider, first, the interest of his company in all transactions and to carry out and believe in its established policies.
2. To be receptive to competent counsel from his colleagues and to be guided by such counsel without impairing the dignity and responsibility of his office.
3. To buy without prejudice, seeking to obtain the maximum ultimate value for each dollar of expenditure.
4. To strive consistently for knowledge of the materials and processes of manufacture, and to establish practical methods for the conduct of his office.
5. To subscribe to and work for honesty and truth in buying and selling, and to denounce all forms and manifestations of commercial bribery.
6. To accord a prompt and courteous reception, so far as conditions will permit, to all who call on a legitimate business mission.
7. To respect his obligations and to require that obligations to him and to his concern be respected, consistent with good business practice.
8. To avoid sharp practice.
9. To counsel and assist fellow purchasing agents in the performance of their duties, whenever occasion permits.

10. To cooperate with all organizations and individuals engaged in activities designed to enhance the development and standing of purchasing.

The Code of Ethics of the National Institute of Governmental Purchasing describes the purchasing agent as follows:

1. He does not seek or accept a position as head or employee of a governmental purchasing agency unless fully in accord with the professional principles of governmental purchasing and unless he is confident that he is qualified to serve under these principles to the advantage of the governmental jurisdiction which employs him.

2. He believes in the dignity and worth of the service rendered by government and his own social responsibility as a trusted public servant.

3. He is governed by the highest ideals of honor and integrity in all public and personal relationships in order that he may merit the respect and inspire the confidence of the agency and the public which he serves.

4. He believes that personal aggrandizement or personal profit obtained through misuse of public or personal relationships is dishonest.

5. He keeps the governmental jurisdiction which employs him informed, through appropriate channels, on problems and progress of the agency which he serves, but keeps himself in the background by emphasizing the importance of the facts.

6. He resists encroachment on his control of personnel in order to preserve his integrity as a professional administrator. He handles all personnel matters on a merit basis. Political, religious, and racial considerations carry no weight in personnel administration in the agency which he directs or serves.

7. He does not seek or dispense personal favors. He handles each administrative problem objectively without discrimination on the basis of principle and justice.

8. He subscribes to and supports the professional objectives of the National Institute of Governmental Purchasing.

SUMMARY

Business is in the process of acquiring a strong sense of social responsibility. In part this seems to be brought about by the higher expectations of the public, expressed through the channel of government control. It is greatly encouraged by the high level of prosperity that has prevailed for an extended period, enabling business executives to concern themselves with such matters as corporate images and ethics rather than sheer survival. It may also be attributed to the fact that most persons seem to have an inherent desire to be better themselves, and this urge induces a concern over their social standing.

Whatever the motivation, there appears to be a significant and growing movement toward the acceptance of a social role by business. Although this change in goals may be somewhat difficult to reconcile with the classical theory of maximizing profit, our system of business organization has always shown more of a tendency to adapt to circumstances than to bear out pure theory. The present adaptation to social needs and demands may well be a response to a new level of affluence and may alter to some extent the nature and operation of our economic institutions. In any case, business managers should be keenly aware of developments in the areas of public relations and ethics, and ethical businesspersons should lend their assistance to many of these changes, which appear to offer the opportunity to practice both sound business and good ethics.

DISCUSSION QUESTIONS

1. Define ethics; business ethics; personal ethics.

2. Should ethics in business be related to an absolute standard or a relative standard?

3. Do you think businesspersons should assume social responsibilities on their own volition when the effect of this action is to reduce the profit?

4. The job of public relations in business is to put the best face possible on the company's behavior. Discuss.

5. Why are the public expectations of business now higher than they were a generation ago?

6. What are the principal external "publics" of the purchasing agent?

7. Show how good internal public relations are essential to good external public relations for the purchasing agent.

8. Name and discuss some of the tools and techniques that a purchasing agent can use in developing good external public relations.

9. How does an association such as the National Association of Purchasing Managers facilitate the practice of public relations by the individual purchasing agent?

10. Discuss the benefits derived from good supplier relations.

SUGGESTED CASES

ABC Corporation (A)

Household Cleaners Corporation

Howell Chuck Company (A)

King County

The Janmar Corporation

Parktown

Utopia School District

CHAPTER 20

PURCHASING REPORTS

No one likes to write reports and almost no one likes to read them. Yet, a large orgainzation is so complex that reporting is imperative if all of those concerned with issues of importance are to be properly informed about them. It is popular today to talk about communications and to observe that many interpersonal problems arise because of a lack of communication. The same is true within organizations. In organizations the problem of communications is increased because a hierarchy exists and the different levels do not easily communicate across the barrier of rank. The officials in the higher ranks tend to issue what those in the lower ranks consider to be arbitrary and uninformed orders. Often such orders result from the fact that those issuing them are working with less than complete information. This inadequate information is often attributable to the fact that those with the greatest knowledge have not relayed it or they may have relayed it in a form that made them appear in a favorable light rather than reporting objective and impartial facts. It is in this light that reports should be viewed—as a form of upward communication in an organization in which such communication is important but difficult.

Business reports are basic means of communication within a firm. Reports typically move from a lower level to a higher level of management and constitute a one-way flow of information. Complete communication requires a two-way, or reciprocal, exchange. Top management has become more cognizant of the need of a reciprocal exchange of information in the enterprise, and is using such devices as written policy statements, newsletters, and staff meetings to communicate downward. All of these can be of value in overcoming the problem of communications, both upward and downward, in a company. In this chapter we shall be dealing with upward communications, through reports from the purchasing department.

Purchasing reports are of three types: (1) intradepartmental reports designed to inform the head of the department about departmental matters, (2) interdepartmental reports directed to other departments, and (3) reports directed to higher levels of management. Informative reports extend the service of the purchasing department to the company by improving interdepartmental efforts and interpreting purchasing's role to management. This chapter will emphasize reports to higher management, since the principles are the same as those involved in other reports.

Primary Purposes of Reports

Three purposes of reports will be discussed: (1) providing information, (2) assisting in evaluation, and (3) aiding self-analysis.

Information

A report is an instrument of managerial control which provides the information on which a person in authority can base a decision or judge an activity. In complex business organizations the top executives must make many decisions on subjects of which they personally have little knowledge. If they are to make sound decisions, they must receive a condensed version of the significant factors affecting the decision at issue. Since their purview ranges over many subjects, higher executives cannot interview personally those who have the detailed facts. Furthermore, oral discussions frequently would be incomplete, since they would not be well planned. Therefore, written reports are best for this purpose, and good reports are a mark of the well-run purchasing department. In performing an information function, management reports interpret the actions, motives, and plans of the purchasing department. Procurement difficulties and market conditions are explained, so that management can make the adjustments necessary to coordinate the efforts of all the departments toward common goals. An important by-product of this informational flow is the development of cooperation through mutual understanding of the operations of the departments.

Evaluation

A second reason for submitting reports to management is that they enable management to evaluate the performance of the department. This is particularly important for the purchasing department, since purchasing is one of the least understood activities within a company. By the submission of reports purchasing agents can edu-- cate management concerning their departments. A report that shows the contribution of purchasing to company profits will do much to gain management recognition of the purchasing function.

Self-Analysis

The third result of reporting is that the preparation itself tends to improve the performance of the department. To prepare a report, the department must, in addition to gathering data on its performance, analyze and interpret these data. In the process of such an analytical review, the purchasing agent is sure to uncover methods and procedures that need improvement. As a consequence the overall efficiency of the purchasing department can be enhanced.

Principles of Report Preparation

Because a report is basically a means of communicating information, the writer should avoid extravagant expressions or any attempt to display his erudition. A report should be as brief and to the point as is possible. It must be remembered that the recipient will be a busy person, and the report will compete for attention with many other administrative matters as well as with other reports. At best the study of reports is unpleasant, and the task should be made as light as possible by making the report easy to read. The following principles will help accomplish this end.

1. *Direct the Report to a Specific Person.* Every report will be of primary interest to some particular person even if it is addressed to several. Prepare the report with this person in mind, considering his motivations, his level with respect to how this influences his need for facts, and his time limitations.

2. *Be Objective.* Emphasize the facts and conclusions presented in the report. Sometimes it will be of value to the reader to present personal opinions but, when this is done, the writer should be careful to present the opinion without injecting emotions. An opinion expressed with undue emotion puts the reader on guard against a hidden bias on the part of the writer and often renders the expressed opinion less than worthless. The writer of a report should always remember that his report is to become the basis for some executive action. The executive will want all the facts possible, logically arranged for easy assimilation.

3. *Be Specific.*   It is the report writer's job to sort out the relevant from the irrelevant facts. The reader wants the essential facts, but will soon lose respect for a report that burdens him with a mass of undigested data only remotely related to the point at issue. The writer should try to tell all that the reader will want to know—not all that the writer knows.

4. *Save the Reader's Time.*   It was mentioned previously that a report is competing for the executive's time—often at a disadvantage. Therefore, the writer should attempt to make the report inviting. This can be accomplished to a large extent through form. If the report begins with a summary and conclusions section, the busy executive can read this over quickly and get the highlights of the report. If the report uses titles and subtitles generously the reader can refer from the summary to any section of the report on which he wants supporting facts. If the reader finds these sections clearly and pointedly expressed, he will subconsciously find himself reading more of the report than he expected to read.

5. *Interpret Data.*   Raw statistics, even when reduced to charts and tables, are hard to interpret by someone remote from the day-to-day operations of a department. Significant facts and relationships should be pointed out to the reader. Whenever possible, comparisons should be made with the figures for previous periods. Frequently the trend is more important than the present status.

6. *Do Not Draw Unwarranted or Unnecessary Conclusions.*   It is usually better strategy to understate than to overstate an issue. Do not say "the facts prove" unless they do prove the point beyond reasonable doubt. A report is not a sales presentation, and the writer should not endeavor to force a decision by the way he marshals his evidence. Also, the writer should not draw more conclusions than are necessary. The report is supposed to provide the evidence on which the reader can reach conclusions. Therefore, the writer should limit the report principally to facts and not try to put conclusions into the reader's mind.

7. *Keep the Number of Reports at a Minimum.*   The number of reports always tends to increase. There are at least ten people inaugurating new reports for every person eliminating them. It has been said that the most useful report is the one that shows how to eliminate one out of three existing reports. All reports should be reviewed at stated intervals to see whether they are still being used and whether they are serving their intended purpose. Report writing is hard and time-consuming work which should be minimized. Reports should be

the purchasing department probably would not report on substitutes found each time it submitted its periodic report. In other instances the purchasing department may have duties not covered by the outline, such as checking incoming invoices. The department would then naturally report on these activities in its periodic reports. Finally, most companies will have certain peculiarities that lead them to want certain information reported, and the periodic report should be designed to conform to such management desires.

Statistical Presentation

Many of the data in a periodic report will be statistical, and such material is very difficult to present interestingly and accurately. It has already been mentioned that bar charts, band charts, pie charts, and graphic curves are very helpful in making statistics comprehensible. However, if one wants to emphasize actual values rather than the trend or rate of change, the ordinary tabular presentation is best.

Mean. Quite frequently a mass of statistics can be greatly simplified for the reader by the process of averaging. One should, however, make judicious use of averaging because it can be misleading if it is not properly done. A very simple instance of this is the averaging of unlike things. It is obvious to anyone that horses and cows should not be averaged, but one finds many cases where slightly different categories of things have been totaled and averaged, and the result has been confusing rather than clarifying. Therefore, it is important to remember, first of all, to average things that are completely alike or homogeneous. A second point to remember is that there are different methods of averaging and that each has its peculiar advantage. The commonest method is known as the arithmetic mean. In fact, this method is so popular that most people identify the arithmetic mean with averaging. Actually there are three different methods of averaging, each of which has its advantages for certain purposes. The three methods are the arithmetic mean, the median, and the mode.

The arithmetic mean is computed by totaling the quantities of individual items and dividing this total by the number of individual items that have been totaled. This method of averaging is best where the individual items to be averaged are all very similar or homogeneous in nature and should only be used where the items fall into a rather normal frequency distribution curve.

Median. If a few of the items differ from the rest of the group by substantial amounts—either above or below—it is usually better to take the median. The median is computed by arranging the items to be averaged, and taking the magnitude of the item at the midpoint of the total number as the average value of the group. This method of averaging is most applicable where there is an extreme range in the magnitude of the items, where the frequency curve is not normal, and where there are a few items far above or below the midpoint. If one were to take the arithmetic average of such a series, the few extreme items would have a disproportionate influence on the average, and such an average would not be a true picture of the main group of items. With the median, these extreme items are each counted as only one item and therefore do not unduly distort the final average.

Mode. The third method of averaging, known as the mode, is to arrange the items into several small groups or classes. This is done by dividing the range from the highest to the lowest item into equal-size group intervals and then recording each item in its proper group. The group that contains the largest number of items is then taken as the average. This method is most applicable to a situation in which the items, by their very nature, fall into certain sizes. What may then be desired is a knowledge of which size is the most frequently used. An arithmetic average would, in all probability, give a figure that did not conform to any standard size. The median, by summing several groups that were not large in themselves, might indicate the average to be a size used but infrequently. Only the modal average would be certain to reflect the most popular group or class interval.

Since businesspersons use the averaging process so extensively in their operations, it is of the greatest importance that they understand the dangers inherent in it and the conditions under which the various kinds of average are appropriate.

Logs. In employing graphic presentations, whether curves, bars, or bands, one should be aware of the possibilities of logarithmic comparisons. It frequently is necessary to compare the rate of growth of two series of quite different magnitudes over a period of time. If two such series are compared pictorially, it is likely to appear that the larger-magnitude series has grown at a faster rate, simply because it deals with larger figures. What is needed is a comparison of percentages of growth of the two series. One can buy graphing paper that has one scale plotted logarithmically rather than arithmetically, and such paper can be used to show a percentage-of-growth comparison between two series of different magnitudes.

Analysis and Interpretation of Data

No report can be very effective unless the reporter has analyzed and interpreted the data. It is sometimes thought that the reporting obligation has been discharged when a mass of facts and figures has been put down on paper. Such an attitude reveals a lack of understanding of the purpose of reporting. Reports are supposed to communicate ideas from the reporting department to management. Undigested facts and figures do not communicate effectively to a superior who is not in daily contact with the activity they picture. Therefore, the reporter should point out significant relationships and trends. Unless this is done, the reporter runs the risk that the report will not be read. Even if it is read, a rambling report will not accomplish the objectives listed at the beginning of this chapter.

An example of analysis and interpretation is to point out trends, comment on their significance, and indicate possible explanations. This may be done for both favorable and unfavorable trends, but ordinarily the unfavorable trends are given the most attention, since they suggest obvious points for improvement. In a specific example, a sharp increase in the cost of transportation per dollar of purchases may result from a combination of higher freight rates and a tendency to order in small lots. Nothing can be done about the higher freight rates, but it might be possible to increase the shipping unit by buying some of these low-use items further in advance of needs or by consolidating two or more small-lot shipments. In another instance, a study of the cost of placing orders may show that the fixed costs of processing an order make the costs of following the usual procedure prohibitively high for small orders. Here the solution might be to reduce the number of small orders and to provide that those under a certain dollar amount be paid for out of petty cash. One purchasing agent observed that many of the material shortages involved items bought in small volume. A study revealed that 80% of the items in inventory represented only 20% of the dollar value of the inventory. His report, therefore, recommended that these small dollar items be bought in larger quantities. The result of the new policy adopted by the company was to reduce material shortages with but a slight increase in inventory investment. An incidental result of the new policy was to permit more concentration of attention on important items which increased the efficiency of buying.

These illustrations indicate the value that can be derived by both the purchasing department and the company from careful analysis and interpretation of periodic reports.

Format of Reports

The principal objective of form should be to secure the initial attention of the recipients and thereafter to hold their interest until throughout the report.

One way of achieving this is to make the report appear light and easy to read. Short sentences, short paragraphs, wide margins, and a liberal use of headings and subheadings all work toward this objective.

Titles. As to order of presentation, it is usual practice to begin with a clear and descriptive title that will immediately tell readers whether or not they are interested in the report. A long title is likely to discourage a prospective reader. If a clear description requires a long title, it is usually wise to give the report a short title with a longer and more complete subtitle. The reader will want to know who prepared the report; hence the name of the reporter should appear in connection with the title.

Summaries. . The first part of the report proper should be a summary or a summary and conclusions. This is an important, but often neglected, part of the report. The summary should contain all of the important points of the report in highly condensed form. They should appear in the summary in the same order in which they will be found in the report, to facilitate reference from the summary to the report. An important rule—and one frequently violated—is that the summary should contain no material that does not appear in substance in the report proper. Although the summary should be written last, it is no place for postscripts and afterthoughts.

Text. Following the summary should come the main body or text of the report. Little can be said about the report proper except that it should be clear, logical, complete, and interesting. This is the part of the report in which the writer's ability, originality, and conscientiousness will show up.

Recommendations. The writer's recommendations should appear at the end of the body of the report if they have not been made a part of the summary. They are most likely to appear as a part of the summary when management has specifically requested the report and has asked for recommendations. One should make sure that he does not recommend when the matter at issue is within his own immediate authority. A report should not be used as a device for shifting responsibility. The writer may wish to report on what action he has taken or intends to take. The proper place for such a statement would be in the body of the report where the subject at issue is discussed.

Appendix. Following the body of the report should come the exhibits and appendixes needed to support the statements in the re-

FIGURE 20-1. Picture diagram illustrating number of vendors.

port. These should be as extensive as necessary, but one should avoid trying to create the impression of thoroughness by overloading the report with irrelevant statistics. The only effect that it is likely to have is to dissuade the reader from studying the relevant figures.

Illustrative Techniques

Illustrations provide the reader with a grasp of significant changes and trends without having to analyze detailed figures. Very often the essential points of the report can be summarized in one or two diagrams. There are six basic illustrative alternatives: (1) picture diagrams, (2) pie diagrams, (3) bar graphs, (4) line graphs, (5) maps, and (6) flow charts. Which device to use depends on the material to be presented and the reader for whom it is intended.

Picture Diagrams. The picture diagram has the advantage of being nontechnical while still achieving a strong presentation. In general the pictures are used to portray changes in quantity by altering their relative sizes or numbers. Figure 20–1 illustrates the use of a change in the number of people to emphasize a reduction in vendors over a 10-year period.

Picture diagrams often include geometric figures such as cubes, triangles, and rectangles in addition to representation of people, buildings, and so on, to illustrate the data. When pictures are used, care must be exercised not to give optical illusions. Picture diagrams are not normally used when precision in reporting of facts is desired.

Pie Diagram. Pie diagrams are frequently used, for example, to show the distribution of purchasing expenditures or to express a whole and the sum of its parts. Pie diagrams should only be used when the number of divisions is relatively small. Figure 20–2 is a pie diagram showing a hypothetical distribution of the purchasing dollar expenditures.

Bar Chart. The bar chart is one of the most effective ways to compare quantities. The length of the bar represents the quantity

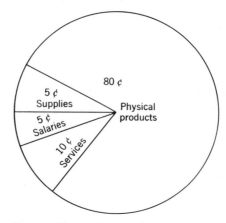

FIGURE 20-2.   Pie diagram illustrating purchasing expenditures.

and the variations in length provide instant comparisons. A bar chart comparing the on-time performance of vendors for two time periods is shown in Figure 20-3.

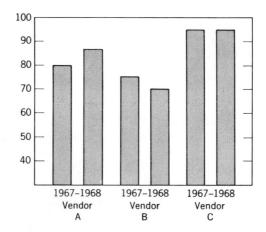

FIGURE 20-3.   A bar chart comparing vendor on-time performance.

Line Chart.   A line chart is particularly useful in presenting data that vary over a substantial period of time. Quantity and time are represented on the vertical and horizontal axes, respectively. Figure 20–4 illustrates a line chart showing a hypothetical relationship between sales and purchasing dollars over time.

Line charts are very useful when attempt is made to project the future on the basis of the past. Such estimates generally use the statisti-

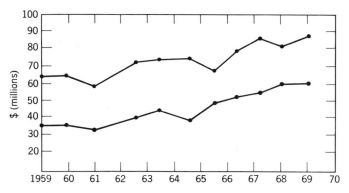

FIGURE 20-4. **Line chart showing sales and purchasing dollars spent—1959-69.**

cal least-squares line to project future estimates. Line charts offer the reader easy comprehension of the relative sizes, and relationships among as many as three or four sets of data.

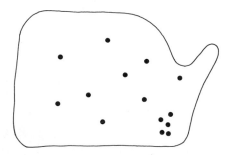

FIGURE 20-5. **Map illustrating vendor distribution.**

Maps. Maps, as an illustrative technique in reports, are used when the data to be presented follow some geographic division. When data appear on a map, the visual effect is instant and clear. Figure 20–5 illustrates the use of a map to indicate the distribution of vendors within a state. Variations can be achieved by letting each dot represented more than one vendor and by expanding or contracting the size of the maps.

Flow Charts. A flow chart can be used to indicate a sequence of operations, series of work procedures, or any similar presentation that involves a series of stages. Figure 20-6 illustrates the use of a flow chart to indicate the procedure followed by an incoming purchasing invoice.

Properly used, these illustrative techniques can add clarity and vividness to any report. Because they summarize in a clear and succinct

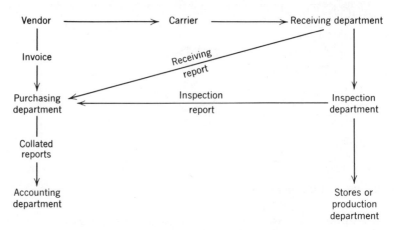

FIGURE 20-6. Flow chart of materials and pertinent forms.

manner, they should be used wherever possible to portray the important data of a report.

Sample reports have not been included in this chapter, because each department will find it necessary to vary its reports in accordance with its objectives and policies. However, the outline that follows is typical of many reports. This outline was derived from a monthly purchasing department operating report submitted to higher management by the director of purchases of a large machine tool manufacturer.

MONTHLY PURCHASING DEPARTMENT OPERATING REPORT

A. Price changes and trends—includes what has taken place during the past month and what is forecast for the next month.
B. Lead time—presented for all major categories purchased and based on expectations for the next 90 days' deliveries.
C. Cost reduction—contains statistics on savings effected by purchasing activities.
D. Progress on current assignments—the report from which this outline was derived contained information on the value analysis program, standardization program, vendor visitations, and departmental expense controls.
E. Unusual occurrences—strikes at suppliers' plants, personnel changes, and so on.
F. Steel—inventory position, amounts received during month, amount currently on order.

DISCUSSION QUESTIONS

1. State and discuss the principal objectives or purposes of reports.

2. Name the three types of purchasing reports and indicate the use of each.

3. What principles should be observed in making reports as easy to read as possible?

4. Discuss the differences between periodic reports and special reports.

5. What various aspects of purchasing should be included in a periodic report to insure its completeness?

6. What basic illustrative techniques are commonly used in reporting? Give an example of the kind of data that would be presented by each of the techniques.

7. The person preparing a report often views it as the culmination of his activities. Discuss.

8. Oral reports are quite common in business. What advantages can you see in oral rather than written reports?

9. Occasionally it is a good idea to omit circulating a periodic report to see who misses it. Discuss.

10. The report may not be an ideal communication device, but it is one of the few ways of communicating upward in a formal organization. Discuss.

SUGGESTED CASES

Davis Mills, Incorporated

Pressure Tanks, Inc. (A)

Smith Electronic Corporation

CHAPTER 21
EVALUATING PURCHASING PERFORMANCE

Evaluation of the purchasing department is essential to the economic health of the firm and to the morale and development of procurement and materials personnel. However, the task is complicated because purchasing as a function must deal with people and ideas; much of its efforts are involved with interpersonal relations with sales, engineering, and other departments within its own and supplying firms. In contrast, other functions are more amenable to objective measurement. The production department, for example, can be evaluated relative to units of output, man-hours of labor, power consumption, rejection rates, and technical product tests.

This is not to suggest that the purchasing department should not be evaluated, but rather that evaluation should be made with full recognition of the inherent problems that exist. Furthermore, the results of evaluation should be interpreted with caution.

Every management function must be measured in terms of its contribution to the basic objectives of the firm. The evaluation consists of developing measurement criteria and then measuring performance against these criteria. The task of evaluation is difficult even in the simplest case because few functions can be accurately or completely measured in quantitative or objective terms.

Evaluation Objectives

Improve Performance. Perhaps the most fundamental reason for evaluating any department is a desire to improve its performance. As a basis for suggesting improvements it is necessary to ascertain the current level of performance. After the level of performance has been determined it is possible to discern the points that need improvement. It is likewise necessary to know the current level of performance before establishing a goal of expected attainment.

Provide Evaluation Data. A second purpose of evaluating performance is to establish an acceptable basis on which to judge the abilities and capacities of the personnel assigned to the purchasing function. Colleagues and superiors are constantly forming judgments about the people with whom they work. This judgment process is necessary and inevitable; hence it is extremely important that those who must make formal judgments about purchasing personnel be given the best data available about their performance. Such data should also become the groundwork for establishing policies on hiring, training, compensating, and promoting personnel.

Improve Morale. A concomitant of the evaluation of purchasing performance is the likelihood of imporved morale and increased efficiency of purchasing personnel. It is recognized that employees do better work and take a greater interest in their jobs when they know that their efforts will come to the attention of their superiors. Good employees do not object to having their work measured by management if they are convinced that the measure is fair and reasonable.

Aid Organization. Evaluation may be used by management as an aid in internal reorganization and the assignment of functions among departments within the company. It has been pointed out in Chapters 2 and 3 that there is substantial variation in the number and kind of activities assigned to purchasing departments. Through evaluation it is possible for management to determine how effectively a given activity is being performed, whether it might be advisable to reassign the activity, or whether related activities should be assigned to the purchasing department.

Facilitate Coordination. A multiplant company that has decentralized purchasing to its several plants will find evaluation an effective tool for controlling and coordinating the purchasing function throughout the company. Through uniform evaluation techniques it is possible to compare the performance of the various purchasing departments. Moreover, evaluation will provide a flow of information from the several plants through which improved methods and techniques in one plant can be transferred to others.

Evaluation Criteria

The difficulty inherent in evaluating people was mentioned in the introduction to this chapter. In this section we consider some of the more common evaluation criteria and some of the problems that arise in using them. Although no one formula exists for measuring all purchasing performance, this does not preclude the possibility of measuring specific aspects of the function. The following evaluation criteria can be combined for an overall picture of purchasing performance.

Cost-Purchase Comparison

A common measurement device relates the dollar volume of purchases to the dollar cost of operating the department. The result is a figure indicating how much it costs to spend a dollar. It is calculated by dividing the annual cost of operating the purchasing department by the dollar volume of annual purchases. Surveys indicate that these costs have a wide range, depending on the complexity of the finished product and the proportion of raw materials to labor costs in manufacturing.

This ratio of departmental costs to purchase volume has significance for evaluating a single department over time, provided that its responsibilities have remained fairly constant. Its greatest limitation is that it represents a measure of total departmental performance and does not indicate points of strength or weakness within the department.

Cost-purchase comparisons between purchasing departments of different companies are not likely to be revealing, since there usually are substantial variations in both factors of the ratio. Different companies buy different proportions of raw materials and processed goods, and this significantly alters the dollar volume of purchases. Different companies assign quite different responsibilities to their purchasing departments, and this influences the costs of running the departments. Thus there is likely to be little common basis for comparison among companies on this criterion.

Cost per Order

Attempts are often made to evaluate purchasing departments in terms of their cost per order placed. The calculation is made by dividing total purchasing department costs by the number of orders placed. This measurement may be criticized because it can so easily be manipulated by those being evaluated. They could greatly improve their showing by ordering smaller quantities more often. Even if a company established controls over the size of orders, the cost-per-order approach to evaluation is becoming less useful because many firms are beginning to buy under open-end and annual contracts. Under such contracts materials releases, sometimes on an automatic basis, replace formal orders for individual shipments. Although this practice decreases the paper work, it raises the cost per order. In such cases the higher cost per order denotes increased, rather than decreased, efficiency.

The difficulty of using cost criteria for intercompany purchasing comparisons is illustrated in Table 21-1, which shows the variations in cost ratios found in a recent survey of purchasing costs.

TABLE 21-1.

Ratio	Variation	Median
Costs/purchase order	$2.20–$68	$10
Dollars/buyer	$240,000–$5,500,000	$1,840,000
Costs/requisition	$0.90–$123	$7.50
Dollars/requisition	$125–$8,080	$610
Requisitions/purchasing person	24–6,860	1,270
Active items/buyer	111–12,500	2,250

Source. Victor H. Pooler, "Measuring the Purchasing Man: TREND," *Journal of Purchasing,* November 1973, p. 73.

Return on Investment

Another approach employing cost data involves the calculation of the net savings per dollar spent on purchasing—referred to as the "return on purchasing investment." Figure 21-1a, illustrates such a calculation.

In this illustration the return is arrived at by multiplying the degree of effectiveness (purchasing savings minus departmental operating costs divided by total purchases) by dollar disbursement (dollars spent per dollar of departmental operating costs). Dollar disbursement can be misleading, since one could cut operating expenditures and thus increase the dollars spent per dollar of operating costs, but departmental efficiency might be seriously curtailed. Return on invested capital (the lower portion of the figure) is a more significant measure of purchasing performance. Return on invested capital (investment turnover times profit margin) emphasizes purchasing's contribution to profits rather than its expense. Figure 21-1b illustrates the effect of a 3% savings for a firm with 20 million sales and an ini-

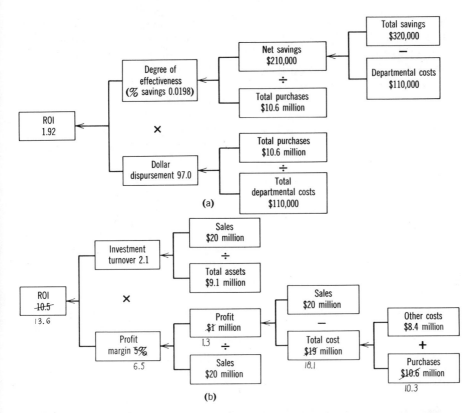

FIGURE 21-1. Comparison of two methods of "return on investment" analysis. Figure b illustrates effect of a 3% savings in purchasing on profits and return on investment. (See Victor Pooler, "TREND," _Purchasing Magazine_, May 1966 and "Measuring the Purchasing Man," _Journal of Purchasing_, November 1973, p. 83.)

tial profit margin of 5%. Purchases are reduced to 10.3 million, profits increased by 300,000, profit margin increased to 6.5%, and return on invested capital improved by 28% (10.5–13.6%).

Other types of evaluation criteria include measures that indicate how well the purchasing department is accomplishing its broad objective of securing the right quality, quantity, price, time, and place.

Quality Criteria

Quality achievement may be measured in terms of the number of rejections of incoming shipments. Defects discovered during the production process should also be considered. The responsibility for defective items must be assumed by the purchasing department because it selected the supplier. Even when the production or engineering departments have designated a supplier, the purchasing department must still share responsibility for poor quality because it should analyze suppliers thoroughly enough to warn the production and engineering departments when they suggest poor sources.

Quantity Critera

Quantity performance can be measured in different ways. One criterion is the amount of "downtime" resulting from a shortage of materials. Another criterion is the amount of rescheduling of production caused by lack of materials. The number of emergency and rush orders processed in a purchasing department also is a measure of the efficiency with which the department is procuring the right quantity. The extent of forward buying to cover production needs and the cost of such coverage both are quantity factors that should be considered in an appraisal of purchasing performance.

Another quantity factor is the relationship between inventory and use. This relationship is known as the turnover rate and is calculated by dividing the value of purchased materials, parts, and supplies by the average investment in such items during the period. A related measure is the inventory losses occurring because of spoilage or obsolescence. A low level of spoilage and obsolescence is a reflection of purchasing efficiency.

Price Criteria

Purchasing performance can be measured by determining how close the department is coming to securing the right price. The long-term relationship between the price paid for purchased goods and the price secured for the company's finished product is an important bench mark. Over time the typical company will find that a reasonably constant proportion of its sales dollar is spent for purchased goods. Short-term performance can then be measured against this long-term standard.

A comparison of the price index of company purchases with one of the standard price indexes can help in appraising price performance. A comparison of the market price at the time of use with the price that was actually paid for that item measures how well a purchasing department is anticipating price changes. Discounts obtained may also be considered in evaluating price performance, but it is difficult to find any basis for comparison other than the past performance of the department.

Time and Place Criteria

Many of the criteria that measure quantity performance are also applicable in determining performance with respect to time and place. In addition to quantity measures, however, it is desirable to compare suppliers' delivery dates with promised shipping dates and to estimate the amount of follow-up required to obtain performance with respect to time and place.

Other Criteria

In addition to the foregoing measures involving dollars spent and saved and quality, quantity, price, time, and place considerations, evaluation can be aided by analyzing performance in terms of the specific steps in the purchasing process.

One such criterion is the total number of purchase orders issued, which is an indication of the work load of the department. One might subdivide this figure into the number of local purchases and nonlocal purchases, small orders and large orders, rush orders and regular orders, and single-item and multiple-item orders.

The number of salesperson interviews conducted, the average time per interview, and the length of time that salespersons are required to wait before seeing the buyer are other factors that can be used in evaluating purchasing performance. The average item required to process an order, from the recognition of need to the mailing of the purchase order, can be measured. The time involved in clearing invoices for payment and the number and amount of discounts lost because of delays in clearing invoices are significant measures of purchasing performance in those companies where invoice checking is a purchasing department responsibility.

Some companies use still another approach in measuring purchasing performance. They evaluate the department in terms of the performance of the head of the department. An attempt is made to classify the department head's workweek into the proportion of time spent on administrative matters and that spent on direct participation in actual purchasing. Frequently such companies tend to overemphasize the administrative aspects of purchasing, on the assumption that a well-run purchasing department requires the head of the department to concentrate on administrative matters. Overemphasis on administration is unwise in that it may divert the efforts of the department head from productive to bureaucratic activities.

An important but difficult aspect of purchasing that should be considered in evaluating performance is the standing of a company with its vendors. This matter must be judged subjectively, since it is one of the intangibles that can be measured only by executive judgment. Its importance should be recognized, for good vendor relations usually make the difference between good and poor purchasing performance.

In evaluating the purchasing department many companies also pass judgment on the relationships between the purchasing department and other departments. Especially important are the relationships among the purchasing, production, and engineering departments. The manner in which the purchasing department plays its part in the overall plan of the company organization should also be examined. Management should consider not only the interrelationships among the various departments but the degree of help and cooperation they afford each other and top management. In this respect purchasing should be particularly watched, since it can uncover data of great help to management on such matters as the trend of the price level, prospective shortages of materials, and new products.

Evaluation Standards

It is in the area of *how* to evaluate purchasing performance that many additional difficulties are encountered. It is perfectly possible to say what should be evaluated and, in the abstract, how performance should be evaluated. However, when one tries to be specific about the techniques to be employed in evaluation, few useful tools are found. Basically, however, evaluation involves a comparison of what is being done with one of four possible standards:

1. Past performance
2. Budgeted performance
3. Performance of departments in other companies
4. An ideal or norm of performance

Past Performances

Perhaps the most widely used standard is a comparison of the current performance of the department with its past performance of those parts of the purchasing function that are capable of statistical measurement. This approach is of particular value where the size of the department and its assignments are relatively stable from year to year. Figure 21-2 illustrates the use of a data chart covering 21 objective criteria over a five-year span. Comparisons are readily made by noting year-to-year changes.

Data Chart for Determining Indicators of Purchasing Efficiency

No.	Factor	Year	1	2	3	4	5
(1)	$ purchases per year (millions)		12.4	16.6	20.4	16.8	18.0
(2)	$ sales per year (millions)		24.3	33.0	41.5	33.6	35.7
(3)	$ purchases/$ sales ratio (%)	(1) ÷ (2)	51.0	50.2	49.0	50.0	50.5
(4)	Purchase orders per year		24,909	25,530	25,655	26,230	26,000
(5)	Number of purchasing employees		19	23	25	24	22
(6)	Ratio of $\frac{\text{purchasing}}{\text{total employees}}$		1/124	1/122	1/126	1/131	1/146
(7)	P.O.'s per purchasing employee per week	(4) ÷ (5) × 52	25.1	21.4	19.8	21.00	22.7
(8)	$ purchases per purchasing employee per year	(1) ÷ (5)	653,000	722,000	816,000	700,000	819,000
(9)	Average $ value per purchase order	(1) ÷ (4)	500	650	793	640	691
(10)	Purchasing employees per $ million purchases	(5) ÷ (1)	1.53	0.90	1.22	1.43	1.22
(11)	$ cost of purchasing per year		120,000	140,000	153,500	150,000	152,000
(12)	$ cost per purchase order	(11) ÷ (4)	4.83	5.69	5.97	5.73	5.85
(13)	Cost of purchasing as % of purchases	(11) ÷ (1)	.097	.085	.075	.089	.085
(14)	Cost of purchasing as % of sales	(11) ÷ (2)	.0495	.0428	.037	.0446	.043
(15)	$ saved per year		125,200	127,000	321,000	353,000	295,000
(16)	$ saved as % of $ purchases	(15) ÷ (1)	1.01	0.77	1.58	2.10	1.64
(17)	Interviews per week		235	217	196	214	225
(18)	$ telephone expenses per month		265	326	369	351	380
(19)	Purchased material price index-% increase (Base-100)		50.1	51.2	55.3	58.1	61.0
(20)	$ direct labor (millions)		1.82	2.07	2.09	2.15	2.25
(21)	Ratio of purchases to direct labor		6.9	8.0	9.8	7.8	8.0

FIGURE 21-2. Objective criteria—historical evaluation. (Adapted from Victor Pooler, "Measuring the Purchasing Man: TREND," *Journal of Purchasing*, November 1973, p. 74.)

Budgeted Performance

If past data are not available, or if procedures or scale of operation have changed considerably, performance can be evaluated against budgeted goals. This approach is a form of management by objective.

At the beginning of the budget period purchasing objectives are established in view of the firm's total objectives. For example, the plans for a purchasing department of a manufacturing enterprise organized for profit might include the following objectives:

1. Reorganize flow of paper work to reduce clerical effort, with anticipated expense reduction of $10,000 annually, to be accomplished by March 1, 1975.
2. Value-analyze our line of pumps during month of April, with a target of 5% reduction in material cost—potential savings $75,000 annually.
3. Negotiate annual agreements for aluminum casting requirements, with a cost reduction target of $35,000 annually, to be accomplished by February 1, 1975.
4. During the month of June, acquire an additional nonferrous metals buyer to satisfy the increased demands for this class of material.

These purchasing objectives will presumably contribute to the profit objectives of the company and are capable of objective measurement. Evaluation by objective can include numerous budgeted criteria. It provides a goal and an incentive for personnel in addition to concrete evaluation data.

Types of Budgets. Two general types of budgets are used for purchasing activities. One is the purchasing or materials budget, and the other is the department operations budget. The materials budget is an estimate of the amount of materials, parts, and supplies to be purchased during the budget period and is derived from production schedules. The department operations budget deals with the estimated costs of running the purchasing department.

Although many companies do not employ budgets, a number of reasons can be advanced for doing so. An operating budget establishes a standard of performance—at least, a standard of a very general nature. A materials budget enables other departments in the concern to coordinate their activities with those of the purchasing department. For example, the materials budget provides the financial division information on the funds needed to meet the commitments that will be made, and it gives the receiving and stores departments the pattern of their work during the forward period.

Another advantage of budgeting flows from the manner in which the budget is made. Implicit in its preparation is planning, and planning encourages coordination and cooperation. In addition, budgeting means that plans have been formalized to the extent of being put into writing and thus becoming a matter of record. This can be important as a means of avoiding mistakes in subsequent periods.

Disadvantages of Budgets.   Although the advantages of budgeting are significant, there are some difficulties in their use as a control device in purchasing operations. This is much more true of the materials budget than the operations budget. The main difficulty arises from the fact that a purchasing agent should buy what is needed rather than what has been forecast. Strict adherence to a budget could lead to overbuying, with its attendant costs. In other instances adherence to the budget might lead to shortages and work stoppages in the plant. In both cases, the department would be given a high rating on the basis of adherence to the budget, but could hardly be considered to be performing its functions well.

Norms

The use of nonbudgetary purchasing norms as standards for purchasing performance has not been very common. This is primarily because there is such a wide variation in the specific duties assigned to individuals within purchasing departments and because of the way in which they perform their duties. One need only consider the variation in salespersons and their concept of how to deal with buyers to understand the difficulty in developing a norm for evaluating a buyer's interview performance.

What is true with respect to the development of norms for comparing buyer performance is even more true of developing norms for the head of a purchasing department. Not only are the duties and responsibilities more diverse but also more individual in nature. A major consumer goods manufacturer has prepared the following listing of *performance standards* for its director of purchases.

Adequate performance consists of:

1. Successful planning which results in establishment and achievement of management-approved goals and programs which (a) improve purchasing operations within budget limits, (b) produce profit for the Company, or (c) increase the ability of the Division to meet new and emergency situations expeditiously.

2. Materials, equipment, and supplies being purchased at prices resulting in the lowest ultimate cost consistent with requir-

ed quality, delivery, and established policies; late deliveries and rejections for quality do not exceed agreed upon levels.

3. Competition among suppliers being encouraged and buying is competitive whenever possible. Whenever competition is not possible or practical, careful negotiation is practiced, and adequate precautions are taken to insure that the best interests of the Company are served.

4. Management being adequately informed of Purchasing activities, significant market conditions, and trends affecting the Company's operations. Recommendations for action are promptly made.

5. An active personnel training program in force, a periodic assessment of abilities and performance of Buyers and Purchasing Agents is made, and counseling results in a satisfactory rate of development toward higher responsibilities, making available adequately trained replacements to fill vacancies.

6. Coordination of Purchasing activities within the Purchasing Division and with other Company activities being effectively carried out, resulting in smooth integration of all functions related to purchasing activity, consolidated purchasing of items used at various locations, and uniformity of interpretation of Purchasing policies and procedures.

7. Purchasing policies which are established and maintained which are fair to all vendors, assure the ability of the Company to make the best purchase possible, and promote good relations with vendors and other outside contacts as well as other Company divisions.

8. Written procedures which are established and revised to insure a standard and efficient handling of purchasing operations.

9. Working relations with those divisions served resulting in mutual cooperation and understanding, confidence in Purchasing's ability to provide services required, and effective communication.

10. Vendor relations, based on mutual cooperation, confidence, and respect, which are established and maintained, resulting in continuing efforts of vendors to provide high levels of quality, service, and technical information and early offering of new product developments.

11. When requested, surplus or salvage materials and supplies being disposed of promptly and at favorable prices.

12. Active participation in purchasing and industry associations.

It is evident that these standards are *qualitative* rather than *quantitative* and that norms in the usual sense of that word cannot be developed.

Evaluation Methods

In practice a large number of evaluation methods are being used relative to the purchasing function. However, there is no consensus as to any one method that is universally preferred. The following discussion will present those considerations which are found in one form or another in most evaluation plans.

Internal Audits

Since the entire next chapter is devoted to a discussion of internal auditing of the purchasing department, it will only be mentioned here that many companies conduct an internal audit of their purchasing department, as they do of other departments, to measure conformity to established procedures and acceptable business practice. Evaluation in the usual sense is not involved, in that the internal auditor is not concerned with how well the purchasing question is functioning but only with whether it is doing things as procedures indicate they should be done.

The internal auditor is usually assigned to the accounting function rather than the purchasing function. Consequently, the internal audit as a method of evaluating purchasing performance is limited by the extent to which management has established purchasing objectives and standards of performance against which the internal auditor can measure the facts he finds.

Purchasing Department Savings

Savings arising from purchasing operations are fairly commonly used as a means of evaluating performance. These savings are concerned with costs of materials, supplies, and services being purchased. Some companies refer to these savings as "cost reductions" and others as "profit improvement."

The problem with using this method is in determining actual savings in cost. If a buyer through negotiations secures a price lower than originally quoted, should this be considered a savings? Is a quantity discount a savings? How does one measure savings on changes of materials or design when the purchasing department only had little or no influence on such changes?

Notwithstanding these questions, there are savings that can be clearly attributed to the purchasing department and used to evaluate its performance, and this technique is gaining in popularity.

Variance from Standard Cost of Materials

Some companies establish a standard cost of the more important materials that they purchase, which is derived from the historical record of prices paid for such materials. Evaluation of purchasing performance then consists of comparing actual costs with this standard cost for the period under evaluation. This method of evaluation is commonly found in companies employing standard costing as a control over manufacturing operations.

To be useful, therefore, the standards must be acceptable to purchasing people. This means prices must be equitably set and established with the complete cooperation and input from the purchasing people involved.

Outside Audit

The outside audit is an audit conducted by a nonemployee of the company whose purchasing department is being evaluated. Management consulting firms typically are employed, although occasionally the company's certified public accountants may conduct the audit.

Auditors usually start with the purchasing procedures or policy manuals, if such exist, and measure adherence to these guides. They attempt to ascertain the extent to which the purchasing department is operating under commonly accepted sound management methods.

Variance from Operating Budgets

Companies that prepare operating budgets, as opposed to materials budgets, may use these budgets as the basis for still another method of evaluating performance. If the operating budget has been realistically prepared, if the head of the purchasing department has had a significant voice in its preparation, and if the department head given the resources to do what management expects the department to do, then judging the department in terms of compliance with the operating budget is fair and reasonable.

Vendor Performance

Evaluating a purchasing department in terms of the performance of the vendors with whom it deals is equitable. The purchasing department is directly, if not completely, responsible for choosing vendors. If it does a good job of selecting vendors, this will show up in good vendor performance.

Methods of evaluating vendors were described in Chapter 5. Unfortunately, in many companies vendor evaluation is highly informal. It is conducted at the time a purchase is made, and no permanent "data bank" of information is maintained, nor are vendors of all commodities evaluated.

Since vendor evaluation should consider quality, quantity, price, time, and place, and since there is variation in the importance of each of these elements for most purchases, few companies have attempted to develop vendor performance formulas. In most cases it would be unsound to employ standard formulas, for each company must develop its own criteria for evaluating suppliers, and these criteria should vary with the commodities being purchased and their importance to the production process.

Appraisal of Personnel

Many companies have established job evaluation and merit rating systems for their personnel. Where such systems exist, they should be applied to purchasing personnel. Forms are usually developed that specify a performance review by one or more of each person's supervisors. Although such evaluation may be sound for individuals in a purchasing department, it is not an adequate evaluation of an entire purchasing department.

Inventory Performance

Performance in terms of inventory levels and turnover may be used to evaluate a purchasing department's performance. This method should be used only where the purchasing department has major responsibility for determining inventory levels and quantities to be bought. Most companies do not give such blanket responsibility to their purchasing departments.

Frequency of Reports

A final concern is to determine the combinations of reports and their frequency. This determination, naturally, depends on the peculiar requirement of the individual firm. The chart on the following page illustrates a record as to type of report and frequency.

Purchasing Manuals

Purchasing manuals aid evaluation by specifying policies and procedures to be followed by purchasing personnel. The policy manual contains approved statements of the policies under which the department operates. The procedures manual contains the procedures to be followed by the department in conducting its activities.

Some purchasing managers believe that manuals should not be prepared because they tend to be restrictive. This attitude is probably

Topic	Reporting Frequency			
	Annual	Semi-annual	Quarterly	Monthly
Total dollar value of purchases	✓	✓	✓	✓
Dollar purchases by commodity class	✓	✓	✓	
Dollar purchases by major item	✓			
Dollar purchases by major suppliers	✓	✓		
Dollar volume of cash discounts	✓	✓	✓	
Dollar value of lost discounts	✓			
Standard cost variances	✓	✓		
Inventory turnover rate	✓	✓		
Scrap and surplus sales	✓			
Number of salespersons interviewed	✓			
Total purchasing department expense	✓	✓		
Purchasing department expense by class	✓			
Total cost savings	✓	✓	✓	✓
Cost savings by buyer	✓			
Cost savings by type	✓	✓		
Long-term contract changes	✓	✓		
Supplier performance	✓	✓		
Problem solving				✓
Current objectives	✓			

based on confusion of policies and procedures. Policies should not be changed frequently, whereas procedures are subject to frequent changes. If policy statements are kept in a separate manual, there should be little difficulty in understanding that they are relatively permanent. Changes should be made in the procedural matters as often as required. Some purchasing agents also question whether small purchasing departments should have manuals. One could argue that small departments need manuals even more than large ones, since only one person in a small department may be familiar with important policies and procedures. If this person is removed for any reason, the department will be seriously handicapped if such matters have not been recorded.

The specific benefits to be derived from the compilation of a purchasing *policy* manual are:

1. A manual eliminates questions as to the position of management on important issues in the administration of the purchasing function.
2. New personnel can quickly be taught the policies under which they are expected to act.

3. A manual can serve for continuous training.
4. A manual tends to ensure greater consistency in the handling of controversial matters such as reciprocity.
5. A manual may be used to inform suppliers of what they can expect in dealings with the company.

The subjects that should be included in a purchasing policy manual will vary with the company. Inasmuch as a policy is a prescribed method of handling a type of situation, matters that seem to be of a nonrepetitive nature should not be included. Policy manuals should have, and clearly indicate that they have, the approval of management.

Everyone in a purchasing department should have access to the policy manual. Copies should also be furnished to the heads of other departments that are affected by purchasing policies. There is disagreement among purchasing managers as to whether copies of the manual should be furnished to vendors. Since purchasing policies often affect vendor-buying relationships, it would appear that vendor knowledge of policies would facilitate sound relationships.

The procedures manual, in contrast, is primarily an internal matter for the purchasing department. These manuals frequently are prepared in loose-leaf form, which makes it possible to insert the frequent changes to which procedures are subject and to separate portions of the manual for forwarding to interested departments without burdening them with detail of no interest to them.

This chapter has emphasized the range of variables involved in the purchasing job, and has illustrated methods whereby these variables could be incorporated into rating systems. Although no one rating system can be used for all companies, application of one of the systems described, or a combination of them, will facilitate purchasing evaluation.

DISCUSSION QUESTIONS

1. What are the objectives of evaluating a purchasing department's performance?

2. How is the cost-purchasing comparison obtained and what is its primary weakness in evaluating purchasing department performance?

3. Why do open-end and annual contracts negate the usefulness of cost per order comparisons?

4. Why is return on capital a more significant measure of purchasing performance than return on purchasing investment?

5. What is the rationale for comparing actual purchasing performance with budgeted performance?

6. What is the essential distinction between policy and procedure manuals?

7. In what ways can quality performance be measured?

8. Compare and contrast the materials budget and the operating budget.

9. What is the main difficulty that arises from use of budgets?

10. Discuss the outside audit.

SUGGESTED CASES

Ajax Sewing Machine Company

Davis Mills Incorporated

Pressure Tanks, Inc. (A)

Smith Electronic Corporation

Sharpe Machine Corporation

CHAPTER 22
CONTROL AND AUDIT PROCEDURES

To assure itself that proper procedures relative to sound purchasing and management principles (as discussed in the previous chapter) are being followed, the purchasing department must be periodically reviewed—a procedure referred to as the internal audit, or purchasing's place in the management audit.

In the past, internal audits were mainly concerned with checking for such things as assurance that proper signatures and approvals were on purchase orders, that material received corresponded to material billed, and that losses were prevented—in a word, checks for integrity rather than checks for efficiency and effectiveness. Today the audit has a much broader perspective.

The discussion that follows will concentrate on the procedures and principles used in one or all of the three types of audits used for the purchasing function. First, the accountant's audit is designed to assure that the purchasing function follows those procedures and controls generally accepted by the accounting profession in formulating certifiable financial statements and reports. The second, the internal audit, is designed to evaluate specific job descriptions and employee performance within the purchasing department. The third type of review, the management audit, evaluates the integration of the department to the total corporate organization and its goals.

Because the major purpose of the management audit is to determine whether the firm is functioning as an efficient whole, it is necessary that someone outside the departmental work areas view the department objectively. In short, an effective audit requires that someone with a concept of the entire operation evaluate each function—someone who can detect strengths and weaknesses that may not be apparent to one confined to a single operation.

In practice, outside consultants with varied training are often charged with the management audit task. The consultant may be a management consulting firm or it may be an internal audit team from the public accounting firm handling the company's account. When the audit is performed by the company itself, the responsibility tends to be assigned to an internal auditing section of the controller's division of the company.

In general the purchasing audit includes study of the following areas:

1. Purchasing organization
2. Purchasing policies
3. Purchasing procedures
4. Purchasing evaluation and reporting

Organization

Effective performance of any function requires good organization, including clearly defined responsibilities accompanied by commensurate authority. In evaluating purchasing, both intra- and interdepartmental organizations should be considered.

Intradepartmental

Within the department the auditor should check to see that there is a defined hierarchy of authority running from the director of purchasing down to the lowest-ranked clerical employees. Typical areas of concern in such an analysis should be:

1. Are line and staff functions clearly defined?
2. Does each department member know his immediate supervisor?
3. Are supervisors given sufficient authority over conditions of work, specific job assignments, and related salary evaluations?
4. Are consistent lines of work assignments established, for example, are buyers assigned by products, such as steel and aluminum, or by service areas, such as engineering supplies and tool and die requirements?
5. Does the organization promote high morale and a feeling of group cohesiveness (often a by-product of definite job promotion possibilities and clearly defined responsibilities)?
6. Are interplant purchasing responsibilities clearly defined?

Interdepartmental

Because purchasing's efforts are so interwoven with those of other departments, it is imperative that the responsibilities be clearly defined. The following areas are representative of those investigated by the auditor:

1. Is departmental authority concerning what to buy clearly understood?
2. Is authority relative to quantity determination clearly understood?
3. Which department controls choice of vendor? Are approved source lists clearly defined?
4. Are any purchasing responsibilities assumed by other departments?
5. Is purchasing consulted by other departments on procedures or changes that affect vendors, order quantities, or specifications?

For each intra- and interdepartmental relationship the auditor should be certain that sound organizational procedures are established to avoid "management by crisis."

Policies

The auditor should begin with a determination of whether policies exist that cover all important aspects of the purchasing process. A normal starting point would be the published purchasing policy manual. Such a manual, if it exists, will reflect what aspects of purchasing are considered important enough to be covered by stated policies. The policies should bear the approval of the top management of the company and be binding on all personnel.

Included should be policies relative to:

1. Altering specifications or requisitions
2. Investigating, approving, and selecting vendors
3. Procedure for obtaining bids
4. Procedures for awarding contracts
5. Policies relating to conflict of interest, gifts, and entertainment

Auditors should concern themselves with whether policies are clear, workable, and enforced. Each audit must cope with the situation that exists in a given company. No standard audit questions can be formulated that would apply to all companies or all the topics that might be covered by a policy statement.

Procedures

An auditor should ascertain that adequate procedures are established to carry out management and purchasing policy, clarify responsibilities, provide and standardize routines, and provide standards of performance. Because a procedure audit is often the area of greatest concern, the following discussion will be quite detailed.

Requisitions

Analysis usually starts with a review of the formal purchase requisition. Auditing will determine who has the defined authority to initiate a purchase requisition and whether the prescribed procedure has been followed in transmitting it to purchasing. The examination may not extend back into determining the effectiveness of the planning on which the requisition was based, but rather the mechanics and the defined authorities involved. The requisition will also be examined to determine whether adequate information is included, so that an intelligent approach can be made to the purchasing transaction.

Purchase Order Control

Control over the issuance of purchase orders or purchase order numbers should be of concern to auditors. They should ascertain whether a prenumbered purchase order system or other control procedure has been established, so that it is not possible for unauthorized people to exercise purchase order authority.

Vendor Investigation

Auditors may examine the apparent ability of vendors to perform, as well as general vendor selection procedures. Financial stability, technical proficiency, and apparent favoritism in the selection of vendors should be reviewed. Limitations upon purchasing personnel in the selection process either through management constraints or trade relations consederations should also be noted.

Transportation and Price

The purchase order should be reviewed by the auditors for decisions that have been made with regard to transportation and prices. In the area of transportation, the auditor should investigate the procedures followed in deciding how materials are to be brought into the plant—F.O.B. points, freight terms (prepaid, collect, or freight allowed), and methods of determining specific routings. Auditing should ascertain whether the transportation cost is included in the bid prices received and whether the appropriate freight terms have been clearly stated on the purchase order. If freight calculations are required in calculating the cost of the material, auditing should review the role of the traffic department in verifying freight rates to assure that the proper economies are enjoyed and that the least expensive shipping mode has been used.

In pricing, the auditors should review the bidding procedure to determine whether competitive bids are solicited and from an adequate number of suppliers. Comparative prices should be examined, as well as the reasons for selecting a specific bidder, particularly if it appears that orders have been awarded to other than the lowest bidder.

There should be an analysis of situations in which price is omitted from the order. This practice could lead to a misunderstanding that might be to the disadvantage of the company. Under certain circumstances the omission of price may be desirable, and therefore, individual cases should be reviewed to determine the reason. Similar analysis should be made of cost-plus-a-fixed-fee or other flexible pricing arrangements to assure that all relevant facts have been considered and that the agreements are clear enough to avoid misinterpretation at some later time. In some cases the cost-plus approach may be desirable, although it usually is wise to include a maximum allowable price.

Auditors usually review the procedure followed in authorizing price changes, as well as the method of recording, evaluating, and transmitting them to the vendors. Difficulties can arise when price changes are not *formally* communicated to the vendor.

Another consideration in pricing that the auditors may check is whether a price for custom-made products includes tooling charges. Where tooling is a consideration, the order should also be explicit about such matters as who holds title to the tools and who has responsibility for their maintenance and insurance.

Discounts

Trade and cash discounts should be checked to see that they have been received at the time of final payment, that they have been properly recorded on the orders, and that they are being realized through the proper handling of approvals. Such items as taxes should be spot-checked by the auditors to determine whether sound procedures are being followed in their handling.

Adjustments

Auditors should examine the method of handling adjustments with vendors when defective materials are returned or when it becomes necessary for the buyer to perform additional operations on purchased parts. Auditors should determine who has authority to authorize such returns or reprocessing, how this is communicated to the vendor, what controls are maintained over the material during its reshipment or reworking, and how the transaction is consummated. Since these can be costly situations, there should be complete coordination within the firm and clearly defined responsibilities.

Make or Buy

Auditors should also examine the procedures established to evaluate "make or buy" decisions. This should include a study of what items are analyzed; the financial considerations, such as the value of money, used in the calculations; and the considerations relevant to the remainder of the firm, including future production plans and the possible effect on future labor negotiations.

Surplus Sale

Since in many companies the sale of scrap and fall-off material is handled by purchasing, the auditors should satisfy themselves with regard to the method of weight control, the method of establishing a price for the material sold, and the control of inventories being held until its sale. Often scrap and fall-off are regarded as undesirable products, to be moved out of the production area as rapidly as possible, with little concern over the method of sale. The auditors should also satisfy themselves that material is not being scrapped when it might be returned to a vendor or that material is not being scrapped by one department when it might be used in another department performing a different operation or making different parts.

Off-Plant Inventory

There are situations when a company may have off-plant inventory, that is, inventory of material owned by the firm but in the possession of a vendor for processing or conversion. It is important that the shipment and receipt of such material be closely controlled and that a procedure be established for ascertaining the accuracy of the physical and the book inventories of such material. Auditors should confirm the existence and suitability of these procedures.

Petty Cash Purchases

Local purchases through a petty cash fund or charge account are common. Controlling these purchases so as to assure proper receipt and lowest cost is a matter for examination.

In somewhat the same category are emergency purchases made by personnel throughout the company for materials required on short notice. The auditors should evaluate the control procedures established for these purchases.

Employee Purchases

Purchasing for employees is a common, though questionable, practice. Auditors should examine the procedures followed for such purchases to determine that proper reimbursement is obtained from the employees. They should also examine the procedures to make sure that there is no legal liability to the company through the practices being followed.

Receipt Procedure

Among associated procedures that should be examined by an auditor are the receipt and inspection of incoming material. Here the auditor is concerned with such matters as whether quantities are checked at some point other than the initial receiving station, the procedure for moving material into and out of the storeroom, the procedure followed in handling receiving reports, and the procedure by which differences between quantities received and billed are handled.

Vendor Payment

The authorization for payment of vendors in some cases is approved by purchasing; however, many companies have an accounts payable section which assembles the documents relating to the purchase, the receipt of the material, and the amount owed for the transaction. Whatever the organizational pattern, auditors should make sure that the necessary checks and balances exist to guard against collusion or slipshod operations.

Ethics

In examining purchasing, auditors should always be on the alert for unusual situations that might indicate ethical problems. Large gifts or unusual entertainment is often evidence of an undesirable situation. Discussions with personnel, examination of records, and spot-checking of vendors are steps taken by auditors to inquire into such stiuations.

In auditing it is customary to employ sampling procedures. The selection of an adequate sample is important if an auditor is to secure a true picture of the operations of the purchasing department. The auditor must examine both usual and unusual purchase transactions. There must be enough transactions to enable the auditor to verify that established procedures and policies are being followed or to reveal situations that call for more intensive examination.

Included in a procedures audit should be purchase of orders of the less usual types, such as the following:

1. Blanket or continuing orders where a number of deliveries are made over a period.
2. Orders where specification of item, quantity, or price is not definite.
3. Orders placed under long-term purchase contracts.

Evaluation and Reporting

The final aspect of an audit is to determine whether objective standards of purchasing performance exist and adequate provision is made for reporting of this performance to management. Even though a department is organized soundly and proper policies and procedures exist, there is no assurance that they are being followed unless the performance of the personnel is periodically reviewed and evaluated.

Specifically an audit should determine:

1. Whether personnel are evaluated regularly on objective bases. (See Chapter 18 for discussion of appropriate criteria.)
2. Whether the department as a whole is objectively evaluated in relation to clearly established goals. (See Chapter 21 for departmental performance data.)
3. Whether periodic reports present the individual and departmental performance to management and whether such reports highlight the significant areas of evaluation.

An accountant in a leading public accounting firm has said:

Any internal auditing program used must be tailored to fit the needs of the specific situation. The internal auditor should not limit himself to determining that prescribed procedures are being followed and that no irregularities exist. He should be able to evaluate the effectiveness and efficiency of the purchasing operation. To do this requires initiative and ingenuity that cannot be guided by a specific audit program.[1]

[1] *Purchasing Policies and Procedures,* Arthur Andersen and Company, 1960, p. 41.

The Institute of Internal Auditors has published a report outlining a recommended approach to an internal audit of a purchasing department.[2] At the time of this report their research indicated that about 25% of the firms with which their members were affiliated were auditing their purchasing departments. Since one would expect internal audits to be made in companies that are affiliated with the Institute of Internal Auditors, it seems probable that there were few nonmember firms conducting internal audits of purchasing. However, more recent informal studies indicate that internal auditing of purchasing is spreading.

It may be that in time a standardized internal-auditing approach for purchasing departments will be developed. If this occurs, it is likely to be based on the recommendations of the Institute and will follow its outline of a typical audit program:

   I. Company policy and organization
      A. Place of purchasing department in organization
      B. Purchasing responsibility and authority
      C. Physical facilities used
      D. Main and branch plant purchasing relationships
  II. Departmental operations connected with basic purchasing activities
      A. Procedures
      B. Forms
      C. Audit sampling procedures
 III. Other purchasing activities
      A. Inspection
      B. Invoices
      C. Receiving and storage
      D. Surplus and scrap disposal
      E. Transportation
      F. Purchases for employees
 IV. Records and reports
      A. Departmental records
      B. Internal reports
      C. External reports

To audit itself, the purchasing department would secure answers to the many questions that can be raised under each of the headings in the outline. The specific questions that a purchasing department

---

[2] *Internal Audit and Control of a Purchasing Department*, Research Committee Report No. 2, The Institute of Internal Auditors, New York, 1955.

could include on its audit will suggest themselves from the materials covered in all the preceding chapters of this book.

The purchasing audit provides an objective analysis of operations that accomplishes two purposes. It provides an outside objective review of the department and its policies and procedures, thereby often suggesting areas for improvement of operations. Perhaps more important, it provides the assurance that this vital activity is synchronized with the objectives and procedures of the entire firm.

Since an internal audit should and will usually be conducted either by a company internal auditor or the public accounting firm with which the company has a relationship, one might think that the purchasing department manager would have little responsibility for the audit. This should not be true. The manager should be aware of what information the auditor will be looking for and should take the necessary steps to make such information readily available. In some purchasing departments, an individual within the department may even be charged with the responsibility of making periodic informal internal audits to ensure that the department's affairs are ready for a formal internal audit.

DISCUSSION QUESTIONS

1. Indicate the major areas of a purchasing audit.
2. In the area of purchasing policy, what should auditors review?
3. What should be included in a procedure audit?
4. How does an auditor check for integrity?
5. What is the essential purpose of a purchasing audit?
6. In audits involving interdepartmental activities, what areas are investigated?
7. What is the auditor's concern regarding trade and cash discounts?
8. Define off-plant inventory.
9. How wide is the practice of internal auditing in purchasing?
10. What role, if any, does the purchasing manager have in the internal audit?

SUGGESTED CASE

John Roberts Manufacturing Company

CHAPTER 23
AUTOMATIC AND ELECTRONIC DATA PROCESSING

Of all the management aids developed during the last several decades, data-processing equipment certainly must rank with the most significant. The collection, storage, retrieval, and manipulation of important control data has been made possible because of such equipment, and correspondingly, organizational changes such as materials management have been permitted, whereby one individual can control by exception heretofore autonomous and functionally independent activities.

However, there has also been a tendency to attribute too much faith and confidence in the system. There is a tendency to forget the limitation that the output is only as valid as human judgment decisions relative to manipulation of the input data. Also, there is a tendency to underestimate overall cost relative to value.

A presentation of the limitations as well as the values and potential applications of electronic data-processing systems is the goal of this chapter. A theoretical foundation as to EDP's role in the automation process will be reviewed along with presentation of basic computer operations and typical applications relative to the materials management functions. Finally, a step-by-step procedure to be followed in "automating" is suggested along with a review of current industry practices.

Automation

Many people do not understand the meaning of automation. The *use* of a computer is not automation. Employees have long made frequent use of the most common of all computers—the adding machine. This may be a form of mechanization, but it is not automation. Mechanization has gone on ever since man invented the simplest tool. The addition of power to tools increased man's mechanization—but this still is not automation. Today man is beginning to design tools that control themselves, and this is the essence of automation.

Machines regulate themselves through *feedback*. Feedback is achieved through a measuring device that continuously monitors a machine's operation by comparing its performance with a desired standard. Through the information that is fed back the machine makes the necessary adjustments to conform to the standard. A household heating plant with its thermostat control is the usual illustration of feedback and adjustment, or automation.

The question of the effect of automation on purchasing must be regarded from two different points of view. Does the automation of production processes affect industrial purchasing? And, can the purchasing function be automated? Before these two questions can be answered one must know what is included in the purchasing operation.

Purchasing includes all aspects of the procurement of material from the time a possible need is known until the material is received and approved for use. While there are variations among companies as to the functions that are assigned to the purchasing department, the following are typically the responsibility of a purchasing department:

1. Determination of possible sources of supply
2. Selection of the source
3. Selection of the most economical method of delivery and routing
4. Issuance of the purchase order
5. Follow-up and expediting

The following are materials management functions but sometimes may be assigned to other departments:

6. Receiving and inspection
7. Invoice checking and payment
8. Material and inventory control
9. Value analysis
10. Salvage and scrap disposal

Can any of these functions within the materials department be automated? They can be partially mechanized, but this is a far cry from feedback and automatic adjustment. The single most important decision made by the purchasing agent is the selection of a supplier. It is difficult to see how this decision can be converted into an automatic process. This is true whether the decision concerns a new procurement or a repeated procurement.

In making a purchase decision the buyer must consider product quality, supplier service, price, transportation costs, reciprocal relationships, and financial responsibility of the supplier. Most of these cannot be quantified, nor can they be programmed so that electronic data-processing (EDP) equipment can perform the decision-making step. The price decision, being essentially quantitative, might be programmed. Quality performance based on rejection and the rates on previous deliveries from a supplier could also be programmed. But how can one program anticipate rates of technological improvements and developments on the part of suppliers? This qualitative process is going on up to the very moment of a decision. Or how does one program the departmental preference for one brand over another based on intangible and changing attitudes?

However, a much higher degree of mechanization of purchasing is possible. For example, the ABC approach to inventory analysis and control, discussed on Chapter 8, is a useful approach to mechanization. It is based on the fact that a small proportion of the items purchased accounts for a large proportion of the dollars spent on purchases, and that the bulk of the purchase transactions involves a small proportion of total dollars spent. Mechanization and EDP equipment can be successfully applied to these small purchases.

Inventory management involves the balancing of the costs of carrying inventory with the risk and cost of a stoppage because of being out-of-stock. Items of low dollar cost can be overstocked at no great expense. These items should not be followed closely by the purchasing agent. The agent's attention should be devoted to type A items. A high degree of mechanization can be used with type C items. The inability to program some of the decision factors will not be too costly to the company. The safety stock level can be inflated to allow for these nonmeasurable factors, and it will not be serious if occasionally a second or third best supplier secures the order.

However, the purchasing agent must devote continuous attention and analysis to the important items to achieve the goals of sound inventory management. The agent may be able to mechanize some of the purchasing steps for such items, but they will involve a large measure of subjective judgment.

EDP and Purchasing

If one thinks of EDP equipment as a means of mechanizing rather than automating the purchase transaction, there is a great potential for its use.

With the development of many kinds of electronic equipment, ranging from the simple to the extremely sophisticated, many business functions in the fields of production, accounting, and marketing have found the equipment useful in an increasing number of ways. But purchasing—the function that spends approximately 50% of a company's receipts—has lagged in the utilization of computers and the less complex data-processing equipment. There are some legitimate and some illegitimate reasons for the delay.

First, in the early stages of data processing, attempts to automate purchase order writing with punched-card systems failed in all but the most repetitive purchasing tasks. Surveys of major national concerns by a manufacturer of EDP equipment lead to a recommendation that purchase order writing not be automated unless such purchases were repetitive. Only when purchasing was a subpart of a broader business "system" was a high degree of mechanization recommended.

Second, ingrained management thinking, abetted by purchasing managers over the years, that purchasing was entirely a nonroutine, decision-making function, often prevented serious consideration of adapting purchasing routines to the computer. To a computer manager it appeared logical to place repetitious and routine business operations on the computer first.

Third, basic changes in purchasing procedures are prerequisite to making any significant use of EDP for purchasing. Even if these changes are made, there must also be changes in a company's data-processing system if it is to be used extensively for purchasing. It is difficult to convince the manager of EDP that such changes will be profitable unless the purchasing manager is thoroughly convinced. Often this has not been the case.

Fourth, lack of knowledge, on the part of purchasing managers, of electronic equipment, its capabilities, and its application to purchasing activities has led to a personal fear of EDP and a reluctance to promote its use. Such managers fail to recognize that its adoption would free them from much routine work, permitting more time for creative planning and action. This would lead to more efficient departmental performance and personal advancement.

Despite these historical obstacles, the constant refinements being made in EDP equipment, the multitude of necessary information, and the continual increases in labor cost, indicate the need for the materials executive to be alert to the possibilities of computerizing all or a part of purchasing activities. Perhaps the typical company should begin by adopting such less-sophisticated mechanization techniques as Flexowriter, Dataphone, and Teletype.

The terms *data processing, automation,* and *computerization* have acquired so much mystery and awe that it is appropriate for anyone occasionally to review a few terms and definitions that are fundamental to an understanding of the automation of the purchasing process and its possible integration into a "total system."

Some Terms and Their Meanings

Data—pertinent facts or statistics that can be processed to provide useful information. Data are the inputs and information is the output on an EDP system. The data are not useful in their raw form in the solution of problems.

Information—knowledge derived from data that have been processed.

Data-processing system—a "conversion unit," which takes in raw data (input) and provides information (output).

EDP (electronic data processing)—a mechanical device characterized by its ability to store large quantities of data and to reproduce such data when "called for," either as data or, when properly programmed, as information.

IDP (integrated data processing)—a system for processing business facts into information for several departments without their having to transcribe it.

ADP (automatic data processing)—any combination of EDP or IDP systems. It is used less often than the more clearly defined EDP and IDP terms.

Program—a set of step-by-step instructions in a language understood by data-processing equipment, covering the retrieval of input data and their sorting, classifying, and computing, so that the results are reported as information.

Punched-card system—a technique for the efficient recording of data on punched cards for automatic or nonautomatic processing.

EDP symbols used in flow charts—programmers and analysts use symbols to represent the sequence of operations and flow of data and paper work. Purchasing personnel working with EDP should be familiar with the symbols used to avoid misunderstandings. A lack of uniformity in the meanings of symbols has led to a proposal by a subcommittee of the American Standards Association that a uniform

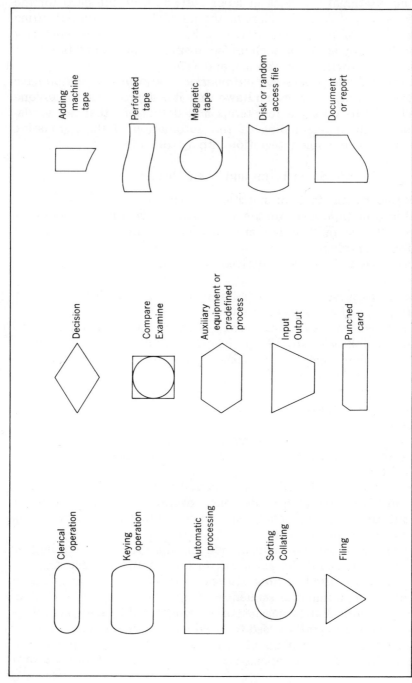

FIGURE 23-1. EDP signposts. The symbols shown are used in flow-charting EDP procedures. They are the most common symbols employed by systems analysts in laying out systems "roadmaps." The fifteen symbols comprise the principal movements and devices that occur in a standard office data-processing setup.

set of symbols be adopted. Figure 23-1 shows a group of commonly accepted symbols.

Equipment

Flexowriter

Flexowriter is an electric typewriter which, among other things, will produce purchase order from prepared tapes or edge-punched cards. It can also produce tapes during the typing of orders, which may provide information to the computer for other purposes or be used in the preparation of purchasing reports.

Data-Phone[1]

Data-Phone is one of the simplest forms of order-processing EDP systems, which also transmits, processes, and stores data. It is basically a punched-card ordering system, which eliminates the preparation of purchase orders, provides data on cards or tapes for purchase analysis, and aids in reducing inventories. In effect it provides direct communication between the purchasing department and the vendor via Bell System equipment.

Computer

A computer is a machine that carries out arithmetic operations on numbers supplied to it in accordance with a program of instructions given to the machine. The instructions create the illusion of intelligence. The incredible speed and accuracy of the computer's mathematical computations add to the illusion. But it is important to understand that, except for its speed, the computer has done nothing but manipulate those figures that have been fed to it.

Most computers are electronic machines whose circuits are made up of resistors, transistors, capacitors, diodes, and so forth. Electrical impulses representing numbers are manipulated by the circuits or recorded on small magnets.

Types of Computers

There are two types of electronic computers—digital and analog. A *digital* computer is one in which digits or symbols (letters or arabic numerals) represent numbers or characters in the data. Digital com-

---

[1] Data-Phone is a registered service mark of American Telephone and Telegraph Company.

puters receive, store, and numerically manipulate data with high speed and precision. Each operation is based on an exact count. Digital computers are used to handle large volumes of data and to perform the necessary arithmetic operations to produce reports, records, and supporting documents such as requisitions, purchase orders, followup notices, and so on. The computer is the heart of the automation of the management of materials, and will be used to illustrate the remainder of the computer applications to the purchasing and materials area.

An *analog* computer is a type of computer in which analogs or physical quantities rather than discrete data represent each number that makes up the input. Analog information is acquired through a measuring process such as a speedometer or electric meters. Data are introduced as electrical charges or physical relationships in the analog computer. It simulates a real-world situation by means of a predetermined equation and solves the same by means of the analog or model produced by the electrical system. As such its use is primarily limited to model building and related scientific applications.

The Systems Approach to Materials Management

The utilization of electronic data-processing equipment has been viewed as the major rationale for incorporating all materials activities[2] under one head, called the materials manager. The possibility of conflicting individual departmental objectives is thus overcome, and the information flow resulting from efficient EDP systems allows one to balance the variables involved in reducing materials costs to their lowest possible levels. What is required is first of all a system, and secondly, the incorporation of an electronic computer.

A system is an orderly way of doing things. Any department has some data-processing system. This is true whether or not electronic equipment is used. In order to achieve its objectives, the department must establish a plan, execute its plan, and then provide a means of evaluating the results. The data-processing system provides the means of handling the clerical aspects of these functions.

A simple illustration is the economic ordering quantity, which is the system for the procurement of the right quantity, at the right price, and from the right source. Purchase order follow-up is the system to ensure that goods are available at the right time and place. A purchase performance index is the system for evaluating performance against preestablished norms for vendors, buyers, and products.

---

[2] Usually inventory control, purchasing, production, receiving, and traffic.

These three systems should be integrated into a unified system for purchasing. Of the three, the purchase order follow-up is the one most likely to be first transferred from manual to mechanical or electronic data processing. It has often proved to be a profitable EDP application and sometimes even the basis on which companies have justified and installed their EDP equipment. This control system employs the principle of management by exception to assure follow-up at each stage of the purchasing cycle—from the time the purchase order is issued until the last payment is made.

The third system, a purchase performance index, is a by-product of the follow-up system. It is a statistical compilation of the data flowing from the follow-up system to provide an objective evaluation of both vendor and buyer performance. Knowledge of its current level of performance is the key to management's effort to improve future performance. Once an EDP follow-up system is operative, the purchase performance index can be implemented as a by-product of the data in the follow-up system.

The economic ordering quantity system is related to the requisitioning and order-writing procedure. Specifically, EOQ is that quantity which results in the minimum annual total cost for the item, considering ordering costs and carrying costs involved for various permutations of quantity. The purchase order is printed by the data-processing system from the completed requisition, with the quantity determined by EOQ formulas programmed into the system.

It is not intended to recommend a single system for every department using EDP. Each company must adopt and adapt a system consistent with its objectives and purchasing procedures. Some companies may find that EDP is not appropriate to their operations. This should only be decided on the basis of a careful study.

Elements of the Digital Computer

In computer terminology the mechanical, electrical, and related components of the EDP system are referred to as the *hardware*, as contrasted to *software* which refers to the instructions or programs that set the hardware in motion relative to specific circumstances.

The principal elements of the computer's hardware consist of a memory, processing and output sections. Information is fed to the memory unit (sometimes called the input unit) in the form of "yes-no" data. The physical form of inputs ranges from punched cards, magnetic tapes or disks, and magnetically treated writing instruments. The latter, referred to as "light pencils or pens," allow the most direct contact between the initiating party and the computer.

Cards and tapes require intermediate preparation before being "fed" to the machine.

The computer then performs its functions on the basis of instructions contained within its memory cells—instructions previously developed by a programmer and logically referred to as the program. This program sets forth the sequence and type of operations that will be applied to the input data. Once programmed, no variations are possible to incorporate last-minute modifications or changes. COBOL and FORTRAN are terms applied to the most popular alternative programming procedures, and represent the particular "language" used to translate input data to the computer.

The processing section consists of the memory, control, and arithmetic units. In the memory unit the programmed instructions for handling the data are stored. The control unit determines how the operator interacts with the machine. In essence the variables are manual or automatic control. Under manual control the operator regulates the input and output units, reads the memory contents, and is alerted by the control panel to operational error detected by the computer. When automatic control is utilized the computer reacts according to the previously determined program.

The arithmetic unit performs the calculations which consist of such chores as addition, subtraction, division, and multiplication, with speeds of one-quarter million operations per second.

Finally, the output unit is concerned with receiving the computed data and reproducing it in a usable form. The output forms range from punched tapes or cards to activated typewriter or television type display units.

The EDP Study

Define Objectives

The objective of applying EDP to any operation is to distill pertinent and timely information for management from the mass of data available as a means of making better decisions. One might then say that the objective of establishing an EDP system in purchasing is to gather, store, analyze, and disseminate pertinent information to ensure an efficient purchasing operation. However, this is too narrow a concept if the maximum value is to be obtained. To confine the EDP objective to the writing of orders, evaluation, and preparation of reports would often fail to justify the EDP system economically.

The greatest benefits of EDP come when all related elements of the business are integrated into a single system. Therefore, the purchasing manager should take a broad view and consider the effects of EDP on purchasing and related functions as inventory, control, receiving, inspection, production control, and production planning. Those making the study should factor in other departments from the start, so that common information from the computer will be of maximum value to all related functions. Purchasing must enter into an integrated system with a realization that the system may present problems that would not occur in purchasing-oriented systems.

Typical computer applications to materials management include requisition writing taking into account projected production, inventory levels, and lead time requirements; historical use data and related information regarding inventory and order status. The following account illustrates a typical application:

When the buyer receives a requisition (which originated with the computer), he checks with the parts history printout to plan his buying strategy. This weekly report tells him the last five orders placed for the item, the vendor, what the price was, and the disposition of shipments. Data is inputted into the computer daily, and buyers needn't wait for the weekly printout if they want more current information. All parts history information is accessible on an on-line basis on terminals located in purchasing. The parts history is only one of several useful by-product reports purchasing receives from the program. Included among others:

—Daily reconciliation sheet, which tells what shipments have been received and how they were disposed of (accepted, rejected, etc.).

—Monthly cash commitment report that tells how much business has been done with each vendor, by part numbers.

—Weekly buyer workload statistics. P.O.'s are coded by buyer number, so the computer can easily calculate how many orders each buyer writes.

—Inspection disposition notice. Buyer accesses this when needed. It tells, by p.o. number and vendor, quantity rejected, accepted, returned, date of disposition, date received in stock. This enables buyers to easily trace errant shipments.

—Weekly stock status. This is basically an inventory report. It tells, by part usage, amount on hand and on order, amount committed and surplus, if any.

—Shortage report. This is broken down by shop order for subassemblies and by individual planner. It enables purchasing to troubleshoot critical items in short supply; really an expediting tool.

—Aged discrepancy report. This is mutually exclusive with the inspection disposition notice. It covers shipments that were rejected but for which the materials review board has not taken action as yet.[3]

The Study Group

The purchase of data-processing equipment and the accompanying "software" (systems and programs) is extremely costly and complex. Considerable study is required before a sound decision can be made. Executives who would not buy capital equipment for the production process without clear cost justification will often authorize the purchase of EDP equipment because of its glamor, "keeping up with the Joneses," or a feeling of inadequacy in evaluating such a complex purchase. Not a few companies have bought equipment even when their studies have indicated that the purchase was not warranted. Such a situation is illustrated by the following quote.

No addiction seems harder to arrest than industry's addiction to the computer. Take any manufacturing operation and management seems to be fascinated by a computer's speed, hypnotized by the reams of paper churned out every day. When the latest printout hits a manager's desk, he tries to justify it by claiming it gives him the information he needs.

Information, yes. But does he need it? Increasingly, purchasing people are saying no, or at least calling a slowdown on the masses of printouts. Says one corporate purchasing director in Massachusetts: "Before I came on this job, there was a push to get all orders on EDP. So far, 58% of the orders written are computer produced and recorded. But my aim now is to reduce this figure. On examining typical printouts, I find computer-placed orders for a one-time purchase of a rare raw material; others for buying specific tools for a project we're never going to repeat. There was even one order for some capital equipment. Programming this order probably took twice as long as hand preparing it, and the computer's ability to repeat instructions was completely wasted here."

In his first three months on the job, one of this man's most urgent functions has been to de-program some orders and restore manual order writing. A step backward? "Not at all. We've just

---

[3] "Production's Computer Helps Purchasing Buy," *Purchasing*, June 4, 1974, p. 45.

been so enamored with the monster that our sense of logic went out the window."[4]

Instead of making a study some companies visit other companies view their equipment and systems with the thought that they can select the best and apply it to their company, thus avoiding start-up problems and expense. This is a faulty assumption, because seldom can one company's system be transferred to another company. Such visits have value, but their value is primarily in acquiring a preliminary knowledge about equipment and systems.

Sometimes purchasing executives, feeling incompetent to evaluate a complex computer, fail to play a significant role in the study. This is a mistake. While the controller and accountants are often in charge of the study because the early applications of EDP equipment concern finance and accounting, it is important that each department whose work could be adapted to the computer be active in the study group. The members of the group should be generally knowledgeable in systems analysis, management objectives and how data processing might be helpful in meeting those objectives, and ways to estimate the benefits of the system and present them to management in a meaningful report.

Systems' personnel and programmers may be impractical and lacking in knowledge of purchasing. An attempt to anticipate every possible condition and to cover every detail creates a system that may prove cumbersome and costly. If certain situations occur infrequently and involve complicated programming, they may be handled manually, at least at the outset. On the other hand, systems people should not dismiss as unimportant certain aspects of the purchasing operation that are important in order to accelerate system design and programming.

The study group must be very careful to ensure that their desire to gain acceptance of the program by higher management does not lead them to underestimate the cost of installing and running the system. Many companies have found such costs to be far above the original estimate.

The study group must be sure that the *equipment* required for running the automated procurement system is available at the proper times. A written schedule should be established and adhered to or trouble will follow. Decisions based on machine information will be delayed and management requests for machine outputs will not be

---

[4] "Slaying the Computer Monster," *Purchasing*, April 16, 1974, p. 32.

met, with consequent friction if schedules are not established and followed.

The computer specialists must appreciate the need for periodic changes in the system because of such things as changes in price, government regulations, and vendor shipping policies. The simpler the system, the easier it will be to change it.

Purchasing must be prepared to stay current with the automated purchasing system so that they can control it once the system is established. If purchasing personnel do not understand the system or if they fail to supply information properly, the data requested by processing department control may pass to the computer specialists by default, and this group may make decisions that affect the purchasing department. To ensure against this eventuality and to promote efficiency, the purchasing department should provide a qualified person as liaison between the purchasing department and the data-processing group. Such a person should be knowledgeable in accounting, purchasing, and related functions and should be someone who is likely to stay with the company until the system is fully operational. Considerable time is required to learn the machine and program technology and to become familiar with the many implications of a complex system.

Personnel

The study group must assure itself that there will be an adequate number of skilled personnel available. Well-planned systems often get off to an unsatisfactory start because programmers or analysts are not available at the time when their work is essential. The attainment of an operational program at an early date does much to convince management of the practicality of the program. The program should be broken down into definable segments, and the information must be properly meshed to meet the priorities established in the timetable.

The Study

In a major metalworking plant the following list of questions provided the framework of the study:

1. Will the automation of Purchasing and related activities result in a lower net cost of performing the function?

2. Will it process all or most of purchasing's clerical functions?

3. Can it handle orders for complex as well as simple parts and materials and multiple items as well as single-item orders?

4.   Will it handle "rush" orders as well as routine deliveries?

5.   Will it be easy to install and operate or will the conversion process and maintenance be difficult?

6.   Will it be compatible with other EDP operations of the company or division?

7.   Does the information provided by the system have value?

8.   Will the cost of obtaining information for management be commensurate with its usefulness, or could it be obtained in a more economical way?

9.   Is the information to be provided by the system already available from some existing secondary source?

10.   What personnel problems and needs will be generated by conversion to automation?

11.   Are many clerks involved in processing data manually at present? (If not—perhaps EDP would be of little value.)

12.   What areas of application should be most rewarding? (This information will assist in the establishment of a priority timetable or conversion schedule.)

13.   What changes in organization, policies and practices must be made?

14.   Will Purchasing be able to use the computer on a regular schedule at a definite time or just "as available"?

15.   What is the volume (percentage) of repetitive work (items ordered, use of same vendors etc.) as compared to non-repetitive?

16.   Will the program provide "management by exceptions" freeing executives of the necessity of working through voluminous reports to determine matters requiring immediate attention?

17.   What are the intangible values that should result from timely information and reports to management, e.g., *goodwill* from "on time" deliveries or report of order status, reduction in "emergency" orders, fewer small unprofitable orders because of grouping of needs by product family, and improved trade relations by virtue of regular monthly report of specific commodity purchases by vendor?

18.   What equipment would provide the desired information at the lowest cost with proper consideration being given to future needs?

19.   Should we consider buying the service at the beginning of the program with an eye to later conversion to our own leased or owned equipment?

20.   What costs and savings will result from automation of Purchasing and related activities? (Be careful not to underestimate but, above all, be sure to be realistic about programming and "going-in" costs.)

21. Are we being coldly realistic about the economic evaluation? Have we compared the advantages of the EDP cost of performing purchasing's clerical work with such systems as stockless purchasing, minimal stock systems, and purchase order check plan?[5]

The Study Decision

The study group will finally recommend to management whether the company should employ electronic data-processing equipment for the purchasing functions. It should support its recommendation with a list of advantages and disadvantages, such as the following:

ADVANTAGES

1. It will make records and reports available from a single recording of information.
2. Peak loads and end-of-month overtime will be minimized or eliminated.
3. Greater efficiency will be attained in purchasing high-volume repetitive items.
4. Better management decisions will result from the speed and accuracy with which information is available.
5. It will permit management by exceptions.
6. It will relieve buyers and purchasing agents of detail, permitting them to spend more time on judgmental activities.
7. It will provide means of ensuring against late deliveries of critical items on major capital projects.
8. The discipline of the computer program will eliminate incompatibilities of systems that now often exist.
9. Exceptions requiring special handling by the computer will lead to the elimination of some bad practices.
10. It will eliminate "defensive record keeping" for government contracts where the government requires a contractor to prove that the buyer obtained adequate "quotes" for items purchased and paid prices consistent with the market.
11. It will reduce cost of accomplishing necessary manual clerical work in purchasing and related activities.

DISADVANTAGES

1. Cost may outweigh the advantages. For example, in many companies the reports are called for but not used.

---

[5] From the consulting files of one of the authors.

Computer Applications	Number
1. Receiving Status Systems	14
2. Schedule Control and Expediting Systems	13
3. Open Purchase Order Status Systems	12
4. Commodity Expenditure Profile Systems	11
5. Vendor Expenditure Profile Systems	11
6. Price and Source History Systems	9
7. Material Requisition Status Systems	7
8. Supplier Delivery Rating Systems	7
9. Department and Buyer Workload Measurement Systems	6
10. Supplier Quality Rating Systems	6
11. Forecasting Systems	5
12. Analysis of Degree of Competition Systems	3
13. Invoice Exception Systems	3
14. Material Price Analysis Systems	3
15. Long-Term Contract Status Systems	2
16. Subcontract Management Status Systems	2

Source: Moore and Fearon "Computer Operating and Management-Reporting Systems in Purchasing," *Journal of Purchasing,* August 1973, p. 27.

2. The procedure is inflexible and must be followed exactly. Manual programs permit deviations.

3. Errors or omissions in putting information into the computer are more likely than they are when the information is manually posted. Checks and safeguards can be designed for computers but the cost of installing them in all areas appears to be impracticable.

4. Since EDP involves special equipment, a company cannot use conventional equipment when the computer breaks down. Some major companies have agreements with Data Processing Centers or other companies for emergency processing of data, but these arrangements are not ideal.

5. A good EDP programmer or department head should be well informed as to company procedures and problems, and it is difficult to hire or replace such employees.

6. Companies often find that vendors who have data-processing systems in their plants are either unable or unwilling to alter their systems to conform to your program.

7. Because of the many mergers and purchases of companies, many invoices are rejected when processed by computer. It is difficult to maintain a vendor file with the required accuracy.

8. All computer entries must be absolutely clear and completely

accurate. Inaccurate input results in inaccurate output which may be accepted as correct unless the error is so large it is evident.

Current Usage

A study of 15 computer users found receiving systems, schedule control/expediting, and open purchase order status reports were the most widely used applications of computers in purchasing operations.

Sophistication in computer programming relative to purchasing department needs has reached the point where such programs can be bought and integrated into existing computers. IBM has developed such a program designed primarily for manufacturing, process and distribution companies, and available for use on the Systems 360 or 370 computers. The functional activities involved are: purchase order planning (calculating net requirements, economic order quantities, and least cost vendors), requisition writing purchase order release and maintenance, and purchase order status and review. Cost for such programs is generally available for under $500 monthly license fees.

SUMMARY

In highly competitive markets with increasing costs of labor, capital equipment, and transportation, management must concentrate on the most important aspects of its responsibilities. An electronic data-processing system can assist purchasing by directing its attention to exceptions that occur in the execution of its responsibilities and by providing an objective base for imporved performance.

While the increasing complexity of business tends to make purchasing personnel "fire fighters," an efficient data-processing system enables them to be orderly and schedule providers of parts and materials, by supplying them with:

1. Organized information
2. Ready reference information
3. Relief from clerical details
4. Management by exception
5. Guide lines for improved performance

In most cases, there are benefits to be gained in partially automating purchasing clerical functions, but maximum benefit is not obtained unless an integrated procedure is adopted which should:

1. Store price quotations, price history records, and vendor performance information
2. Calculate the "economic order quantity" (EOQ) and determine whether the quantity should be increased or decreased over the amount ordered
3. Evaluate price and delivery information and requisition from the supplier offering the best price and delivery for the quantity ordered

DISCUSSION QUESTIONS

1. Distinguish between data and information as they relate to an EDP system.

2. What is the basic objective of establishing an EDP system in purchasing?

3. What benefits should an efficient data-processing system provide to purchasing personnel?

4. Why has there been so much delay in the use of data-processing equipment in the purchasing department?

5. Indicate major difficulties involved in automating the functions of the purchasing department.

6. Define EDP.

7. Distinguish between two types of electronic computers.

8. Indicate the general means whereby an EDP system can assist purchasing.

9. What has been the role of EDP in promoting the materials' management concept?

10. What is the EDP study?

SUGGESTED CASE

John Roberts Manufacturing Company

CHAPTER 24

CAPITAL EQUIPMENT

Capital equipment refers to those items of machinery and equipment whose long life and high value require that they be carried on the balance sheet and depreciated over a period of time. Capital equipment differs from materials and supplies, which are charged immediately to expense and are a cost of current production.

Accounting practices for capital equipment vary from firm to firm. Some companies capitalize most equipment purchases, whereas others are inclined to charge the less costly and shorter-lived items directly to expense accounts. Therefore, although the criteria of long life and high value do not precisely characterize capital equipment, the criteria are accurate enough for the purpose of this chapter.

Examples of capital equipment are boilers, pumps, electric generators, machine tools, can- and bottle-capping equipment, mechanical conveyors, railroad engines and cars, steel rolling mills, and generators. It will be observed that some of these items are used for a single purpose in a given industry, whereas others are used in a variety of ways in many industries. The first class is frequently described as special-purpose equipment and the second class as general-purpose equipment. This distinction makes for important differences in purchasing methods as will be indicated throughout the chapter.

Distinguishing Characteristics of Capital Equipment Purchasing

Extended Negotiations

The purchase of capital equipment differs from the purchase of raw materials, supplies, and other items in that each purchase is the result of careful negotiations, requiring the consideration of many more vendors than is usual for other purchases. With raw materials such as coal or chemicals, after the vendor has been selected, on the basis of price, quality, location, and similar factors, subsequent purchases are ordinarily made from the same vendor until some strong reason for change arises. With major equipment, however, each transaction is likely to result in separate and extended negotiations. Occasionally, satisfactory experience with the first purchase may result in an automatic reorder, but this is the exception.

Lead-Time Requirement

Another difference between capital equipment and other purchases concerns lead time. Lead time is the interval between the placing of an order and the delivery date, and, as a general rule, the lead-time requirement for capital equipment is much greater than for other materials and supplies.

This is particularly true for capital equipment that is special or custom-built and for which considerable engineering is required. Even though the item is of standard design, there usually are options available for the buyer to select. Standard-equipment items also are sometimes of such size and value that it is impracticable for them to be made up and stocked by the manufacturer.

Multiple Purchasing Influence

Because of its importance to the manufacturing process of a company and its usual distinctiveness, a capital equipment purchase attracts the interest of several members of a buying firm. Primary interest is always centered in the using department. In the case of raw material and supplies, the using department may be the only one concerned. This is not true of capital equipment, since such transactions have wide ramifications. Often the machinery is part of an expansion or modernization program. In such a case the project itself has been under consideration by top management long before discussions about the equipment were begun with vendors. Engineering work also is required to determine the specific items to be purchased. Because of the financial outlay involved in the purchase, the financial officer must be consulted. Installation and maintenance of the equipment will involve others in the equipment selection. Finally, whoever has charge of the power plant will be concerned about the purchase as it affects the power load within the plant.

The purchase of a new turbine generator illustrates the widespread interest in the acquisition of capital equipment. Top management will first consider the matter, based on reports it has received of the need for the equipment, its estimated cost, and the savings to be expected from its use. After top management authorizes the purchase, much engineering work must be done to determine the exact size of the unit, the particular type to be bought, its location, its installation, and similar matters. When proposals are received from vendors, the interested persons will check the offers in the light of their own interest before a final decision is made. Contrast this with the order for the car of fuel oil where the need exists only in the one department and the concern of other departments is merely that common to routine business transactions.

Flexible Specifications

The specifications for standard capital equipment frequently are not so inflexible as the specifications for raw materials and supplies. One important reason is that equipment designed by different companies for the same purpose may vary significantly in characteristics. Many manufacturers of pumps, for example, may be able to offer pumps to meet certain conditions of capacity and head, but not all the pumps would meet òne set of specifications. If the buyer were to insist on rigid specifications, he would reduce competition and probably pay a higher price as a consequence.

One of the dangers of relying too heavily on engineers in purchasing major equipment is that they tend to insist on unnecessarily restrictive specifications. Such specifications often require the maker to alter the design at a higher cost and with delayed delivery.

Detailed Records Required

A further difference between capital equipment and most other purchases is that the buyer preserves the identity of major-equipment items through detailed accounting and statistical records. This is not done for raw materials and supplies, since one unit is like another. An equipment item is usually given a serial number by its maker, and the buyer uses this number to preserve an individual record from the time of purchase.

This equipment record is useful for several purposes. The accountants use it as a basis for depreciating the equipment for tax and income determination. Those responsible for the operation and maintenance of the equipment need records, including all the necessary identifying numbers, for ordering spare parts and for operating and lubricating instructions. The records are also important because of the possibility of later changes in the design of the equipment by the manufacturer. The maker frequently offers the buyer the opportunity of altering the design of a machine when design changes are introduced after its purchase. At times it is enough to know that changes have been made as a guide in future purchases of such equipment. In any case it is important to be able to identify the equipment from company records.

High Value

The unit value of capital equipment is high because equipment contains a higher proportion of labor to raw material than almost any other kind of purchase. The high unit value is most significant for financing. Top management must usually budget and authorize such expenditures before they can be made. Most other purchases can be made without such specific authorization.

Nonrecurring Purchases

Large companies may purchase capital equipment items frequently, but even in these companies a specific type of equipment will be bought only at infrequent intervals. This infrequency of purchase is one of the reasons that a careful evaluation and study must be made of each transaction. Past history of previous purchases is so limited as to afford little guidance for a new purchase.

The nonrecurring nature of equipment purchases also makes it important that the purchasing department keep alert to changes and new developments in the field. While progressive suppliers can usually be depended on to keep their customers posted on design changes and improvements, the alert purchasing agent makes a determined effort to keep abreast of such developments.

One policy determination concerns whether a company shall purchase its capital equipment abroad or in the United States. Arguments usually made in favor of purchasing in the United States include the creation and preservation of jobs, the preservation of buying power for domestic products, and the payment of domestic taxes that otherwise would have to be borne by fewer firms. On the other hand, the price of foreign-made equipment may be less and quality is often comparable. Unavailability of emergency repairs, difficulty in securing qualified service personnel, and costly communications are sometimes considerations against purchasing foreign-made equipment.

Governmental Inducements

Over the past several years the federal government has sought to encourage investment in capital equipment as a means of stimulating productivity or the level of economic activity. One way of doing this has been to allow the investing company to depreciate capital equipment at an accelerated rate. Another way is through what is called an investment tax credit. This permits the investing company to deduct a percentage (7% and 10% have been allowed) of the value of the investment from taxable income in the year of purchase. The government can regulate the amount of the tax credit or even suspend it entirely to stimulate or curb economic activity and inflation as the situation warrants.[1]

Allied Purchases

Another contrast between the purchase of capital equipment and that of other items is that the purchase of capital equipment frequently entails the purchase of related equipment, materials, or supplies. The purchase of one new machine may make some other piece of equipment obsolete and necessitate its replacement. In the same way, it may be necessary to find a substitute raw material in order to utilize the new machine, or new supplies may be needed for its operation. Therefore, it is important to recognize that the purchase of a major equipment item may start a chain reaction. In many firms the persons responsible for buying capital equipment are not those who buy raw materials, and unless good coordination is maintained serious maladjustments may result.

Another important facet of capital equipment purchases is the value of the accessories that go with the main unit. Sometimes these "extras" equal the price of the basic equipment and therefore special care must be exercised in their procurement. Often it is not advantageous to buy such accessories from the manufacturer of the equipment as he may purchase the accessory equipment for resale and add a middleman profit. In other cases competitive materials may be available at a lower price.

Service as a Factor in Equipment Purchases

While service is a factor in the purchase of materials and supplies, it is a particularly important consideration in the purchase of capital equipment. There are four varieties of service available to a buyer, and their relative importance varies with the type of equipment involved. Often the service is as important as the equipment.

[1] Monroe M. Fird, Jr., "Remove or Suspend Investment Tax Credit to Curb Inflation," *Financial Analyst Journal*, March-April, 1969.

Prepurchase Survey by Vendor

Because it is possible to buy equipment with varying characteristics from different manufacturers for the same job, it is frequently necessary to have a survey of the buyer's needs made by each potential vendor. Suppliers may insist on making such a survey so that they can ascertain that the proposed use is a proper application of their equipment. If a survey is not suggested, it is often wise for the buyer to ask for it so that the responsibility for correct application can be placed with the vendor.

The benefits of prepurchase surveys are illustrated in the purchase of a pump in the chemical industry. The materials used in making a pump are important because of the chemical and physical properties of the substances to be moved. Manufacturers have varying metal alloys to handle the different chemicals and special names are used to designate these alloys. Since the buyer does not know the composition of these alloys, it is impossible for him to specify what is required even if he has detailed knowledge of the application. While the material to be moved is studied the problems of capacity and head of the pumping specification are also analyzed. With the results of such a survey the buyer and seller can be reasonably sure that the equipment will be properly designed for its use.

Another important reason for a prepurchase survey is that the vendor can often suggest economies regarding the application. For example, a chemical plant had a materials-handling problem involving the movement of bulk chemical from one building to another. The plant engineers suggested the introduction of water into the material and pumping it to the distant building. Because the material was highly corrosive special alloy pumps and special alloy piping were suggested. The engineer's solution presented the problem of removing the water from the material after it had served its purpose as a vehicle. Representatives of various pump manufacturers were called in to survey the situation and to recommend equipment. As a result of the survey a much more economical solution was suggested—that a special type of mechanical conveyor system be installed to move the dry material between the two buildings at a saving of 25% under previously recommended alloy pumps and piping.

Installation Service

The installation of a large machine is usually handled by personnel from the buyer's plant under the supervision of the vendor's representative. When such service is essential from the seller's point of view, the cost of installation supervision is included in the purchase price. When supervisory installation service is optional, the charges are usually assessed on the basis of the actual time and expenses incurred. When highly specialized equipment is involved, sales engineers usually provide a limited amount of service in conjunction with installation, start-up, and general "troubleshooting." There is usually no explicit charge for this type of service.

Demonstration and Training Service

The demonstration of equipment and training of operators may be an integral part of the installation service. Usually the service engineer who supervises the installation also oversees the start-up and assists in training the operating personnel.

Proper training of operators is important to the buyer because vendors frequently include a provision in their warranty relieving them of responsibility for damage to equipment caused by improper operation. If the vendor's representative has trained the operator, it is hard for the vendor to avoid the warranty obligation by claiming that the operator was incompetent.

Postsales Service

Service on equipment after it has been installed and is in operation is of two types—service during the warranty period and service after the warranty period. On most items of capital equipment there is a written guarantee against failure of the equipment from faulty design or from defective parts or assembly for a stated period, frequently one year. During that period the buyer can obtain free service on the equipment if any trouble develops.

After the warranty period the buyer must usually pay for service calls on the basis of the hours spent and travel and living expenses of the service representative. Sometimes, in order to build or preserve goodwill, a seller will give "free" service after the guarantee period is past. If trade practice necessitates that a seller perform a large amount of such postguarantee service, the price will have to cover these costs. Ultimately all customers will be paying an average share of such costs, and those who use less than an average amount of service are penalized. In view of this inequity it is better for both buyer and seller to have a reasonable guarantee period and to adhere strictly to its terms.

Procedure for Purchasing Capital Equipment

The precedures followed in purchasing major equipment are obviously guided by the same common purchasing principles—the right equipment at the right price, quality, and service—as guide the purchasing of any other material or supply item. In some companies special central teams or groups at the corporate level are charged with equipment purchasing responsibility. In other companies local plants handle their own equipment procurement. A common variation is to have the local purchasing manager originate such transactions subject to approval at the corporate level.

Because of the nature of equipment purchases in terms of sums involved, relative infrequency of purchase, and capitalization of the purchase, it is not surprising that detailed procedures have been developed to facilitate and control equipment purchasing. One such approach is based on the critical path (CPM) techniques that evolved in defense contracting.[2] The cited approach involves a 24-event critical path from the request for investigation to the receipt of the equipment.

Need

Evaluation of need is the first step in the purchase of capital equipment. The recognition of the need originates with the using department, and the evaluation of this need requires the study of alternative methods, a cost analysis of the alternative methods, a search for equipment that will do the job, and a second cost study to determine the savings made possible by the use of the proposed equipment. A number of other departments cooperate with the using department in this evaluation. The function of the purchasing department is to provide information on available equipment, its cost, and the probable delivery schedule.

Specifications

After the need has been confirmed and the basic type of equipment determined, it is necessary to establish the specifications. There are basically three types of purchases possible. Most common is the purchase of equipment that is standard or common to an industry. Such equipment is available from a number of sources serving the industry. Standard equipment which requires no engineering modifications or changes can generally be purchased at a more favorable price and with minimal delivery-time problems as compared with any special requirements or modifications of standard equipment.

In some situations it will be necessary to customize standard

---

[2] "Critical Path to Equipment Buying," *Purchasing Week*, May 10, 1971, p. 34.

equipment to meet the specific needs of the buyer. It is important for the special feature to be clearly defined and its price impact on the basic cost of the equipment delineated.

At times it may be necessary to buy equipment that is unique to the buyer's specifications. Such equipment will be purchased on the basis of clear and complete specifications and may involve many meetings between buyer and seller until the specifications are agreed to by both parties. It the buyer does not have the necessary engineering staff capability, he may have to rely completely on the seller's design and engineering capabilities. In such cases, it is normal to select a single supplier and work with him rather than to secure competitive bids.

Negotiation

At this point the purchasing department, which has so far arranged the contacts with vendors, determines which vendors to solicit for quotations. Specifications are presented to the selected vendors, and they are invited either to quote or to send a representative to survey the job before quoting. Because there may be important differences in the ability of manufacturers to deliver the equipment which do not show up in the quotations, it usually is not advisable to accept quotations without some discussion with the vendor.

Ordering

After deciding upon the supplier, it is necessary for the purchasing department to work out with that vendor all details of the purchase order. Perhaps the vendor offered several optional methods of payment, or the buyer may prefer certain transportation routings or carriers. It is wise to impress on the vendor the fact that the delivery date quoted must be adhered to and that the vendor will be held strictly to the specifications. One should not assume that a seller's acceptance of an order automatically guarantees that he will live up to all the conditions in the quotation. An experienced buyer knows that, although he may be reimbursed in money for any damages incurred, he can save himself much trouble, cost, and work by taking precautions before placing the order.

Follow-Up

Because the purchase of capital equipment usually covers an extended period of time, follow-up of the order is an important responsibility of the purchasing department. Often engineering work is necessary, and this must be approved by the buyer before fabrication can begin. All the various stages of the transaction must be carefully followed to make certain that the delivery is not delayed. A recommended procedure is to have the vendor specify time intervals for each of the steps in the process so that any delays can be spotted as they occur. It is much easier, for example, to overcome a delay in the preparation of drawings while they are being worked on than months later when the machine should be delivered but is not ready.

The follow-up of an order should be performed by the person who placed the order. The detail work of keeping track of the order in the purchasing department can be handled by others, but dealings with the vendor should be conducted by the person who negotiated the order. Better results will be achieved by personal dealings than by a more impersonal approach such as a form letter or card.

New or Used Equipment

When an item of major equipment is required, one of the first possibilities to consider is the purchase of used equipment. The used-equipment market is large, and in every industry there are many firms that specialize in the buying and selling of used equipment peculiar to that industry. We shall consider some of the reasons for buying both new and used equipment.

Considerations Favoring the Purchase of New Equipment

Long Life Expectancy.   One of the important reasons for buying new equipment rather than used is that the life expectancy of new equipment is longer. If the equipment is a substantial item that will be needed for many years, a new machine would be indicated. Equipment such as earth movers and construction equipment which are subjected to extremely hard use are usually bought new because, at best, their life expectancy is not long.

Uniform Life Expectancy.   The nature of a particular project may justify the purchase of new equipment. For example, some company may be modernizing an entire department of its plant. In such a case it is important that all components of the process be new equipment so that the facility, when finished, will have a uniform life expectancy. It would be unwise to install an item of used equipment with an uncertain life which could cause a shutdown of operations.

Technological Innovations.   New equipment is usually of more modern design. Manufacturers are constantly striving to improve their products, not only because of competition for the market, but also in an effort to improve their own manufacturing efficiency. The buyer of major equipment is therefore interested in getting the most modern design. Sometimes a choice must be made between buying a duplicate of the machine currently in operation or a more modern design of the same unit. As a general rule it is better to buy the modernized version, but at times the new design may require additional and costly changes in the balance of the production line. Thus an old design may be preferable.

Reduced Maintenance. New equipment quite naturally requires less maintenance than used equipment. This is a strong argument for the purchase of new equipment. Maintenance is a factor often overlooked when alternative purchases are being weighed, but in view of the importance of maintenance costs its omission is a serious oversight.

Lower Parts Inventory. Related to the lower maintenance cost for new equipment is the fact that a smaller stock of spare parts is needed for new equipment. The cost of the spare-parts inventory is a seldom-discussed but nevertheless significant item of expense. Inventory requires capital investment, storage space, and a detailed accounting procedure. The decreased cost of maintaining spare parts therefore should be taken into account in considering the advantages of new equipment.

Bid Comparisons. It is much easier to evaluate competitive bids for new equipment than to compare bids on used equipment or bids that involve some of each. This is so because two items of used equipment are never in exactly the same basic condition or state of repair. The buyer then must compare both price and the much less tangible element of residual service.

Specification Considerations. As previously stated, specifications play a very important part in the purchase of major equipment. Once careful specifications have been worked out, it is a relatively simple matter to relate them to new equipment being considered. This is not true for used equipment. The only used equipment that can be considered is that which is available for sale, and therefore it is difficult to match the available equipment with a set of specifications. As one departs from specifications, it becomes increasingly difficult to evaluate competitive bids.

Warranties. Although it is sometimes possible to secure a limited performance guarantee with the purchase of used equipment, this is the exception rather than the rule. By contrast, all reliable manufacturers guarantee new equipment to produce up to a specified level of performance. In many cases the installation of machinery changes the processes of a plant and a transition period ensues during which minor difficulties are encountered. Even when a performance guarantee is given on used equipment, it is for a short period. When no guarantee is given with used equipment, the buyer, during the transition period, might discover that the equipment will not work into the production process. In such cases the buyer not only has purchased something of no value, but will have additional expenses to regain his original position.

Considerations Favoring the Purchase of Used Equipment

Cost. Perhaps the major consideration favoring the purchase of used equipment is its lower cost. This is difficult to establish, however, because of the imponderables involved in determining the worth of used equipment. Prices of used equipment vary with the supply of used equipment, and with the prices and delivery schedules of comparable new equipment. At times substantial savings can be made by purchasing used equipment. Often the high cost of a large project forces the company to economize by purchasing some used equipment. If the choice is between not going through with the project and buying used equipment, the second alternative may be preferable.

Delivery. Sometimes a compelling reason for the purchase of used equipment is its immediate availability. Frequently production is required on short notice, and the only possible way to achieve it is by the purchase of used equipment. When one unit of an elaborate manufacturing process breaks down, the cost of a shutdown of the entire process, even for a short time, is often much greater than the purchase price of a used unit. The immediate availability of used equipment makes it a bargain at any reasonable price.

Design Considerations. There are times when a project calls for certain equipment that duplicates equipment presently in the plant. The manufacturer may feel that the current design is desired over the outmoded design now in use. However, the buyer may rightly contend that it would be better to duplicate the older design by purchasing used equipment, especially when there are several of the older designed units in service. This permits the addition of another unit without requiring an increase in the spare-parts inventory. Also, the maintenance staff of the plant is familiar with the old model, and its operation presents no new problems.

Temporary Need. There are occasions when it is satisfactory to buy used equipment because long life is not required. Often a rather elaborate temporary process must be set up and operated for a short term. Under these conditions used equipment is likely to be more economical. When pilot plants are set up for experimenting with the production of new products, the short duration will dictate purchase of used equipment.

In certain cases the problem of maintenance may *not* be a significant factor in deciding between new and used equipment. Some items of equipment in a manufacturing operation are so important and operate so steadily that they receive maintenance attention according to a carefully prescribed schedule. Here used equipment might be satisfactory, because it would get as much attention as it required.

Inspection.   A final argument for the choice of used equipment is that one can inspect the equipment before purchase. Closely related to inspection there is frequently the possibility of being able to see a used machine in operation. For many people, particularly operating personnel, this is a major reason for buying used equipment.

Difficulties in the Purchase of Used Equipment

One of the foremost difficulties in buying used equipment is assessing the severity of previous service. There are as many ways to rejuvenate a used piece of equipment as to rejuvenate a used automobile. It is common practice to clean up the machine, paint it, and make it look as much like new as possible. Unscrupulous poeple dealing in this type of equipment do many other things to hide the true condition of a machine in order to trap the unwary. If one can determine why the equipment was withdrawn from its former service, that information may greatly aid in assessing its worth. Frequently, equipment is found unsuited for the task for which it was purchased through no fault of its own. In all probability it would then be in good condition and represent a bargain for the right buyer.

One of the most serious difficulties in buying used equipment is that it often is necessary to deal with unfamiliar sources. When equipment is offered by strangers, even when guaranteed, the buyer must evaluate the guarantor as well as the equipment.

The terms of sale for used equipment are usually restrictive, with most sales on an "as-is and where-is" basis with terms of "net cash." The machine is purchased where it stands and in its present condition. The buyer must arrange for transportation, which often adds as much as 10% to the purchase price. If the machine is large and must be dismantled before moving and assembled when received, the extra cost may run as high as 20%. The net cash terms are often supplemented with sight draft bill of lading which requires the buyer to pay the draft before securing delivery of the equipment.

Leasing

Many items of major equipment may be leased instead of being purchased. Much the same study of requirements and negotiation with vendors is necessary in leasing equipment as in outright purchase. The principal difference between the two types of transactions is that title to the equipment remains with the original owner.

Reasons for Leasing

One of the common reasons for leasing equipment is the temporary nature of certain needs. For example, construction work often necessitates items such as metal scaffolding, wheelbarrows, and air tools whose life is longer than the particular project calls for and for which the user will have no need after the building is completed. Since there are companies that specialize in the rental of this type of equipment, leasing is more economical.

Another example of leasing for temporary use is the rental of power equipment, such as a transformer, for emergency service until other equipment can be delivered or repaired. The rental charge for leased equipment for the short period involved is relatively low. Therefore, leasing is an excellent means of satisfying such a temporary requirement.

In some cases leasing may be the only way equipment can be acquired. If a seller has a unique item of equipment, he may decide that it is in his financial interest to offer only the lease option. This practice may not only maximize his income, but it gives the seller greater control over the resale market as well. The refusal to sell equipment outright may be a violation of Section 3 of the Clayton Act, if practiced by a large company, because the course would be likely to hold that such a policy would "substantially lessen competition." However, small companies would not risk that danger and could, therefore, legally lease their products rather than sell them.

Some companies manufacture rather complicated equipment such as data-processing machines, which are continually being redesigned. The buyer would suffer if newly purchased items were rendered obsolete soon after purchase. On the other hand, the seller cannot delay improvements because of competitive pressures. In such situations, both parties may be satisfied with a lease arrangement.

Another reason for leasing is the buyer's desire to have the title remain with the manufacturer or the rental agency, thereby shifting responsibility for service. This is particularly true of equipment requiring frequent adjusting, cleaning, and repairing by highly skilled service people.

Lift trucks are a good illustration of an equipment item whose maintenance requirements are so great that leasing may be the most economical and expeditious means of accomplishing such service.[3]

> The average lift truck operates efficiently for five years or 10,000 operating hours—the equivalent of 350,000 automotive miles. It is no wonder that a lift truck requires great maintenance. Yale studies indicate that during its five year, 10,000 hour economic life a lift truck is down for repairs for 900 hours or 22 weeks, and maintenance accumulates to 90 percent of acquisition price. And these studies are premised on doing everything right: proper lubrication, maintenance and preventive maintenance.

Sometimes the nature of the equipment may make outright purchase impracticable. For example, a company requiring a railroad tankcar, to operate between its own plants, would probably not have facilities for maintaining the car and, furthermore, the car will be out of its direct control for most of its active life. Since there are companies that own large fleets of tankcars, it is a simple matter to lease a car and have the lessor take care of all the details of repair, maintenance, and accounting necessary in conjunction with its movement over various railroads.

The fact that certain equipment has a high rate of depreciation is another reason for leasing. Companies operating fleets of trucks and passenger cars often resort to lease for this reason. It has been found that, because of the high depreciation of such automotive equipment, it is often more economical to rent the fleet and leave the problem of replacement to the lessor. Many companies formerly kept such equipment for 3 or 4 years because the mileage was low. When these units were replaced, the trade-in allowance was smaller than was thought to be fair in view of the low mileage. Actually, the age of the vehicle was the determining factor in the low trade-in. Under a lease arrangement the owner can transfer cars among users to keep their age and mileage at the level that will secure the highest trade-in value.

Many firms turn to the lease arrangement for items of equipment with a high unit price because they believe it is favorable from the point of view of income-tax determination. The cost of leasing may

[3] "Lift Truck Leasing," *Modern Plant Operation & Maintenance*, Summer- - Fall, 1973, p. 11.

be deducted from income in its entirety, whereas the cost of purchased equipment can only be charged against income according to government-approved depreciation schedules. Therefore, deductions permitted under a lease arrangement may be more liberal than those permitted if equipment is owned. However, the government has approved various methods of increasing the rate of depreciation for owned equipment, and in these cases the tax issue may no longer favor leasing.

It should also be observed that, by leasing equipment, the buyer is spared the large cash outlay required for outright purchase. This is an important consideration for companies of limited resources, those that may be short of working capital, or those with favorable opportunities for expansion.

Notwithstanding the rather rapid growth of leasing of equipment in general, there is one field where this does not appear to be the case. That field is production equipment or machine tools. There are three possible reasons for this lag.

The first is tradition. Machine tool manufacturers have traditionally sold their products for cash; machine tool users have traditionally clung to the "pride of ownership" mystique that surrounds production equipment. Second, machine tools generally have a long life and high resale value. There is an apparent sharp contrast between the short-term lease and the long life expectancy of machine tools. The third, and perhaps most basic reason, is lack of familiarity with leasing on the parts of both machine tool makers and machine tool buyers.

Limitations of Leasing

There are some unfavorable aspects of leasing that should be taken into account before a decision to lease equipment is made. Over an extended period of time it probably will cost a company more to lease than to buy equipment. This is so because the lessor expects to make a profit proportionate to his risk, and the risk to a supplier is greater from leasing than from selling. On the other hand, one can argue that the supplier is able to minimize risks of obsolescence through design changes and new techniques and, therefore, can perhaps assume such risks at a lower cost than could a using company that bought the equipment outright. This is a point that can never be settled to the satisfaction of everyone.

A lessee should also recognize that he will have to grant the lessor access to leased equipment for repair and maintenance. Such free access can prove embarrassing to a company that has methods and processes which it desires to keep private.

Another factor to consider is that the lessor frequently hopes to use leased equipment as a means of inducing the purchase of supplies for the equipment. The lessor cannot legally force the use of such supplies through a "tying contract," but he can, and often does, use persuasion and ignorance of the user to further such sales.

Mechanics of Leasing

Equipment available under lease may be available directly from the manufacturer, an outside sales agency, and firms specializing in financing and leasing equipment.[4] Lease arrangements are evidenced by a contract. The contract describes the equipment so that it can be positively identified, defines the duration of the lease, sets the rental rate and terms of payment, and defines the responsibility for maintenance of the equipment. Frequently the lease agreement includes an option of outright purchase with the provision that rental payments may be applied against the purchase price.

Financing Major-Equipment Purchases

The financing of major-equipment purchases often involves such large amounts that special methods of payment are utilized.

Financing by the Vendor

Frequently the financing of a high-unit-price item of equipment is handled directly with the vendor. Manufacturers of this type of equipment usually are financially able to assist their customers in such financing. The fact that equipment requires a long lead time for designing, engineering, and manufacturing is an aid to these financing arrangements.

One of the commonest methods of financing is the payment of a percentage of the purchase price when the order is placed, with the balance payable either at the time of shipment or partially at the time of shipment, with the remainder due 30 days after shipment. The percentage paid with the order is usually 25 or 33-1/3%. This down payment gives the manufacturer money with which to finance engineering work and raw materials. Vendors also insist on a percentage down payment with the order to insure themselves against serious loss if the order should be canceled.

---

[4] See "Equipment Leasing: Before the Cash-flow Analysis, What Else?" John P. Matthews, *Journal of Purchasing*, February 1974, pp. 5–11, for a description of the various types of lessor firms.

Control of Purchasing Activities

A similar and quite popular method of equipment financing is the installment plan, with payments beginning when the order is placed and continuing either until shipment is made or some later specified date. The total price of the equipment is divided into an equal number of periodic payments. If, for example, the price is $600,000 and delivery is estimated to take 20 months, the monthly payments might be set at $30,000 plus carrying charges. If delivery is made on schedule, the final payment would coincide with shipment. If the delivery date is uncertain, it might be decided to schedule the payments over 30 months with monthly payments of $20,000. Under this plan, if delivery were complete in 24 months, the payments would continue for 6 months beyond delivery.

For very large units of equipment a percentage may be paid with the order and progress payments stipulated at certain intervals based on an engineering estimate of the percentage of completion.

These are the usual payment procedures—others are only variations. In some cases 10% of the purchase price is paid every 60 days, beginning when the order is placed and continuing until 50% has been paid. The balance is then payable at the rate of 50% upon shipment, another 40% thirty days after shipment, and the final 10% sixty days after shipment. Frequently the payment of the balance due on shipment is postponed until after installation and testing. Some equipment, such as boilers, has acceptance tests after completion, with the final payment made after the tests have been satisfactorily completed.

Financing through Outside Agencies

When the cost of equipment is very high it is often necessary to secure funds from outside sources. The simplest and probably the commonest method is the direct loan from a bank or insurance company.

A common method of financing large-equipment purchases, used mainly by the railroads, is the issuance of equipment trust certificates. In this case the buyer gives a mortgage on the equipment to some financial institution which advances the money for the purchase. Usually some identifying device is attached to the equipment to show to whom it has been mortgaged. This financing arrangement is also used by the commercial airlines to finance their planes.

Another common method of financing large-equipment purchases is the rental agreement with an insurance company. The insurance company actually purchases the equipment according to the buyer's specifications and leases the equipment to the buyer on a long-term rental agreement. Usually these agreements provide that the rental payments shall be applied to the purchase price, so that at the expiration of the term the buyer takes title to the equipment. This method of financing sometimes has an income advantage in that the full amount of the rental paid can be deducted from income as expense. Its status appears to be the same as that of the lease in this respect.

Disposal of Surplus or Obsolete Equipment

Responsibility of Purchasing Department

The disposal of surplus or obsolete equipment is commonly the responsibility of the purchasing department, because the purchasing department is likely to be best informed about possible buyers and usually has complete records regarding the equipment and its maintenance. The purchasing department is also familiar with used-equipment prices and is therefore able to set a fair price on the equipment for disposal. Thus the purchasing department is usually best equipped to dispose of surplus and obsolete equipment.

Channels of Sales Available

One of the easiest methods of disposal of surplus equipment is the sale to used-equipment dealers. If the item is a piece of equipment peculiar to the industry, as, for example, a complete paper machine, the dealers who specialize in papermill machinery would be the likely people to approach.

Other prospects for the disposal of surplus equipment are companies in the same field. It is usual for one paper manufacturer to locate another who may be interested in special equipment. Purchasing agents of various companies in the same industry are acquainted with each other and in their frequent contacts can often facilitate the disposal of surplus equipment.

For certain types of equipment, the disposal is made as a trade-in on new equipment. This is usually restricted to equipment that is not peculiar to one industry but can be used by many industries. Trade-ins are most common in the construction, automotive, and machine tool fields. Dealers in these types of equipment frequently do a large share of their total business in the secondhand field. If new equipment is purchased direct from the producer, it is likely to be more difficult to negotiate a trade-in than if the purchase is made from a dealer. Manufacturers are not organized to handle used equipment. However, some manufacturers purchase used equipment of their own manufacture, rebuild it, and sell it with a guarantee to augment sales of new units.

Peculiarities of Selling Used Equipment

Because of its sporadic nature, it is difficult for purchasing personnel to become particularly skilled in the sale of used euqipment. The items to be sold vary greatly from one occasion to the next, and consequently the seller does not deal with the same buyers on successive transactions. Every piece of equipment has different characteristics of age, condition, and usefulness, and there can thus be no set pattern for sale. Price levels for used machinery also vary greatly from time to time and from dealer to dealer. All of these facts make used-machinery sales interesting but difficult.

Economic Analysis for Capital Equipment Purchase

In this chapter we have mentioned several times that a company considering the purchase of new equipment makes a careful cost analysis to compare the operation of the proposed equipment with its present equipment. Some companies base such purchasing decisions on little more than intuition or hunches. Others use ranking procedures to establish investment priorities.

However, because of the large size of capital equipment expenditures, most firms use detailed economic analysis procedures to calculate the expected return from the purchase against the expected cost. The validity of these calculations can determine the difference between a firm's operating success or failure when many millions of dollars are involved. The purchasing agent will be expected at least to be familiar with the concepts involved, and in some cases will be the party making the determination. An early study of the methods used by firms to evaluate new capital expenditures indicated that a number of firms use more than one method.[5] A recent article reported on a study of the criterion that enters into the decision as to which of several alternative models that are available for equipment replacement decision-making is favored.[6] The authors concluded that the latter ranked low because the model is "difficult to understand and apply."

[5] James H. Miller, "A Glimpse at Practice in Calculating and Using Return on Investment," *N.A.A. Bulletin,* June 1960, p. 73.

[6] Everett E. Adam, Jr. and Michael F. Pohlen, "Equipment Replacement Models: User Evaluation," *Journal of Purchasing,* February 1973, pp. 48–56.

Payback Period

The payback method is the most widely used method of analyzing the economics of major equipment purchases. Its use stems from its relative simplicity. The objective of the payback approach is to determine the number of years that would be needed before the cost of the equipment would be recovered from the savings generated by the equipment.

In its simplest form one assumes that the return each year from the use of the equipment is constant, no allowance is made for depreciation or taxes, and the return after the payback is computed on an after-tax basis by using in the denominator annual operating savings after taxes. The numerator consists of the net investment in the equipment.

Many firms have established policies relating to the maximum number of years over which they plan to recover the cost. A common payback period is three years. It is reasoned that if the equipment does not pay for itself within that time, the dangers of obsolescence are so great that purchase of the equipment would not be feasible.

There are two specific advantages, in addition to simplicity, to the payback approach. It shows the rate at which cash will flow back in to the business after an equipment purchase is accomplished. In addition, where rapid obsolescence of the new equipment is likely, it provides the necessary short-run emphasis to the investment decision.

The criticism leveled against this approach is that it does not pay attention to the total profitability of the equipment investment after the payback period is finished. The method also makes it difficult to compare alternative equipment with varying useful lives.

Present Value

Essentially any investment calculations involve two things: the expected payoff, or savings, which extends over many years, and the cost of the capital invested. Because capital equipment will usually produce savings over a long period of time, it is necessary to determine the worth of the future savings *today*. The so-called present value of anticipated savings can be obtained by several means, the simplest of which is:

where V = present value
     i = the interest rate on capital
    $R_1, R_2, \ldots, R_n$ = cash inflow after taxes in years 1, 2, . . . , n
    n = life of asset
    S = salvage value in year n

If the present value of the investment, V, exceeds the cost of the equipment, the purchase is economically sound. The determination of the present value of estimated future savings is an integral part of any capital equipment economic analysis.

The difficulties in this approach are that it may be impossible to estimate the life of the equipment (not knowing when it will be obsoleted by new inventions) and the accuracy of the cash inflows is subject to question.

Discounted Cash Flow

The discounted cash flow refers to the rate of discount which when applied to the future cash flows will equate their sum to the supply price of the assets. It is given by the following formula:

$$C = \frac{R_1}{1 + r} + \frac{R_2}{(1 + r)^2} + \cdots + \frac{R_n}{(1 + r)^n} + \frac{S}{(1 + r)^n}$$

where r = discounted rate of return
    $R_1, R_2, \ldots, R_n$ = cash inflow after taxes in years 1, 2, . . . , n
    n = life of association
    S = salvage value

After the discounted rate of return on the investment has calculated, it is compared with the cost of the capital to be invested. If the return is greater than the cost, the purchase is economically sound, because the discounted return is greater than the return that could be obtained from the invested capital in alternative uses. This approach again requires that estimates be made of future returns and the estimated life of the equipment. The limitations involved in accurately making these determinations have already been presented.

Return on Assets

This approach relates the cash savings anticipated to result from the purchase to the amount of money invested. Simply stated, it is:

$$\frac{\text{Present value of savings}}{\text{Dollar investment}} \times 100$$

The result is a rule-of-thumb figure indicating a profitability figure on the basis of which all alternative investments can be analyzed.

Current liabilities are sometimes deducted because they are a normal source of short-term funds for any business and are not considered a part of the investment base by some managements.

This approach is subject to all the conceptual difficulties already mentioned: estimated life of equipment, estimated future returns, and so on. However, it is a simple approach and does allow comparisons of alternate investment possibilities.

MAPI Formula

The Machinery and Allied Products Institute developed a formula that compares investing in a project with going without it for one more year. It attempts to evaluate replacements, recognizing the fact that a machine ages and, therefore, loses some of its efficiency, in addition to becoming obsolete. The formula is:[7]

$$r = \frac{(R_1 + y)(1 - x) - (z - Tx)}{C}$$

where r = rate of return

R_1 = first year operating advantage of the proposal before taxes

y = loss in salvage value the present project will incur next year plus capital additions planned for the existing project

x = tax rate

Z = next year's capital consumption of the proposal

T = next year's tax deduction on the new project

C = cost of the proposal

Analysis charts can be prepared that allow one visually to calculate the return without going through the detailed calculations of the formula. Figure 24-1 illustrates the equipment analysis form, using next-year operational comparison of the old and new machines. Figure 24-2 illustrates the diagrammatical determination of the "adverse minimum" rate. This is defined as the annual inferiority of the old machine (or the superiority of the new machine) plus the capital cost of carrying the old machine another year.

[7] W. W. Haynes, *Management Economics*, The Dorsey Press, Homewood, Ill., 1963, p. 539.

EQUIPMENT REPLACEMENT ANALYSIS
(As Determined by the MAPI Formula)

EQUIPMENT UNDER CONSIDERATION

PRESENT EQUIPMENT	PROPOSED EQUIPMENT
Builder _____ Howadore Company	Manufacturer _____ Howadore Company
Model _____ AC Milling Machine	Model _____ HCLP Milling Machine
Year _____ 1939	Proposal No. _____ 5261
Serial No. _____ 97642-A	Estimate No. _____ 2782
Location _____ Milling Dept	Date of Proposal _____ December 17, 1954

ANALYSIS OF THE JOB
(MAPI — "Operating Advantage — Next Year")

FACTOR	PRESENT	PROPOSED
(1) Superiority of Product	$	$
(2) Increased Output		1764.00
(3) Other Product Factors		
(4) Direct Labor		5880.00
(5) Indirect Labor _ 10% of (4)		588.00
(6) Fringe Benefit Costs _ 20% of (4)+(5)		1293.60
(7) Maintenance		925.00
(8) Supplies	150.00	
(9) Tools	2000.00	
(10) Spoilage		45.00
(11) Down Time		
(12) Floor Space		70.00
(13) Power		
(14) Property Taxes & Insurance	542.92	
(15) Other Manufacturing Factors		
(16) TOTAL OPERATING ADVANTAGES	$ 2692.92 (A)	$ 10,565.60 (B)

(17) *Net Operating Advantage of PROPOSED Equipment (B-A) _____ $ 7872.68

ANALYSIS OF THE EQUIPMENT
(MAPI — "Adverse Minimums")

PRESENT EQUIPMENT	PROPOSED EQUIPMENT
(18) Salvage Value — Now _____ $ 5000.00	(27) Cost Installed _____ $ 20,000.00
(19) Salvage Value — Next Year $ 3500.00	(28) Service Life _____ 20 Yrs.
(20) Loss Salvage Val. — Next Year $ 1500.00	(29) Salvage Value _____ $ 500.00
(20) Loss Salvage Val. — Next Year $ 1500.00	(30) Salvage Ratio _____ 0.025 %
(21) Interest — Salvage Val. _ 10% 150.00	(27) Cost Installed (D) _____ $ 20,000.00
(22) Proration — Cap. Addition _ 250.00	(31) Chart % _____ 0.07
(23) Interest — Cap. Addition 10% 25.00	(32) Interest % _____ 0.10
(24) Annual Fixed Cost _____ $ 1,925.00	(33) Total % (E) _____ 0.17
(25) * Net Opertg. Disadvantage _ 7872.68	(34) Annual Fixed Cost (D x E) _____ 3,400.00
(26) Annual Operating Cost (C) _ $ 9797.68	(35) Annual Operating Cost (F) _ $ 3,400.00

(36) GAIN FROM REPLACEMENT NEXT YEAR (C − F) $9,797.68 − 3,400.00 $ 6,397.68

Signed _____ James J. Jones _____ Date 12-17-54

FIGURE 24-1. Equipment analysis form.

Guaranteed Maintenance (Life-Cycle Costing)

Because purchases of equipment and other major installations involve large sums of money and relatively long-term usage, capitalization and depreciation over a period of years are the proper approach for handling such expenditures on the books of the buying company. More often than not there may be alternative pieces of equipment

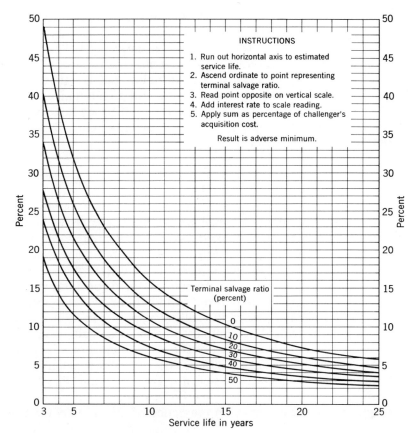

FIGURE 24-2. "Adverse minimum form"—chart for deriving challenger's adverse minimum by the MAPI formula.

available with different projected lives as well as somewhat different features that may result in variations in price quotations.

As one means of developing greater comparability among alternatives the concept of "life-cycle costing" was developed. Under this concept the total cost of the piece of equipment for its entire life is computed, that is, the initial cost plus the cost of maintenance and service during its projected life. One of the earliest users of this approach was the city of Chicago Purchasing Department.

This approach in turn led to the development of guaranteed maintenance contracts which place the responsibility for servicing and maintaining equipment during a predetermined life cycle with the manufacturer or seller. The seller establishes the price quotation as a composite of the original cost of the equipment and the cost of maintaining that equipment.

A price for equipment that is based on guaranteed maintenance provides for greater comparability among alternative pieces of equipment. It has the further advantage of bringing into consideration all of the costs of equipment, both ownership and maintenance.

In 1970 the Department of Defense adopted procedures designed to implement life-cycle costing for procurements below the level of the complete weapon system.[8]

SUMMARY

The variety of economic analysis techniques is great, and they often involve quite detailed and complicated procedures. Only a few have been presented, as the intent is merely to acquaint the reader with some of the techniques used and to provide a starting point for future study. There are many refined formulas available; to be useful, they must be tailored to individual company needs.

It is well to keep in mind the following points in evaluating any replacement formula. The comparisons that are made must be reasonable. A formula that compares the performance of new and old machines over the estimated life period of the new machine is unreasonable. The old machine will not last that long. For this reason anything other than a one-year comparison is dangerous.

One must recognize that obsolescence of an old machine to the point in time at which a new investment decision is being made can be established. However, one cannot establish the *future* obsolescence of the new machine. To some extent the same is true of salvage values. Yet both of those factors may be included as parts of any formula approach to a capital equipment purchase decision.

Sometimes replacement analyses are made on the assumption that the services rendered by the new and the old machine are identical or that the quality of the output of the two machines is the same. This frequently is not the case, and minor differences can be expected. The problem is one of assigning a dollar value to such differences.

If the new machine has a greater output or a faster rate of operation, one might assume this to be a greater value. But this is not necessarily true if there is no need for the faster or greater output.

---

[8] *Life cycle Costing Procurement Guide*, Department of Defense, July 1970.

DISCUSSION QUESTIONS

1. Discuss the ways in which purchase of capital equipment differs from other types of purchases.

2. What are the advantages of maintaining an equipment record?

3. What are the advantages of purchasing new equipment?

4. Discuss the difficulties involved in the purchase of used equipment.

5. What are the advantages to the lessee in leasing equipment?

6. Why has leasing not made much headway in the machine tool field?

7. Discuss the various means of financing major equipment purchases.

8. What are the means available for the disposal of used equipment?

9. Discuss the use of the "payback" approach to equipment purchase analysis.

10. Describe the life-cycle costing concept.

SUGGESTED CASES

Howell Chuck Company (B)

Megalopolis City

Roberts Fibre Products Company

Stephen Motor Company Incorporated

PURCHASING CASES

FIELD OF PURCHASING

EXPEDITING PROBLEMS

The subject of expediting was covered in the predinner professional development session of the Madison Purchasing Managers' Association during its March meeting. Three members presented short case descriptions of recently expedited purchases with which they had been involved.

In introducing the subject the panel moderator suggested that expediting of purchases could be accomplished by a wide variety of techniques. Among those listed were:

1. Purchase of delay-causing materials or components for the supplier or, alternatively, the furnishing of such items from the buyer's own inventory
2. Cancellation of contracts or threatening to do so
3. Stationing of field expediters at supplier's plant

Mr. Jones of the Medical Instruments Corporation reported that his expediting organization consisted of six expediters assigned individually to specific buyers to operate as a team. The expediters also are authorized to place routine repetitive orders and are required to perform special assignments.

He said: "The company entered into a procurement contract to purchase an electronic sub-system from a small, newly organized company. The sub-system was designed, developed, and sold to us for use. Samples were submitted and approved by Engineering. Purchase was made with a minimum of drawings in order not to delay delivery of the sub-system.

"The first order for 1000 units was delivered at a reasonable rate, considering start up by a new company. Quality problems were encountered, but generally were resolved with a minimum of production interruption.

"The second order was placed; also for accelerated delivery as experience with the first units proved the unit did help sales of one of our instruments. The shipment of units received against the second order was found to be 50% defective because of an electronic component. An examination of the units revealed substitute components had been inserted to save money. Many of these components were believed to be unacceptable for our product based on previous independent testing. Production was immediately halted.

"The vendor flew in to resolve the problem. He said he could not obtain the components originally used for four weeks and besides, just starting up the line again once it was shut down would take four days. Our Engineering Division replied that in order to obtain data that might permit us to grant approval for the untested components would take 1000 hours (45 days) of environmental and reliability testing.

"Management insisted on having the products for shipment before the end of the fiscal year but would not authorize use of substitute units. How would you proceed to get delivery of acceptable units in time to meet sales and profit objectives?"

Mr. Roberts of the Steel Machinery Company reported that several months ago his company had been faced with the problem of locating quickly a new source for shell molded steel castings. The company they were dealing with at that time had taken more government orders than it could handle, and the government had taken over almost its entire production by enforcing priority ratings. Even though most of the 3700 castings on order were considerably overdue, the company could not promise to produce any and further requested that the tooling be removed from its shop.

Mr. Roberts particular problem was that he needed castings in 6 weeks to meet production requirements of hand-strapping tools. Weekly usage of these castings was approximately 80. Mr. Roberts was not aware of any foundries within a reasonable distance that could produce similar castings.

Mr. Wier of the Electronic Testing Corporation reported that his expediting department consisted of seven people and that expediters were assigned according to products. They followed these basic expediting procedures:

1. Supplier order acknowledgment
2. Routine follow-up for delivery promise

3. Promise referral to shop
4. Acceptance or additional expediting

An order for an Electron Test Set (value $150,000) was placed in October 1967, with a June 1968 delivery promise.

This was a new kind of testing machine which would result in significant manufacturing cost reductions. Therefore, his company was quite anxious to obtain early delivery.

In January the supplier said that he could not meet the June delivery date because of extended delivery from vendors on purchased components. The longest interval items were components from General Tool promised for September with a value of $340. A visit to General Tool showed that its production capacity was booked solid, with no overtime available. Electronic Testing's expediter was unable to improve the delivery date of the component even after discussions with General Tool's top management.

1. Can any of the moderator's suggested approaches to expediting be employed in these cases?
2. Are there any other approaches that might be tried to get delivery of required items on time?

JOHN ROBERTS MANUFACTURING COMPANY

The John Roberts Manufacturing Company is an air-conditioning equipment manufacturer in Houston, Texas, employing 800 people. It manufacturers both window-type and large industrial air-conditioners. It also has a line of automobile air-conditioners.

The purchasing department is headed by Allen Harrison, Director or Purchases. Reporting to Mr. Harrison are four purchasing agents and one full-time expediter. The purchasing director has a secretary who handles his filing, takes dictation, and types his correspondence. There are two typists who type approximately 2000 purchase orders and change orders each month. Approximately 65% of the items purchased are repetitive in nature; the balance are nonrepetitive and generally require considerable buyer attention. Practically all of the maintenance, repair, and operating supplies (MRO) are purchased from local vendors.

The MRO stores and the receiving and shipping functions report to the director of purchasing. The company operates its own printing shop, which includes the stationery and office supply inventories. The supervisor of the printing and stationery department also reports to the director of purchasing. Responsibility for maintaining adequate inventories of stationery and office supplies as well as MRO supplies rests with the director of purchases.

An internal audit team has "spotlighted," and management has asked the director of purchases to present a plan for correcting the following problems:

1. A considerable number of items are delivered to the receiving department by local vendors before the receiving copy of the purchase order has reached the receiving department. This happens because deliveries are made within 4 to 6 hours on telephoned orders, whereas the typed copy of the purchase order is not received until the next day. This causes confusion, wasted effort, and delays in delivery to the requisitioner who may have an urgent need for the specific item.

2. The typists are unable to handle the peak loads of purchase order typing. The adoption of traveling requisitions has reduced requisition writing but not the number of purchase orders. The use of "blanket orders" on large-usage items provided some relief for the typists when adopted one year ago. In order to avoid serious delays in the typing and mailing of purchase orders, considerable overtime expense is incurred.

3. Although the expediter appears to be competent, many items are received late, some of which cause serious production delays or hold up construction of needed facilities. Deliveries of capital equipment have been as much as 4 to 5 weeks late in some instances. This has seriously delayed the start-up of some production lines. Upon investigation by the buyer, it was found that the vendor had not been expediting all items from its own suppliers and subcontractors because it had been the vendor's practice only to expedite what it considered "critical items" based on past experience or pressure from their customers.

4. The company's Value Analysis Program has "bogged down" because the buyers say that they are so busy placing orders and expediting that they do not have time for analyzing costs and devising ways to accomplish the desired functions at a lower cost while preserving or improving quality and reliability.

5. The auditors found several instances of vendor's products that did not meet specifications of physical qualities, and in some cases there were dimensional deviations. Although the suppliers replaced the material, they did not compensate the Roberts Company for labor expended up to the point of rejection, nor for the loss of production time.

The vice-president, to whom the director reports, has suggested that it might be possible to utilize the recently installed computer to overcome some of the problems. The controller supported the vice-president's suggestion because of the accounting department's successful use of EDP.

1. What recommendations can you make to correct the problem facing the Roberts Company purchasing department?

NELSON AUTO PARTS CORPORATION

The Nelson Auto Parts Corporation is one of the largest suppliers of automotive parts to original equipment manufacturers. Several years ago, the product engineering department within the company developed an automobile hub cap that would not rattle. The key feature of the new product was a shaped spring steel clip. Specifications for the clip were drawn up, and the Nelson Corporation's purchasing agent found two nearby suppliers willing to produce the clips. Samples were procured and tested and orders were placed.

After approximately 90 days both suppliers requested an increase in the contract price of 50 cents per thousand units. Since the average daily use of the clips was 150,000 units, the increased cost per year would be between $15,000 and $20,000. Both suppliers argued that the increase was necessary because of the rigid standards that the Nelson Corporation had imposed in the specifications for the part.

The purchasing agent for the Nelson Corporation also found that his inspection department was rejecting incoming shipments of the part at an unusually high rate. After talking to the head of the inspection department he learned that the rejections were primarily because of the hardness test. Specifications called for only a three-point spread in hardness. The inspection department superintendent, who was an engineer, said he could prove that a six-point spread would be satisfactory. He pointed out that, if the specifications were changed to allow the six-point spread, the rejection rate would drop to almost zero.

The purchasing agent also conferred with the head of the engineering department. He pointed out to the purchasing agent that during the 90-day period thousands of satisfactory clips had been supplied, and, in view of this, he argued that the suppliers could just as well make millions of satisfactory clips. In addition, the head of the engineering department stated that the tests employed by the inspection department were far more extreme than the abuse that a typical consumer would give the product during the life of his automobile.

1. Should the supplier be granted the 50-cent increase?
2. What should the purchasing agent do about the apparent conflict in viewpoints within his company?
3. Could this situation have been avoided or alleviated sooner?

ROBERTS FIBRE PRODUCTS COMPANY

The Roberts Fibre Products Company operates 20 plants throughout the Midwest. The company manufactures fiberboard and, in some plant locations, also manufactures corrugated paper containers. Management is decentralized, each plant being under the control of a vice-president in charge of manufacturing. Mr. Ward, Purchasing Agent for the plant in Capitol City, reports directly to the vice-president in charge of manufacturing.

Mr. Ward's most important responsibility is the purchase of straw and wastepaper, the two principal raw materials used by the plant. In purchasing these commodities he is guided largely by market prices as published in trade papers in the two fields. Mr. Ward also processes all purchase requisitions involving expenditures in excess of $25.

Reporting to Mr. Ward are Mr. Bond, Inventory Control Clerk, and four clerical employees. Mr. Bond is authorized to purchase items not exceeding the $25 limitation. It is also his responsibility to requisition materials and parts on which he maintains inventory control cards whenever he notes that the supply of an item is too low. It is left to his discretion to determine the reorder point.

As insurance against plant shutdowns and slowdowns in the plant the company maintains an inventory of replacement parts and fittings for its machinery and equipment. Each replacement part is tagged as it is received with such information as the part number and the supplier's identification. When a part is issued from stock, Mr. Bond is expected to make an entry on the tag, which is removed, noting the date and the equipment for which it is being used. He is then required to forward the tag, along with a requisition for replacement, to the purchasing agent.

Stock items may be requisitioned by any employee, and the requisition is then sent to the purchasing agent for his processing. Requisitions involving purchases in excess of $1000 are treated as capital expenditures. Requisitions for capital expenditures can be initiated only by the purchasing agent, the plant manager, or the plant superintendent and must be approved by the vice-president. All such requisitions must be accompanied by a form showing the estimated costs, the reasons for the expenditures, the annual savings anticipated, and the proposed disposition of any old machinery or equipment.

A recent purchase of forklift trucks illustrates the procedure of the purchasing agent, Mr. Ward, with respect to the selection of a supplier for such items. The plant superintendent initiated the approved requisition. Mr. Ward then visited several fiberboard plants to determine the type of trucks they were using. He next arranged for three suppliers to send in demonstrator models so that his workers could try them. His choice of supplier was based largely on the preference expressed by the workers who used the forklift trucks.

Mr. Ward says that he likes to keep paper work to a minimum because of the small size of the purchasing department. The two most frequently used forms are the purchase order requisition and the purchase order form. The requisition form has space for identification of the item, quantity desired, the department initiating the requisition, the purpose for which the item will be used, and the date by which the item is required. The individual initiating the requisition fills in all of this information. There is also space on the requisition for the purchasing agent to fill in the name of the supplier, the purchase order number, the price, terms of sale, and shipping information.

The purchase order is typed in triplicate by one of the clerical employees from the requisition form. One copy is sent to the supplier, one to the receiving department, and one is kept for the purchasing department files.

A postcard is used when follow-up of an order is indicated. The printed card contains a simple request for information as to the expected shipment date of an order which is identified by purchase order number.

A special form is used when a fixed asset is being requested. This form is called the Fixed Asset Expenditure Recommendation. In addition to identifying the asset and its proposed plant location, the form provides space for a description of the item, the reasons for making the acquisition, the estimated costs, detailed information about any assets that will be retired because of the purchase, and the recommended supplier.

1. Evaluate the purchasing procedures used by the company. Would you suggest any changes in procedures?
2. Evaluate the procedure followed by Mr. Ward in selecting the supplier of forklift trucks.
3. Can the follow-up procedure of this company be improved?
4. Should the company make use of the Fixed Asset Expenditure Recommendation form for all purchases of fixed assets?

THE GEER COMPANY

The Geer Company, a manufacturer of heavy-duty road-building equipment, was established in 1920 and grew slowly until 1962 when its sales volume was slightly in excess of $35 million. At that time the company "went public," and nonfamily management came into power. Aggressive management led to a tripling of volume by 1974.

During the period of slow growth the company's purchasing department consisted of a purchasing agent, who reported to the vice-president, and three buyers. One buyer bought only steel. The other two buyers bought all other items. One expediting clerk, as well as the necessary clerks and typists to write purchase orders and check invoices, were also assigned to the department. Inventory control was not a part of purchasing but rather reported to the production manager.

The Geer Company had operated a small foundry until 1956. When this facility was closed, the responsibility for buying ferrous castings was assigned to the production manager's office and was handled by a person who had been a supervisor in the foundry.

During the period of rapid expansion the company's manufacturing facilities were inadequate and it became necessary to subcontract a significant volume of machining operations. Two buyers who were responsible for subcontracts were assigned to the production manager. During the same period five new buyers and two expediters were added to the purchasing department.

The added work load in purchasing, the divided buying responsibilities, and the number of inexperienced buyers created many problems and brought complaints from the operating divisions of the company. Delays occurred in placing orders because of inexperienced employees in inventory control. Frequently late deliveries and incorrect ordering quantities led to shortages and excesses in inventories, both of which were costly to the company.

Management finally decided to engage a consulting firm to aid in reorganizing the purchasing operation and to make recommendations as to assignment of responsibilities connected with the various buying functions.

1. As a consultant, how would you proceed to analyze this problem?
2. Prepare a recommended organization chart for the purchasing department.
3. Indicate how you would assign those functions that, while not direct buying activities, nonetheless are closely related.

THE JANMAR CORPORATION

The Janmar Corporation was created in 1974 through the merger of Janson Company and the Mary W. Foods Corporation. Janson operated two large flour-milling plants—one in St. Paul and the other in Buffalo. In addition the company had 11 feed-mixing plants scattered throughout the Midwest and Plains states. Mary W. Foods produced various consumer-food products in 12 plants as well as a frozen-foods plant and a plant producing pet foods. These 14 plants were scattered throughout the United States.

Janson, with sales of approximately $100 million, was headquartered in St. Paul, and Mary W. Foods, with approximately the same sales volume, was headquartered in Kansas City. Prior to the merger, each plant of the Janson Company had responsibility for purchasing all required materials and supplies. Major equipment and a few common-use items were purchased centrally by a purchasing agent at the St. Paul headquarters.

Mary W. Foods operated with a centralized corporate purchasing department. The only buying permitted at the 14 plants was for orders of less than $500. The company believed that such orders were important in developing local public relations in the plant communities. Responsibility for such purchases was assigned either to the plant office manager or the plant production manager. All local purchases were made on bank-draft purchase orders. The individuals placing such orders were under instructions to attempt to secure an extra discount by reason of payment through the bank draft when the order was received by the vendor.

At the time of merger it was decided that the corporate headquarters would be located in St. Paul. It was planned that over a period of 18 months the Kansas City headquarters would be closed and a consolidation of staffs would take place. In some instances the Janson Company individual in charge of a department or staff function was named to the corresponding position in the new corporate organization, and in other instances this individual would come from Mary W. Foods. This person's counterpart was frequently made an assistant.

The director of corporate purchasing had been the chief purchasing agent of the Mary W. Foods Corporation. The senior purchasing agent, who came from the Janson Company, was given the title of assistant director of corporate purchasing. Purchasing activities were to be moved to St. Paul on July 1, 1975. The director believed that in the process of combining a centralized operation with a decentralized one, conflicts would arise, and also that it would be easier to gain cooperation from the purchasing personnel in both of the former firms if an outside specialist were hired to draft a purchasing department organization chart and policies manual.

Mr. Victor, who was engaged in this capacity, met with the director of corporate purchasing and the immediate superior. At this meeting Mr. Victor discovered that traffic and transportation matters were to be assigned to a transportation manager who would have complete responsibility for the purchasing of tractors, trailers, and all transportation equipment in addition to matters usually assigned to a traffic manager. He was also informed that grain buying for the milling operations would be under the direct control of the vice-president for manufacturing. It also developed that various departments and divisions within the company would continue to make such purchases as advertising and promotional materials, service contracts, and printed forms.

In the discussions it developed that there was some doubt as to the capability of the senior Janson purchasing agent to assume the position of assistant director. It had, however, been decided that the agent would have responsibility for the buying of biological and pharmaceutical chemicals, important additives in the feed manufacturing process. Mr. Victor also found that central receiving for the St. Paul milling complex had been a responsibility of this individual in the past.

The Janmar executive board had decided that the Buffalo milling plant was such a large operation that purchasing for the plant should remain decentralized except for basic grains. The board also decided that for the present it would continue the bank-draft purchasing system for each one of the Mary W. Foods and expand it to the Janson plants.

On May 1, 1975, Mr. Victor submitted a proposed organization chart for the purchasing department along with a number or recommendations, some of which are summarized below:

1. The company is too large for the position of assistant director to be eliminated. If there is doubt as to the ability of the biological and pharmaceutical chemicals buyer, that individual should be assigned as acting assistant director and retain the chemical buying responsibilities.

2. The amount of purchasing being done locally under the bank draft system suggests that serious consideration be given to consolidating such buying at the corporate level for all but emergency needs. Blanket purchase agreements and national contracts against which the individual plants can requisition direct from the vendor should be entered into as rapidly as possible.

3. The director of corporate purchasing should have a greater de-

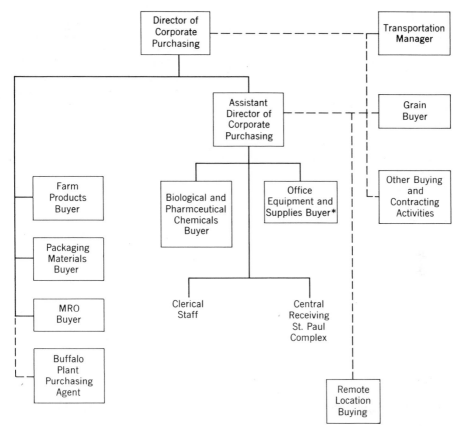

*The Office Equipment and Supplies Buyer handles also local small-order purchasing and materials release orders for St. Paul organization.

FIGURE 1. Proposed purchasing organization—Janmar Corporation.

gree of contact with and control over the buying activities not now assigned to purchasing.

1. Evaluate the proposed organization, shown in Figure 1.
2. Will reduction or elimination of local purchases at local plants affect community public relations? Should Mr. Victor's suggestions on local buying be adopted?
3. Is the policy of seeking an extra discount on purchases made by bank-draft purchase order sound? Should a similar procedure be adopted for larger corporation purchases?

PURCHASING ACTIVITIES

AJAX SEWING MACHINE COMPANY

The Ajax Sewing Machine Company has just received a large over-seas order and has put production on a three-shift basis to meet it. But inventory has fallen to a minimum, and Ajax is considering re-assigning its expediters to ensure that critical materials will come in on time.

Four key parts are purchased, respectively, from the Arkwright, Benton, Crowley, and Danielson companies. The four suppliers give rather poor service on deliveries, although they are more than satis-factory in other respects. Ajax, therefore, has made a practice of assigning one of its crack expediters to each of the four accounts.

On the basis of the past 5 years' experience, Ajax is able to tabu-late the average days of delay experienced when each expediter is assigned to a particular supplier, as shown in Table 1.

TABLE 1.

Expediter	Supplier			
	Arkwright	Benton	Crowley	Danielson
Jones	12	40	30	11
Smith	24	60	7.5	9
Peters	21	42	20	24
Hammond	16	36	12.5	8

Thus if Jones is assigned to the Danielson account, we may expect Danielson to be 11 days late in making its shipments. If Smith is given this assignment, the delay is reduced to 9 days.

An analysis by Ajax management shows that a delay at Arkwright will cost $125 per day; a delay at Benton, $50 per day; a delay at Crowley, $80 per day; and at Danielson, $100.

Ajax Sewing Machine has to assign four additional inspectors to handle the increased volume from the four suppliers. The cost of an inspector's mistake is $10 on an Arkwright part, $20 on a Benton part, $30 on a Crowley part, and $40 on a Danielson part.

The four inspectors—Herman, Abrams, Adams, and Johnson—vary considerably in their ability to catch errors. Herman has a 10% chance of letting an error go through in the course of a day, Abrams 20%, Adams 30%, and Johnson 40%.

These estimates are based on the overall records of the four inspectors. However, when the records are analyzed by type of job, we see that Abrams has a bad record on the Benton parts, so that Abrams' chance of making an error on a Benton job is 25%. On a Crowley part, his record is very good, and his chance of error is only 10%. By the same token Adams has a particularly good record on Danielson-type jobs, with only one chance out of ten that he will make an error.

For the others, the job analysis supports the original estimates. Table 2 shows the chances of a daily error.

TABLE 2.

| | Chance of Error (%) on Part of | | | |
Inspector	Arkwright	Benton	Crowley	Danielson
Herman	10	10	10	10
Abrams	20	25	10	20
Adams	30	30	30	10
Johnson	40	40	40	40

1. How should the four expediters be assigned to minimize delay costs?
2. How should Ajax assign its inspectors so as to minimize the dollar value of its inspection errors?

BERG RAINGEAR, INC.

The Berg Raingear company manufactured a complete line of men's, women's, and children's raincoats as well as umbrellas and other types of raingear. Its annual sales were $12 million in 1966. The raingear was of two types: (1) a rubberized fabric and (2) chemically treated fabrics. Sales were evenly divided between the two types.

Annual purchases of "Wein's rain repellent," a chemical used in treating the fabrics to produce the rain-repellency characteristics, were approximately $100,000. This product was sold by its manufacturer both to clothing manufacturers and direct to the consumer in an aerosol spray can. The latter sales were backed by heavy consumer advertising, and broad consumer acceptance of the brand name had been achieved. Berg Raingear, Inc. was authorized by Wein to attach a special label to all of its garments on which the solution was used.

Shortly before a new contract was to be negotiated with Wein, Ms. Frank Adams, chemicals buyer for Berg, was approached by a salesman of the Madison Chemical Corporation. He stated that his company had developed a new waterproofing compound for textiles that was better than anything then on the market. Madison Chemical was planning to introduce it to the industrial market first, but hoped to begin to move the compound into the consumer market through an extensive advertising campaign within 12 months. The price of this new product was competitive with the Wein product.

A sample of the new product was delivered to the company research chemist for testing purposes. He reported back to Ms. Adams that this new product was the equal of that currently being purchased. However, he suggested that without much trouble he could develop a similar chemical compound that would be satisfactory and could be manufactured in the Berg plant at a saving of 15% over price being paid to Wein. He estimated that, if this course of action were adopted, the necessary equipment could be purchased new for $11,500 or used for $5000 or less.

Ms. Adams asked the chemist to give her a list of the chemical ingredients, and their proportions, in the product. She then called on two small local chemical plants and solicited bids for a waterproofing compound made to the Berg company specifications. One bid was received at a price of 5% below that then being paid to Wein.

1. Should Ms. Adams change suppliers?

2. Should Berg Raingear produce its own waterproofing compound?

EVANS CORPORATION

Evans Corporation is a relatively small company specializing in the design and manufacture of suspension seats for tractor and truck use. Traditionally the company has been engineering-oriented, but a recent change in ownership resulted in an intensive analysis of all departments, attempting to integrate more efficiently the various functional areas.

The purchasing department, which spends approximately $30 million for purchased materials, supplies, and services annually, presently consists of the purchasing manager, Mr. Gray, nine buyers, and seven clerks. An analysis of the purchasing function revealed 25% of the total purchases to be steel, comprising over 200 separate items purchased from ten different suppliers. Six steel suppliers represented direct mill purchasing, two were odd-lot, local steel warehouses, and two were national steel warehousing firms. The majority

TABLE 1.

Number of Compressors Ordered	Actual Demand for Turbulators	Cost of Lost Sales ($1000)	Cost of Scrapping Compressors ($1000)	Overall Costs ($1000)
60	60	0	0	0
	70	100	0	100
	80	200	0	200
	90	300	0	300
70	60	0	50	50
	70	0	0	0
	80	100	0	100
	90	200	0	200
80	60	0	100	100
	70	0	50	50
	80	0	0	0
	90	100	0	100
90	60	0	150	150
	70	0	100	100
	80	0	50	50
	90	0	0	0

of the suppliers had been supplying the Evans Corporation for many years.

When asked about the possibility of reducing the present number of suppliers, Mr. Gray admitted that the number could possibly be cut in half. However, he was quick to add that one of his main justifications for not doing so was insurance against the failure of a single supplier to meet his requests during a period of high demand or supply shortage.

Historically, Evans Corporation had encountered quality problems with several of the smaller-volume steel items purchased. Problems in delivery were also associated with several such items. Though Mr. Gray felt that Evans' suppliers were quite competitive on price, he thought that their quality and service standards left much to be desired. In the past no supplier changes had been made unless substantial cost savings could be proved.

1. Should Evans Corporation consolidate its steel purchases?
2. Should it develop a set of policy guidelines for use in steel source selection?
3. Should such a policy be applied to purchase of the other items needed by Evans?

GAMMA CORPORATION

Al Beta, Purchasing Vice-President for the Gamma Corporation, was called into a top-management conference to hear about a new market being opened for the company's turbulators.

These were very high-priced items, manufactured to order, and it was anticipated that demand would be pretty much of a one-shot affair. Sales office surveys indicated that the level of demand might range anywhere from 60 to 90 items.

Among the most important subassemblies for the turbulators were compressors. These were vendor-supplied on special order. Because of the job-lot nature of compressor production, reorder and setup costs were prohibitively high. Thus Gamma would have to order all its compressors in one lot.

Since the demand might range from 60 to 90 turbulators, there was the danger of sales lost because of insufficient production if Gamma ordered only 60 compressors. But if more were ordered than were needed, there would be the possibility of having to scrap unused compressors.

The sales office claimed that each lost sale represented $10,000 down the drain. Al estimated that a loss of $5000 would be involved for each compressor scrapped. The question then was: How many compressors should be ordered?

So Al did some figuring. Since packaging, shipment, and other considerations made it necessary to order compressors in units of 10, he reasoned that the question really was: Should 60, 70, 80, or 90 items be purchased? Now, if 60 compressors were bought and 60 turbulators manufactured, this would turn out to be ideal—if sales amounted to 60 items. But if there was a demand for 70 items, a loss of $100,000 would be incurred. And if the market actually could absorb 90 units, the loss would be $300,000.

On the basis of such he constructed the chart shown in Table 1. Studying this chart, Al found the answer to his problem.

1. What was the solution, and how did Al find it?

GOLDEN CITY

Early in 1968, the Golden City purchasing agent solicited bids for refractors. The specification provided that an aggregate award would be made to the low bidder. Bids were received from five firms interested in this contract. The bids were tabulated, along with the most recent price paid by Goden City (Exhibit A, page 539). The purchasing agent, in reviewing the bids, noted that there had been significant increases in items 1 and 4. He discussed this with all the bidders and was not completely satisfied with their explanation of the price changes.

The purchasing agent believed that it was in the city's best interest to request new bids on these two items and to make individual awards to each low bidder on the other items. All bidders were agreeable to this approach.

1. Should the purchasing agent carry out his plans?
2. Would your response be the same if this were an industrial buyer rather than a city buyer?

HOUSEHOLD CLEANERS CORPORATION

Folding cartons for the "Soap Pads" and Scouring Cloths" that Household Cleaners Corporation produces are manufactured in production runs of about 5 million units, valued at $50,000 to $120,000 per run. This is very attractive business for the carton industry,

		Anderson Electric Corporation	Jones Supply Corporation	National Electric Company	Smith Electric Company	Stevens Supply Company	Previous Experience
(1) 200 each	Refractor, #4377E, complete with endural insides	each	9.18	9.19	9.33	12.30	9.19	8.07 (1963)
(2) 50 each	Refractor, #4334 CL, complete with endural insides	each	4.95	4.93	4.89	4.96	4.94	4.96 (1963)
(3) 100 each	Refractor, #4387 CL, *outside only*, for 4377 unit	each	4.09	4.07	4.04	4.39	4.08	3.97 (1962)
(4) 150 each	Refractor, #4189 VF, *outside only*, for 4179 unit	each	7.05	7.04	6.97	6.93	7.04	5.60 (1963)
(5) 25 each	Refractor, #4937, complete except *without* casting, for park unit	each	29.25	29.08	28.86	24.96	29.19	25.36 (1960)
(6) 25 each	Canopy, Refractor, #4957 S.F., for #4937 Park Unit	each	1.93	1.93	1.91	1.84	1.91	2.04 (1963)
	TOTAL NET AGGREGATE AMOUNT (after cash discount)		4286.20	4279.52	4285.96	4856.50	4283.23	
	CASH DISCOUNT		1%	1%	1%	Net	1%	

EXHIBIT A.

which is highly competitive. The volume of business available in these two types of cartons has increased over the last 4 years from $500,000 to about $2 million per year. Cartons represent 20% of product cost.

Rinkle Company has been the principal supplier. A careful check of the market indicated that the industry was protecting the Rinkle price list by submitting prices no lower than its schedule. In view of this situation, Cartoncorp was picked as a second source for "Soap Pads" cartons and Singer as a second source for "Scouring Cloths" cartons, both at the price levels established by Rinkle.

In the last few months of 1975 a more aggressive interest was shown by other sources of supply. Active Carton, through its sales vice-president, requested to be allowed to quote on a specific requirement for "Soap Pads" cartons, and North Industries made a similar request to quote on "Scouring Cloths" cartons through its president, Charles North.

Each of those companies quoted prices that were competitive with the prices paid Rinkle. They were told that they were competitive, but that it was not good enough to generate any business. Subsequently, they each indicated that they would quote a lower price if they were told what price was necessary. Such a situation, of course, would put Household Cleaners Corporation in the position of pricing their product. It puts Household in the position of protecting the Rinkle quote up to the point where it establishes the price at which it would bring others in as an alternate source. Cartoncorp and Singer indicated a desire to have a share of the business at a lower price level, but were unwilling to be labeled as a price cutter. They wanted to transmit this bonus to Household Cleaners Corporation.

The major attraction was not merely the $5000 or $10,000 saving on specific orders, but the price competition it would provide over time to the carton program for the two kitchen cleaner products. Household would not have to use the lower prices as leverage to lower Rinkle's prices, but it would be available if Rinkle attempted to increase prices. The folding carton industry is competitive on prices, but all manufacturers think they are operating with depressed prices so that they are constantly alert to the opportunity to raise their prices. Price increases are usually effected by announcement in the trade journals that prices have been increased by 3–5% and then presenting it as if it were a fact. It is reasonable to assume that Singer and Cartoncorp would welcome any leadership taken by Rinkle in this regard. The lower-price second suppliers could very well contribute to the avoidance of a $100,000-a-year cost increase.

Should Household Cleaner, however, set the price when it believes that its action will be publicized throughout the industry? If they really want these companies as alternate sources, should they be told:

Household Cleaner will not give them any further price information.

Household Cleaner does not intend to price their product for them.

They have enough information to quote a price that would interest Household Cleaner.

Any price they established must be based on how the business fits into their plant operations.

Any price they quote will be held in confidence.

HOWELL CHUCK COMPANY (A)

The Howell Chuck Company is a manufacturer of chucks and similar accessories for original machine-tool equipment and replacement purposes. Approximately 500 employees work for the company. The purchasing department consists of the purchasing agent who also functions as treasurer, two buyers, and two clerical employees. Inventory records for raw materials and stores items are maintained in the purchasing department.

The purchasing agent and the two buyers make all final decisions as to sources of supply, although heads of operating departments are permitted to recommend suppliers and the buyers often follow their recommendations. All salesmen are interviewed in the purchasing department. Where the situation seems to warrant it, the buyers arrange for the head of a department to interview a salesman.

Over the years the Howell Chuck Company has developed and followed a policy of loyalty to established suppliers. The experience of the company during periods of short supply convinced the purchasing agent of the wisdom of this policy. On many occasions the agent was able to secure deliveries of items that competing firms had difficulty in securing because they had patronized many suppliers. The purchasing agent felt so strongly on this point that the buyers were instructed not to shift from an established supplier unless a price differential of more that 10% existed. If products were defective or unsatisfactory, the agent would notify a supplier that he was "on probation." If no additional problem shipments were received during the next 6-month period, the supplier was retained. If a second unsatisfactory shipment was received, the supplier was called in for an interview before a decision to drop him was made.

During May 1975 a requisition was received from the foreman of the heat treatment department for a new welding outfit. The requisition recommended the make and model, which was priced at $360. The proposed supplier was a recognized firm in the field, although the company had not previously bought from it. The company bought similar equipment from Ace Welding Company, a local firm with whom it had dealt for more than 20 years. The proposed supplier did not sell the gas used by the welding equipment, but such gas was available from five local suppliers, including the Ace Welding Company.

The buyer who was processing the requisition called in the foreman of the heat treatment department and asked why the new supplier was recommended. The foreman said that inspection of the new equipment and discussions with the salesman convinced him that the equipment was clearly superior to that sold by Ace Welding Company. The new equipment sold for $30 less than the equipment available from the old supplier. During the discussion it developed that the new salesman had gone to the heat treatment department foreman without the consent of the purchasing department.

The purchasing agent had never made visits to supplier plants but had recently decided to change this policy. After discussions with his buyers the purchasing agent had prepared a policy statement to govern plant vistiations of which pertinent excerpts are quoted:

1. Visits shall only be made to suppliers who receive orders totaling more than $20,000 annually.
2. Usually each supplier shall be visited annually.
3. Supplier visits shall be made by purchasing department personnel only.
4. Potential suppliers shall only be visited if the proposed volume of purchases exceeds $20,000 annually.
5. Initial contact for a plant visit shall be made through the supplier's sales representative.
6. No undue entertainment or favors shall be accepted by purchasing personnel during a plant visit.

1. What should the buyer do about the requisition for the welding equipment?
2. Should steps be taken to prevent direct contact of salespersons and operating personnel within the company?
3. Is the Howell Chuck Company policy with respect to supplier loyalty sound?
4. Evaluate the proposed policies dealing with plant visitations.

KING COUNTY

Bids for ten 85-pound concrete breaker pneumatic tools were requested by King County for delivery to the County Highway Department Service Center. Bids were to be opened at 2 P.M. in the county purchasing department.

The representative of the Speedy Contractors Supply Company arrived with their bid, which was time-stamped 2:01 P.M. He was infuriated about the parking conditions in the vicinity of the Court House and told the purchasing agent so. He had been riding around for more than 15 minutes, trying to find a place to park. He also questioned the accuracy of the time stamp as his watch showed that it was 1:59 when he submitted the bid. With this plausible explanation, the purchasing agent waived the one minute and accepted the bid for consideration.

When the bids were read, it was noted that the bid of the Speedy Contractors Supply Company was not signed. The representative said that he had intended to do this before submitting it; however, in the excitement caused by his difficulty he neglected to do so. The purchasing agent felt that this was related to his trouble in not getting the bid in on time and allowed him to sign the bid.

When the bids were opened and read, that of Speedy Contractors was low. Later in the afternoon, the next to the low bidder protested to the purchasing agent about the acceptance of this bid and its late signature.

1. Should the Speedy Contractors bid have been accepted and entered into the competition by the purchasing agent?
2. Should Speedy Contractors receive the award?

MEGALOPOLIS CITY

Ward F. Johnson, Purchasing Agent for the city of Megalopolis, recently presented a talk at a national meeting of governmental buyers on the subject of purchasing research. Excerpts of his talk are presented below:

"We use value engineering in connection with our purchasing. This is an approach in which we analyze the component parts that enter into the makeup of an item in relation to its component costs in an attempt to learn its lowest cost denominator. We look at costs of labor, materials, amortization, overhead, and profit.

"A recent example was our installation of street lighting. The value engineering study showed that it would be advantageous to buy the materials and contract for the labor. Our engineers estimated labor costs at $31 per unit. We were contracting for 50,000 units. Six bidders responded to our request for bids with quotations ranging from $59 to $63 per unit. This was one and one-half million dollars more than our engineering analysis indicated. We rejected all bids and again advertised for bids. The new bids were approximately one-half million dollars lower. We decided to do the work ourselves. . . .

"We introduced the concept of Life Cycle Costing on equipment purchases. Life cycle costing is the determination of what an item would cost to perform its designated function through its total normal life. This covers the original cost of the equipment plus the total cost of maintenance of the equipment during its lifetime. We recently purchased garbage trucks on this basis. Suppliers requested to quote original cost of the trucks plus the total cost of maintenance for six years. Equipment cost would be paid immediately and maintenance on a monthly basis for six years. The low bidder did not have the lowest truck cost of the eight bidders who responded. . . .

"We now apply value analysis cost engineering to the disposal of so-called "Junk." Formerly we sold used fire department hose to waste paper and bag dealers for less than $4 per ton. Our analysts applied value analysis techniques and we now receive more than $300 per ton for the hose which is sold for end use purposes such as boat bumpers, making drop pads for beer kegs and to irrigation farms which are not too concerned with a few leaks in the hose.

"One additional illustration of purchasing research in the salvage field is illustrated by the fact that we buy guinea pigs for $1.50 alive and sell them for $2 dead. We buy these animals for tuberculi research at the City Sanitarium. Formerly, when the animal died it had to be incinerated and destroyed according to city health laws. Value analysts found a market at one of our local teaching hospitals which buys the animals for purposes of student medical research. The only problem is that we have to freeze the animals as soon as they die. For an investment of $200 for a deep freeze we are able to secure a significant return on what was formerly of no economic value. . . ."

1. Do you consider each of these illustrations to be purchasing research?
2. Can value analysis have applicability to the purchases of a government agency, which must advertise for bids publicly and then accept the lowest responsible bid?
3. Should life-cycle costing be used by industrial purchasers?

PARKTOWN

A large supplier opening a branch in the city of Parktown invited the city purchasing agent to an "open house," which included a display of the supplier's new products. Drinks and food were served and attendance prizes awarded. The city purchasing agent believed he owed it to his agency to keep abreast of new products and sources of supply, and hence accepted the invitation.

After the "open house," he decided to purchase one of the new products for an application that had been troublesome for many years. The previous supplier, a local firm, upon hearing of this and realizing that it would lose the business, called the city purchasing agent and said he thought that the purchasing agent was grossly unfair in securing these products from an out-of-town firm. He argued that Parktown did not pay taxes in the city while he did and had about the same products. He said that all the other cities he knew favored local merchants in their purchases.

1. Should the purchasing agent have accepted the invitation from the supplier? Why or why not?
2. How should the purchasing agent reply to the irate local supplier?

RADMER COUNTY

Radmer County is located in northern Wisconsin. The population in 1973 was estimated to be 12,000. The county seat, Hayson, had a population of 1900. Mr. Pippert was county purchasing agent. He had two clerks who took care of files, records, and typing for the department. There was also an assistant purchasing agent who handled purchasing matters of lesser importance and those of little interest to the purchasing agent.

The purchasing department was part of the county treasurer's office and did the purchasing for all county departments, including the consolidated school district which was slightly larger than Radmer County itself. All purchases above a value of $10 had to be bought through open, competitive bidding.

Gasoline, oil, and tires for the county road-maintenance equipment, the county conservation department vehicles and boat motors, and county patrol cars accounted for one fourth of all expenditures. For items of this type, an announcement was made in the local weekly newspaper and, upon inquiry, a potential supplier was given a specification sheet. Specification sheets were not unduly detailed. For example, a recent specification sheet for gasoline had octane rating, market grade, and two additives to establish the desired quality. Also included on the specification sheet were delivery date, point of delivery, and the quantity to be bought.

A major problem was the fact that Radmer County, being sparsely populated, had few potential suppliers for many items. Price was the most important factor in all purchase decisions.

The emphasis on price resulted from the fact that the department operated under a materials budget. An idea being considered to bring down prices further was cooperative purchasing. Meetings were being held to determine how many northern counties would sacrifice enough of their independence (legal obstacles, preferences among brand names and local dealers) to agree on a common standard for such items as gasoline and tires. According to Mr. Pippert's estimates, this would reduce the price of premium gasoline from 29.8 to 28 cents per gallon.

One other problem that arose from emphasis on the low-bid awards was that of "orphan equipment." Because the supplier may, and often does, change from year to year, the inventory of equipment consists of a mixture of brand names. The conservation department's outboard motors, for example, consisted of Evinrude, Johnson and Mercury, and a few other brands. This naturally poses a maintenance and spare-parts problem. Other county departments purchasing in the area avoided this problem by long-term contracts, but, according to Mr. Pippert, this was impossible in Radmer County because of political "wrangling higher up."

1. What differences, if any, might one expect between a small governmental purchasing operation and that of a small industrial concern?
2. How can an isolated buyer, government or private, develop sufficient suppliers so as to ensure competition?
3. How might one establish cooperative buying among several counties in the light of such factors as political influences and demands by local suppliers in each county?

SELMA INSTRUMENTS COMPANY

The Selma Instruments Company was the successful bidder on a contract, offered by the prime contractor, for a component of an intercontinental missile. Two important items for this component had to be purchased from outside suppliers. These were for 5000 instrument housings and 100,000 transistors. In bidding on this contract the company had cut its quotation approximately to cost. As a result, after the award, instructions were sent to all departments to increase their efficiency in every respect in order to meet the price commitment.

The purchasing agent discovered that the contract provided large progress payments during its 2-year term. Therefore, the financing of inventories, one of the usual considerations in setting inventory levels, could be disregarded. Under these circumstances the company could place orders for immediate delivery of its entire requirements rather than spacing shipments over the 2-year period.

Competition to supply the transistor and the instrument housings was keen, and the Selma Company was able to negotiate considerably lower prices than those originally estimated. The transistor order was given to a single supplier, and the housing order was split between two suppliers with whom the company had had a long and satisfactory relationship.

The transistors were purchased subject to the manufacturer's standard warranty. The packages stated plainly that replacement would be made for any transistor found to be defective within one year from the date of delivery. The Selma Company inspection department followed a different inspection practice depending upon the product. In cases where transportation costs were large, inspection was conducted at the supplier's plant. Statistical acceptance sampling techniques were used for high-volume technical items with close tolerance levels. When an item was procured that carried a guarantee (mostly shelf stock items), a visual identity inspection by the receiving department was deemed sufficient.

After a period of 16 months, it was discovered that there had been an undue proportion of defective transistors. By that time about 30% of the transistors had gone into production.

Because the Selma Company had realized that all of its departments would be working at or beyond their capacity, its contract with one of the housing suppliers had specified that inspection would be done at the supplier's plant by a Selma Company inspector. In this way the pressure on the Selma Company's inspection facilities would be reduced. Each housing required 45 minutes for inspection because of the close tolerances specified. The purchase from the second supplier of housings was governed by the standard clause on the Selma Company's purchase order, which stated that "Material is subject to inspection for a period of 75 days after delivery."

As material was received from the source-inspected supplier, it was moved directly to the production line. Housings from the other supplier were stored for later use. This procedure was followed by the inspection department because of the many activities it had to perform during the initial stages of the contract. Delivery by both housing suppliers was completed within 4 months. It was not until after 7 months that housings from the second supplier moved onto the production line. The first ten housings inspected were immediately rejected because holes had been drilled in the wrong places.

The supplier was called in at once, but he refused to take responsibility for replacement. He pointed out that the Selma Company had had adequate time to inspect the housings and that if they had inspected them within the prescribed period, the error could have been corrected before the order was completed. Since he had already been paid, he assumed that his shipments had been satisfactory. He agreed that the holes were slightly misplaced, but pointed out that the Selma Company had dealt with his company for years and had frequently specified closer tolerances than necessary and had not previously rejected goods when he had exceeded tolerances. He felt that he should have been warned if this contract was to be subject to different standards of acceptance.

1. What courses of action are open to the purchasing agent of the Selma Company in these two cases?
2. Could this situation have been avoided?
3. Should shelf stock items be inspected as received if they are procured in such quantities that they will be used before the guarantee period has passed?

SHARPE MACHINE CORPORATION

The Sharpe Machine Corporation was located in Michigan, with branch plants in Canton and Cincinnati, Ohio. Annual sales were in excess of $200 million. The company's major product line consisted of milling machines and lathes.

Mr. Fred L. Consel, Vice-President in charge of purchasing, had established a basic policy calling for annual review of all suppliers of major items. It was company policy that for such items there be an approved list of four companies who would share in the business available. At the time of the annual review, the buyers were expected to evaluate potential new suppliers who might replace one or more of the current suppliers. A special evaluation form had been developed for this purpose. (See Exhibit A.)

| Product | Supplier | Financial Status | Location | Inventory | | Physical Layout | Administrative Talent | Engineering Talent | Delivery Service |
				Breadth	Depth				
16″-3 Jaw Chuck	Adams Co.	E	E	E	E	G	G	G	E
	Ernst Bros.	E	P	E	E	C	F	E	G
	Ennis Corp.	E	E	G	G	N	E	E	E
	Tooling, Inc.	F	E	E	P	G	G	E	E
	General Tool Co.	F	E	E	E	E	E	E	P
	Murray Co.	E	E	E	E	G	P	P	E

Legend: E = excellent; F = fair; C = correctable; G = good; P = poor; N = noncorrectable.

EXHIBIT A. Sharpe Machine Corporation New Supplier Evaluation Form

Financial status was determined from study of Dunn & Bradstreet ratings and the most recent annual report of the prospective supplier. A supplier located within 200 miles was considered to be in an excellent location. Inventory breadth was determined by studying the supplier's catalogs. Depth of inventory physical layout, administrative talent, and engineering talent could not be fully evaluated without making a plant visitation. Delivery service ratings were based on the highway system between the supplier's plant and the Sharpe plants and on the availability of good common carrier service between the two points.

The annual review of chuck suppliers had indicated an unsatisfactory condition to exist with two of the current suppliers, and Mr. John Ozanne, tooling buyer, decided that he should replace both suppliers. He was uncertain which two new suppliers should be added. (See Exhibit A.) In talking this problem over with Mr. Consel, he pointed out that he thought the Adams Company was best and should be added to the approved list. However, he thought there might be problems with each of the others.

1. Which two suppliers should be added to the approved list?
2. What is the relative importance of the various evaluation factors?
3. Should any other factors be used in the evaluation?
4. Can this form be used or adapted for the evaluation of existing suppliers?

SMITH ELECTRONIC CORPORATION

The Smith Electronic Corporation is a large manufacturer of component parts for radio and television sets. The company purchases total about $5 million annually and are composed of more than 10,000 different items purchased from approximately 3000 suppliers. To improve the buying process, the purchasing agent developed a system for rating suppliers. He stated that the purpose of the system was to introduce an element of objectivity into an area of purchasing that is basically subjective.

The rating system was based on analysis of the inspection reports, adherence to delivery commitments, and the service provided by the supplier. Data for rating a supplier were recorded on a rating form developed by the purchasing agent (Exhibit A).

The volume of purchases for the current month was secured by tabulating invoices. The 3-month average was derived from the vendor cards that the company maintains. No attempt is made to rate suppliers by individual types of products purchased. All pur-

			Dollar Volume of Rejections				
Supplier	This Month	3-Month Average	This Month	3-Month Average	Average Monthly Rejection* (%)	Delivery	Comments
Adams Co.	3722	2500	1210	505	20	Excellent	Very adaptable—accepts small orders
Baker Manufacturing	202	1420	—	160	11	Fair	Decrease percentage of business
J. I. Smith	9200	8500	980	2000	24	Good	Rejection rate still too high
Selma Instruments	6480	5500	2020	930	17	Good	Watch rejection rate closely

* Includes passed on exception.

EXHIBIT A. Supplier Rating Form.

chases from one vendor are recorded on one line of the Supplier Rating Form.

Inspection reports provide the dollar volume of rejections and the percentage of rejections figures on the rating form. The percentage of rejections is not based on units, but rather on the value of the materials rejected divided by the value of the materials shipped by the supplier.

The expediting section rates the supplier in terms of adequacy of delivery. Four ratings were established for the evaluation of this factor:

1. Excellent—a supplier receives this rating only if there has been no need for expediting and if he has returned acceptance copies of the purchase order within 7 days.
2. Good—a supplier receives this rating if the need for expediting or follow-up to secure order acknowledgments has been occasional rather than regular.
3. Fair—a supplier receives this rating if frequent expediting is required.
4. Unsatisfactory—a supplier receives this rating if he seldom acknowledges orders, frequently misses delivery dates, and/or ships incomplete orders.

The buyer who placed orders with the supplier fills in the last column on the rating form. He bases his comments on the services provided by the supplier's representative, the willingness of the supplier to handle rush or emergency orders, the ability and willingness of the supplier to assist in the design and development of products to meet new requirements, and the supplier's productive capacity.

Each month the purchasing agent sends a letter to each supplier informing him where he stands in relation to competitive suppliers. This letter is addressed to the sales manager of the company rather than the local salesman. The purchasing agent feels that the salesman should know the situation without being informed. In addition, if improvement is needed, the purchasing agent believes it will more likely be forthcoming if the customer informs the supplier of his deficiencies rather than relying on his salesman to inform him.

1. Can vendors be rated objectively?
2. Should any other elements be included on this rating form?
3. Is the practice of rating the supplier in total, rather than by individual items purchased, sound?
4. Should suppliers be informed of their ratings?

SPACE SYSTEMS, INCORPORATED

Space Systems, Incorporated is a major supplier of missile guidance systems for the United States Air Force. It received an initial contract for 50 guidance systems for a new missile on a cost-plus-fixed-fee contract. Many of the system components were purchased for subcontractors. One such subcontract was for a specially designed electronic component at a firm price of $1000 each for 50 units.

The guidance system proved to be effective, and the Air Force began new negotiations for 300 additional guidance systems. The new contract was to be on an incentive contract. Under this contract cost savings are shared on an agreed-upon basis between the government and the prime contractor, and costs above a target figure are not fully paid by the government. These terms provide an incentive to maintain or reduce costs.

Through auditing the production costs of its subcontractor for the electronic component, Space Systems became convinced that its manufacture was subject to an 80% learning curve. Because of the need for the 300 new units and additional ones for replacement purposes, it was decided to buy 350 of these electronic components. Using a log-log paper, Space Systems arrived at an average price that it would pay the subcontractor. The subcontractor, not understanding the learning curve concept, argued against this price.

1. Applying learning curve assumed by the buyer, what price should be paid for the 350 electronic components?
2. How should the supplier's objections be met?

UTOPIA SCHOOL DISTRICT

The purchasing agent of the Utopia School District solicited bids on new furniture for the high school. The sealed bids were opened and read publicly at the designated time, and the Riverview Office Equipment Company seemed to have submitted the low bid. Later when it did not receive the award, Riverside Office Equipment, which was located in one of the villages of the district, complained to a member of the Board of Trustees. "What goes on here? I am the low bidder and I should get the order." The trustee relayed the inquiry to the purchasing agent.

The purchasing agent explained to the trustee that the specification required delivery to the Utopia High School, and the low bidder had specified that his bid was "f.o.b. shipping point with transportation charges prepaid and allowed." The trustee argued, "They are delivering the equipment to you at the price stated on the bid—what more do you want?"

The purchasing agent next explained that the Riverview bid also contained the statement: "Price in effect at the time of delivery." The trustee explained that most of this firms' bids are made in this manner, as the manufacturer will not give them a firm commitment, and he pointed out that so long as delivery is made immediately this is an unimportant question.

1. May the purchasing agent award the contract to the second low bidder?
2. What would you tell the low bidder and the village trustee?

THE WAGNER CORPORATION (A)

The Wagner Corporation is rated among the top five television set producers. Approximately 30% of its volume is obtained from government purchases of electronic components. With the appointment of a new director of purchases, a purchasing policy manual was prepared for the first time. A university professor with experience in purchasing was employed as a consultant to prepare this manual. Before writing the manual he interviewed key personnel in purchasing and other departments of the company and visited plant buyers at each of the branch plants.

In connection with the formulation of a policy on local purchasing he realized that the new director of purchases was of the opinion that development and maintenance of "community spirit" were a responsibility of the industrial relations division and not purchasing. The director stated that price was the most important consideration in selecting sources. "Local sources offer convenience but one should not pay a premium unless such convenience is crucial" seemed to represent the director's position. Professor Frank was uncertain as to whether he should include a policy statement on local purchases.

Because of the relatively large number of government orders received by the company and the frequent audits of such contracts, the director was insistent that three quotations be obtained on all purchases. Professor Frank therefore prepared the following policy statement:

THE WAGNER CORPORATION PURCHASING POLICY
POLICY ON CHOICE OF VENDOR

GENERAL POLICY
It is the policy of the Purchasing Division to buy materials and services from the lowest of at least three qualified bidders or to have an acceptable reason for doing otherwise.

APPLICATION OF POLICY

Due to the highly specialized nature of our business, the general purchasing policy must be modified to fit many special situations. These special situations are considered as acceptable reasons for deviating from the general policy on placement orders.

A. *Engineering Approval of Sources*

In order to meet contract requirements and also Wagner specification it is necessary that all parts of a critical nature be purchased from vendors who are approved by the Engineering Department. Only those vendors who are on the approved list (referred to as WAL) can be considered as eligible bidders for an individual part.

A one or two quote requisition may be satisfactorily explained as, "only approved source/sources" or by "WAL."

The buyer may develop additional sources to those originally approved by Engineering if warranted by consideration of cost and time. No parts can be accepted from such a source until Engineering approval is granted.

B. *Special Tooling Requirements*

Parts of a mechanical nature which require the purchase of special tooling are handled as follows:

1. Original order for parts and tools is placed on basis of three competitive quotes. In the case of some specialized operations such as impact extruding, it may not be possible to find three capable vendors.

2. Repetitive orders for the part will be placed with the tooled vendor as long as the quoted price remains compatible with that established on the competitive basis. The price may also be checked by obtaining an estimate for Wagner fabrication.

A requisition with less than the desired three quotes may be explained by the comments "only tooled source" or "tooled competitively."

C. *Short Lead Time Requirements*

If a part is required in less than normal lead time the purchase order for same may not be based on three quotations or it may possibly be placed with other than the low bidder.

If the lead time is too short to allow for normal quotation processes the buyer may place the order on the basis of previous price experience with the qualified vendors with consideration given as to the vendors delivery cycle and past record of performance. In certain emergencies small quantities of parts may be purchased from distributors at wholesale prices rather than direct from a vendor.

Consideration must be given as to the cost of a line stoppage versus the added cost of the individual part.

D. *Vendor Quality Level*

In some instances, certain price differentials may be outweighed by a difference in quality level between the bidders. This would be true where the cost of additional inspection and cost of handling rejected parts would be greater than the original savings.

E. *Vendor Financial Stability*
In certain instances a lower bid may be disregarded due to financial insecurity of the vendor. Membership in two credit organizations provides up to date information on such matters.

F. *Purchase of Standard Catalogue Items*
Quotations are not listed on those items which are of such a standard nature as to be covered by price lists which are published by the vendor. Buyers will purchase from the vendor with the lowest price listing which is compatible with the considerations of delivery, quality, etc.

G. *Industry Standard Price*
No quotations will be listed on those requisitions which are for items for which there exists a single industry wide price. Such requisitions are to carry a notation to this effect.

H. *Sampling Plan for Receiving Inspection*
In certain instances a low bid might be disqualified because the vendor would not accept our sampling plan for receiving inspection.

I. *Vendor Loading*
In certain instances an order may be directed to other than the low bidder due to overloading of the vendor with lowest bid. This is especially true where there are only two or three qualified bidders for a variety of part numbers. In situations of this nature the buyer allocates the various parts in a manner to minimize the added costs.

J. *Double Source Protection*
In the instance of high production rates or in the case of parts of a highly critical nature, requirements may be divided between two bidders. Here again the buyer must allocate the parts in a manner to get the desired protection at the least additional cost.

K. *Transportation Costs*
In some instances differences in transportation cost may direct an order to other than the low bidder.

L. *Proprietary Items*
Proprietary item is used here to identify those parts which, because of patent rights or other reasons, are available from only one source. Only one price is available for such items.

DOCUMENTATION VENDOR SELECTION
Bids shall be posted on the reverse side of the requisition to which they apply. In those cases where the lowest bid is not selected or where less than three bids were obtained, one or more of the previously stated reasons for such action shall be indicated on the reverse side of the requisition to which it applies.

REGULATION AND CONTROL OF POLICY
All requisitions shall be checked by the Administrative Buyers to determine that vendor selections were made on a competitive bid basis or that an acceptable reason for doing otherwise has been indicated. Only after this

approval may requisitions be forwarded for the preparation and issuance of Purchase Orders.

1. Evaluate the director's position on local purchases.
2. Should Professor Frank draft a policy statement on local purchases? Prepare such a draft.
3. Evaluate the policy statement on vendor choice.

THE WAGNER CORPORATION (B)

In preparing the proposed purchasing policy manual Professor Frank secured copies of correspondence with suppliers relative to Holiday Season gifts that had been mailed in December 1974.

One letter went to all purchasing department employees, the other to all suppliers. The letters follow:

SUBJECT: Gratuities

I find it timely to direct a word to you on the subject of gratuities and to restate the policy under which all employees of The Wagner Corporation are to be governed in this regard.

1. It shall be the policy of the Wagner Corporation employees to be fair and impartial toward all with whom we do business and to select our sources of supply solely on the basis of merit. Vendors are to be selected strictly on the basis of price, quality, and delivery. Their appreciation for past and expected future business can best be shown by their continued efforts to excel in supplying the best quality material at the lowest prices and meet required delivery schedules.
2. No employee of the Company shall accept gifts of any form or value from anyone with whom he does business on behalf of the Company, because such acceptance may place him in a difficult, prejudicial, or embarrassing position, or interfere in some way with the discharge of his duties with impartial consideration for the interest of the Company. This policy merely requires the application of common sense, simple honesty, and intelligence and does not, for example, require the nonacceptance of advertising novelties.

The approach of the Holiday Season will no doubt bring thought to many business firms that they must do something to show their appreciation for business received. Any thoughts in the direction of The Wagner Corporation employees in this regard should be discouraged, and you, as our first line contact with the vendors, are to discourage any such thoughts. You are to carry out the principles of our company policy on the matter of gratuities by word of mouth to back up the letter (copy attached) that will be sent to all vendors again this year.

L. M. Smith

December 4, 1974
To Wagner Suppliers:

The approach of the Holiday Season prompts us to reiterate the policy of The Wagner Corporation with regard to the ethical code expected of our employees in their relations with our suppliers. This policy forbids the acceptance of gifts or favors of any form or value by our employees from anyone with whom he does business on behalf of the company.

We view with pride the cooperation and valuable services our many suppliers have extended in the past to help us meet our objectives. In order to carry out these objectives on an impartial basis we ask that you continue your cooperation by respecting our policy on gratuities. This will save embarrassment to our employees as well as to your company. We shall appreciate your careful consideration and adherence to this policy in all transactions with our company.

We extend our very best wishes for a Merry Christmas season and a Happy and Prosperous New Year.

Very truly yours,
THE WAGNER CORPORATION
L. M. Smith
Director of Purchases

In discussing this subject with Mr. Smith, Professor Frank was told of a unique suggestion made by a major supplier. After receiving the letter on gratuities, he called on Mr. Smith and asked for permission to stage a Christmas party at a local hotel to which all of the Wagner purchasing department personnel would be invited. He said that his company wanted to show appreciation for the many courtesies extended to his sales representatives. He further stated that he wanted all purchasing people to attend, not just those buyers and expediters with whom his company dealt. There would be no gifts given at the party.

1. Evaluate the letter to employees and the letter to suppliers.
2. How should Mr. Smith have handled the party request?

RELATED PURCHASING ACTIVITIES

AMERICAN ARBITRATION ASSOCIATION

The American Arbitration Association is a private, nonprofit organization established to aid businesses in finding solutions to legal disputes. Contracts between buyers and sellers sometimes contain what is called a "future dispute clause." This clause establishes an agreement to settle disputes and claims in accordance with American Arbitration Association rules. Arbitration is invoked in lieu of a formal lawsuit.

The following five recent disputes were submitted to arbitration:

1. The Purchasing Manager contracted to buy a large supply of corrugated boxes in a size for shipping a new line of merchandise his company had in production and would begin marketing in about four months. The delivery date was set at two months from the time of the agreement. Several days after he had submitted a purchase order, the P.M. received the order confirmation, and the deal was completely set.

Then the salesman from the packaging company called about a week later, with a special request. "Listen, we've got a warehousing problem here. We're about to rent some new space and it would make our inventory control a lot easier if you can take delivery on that order now."

The buyer was willing, since he happened to have space to store the boxes till he needed them. However, he pointed out to the salesman "I can take that shipment now, if I'm not required to make an inspection of the merchandise until I need it." Their agreement called for any defects to be reported within 14 days, and he didn't want to have to unpack all the boxes, then repack them for storage.

"That's no problem," the salesman told him. "Your 14 day inspection time won't begin until the original delivery date."

They accepted shipment of the order and stored it on their premises. Two months later, when the shipment was opened, damage apparently caused by water, was discovered.

The P.M. immediately called the supplier and learned that the salesman he had dealt with was no longer with the company, so he spoke to the sales manager. "These boxes we ordered from you are water damaged and can't be used."

"There's nothing I can do about it now. You've had that order for two months."

"Wait a minute," the buyer said. "We agreed to take that order early for your convenience, and your salesman said that the inspection time didn't start until the original delivery date."

"Well, he shouldn't have made a verbal agreement like that. Look at the order confirmation. It specifically says no changes can be made except in writing."

"Well, he did make an agreement and since he was your salesman, you're bound to it."

"Nothing doing," was the supplier's reply. "How do we know that you didn't damage those boxes yourselves? I'm afraid it's just too late to make a claim." Both parties repeated basically the same arguments before the arbitrator.

2. Stan Franklin, the purchasing manager for Graphics, Inc. one day felt the need for some advice on an order of paper, and went to a wholesaler for help. He discussed his needs in full, explaining that the paper he wanted was to be printed and varnished and used as box wraps. The supplier was ready with quick advice. "Got just what you need," he piped.

Following the agent's recommendation, the purchasing manager ordered 27,000 sheets of a certain 34" x 57" paper. The cost was $1,500.

Soon after, the order was delivered and Stan's company put the paper through the various processes to prepare it for final gluing. When the company started gluing the paper to the boxes, the results were unsatisfactory. The paper blistered and could not be made to stick.

Pressed for time, Stan went to another supplier and got paper that proved satisfactory for the purpose, and his company was able to meet its obligation to the customer. Afterward, Stan totalled up expenses of $4,000 in reprinting, finishing, and trucking the substituted paper. Then he let the first supplier know that his company had no intention of absorbing the cost. The tactic chosen by Stan's company was to deduct the expense from other invoices owed the supplier.

"You can just deduct $4000 from what we owe you," said Graphics officials, "and next time don't promise that a product can do a job unless you know what you're talking about."

"Who promised anything?" replied the supplier. "What I said amounted to no more than an opinion that the paper *might* be suitable."

"In fact," he went on, "the sales contract specifically states that *"Seller makes no warranties whatsoever, express or implied, as to suitability."* That proves that you've got no gripe with me. If you couldn't make the paper perform satisfactorily, it wasn't due to any fault or defect in the paper. This is a case of bad judgment on your part and you can't hold me responsible for that!"

Stan's company decided to bring the matter to arbitration in accordance with the dispute settlement clasue in the sales contract.

3. The sales manager of Eastville Specialty Cabinets was not in the habit of turning away business, but one day it looked as if he might have to.

The prospective customer, a life insurance company, had sent in a purchase order for a large supply of metal filing cabinets for a suburban branch under construction. To prevent duplication of moving costs, the insurance company had requested that the goods be shipped directly to the new office during the last week of May when construction was to be completed. But Eastville officials were not happy about that kind of arrangement. They did not like the possibility of having their already limited storage space taken up by the insurance company's goods, should the new quarters not be ready on schedule. When all was taken into consideration, Eastville's sales manager felt that the order wasn't worth the trouble if his company had to risk jeopardizing the movement of other orders.

He explained the situation to the insurance company's purchasing manager and after some discussion they worked out a solution. It appeared in the sales agreement as Section 14: If the buyer does not accept delivery on date requested, then the goods will be stored at the buyer's expense.

The construction work progressed smoothly and to the relief of both the insurance company and the supplier, the building was ready on time. Eastville was notified and the goods were shipped. But upon their delivery the purchasing manager found them less than satisfactory. Apparently when they were crated the cabinets had gotten pretty badly banged up.

"Take them back," the purchasing manager told the driver. "We can't accept them in this condition."

The goods went back and the deficiencies were corrected. When Eastville asked the purchasing manager for shipping instructions, the firm was told that the local building department had closed the office down pending certain repairs by the contractor. Six weeks later, the manager called Eastville's sales office back. "We're in business again. Send the goods," he said.

Eastville did just that, but along with the cabinets came a bill for six weeks' storage.

"We won't pay," the purchasing manager's company replied. "That storage provision in the contract applied only if for some reason we were unable to receive goods on the date we requested. We did not intend to pay storage if the goods went back because of defects."

Eastville was adamant, however, and the case eventually found its way to the American Arbitration Association.

4. The buyer estimated that he needed 3600 bundles of tile to complete a land-sea trucking terminal. His supplier gave him a price of $14,400—$4 a bundle.

When the shipment arrived, the invoice was for 4800 bundles, not the 3600 ordered. He thought about it briefly, and then decided to accept the shipment. "We decided to accept this shipment. "We might need the extra tiles," he reasoned. "Some of the men might be careless, there might be some pilferage—I'll keep the whole batch and see how many we use."

When the job was finished, the buyer discovered that his workmen had used 500 extra bundles. He called the supplier to ask him to adjust the bill accordingly, charging the company for 4100 bundles. He was going to return the remaining 700 bundles.

The supplier was amenable to the return, mentioning in passing that as long as the tiles were still in factory sealed cartons, he always allowed returns.

The buyer checked with his foreman and learned that the cartons had all been opened at the beginning of the job. The workmen had culled the damaged and broken tiles from the shipment, and these made up a great many of the remaining tiles. He went back to his supplier with this news, but still claimed that he had the right of return.

"After all," he said, "we only ordered 3600 bundles in the first place. The extra ones were your responsibility. Since we did use more than we anticipated, I'm perfectly willing to pay you for those. But it's ridiculous for me to have to pay for tiles that I didn't order and didn't use."

"If you had rejected the shipment on delivery, or told me that you might use some extra tiles at that time, I could have made it clear to you that I only accept returns if they are unopened," the supplier replied. "If you had found broken tiles in the shipment when you first received it, I would have given you credit for them; but now, since the cartons have been opened, there's every reason to believe that the tiles were damaged by the carelessness of your own workmen. You have no way of proving to me that those tiles came to you in a damaged condition.

He decided to invoke the arbitration clause on the purchase order his company used, and he and his supplier met a month later in front of an arbitrator to tell their stories.

5. The Whirlpool Corp. had purchased from a company in North Carolina an expensive piece of machinery. It was apparently loaded onto a truck of the McLean Trucking Co. in good condition, but when it arrived at its Minneapolis destination, the shipping case was broken. Whether the equipment was damaged could not be determined immediately, but the receiving clerk took the precaution of noting the defect on the receipt.

The original bill of lading contained a nine-month time limit for filing claims, and the Whirlpool executive apparently thought he had acted well within that limit when, a few weeks later after the shipment arrived, he sent to McLean's depot a straight bill of lading on which he had written "Clain to be filed."

Believing he had preserved his rights to assert a claim, the Whirlpool executive took his time about expressing his claim in detail. He finally did so about a year after the shipment was received. The claim was for $488.86.

McLean's response must have come as a surprise to Whirlpool. The trucking company stated that, as no claim had been filed within nine months, it was too late to do so. Whirlpool replied that the notice expressed on the straight bill of lading did constitute a claim, but McLean refused to accept that interpretation.

So the question went to arbitration.

1. How should the arbitration panel rule in each case?

2. Was there anything that could have been done to lessen the likelihood of each of these dispute's arising?

THE ANSON COMPANY

The Anson Company is one of the largest manufacturers of electrical generating equipment. Periodically over the last 20 years the company has booked more orders than its productive capacity can supply. At such times the company has resorted to subcontracting part of its work. This subcontracting has not only included the making of component parts but also some of the steps in the machining of parts which are to be finish-machined, tested, and assembled at the Anson plant.

Most of the subcontracting of machining operations involve heavy, cast-steel parts, some of which weigh more than 100,000 pounds. The Anson Company has three boring bars and milling machines with the capacity to handle pieces of this size. During periods of peak production, these machines operate on a three-shift basis but still are unable to keep up with the needs. The purchasing agent has arrangements with other metalworking firms using the same types of machine tools under which he has been able to place such subcontracts with one of two firms located within 100 miles of the Anson plant.

Although Mr. Lightman, the purchasing agent, had never had occasion to make use of them, he knew of two other firms with machines of proper capacity for this type of work. These firms were located in Johnson City, 125 miles from the Anson plant and 80 miles from the city where the present subcontractors were located.

In the spring of 1974 it became apparent that the work at the Anson plant was building up to the point where machining capacity for large pieces would be inadequate. Mr. Lightman, therefore, contacted the two subcontractors who had done this type of work before to inquire if they could fit the jobs into their scheduled machining capacity. In the past there had been but minor differences in the prices quoted for this type of work. The prices were quoted in terms of the estimated number of hours of machining involved. The estimated hours were those determined by Anson engineers and used in its own cost calculations. If a subcontractor was able to machine a piece to specifications in fewer hours, he benefited from his efficiency. If it took him longer, he received no additional compensation.

The two subcontractors quoted identical prices for the machining of six castings, which were estimated to require 250 hours each. The castings were to be shipped directly from the foundry that cast them for the Anson Company. In this way the transportation costs, which were substantial because of the weight involved, would be minimized. Each casting was to be shipped by the foundry after it had passed an x-ray inspection. It was anticipated that the first casting would arrive at the subcontractor's plant on May 1 and that the other five would follow at 10-day intervals. It was necessary that all six castings be machined and delivered by July 15.

Bates Machinery Company, one of the subcontractors, had two boring bars large enough to handle the work. The Bates Company informed Mr. Lightman that it would schedule the Anson work on a three-shift basis on one of the machines and use the other for its own manufacturing purposes. The Benson Machinery Company, the other subcontractor, had six machine tools in its plant capable of handling the work. The company believed that it would experience no problems in meeting the July 15 completion date.

In view of the fact that the subcontract would require the Bates Company to work at capacity and allow for no disruptions if the deadline was to be met, Mr. Lightman decided to subcontract with the Benson Company. Because of the tight schedule, a senior expediter was assigned to the contract and instructed to check once a week on the status of the work. On May 21 the first machined casting was delivered from the Benson Company; the second was delivered on June 4. The Benson Company regularly assured the expediter that the final deadline would be met. On June 12, Mr. Lightman and the expediter visited the Benson plant and discovered that only one machine had been scheduled to work on their castings. Several days of machining time had been lost through a breakdown of the machine. Mr. Lightman attempted to induce the Benson production manager to assign two machines to his job. However, Mr. Benson, the owner of the company, was on a 2-week fishing trip in Canada and had set up production schedules for the plant before leaving. Neither the production manager nor the other executive wanted to countermand Mr. Benson's instructions. Mr. Lightman realized that if four of the six machines were put to work on his castings after Mr. Benson returned from his vacation, the deadline could still be met. However, he had no way of knowing whether Mr. Benson would take this action.

Mr. Lightman returned to the Anson plant and conferred with company executives. He pointed out that there were alternative courses of action available. They could leave the job with Benson and apply pressure to speed up the work. They could remove all or part of the work from the Benson plant and try to induce the Bates Company to machine some of the castings and have the others machined elsewhere. It appeared that there was no possibility of finding machine time at the Anson plant. Mr. Lightman was reasonably sure that he could place the work with one of the potential subcontractors in Johnson City. However, he noted that there would be substantial costs involved in moving the castings from the Benson plant to Johnson City.

Mr. Lightman's recommendation was that they permit the Benson Company to work on two of the castings and move the other two castings to the Bates Company plant for machining.

1. What action should Anson Company take to meet the July 15 deadline?
2. Was there anything that could have been done to prevent this situation from arising?

BIELAW COMPANY

The Bielaw Company manufactures a varied line of industrial equipment and installations. Over the last 15 years the company has gradually been increasing the size and weight of many of the installations that it makes in order to meet customer requirements. A problem facing the company is the scarcity of special equipment to transport these large and heavy units. The company often had to sectionalize big units and reweld them on the job site. This was both time-consuming and costly. The cost added appreciably to the prices the company quoted its customers.

The railroad equipment used for such shipments were depressed-center cars, wellcars, and heavy-duty flat cars. Because such equipment was in short supply, it was necessary to make arrangements with carriers at least 6 months in advance of requirements. The railroads distribute such special equipment through the Car Service Division of the Association of American Railroads, since many lines do not own cars of these kinds.

When a shipper required special equipment, he placed an order with the originating carrier. If this carrier was not able to furnish the car from its own equipment, it placed an order with the Car Service Division, which attempted to secure the equipment from another carrier. This procedure tended to make the shipping schedules of the Bielaw Company uncertain. There were occasions when the company had to make penalty payments under its contracts because of delays occasioned by the unavailability of rail equipment when needed. In addition, prompt loading and unloading of cars was necessary to avoid demurrage charges, and this was hard to arrange when the cars had to be requisitioned 6 months in advance of use.

The traffic manager of the Bielaw Company prepared a special report for management on his problem. The report recommended the purchase of three specially designed railway wellcars at an estimated cost of $250,000 each. As part of the report he made a compilation of all charges paid during the previous 12 months for the rental of special equipment, which totaled $498,561. In addition, the report held that it was possible to design a car so as to permit larger dimensions of the pieces shipped, which would reduce cutting and welding costs. However, at the time the report was submitted, engineering feasibility studies on larger sectionalization had not been made.

Additional advantages stressed in the report included the competitive advantage of owning cars, which would permit guarantees to customers with respect to delivery dates. The two principal competitors of the Bielaw Company did not own special railway cars. The report pointed out that if Bielaw equipment could be redesigned to be shipped in larger sections, the savings could be used to quote lower prices than the two competing firms could offer.

An additional saving to the company was through the reduction in blocking and tie-down costs. When the company used railway-owned cars, it frequently incurred costs in excess of $1000 per car for lumber and dunnage materials needed to secure the item against the hazards of travel. The report observed that such dunnage was completely lost, since the car moved on to another user after it was unloaded. With company-owned cars it would be possible to install permanent blocking and tie-down equipment that could be reused.

The report concluded that the payoff period on special rail equipment would be approximately 20 months, disregarding the sales advantages that might accrue to the company.

Mr. Lester, president of the company, discussed the report with his executive committee. He was of the opinion that the company should purchase the special cars as soon as possible. He planned to use this as a basis for underbidding competitors on a large government contract for which bids were due in 20 days. Mr. Lester thought that the savings would justify a substantially lower bid and that his competitors would be at a loss to understand the low bid until the special cars were placed in service. This could give the Bielaw Company a 9-month period during which it could underbid competition.

The executive committee discussed, without reaching a conclusion, whether this special equipment should be reserved for company use or made available through the Car Service Division to any user. The treasurer pointed out that the latter approach would increase the return to the company on its investment. He believed that conditions could be established which would permit all but the Bielaw Company's direct competitors to rent the equipment. The advertising manager thought that this was a good idea, since it was proposed to paint the cars the distinctive colors used on all Bielaw products and to emblazon the company name on the sides of the car.

The production manager and the purchasing agent felt that there should be further study before a decision was reached. They argued that engineering studies on sectionalization should be completed and firm bids should be secured from the manufacturers of the special cars before actions were taken that assumed the final profitability of this move. The traffic manager countered with the argument that the availability of the cars when needed was sufficient reason for their purchase even if no larger sections could be carried and that they would pay for themselves even if the cars cost twice as much as he had estimated.

1. What decision would you make on the procurement of the special cars?
2. Is Mr. Lester correct in assuming that he will enjoy a 9-month price advantage over competitors?
3. Would you reserve the special cars for Bielaw Company use?

COURT DECISIONS ON PURCHASING ISSUES

The following cases from the courts of various states illustrate legal issues with which a purchasing agent should have some familiarity. Though the typical purchasing agent cannot have a lawyer's knowledge of the law, the agent should be aware of the legal implications of certain purchasing decisions that are made.

Digests of several cases are related below and the reader is asked to analyze the facts, determine the point of law at issue, and make a decision.

1. The buyer entered into a contract with seller for the purchase of scrap copper and agreed to secure the necessary government export licenses during the period preceding delivery. When the scrap was ready, the seller notified buyer, requesting shipping instructions and the necessary export licenses. But the buyer was unable to furnish the licenses then because of a federal government embargo on the scrap metal. The seller held the material at his plant, and when the period prescribed for delivery had elapsed, he notified the buyer that he would not sell the material because of the buyer's failure to comply with the terms and conditions of the agreement.

The buyer sued the vendor for $10,725 damages for breach of contract, claiming that the price of copper had gone up since the date the contract was entered into. (*Bay State Smelting Co.* v. *Ferric Industries, Inc.*, 292 F 2d 96.)

2. The seller sent a letter to a purchasing agent at his employer's address, offering to sell a hydraulic power cutter. The purchasing agent returned the letter to the seller with the notation: "We wish to order the equipment as specified above." The purchasing agent signed his name below the notation.

The deal fell through, and the seller later sued the purchasing agent personally for the price of the cutter. The purchasing agent's defense was that he had signed as an agent for his company and was not personally liable. (*Sago* v. *Ashford*, 358 p2 599.)

3. Buyer bought circuit breakers from seller on C.O.D. terms. Before the seller unloaded the breakers at the buyer's plant, the buyer handed the seller's deliveryman a check in payment. While the unloading was in process, the truckman noticed that the check was not signed and returned it to the buyer. The buyer promised to get the check signed and delivered upon completion of the unloading. After the circuit breakers had been unloaded, the buyer refused not only to sign the check, but also to return the circuit breakers. (*Gallagher* v. *Hockler*, 229 N.Y.S. 2d 623.)

4. Randy Knitwear, a clothing manufacturer, purchased fabric from a textile manufacturer and finisher. This firm treated the fabric purchased by Randy with "Cyana," a chemical resin made by American Cyanamid Company. Treatment with this trade-marked resin was designed to prevent shrinkage, and textile manufacturers who used the product were authorized by American Cyanamid to sell them under the "Cyana" label and with the statement that they were "Cyana"-finished.

After Randy Knitwear had made and sold garments with "Cyana"-treated fabric to its customers, the company claimed that ordinary washing caused them to shrink and lose their shape. Randy Knitwear sued American Cyanamid for breach of warranty. Cyanamid maintained in court that the case should be dismissed because of lack of privity of contract between it and Randy. (*Randy Knitwear, Inc.* v. *American Cyanamid Co.*, New York Court of Appeals, 2-22-62.)

GORMAN PRODUCTS, INC.

The Gorman Products company was created in 1966 by the merger of Gorman Cookware, a small Midwestern manufacturer of kitchen utensils, and the Electronics Products Company of Houston, Texas. The latter had annual sales of approximately $20 million, most of which consisted of subcontracts of missile components for the company, which held the prime contractor from the Defense Department. Gorman cookware sales in 1965 were $10 million.

The executive board of the merged company had directed that unified corporate policies and procedures be established to the maximum extent possible. Mr. Ritchey, corporate purchasing manager, was uncertain how to proceed in establishing policies dealing with controlling the quantity of purchased materials and supplies. His problem can be illustrated by describing a major purchase of each of the two original companies.

One of Gorman's principal purchases is the chemical Teflon, used in coating its pots and pans. Fluctuations in teflon usage had been as high as 70% from one period to the next, and future usage was predicted to increase greatly, thus accentuating the problem of purchasing the correct quantity. A further problem was presented by the fluctuating price of teflon. In the past, Gorman had followed a policy of holding a 90-day supply of such items as a hedge against large price fluctuations. The generally accepted reordering period for all inputs was set at 2 weeks.

The purchasing department was in charge of inventory control. Storage space was a problem, and even though no critical shortages had resulted in the past, any sudden changes in the production rate could lead to such a problem. No physical inventory was taken, but the purchasing department felt that this was unnecessary so long as accurate records were kept.

Two of the most important purchases of Electronic Products were printed circuits, costing approximately $0.02 each, and transistors, some of which cost as much as $500 each. Approximately 80 transistors were needed monthly, and printed circuits were used at the rate of 600 per month. Management policy had been to reorder these items every 2 months. The delivery cycle on both items had ranged from 2 to 5 weeks over the past 4 years. Quantities of printed circuits and transistors ordered were based on carrying one-week's supply as a safety factor.

Mr. Ritchey was informed by the corporate controller that an inventory carrying charge of 24% was being assessed by management and that the average ordering cost was $6.

1. Should there be uniform policies relating to purchasing quantities?
2. What should be done about the difference in reordering periods between 2 weeks and 2 months?
3. Should EOQ formulas be applied to printed circuits and transistor purchases?

4. Set up a maximum-minimum inventory control model for the printed circuits and transistors. Would you recommend its adoption?

HEARONS COMPANY

Mr. Fred Walker, purchasing agent for the Hearons Company, has engaged the services of a business consulting firm to advise him on a problem that he suspects exists. He believes that he is paying a higher price than necessary for a major raw material because of the way in which he buys it. His suspicions have developed because there have been no significant price variations over a period of several years for the commodity and because the several suppliers quote prices that are remarkably close.

The Hearons Company is a large paper manufacturing and converting firm with annual sales of $80 million. Among its major items of raw material it buys large quantities of fiber glass yarn for use by one of its converting departments as a reinforcing medium in laminated combinations. The yarn is buried in the laminate between the two sheets of paper.

The company manufactures a number of grades of laminated combinations, some of which do not use any reinforcement, but all of which are processed on the same machinery. The company has six processing machines, and the yarn may be used on all, none, or combinations of them. There are periods when no fiber glass yarn is required and periods when it is consumed in large quantities. This results in swings in consumption of fiber glass yarn, depending on the product mix and machine schedules.

To further complicate the problem of maintaining an adequate, but not excessive, inventory of fiber glass yarn, it is used in two different types which must be ordered and stored separately. In addition the company can only buy both types from one of its three principal suppliers. Thus the planning and scheduling of shipments of the two types from the three suppliers present some problems.

As a means of meeting these problems the company estimates at the beginning of each year the total amount of yarn of each type that will be required. A determination is then made as to the amount that will be purchased from each of the three suppliers. A blanket order is then placed with each supplier in multiples of 30,000 pounds, the quantity required for a single truckload.

As the year progresses, frequent inventories are taken to keep track of usage, and releases are issued in truckload quantities, with as much advance notice as possible to the supplier. By keeping accurate usage records it is possible to spot trends in the usage and modify the original quantities covered by the blanket orders if necessary.

1. How can the consultant determine if price competition exists for this commodity?
2. Is the method of purchasing a form of forward buying, since it does not involve protection against price fluctuations?
3. What steps can be taken to develop greater price differences among the three suppliers?

POWERS COMPANY

Mr. Abel, Manager of Purchases for the Powers Company, a rapidly expanding firm whose main line was manufacturing household and commercial appliances, was faced with the difficult problem of reorganizing his department. Because of the extremely rapid growth of the Powers Company during the past 10 years, he had noted that his buyers were becoming overloaded with the repetitive details of buying. Since his department had not grown in size during the past 10 years, the personnel were becoming so involved in their routine operations that they were not accomplishing his goals, which assumed that purchasing was a "profit-making" function of his company.

Because of public acceptance of the company's products, which were manufactured to high quality standards and sold at competitive prices, as well as the improved economic conditions in the country, the sales of the company had expanded fivefold during the past 10 years. The dollars spent for purchased materials had expanded at the same rate. Despite this growth the number of persons in the purchasing department had not expanded during these 10 years except for the addition of two clerks who maintained purchase records. In addition to Mr. Abel, the department consisted of ten men, all of whom were responsible for buying activities, eight secretaries, and the two clerks.

Although the personnel of the department were not sectioned formally, the buying personnel were in effect specialized. Their specializations were as follows:

1. Two buyers purchased raw materials. One, a 25-year veteran with the company and classified as a purchasing agent, purchased all forms of aluminum and stainless steel. The other, an employee for 10 years, purchased all of the carbon steel, copper, and brass, as well as tool steel for the machine shop. The two metals buyers shared a secretary.

2. Another buyer, an 18-year employee with the company, 13 of which had been in the purchasing department, who was now classified as an assistant purchasing agent, bought all of the foundry products used, including die castings, permanent mold castings, and sand castings. Aluminum, zinc, and stainless steel castings were also purchased. This buyer was also responsible for a modest quantity of forgings purchased for the larger appliances. A secretary was assigned to this buyer.

3. One buyer, who had been in the purchasing department 17 years, purchased all of the switches, controls, and other electric and electronic components used in the company's products. He carried the title of assistant purchasing agent and had a full-time secretary.

4. Two men were responsible for purchasing capital equipment and MRO supplies. One, a 20-year employee, was classified as a purchasing agent whose major responsibility was the purchase of tools and equipment, including building additions, furniture, and similar items. A young buyer, with the company 5 years, purchased the MRO supplies used by the shop. His purchases included small tools and dies, fixtures, and other materials required for maintenance and repair. He was classified as a buyer and shared a secretary with the capital equipment buyer.

5. A 12-year veteran of the company, originally hired for the advertising department, has spent the last 8 years as a buyer of packing materials. He purchased all of the containers, folding boxed, packaging supplies, and accessories used. He carried the title of buyer and had a full-time secretary.

6. Two members of the purchasing department were responsible for the purchase of all stampings and components required for production. One, a member of the department for 13 years and classified as an assistant purchasing agent, was responsible for the purchase of all molded plastic materials, as well as specialty stampings not fabricated by the company. The other, a member of the department for 5 years, was classified as a buyer and purchased all the fasteners, glass, ceramic, and rubber and wood components used for production requirements. Each had a secretary.

7. Although the company was equipped to do mechanical as well as organic finishing, it was not set up for chemical finishing. For this reason one man listed as a buyer was responsible for the processing and anodizing of aluminum, decorative plating of steel, and electropolishing of stainless steel components and subassemblies. He had been with the company for 6 years and had a full-time secretary.

Each buyer was completely responsible for the work in his area. He processed all requisitions from the planning department, initiated inquiries, evaluated quotations, entered orders and expedited them, negotiated settlements regarding complaints on reject material, approved invoices, interviewed salesmen, and made inspection trips to new sources. All of his letters and reports were dictated to the secretary assigned to him.

In addition to receiving and transcribing all dictation, the secretaries were responsible for maintaining the buyers' inquiry files, recording acknowledgments of purchase orders and receipts of materials, clearing invoices, and providing the buyer with daily follow-ups. The more experienced secretaries were competent to do some expediting for the buyer.

A records section was maintained in the department where all orders were recorded on a Kardex system showing order number, item, quantity, price, F.O.B. point, and delivery schedule. In addition, after the invoices were received and recorded on the expediting copies of the purchase orders for use by the buyers, the invoices were recorded by date and quantity on the Kardex. The invoice date and quantity were checked against the receiving report date and quantity, and if they did not agree, were referred to the buyer, who was responsible for handling the discrepancy. After entry on the Kardex, the invoices were forwarded to the accounts payable department for payment. Two clerks handled the records section.

Mr. Abel's problem stemmed from the fact that, except for some minor variations, department personnel were doing exactly the same thing today that they had 10 years ago. With the greatly increased sales volume, the sheer quantity of paper processed by the purchasing department minimized the effectiveness of the buying personnel. The buyers complained that they were becoming "paper pushers" and that because of the volume of work they were becoming less effective in "creative purchasing."

For some time, Mr. Abel had been proud of the fact that despite the increasing volume of new products and the work load in the department his staff was able to handle the job, whereas engineering personnel had increased approximately threefold and sales department personnel approximately fourfold over the decade.

Mr. Abel observed that with the heavy load on each of his buyers he was unable to obtain the profit potential possible through creative purchasing. Buyers were reluctant to explore new sources, either by plant visits or by giving a new company an opportunity to quote on new items. To accomplish their daily routine, interviews with salesmen were frequently shortened to the point where the salesmen were reluctant to discuss new materials or processes.

Following a purchasing research seminar at the state university,

Mr. Abel realized that he was not using the personnel of his department as effectively as he could. Although he had always considered himself to be progressive in his thinking, he finally realized that he was not using the tools available to his department to create profits for his company.

What purchasing research ideas would you introduce in Mr. Abel's department to restore morale and purchasing efficiency and to bring the department back to a profit-producing operation?

ROAD EQUIPMENT MANUFACTURING COMPANY

Road Equipment Manufacturing Company is one of the largest firms in its field. It manufactures a complete line of equipment used in road construction and maintenance. Since it sells to units of government which must buy on a low-bid basis or to contractors who in turn bid on construction jobs in the same manner, there is constant pressure from management on the purchasing and engineering departments to keep costs of materials and parts at a minimum.

Management repeatedly asks both the purchasing and engineering departments whether they have weighed the alternatives of making and buying the components that become a part of the equipment.

The purchasing policy manual contains the following statement concerning make or buy:

POLICY ON MAKE OR BUY

In arriving at the "make" or "buy" decision, Purchasing will generally be best equipped to counsel in regard to the "buy" side of the decision-making process. Since Purchasing is the contact with outside suppliers, Purchasing efforts should be directed toward obtaining all necessary information in this regard and should concern itself not with the details of costs of "make" but only that the appropriate departments have given adequate attention to them.

Specific assignments of responsibilities to the Purchasing Division which relate directly or indirectly to Make or Buy are as follows:

1. One buyer serves as a member of the Make or Buy Committee which controls parts in the Fabrication Inventory.

2. The Director of the Purchasing Division acts as a member of the Senior Committee on pricing.

3. A Purchasing Division Subcommittee on pricing is composed of the Purchasing Agent, Supervisor of the Purchasing Cost Estimating Department, and the Administrative Buyer in charge of the Subcontracting Department.

4. The Director of the Purchasing Division and the Purchasing Agent serve as members of the committee which controls the outside procurement of end items which are destined for replacement parts sales activity.

5. The Supervisor of the Subcontract Buying Section serves as a member of the Make/Buy Committee for control of manufactured assemblies.

The chief aims of Purchasing in this area of activity are as follows:

1. Insure that all facts are available which are needed to evaluate each situation from the standpoint of overall economy to the Company.
2. Provide information on availability in industry of any specialized services or products which would be of value in the operations of the Company.
3. Encourage company activity in need areas inadequately supplied by industry and insure that due consideration is given before entering areas of activity which are already well supplied on a competitive basis.
4. Attention shall be given guarding against any decision, either "make" or "buy," which will cause unnecessary or unjustifiable duplication of tooling or facilities.

When operating in the areas of "make" or "buy" Purchasing Department personnel will at all times give consideration to the fact that decisions of this type must never cause the end product to suffer in regard to specified quality, reliability or delivery.

The two make-or-buy committees referred to in the policy statement each have a permanent representative from engineering and from general management. The committee's decision is final. The works manager, production manager, and controller receive a copy of each Manufacturing or Purchase Analysis sheet prepared. Any comments they have are written in the "remarks" section of the form for the guidance of the three-man committee.

Three recent make-or-buy analyses are presented as Exhibits A, B, and C on pages 577, 578, and 579.

1. Evaluate the make-or-buy policy statement of the company.
2. Evaluate the committee structure used for make-or-buy decisions.
3. What decision should be made on the Locking Nut Wear Ring?
4. Do you agree with the decision regarding the other two items?

WELDON COFFEE ROASTERS, INC.

Mr. Williams is purchasing agent for Weldon Coffee Roasters, Inc., one of the five largest coffee roasters in the United States. One of his most important responsibilities is to keep informed of the daily fluctuations in the price of green coffee beans. To do this, he is in frequent communication with several commodity brokers.

When he believes that a significant price change is about to occur,

ROUTE TO: INITIAL AND FORWARD 3. PRODUCT DIVN. _____
1. WORKS MANAGER _____   4. CONTROLLER
2. PURCHASING _____   5. RETURN TO ORIGINATOR

MANUFACTURING OR PURCHASE ANALYSIS

PRODUCT	DESCRIPTION	DRAWING NO.	EFFECTIVE DATE 9-15-65	PART NO. 4210-3011
MOWER	LOCKING NUT WEAR RING	B-5095	Make Buy Review *	EFFECTIVE WITH WORKS ORDER NO. NEW ORDER

USAGE / YEAR: NEW 1965

HISTORY / IF PURCHASED

DATE	ORDER NO.	QUAN.	MADE AT	MATERIAL	DIRECT COST
9/15/65		1 to 3	VENDOR (ABC CO.)		42.70
9/15/65		1 to 3	OUR FOUNDRY	4.00	

OTHER COST INVOLVED

IF MANUFACTURED

	MATERIAL	DIRECT LABOR	DIRECT COST	MFG. COST	ACTUAL DIRECT COST OF FIRST ORDER AFTER ABOVE DECISION
		27.33	31.33		

TOTAL DIRECT COST PER EACH	42.70		31.33

AVERAGE YEARLY USAGE: NOT KNOWN

MIN. QUANTITY FOR REORDERS:

SAVINGS PER: EACH 11.67 YEAR

REMARKS: THIS IS A NEW PART RELEASE
SAVINGS EACH OF $11.67 IS BASED ON QUANTITY 1 TO 3
AVERAGE YEARLY USAGE IS NOT KNOWN AT THIS TIME.
THIS IS ROUGH CASTING ONLY.

ORIGINATOR	DATE	APPROVED	DATE	METHODS DEPT. APPROVAL OF HOURS	DATE	DECISION NOTED ON LEDGER	DATE	REVISION	DATE

AFTER NOTATION RETURN ORIGINAL COPY TO COST DEPARTMENT

86

FORM 2412 REV. 1

EXHIBIT A. Mower.

ROUTE TO: INITIAL AND FORWARD
1. WORKS MANAGER
2. PURCHASING
3. PRODUCT DIVN.
4. CONTROLLER
5. RETURN TO ORIGINATOR

MANUFACTURING OR PURCHASE ANALYSIS

PART NO. 1234-5678

PRODUCT	DESCRIPTION	DRAWING NO.	USAGE / YEAR	EFFECTIVE DATE 8-3-65				EFFECTIVE WITH WORKS ORDER NO.
					Make	Buy	Review	
DITCH DIGGER	ROPE – WIRE	I 1234-5678	20 / 1964			*		AFTER X-1020
			79 / 1965					

HISTORY

DATE	ORDER NO.	QUAN	MADE AT
7/65	2612-1131	20	OUR PLANT
8/2/65	Quote	25	* Vendor (specific)

IF PURCHASED

MATERIAL	DIRECT COST
	10.73

IF MANUFACTURED

MATERIAL	DIRECT LABOR	DIRECT COST	MFG. COST	ACTUAL DIRECT COST OF FIRST ORDER AFTER ABOVE DECISION
11.00	1.60	13.24		

OTHER COST INVOLVED

TOTAL DIRECT COST PER EACH		
10.73		13.24

AVERAGE YEARLY USAGE: 50	MIN. QUANTITY FOR REORDERS: 25	SAVINGS PER: EACH 2.51 / YEAR 125.50

REMARKS: IT IS THE CONSENSUS OF OPINION THAT WE HENCEFORTH PURCHASE THE SUBJECT ROPE CUT TO LENGTH AND WITH THE ENDS WELDED AS PER OUR DRAWING. THIS ROPE WAS FORMERLY PURCHASED IN REEL LENGTH OF 1,000 FEET AND PIECES WERE CUT AND THE ENDS TAPED TEMPORARILY, STORED AND THE ENDS WERE FINALLY WELDED. THESE OPERATIONS WERE FOUND TO BE VERY AWKWARD.

* VENDOR – JOHN JONES CO.
1080 BLANK ST.
CHICAGO, ILLINOIS

ORIGINATOR	DATE	APPROVED	DATE	METHODS DEPT. APPROVAL OF HOURS	DATE	DECISION NOTED ON LEDGER	DATE	AFTER NOTATION RETURN ORIGINAL COPY TO COST DEPARTMENT	REVISION	DATE

FORM 2412 REV 3

87

EXHIBIT B. Ditch digger.

MANUFACTURING OR PURCHASE ANALYSIS

PART NO. 5061-7801

PRODUCT	DESCRIPTION	DRAWING NO.	USAGE	YEAR	EFFECTIVE DATE 8-24-65			EFFECTIVE WITH WORKS ORDER NO.
					Make	Buy	Review	
EXCAVATOR	FABRICATED SWIVEL	D-1066	74	1965	*			NEXT ORDER
			36	1964				
			73	1963				

HISTORY

DATE	ORDER NO.	QUAN	MADE AT
1/31/65	1645-2030	8	OUR PLANT
8/24/65	NEW QUOTE	12	VENDOR (FAB. ONLY)

IF PURCHASED

MATERIAL	DIRECT COST
	118.50
	* 375.00

OTHER COST INVOLVED

	MATERIAL	DIRECT COST
OUR MACHINING		25.12
OUR MISC.		7.94

TOTAL DIRECT COST PER EACH	408.06

IF MANUFACTURED

	DIRECT LABOR	DIRECT COST	MFG. COST
	69.18	248.49	
		248.49	
		159.57	
		9574.20	

ACTUAL DIRECT COST OF FIRST ORDER AFTER ABOVE DECISION

88

AVERAGE YEARLY USAGE: 60   MIN. QUANTITY FOR REORDERS: 12   SAVINGS PER: EACH / YEAR

REMARKS: * TO DATE QUOTATIONS $375.00
415.00 } MATERIAL & FABRICATION ONLY
470.00
510.00

IN VIEW OF THE ABOVE EVALUATION, CHANGE LEDGER TO "DEFINITELY MAKE"

ORIGINATOR	DATE	APPROVED	DATE	METHODS DEPT. APPROVAL OF HOURS	DECISION NOTED ON LEDGER	DATE

AFTER NOTATION RETURN ORIGINAL COPY TO COST DEPARTMENT

REVISION	DATE

EXHIBIT C. Excavator.

he notified Mr. Alberts, the company president. Mr. Alberts immediately calls a meeting of the executive committee. This committee consists of the executive vice-president and the treasurer as well as Mr. Alberts and Mr. Williams.

The committee evaluates market trends in terms of the company's inventory position, official crop forecasts, past trends, "feel of the market," and political trends in coffee-producing nations. A decision is then reached whether to take a position in the futures market and how much to buy or sell. If the decision is affirmative, the purchasing agent is responsible for initiating the futures transaction. If inventories are high and the committee expected a price decline, he sells futures. If, for example, there has been a killing frost in Brazil, he would buy futures.

Weldon seldom uses the futures market for procuring green coffee beans. This is true even if there has been a sharp price increase in the "spot" coffee market so that "spot" prices are higher than might have to be paid for near-term futures contracts.

An example of one transaction follows. In early January the company bought 5000 bags of Columbia (high-quality) coffee at 45 cents per pound, to be delivered during the January-March period. This purchase was made to ensure an adequate supply of that particular type of bean and because the seller offered a half-cent per pound discount from the current spot price.

In early February, Mr. Williams feared a price decline, and the committee gave approval to sell a March "futures" contract for 3000 bags, the amount not yet used of the earlier purchase. Late in February the price declined about 2 cents on both the spot and futures markets. Weldon then got out of its futures contract by buying a 3000-bag March "futures" contract.

1. Is Weldon using the futures market for price protection or is it speculating?
2. Compute the profit or less on the illustrated transactions.

CONTROL OF PURCHASING ACTIVITIES

ABC CORPORATION (A)

ABC Corporation, a manufacturer of electrical equipment, is in a segment of its industry that is highly competitive. For this reason, it has become necessary to search energetically for better and, frequently, radically different ways of performing standard operations in the manufacture of the product. Often it becomes necessary to develop special-purpose equipment, which bears little or no resemblance to any other machine or device, either in its plant or in competitors' plants. This course of action has been dictated by the absolute need to eliminate every item of cost possible to ensure a profit.

Joe Hammel, the plant engineer, had an idea for such a radical device and was successful in selling his idea to management. Joe was authorized to discuss his idea with a number of firms engaged in the design and manufacture of special automated machinery. After a thorough search, one manufacturer was selected because he corroborated Joe's supposition that a machine built on Joe's principle would produce sizable savings.

A cost projection was made to establish rather firmly the cost of this equipment, and an involved method of payment was decided upon. One of the unusual features was premium payments for early delivery of the equipment, and penalties for late delivery. The contract was undertaken in an aura of great optimism. However, despite the incentive of premium payments, the machine was not delivered on time. In fact, delivery was not made until several months after the penalty date. During this entire period, both ABC and the machine manufacturer, encountered unexpected problems, and it became obvious that the design requirements exceeded the capabilities of the machinery manufacturer. To compound the problem, the man who developed the original electrical circuitry and had done much of the basic research left the employ of the machinery manufacturer.

When it became obvious that progress was not being made, the impasse was resolved by taking delivery of the machine despite the fact that the original contract called for satisfactory performance under production conditions while still in the machine manufacturer's plant. The decision to take delivery was made in the hope that the technical resources of ABC could be successfully applied to the problem. After investing much additional time and money, the machine finally began to operate as Joe originally had anticipated.

ABC was aware of its legal responsibilities in breaching the contract by taking delivery of equipment that failed to meet specifications. It did so because of the more difficult alternative arising from the fact that the machine manufacturer was near bankruptcy and could not invest further money in this piece of equipment. Had ABC forced the issue, it might have led to the liquidation of the machine manufacturer. This would have exposed ABC to the hazard of loss of many of its ideas incorporated in the machine. The device was protected by a gentleman's agreement between ABC and the machine manufacturer, and the machine manufacturer had customers who were competitors of ABC.

This involved situation created many problems in public relations for ABC. Among them:

1. How to deal with a supplier verging on bankruptcy on a matter involving costs in excess of contract.
2. How to arrange to supply know-how replacing that already contracted for.
3. How to protect design ideas that were mutually developed against becoming competitors' property.
4. How to deal with this supplier in the future so as to draw upon his knowledge without running undue risks; or, as an alternative, educating another supplier.

How would you handle each of the public relation problems listed?

ABC CORPORATION (B)

After 2 years of developmental work, the special machine referred to in ABC Corporation (A) began to function as originally anticipated. Labor costs had been minimized to a degree not previously realized in the industry.

There was one problem, however: raw material from one manufacturer seemed to work well in the machine, whereas material from another manufacturer (there were only two suppliers of any consequence of this material) seemed to perform erratically and at times could not be used at all.

Much time was devoted to finding the reasons for this variation in performance. After months of investigation and trial it appeared that some manufacturing procedure in the second vendor's plant made his product less acceptable.

Discussions were held with the supplier, but it was difficult to convince him that the processing of the product in his plant would have any bearing on its performance in the special machine. However, it was finally arranged that representatives of ABC's purchasing and quality control departments would view the manufacturing processes in both supplier's plants.

The visiting team was given a step-by-step view of the material from the melt to the final slitting operations so that comparisons might be made. It was discovered that two steps in the manufacturing process accounted for the difficulties.

Although the offending manufacturer grudgingly agreed that his processes accounted for the problems on ABC's machine, he observed that his product was found to be acceptable by other customers. It was, therefore, the uniqueness of ABC's machine that created the manufacturing differences. The unstated question was: Why change a manufacturing process that provides an acceptable product to all but ABC, and gives ABC difficulties only because it insists on using the material in a unique device?

It was obvious that changing the manufacturing process was going to be a rather costly undertaking. The supplier did admit, however, that some changes were being contemplated in its processing for reasons other than accommodating ABC. The company indicated that consideration would be given to ABC's problem when these changes were being planned if they would not greatly increase manufacturing costs.

A number of factors had to be considered at this point in the problem:

1. ABC is a sizable user of this expensive material. Its rate of use is increasing at more than industry-average rate. This makes ABC a better-than-average account and lends a degree of leverage to its bargaining.
2. At least two sources of supply for a material of this importance are highly desirable.
3. A third source is on the horizon but, although this source has spent millions of dollars in getting into this business, it has not yet succeeded in establishing itself as a dependable supplier.
4. In either the second source (the one with the product-producing problems for ABC) or the third (potential) source additional expenditures in mechanical processing equipment will need to be made by the suppliers.
5. Should ABC's process be successful in producing a satisfactory product at lower costs it is almost certain that ABC's competitors will discover a similar approach.
6. An alternative would be the development of another machine by ABC, designed to overcome the present limitations. This would not be easy, since many of the possibilities explored have proved to be unsatisfactory.

How should this problem be handled?

DAVIS MILLS, INCORPORATED

The Davis Mills, Incorporated is one of the largest manufacturers of cotton fabrics and products made from cotton fabrics. The company has 16 plants scattered throughout the country. Headquarters are in Philadelphia, although the nearest plant is approximately 100 miles away. The company follows a policy of decentralized operations, with a general manager at each plant responsible for the profit showing of his plant. The home-office staff departments formulate company policies that are to be followed by their counterpart departments at the various plants.

The director of purchases has found it desirable to hold an annual meeting with his several plant purchasing agents to discuss company policies and procedures. The major topic for consideration at the meeting held last year was purchasing reports. Up to that time there had been no requirement for the submission of reports by the various managers to the director of purchases or to their own general managers. Nor had there been any requirement for internal purchasing department reports at any of the works.

At the meeting each purchasing agent was asked to give his opinions on the value of a reporting system and what types of reports, if any, should be required on a company-wide basis. Those who had developed reporting systems were asked to describe them to the group.

The purchasing agent of the Chicago plant reported that he had developed a plan of reporting on the operations of his entire department to the general manager. He claimed several advantages for this type of reporting. In the first place, it provided an incentive for his assistants and employees to maintain a high level of performance, since they knew that their actions would be measured and reported upon annually. It had the virtue of requiring the purchasing agent to review the operations of his entire department in a thorough and quantitative manner, since this was the only way in which a useful and comprehensible report could be prepared. The process of preparing the report frequently brought to light procedures and methods that could be improved, and the purchasing agent felt that such matters were less likely to be observed in the ordinary course of business. Finally, he felt that the report served to call the contributions of the purchasing function to the attention of the general manager in an explicit way at least once each year. This, he believed, served to make the general manager more sympathetic with the needs of the purchasing department and gave the department a basis for requesting good treatment at budget time.

The purchasing agent of the St. Louis plant said that he had tried submitting an annual report to the general manager for a few years, but found that after the first year or two it received little attention. He attributed this to the fact that the report was essentially a series of statistical tables, which looked about the same from year to year unless they were studied more carefully than the general manager seemed willing to do. Consequently, he had come to the conclusion that the primary purpose of reporting was the internal discipline it required of departmental personnel. Therefore, he had shifted reporting to an intradepartmental basis. Each of the men reporting to the purchasing agent knew that his report would be completely reviewed and understood by the purchasing agent and, consequently, each man reported fully to make a good impression on his superior. The purchasing agent said that he then reported any unusual matters to the general manager informally when the occasion seemed right. The St. Louis purchasing agent argued that this method of reporting had the virtues of a departmental report without its stultifying effects.

The Denver purchasing agent argued in favor of formal, oral reports. He contended that written reports inevitably fell into a pattern of reporting on the routine affairs of the department which fit neatly into statistical form, whereas the significant things were usually those out-of-the-ordinary things that would not occur to a person in the process of preparing a written report. The purchasing agent therefore held monthly meetings of his employees at which they were asked to report informally on anything of consequence that had happened in his area of work. In order to preserve the informal nature of the meeting no minutes were kept or notes taken. However, after each meeting the purchasing agent made notes on the significant items. The general manager of the Denver plant, in turn, had quarterly meetings of the functional plant executives at which each executive was expected to report orally on the operations of his department. The purchasing agent reported to this meeting on the basis of the notes he had made on his own monthly meetings. He believed that this method of reporting brought to light the worthwhile things and saved his men the time and trouble of preparing written reports.

Some of the purchasing agents from the smaller plants argued against any form of reports. They thought that the important matters of purchasing performance were known to the general manager on the basis of his daily contacts with the departments under his control. They argued that a purchasing department that could not justify itself without reports was not operating effectively and that their time could be spent more productively in improving performance than writing reports.

1. Evaluate the arguments in favor of each of the forms of reporting.
2. Design a reporting plan for Davis Mills, Incorporated that would meet the needs of the company at the various levels of its purchasing operations.

FERNER COMPANY

The Ferner Company produces electrical control equipment. Although a portion of its production is devoted to standard components, the bulk of its sales volume is derived from complex, custom-built installations. Annual sales in 1973 were $30 million and had been rising at a 10% rate for the past 5 years.

The entire Ferner Company has for many years followed the policy of filling vacancies, whenever possible, by advancing personnel from within its organization. Shifts between functional areas were common.

When an opening for two expediters in the purchasing department developed in February 1974, word spread quickly through the company. In addition, the employment manager was asked to secure applications from outside sources. He ran a classified advertisement in the local evening newspaper for a one-week period.

A number of applications were received, some of which were immediately discarded because there was no indication of the applicant's fitness for the position. After this screening, eight applicants were interviewed for the two expediter positions by the assistant director of purchases. He narrowed the list to four finalists:

1. Mr. Jones, employed as an expediter for 2 years by a company in the textile business. Mr. Jones was 22 years old, a high school graduate, and had completed his military service.

2. Ms. Spence, employed as a materials controller (storekeeper) by the Ferner Company, with 4 years of experience. One of her major responsibilities was the issuance of requisitions to the purchasing department for the purchase of materials when inventories dropped to predetermined order points. Prior to working for Ferner she had held employment as a retail clerk.

3. Mr. Wesley, a young man working for another company as a shipping clerk, with no experience in expediting or purchasing. He was in the process of completing a two-semester evening course in industrial purchasing at the local university.

4. Ms. Harvey, a sales correspondent in the Ferner Company service department who wanted to "get into purchasing." Ms. Harvey was a college graduate.

All of these applicants were in the desired age bracket and all seemed alert and personable. After reviewing the application forms, studying the work records of each, and evaluating the personal interviews, the assistant director of purchases decided to promote Ms. Spence to one of the two positions. He was uncertain about the best prospect for the other vacancy.

In talking the matter over with his superior the assistant director pointed out that he was being guided by four factors:

1. Company policy on promotion from within
2. Character, knowledge of job procedures, and work habits
3. The applicant's knowledge of company policy, products, and personnel
4. Prospect's potential for growth

1. Do you agree with the promotion of Ms. Spence? Give reasons for and against.
2. Choose one of the three remaining applicants to fill the vacancy, and present your reasons for selecting him/her and for not selecting the others.

HOWELL CHUCK COMPANY (B)

All purchases of major equipment made by the Howell Chuck Company were decided upon by the executive committee of the company at the time that the annual capital budget was prepared. Members of this committee consisted of the president, executive vice-president, secretary-treasurer, production manager, sales manager, and purchasing manager.

Requests for purchase of new equipment to meet new production requirements or to replace old equipment could be originated by the production manager, chief maintenance engineer, or the engineering and design section. It was expected that whoever initiated such a request would provide the executive committee with adequate information on which to act. A memorandum received by the executive committee prior to its 1973 capital budget session contained the following information:

November 19, 1973

To: Executive Committee
Subject: New Lathe

1. Recommend the purchase of a new 16-inch automatic lathe.

2. One of our lathes was purchased second-hand in 1966 and is giving the production scheduling department considerable difficulty due to frequent breakdowns. I have checked this lathe over and believe that it will require a complete overhaul. My estimate of the costs of such an overhaul is $8,700 in direct labor and parts. Such an overhaul will prolong the life of this lathe by six years.

3. In checking through the catalogs of the various lathe manufacturers I have come to the conclusion that we can buy a new 16-inch automatic lathe for $32,000.

4. The new machine will have a 15-year life before it would require a complete overhaul. It would provide us with an increased production potential of 25% for this one piece of equipment. I estimate that with the improvements this lathe contains we can save $3,700 in direct labor costs based on the same number of units of output which is all that we require at this time. I believe that normal maintenance on this new lathe will be approximately $800 less per year than on the present lathe.

5. The new lathe will require an additional $1,100 of special tooling and spare parts since it differs from any of our present lathes.

s/Fred Jones
Chief Maintenance Engineer

When the executive committee met, each member was given a copy of the memorandum and after a brief discussion the decision was tabled and the memorandum sent back to Fred Jones with the request for additional information.

1. What additional information should Mr. Jones have furnished to the executive committee?
2. Can an equipment replacement formula be used in this situation?
3. Is the procedure followed for major equipment purchases by the Howell Chuck Company sound? Can you suggest improvements?

PRESSURE TANKS, INC. (A)

Pressure Tanks, Inc. manufactures compressed gas cylinders, bulk storage tanks for liquefied gases; chemical drums of stainless steel, nickel, or Monel; air receiver tanks; transport truck bodies for compressed liquefied gases; and seamless deep-drawn shells. Pressure Tank, Inc. has three plants. The main plant, including corporate headquarters, is located in New England. The other two plants are located in Pennsylvania.

Management has asked Mr. Holmes, the Corporate Purchasing Agent, to prepare an operating budget for his department. Prior to 1973, management had not expected departments to prepare or operate according to approved annual budgets. Concomitant with the preparation of the operating budget, Mr. Holmes decided to prepare a procedures manual for his department. He had been contemplating this step for several years and had accumulated much information but had never organized it.

When he came to the section dealing with reports he realized that he had not required any written reports from his subordinates in the past. There were many verbal reports made to him, and in the past many business decisions had been made on the basis of informal written reports and oral discussion with buyers.

Recently Mr. Holmes had been submitting the following written reports to other executives in the company:

PERIODIC REPORTS

1. *Purchases, inventories, and disbursements of steel report.* This report, which was sent to the officers of Pressure Tank, Inc. and all department heads, subdivided steel into flat-rolled sheets, billets, and products. This report gave a forecast of expected usage, inventories, and purchases 3 months into the future as well as current usage, inventories, and purchases. Mr. Holmes, who was also the steel buyer, issued this report.

2. *Monthly mill steel performance report.* This quality-evaluation report was initiated by the product engineering department. The

report was forwarded to Mr. Holmes who analyzed it and wrote the cover letter for the report. The purchasing department then sent copies of the report to officers of Pressure Tank, Inc. and copies of sections of the report to the steel-vending companies involved. This report was concerned with the grades of steel received, the quality of the steel, scrap caused by defective material, and the nature of the defects.

The sections sent to the steel companies were about the performance of that company's steel; that is, what percentage of their steel was defective, the nature of the defects such as tears, voids, and so on.

3. *Yearly mill steel performance report.* This report was the annual composite of the monthly reports. Prepared by the purchasing department and the product engineering department, it also contained a vendor evaluation in the form of comments on the vendor's performance for the year. The vendors were not sent a copy of this report, but it was sent to the president, vice-president of manufacturing, and secretary-treasurer, and copies were kept by the purchasing department and the product engineering department.

4. *Monthly supplies report.* The monthly supply report was prepared by the purchasing department to report on the inventories, usage, and purchases of coal, gas, and butane. This report was not sent to the Pressure Tank, Inc. officers, but only to "interested" department heads and plant managers.

SPECIAL REPORTS

1. *Casting requirements report.* This report was prepared by the purchasing department on all castings needed for cyclical orders where the procurement time was 3 months or longer.

2. *Reciprocity report.* A reciprocity report was prepared by Mr. Holmes before any reciprocity contracts were negotiated. Mr. Holmes prepared a report of the proposal and sent it to the vice-president of sales. A review of the reciprocity report was made by Mr. Holmes, the vice-president of sales, and the market analyst before the vice-president of sales negotiated the contract.

Reciprocity agreements were made on a one-year basis. No review was made of the cost of reciprocity, nor was a study made when the contract expired and was renegotiated for the next year. Investigations and reports were made only for initial proposals. If a competing vendor came in with a lower price during the contract year, a mental note was made of this and it would be mentioned to the vice-president of sales when the existing reciprocity contract came up for renegotiation.

1. How should Mr. Holmes proceed in preparing an operating budget for the department?
2. Should he require written reports from his subordinates? If so, what subjects should they cover?
3. Do the reports now being made by Mr. Holmes provide a basis for the evaluation of his department?

PRESSURE TANKS, INC. (B)

Pressure Tanks, Inc. used a standard employee evaluation for all salaried employees. Employees were evaluated annually, the evaluation being scheduled one year from the date of hiring for or promotion to a new work assignment. The supervisor was supposed to prepare his rating on the basis of a personal interview. He used the interview form shown below.

EMPLOYEE PROGRESS & PERFORMANCE REVIEW

Name _____Date _____

Dept. _____Job Title _____

Date Prior Report_____ Tentative
Date Next Review_____

CODE

PROGRESS REVIEW

Columns indicate merit or change in qualities listed, based on rater's own knowledge of specific acts which justify rating.
S —Absence of normal growth; must improve to hold own on job
N—Normal growth and progress on job through experience
G—Good progress; better than average through special efforts

PERFORMANCE REVIEW

Columns indicate where employee stands related to job standard or expected performance. Be sure to rate each quality independently of others to avoid 'halo effect.'
O   Outstanding; falls in top 8% in any large representative group
A+ Adequate plus; above average
A   Adequate; average performance
A— Adequate minus
I   Inadequate; must improve to hold job; failing in this category

CATEGORIES

(First 9 factors for everyone; last 5 for supervisors only)

Mark "X" in appropriate column for PROGRESS and PERFORMANCE in each of the categories available to employee. Prepare this list rating carefully, accurately, independently of any other rater. Its value lies in impartiality and sound judgment used by rater. After two or more preliminary rates have been prepared, compared, and adjusted the final rating will be discussed with the employee involved, suggesting areas and means of improving his job performance.

ADDITIONAL comments, explanations, suggestions to justify your ratings or to aid employee in understanding "how he stands" at this time.

_____

_____

_____

_____

I have been shown this review. (I do not necessarily indicate agreement with it by signing)	I have counselled with this employee in accordance with this review and have suggested ways to improve.
_____ Employee	_____ Counsellor

NINE NEEDS COMMON TO ALL EMPLOYEES
(place checkmark in appropriate column for each category)

PROGRESS				PERFORMANCE
S N G		*Quality*		O A+ A A— I

O   Very accurate, completes job well

A+   Well above average, good accurate worker

A   Accepted percentages of errors, good work

A—   Sometimes careless, sub-standard quality

I   Excess carelessness, work must be checked thoroughly

PROGRESS				PERFORMANCE
S N G		*Quantity*		O A+ A A— I

PROGRESS			*Quantity*	PERFORMANCE
	O	Produces exceptional amount		
	A+	Usually does more than expected, works steadily		
	A	Normal output		
	A—	Below standard, slow producer, needs prodding		
	I	Unacceptable, wastes motions, no ambition		

Initiative

	O	Always alert, advances ideas, hunts work
	A+	Plans work well, acts voluntarily on job
	A	Needs average guidance, acts voluntarily in routine matters
	A—	Shows occasional 'flashes,' not consistent
	I	Need 'push' continually

Cooperation

	O	Goes out of way to work with others
	A+	Always congenial, helpful, group conscious
	A	Fulfills obligation to meet others halfway
	A—	Reluctant to cooperate, difficult
	I	Irritates, causes friction, quarrelsome

Personality

	O	Very pleasing, inspires confidence, leader
	A+	Outgiving, friendly, good habits, respected
	A	Well adjusted, average friendly
	A—	Does not make friends easily, poor habits
	I	Negative, lacking, antagonizes, arouses resentment

Job Knowledge

	O	Expert in his job, excellent understanding of related jobs
	A+	Thoroughly understands own and related jobs
	A	Adequately understands own and related jobs
	A—	Narrow concepts of own job only
	I	Limited 'know-how,' inadequate training

PROGRESS				PERFORMANCE
S N G				O A+ A A— I

Learnability

O   Learns rapidly, excellent memory
A+   Requires little instruction, grasps well
A   Normal help only is needed to learn
A—   Needs careful repetitive instruction
I   Very slow, poor memory, cannot grasp ideas

Dependability

O   Extremely reliable, minimum supervision
A+   Dependable, seldom needs follow-up
A   Average guidance, usually dependable
A—   Requires more than normal supervision
I   Unreliable, needs constant supervision

Judgment

O   Shows excellent judgment, sound decisions
A+   Uses common sense, most decisions accepted
A   Judgment dependable in routine matters with little trouble resulting
A—   Jumps at conclusions, frequently in error
I   Poor sense of value, constantly in trouble because of poor judgment

FIVE NEEDS AT SUPERVISORY LEVEL

PROGRESS				PERFORMANCE
S N G				O A+ A A— I

Coordinate, Plan

O   Exceptional planner, long and short range company concepts
A+   Lays out work to match own and other groups
A   Able to layout and coordinate work in own department
A—   Takes short range view, gets flustered easily
I   Inadequate planner, no sense of organizational relationship

PROGRESS				PERFORMANCE				
S	N	G	*Control*	O	A+	A	A—	I

O   Exercises exceptional control with his responsibilities

A+ Rarely lets matters get out of hand, seldom needs to impress with authority

A   Requires normal follow-up to accomplish results within area of responsibility

A— Plans not always carried out, needs substantial supervision

I   Control inadequate, matters usually out of hand

Delegation

O   Exceptional skill in knowing what and how to delegate, and doing it

A+ Usually delegates properly and effectively

A   Occasionally does work which should be delegated

A— Frequently does work which should be delegated

I   Incapable of delegating authority and responsibility

Development of Others

O   Excellent teacher, fully understands needs for improving subordinates

A+ Does good job training subordinates

A   Does adequate job training, scope may be limited

A— Occasionally lacks patience, limited concept of value of development

I   Makes little effort to improve subordinates, lacks training techniques

Communication

O   Exceptionally capable and effective in communication

A+ Usually does good job in communication, good listener

A   Communicates adequately (much of time), usually listens patiently

A— Frequently fails to communicate, tends to listen impatiently

I   Unwilling or unable to communicate

Prepare rating carefully and accurately. Its value lies in the impartiality and sound judgment used by the rater. Judge each characteristic or trait separately or independently, that is, you should not let your evaluation of one trait unduly influence you on another. Place an "X" in the appropriate space.

Personal Criteria

When interviewing an employee we suggest the supervisor look for certain qualities in each person. You will find a short description of what to look for in the nine categories common to all employees listed below and so that you have a better idea of the meaning of each of the five categories "For Supervisors Only" we list below the "Webster Dictionary" definition in each case together with a brief description and application.

QUALITY OF WORK—consider neatness, accuracy and general efficiency of work; does he maintain high workmanship in this respect?

QUANTITY OF WORK—consider the quantity of work turned out and promptness with which he completes it.

INITIATIVE—consider ability to act on own responsibility in the absence of instructions. Can he start needed work and go ahead, or is he the type that has to be told what to do?

COOPERATION—consider willingness to work with and help others. Is he willing to assume full share of work and responsibility? Does he cooperate in manner as well as act?

PERSONALITY—consider appearance, tactfulness, self-confidence, integrity, loyalty, and the impression he makes on others.

KNOWLEDGE OF JOB—consider how much he knows about present job and of other work closely related to it and work in other departments.

APTITUDE & ABILITY TO LEARN—consider how quickly he learns new work, retains what he has learned, and ease with which he follows instructions.

DEPENDABILITY—consider the amount of supervision required. Can you depend on his work? Is he punctual? Is his attendance record without fault?

JUDGMENT—consider the intelligence and thought he uses in arriving at decisions. Does he have the ability to think and act calmly, logically, and rapidly under stress?

COORDINATE—to arrange in due and relative order; to harmonize. (Description:—consider effectiveness in planning and carrying out his work and that of his subordinates in light of interdepartmental relationships and of company goals.)

CONTROL—to hold in restraint; to regulate; to govern; to subject to authority. (Description:—consider ability to insure that his plans and work assignments of his subordinates are completed effectively, timely, and economically.)

DELEGATE—to intrust, commit or deliver to another's care and management; to send with power to act as a representative. (Description:—consider effectiveness in delegating authority and responsibility in order to afford himself time to plan, control and otherwise effectively supervise his department or group.

DEVELOPMENT OF OTHERS—gradual growth or advancement through progressive changes. (Description:—consider his interest in improving the performance of his subordinates through training and his effectiveness as a teacher. Is he aiming to have one or more subordinates who could fill his shoes?

COMMUNICATION—information or intelligence imparted by word or writing. (Description:—consider his recognition of value of conveying information, discussing ideas, and being a good listener. Do people clearly understand what he is trying to convey?

CONCLUSION—It is intended that this report be prepared once each year. It may be necessary more often for certain persons. Reports are to be prepared by his supervisor and reviewed by his immediate supervisor.

Forms must be prepared in duplicate; original for office manager, copy for future reference for person preparing report.

1. Should a standard form be used for all salaried employees?
2. What are the advantages and disadvantages of reviewing the completed form with each employee?
3. Is the annual scheduling of these evaluations appropriate?
4. Evaluate the form as to its suitability for purchasing personnel.

STEPHEN MOTOR COMPANY, INCORPORATED

The Stephen Motor Company manufactures a diversified line of motor-driven vehicles. It has three operating divisions: (1) Outboard Motors, (2) Road Construction Equipment, and (3) Garden Equipment. The vice-president in charge of each division has responsibility for both the manufacture and sale of the products in his division. Certain departments in the company that serve all three divisions are grouped under a vice-president in charge of staff activities. Included in this group is the purchasing department.

All purchases of major equipment and installations must have prior approval of the board of directors. Each of the three divisions follows a slightly different approach in determining what equipment shall be purchased for replacement of existing equipment. In each of the divisions responsibility for equipment maintenance is assigned to a superintendent of maintenance. In the Outboard Motor Division the superintendent reviews the condition of each piece of equipment during November and prepares a list of the equipment needing replacement for the board of directors the following January. When approval is given, he initiates the purchases through the purchasing department.

In reviewing the condition of equipment the superintendent prepares an analysis of each item under his control on forms that he has adapted from the standard form developed by the Machinery and Allied Products Institute (MAPI). In his adaptation of the form he has included only 5 factors of comparison instead of the 12 or more factors suggested by MAPI. His 5 factors are direct labor, power, floor space, taxes and insurance, and normal maintenance. He justifies his exclusion of indirect labor by pointing out that indirect labor is generally computed as a percentage of direct labor. Thus its inclusion for both the old and the new equipment would not change the outcome. Defects and downtime are excluded because he says that all equipment in his division is kept in perfect order and, therefore, there can be no difference in these two factors between new and old equipment. Tooling is excluded as are supplies in the belief that these items will be used in approximately the same amounts for new and old equipment.

The Equipment Analysis Forms are reviewed with the vice-president in charge of the division, and any analysis that then shows a cost advantage for new equipment is submitted to the board of directors. The board then determines which of the requests are to be approved for the ensuing 12-month period.

The superintendent of maintenance of the Road Construction Equipment Division does not believe that the MAPI formula provides a sound approach to the purchase of equipment. He argues that it is impossible to measure accurately the various factors of comparison. Furthermore, he believes that reliance on a formula approach to business decisions tends to inhibit the exercise of executive judgment. Therefore, he reviews his equipment annually and submits requests for board approval at the January meeting which are supported by data relating to age, downtime, rejection rates, and so on, on the equipment involved.

Requisitions for the purchase of equipment for the production lines in the Garden Equipment Division are initiated at any time during the year when the superintendent of maintenance believes such action is indicated. At times he uses the equipment replacement formula and at other times he does not. He refuses to make an annual review to determine equipment needs for a 12-month forward period. He believes that this procedure is wasteful in that, once the board has approved a request, orders are placed immediately even though there may still be some months of useful life in the old equipment. Furthermore, he contends that competitive developments in garden equipment are such that changes in design may occur at any time during the year and require equipment changeover. If a division has used up its allocation of funds for equipment, it may experience difficulty with the board when it submits a supplementary request.

Mr. Ronald, Purchasing Agent for the Stephen Motor Company, has board of directors' approval for a policy of not leasing any production equipment. In securing approval, he cited as justification for his position the fact that in the long run costs of equipment are higher under a leasing plan. Furthermore, he contended that only companies with limited resources use the leasing method of procurement. If the Stephen Motor Company were to lease, he thought it might reflect adversely on the company's credit standing in the money markets.

Mr. Ronald does not approve of the purchase of used equipment for the company. He believes that if the company invests in equipment, it should be based on long-range plans and requirements. Used equipment is of value for a short-run producer who does not intend to remain in business for very long. Furthermore, it is almost impossible to evaluate a piece of equipment that has been in use for some time, according to Mr. Ronald.

1. Compare the positions of the superintendent of maintenance each of the divisions. Which position appears soundest?
2. Is Mr. Ronald correct in his policies on leasing and the purchase of used equipment?
3. Can variations in policies between divisions of a company be justified?

INDEX